NEGRO WITH A HAT
The Rise and Fall of Marcus Garvey

NEGRO WITH A HAT

The Rise and Fall of Marcus Garvey

COLIN GRANT

OXFORD

UNIVERSITY PRESS

OXFORD
UNIVERSITY PRESS

Oxford University Press, Inc., publishes works that further
Oxford University's objective of excellence
in research, scholarship, and education.

Oxford   New York
Auckland   Cape Town   Dar es Salaam   Hong Kong   Karachi
Kuala Lumpur   Madrid   Melbourne   Mexico City   Nairobi
New Delhi   Shanghai   Taipei   Toronto

With offices in
Argentina   Austria   Brazil   Chile   Czech Republic   France   Greece
Guatemala   Hungary   Italy   Japan   Poland   Portugal   Singapore
South Korea   Switzerland   Thailand   Turkey   Ukraine   Vietnam

Published by Oxford University Press, Inc.
198 Madison Avenue, New York, NY 10016

www.oup.com

First issued as an Oxford University Press paperback, 2010

Oxford is a registered trademark of Oxford University Press

Library of Congress Cataloging-in-Publication Data
Grant, Colin, 1961–
Negro with a hat : the rise and fall of Marcus Garvey / Colin Grant.
p. cm.
Includes bibliographical references and index.
ISBN 978-0-19-539309-5 (pbk.)
1. Garvey, Marcus, 1887–1940.   2. African Americans—Biography.
3. Black nationalism—United States—History—20th century.
4. African Americans—Race identity.
5. Back to Africa movement.
6. Universal Negro Improvement Association—History.
7. Jamaica—Biography.   I. Title.
E185.97.G3G73 2008
320.5'4092—dc22   2007045681

Printed in the United States of America
on acid-free paper

to my mother, Ethlyn

CONTENTS

ILLUSTRATIONS

Section 1

1 Kingston Earthquake, 1907 (© National Library of Jamaica) 2 Cowtail and hoe brigade (PBS) 3 Jamaicans preparing a compressed air drill (General Research and Reference Division, Schomburg Center for Research in Black Culture, The New York Public Library, Astor, Lenox and Tilden Foundations) 4 Marcus Garvey wedding photograph (Photographs and Prints Division, Schomburg Center for Research in Black Culture, The New York Public Library, Astor, Lenox and Tilden Foundations) 5 Edward Wilmot Blyden (New York Public Library, Schomburg Center) 6 Robert Love (© National Library of Jamaica) 7 Dusé Mohamed Ali, African Times and Orient Review, September 1913 (Adam Matthew Publications) 8 A. Philip Randolph (PBS) 9 Amy Ashwood, c.1920 (UNIA Papers Project, James S. Coleman African Studies Center, University College Los Angeles) 10 Hubert Henry Harrison (Photographs and Prints Division, Schomburg Center for Research in Black Culture, The New York Public Library, Astor, Lenox and Tilden Foundations) 11 The Reason Cartoon, 1920 (General Research and Reference Division, Schomburg Center for Research in Black Culture, The New York Public Library, Astor, Lenox and Tilden Foundations) 12 A Negro Family Just Arrived in Chicago from the Rural South (Photographs and Prints Division, Schomburg Center for Research in Black Culture, The New York Public Library, Astor, Lenox and Tilden Foundations) 13 Marcus Garvey, 1920 (Getty) 14 UNIA Parade, Harlem, 1924 (Getty) 15 W.E.B. Du Bois (Getty) 16 Booker T. Washington (Getty) 17 The Birth of a Nation, 1914 (Getty) 18 Silent Protest, 1917 (Photographs and Prints Division, Schomburg Center for Research in Black Culture, The New York Public Library, Astor, Lenox and Tilden Foundations) 19 Liberty Hall during 1921 UNIA convention (UNIA Papers Project, James S. Coleman African Studies Center, University College Los Angeles)

NEGRO WITH A HAT
The Rise and Fall of Marcus Garvey

PROLOGUE: A PREMATURE DEATH

In death I shall be a terror to the foes of Negro liberty.
Look for me in the whirlwind or the song of the storm.
Look for me all around you.

Marcus Garvey, Atlanta Penitentiary, 1925

AT the end of May 1940, Marcus Garvey sat cold and forgotten in a tall draughty rented house at 53 Talgarth Road in West Kensington, London. Recovering from a stroke which had left him partially paralysed, he was sorting through the newspapers that his secretary, Daisy Whyte, had placed beside his bed when he came across a headline which he knew could not be true: 'Marcus Garvey Dies in London.'[1] He scanned the other papers, some of which also carried notices of his death. They were not kind obituaries. It took almost a week for many of the papers to issue corrections. By then, wakes and memorials had been held for Marcus Garvey in the Caribbean and the United States. Garvey found himself eulogised by a number of people whom he'd considered enemies and vilified by others who had not forgiven him for his alleged exploitation of black people. Miss Whyte tried to shield her boss from some of the more uncharitable news stories but he insisted on seeing them all. Garvey was still weak from the stroke, but more than the distress and embarrassment of his disability, he was deeply upset by his public and private impotence, by his inability to arrest the decline of his mass movement, and by his estrangement from his family: two years previously, his wife had left him and returned to Jamaica with their children; he hadn't seen them since. Even if he'd been physically able to travel, there were few transatlantic passenger ships prepared to run the risk of being sunk by the German U-boats patrolling the high seas.

Marcus Garvey was now 'faced with clippings of his obituary [and] pictures of himself with deep black borders,' wrote Daisy Whyte, '[and] after the second day of this pile of shocking correspondence, he collapsed in his chair.' Reading through the damning accounts, written by former friends and enemies, Garvey had suffered another massive stroke: he died two weeks later, on 10 June 1940.[2]

In those last weeks of his life, Garvey might also have been caught off guard by the surprisingly balanced coverage of papers such as the *New York Times*, the *Daily Worker* and the *Chicago Defender*. Back in the 1920s the *Chicago Defender* had led a pack of Negro papers in shrilly denouncing Garvey as a menace and disgrace to the black race. Now, on 22 June 1940, the *Defender* wrote, 'Endowed with a dynamic personality, with unmatched oratorical gift, Garvey was easily the most colourful figure to have appeared in America since Frederick Douglass and Booker T. Washington. From 1914 to 1921 he dominated the scene with . . . the powerful Universal Negro Improvement Association. Had Garvey succeeded in his undertakings, he would have been incontestably the greatest figure of the twentieth century. Having failed, he is considered a fool.'

A whiff of hypocrisy rose from its pages as it was the *Defender*'s London correspondent, George Padmore, who had initially spread the rumour of Garvey's death. Amongst the small circle of exiled Caribbean intellectuals in 1930s London, the rising stars, George Padmore and C. L. R. James, had mounted a running campaign against the older man, heckling him at Speakers' Corner and at political meetings, and seizing every opportunity to harass him and pour scorn upon his head. In the 1920s, J. Edgar Hoover had considered Marcus Garvey to be one of the most dangerous black men in America, but by the time of his death Garvey had retreated from the radicalism and militancy that the Bureau of Investigation boss had so feared. Garvey's critics in London could not forgive his sharp turn to the right, nor his denunciation of Emperor Haile Selassie for fleeing Ethiopia during the Italian invasion of 1935.

If this tiny coterie of black intellectuals in London, including Garvey, had paused to reflect, they would have realised that they shared a commonality of purpose. Instead, they circled round each other in a narcissistic battle of minor differences. Theirs was a mirror of the many skirmishes Garvey had fought with other black leaders in Jamaica and Harlem throughout his unusual career.

C. L. R. James came publicly to regret his role in Marcus Garvey's final demise, but it would take two decades before Garvey's label as a fool was replaced officially with a badge of honour.[3] In 1964, Edward Seaga (a future Prime Minister of Jamaica) arranged for Garvey's remains to be returned for a state funeral and for the visionary, the man they called the Black Moses, to be honoured as Jamaica's first national hero and one of the most radical and enigmatic figures in twentieth-century history.

BURY THE DEAD AND TAKE CARE
OF THE LIVING

*And, behold, the Lord passed by, and a great and strong wind rent the
mountains, and break in pieces the rocks before the Lord; but the Lord
was not in the wind. And after the wind an earthquake. And after the
earthquake a fire; but the Lord was not in the fire. And after the fire a
still small voice.*

1 Kings 19:11–12

ON 14 January 1907, the nineteen-year-old Marcus Mosiah Garvey
anxiously picked his way through the corpses, rubble and fires that
raged beyond control over 10 square miles of Jamaica's capital,
Kingston, in search of his mother and sister. Hours earlier, the Caribbean
island had been hit by a massive earthquake. It was most severely felt
along a line from Port Royal to Buff Bay with the epicentre below the
sea, a few miles south of Kingston.¹ Just after 3 p.m. it erupted with
such ferocity that in a short time it had left a trail of more than 600
dead, thousands injured and much of the capital in ruins. The English
journalist, Ralph Hall Caine, who had arrived on board the twin-screw
steamer, *Port Kingston*, which had sailed into harbour just days before
the quake, catalogued the pitiful sights and occasional lucky escapes.
From the fallen wall of the railway station, Caine heard that a rail-
worker 'was thrown and impaled on the railings below, [but managed]
to regain complete recovery notwithstanding his punctured lung'. Ralph
Caine recorded the endless bodies, the bloated 'human flotsam and
jetsam (from which I must avert my eyes)' drifting out to sea, and the
desperate attempts at 'putting out of the fires, the . . . lighters in the

harbour receiving the dead bodies, the Parade Gardens in a mess, with families encamped there, and American blue-Jackets to the rescue'.[2]

A cloud of dust from the rubble eclipsed the sun; Kingston was cast in an eerie darkness. Much of the infrastructure and many of the businesses were destroyed: the great merchant houses which supplied the sugar plantations, dingy one-produce shops, government offices and factories were wiped out; flames jumped between buildings, and warehouses, packed to the rafters with sugar and rum, exploded. The biggest single loss of life came at the Machado Cigar Factory where up to 120 Cuban workers were killed when the building collapsed on them. No brick edifice was spared: almost all were wrecked including the printing plant and offices of the island's principal newspaper, the *Daily Gleaner*; in the following weeks, newspapers around the world would reproduce the one iconic photograph that captured the calamity of the Kingston earthquake: the ghostly apparition of a young woman in starched white dress and straw boater stepping gingerly over the rubble in the heart of the commercial district on King Street. Fire had raged the length of the street and all the buildings including number 68, the site of P. A. Benjamin's printers, where Garvey worked as a compositor, had disappeared.[3]

The power and devastation that nature could unleash was not unfamiliar to Marcus Garvey. Four years earlier he, his mother and sister had been trapped in the countryside of his birth, following a great hurricane that thrashed through the north coast at more than 200 miles an hour and destroyed all of their crops of bananas, pimento and coffee. Local people would so often resign themselves to their fate and the fact that 'God is not in the wind'. But hurricanes were commonplace in the Caribbean, earthquakes were not. And the earthquake of 1907 was on a scale of unimaginable horror.

Kingston had been founded after a previous earth-shattering quake of 1692 that had destroyed Port Royal, described then as the most wicked place on earth: a playground for picaroons, pirates and prostitutes, and a haven for the notorious state-sponsored rogue, Captain Morgan. Popular folklore recorded how God's wrath had been visited on this licentious den of iniquity when most of Port Royal and its fabulous riches were swallowed up by the sea. Such superstitions rose again from the fires of 1907. Church-going Jamaicans, more given to an Old Testament vision of the world, and yet to be touched by the compassion and tenderness of the New Testament, believed Negroes to be cursed. At 3.30p.m. on

Monday 14 January, Christian fundamentalists were vindicated as the new seismologists: their much foretold chronicle of the 'Last Days' had finally arrived. The revivalist sect, the Bedwardists, shrieked the loudest, wrote the *Gleaner*. Minutes after the quake, 'one could hear along the streets the cry of "Judgement!"' Remorse gave way to penitence. The Anglican Church reported that over the next two days, 300 couples previously 'married but not parsoned' rushed to tie the knot. The novelist, Anthony Trollope, who had visited Kingston 50 years earlier, drew attention to the topography of the capital, noting that 'the streets all run in parallels. There is a fine large square, plenty of public buildings, and almost a plethora of places of worship.'⁴ But now the streets were all buckled, rubble filled the squares and hardly any of the churches escaped unscathed: the 300 wedding ceremonies were conducted outdoors.

Reunited with his family, Garvey, along with most of the 46,000 surviving Kingstonians, spent months out in the open, grateful that the rains did not fall. Their desperate condition was not helped by the callous and brittle Governor Alexander Sweetenham, who was soon distracted by a perceived challenge to his authority which threatened to take precedence over the more pressing needs of feeding, clothing and sheltering a shocked population. The Governor summarily rejected a compassionate offer from a regiment of US Marines, whose battle-ships *Missouri* and *Indiana*, together with the gunboat *Yankton*, had steamed from Cuba just days after the earthquake struck. The Marines hadn't paused to reflect: instinctively they had disembarked at great speed and fanned out over the city administering to the needy but also shooting at suspected looters. Affronted by the breach of diplomatic protocol – never mind the assault on British sovereignty – the Governor wrote tersely to the American admiral:

Dear Admiral Davis,

While I must fully and heartily appreciate your very generous offer of assistance, I feel that it is my duty to ask you to re-embark your working party, and all parties, which your kindness has prompted you to land . . .

It is no longer any question of humanity; all the dead died days ago; and the work of giving them burial is merely one of convenience.

I should be glad to accept delivery of the safe, which the alleged thieves were in possession of from the jeweller's shop. The American Consular Agent has no knowledge of it; the shop is close to a sentry post, and the officer in charge of post professes ignorance of the incident; but there is a large safe on the premises, which has been opened by the fire, and also by some other.

I believe Police surveillance of no city adequate to protect private property. I may remind your Excellency that not long ago it was discovered that thieves had lodged and pillaged the town house of a New York millionaire during absence of the owner for the summer. But this fact would not have justified a British Admiral in landing an armed party to assist the New York Police.

I have the honour to be, with profound gratitude and highest respect.

Your obedient servant, Alexander Sweetenham, Governor.[5]

Later Sweetenham would be recalled to London in disgrace and the British would come to the island's aid with the pledge of a massive loan to reconstruct the city. HMS *Indefatigable* was dispatched from Trinidad with provisions and clothing. Help also came from a French cruiser that hurried from Martinique, and the Mansion House relief fund was started. In the meantime, claimants battled with dry-eyed insurers who directed them to the small print of their home-insurance policies: fires were covered, earthquakes were not. The price of everything, already extravagant, would become even more so.

Jamaica was not a cohesive society. Its population of just under a million was cleaved along lines of race and colour. More than 800,000 black citizens were the descendants of enslaved Africans; about 5,000 white people constituted the ruling elite, buffered by 15,000 brown folk of mixed race. The Browns might take tea with the Whites, but certainly not with the Blacks. As the early historian of Jamaica, Edward Long, noted at the end of the eighteenth century, 'the rich are the natural enemies of the poor', and if that state of affairs hadn't much changed a century later, there were optimists who reflected Edward Long's great hope: 'Yet if both parties could compose themselves, the faeces would remain peaceably at the bottom, and all other parties range themselves in different strata, according to their quality, the most refined floating always at the top.'[6]

The great problem was that a culture of social service had not yet evolved in Jamaica. The majority of people were too concerned with survival to think along selfless lines and those idle rich who could afford to, remained idle. When, a little while later, the young lawyer (and future Prime Minister) Norman Manley was approached by the directors of the charitable agency, Jamaica Welfare Ltd, and asked to volunteer his service, he looked bemused and answered, 'in my sweet young life, I never once heard mention of the word "service" [in that context]'.[7] In such a climate, the population of Kingston looked to friends and family outside the capital for support. But for the young Garvey there would have been little sense in sending a message to his birthplace, St Ann's Bay, for aid from his father. Garvey senior – Malchus – was a cantankerous and bookish loner. From birth he'd been apprenticed to a former slave-owner, his own father and grand-father having been born into slavery. The parish records only showed a break in this pattern following the slaves' emancipation in 1834. The British implemented a four-year period of transition, as much to process the claims for compensation from the slave-holders, as to allow the formerly enslaved to acclimatise to the peculiarities of being 'fully freed'. The formerly enslaved were expected to work without pay for their former slave-owners for 40 hours a week; payment for extra work was to be negotiated. This period was quaintly called 'The Apprenticeship System'. As well as adults, a child whose parents died within the four years of transition or whose parents gave approval (as it appears did Malchus Garvey's) could also be apprenticed to their former master.[8]

A class apart from the peasant farmers in the area, Malchus Moziah was a stonemason and rum-shop scholar who'd occasionally pronounce from the pulpit of his encyclopedic mind. Garvey senior drew a very important distinction between himself, an artisan, and his neighbours who were primarily labourers. His son, Marcus, was born at 32 Market Street. Typical of the area, it was, recalled an early boyhood friend, Isaac Rose, a functional and unprepossessing wooden 'old board-up house'. But Garvey's father was an ambitious man who bought land up on Winders Hill. He turned his trade to good use and, with great satisfaction, built a 'Spanish wall' house for his family on the outskirts of town in the St Ann's district – commonly referred to as the 'Garden Parish' because of its outstanding natural beauty. The property on the hill backed onto the Cloisters, once the home of the Anglican Rector, George Wilson Bridges, one of Jamaica's most ardent and vocal oppo-nents of the emancipation of the enslaved; during Garvey's time the Cloisters had been purchased by the Wesleyan Methodist Church. Garvey senior was a master mason whose service, though not always affordable to local people, was much in demand.[9]

Garvey's mother, Sarah Richards, a sincere and gentle woman, was the daughter of peasant farmers. Relatively late in life, at the age of forty-two, she had married Malchus Garvey. Their son, by then a toddler, had been born two years previously on 17 August 1887. Though the marriage certificate registered Malchus as a bachelor, Sarah was purported to have been his third partner; the previous two women, Caroline Trail and Charlotte Lawrence, had borne him six children between them. When Malchus Garvey moved on to Sarah Richards he fathered four more children with her: Trueman, Indiana, Rosana and finally Marcus. Trueman and Rosana both died in infancy.

Though wealthier than his peasant neighbours, Garvey senior still required his wife to work. As well as growing crops on a small plot, Sarah worked as a domestic servant, cooking for their neighbours, the family of the Wesleyan minister, Reverend Arthur F. Lightbourn. Marcus Garvey grew up playing with the children of Reverend Lightbourn. His best friend at this stage was Isaac Rose, whose family lived and worked on the Seville sugar estate, known locally as 'Nigger House'. Isaac Rose recalled that, in contrast to the Garveys' substantial and robust 'Spanish wall' house, his own family lived in a property 'made out of thatch, wattle and daub, paved inside with marl'. Isaac Rose's father fed the sugar mill with cane, crushing them and extracting the liquor which then flowed through bamboo troughs to the boiler; his mother worked in the refinery boiling down the sugar in large vats. Husband and wife saved and prospered. They were able to move out of their humble dwelling to become neighbours of the Garveys at Winders Hill, once Marcus's father had built a house for them. Though the Roses were not the class of company whom Mr Garvey would want to keep, no impediment was placed in the way of his son befriending whomsoever he chose.[10]

A generation up from slavery, Mr Garvey, as he insisted on being referred to by everyone, including his wife, was an extravagantly proud, self-educated man who had amassed an impressive collection of precious books. In later life Marcus Garvey would recall how he'd steal into his father's library and luxuriate in the knowledge contained therein. Outside of the library and local school, Marcus displayed only an intermittent reverence towards the other traditional seats of learning. The local church and Sunday school came with an extra hazard, as Garvey senior was an occasional layman – though, by his son's account, whenever in attendance, Mr Garvey was most likely to be found asleep in the gallery. Isaac Rose recalled a bruising encounter with Marcus when Rose and the other local boys rolled up some paper, fashioned a makeshift cigarette for the sleeping Mr Garvey, placed it between his lips, lit it and ran. The ringleader was caught by the furious and protective junior Garvey and thrown down the stairs of the church.

When his father wasn't the chosen victim, Marcus was not averse to joining in the pranks and high jinks of the gang. Sunday school seems to have served primarily as a venue for the local boys to try to impress the girls, and for Garvey to hone his mimetic skills. Amy Ashwood, whose life was to become intensely linked with Garvey's, wrote that 'Marcus was barely seven years old when he began to play the role of priest, guiding his flock composed of his village playmates . . . preparing his own "divine service", his own hymns and prayers and [would] close the meeting with a rousing sermon'.[11]

By the age of twelve, Marcus had developed a talent to amuse his peers and irritate his sixty-two-year-old father. Wife- and child-beating were commonplace on the island among the peasant and artisan classes. Mr Garvey did not depart from the script of Jamaican fathers' conventional approach to the imparting of wisdom and lessons to their sons, succinctly characterised by the local expression 'if you can't learn you will feel [the consequences]'. He was an intolerant and punitive husband and father. His self-righteous indulgence in the brutality of fact was aptly demonstrated when his young son Marcus and his idle, semi-delinquent gang were arrested after they were seen throwing stones that broke all of the windows in the local Wesleyan church. The boys were brought before the Juvenile Court on a charge of wilful destruction. Amy Ashwood recalled that when Marcus was found guilty, the magistrate turned to his father and gave him two options: he could either pay a fine of £1 or the boy would be imprisoned. 'In his wrath, [Mr Garvey] wiped his hands of his son and urged the Bench to send his son to a reformatory,' said Ashwood. Despite pleas from his wife Sarah, Garvey senior would not relent. The brutal fact was that the boy had broken the law and he, not the father, should suffer. Marcus was only spared imprisonment when Sarah 'came forward and promised to pay the fine out of savings she could ill afford'.[12]

The incident strained relations between father and son. Even if Marcus Garvey had been able to move away mentally from such an act of paternal betrayal, there were other examples of brutality that would be stored up for adulthood. Perhaps the most bizarre took place under a backdrop of a seemingly tender moment of maturing co-operation. Mr Garvey had been commissioned to build a vault by a wealthy landowner whose son had died from pneumonia, and he asked the adolescent Marcus to help. After several hours down in the vault, digging, shovelling and pounding, it was time for a lunch break. Mr Garvey proceeded up the ladder, and immediately pulled it up, leaving Marcus in the unfinished vault, ignoring his tearful protests. After several hours Marcus fell asleep, and in a half-reverie imagined that he saw the dead man peering down on him. When Mr Garvey eventually woke his son and rescued him from the vault, he explained that he'd given Marcus a valuable lesson in conquering fear. In later life, Marcus Garvey recounted this story when seeking to explain his fearlessness. However, it is hard to imagine the experience inducing anything other than the opposite effect.

Garvey junior took refuge in the company of his maternal uncle, Joseph Richards, working on his small 50-acre farm. The turn of the twentieth century had brought a huge expansion in the number of peasant farmers. The vast majority of the more than 100,000 in Jamaica carved out a subsistence existence on smallholdings of 5 acres or less, growing fruit and vegetables for their own households and selling bananas, coffee and pimento. The bottom had dropped out of the sugar market soon after the emancipation of the enslaved in 1834. Even if it had been viable, few Jamaicans of African descent would have relished turning their land over to a crop that was associated with the brutalities of slavery on the plantations. This was much to the chagrin of the essayist, Thomas Carlyle, who equated the former slaves' abandonment of the plantations as a sign of indolence. The archetypal Jamaican 'Quashee', Carlyle believed, was 'sunk up to the ears in pumpkins, imbibing sweet pulps and juices . . . while the sugar crops rot round them uncut, because labor cannot be hired'.[13] The actual model for such a description was hard to find and certainly did not fit Joseph Richards.

To the adolescent Marcus, Uncle Joseph ('Ba Joe') was the picture of benevolence. He was a hard-working Christian whom Garvey fondly remembered: 'between his Bible and his [hoe] you could not separate him'. The land in the 'Garden Parish' was particularly fertile and Uncle Joseph prospered: 'one farm brought him an income of about £100 per year. He was expanding and he was intelligent and he was able to educate me because my father would not do it. I helped to keep his books and so at the week end I got a commission of 13/- for selling bananas.'[14] It might have been small change but it was income that would soon be necessary to bolster the family coffers.

Garvey senior's miserliness had ultimately tripped him up. From early adulthood Malchus Garvey had regularly received a journal from a publisher, on the assumption that the subscription was a gift. Decades later, when the publisher died, the executors of his estate sent Mr Garvey an unexpected bill for twenty years' supply of the newspaper. Incensed, he withheld the back payment of £30; he was sued by the creditors, contested and lost the case. Even so he stubbornly refused to pay; he was penalised and one of the family's properties was attached to the court to meet the costs. It was a pattern that would be played out with increasing regularity. Cussed bloody-mindedness led to a series of petty disputes with neighbours over land boundaries and property rights. The arguments escalated quickly and culminated in litigation which Malchus seemed to specialise in losing, so that little by little, in a series of court rulings, the Garveys saw all of their plots of land disappear until they were left with just the rump few acres where the family home stood. Perhaps not surprisingly, Mr Garvey's spirit darkened thereafter. His withdrawal was now more pronounced, typically characterised by a locked-jaw retreat behind a bolted door to fester in his library, burning his kerosene lamp long into the night. In an attempt at autobiography some years later, Garvey recalled, 'My father was a man of brilliant intellect and dashing courage. He was unafraid of consequences. He took human chances in the course of life, as most bold men do, and failed at the close of his career.'[15]

The lesson would be well learnt. Garvey senior's recklessness had succeeded in depleting the family fortunes beyond penury. His recourse then was to abandon his wife, leaving his adolescent son to provide for her and his elder sister, Indiana, when he was just fourteen.

Uncle Joseph was in no position to help. He leased his farmland from the wealthy land-owning Pratt family in Mammee Bay. In line with the precarious fortunes of tenant farmers reliant on the benevolence of their landlords, Joseph Richards had, after he'd 'cleaned and cultivated' the 50 acres, been forced off the land at the landlord's whim. Edward Carol Pratt had other designs on Richards' leased acres. Cattle were to be given preference over people. The shock of losing his home and livelihood induced a kind of catatonia, draining Garvey's uncle of all his resourcefulness. Even the strength of his Christian faith and his profound sense of vocation towards his stewardship of the Laurinston Presbyterian Church, could not help. Marcus Garvey would later write with aching tenderness about the injustice of 'Ba Joe's' loss which so broke his uncle's spirit that he never recovered.[16]

It was at about this time that Garvey recorded yet another emotional blow in a scene reminiscent of his future rival William Edward Burghardt Du Bois's early brush with the colour line. Garvey was friendly with Reverend Lightbourn's daughter; though she was white and he black, they had played throughout childhood with no regard for the difference of their races. All that changed when the girl reached fourteen. She informed him that she would be leaving shortly to continue her education in Scotland, and that, though there was every possibility that she would return to the island later, her departure marked the end of their friendship. Garvey was perplexed as to why this should be; when he pressed her for an explanation, she confessed that the decision had been made for her by her father. The minister had instructed his daughter that 'she was never to write or try to get in touch with me, for I was a "nigger".' As told by Garvey, it had never occurred to him before that he was such a thing.[17]

St Ann's Bay was a seaside town of 2,000 souls. Marcus and Isaac both attended the local church school until they were fourteen. Lack of finances meant that further education was not an option. The teenage Garvey bemoaned the cultural climate in which peasant families believed there was 'nothing practical to be gained by irrelevant brainwork. After all, one was slated to be a cowhand or labourer, a blacksmith or shoemaker.'[18] Even so, in 1901, he gratefully accepted the offer of an apprenticeship to a local printer, Alfred 'Cap' Burrowes. Apprenticeships were much sought after and rarely attained; fortunate boys of Garvey's class would normally have had to pass a trade scholarship examination set by the government. But Alfred Burrowes was a friend of the family and saw himself as acting in the role of the boy's godfather. So, whenever the young apprentice asked for an increase in his wages he was wryly reminded of his debt of gratitude towards his godfather. The learning of a trade was, surely, more valuable than any pecuniary considerations. Garvey was a conscientious and enthusiastic student; he experienced all aspects of printing and seemed to have a special talent for the art of the compositor. Although he learnt quickly, he was always restless and harboured greater ambitions than his immediate prospects seemed to warrant, remembered Isaac Rose. Even now Garvey was beginning to frame a picture of himself that was bigger than his surroundings.

'Marcus Garvey was a fellow like this: all the time when I meet him he wear jacket and every time, his two jacket pockets full of paper,' Isaac Rose recalled. He was forever 'reading and telling us things that happen all over the world. Him know I don't know but him telling us. He was very interested in world affairs.' So with a jacket packed full of papers adorning his proud shoulders, and with his nose constantly in a book, Garvey ambled round the town square as if he were an undergraduate in the quad of an imaginary university, offering worldly tutorials to his bemused peers. Though they sometimes exchanged blows, Isaac Rose was clearly enamoured with Marcus Garvey. For the want of a better idea, Rose found himself shadowing Garvey as he edged ever more away from the countryside.[19]

Two years later in 1904, Garvey jumped at the chance to relocate to the town of Port Maria where Alfred Burrowes had set up another branch of his print works. Setting off in the morning from St Ann's Bay, Garvey would have travelled along a coastal route and, depending on the serviceability of the horse and cart and the quality of the red clay road, might have reached the self-important town of Port Maria by nightfall. Only 25 miles away, Port Maria (though smaller than St Ann's Bay) prided itself on being a key centre of operation for the United Fruit Company. It even boasted secure phone connections to Boston. Adding to the glamour were the numerous ships, their foreign flags snapping in the wind, that plied the harbour; conches sounded excitedly whenever an empty banana boat came in, summoning the loaders from the hills, who swarmed down to the wharves. They worked through day and night, 'carry-go and bring-come', loading the bananas until the ships, pregnant with their precious perishable cargo, departed. As well as serving the North American market there were fortnightly trips to England with the bananas kept cool and delayed from ripening on specially refrigerated ships. But no amount of big-city pretensions could disguise the provincial feel of the town. Marcus Garvey hungered for the excitement of a metropolitan centre, but it would take another year before the country boy could save up enough money to try his luck in the capital. Promising to send for his mother once he'd secured a good enough job and established himself, he moved to Kingston.

Garvey headed for the busy market district of Smith Village, where he boarded with the family of Thaddeus McCormack (a tailor who was to become a lifelong friend of Garvey) at 13 Pink Lane; he occupied a tiny room, attached to the main house, which, had the family been able to afford it, would have been set aside for a servant. Though the McCormacks aspired to a life commensurate with the educated classes, they actually lived in an impoverished working-class district. Residents had asked the council to provide gas lamps for the streets and concrete drains; and on 25 September 1905 their request, along with the general state of affairs in Smith Village, was discussed at the regular fortnightly meeting of Kingston City councillors. Rising to his feet, Councillor Davis complained that he 'had occasion to drive through the district [of Smith Village] recently and on occasion the sanitation was absolutely disgraceful . . . If an epidemic broke out . . . the people of the village would die like rotten sheep.' Mr Davis warned his fellow councillors that the situation was urgent as yellow fever was so close to the city's borders. 'But,' countered the Mayor coolly, 'where is the money to come from?' And in any case, he reminded Councillor Davis, 'that class of people don't get Yellow Fever'. On the same page as the report of that meeting, the *Daily Gleaner* carried an advert aimed at the paper's more affluent readers: 'A Parisian Social Event is often a failure for the want of discretion of the hostess in the choice of perfume. No mistake, however, can be made or offence caused if "Rigand's White Violet" is selected which is the most grateful and delicate flower perfume.'[20]

But it was the advert for the popular 'Stearn's Electric Rat and Roach Paste' which would more likely have caught the eye of residents of Smith Village. Garvey had only to venture a few yards from Pink Lane to witness the local constabulary handing out fines and making arrests for soliciting, vagrancy, loitering and indecent language. Smith Village was also known as a perfect hangout for a hard core of criminals and for God. Garvey's neighbours at number 25 had been particularly vexed by the noisy incantations to the Almighty round the corner on Beeston Street. The swell of singing and preaching from the local revivalist church had recently earned the pastor an audience with the courts. As reported in the *Gleaner* the plaintiff at 25 Pink Lane had been driven to the peak of distraction by 'about twenty people in the [pastor's] house who indulged in yelling, clapping their hands, stamping their feet and moving their bodies to tunes in a vulgar way'. Their numbers had swelled, complained the neighbour, after a recruiting drive heralded by the beating of drums, tambourines and blowing of horns, netted 'a crowd of the unwashed', recent arrivals to the area. The great drift of migrant workers from the countryside to the town had surged amid rumours that United Fruit, one of the island's largest employers, planned severe cuts to its workforce. Anxious labourers descended on Kingston in search of work. In the poorest districts, like Smith Village, accommodation was just about affordable. Once there, unlucky job-seekers joined the ranks of the yard-boys who idled away their under-employed hours in yards, occasionally attending to their teeth with toothpicks or, when particularly energised, swatting mosquitoes.

Garvey was more fortunate. Brandishing a note of recommendation from 'Cap' Burrowes, Garvey soon found work at the printing division of P. A. Benjamin Manufacturing Co. – a job that, while not guaranteeing him clean fingernails, came with the expectation that he would wear a suit. It might not have attracted the awe and reverence the black population held for even the humblest white-collar position, but he was surely on his way. By the age of eighteen Garvey said that he had already begun to feel 'a yearning for service of some kind, because of [my] training in the first government – government in the family home'.[21]

At five feet and seven inches, Marcus Garvey was not particularly short. He had a broad chest, an overall stocky build, and a head that was slightly too large for the rest of his body; he did not have the kind of stature that would make him stand out from the crowd. Garvey's eyes, though, were what people most often commented on. Resembling the stone from the fruit of an ackee, very dark, almost black, but sparkly and intelligent, they were said to explain his decisiveness of thought and action. Having caught the attention of his employer, Garvey advanced rapidly, promoted through the lower orders to the unprecedented position of foreman – a post which had, until then, been reserved for Englishmen. Jamaica lacked the facilities for training artisans and engineers locally, and industry was therefore dependent on foreign technical know-how. Hence the English foremen, shipped over as prized specimens from the motherland.

Life for the majority of Jamaicans was not so promising. The aftermath of the quake brought in an unpleasant and uncertain new order. Physical and social aftershocks were still being felt as late as April. Amidst the rampant looting and subsequent curfews the city teetered on the edge of economic collapse. As a result, businesses dismissed workers and enforced lower wages. Commonly, managers employed baton-wielding thugs to settle disputes with labourers who had the temerity to ask for more; not far removed from the way overseers were used to subjugate plantation workers in slavery days, the memory of which was built into the cultural DNA of the island. Garvey loved an argument. By his own admission 'strong and manly', he was already garnering a local reputation of thrusting himself uninvited into volatile environments and, according to his fans, with a verbal talent to resolve conflicts. His handling of a local henchman of the employers, Tom Prang, a renowned waterfront bruiser, served as further encouragement. 'Tom Prang was a big fat fellow,' recalled Isaac Rose. 'When any of the waterfront workers went to speak hard to the managers, the employers would get Tom Prang to beat them.' One day Garvey confronted Prang and asked, 'Did he think any white man would [ever] beat him friend for a nigger?' Soon after Prang slunk out of town, and headed north to Montego Bay and obscurity.[22]

In 1908, Isaac Rose left Kingston to go back to St Ann's Bay. A return to the north coast, to the simplicity and beauty of the 'green parish' of St Ann's, was something that Garvey's mother, Sarah Jane, also pined for after the quake, with greater intensity than when she had first been lured to the metropolis by her son. Going back would have made practical sense: town (Kingston) was rough and unrelenting. Sarah Richards left little trace of her time in the capital. She lived there for over a year but the tiny room on Pink Lane would have been too small to accommodate Garvey's mother and sister. In Kingston both Sarah and her daughter, Indiana, struggled to find regular employment in a city saturated with domestic servants. Their life was harsh. At least in the country, when times were difficult and money hard to come by, you could go to your plot of land and reap the yam, cassava and callallo you'd planted the season before, or you could place your pan or basket at the end of the roaring river and when the river 'come down' catch the janga, snappers and crayfish. In town there was no outlet for poverty; people lived on top of each other in diminishing prospects. Not so for Marcus Garvey. Sarah's son had great expectations at P. A. Benjamin's. The pay, though modest, was reasonable.

The apprenticeship at Alfred Burrowes had been a good investment; Garvey thrived but his mother could give no shape to her life in the city. At the beginning of 1908, Sarah Richards turned her face to the wall, withered and, with characteristically little fuss, died suffering cerebral apoplexy on 18 March at the age of fifty-six – not far off the life expectancy of a Jamaican at the turn of the twentieth century. Garvey eulogised his mother as a 'sober and conscientious Christian, too soft and good for the time in which she lived . . . always willing to return a smile for a blow, and ever ready to bestow charity upon her enemy'.[23] Sarah was survived by her estranged husband and two children who'd made it into adulthood, Indiana and Marcus.

Brother and sister dug in in Kingston. Indiana went to work as a live-in maid for the family of the Kingston city engineer George Fortunatus Judah, who, though a prominent member of the 2,000-strong Jewish community, was closely associated with the Catholic Church.[24] Over the next few years Garvey, also, would forge strong links with the Roman Catholic diocese of Jamaica, and would convert to Catholicism. Now, with his sister financially secure, he concentrated on his own ambitions. Pretty soon Marcus Garvey was boasting of his promotion at P. A. Benjamin's to the 'excellent position as manager of a large printing establishment'.[25] Yet, in this climate of every man for himself, where he confessed, 'I had not much difficulty in finding and holding a place for myself, for I was aggressive,' Garvey found that his loyalties wavered between self-advancement and communal justice. It was perhaps a mark of his social and political sensibilities that, even as he progressed up the lower rungs of management, he retained his trade-union membership. Towards the end of 1908, the card-carrying foreman of the Kingston Typographical Union found himself in an impossible position.

Print workers' demands for better wages and working conditions were ignored by managers throughout the capital. When the workers went out on an island-wide strike on 28 November 1908, Garvey defied expectations by not only joining the strike but also taking a leading role amongst the strikers. The year before, he'd been elected vice-president of the compositors' branch of the union; but few young men, at the age of twenty, would have demonstrated the maturity needed to organise and motivate the masses. The strike force found support amongst the American affiliation of the International Typographical Union and, for several weeks, the men weathered the hardship of no wages. In the interim, their resolve was severely tested by two undermining pieces of news: firstly, that Jamaica's newspaper proprietors had ordered new linotype machines from New York, thus reducing the number of workers required for printing plants; and, secondly, that the union's treasurer had absconded with the strike fund. When the strike was eventually broken and the workers returned, Garvey, along with the executive members of the union, was sacked by the management. Found guilty of the Jamaican adage, 'you can't sidown pon cow, so cus cow kin' (you shouldn't bite the hand that feeds you), and subsequently branded a troublemaker, Garvey was unable to find any other work in the private sector.

Garvey knew of the vindictive nature of Jamaican employers, yet he walked out on a point of principle, and aligned himself with the working class. When he later wrote about that period, he seems to have surprised even himself; good opportunities for someone from Garvey's background were extremely limited and 'it was not easy to pass on to office and position'. It was a measure of his single-minded determination to succeed, that he held up for public admiration his achievement at P. A. Benjamin's of 'having under my control several men old enough to be my grandfathers'. The decision to come out with the men had been taken on instinct rather than sober reflection. Later attempts to explain that bold action were reduced to the frank and un-analytical, 'I got mixed up with public life.' Garvey found that he was shocked by what he saw: 'the politics of my country . . . disgusted me.'[26]

For all of Garvey's talk of being aggressive, Amy Ashwood recalled that though he 'possessed an overwhelming quota of physical courage', Garvey was also an extremely sensitive young man who was no stranger to tears.[27] Moving from a rural area to the capital, he could not fail to notice how the differences between the classes were accentuated. Garvey was not misty-eyed about the romanticism of simple country life: St Ann's Bay and Port Maria were both marked by social stratification that was partly obscured by the egress offered by the green hills, the wilderness and expanse of the countryside; but in the oppressed cauldron of Kingston, the vulgarity of wealth butted up against the perfect squalor of Smith Village. Garvey was steeped in the reeking, pestilent poverty of a neglected people, apparently immune to yellow fever and untreated sewage, whose surroundings offered little dignity and certainly no grace. 'I started to take an interest in the politics of my country,' Garvey recalled, 'and then I saw the injustice done to my race because it was black, and I became dissatisfied on that account.'[28]

Up until then, he'd been well on the road to a respected and respectable career. Looked at coldly, he'd made an egregious and reprehensible mistake. But in Kingston, Garvey was developing a fierce hatred of the iniquities of Jamaican society – even as he craved respectability. At the age of twenty, he had taken a huge gamble with his career and his livelihood and lost. Jamaica wasn't the kind of society that allowed for second chances. Marcus Garvey counted himself extremely fortunate, therefore, when he eventually found temporary employment at the government printers.

Britain ruled Jamaica as a Crown colony. It was a strange hybrid system in which half of the members of the local legislative council (including the Governor) were executive appointments and the other half elected officials – collectively this group presided over an assembly commonly cursed as 'the house of 40 thieves'.[29] Critics argued that in replacing the quick-tempered Governor Sweetenham with the acerbic Sir Sydney Haldane Olivier after the earthquake in 1907, the British had swapped like for like. The compass that had guided Olivier's Fabian principles in England seemed to have gone awry somewhere between the Colonial Office and King's House, as it often did when civilised men went out to the colonies. Olivier was perhaps not as brittle as his predecessor but he could be equally autocratic. Local antipathy towards the new Governor was not universal. The island's burgeoning poet, Claude McKay, was so pleased with the encouragement of the poetry-loving chief executive that he dedicated his first book of poems to him. Sydney Olivier had shown his appreciation by donating books to the Literary and Improvement Society of which McKay was secretary. But, arguably, Olivier's acts of individual kindness were not matched by his overall approach to the workforce.

In his book *White Capital and Coloured Labour*, Olivier gave a bleak prognosis for sugar production on the island, given the inefficiency of the emancipated African who was 'no longer exercised by fear of the Driver and the whip'. In so doing, he upheld the common belief that 'the strenuousness of the inhabitant of the temperate zone must not be looked for'.[30] His appointment further fuelled discontent amongst the masses who occasionally roused themselves to demonstrations in the heat of the night. By now Garvey was growing weary of the unfocused rage and meaningless verbal skirmishes that served as Saturday evening's entertainment down at the Victoria Pier. There he was amongst the reformist pamphleteers who sought vainly to politicise jeering, rum-soaked ragamuffins. Ultimately it was little more than schoolboy grandstanding and a trifle undignified. Garvey had outgrown it. In a period of accelerated political education, the young man aligned himself with the National Club, where in a 'tumultuous meeting' he was elected first assistant secretary on 20 April 1910, along with the equally youthful Wilfred Domingo, an apprentice tailor who became the second assistant secretary. Domingo and Garvey were both natives of St Ann's Bay (though as Domingo was the child of a much more prosperous family the two had never met). Another member of the National Club recalled being impressed by Garvey, especially by the intense young man's continuing self-education: 'He carried a pocket dictionary with him and said he studied three or four words daily, and in his room, he would write a paragraph or two using these words.'[31] By night he learnt and by day he put into practice, as Garvey lent his expertise in the printing and publication of the group's fortnightly journal, *Our Own*.

The club, Jamaica's first nationalist political organisation, sought to challenge the abuses of the Crown government and campaigned actively for the removal of Governor Olivier and an end to the 'coolie' immigration (the influx of indentured Indian labour brought in to replace blacks who, after their emancipation, refused to work on plantations). In some quarters this rise in immigration bore significant responsibility for the commensurate rise in native unemployment. The objectives of the National Club rested on the shoulders of Solomon Alexander Cox who had gained a seat on the Legislative Council. Cox complained that the 'coolies were brought in to help the planters [and] . . . large companies such as the United Fruit Company who . . . consisted for the most part of Americans who would simply place the Jamaican to a pile and set them on fire if they had a chance to do so.'[32] Cox's was a lone voice amongst a council more given to the concerns of planters than labourers, and his tenure was short-lived. He was unseated – much to the relief of the authorities – through deft machiavellian manoeuvring. The *Jamaica Times* noted the outrage of one Marcus Garvey, a junior member of the National Club, who had collaborated with Wilfred Domingo in publishing *The Struggling Mass,* a 'sedulous pamphlet in which he upholds the policy of Mr Cox and deals severely with the Press which he declares is now an enemy of the people'. Although not so remarkable, it did signal perhaps the first island-wide public recognition of the young man from St Ann's Bay. Garvey did not rush to correct the flattering misperception that he was the sole author and not, more accurately, the co-publisher along with Wilfred Domingo.

This phase of Garvey's life was characterised by a stringent regime of self-improvement; he enrolled for elocution lessons, with the aim of recasting his thick country accent into the kind of neutral Standard English spoken in music-appreciation and debating societies. On the

face of it Garvey's choice of occasional tutor was an odd one. Robert
J. Love was celebrated as a natural orator of great ability, capable of
an effortless swaying of the emotions of those lucky enough to hear
him. But even if he'd been so inclined, Love's ability to offer elocution
lessons would have been impaired by a recent stroke. It didn't stop the
young pretender, with heroic potential, seeking out the man many in
Jamaica thought of as an oracle. For Robert J. Love did not confine
himself to the rendition of clean seductive sounds and aural perfec-
tion. As well as being a doctor and preacher, Love was a proud
'decidedly black' radical journalist and aggressive campaigner for social
reform. From the public platform he used his tongue as a tomahawk,
provocatively advocating, for example, the erection of a memorial to
the black Baptist preacher, William Gordon, executed for his part in
the Morant Bay uprising forty years earlier, in 1865. Such sentiments
alarmed the authorities and prompted sombre warnings from agitated
editorial writers who chastised Love and prophesied that his careless
talk would lead to a resurrection of racial animosities on the island; a
claim largely overstated as Love lacked any mass movement or the
engine of a political party to push his ideas through.

In young men like Garvey and Domingo, though, Robert Love found
disciples radicalised and racialised by the sermons in his weekly journal,
the *Jamaica Advocate*. The paper not only spelt out the glaring inequities
in Caribbean society but was an early champion of the Pan-African
idealism that would soon infect its most avid reader. Although evidence
of the correspondence between the two men is patchy, it is clear that
Garvey revered the great man and considered him a mentor.[33]

The young elocutionist's next move was to put his new-found private
voice on public display. The road test was his entry into a number of
public-speaking competitions, culminating in a grand finale where
recitations of leading authors would be given by various parishes of
the island. The *Gleaner* of 20 August 1910 announced that the Garden
Parish of St Ann would be fittingly represented by 'the energetic elocutionist, Mr M. Moziah Garvey'. Midway through Chatham's speech
on the American War of Independence a wag in the audience threw
out a witty remark about Garvey's sometimes squeaky voice and the
rows of Collegiate Hall resounded with laughter. Not surprisingly, St
Ann's favoured son did not figure amongst the winners. By his own
estimation, though, Marcus Garvey should have ended the night in
first place. So seriously did he take this setback in the competition that

a month later, in the first foray into a lifetime of litigation, he sued the heckler who had put him off his stride.[34]

Garvey's voice may have wobbled on the platform but it struck a surer note in print. A natural exuberance and self-conscious zeal fired the pages of *Garvey's Watchman*, his first weekly journal that rolled off the printing presses in early 1910. There was much to admire in newspaper columns that crackled and fizzed with the certainty of youth. Garvey had announced his ambition from the outset with the title *Garvey's Watchman*, for though the paper might have seemed like an exercise in vanity, it actually bore earnest homage to *The Watchman* published by George William Gordon. In 1865 the authorities claimed this militant journal had incited the violent rioters of Morant Bay. Their murderous call of 'Colour for colour and blood for blood!' resulted in the death of a dozen white men and was followed by swift and brutal British retribution with 400 rebels executed and more than a thousand flogged.[35]

Garvey's Watchman claimed a circulation of 3,000, but given that the population of the city did not exceed 50,000 (the majority of whom were only semi-literate) and the fact of Garvey's limited funds for promotion, that figure is unlikely. The hard-working publisher struggled from the outset to sustain his weekly paper. By the middle of 1909, recession in Jamaica was beginning to cut deep, and with their bellies knocking on their backbones, fewer citizens were prepared to take a punt on the expense of a journal. Garvey was forced to suspend publication after the third issue. Unsold copies of *Garvey's Watchman* went the way of the pamphlets at Victoria Pier the previous year, distributed like confetti on the water. *Garvey's Watchman* was the bold experiment of a twenty-two-year-old man. In its short life, the paper had briefly mounted a campaign over the lack of relief for the poor, and the tendency to cast the unemployed as agents of their own misfortune as 'Quashees' who continued to doze under the shade of palm trees, spitting out pumpkin seeds. The indifference of the authorities to the population's hardships was a common complaint and a theme later take up by Claude McKay when he wrote bitterly:

> Gov'mint seem no hea' de cry
> Dat de price o' food is high,
> Not a single wud is said
> 'Bouten taxes to be paid;

Same old taxes ebery year,
Though dere's hunger in the air.[36]

Though figures suggested an increase in the island's workforce, this
was largely the result of splitting the work of existing jobs. More than
one in ten workers were now in domestic service, but the swell in their
numbers did not come from a greater middle-class demand for cooks,
cleaners, gardeners and handymen but rather answered the urgent need
to create employment for a surplus rural population. 'Every house and
shop is filled with black servants,' J. Bigelow observed when visiting
the island in 1850, and the situation had not changed much sixty years
later when even modest homes had 'four to five domestic servants . . .
and the amplest provision is always made to prevent the possibility of
the ruling race being compelled to do anything themselves which can
be done by servants'.[37]

During the days of plenty Jamaica's plantocracy had reaped fantastic
rewards from the hundreds of sugar-cane plantations (at its most profitable the pearl of the Antilles was the jewel of the British Empire),
but by 1910 sugar production had been scaled down in favour of
bananas; and though there was a boom in the planting and harvesting
of bananas (more than 10 million bunches were exported annually),
their production was not as labour intensive and required fewer
workers; competition from cheaper 'coolie' migrants forced an already
mobile working population to consider looking for jobs beyond the
island. In 1910, Colonial Office records charted a great exodus of
13,109 Jamaicans; more than 10,000 of these economic migrants
headed for Central America.

In the middle of 1910, Marcus Garvey cleared out his savings and
approached steamship agents for a ticket to Costa Rica. He was one
of hundreds of hopefuls who gathered at the wharves each week, united
in a singular belief that the bananas cultivated by the mighty United
Fruit Company in Central America were 'green gold'. Such was the
demand amongst Jamaicans for work that the United Fruit recruiters,
accompanied by doctors, could afford to be exacting in their choice.
As well as harvesting bananas, the Jamaican labourer would need muscles
of rope to clear the forests in the never-ending drive for new land. There
was no policy of crop rotation, and bananas would be grown until the
land was exhausted; planters then moved on to the next fecund and

fertile patch made ready by an army of gasping and sweating machete-laden labourers. Marcus Garvey would be spared the indignities and more unpleasant aspects of plantation life; another uncle, Henry Richards, had secured him a job on one of the larger plantations in the Limón division, in the privileged position of timekeeper.

Contract labourers had ventured to Costa Rica since the 1870s, first to build the railway lines through an unforgiving landscape of tropical rainforests (the daily rains typically measured over 2 metres in the course of a year). Men worked all day in the mud up to their knees. Landslides were terrifying and routine; work was always hazardous and sometimes fatal. On 22 August 1886, the *New York Tribune* reported a spate of accidental burials, of makeshift graves of black workers buried under piles of rubble: 'It was the same every day – bury, bury, bury, running two, three and four trains a day with dead Jamaican niggers all the time.' Labourers ran the risk of personal injury and death whilst investors baulked at the cost of the railway-line projects and the depressing prospect of no financial returns. To dissuade entrepreneurs such as Minor Keith from abandoning their half-built railway lines, the government in San José had offered generous land concessions. Hundreds of thousands of acres were transferred, and as the laying of the track progressed, Keith organised for banana trees to be planted all along the route of the line to feed his workers. When the various railway lines neared completion and the passengers for whom they were conceived failed to materialise, Keith and his associates began to adapt their carriages and rolling stock, and gradually converted their use to the transportation of freight, primarily bananas. The so far luckless entrepreneur had unwittingly stumbled on a produce whose harvest would soon transform his company into one of the richest in the world: green bananas were gold.

In the autumn of 1910, armed with the permit (having paid the dollar deposit that the Treasury required to cover the potential cost of repatriation), Marcus Garvey set sail for Costa Rica. Minor Keith's United Fruit steamers regularly ferried bananas from Central America to North America, and mail and passengers to and from Caribbean islands (primarily Jamaica) to Costa Rica, Cuba and Panama. The cost of a steerage-class ticket would be offset by the salivating prospect of wages several times higher than the passenger could expect for similar work in Jamaica. The Right Reverend Herbert Bury recorded the great swell of excitement as the departing men boarded the ships. Defying the fierce morning heat, friends and relatives accompanied the men who struggled aboard with 'the most extraordinary collection of personal property . . . friends on shore handed over the side, and those on board received and stowed away, pathetic little bundles . . . imposing tin boxes and portmanteaux, pillows, beds, chairs, cooking vessels . . .' They were deck passengers, and as soon as the ship cleared the harbour, Herbert Bury, the self-styled 'bishop amongst bananas' observed how 'everything was now neatly arranged and in order, for their two days and nights at sea had to be spent just where they had put down their belongings when coming on board'.[38] It was Garvey's first time off the island; a huge gamble but also a great adventure. He aimed to stay, in the first instance, with his maternal uncle in the Caribbean enclave of Port Limón (home to an estimated 20,000 British West Indians). Limón was an isolated region of Atlantic coast where the bullish United Fruit Company dominated the banana industry, and acted largely with impunity as if it were an autonomous government. Not satisfied with its near-monopoly of the North American market, the transnational United Fruit Company, which local people called '*el pulpo*' (the octopus) because of its aggressive competitiveness and all-pervading reach into its workers' lives, continued to expand its production and distribution. Each week its ships, the 'Great White Fleet', laden with perfect bananas, struggled to keep up with demand.

Disembarking from the steamers that brought them to Port Limón, the first thing passengers noticed was the smell – the cloyingly sweet smell of rejected, rotting bananas – and then the sight and sound of the workers summoned to load the boats. All day long women, poised with heavy loads of banana bunches on their heads, strode up and down the gangplanks of the company's steamers. Dark stains of banana juice decorated their ragged garments that were once Sunday gowns. The 'knee-dipping canter of the bearers' would have been a familiar sight to Garvey. The work rendered the women indistinguishable from their Port Maria and Port Antonio counterparts back home, whom Governor Olivier was to describe 'in all the imaginable shades of dinginess'. Banana loading was primarily women's work. Almost every other aspect of banana cultivation was carried out by men. There was no banana season; work was an unbroken cycle. But employment was competitive and irregular; United Fruit preferred to pay wages in the form of coupons that could only fully be exchanged for provisions in United Fruit shops (partially redeemed in non-UF shops).

Though the majority of West Indian workers were labourers (single men housed in barracks and labour camps) and small-scale farmers (with their families), there had evolved over three decades of their presence in Costa Rica, a degree of upward mobility. The North American managers of United Fruit generally showed a preference to West Indians over the local Hispanic population, primarily because the West Indians spoke English and were more literate. After a while, the Hispanic peasants were relegated to the more unpleasant tasks of digging ditches and draining swamps. West Indians became foremen and timekeepers; they had a monopoly on the docks and worked in the corporate offices as clerks. However, the United Fruit Company's heavy-handed control of the workforce, especially out on the plantations, was, as Governor Olivier would later report, 'uncongenial to the Jamaican temperament'.[39]

Marcus Garvey arrived in the midst of a rancid dispute between Jamaican labourers and their North American managers: the Costa Rican government had recently proposed a tax on banana exports (2 cents per stem), and rather than absorbing the losses, the United Fruit Company had attempted to pass on the burden to its employees in the shape of a 12 per cent reduction in the wages. Earning 85 cents a day was bad enough, but when straight-faced managers insisted on a cut that would reduce their wages to 75 cents a day, resentment among the workforce, already running high, exploded into angry demonstrations that centred on Port Limón. The Jamaicans' conflict with United Fruit was exacerbated when the newly formed Artisans and Labourers Union had the temerity to request that 1 August, the anniversary of emancipation, be recognised as an annual holiday. The company responded precipitously. It selected 600 union members – as an example to the others – and extending their leave indefinitely, locked them out from all United Fruit plantations. The fledgling union (more a mutual-aid society than hard-core labour movement) observed 'el pulpo's' approach to conflict resolution with equal horror and dismay: company recruiters were dispatched to St Kitts and, after a speedy trawl through the countryside, shipped in several hundred Kittitians to take the place of the recalcitrant Jamaicans. On 23 November 1910, the British Consulate in San José sent an urgent telegram to the Governor in Panama:

[Artisans and Labourers] Union strikers have been replaced by other working people. 600 from Nevis and St Kitts under contract arrived all right last week. Today 180 intimidated by Union agitators – Riot suppressed without loss of life. Rioters detained under arrest . . . For the present all quiet. Deportation ringleaders probable. [Vice-Consul] Macgrigor remaining Limón.'[40]

The men from St Kitts would have been aware of the ambiguous role intended for them. The company frequently made a policy of exploiting inter-island rivalries, but, though there was initial friction with the Jamaicans, the Kittitians were soon alerted to the real enemy: the United Fruit Company for whom they were contracted to work at 10 cents a day less than the Jamaicans. Duped by the transnational, the new men also went out on strike, with the North American managers looking on anxiously, anticipating the violent backlash that they feared was bound to follow. When United Fruit appealed to the Costa Rican government, the authorities sent in troops to enforce vagrancy laws (contracted workers who refused to work could be considered vagrants and arrested) and to prevent more farm labourers descending on the port. Even the conservative *Limón Times* thundered at the injustice, its outrage mixed with a plaintive SOS: 'We are all British . . . we all belong to a world-wide Empire, and on the strength of that assertion all British Subjects have every right to be treated with the greatest amount of respect; and should not be so subjected to American aggression.' But the appeals of these Caribbean sons and daughters of a distant Albion for intervention met with little sympathy from local consular officials who believed them 'vainly influenced by agitators'. In further telegrams, the British consul, Frank Cox, sounded a note of rising panic:

It is quite likely that martial law will be declared in Limón and unless things go well tomorrow I anticipate serious trouble. Government has 250 men here sufficient to maintain order in the town . . . There is uneasiness nevertheless which would be relieved by the presence of a warship.[41]

On 29 November 1910, Cox addressed the strikers and warned that they risked being drafted to Cartago to work by armed force: 'You are hereby directed to return, as free men, to work at the farms of the United Fruit Company . . . I advise you to work as free men, and save money, rather than to be forced to work, and have nothing.'

Added to the hazards of duplicitous managers, officious British consular representatives, snakes and swamps, were the local bandits who regularly ambushed the bewildered immigrants on the edge of the jungle and relieved them of their wages. Still, once the strike was over, 75 cents a day seemed preferable to near-starvation in Jamaica and St Kitts. The immediate dispute was settled but the recriminations and grievances rumbled on. The newly appointed timekeeper, Marcus Garvey, found himself in an invidious role; his predisposition towards supporting his countrymen conflicted with his job description. Whilst the labourers desired to work speedily to meet their required daily targets, the overseers, foremen and timekeepers were charged with ensuring that maximum efficiency did not come with the cost of bruised or scarred bananas. Timekeeper Garvey was employed to oversee the smooth running of the 'factory in the fields' (as banana plantations were commonly known) that left workers with the conviction that United Fruit were more concerned about the welfare of the bananas than the people who harvested them. Marcus Garvey only spent a few months on the plantations and though the bullying and belittling of his compatriots that he witnessed at close hand sickened him, it also heightened his sense of identification with the group.[42]

The labour dispute had highlighted the precarious and unprotected state of the Caribbeans in Costa Rica; ultimately, the host nation restricted citizenship and citizens' rights to the descendants of Spain who had settled there over three centuries. The men had been forced back to work but the cynical attempt to drive a wedge between West Indian labourers had failed. The migrants may have come from diverse islands but they shared a common language and allegiance to Britain; the fraternal lodges and friendly societies that they established provided some succour; though they might organise petitions and seek the protection of the British Crown, the Artisans and Labourers Union, the Jamaica Burial Society, the St Kitts Sports Club Committee and the West Indian Immigration and Protection Club, were not marked by militancy. At the top of these organisations were elders who recognised their vulnerability and eschewed conflict. The unfortunate dispute with United Fruit had demonstrated the futility of any other approach. By the end of 1910, a handful of strike activists had been expelled from the country and the more conservative element of the expat society had reasserted itself.

Garvey was soon upsetting the new, old order. In the spring of 1911, he established a bilingual newspaper, the *Nation* or *La Nación*. Its potential readership would have been drawn from the captive audience of British West Indians in and around Limón. Up until the *Nation's* launch, the long-established *Limón Times* had cornered the expat market. The *Nation* immediately displayed its colours as a small but feisty paper capable of punching above its weight in targeting the local West Indian leadership and its timid cap-in-hand response to the abuse of its compatriots. Every time these elders in Costa Rica opened the pages of Garvey's paper, they had cause to wince. Although they couldn't possibly argue with the sentiment behind the *Nation*, they baulked at its un-diplomatic language. Like self-conscious guests at a powerful host's party, the West Indian elite muttered tetchily amongst themselves that Garvey's complaints were ill-mannered and only served to make things worse. 'How much longer,' wondered an irate letter-writer to the *Limón Times*, 'must . . . a respectable community be offended by the scurrilities of a vile penny-a-liner.' That outburst was prompted by Garvey's attack on the 'notorious demons', the Millennial Dawnists (precursors of the Jehovah's Witnesses) who flourished amongst sections of the West Indian population and who, having 'discarded the Old Testament, are expounding the doctrine of an ambitious American grafter'. To criticise the group's figurehead, the venerable Charles Russell was an affront perhaps not beyond the bounds of fair comment, but it was the young upstart's hijacking of preparations for the celebration of King George V's coronation that particularly irked. In blitzing Port Limón with posters 'calling on British subjects to unite and celebrate the Coronation', Garvey had stolen a march on the coronation committee and ensured disunity. He raised substantial funds – contributions that, at any other time, his rivals of longer-standing reputation in the community might reasonably have been expected to collect. Aggrieved members of the official committee mounted a whispering campaign that this 'Johnny-come-lately' had misappropriated several thousand dollars – accusations which were never substantiated but which gave some of Garvey's supporters pause for thought.

Three months on, the editor of the *Nation* appeared to have gone too far – even by his extreme standards – when making unguarded comments about a fire that had consumed several West Indian-owned small businesses in the centre of Limón. Garvey questioned the motives and priorities of the fire brigade who'd given so much effort to saving the luxurious home of Cecil Lindo, a wealthy white Jamaican, that when they turned their hoses on the flames lapping at the smaller businesses, there was no more water. That report earned him a brief audience with rough-handling police, foreshadowing the trouble that was heading his way. But the retribution when it came was accidental: days after the fire an important component broke on Garvey's printing press. The only business that could cast a replacement was owned by United Fruit, which had lately borne the brunt of the *Nation's* criticism. The printing press would not be fixed and ceased to turn. Under the heading, 'A "National" Disaster, RIP', the rival paper barely contained its grief over the news that Garvey's flysheet 'has now retired into private life'. Marcus Garvey, noting the valuable lessons he had drawn from Limón, had little option but to get out of town. The *Limón Times* was not so generous in its assessment of a young man 'seeking prominence . . . [who] must be first humbled before he can be exalted'.[43]

Itinerant Jamaicans were the staple of much of Central America's temporary workforce. Over the next few months Garvey garnered something of an unsentimental education as he picked up enough casual work to make his way through Panama, Honduras, Ecuador, Colombia and Venezuela.[44] His experience of life in the zone of the Panama Canal was both disturbing and exhilarating. Over thirty years in the making, in fits and starts, and still three years from completion, the Panama Canal was an explosive crucible of ambitious men, dangerous materials, promissory notes of wealth and blatant exploitation. First in Bocas del Toro and later Colón (where he started another paper, *La Presna*), Garvey charted the fortunes of men flung together in this Creole culture: the oppressive humidity and heat which meant that nothing was ever dry; the gangs of labourers who cleared landslides; the porters who balanced dynamite boxes on their heads; explosions that went wrong; the stench of the malaria-infested hospital wards; and the fights over petty insults and the favours of prostitutes.

British West Indians had been travelling to Panama since the 1850s, first to construct the railroads, then to begin work on the initial French efforts to carve out the great canal. As communities were established and the cost of migration rose the ranks of construction labourers had been swelled by professionals and craftsmen. Latterly, during the American construction from 1904 onwards, another great wave of Jamaicans had gone over. Back home these adventurers were famed as Colón Men, who had braved the high seas, disease and discomfort and returned with renewed confidence, with gold in their teeth, gold rings on every finger, gold-capped walking sticks, and waistcoats adorned with gold watches and chains (though, it was said, if you stopped such a man in the street and asked him the time, he'd look to the sun). Every Jamaican village boasted a glamorous Colón Man and even those who spurned ostentation were still noted for their smart tweed suits, the snap of a North American twang on their lips, and the swagger in their step. The burgeoning dandy in Marcus Garvey would not have been out of place in such company. But there was a catch. Once in Panama, to qualify for his Yankee dollar the Caribbean worker entered into a Mephistophelean pact. USA contractors implemented 'Jim Crow' standards of segregation and introduced a two-tier system of payment: white workers benefited from gold roll, while blacks had to settle for silver. The compromise to his pride, together with the debilitating assault of bacterial infections on his asthmatic lungs, reduced Garvey to a fever and forced his return to Kingston at the end of 1911.[45]

It was not an opportune time to be returning to the island. The largesse of the Colón men was apparent but even their remittance made little dint on the wealth of the country: poverty and desperation were the only growth areas. And if signs were needed that things were getting worse, one only had to look to the brutality of the nationwide strike that led to the first inadvertent encounter between the recovering time-keeper and Governor Olivier. On 26 February 1912 the capital, Kingston, erupted into violence during protests over a hike in tramcar fares. Governor Olivier decided to leave his official residence to assess for himself reports of the riot. He stopped outside a bar where two policemen were trapped by rioters, and instead of heeding his command to disperse, the rioters turned and started to hurl debris and stones at the Governor who was struck on the head with a brick. Luckily for Governor Olivier, the recent returnee Marcus Garvey, now recovered from his fever, happened to be in the vicinity. Decades later, Garvey reminisced with reporters from the Daily Gleaner that 'he was an eyewitness, and was one of the two men – Mr Elliot the photographer being the other – who shielded the Governor on the day from attack'.[46]

Unusually, given Garvey's tendency to overstate his achievements, he doesn't seem to have dined out too heavily on the anecdote at the time. There would have been little point as he was soon planning on company of a very different kind of class and race of person.

When he'd saved enough money for another berth, Garvey began making preparations for a further expedition. This time he'd test his mettle in a more temperate climate. Three weeks later the steamship would dock in the place which every British West Indian considered the cradle of civilisation: England.

2

ALMOST AN ENGLISHMAN

I've a longin' in me dept's of heart dat I can conquer not
'Tis a wish dat I've been havin' from since I could form a t'o't
'Tis to sail athwart the ocean an' to hear the billows roar
When dem ride aroun' de steamer, when dem beat on England's
 shore

          Claude McKay, 'Old England'

AFTER seventeen days at sea, Garvey arrived in London in the spring of 1912. The record of his passage to England has not been found but the cheapest route would have been aboard one of the bi-weekly Elder Dempster banana boats that set out from Jamaica with a crew of just under 60, a maximum of 12 passengers and 50,000 bunches of bananas.

 After the experience of discrimination – which he characterised as the 'stumbling block [of] "You are black"' – together with the conse-quent limitations imposed on Caribbean people that he witnessed in Panama and Costa Rica, Garvey had set out for Europe 'to find out if it was different there'.[1] Like the few young men and women who'd ventured from the colonies, he was greatly excited about being in the metropolis, at the heart of empire. For someone of Garvey's educa-tional and social background, Jamaica's rigid society provided only limited opportunities; Jamaica was somewhere you left. Garvey never spoke of any apprehension about what he was embarking on, but in many respects he was a pioneer. England for the vast majority of its imperial subjects was an abstraction. Jamaica's newspapers often repro-duced articles from the English papers on some of the wondrous but inconceivable tales of the daily working of the mother country; peppered with gorgeous accounts of society weddings and fashion tips for Derby day or the Ascot races. Sometimes, the *Gleaner* would print lively exchanges between readers in its letters pages on events taking place in London like the 'Universal Races Congress' of 1911 as pertaining to Jamaica's Creole culture. But apart from the mariners' tales of ordinary Jamaicans who traversed the Atlantic on the Elder Dempster Line, there had only been occasional celebrated news stories in the island's papers about Jamaicans who had visited England. The ten members of the Kingston Choral Union who toured Britain in 1906 met with much acclaim. Their triumphs, typified by the *Fruit Trader's Journal*'s appreciation of 'their quaint enunciation and strict attention to light and shade', were followed gleefully by readers of the *Gleaner* and the *Jamaican Times* back home.

In an interview with the *Times*, the bassist Carlton Bryan lauded his hosts who, thank God, did not have 'the American colour prejudice. It does not matter in England if a man is black, white, blue, green or yellow.'[2] Jamaican readers of the *Times* had even purchased souvenir posters of the troupe, photographed in studied dignity: the bow-tied men in evening suits and the women in long and frilly white gowns. But a reader could spend a lifetime scouring the archives of the *Gleaner* and still not find news of a Jamaican printer ever being welcomed or established in England. That, though, is not what Garvey had in mind. In many respects, he saw his time in England as an opportunity to complete his informal education. Garvey had no university education: there was no university in the West Indies, and though it would have been unlikely he'd be able to afford a college place in London, at least he might benefit from exposure to its great libraries and the lectures of men and women on the public circuit. Garvey harboured a burgeoning thought that public speaking might be the key to his future life. In any case, he was determined to find his place in the world; and the centre of the world, for all British colonials, was London. 'Viewing the Mother Country with an adoring eye,' wrote Eric Walrond (a future associate of Garvey), 'the Negro in the British overseas colonies is obviously at the mercy of a rainbow ... This deception, common to the virgin gaze of African and West Indian alike, is partly a case of "distance lends enchantment," partly a by-product of the black man's extraordinary loyalty to the Crown.'[3]

Marcus Garvey's adoring eye yearned for such wonders that his compatriot Claude McKay had anticipated in his dialect poem, 'Old England', and to see 'de ancient chair where England's kings deir crowns put on'. Number 176 Borough High Street, south of the river, was close enough and renting a room there was just about affordable. Garvey was as delighted as Carlton Bryan with his first impressions: 'When we visited England,' he would later write imperiously of his time in London, 'we found a different state of affairs. We of ourselves, who are not coloured but black, found no difficulty in securing lodgings.'⁴ Any doubts about how far this black, country boy from St Ann's Bay had come were dispelled by the peels from the bells of Big Ben, a brisk walk away over Vauxhall Bridge.

To obtain a gallery pass to the House of Commons one simply needed to queue. David Lloyd George was the British politician whom Garvey most admired. As well as great parliamentary speeches, he seems to have been just as much enamoured of the traditions and symbols of power invested in the House of Commons and Lords. The pomp and ceremony, robes and pageantry appealed to him. Joel A. Rogers, a Jamaican who made a study of his compatriot in later life, believed that Garvey was 'never able to throw off the impression British folderol and glitter had made on him in his childhood'.⁵ When Lloyd George was not on the floor, the House was in recess, or the debates proved lacklustre, the twenty-five-year-old admirer of the cut and thrust of a good argument might soon wend his way to Hyde Park, drawn by the impassioned and irreverent opinions at Speakers' Corner, that were not too far removed from the roiling arguments outside the rum shops of Kingston. To the uninitiated, this people's parliament would appear the site of a dizzying array of competing voices, both toxic and benevolent: Latvian anarchists, millennial doom-peddlers, Sinn Feiners, stalwarts of anti-imperialism, crusading protectors of aboriginal peoples, eugenicists and suffragettes; but not many, if any, black notables. Commandeering a soapbox, Garvey energetically made his first faltering attempts at extempore public speaking, pitting himself against the regulars, vying for the attention of the curious, the committed and the cynics who gathered in great numbers each Sunday.

Colour was his unique calling card; British citizens were largely ignorant about life in the outposts of empire. There were so few black people in England that they were considered exotic. As the London-based Sierra Leonean humorist A. B. C. Merriman-Labor wittily observed of Edwardian Britain, 'credulous people . . . believe that every Negro with a decent overcoat and a clean collar is an African prince'.⁶ There were some outstanding black men and women in London. The composer Samuel Coleridge-Taylor, fêted for his recent operatic success, *The Song of Hiawatha*; John Richard Archer, soon to be appointed Mayor of Battersea; and the journalist and proprietor, Dusé Mohamed Ali, were perhaps the most prominent. But they constituted tiny specks on the cultural landscape. That such men thrived was not a testament to the liberal cosmopolitanism of early twentieth-century Britain but rather confirmation of a long-standing curiosity about exotic and noble Negroes who confounded the popular conception of Blacks as infantile. If the masses at Speakers' Corner were to close their eyes as Garvey spoke, they might have imagined themselves in the presence of almost a gentleman – an English gentleman no less. But, as yet, there was little profit in it for a young Jamaican mimic who carried no letters of introduction to the traditional patrons of social engineering who might have been able to help.

There were only a few thousand black people living and working in London in 1912. According to David Killingray, census returns for 1911 suggested that 4,540 'Africans' were estimated to be living in the UK, with West Indians included amongst the 'Africans'. The population of London was more than 4 million (4,521,685) at the time. There was no concentration of black people; they were scattered around the capital. The *African Times and Orient Review* was especially keen to capture the success stories, like that of the two Nigerian brothers, Adeyemo and Olayimka Alakija who, along with Debeshin Folarin, were called to the bar in 1913. From his office in Manhattan, the black American editor, William Du Bois, also monitored stories that he characterised as credits and deficits to the race. In the September edition of the *Crisis* (a magazine providing a record of the darker races) for 1912 Du Bois was delighted to inform readers that '[Clement] Jackson, a colored student at Oxford University, won the 1,500 metre race at the Olympic games. The credit for this victory goes to England and the Negro race has scarcely been mentioned.' In later editions of the magazine, Du Bois also pointed to the hypocrisy at large in English society. The story of the coloured physician refused an appointment in Camberwell on the grounds that 'the fastidious poor would refuse to be attended by a Negro', particularly enraged Du Bois. However, the majority of black people in London were not professionals. They were labourers. On 26 November 1903, the *Anglo-African Argus* cited the example of railway engineers and blacksmiths amongst the workers who had made their way to England. But there were also dockers, nannies, entertainers and sometimes impersonators. A man called Isaac Brown caused a brief sensation when he was arrested and convicted of impersonating the Jamaican military hero, Sergeant William James Gordon, who had been awarded the Victoria Cross in 1892.[7] Con-men like Isaac Brown, though, were as likely to share the tabloid headlines with eccentrics like the amateur Afro-Guyanese inventor, Mr Williams, who on the money he made from the sale of his motorised horse was able to relocate to the more fashionable Marylebone High Street.

The metropolis was a bewildering place to navigate, and the prospects for paid work among London's black population was even bleaker than for the white working class. Within a couple of months Garvey was reduced to applying for assistance from the Colonial Office. Pride or luck seems to have intervened, though, because eventually Garvey found piecemeal work at London's dockyards, where black labourers, who were prepared to accept less than the East End dockers, were blamed for driving down wages.[8] There the enigma of Garvey's arrival was compounded by the sight of these African and Caribbean merchant seamen who, worryingly, having given up on their own adventures, stuck close to the Thames and the harbours of Liverpool, Bristol and Cardiff, on constant lookout for berths on ships back home.

It was one of these brother seamen who tipped off Garvey about the intriguing prospect of alternative employment at the newly launched *African Times and Orient Review*. The paper was run by the Egyptian-born Dusé Mohamed Ali, a man of many talents who was a returning columnist on the Fabian journal, *New Age*, as well as a former theatrical impresario, renowned for his productions of *Othello* and *The Merchant of Venice*. The year before Garvey's arrival, Dusé Mohamed Ali had forsworn the stage and embarked on yet another transformation, lending his support and organisational skills to a unique experiment in inter-racial cooperation – the Universal Races Congress which met in London on 26 July 1911. *The Times* reported approvingly on the elitist international gathering of 300 delegates that brought together such eminent scholars as the African-American editor of *Crisis* magazine, W. E. B. Du Bois, the ethnographer Sir Harry Johnston of the Royal Geographical Society, and Sir Sydney Olivier, the Governor of Jamaica. There were papers presented on a range of subjects from 'the hierarchical classification of the races' and 'the benefits of mixed marriages'. Sydney Olivier, warming to a subject dear to his Fabian heart, expressed the view that mixed marriages and their mulatto offspring were indispensable to the development of the West Indies because it 'saves the community from any cleavage between black and white and helps form an organic whole'.[9] *The Times* in London devoted considerable attention to the debates at the Universal Races Congress. But there were some critics, recalled Du Bois, who mockingly 'professed to think it had something to do with horse-racing'.[10] Discussions on racial matters were of minor interest in unenlightened Edwardian Britain. But speaking at a luncheon held at the Lyceum Club the month before, the noble-headed Du Bois had been gratified by the quiet applause of the calibre of guest befitting the high purpose of the forthcoming congress. They included 'a bishop and two countesses; several knights and ladies and men like Maurice Hewlett and Sir Harry Johnston'.[11] Buoyed by the dignity conferred upon it, Du Bois had addressed the opening of the congress, in the great hall of the University of London, and delivered his 'A Hymn to the Peoples', especially composed for the occasion. It ended with:

> Save us, World-Spirit, from our lesser selves!
> Grant us that war and hatred cease,
> Reveal our souls in every race and hue!
> Help us, O Human God, in this Thy Truce
> To Make Humanity divine![12]

Such sentiments were to inspire Dusé Mohamed Ali later that same year when he turned his considerable energies to print journalism with the *Review*. The Colonial Office took a dim view of the whole enterprise, marking Ali down as 'a rather doubtful character whose paper was *suspect*, being inclined to the Ethiopian movement and in touch with undesirable elements in India and Egypt'.[13] His love for his father's homeland was evident in a 300-page history of Egypt that Dusé Mohamed Ali had recently published. The journey to its publication was strange and unexpected. The former president of the USA, Theodore Roosevelt, should, in no small way, have been included in the credits and acknowledgements. On a much publicised visit to the UK in 1910, Roosevelt stepped into the increasingly rancorous debate on the Egyptian agitation for home rule. Roosevelt had encouraged his British hosts to take any means necessary to suppress those 'uncivilised Egyptians' who were advocating a kind of self-government in Cairo which he considered 'a noxious farce'.[14] Ali had first tried to shrug off the comments, but had then become extremely vexed; and one day, as he fumed in the offices of the *New Age*'s editor, A. R. Orage had put it to him that writing a history of Egypt would serve as a vengeful corrective to the former president's obnoxious remarks.

In the Land of the Pharaohs was the result. With its emphasis on earlier civilisations, Ali's book was craftily conceived to redress the belief in oriental inferiority – then widely held in Britain. That he was a genuine Egyptian lent the book added gravitas and validity, and with it Dusé Mohamed achieved national and international fame. The book had been cheered to the rafters by the informal club of Pan-Africanists in London and had silenced peddlers of Rudyard Kipling's 'The White Man's Burden' view of history. But the routing of his enemies was soon reversed. Though well received at first, *In the Land of the Pharaohs* went on to scandalise literary London when the scale of its unattributed reliance on the work of Arab scholars such as Wilfred Blunt was revealed. The respectful applause of respected Englishmen came to an abrupt end, but the disgrace of plagiarism did not dint his reputation amongst the British colonial subjects throughout the empire. In the space of a year, the redoubtable Dusé Mohamed Ali had apologised, shrugged off further criticism, and rebuilt his acerbic reputation as an unrepentant chronicler of the era in the *African Times and Orient Review*.

In its inaugural edition, Ali had called for contributions from the 'young and budding Wilmot Blydens, Frederick Douglasses and Paul Laurence Dunbars' (all notable black writers). The advert appeared tailor-made for the young Garvey, and in early 1913, after laying siege to its offices at 158 Fleet Street, he was taken on, not yet as a writer, but as a messenger and handyman.

Less than a year old, the *Review* had quickly found its voice in the certainty of its cause, summarised by the editor, Dusé Mohamed Ali, as a 'monthly devoted to the interests of the coloured races of the world'. The first volume proclaimed that 'the recent Universal Races Congress, convened in the Metropolis of the Anglo-Saxon world, clearly demonstrated that there was ample need for a Pan-Oriental Pan-African journal at the seat of the British Empire, which would lay the aims, desires and intentions of the black, brown, and yellow races at the throne of Caesar'.[15]

The paper's continued advocacy of Egyptian home rule and Ethiopianism (the generic term for the promotion of a Negro ethical ideal and African autonomy) caused greater irritation as the European imperial powers and therefore, by extension, their colonial possessions, flitted and fidgeted towards the cataclysmic conflict that was just a year away from engulfing the continent. In the lead-up to the Great War there was a reduced appetite for tolerance. Rumours abounded of secret agents; streets, parlours and parliament crackled with excited talk of the need for an alien register. Dusé Mohamed, despite his protests, was forced to comply. He presented himself at Brixton police station where he was registered as an Ottoman alien. The authorities doubted his origins and kept him under surveillance. Nonetheless, the *Review* did not fight shy of polemic and on a bad day its editor would be upgraded by British colonial officials from 'suspect' to 'of doubtful loyalty' – a euphemistic assessment which, stripped of its diplomatic language, could be translated as 'of borderline treachery'. Even so, Ali escaped official censure and although his security file remained open, it was never acted upon.[16]

More than through a reading of the pages of the *Review*, the reputation that clung to him was owed to his writing in the *New Age*. Ali had cut his teeth on the Fabian journal. The editor, A. R. Orage, had encouraged – indeed was quietly thrilled by – Ali's righteous smiting of the promulgators of cant and hypocrisy in perfidious Albion. For example, he singled out those concerned Englishmen who, whilst deploring the growing number of incidents in London of 'marital and sexual relationships between white women and "half-civilised" oriental men', went on to slake their thirst for the mysterious orient 'in brothels in Eastern seaports'.[17] Time and again in the *New Age*, Dusé spelt out the case for the prosecution in the trial of British imperialism. And yet it is evident that he courted, and was flattered by, the attention of aristocratic acquaintances who 'belonged to the good old days when a man of breeding was respected in England – and there was no colour bar'. And therein lay the rub, because there were some among those men of breeding who, having smelt the smoke in his plagiarism, began to look for the fire. Surely a gentleman would never have committed such a heinous act as putting forward the scholarship of another as the work of his own. Except for the amateur aristocratic sleuth, Ali's peripatetic life was hard to follow and the trail of his genealogy soon ran cold.

Dusé Mohamed Ali maintained that he was the son of an officer in the Egyptian army killed in the trenches of Tel-el-Kebir during the land invasion that followed Britain's naval bombardment of Alexandria in

1882. Much of Dusé's education had been in England. Nonetheless, what aroused the suspicions of his critics was his inability to string two sentences of Arabic together. He claimed to have forgotten it through lack of use, but as one sceptic said of his inability to even recite the Muslim declaration of faith, it was rather like 'a Catholic being unable to recite the "Hail Mary"'.[18]

His association with the raffish 'profession' of the stage only confirmed their doubts about him. In the decades before, Dusé Mohamed Ali had trodden the boards of theatres from Glasgow to London, and had even managed his own company in Hull. Although he was undeniably black, critics sneered that this was only conveniently so – on closer inspection, you might get a whiff of the burnt cork and greasepaint of the minstrel on his skin – and that of course the fez (which rarely left his head) was more of a stage prop than a badge of authenticity. For Garvey though, Ali was the real thing: the embodiment of culture and commerce. He looked on in admiration as his employer managed the extraordinary trick of irritating the authorities with his thinly veiled attacks and, at the same time, securing patronage from senior establishment figures like Lord Cromer.

That the *Review* boasted contributions from the A-list of intellectual and public life was largely down to a sly process of literary entrapment. Mohamed Ali had simply written to the elite of the British establishment – canvassing their opinion about whether such a literary venture 'operated by coloured people could succeed in promoting goodwill between Orient and Occident'[19] and then published their responses in the first edition. In this way the editor could justifiably claim the Countess of Warwick and Sir Sydney Olivier among the writers of the *Review*. Indeed, Dusé Mohamed Ali never overlooked an opportunity for promotion, even enlisting the support of the recently deceased Samuel Coleridge-Taylor: the *Review*'s obituary of the composer carefully included a letter from him praising the fledgling paper a little while before his death.[20]

Garvey too was learning how to maximise every possibility. He had few leads or contacts but he made sure to track them down. Sir Sydney Olivier's tenure as Governor of Jamaica had come to an end in January 1913, and he had taken up a new post as secretary of the Board of Agriculture in England. No record has been found of their meeting (though Garvey would later brief journalists back in Jamaica), but the road to Olivier inevitably continued on to politicians who had already shown an interest in how the colonies in the British West Indies were run. Men such as Lord Balfour of Burleigh and the Labour politician, Joseph Pointer, were successfully courted and added to his book of contacts. Those meetings did not translate into tangible or immediately beneficial results but, in a small way, Garvey believed that he was taking steps towards establishing, if only in his own mind, a sense of himself as a public personality.

After almost a year of fetching and carrying down at the docks, Garvey had been taken on by Dusé Mohamed Ali, and he could sense his luck was changing. It was an extraordinary piece of good fortune to have arrived at the birth of one of the most exciting journals to come out of London in decades. In Dusé Mohamed Ali, he was to find a black man who, in doing something for the race whilst advancing his own self-interest, espoused a philosophy that the younger man had not yet articulated but most heartily felt. If under Alfred 'Cap' Burrowes Garvey had learnt the practical skills of printing from a master, then his time at the Review would serve as another kind of apprenticeship: a close study of Ali would reveal the secrets of a master propagandist.

Recalling his days at the Review, Garvey later glossed over his humble status and drew attention to the time when, after a few months of relentless lobbying, he managed to badger his way to a journalistic commission and moved temporarily from the back room to the freelance desks. In the October 1913 issue, he wrote a historical essay, 'The British West Indies in the Mirror of Civilisation', which was an unflattering account of European excess and rapacious greed in the Caribbean. Focusing on Jamaica, Garvey voiced a resentment of the way in which, in the outpost of civilisation of the British Empire, colour was an impediment to advancement. A system by which the much-coveted jobs in the civil service had previously been awarded on the strength of an examination, had been abandoned by the time Marcus Garvey reached adulthood. In open competition black youths excelled and had filled every position, whilst their white compatriots trailed behind. Within a few years the government was persuaded 'to abolish the competitive system and fill vacancies by nomination, and by this means kept out the black youths. The service has long been recruiting from an inferior class of sycophantic weaklings whose brains are exhausted by dissipation and vice before they reach the age of thirty-five.' Nonetheless, in a tone of youthful sobriety, Garvey prophesied a turning point in history when 'the people of [the West Indies] will be the instruments of uniting a scattered race who, before the close of many centuries, will found an Empire on which the sun shall shine as ceaselessly as it shines on the Empire of the North today'.[21]

Praise for his essay came from as far as the USA, where the black scholar William Ferris (the author of *The African Abroad*) held it up as 'a powerful and telling summing up of the History of the West Indies'.[22] That kind of dialogue between black populations in the diaspora was just the kind of development that Dusé Mohamed Ali had hoped for. Though copies of the journal were shipped to black conurbations in the USA like Harlem, and a handful of cities on the African continent, the majority of its readers were still to be found in Britain.

At twenty-six, Marcus Garvey was twenty years Ali's junior. In an audit of his achievements to date, he could only count on having lived a fraction of the life of his latest mentor. The *Review* served as a hub for black intellectual life. The trainee journalist took his place in the line of colonial admirers who thronged the offices at Fleet Street, and over whom Dusé Mohamed cast a long shadow. Essays by black leaders and thinkers such as the American educationalist, Booker T. Washington, and the Liberian scholar, Edward Blyden, jostled for space with satirical cartoons. Also included were reviews of recitals by African chamber musicians in London and the poems of at least one Indian poet, Sarojini Naidu, who was associated with Yeats's 'Monday Evening Circle'.[23] For students of the black condition – and Garvey was beginning to see himself in this way – the *African Times and Orient Review* was regarded as a manual of black malaise and a road map for the redemption of the race.

Wages at the *Review* were modest but kudos made up for some of the shortfall. Garvey prided himself on his proximity to Dusé and the black intellectuals who swung though the doors at 158 Fleet Street. Never mind that others mocked Dusé Mohamed as 'the pushing journalist', he congratulated himself on his association with the white ruling class. Throughout 1913 Marcus Garvey hung around the offices of the *Review* but he had no entrée yet into the circles in which Dusé Mohamed Ali moved. Only a man fooled by his fictive persona would fail to glean that, measured alongside the great Dusé Mohamed, the young Jamaican was a mere minion. In between fetching and carrying for Dusé Mohamed Ali, Garvey spent all of his free time striving to make up for the shortcomings of his formal education. Despite a later fondness for being photographed in academic robes, complete with mortar board, Garvey had little hope of the finances needed to obtain a degree. He did, however, attend lessons in law at Birkbeck College, founded in 1823 as the London Mechanics Institute and predicated on the needs of working-class students without formal qualifications. The crest on the college arms – a lamp and owl alongside its motto, *In nocte consiliem* ('Study by night') – recognised that its undergraduates, like the newly registered Jamaican, could only afford to study part-time. And Garvey just about managed to scrape together enough for some evening classes. With some pride and justification, he now identified himself as a student and journalist.

Ali proved only a fleeting mentor to Garvey who took rather less note of his overblown literary style. He was more intrigued by Ali's ambitious business schemes, which included the setting up of an independent bank in Britain's West African possessions to circumvent trade barriers erected by European competitors; and numerous import–export dealings. Invariably, they attracted more derision than serious consideration, as each project failed to win the blessing of the Colonial Office – without which they could not proceed. Many of these business ventures rode on the back of the *African Times and Orient Review* through which he sought potential partners but Dusé Mohamed Ali was ultimately a venture capitalist without the capital. Later, in 1921, he left England for America, making his way to Harlem where he was reintroduced to Garvey by a mutual friend, the veteran African-American journalist, John E. Bruce. Though Ali smarted somewhat at his former pupil's success, he was humble enough to take up a column on Garvey's own paper, the *Negro World*.

For now though, it was Garvey who had cause to be grateful. With the security of a small but regular income from his work as a handyman, he prepared to set off on a grand tour of European capitals. At this point, his sister Indiana had followed him to England.[24] Garvey had written to her employer, George Judah, in Kingston, Jamaica, requesting that Indiana be allowed to accompany his family on a visit to England. She sailed from Jamaica with the Judah family on board the *Barranca* and docked at Avonmouth in August 1912. Indiana was employed in a job best described as a hybrid of domestic servant and companion to the children. Indiana failed to thrive in England. Though she was a simple and retiring woman, in London she was conspicuous. Sitting alone amongst a sea of white faces in the local church, she suffered quietly in her discomfort; after the service, she attracted the unsubtle attention of the congregation who were delighted with the opportunity she presented to test their pseudo-scientific racial theories. At the end of one service, 'the minister's daughter asked where she had hidden her tail!'[25]

Her brother, by contrast, courted attention. A tour of the capitals of Europe would be his next venture. Marcus Garvey settled his account at his lodgings in south London and arranged for his correspondence to be forwarded, care of his sister at 14 Durley Road, Stamford Hill.

One of his first journeys was on board the overnight train to Scotland where he stayed at least one night at the Cecil Hotel in Glasgow. On 10 December 1913, Garvey wrote excitedly to Thaddeus McCormack back in Smith Village, Kingston, Jamaica that the next time he heard from him, Garvey would be in Paris. Monte Carlo, Boulogne and Madrid were also on the itinerary. On mainland Europe, Garvey ticked off the great architectural wonders and soon fell in with some travelling missionaries. Not quite believing his good fortune, he was quietly pleased with the impression he seemed to make along the way. 'I have seen wonders,' he wrote enthusiastically to McCormack, 'at some places . . . I have been the only black man seen for a good time . . . some of the tourists are wondering how a black man can travel about so much, some take me for an African millionaire.'[26] In subsequent letters, Garvey cited his popularity amongst his aristocratic lady fellow travellers and playfully speculated that he might one day return to Jamaica with a white heiress on his arm. Two months later, it was apparent that it wasn't just Europe's great architectural sites that caught the young man's attention. On 2 March 1914, Marcus Garvey confided bashfully to Alfred 'Cap' Burrowes, 'I am engaged to a Spanish–Irish heiress whom I had the pleasure of meeting on the Continent.'

Providence had waved her magical wand, and an heiress had materialised. He had mused on the fantasy of a union with just such a creature. Remarkably, it now seemed a distinct possibility. It was a spectacular volte-face. Love had triumphed over his often stated and violently held belief that any union between blacks and whites was repugnant. 'It is somewhat destructive of my principle,' he conceded, 'yet I hardly think I can change my mind in marrying her.'[27] There had been marriages between black men and white women but they were rare in the extreme and, when subject to public scrutiny, were considered abhorrent. Stranded African seamen in Liverpool, whose romantic attentiveness was preferred to the drunken neglect of their white counterparts, had made lives and homes with local women without much censure. But just a few years earlier, polite Edwardian society had been scandalised by the engagement of an African prince, Peter Lobengula, to Kitty Jewell. Prince Lobengula was purported to be the son of the Matabele Chief, but his inability to speak the Ndebele language was evidence enough, for some, of his fakery. His credentials were not enhanced by his day job, at the centre of *Savage South Africa*, a bizarre show performed at Earl's Court, which twice a day reenacted scenes from African life.

The *Evening News* just about summed up tabloid opinion on romance between Kitty and Peter when it wrote, 'There is something inexpressibly disgusting in the idea of the mating of a white girl and a dusky savage.' It was not a propitious time to be breaking with convention.[28]

Back in London, the good times were quickly coming to an end. Although he had been employed for the better part of a year, further work for the *African Times and Orient Review* failed to materialise. Dusé Mohamed Ali complained that he was lazy. It seems that Garvey's estimation of himself (a journalist with a favourably reviewed essay) ran counter to the practical demands of his actual job description of messenger and handyman – albeit one who'd been released temporarily from such chores.

Marcus Garvey found himself close to destitution. His fortunes plunged even further when he was robbed of the little money that would have carried him over in lean times. Garvey's dilemma was not atypical of young colonial subjects without means who had come to England. On 18 April 1913, Dusé Mohamed Ali had helped the Anti-Slavery and Aborigines' Protection Society to organise a conference to look into ways of helping young Africans in London. The conference, convened at the Westminster Palace Hotel, resolved that an African Club be established to provide both a physical shelter and a psychological shield from 'harmful influences'. The resolution was circulated widely amongst sympathetic MPs and also sent to the Colonial Office for its perusal.[29] No such provisions were yet in place by the middle of 1914, and Garvey was reluctant to inform the heiress of his impoverished condition.

When he was eventually forced to seek financial help, he knew which charitable organisation to approach. To the cynic, Garvey's account of being robbed (he does not seem to have been injured) might have appeared convenient and apocryphal, but Travers Buxton of the Anti-Slavery and Aborigines' Protection Society was sympathetic. The society composed a letter to the Colonial Office 'to enable him [Garvey] to raise his passage money [to Jamaica] and pay off a few debts . . . He is willing in part to work his passage back.' Travers Buxton offered to put up a guinea if the same (amount) might be matched by the Colonial Office.[30] But the Colonial Office was not inclined to rescue adventurers who had turned into supplicants. To do otherwise would be to establish a precedent that would be cited by the very next colonial subject who was brave or foolish enough to gamble on journeying to the metropolis. Local parishes had a duty of care towards citizens who found themselves down on their luck in other cities; an unemployed Liverpudlian in London was encouraged to return to Liverpool. But relief was more problematic for the luckless colonial who found himself or herself without work abroad. When approached, officials pointedly directed applicants to the workhouse, although women, who found themselves amongst the 'distressed natives', were treated with greater compassion. Towards the end of 1910, the Colonial Office did lend a helping hand to the appropriately named Mrs E. Virtue and her daughter from Liverpool, paying half their fare on an Elder Dempster steamship bound for Jamaica.[31]

Marcus Garvey's correspondence was still being delivered to Stamford Hill but he could not count on charity from his older sister. Though she might consider herself a governess, Indiana was paid the meagre wages of a domestic servant. She too found herself trapped in London, earning enough to survive but insufficient to return to Jamaica. In her straitened circumstances, she would soon be following hard on the heels of her brother, through the doors of the Colonial Office, in a desperate search for patronage and funds towards her own repatriation.

Whilst awaiting a more favourable response, Garvey mustered one last effort to raise funds; he'd obviously discovered the freelancer's skill of recycling old material because most of the content from the *African Times and Orient Review* article later appeared in the *Tourist*, albeit a distilled and diluted version, with much of the polemic softened. Swallowing hard, Garvey had bartered awkward principles against the practical need to pay for his food and lodgings – his article for the *Tourist*, euphemistically entitled 'The Evolution of Latter Day Slaves:

Jamaica, A Country Of Black and White', reads in part like a conflicted (smiling through gritted teeth) but ultimately inoffensive tourist advert for the island where 'white Americans have come to realise that all negroes are not pugnacious and vicious, for when they go over to Jamaica to spend their winter holidays they befriend the black natives just the same as they do with people of their own race'.[32] But he ended with a bitter note of remembrance: 'Jamaica of the present time is partly forgetful of the past. Although the 1st of August each year is observed as Emancipation Day . . . "It's a holiday, and we must get merry," is the only thought that is given to that historic day when their forefathers' shackles fell off and liberty was proclaimed.' At the beginning of the nineteenth century, the *Tourist* had been instrumental in disseminating abolitionist sentiment throughout Britain; in part Garvey's essay idealised race relations in Jamaica, and would have left its British readers, as perhaps intended, with the self-satisfying thought that Jamaican harmony was the fruit of their endeavour.

Shuffling uncomfortably between the Anti-Slavery and Aborigines' Protection Society and the Colonial Office, Garvey – like his father before him – took refuge in the safe, unjudgmental world of books. Earlier, Dusé Mohamed Ali had vouched for his employee's honesty and integrity in his request for a reader's pass to the British Museum. In support of his application, Garvey had cited a need to examine the works of the Liberian scholar, Edward Wilmot Blyden. The museum, whilst not fully granting his wish, offered the consolation of a month-long ticket. Nonetheless, his reverence for a house of knowledge would never be greater. Clutching his temporary pass, Garvey set up camp in the great domed library and tenderly turned the pages of black history texts and other wondrous manuscripts therein. He was an explorer on the threshold of a great discovery and would not be disappointed. It was during this period that he discovered the book that would prove the most influential on his life: *Up from Slavery* by Booker T. Washington. 'I read *Up from Slavery*,' Garvey was later to write, 'and then my doom – if I may so call it – of being a race leader dawned on me.'[33] He prepared to leave London, boarding the SS *Trent* on 17 June 1914. The crew and passenger list records that he was only one of three third-class passengers. Over the next three weeks Garvey would have plenty of time and little distraction to reflect on which great expectations had been met in England and what might yet be met in Jamaica.

In his two years abroad, in London and the other European capitals, Garvey's thinking had undergone a profound shift. His passport identified him as journalist and student, but on the Continent he had been mistaken for an African prince. The cycle of fake African princes was yet to be played out in Europe and America, but Garvey had not set out to defraud anybody. The error gave testament to the fact that the black man was both visible and invisible. Through Caucasian eyes the Negro could not be confidently read: the peasant might just as well be a prince.

In Europe, Garvey had made his way, haltingly, through a world that was foreign to him. In Jamaica he would be returning to familiar territory, but he would not be bound by its small-mindedness and the lowly expectations of the Negro; he had advanced into a 'higher state of enlightenment'. As the SS *Trent* steamed across the Atlantic, he began to compose and order his thoughts, and sketch out arguments that would form the basis of essays and letters once he'd reestablished himself back home. The draft of the pamphlet 'A Talk with Afro-West Indians', which appealed to his compatriots to shake themselves from their slumber, had all the fire and urgency of the evangelist, worthy of Blyden, Du Bois, Booker T. Washington and all the other champions of the race that he had studied in London:

> Sons and daughters of Africa, I say to you arise, take on the toga of race pride, and throw off the brand of ignominy which has kept you back for so many centuries. Dash asunder the petty prejudices within your own fold; set at defiance the designation of 'nigger' uttered even by yourselves, and be a Negro in the light of the Pharaohs of Egypt, Simons of Cyrene, Hannibals of Carthage, L'Ouvertures and Dessalines of Hayti . . . Blydens of Liberia . . . and Douglasses and Du Boises of America, who have made, and are making history for the race, though depreciated and in many cases unwritten.[34]

As yet, the name 'Marcus Garvey' did not figure on that list of black heroes. But he reflected, now, that perhaps it soon would. England had sharpened Garvey's belief in his own destiny, and heightened his sense of racial awareness. As he was soon to write, Europe was a place where 'the Negro is identified by his colour and his hair, so it is useless for any pompous man of colour to think because his skin is a little paler than that of his brother that he is not also a Negro. Once the African blood courses through the veins you belong to "the company of Negroes".' Garvey had come to a broad understanding of himself and reached an irrevocable conclusion: he had decided to hitch himself to the Negro race. The intent was clear and the details would soon be worked out.

3

IN THE COMPANY OF NEGROES

In Jamaica, indeed, they talk of one Negro as a man of parts and learning; but 'tis likely he is admired for slender accomplishment, like a parrot who speaks a few words plainly.
David Hume, 'Essay on National Characters', 1758

SAILING back to Jamaica in 1914, Garvey fell in with the other two third-class passengers, a Caribbean missionary returning from Basutoland and his Basuto wife.[1] Marcus Garvey was shocked by the missionary's description of life there. When he reflected on the missionary's account of the 'horrible and pitiable' abuse of Africans, Garvey was so moved that he seems to have undergone an epiphany. 'Where is the black man's government?' Garvey asked himself. 'Where is his President, his country, his ambassador and his army . . . ? I could not find them.' Capturing the feverish urgency of the time, Garvey later wrote that his brain was afire, that he had a vision of 'a new world of black men, not peons, serfs, dogs and slaves, but a nation of sturdy men making their impress upon civilisation and causing a new light to dawn upon the human race.'[2]

Each night, lying on his back in his tiny cabin, Garvey had the same dream. And by day, pacing up and down the empty decks as the ship steamed across the oceans, Garvey began to formulate a plan in his fertile imagination of a radical movement that would unite black people the world over.

But Marcus Mosiah Garvey was little known in Jamaica – outside of a small circle of admirers to whom he'd communicated his European adventures. His sister might have been there at the docks to embrace him but it would be another six months before Indiana could save up enough money for her passage to Jamaica. So there was no welcoming committee for Garvey save for the vagabonds who kept a vigil for returning vessels, and the silver coins that might be tossed by Colón men in a flush of ostentatious largesse. As far as the disappointed beggars – whose outstretched palms Garvey could not cross – were concerned, there was little to mark him out from the horde of young hopefuls who had set out penniless from the pearl of the Antilles and returned in a similar state: empty but for zeal and great ambition.

Within five days of landing in Kingston on 7 July, Garvey would take on the role of recruiting officer and set himself the unenviable task of enticing the sceptics to his banner. He formed the Universal Negro Improvement Association and African Communities (Imperial) League (usually rendered UNIA).³ The gestation of this new confraternity appeared to be astonishingly short but Garvey's account is, typically of him, a truncated version of events.

The actual germ of the idea had been sown much earlier in London. The source of Garvey's emergent Pan-Africanist thinking could be gleaned from the pages of *Ethiopia Unbound – Studies in Race Emancipation* by the Gold Coast lawyer, J. E. Casely Hayford. In the salvation of the race – the cause in which Marcus Garvey now cloaked himself – and in the path he mapped out for its execution, Garvey bore more than a passing resemblance to the fictional and heroic protagonist of *Ethiopia Unbound*. Published in 1911, the novel focused on an African student whose intellectual consciousness is awakened in London and who then returns to lead a political struggle in his native Gold Coast. *Ethiopia Unbound* may have provided the template for Garvey's new character but the script would be drawn from his study of the seminal works of African and West Indian writers in the pages of the *African Times and Orient Review*: men like the coruscating and intense Liberian scholar, Edward Wilmot Blyden, who was internationally respected for his work on *Christianity, Islam and the Negro Race*.⁴ Blyden's text was a modern and fractured book of notes, history, philosophy and other reflections on the reduced state of black people the world over. On the subject of religion, Blyden suggested that Islam, with its lack of colour distinction, was more attractive to black people than Christianity. Blyden, who'd migrated from the Virgin Islands to Liberia as a young man, was also an advocate of repatriation schemes which encouraged the return of blacks from the diaspora to Africa.

In his relatively brief period in London, Garvey had shown an amazing capacity to absorb political tracts, theories of social engineering, African history and Western Enlightenment. A prelude of his macroscopic vision was to be found in the detail of that first ambitious article for the *Review* in which Garvey had laid out, in part, his belief in a future of 'unmolested liberty' for the West Indies.

The Universal Negro Improvement Association's stated aim was 'to establish a brotherhood among the black race, to promote a spirit of race pride, to reclaim the fallen and to assist in civilising the backward tribes of Africa'. Its motto, printed proudly on the letterhead, proclaimed, 'One Aim. One God. One Destiny'. Garvey – acknowledging kinship with the Vatican – suggested that 'like the great Church of Rome, Negroes the world over must practise one faith, that of confidence in themselves with One God! One Aim! One Destiny!'

The motto was open to interpretation: the actual title of the nascent organisation was not. The UNIA was a name that many refused to embrace. Those in opposition to Garvey's organisation were the descendants of white planters and raped slave women, the light-skinned Jamaican elite. They constituted the vast majority of the decision-makers in Jamaican society, and who were most outraged by one word: Negro. No one, least of all the aspiring brown artisans, bank clerks and civil servants, would have willingly ticked such a box denoting their racial classification. Negro might sound scientific and denuded of negative connotations but in practice it was an insult. And light-skinned blacks recoiled at Garvey's presumption to herd them together with their unfortunate darker brethren. As Vivian Durham, a contemporary of Garvey, later said, 'It was a time when it was the ambition of every black man to be white'.[5]

Over the 300 years of British rule, the population of Jamaica had evolved its own prejudicial stratification of class, with a twist: the subtle and sophisticated British system was compounded in the Caribbean by colour. So that, if you craved social mobility and were shrewd, you not only married out of your class, but out of your colour.

By 1914, Edwardian Jamaicans had developed an almost clinically discerning eye for gradations of colour. Such was the premium placed on fairness of skin that there was manifestly an unspoken division in society even within the various sub-groups of brownness. So, a half-black child – the progeny of an 'unadulterated' black and a fully white parent – was described as a mulatto; a quarter black was a quadroon; an eighth an octoroon; and so on down the line until one might virtually 'pass' for white. It was a code that everyone adhered to, from the playground to the chambers of commerce, and was succinctly encapsulated in the folk song 'There's a Brown Girl in the Ring':

> There's a brown girl in the ring
> Tra la la la la
> For she loves sugar
> And I love plum

Society was engineered for the greater benefit of the brown girl dancing merrily in the ring of black girls who held hands and formed a circle around her. She would invariably be offered the sweeter things of life – the sugar – whilst the mass of less fortunate Blacks would have to make do with the sour plum.

Garvey identified the central plank of the problem he would face in Jamaica: 'The prejudice in these countries is far different from that of America. Here we have to face the prejudice of the hypocritical white men who nevertheless are our friends as also to fight down the prejudice of our race in shade colour.'[6]

But Jamaica's wasn't an entirely rigid caste system. There was still room for manoeuvre. Even if you were 100 per cent black, like Garvey, you could still slide up the social scale by dint of hard work and education. It was clear that a man of energy and intelligence need not be bound to the lower orders. Garvey *was* determined to make a name for himself, and he was acutely aware of the need to capitalise on the boon from his stay in England before it became too distant to merit comment. At least his old printing skills might be put to use and press releases profiling Mr Marcus Garvey 'who left Jamaica last year for the purpose of taking a BA degree at the University of London', were sent out to the island's newspapers.

An almost immediate and welcome return came courtesy of the society pages of the *Gleaner* which concurred with the youthful traveller in believing his homecoming worthy of record. The *Gleaner* printed a brief appraisal of his sojourn abroad, along with an impressive list of the notables he had met on his travels, including the former Governor of Jamaica, Sir Sydney Olivier, and Lord Balfour of Burleigh.

Nevertheless, name-dropping aside, Garvey seemed bent on forfeiting the opportunity of joining the right set. 'I had to decide,' he later wrote, 'whether to please my friends and be one of the "black-whites" of Jamaica, and be reasonably prosperous, or come out openly and defend and help improve and protect the integrity of the black millions and suffer.'⁷ This bold statement was nothing more than the ranting of a Janus-faced hypocrite, according to letter-writers to the *Gleaner*, who took him to task over the small matter of his previous saccharine article for the *Tourist*. On his return, Garvey had persuaded the *Gleaner* to reprint that article under the caption 'What Freedom has done for the Natives of this Island', leading one fellow black correspondent to suggest that he had momentarily parted from sanity. Yet another complained that Garvey gave the impression to 'folks who don't know anything about conditions in Jamaica, that the black man's bread is buttered . . . [when] not only is his bread not buttered on any side, but he hasn't any bread to be buttered'. With magnanimous aplomb, Garvey accepted that 'all people engaged in particular ideals do not always "travel" the same way.' He countered that his conscience was clear and that, as Jamaicans so often got a bad press abroad, he wasn't going to provide further ammunition.

That seemed to silence the snipers for now; they would mount more serious challenges in the year ahead. At present though, his detractors were no more irritating than the island's overfamiliar mosquitoes that you learnt to swat away as you got on with your life, or in Garvey's case, with laying down the foundations of his fledgling organisation. On 20 July 1914, just two weeks after his return to Jamaica, he had convened the first-ever meeting of the UNIA and elected officers who, in turn, appointed him the president and travelling commissioner.

The organisation's modest funds meant that the operational headquarters of the UNIA was confined to 12 Orange Street, Kingston – a central location which, to those unfamiliar with the topography of the capital, might suggest a confident beginning and some success. On closer inspection, however, it turned out to be Garvey's cramped hotel room, complete with a small bed jammed into the corner.

From the start the UNIA made clear that it was not a political organisation but a charitable club built around the nucleus of a literary, music-appreciation and debating society, to which all were welcome.

Such debating societies had mushroomed in the capital, partly in compensation for the island's limited formal educational system. The educationally aspiring had a plethora of groups to choose from: Spaldings Literary and Social Society, the Queen Street Baptist Literary and Debating Society, and a host of other genteel associations competed for members; James Hills's Literary and Improvement Society, with its extensive library, was perhaps the most alluring. It was over tea and johnny cakes at the Queen Street Baptist Literary and Debating Society at the start of August 1914 that Garvey met a formidable seventeen-year-old girl (ten years his junior) who had recently graduated from Westwood High School for Girls. Even at so young an age, Amy Ashwood's elegance and regal bearing were remarked upon. She had a haunting and mischievous face.

Decades later, in her unpublished manuscript, *Portrait of a Liberator*, Amy Ashwood wrote glowingly of an unexpected encounter with a member of the audience at the end of the debate. Garvey had followed her out into the wine-dark night to the tram shelter where she stood waiting for the streetcar to take her home. They struck up an immediate friendship and 'the very next day at eight in the morning he [Garvey] was knocking on the door of my home'.[8]

The honourable leader of the UNIA invited Amy to a committee meeting at Orange Street. But as he strode forward into the office, she held back at the door, alarmed at the signs of domesticity. Under cross-examination, Garvey admitted that, given the convenience of its central location, he 'sometimes rested there'. It was evidently an unsatisfactory answer. Amy Ashwood promptly informed him that it was not appropriate for a young unaccompanied lady to be calling at the home of a gentleman, and she 'would not be able to return there to attend any meeting and . . . mother was very dubious about the whole affair'.[9] Alternative premises needed to be found.

If Garvey, like Ashwood's mother, had doubts about including a member of such tender age, then Amy's subsequent offer a week later – of a large rented house in new Kingston divided in two so that one half would serve as UNIA offices – settled the matter. The organisation's fortunes would improve substantially with the admission of Amy Ashwood.

Amy was extraordinarily mature for her years. Her precocious brilliance dazzled all those who came within her sphere. Her personality seems to have been an appealing concoction of high intellectual seriousness and convivial mischief: a formula that drew people to her and, by extension, to the nascent movement.

The rental of the new HQ at 30 Orange Street had been secured on her father, Michael Ashwood's, credit. He thought highly enough of Amy to have made her treasurer of the family fortunes in his absence. A baker by trade, Michael Ashwood had stayed on in Panama City, having migrated there with the family at the height of the canal's construction, and set up a restaurant and food-catering service. The nostalgia of his fellow Caribbean émigrés – or at least their palates – was sated by Michael's cuisine of rotis, ackee and salt-fish, and jerk chicken; business had boomed, so much so that the decision was made, after a few years, for his wife and daughter to return to Jamaica, where Amy was enrolled as a boarder at the pioneering Westwood High School – 'a school for the training of native girls along with others regardless of class or colour'.[10]

She was as passionate as Garvey, sharing his belief in the need for the salvation of the race. The miracle of her education bore testimony to the pathology of Jamaica and the desire for its redemption. Westwood had been founded in 1880 by a Baptist minister who abhorred the prejudices exhibited by the parents of light-skinned students, fretting over their possible contamination by too close a proximity to blacks. When admissions policies proved lax enough to let in darker-skinned girls, these anxious parents simply withdrew their brown children from the schools.

Westwood High School closed its doors to no child, no matter her colour. Buoyed by the financial support of a committee of philanthropic English ladies, the school charged moderate fees, and aimed to compete with more prestigious institutions offering 'all the advantages of a fair English education, residence in England only excepted'. In practice this was rudimentary. And yet the ebony-skinned Amy Ashwood excelled, despite the constraints of a prospectus – French, drawing, painting and music aside – that prided itself on guaranteeing 'a thorough instruction in all matters pertaining to household management'.

On 31 October 1914, the smartly turned-out audience in the wooden-panelled chambers of Collegiate Hall, rented that evening by the UNIA, warmed to her recitation of Paul Laurence Dunbar's 'The Lover and the Moon' during the weekly meeting of the society; she also wrote and performed in charming dialogues, and was the equal of any UNIA member on the debating platform. Its titular head put Ashwood forward for election as secretary of the UNIA's ladies' division – not that there was much competition. At present, there were almost as many titled officers as there were members. Garvey's sister Indiana made up the numbers, and each new convert was pressed into evangelical service, to return with a family member or friend. Remarkably, the island's newspapers seemed to chronicle each stage of the association's development with the affection of a doting parent. In an article entitled 'Some Worthy Efforts', the *Jamaica Times* reported, 'Marcus Garvey has started here the Negro Universal Society which has excellent aims and has made a promising beginning.'[11] The admiration of these conservative journals reflected an approval of Garvey and his organisation's patriotism – not only apparent in the lusty singing of the national anthem at the end of each meeting, but also in their leader's breast-thumping avowal of allegiance to the Crown in letters to the Prime Minister and senior figures of the establishment, supporting the war effort. Garvey was in step with the brave sons of empire marching towards the Somme in the deathly struggle with the Kaiser's army.

In a much-touted resolution passed by the UNIA, Garvey wrote to George V that, 'being mindful of the great protecting and civilising influence of the English nation . . . and their justice to all men, especially their Negro subjects . . . [we] hereby beg to express our loyalty and devotion to His Majesty the King, and Empire . . . We sincerely pray for the success of British arms on the battle fields of Europe and Africa, and at Sea, in crushing the Common Foe.'[12]

The authorities were delighted. Sir Gilbert Grindle of the Colonial Office was gratifyingly surprised by such loyal sentiments and went on to confess, 'I blush to think that I once suggested to Mr Marcus Garvey that he should go to the workhouse.'

No one doubted the expression of unrivalled affection laid before the King. It captured the fervour of Jamaicans who, in their thousands, threw off 'the influence of the deadening tropical languor', and, answering 'the canon's summoning roar', were soon volunteering to serve the empire.[13] Not least because the honour of military engagement would surely be recognised at the cessation of hostilities, and equally, sincere and devout pronouncements on behalf of the UNIA might also prove expedient. In the short term, such uncomplicated devotion meant that significant figures in the colonial administration were more kindly disposed towards the movement. It was a down payment of goodwill. But patience and caution were virtues yet to take root: Garvey was a man in a hurry. The *Jamaica Times* was right. He'd made an excellent start, and very soon was pressing home his advantage; one by one the gatekeepers of every facet of Jamaican society were charmed. The Mayor of Kingston was a sizeable prize. A sweep of the business community netted scores of philanthropic patrons, but Garvey reserved his greatest skills for the courtship of the Governor. Sir William Manning wrote a cheery letter to Garvey on 7 December 1914 pledging his support and adding a respectable £2.00 to the collection basket. As well as charitable work for the relief of the poor, Garvey also began to conceive a bigger scheme. At this stage of his and the movement's development, Garvey had visions of founding an 'industrial farm', a vocational training college in Jamaica modelled on the Tuskegee Institute, that was underpinned with its founder, Booker T. Washington's, practical conviction that 'there is as much dignity in tilling a field as in writing a poem'.[14]

Were Marcus Garvey to have undertaken an audit of the year, then the credit sheet, with its roll call of the great and the good of mostly white Jamaican high society, looked greatly encouraging. Work still needed to be done on the resistant strain of his race but even Amy Ashwood's mother, Maude, showed signs of succumbing to the UNIA maestro's Midas touch. If 'dubious' Maude Ashwood could be coaxed out of her living quarters – the other half of Orange Street – and converted to the cause, then anything was possible.

Mrs Ashwood can't, though, have failed to notice the trilling in her daughter's voice when she stepped out in Garvey's company: a mutual appreciation of intellect was daily blossoming into an amorous attachment, which was all the more apparent for their attempts to hide it. Maude's resolve to separate the paramours was more than matched by her daughter's ingenuity in circumventing the restrictions. When Amy was locked in her room and banned from attending UNIA meetings, she schemed with the maid to swap places with her while she slipped out through the bedroom window. The ruse worked well enough for a while until one evening as Amy spoke from the platform of a UNIA event at Collegiate Hall, she looked up to see a frowning Maude in the audience. Maude would keep her own counsel no longer and immediately sent a telegram to her husband in Panama City. Alarmed by the reports coming out of Kingston, and suspicious of Garvey's intentions towards his now eighteen-year-old daughter, Michael Ashwood was soon on the high seas, rushing back to Jamaica. In the baker and restaurateur's estimation, the young Marcus Garvey was not ostensibly a man of great prospects. Mr Ashwood had something better in mind for Amy than a suitor who, despite his growing stature, presently eked out a living selling greeting and condolence cards (a large stock had recently been shipped over from Britain). When that enterprise proved less than lucrative, Garvey had tried his hand at selling monumental tombstones.[15] Amy would not retreat – she would not give up her Napoleon, nor he his Josephine. Her father's protests served only to fan the flames of the romance, and in 1915, Amy Ashwood and Marcus Garvey were secretly engaged.

The Spanish–Irish heiress needed to be notified that his affections were now directed elsewhere. In any case his resolve to defy convention had dribbled away. In her memoir, Amy Ashwood related that Garvey wrote to his fiancée soon after, breaking off the engagement. Garvey's letter has not been found and Amy Ashwood's account is almost certainly a paraphrase of the original in which Garvey makes the sober observation, 'Marriage between us is now impossible. You will be far happier with a member of your own race; so will I be with one of mine.' According to Amy Ashwood, Garvey begged forgiveness from the heiress. He told her, 'I have seen a girl, blood of my blood and of my own race.'[16]

As Amy Ashwood was to recall, theirs was a partnership steeped in the movement: there was no separation between love and labour, so that a hand-holding, moonlit stroll down by the bay was immediately followed by the more pressing business of planning the running order of speeches for the next UNIA meeting. 'Your Napoleon is longing to see you, longing to gaze into your beautiful eyes,' Garvey wrote breathlessly, only to continue, on a more sober note with, 'Let no mother, no father, no sister, no brother stand in the way of the redemption of Africa. I will always worship at your shrine.'[17] Garvey's relationship with Amy Ashwood was intense and passionate and, occasionally, melodramatic. 'He loved in the grand manner,' wrote Ashwood, 'and was soon urging me to announce our engagement openly . . . I took the precaution of only wearing the ring when my mother was out of sight.' Only weeks later Ashwood decided that their relationship was too intense and problematic, and decided to suspend their engagement. 'Returning home, I discovered a note from Marcus. He poured out such a torrent of feeling that my youthful sensibilities were almost overwhelmed.' At the end of the letter Garvey warned that he was going to commit suicide by 'throwing himself into the sea'. Ashwood hailed a taxi and 'rushed to that section of the beach where Marcus was accustomed to promenade. There he was and I almost collapsed with relief at finding him on time.' The engagement was renewed.[18]

The UNIA-sponsored musical and literary evenings at the Collegiate Hall could now count on a regular and loyal following but membership was still modest and stuck below the 100 mark. To attract a larger audience the board settled on the popular idea of a competition, a biannual elocution contest. There was, however, little chance of certain officers holding back to allow the public to come to the fore. As the young competitors took to the rostrum, the pedigree of one man in particular was most apparent: a beautiful gold watch adorned the breast pocket of the UNIA president when he took first prize on 23 February 1915 for his party piece, a recitation of 'Chatham on the American War'. Garvey had long been inspired by the 'trumpet of sedition' – as the King referred to the Earl of Chatham. Garvey's rendition of Chatham's passionate House of Lords' speech, which attempted to avert the American War of Independence, served a double purpose: to remind the audience of the need to free itself from 'mental slavery', and of their own, much overlooked involvement and fortitude in key historical moments. In that War of Independence, large numbers of black slaves in the Americas – seduced by the promise of freedom held out by the British – hedged their bets and sided with King George III. But whether they crossed the lines or stayed loyal to their slave masters, the gallantry of Negro infantry had been recorded for posterity.

The subject of sacrifice and its reward was one that Garvey would default to at almost every opportunity in the coming months. Though the German threat to British sovereignty in the Antilles warranted little more than the vigilant bicycle patrols around the island that kept watch for spies and enemy ships, like the recently captured *Bethania*, the war in Europe inspired Garvey to reflect on previous military conflicts in which the black sons of empire had comported themselves with honour. It was a theme guaranteed to resonate with an audience who hungered after any recognition not determined by the colour of their skin. Most keenly felt were memories of British military campaigns of the 1890s, when volunteers of the first and second battalions of the West India Regiment – almost entirely recruited from Jamaica – gave further proof that, in suppressing rebel tribes in Gambia, the Caribbean colonial was just as willing and capable of dying for imperial integrity.

Twenty years later, Jamaicans were still celebrating the achievement of Lance-Corporal William J. Gordon, awarded the Victoria Cross for valour in the field on 13 March 1892, during a British army offensive at Toniataba in Gambia. Gordon had saved a major's life, pushing him out of the line of fire and throwing himself in front of enemy musket muzzles. In the margins of the British Empire – where there was little to shout about – these individual acts of bravery were emblazoned on the hearts of black subjects.

But Jamaica was only a subplot. In 1915, the bigger story was, as always, elsewhere. Daily, the local newspapers carried rousing bulletins of virile manhood in the carnage of Flanders Fields. Garvey, the patriot, was preoccupied with the notion of a war full of noble deeds, in which Caribbean men might be denied the opportunity to show that they too were brave enough to face 'an appointment with a bullet'.[19]

In April, the UNIA invited Brigadier General L. S. Blackden, commander of the local Jamaican forces, to deliver a lecture on the war. Garvey would later endorse the brigadier's call to arms, for the most able men to come forward and take up the privilege of military service in forming a Jamaican contingent. Indian troops, shipped over in their thousands to plug the gaps left by the enormous number of casualties suffered among the British Expeditionary Force, had already been valiantly engaged in battle on the Western Front. Whilst Jamaicans took pride in these Indian triumphs, there was a danger that they themselves might miss out on the glory. The thousands of volunteers presented an awkward dilemma for the local authorities who were protective of the racially stratified social order that had served them so well. What lasting lesson might be learnt by those deferential colonised people once granted the qualified privilege of killing a *white* enemy? It needed to be stressed that though the German was undeniably coarse, he was surpassed only by the Englishman in evolutionary development. And were it not for the absurd and hateful imposition of Prussian militarism on his character, then he might still be redeemed to civilisation. Foe that he was, one killed him reluctantly; he was not to be confused with the African blacks upon whom the West India Regiment had been unleashed during the Asante Wars of 1873–1874.

Brigadier Blackden, whom the Negro Society had earlier received so warmly, was soon complaining about the quality of the recruits, and that military prestige was being dispersed to the wrong sort, who all too often were 'an undersized, ragged, barefooted set of fellows, who came forward probably to get a meal'. Blackden conceded that whilst there was 'room for the muscle that drives the bayonet home, there is more room for the brain that can use the complicated weapons of modern warfare'.[20]

Garvey and his society had much more time for the ragged and bare-footed populace and, as the title of its organisation suggested, harboured great ambitions for their improvement. Perhaps emboldened by the success of the first year, Garvey now made a false move. Setting out his agenda for the new improved Negro, he gave a blunt assessment of the scale of the problem in a speech delivered at Collegiate Hall which was subsequently reproduced in the pages of the *Daily Chronicle*: 'To the cultured mind the bulk of our people are contemptible,' wrote Garvey. 'Go into the country parts of Jamaica and you will see there villainy and vice of the worse kind, immorality, obeah and all kinds of dirty things . . . Kingston and its environs are so infested with the uncouth and vulgar of our people that we of the cultured class feel positively ashamed to move about. Well, this society has set itself the task to go among the people . . . and raise them to the standard of civilised approval.'[21]

The overall sentiment may have been encouraging and sincere, but the detail of the script read like something penned by Brigadier Blackden. Such unsparing and unflattering language, reprinted in a national newspaper, was bound to provoke. Garvey was taken off guard by the severity of the response, especially from sections of the brown middle class whose resentment towards him had been festering for more than a year. Dr Leo Pink was particularly incensed on behalf of the 'contemptible, filthy and vulgar' compatriots. Dr Pink warned Garvey that 'the Jamaican Negro can not be reformed by abuse', and went on to ask sarcastically, 'Were he [Garvey] appointed missionary to the penitentiary, would he go into that institution and call the inmates thieves?' Garvey answered that Pink's complaint was mere camouflage. The real source of Pink's ill-temper was that 'nearly every high official (including the Colonial Secretary and Brigadier General) had given them [the UNIA] words of cheer.'[22] The UNIA president had indeed trespassed on the natural turf of men such as Dr Pink, ingratiating himself, as they saw it, with the Governor, and writing fawning, congratulatory telegrams to the King on the occasion of his birthday.

To further enlarge on his acquaintance with persons of influence, he'd even managed to get himself on the guest list for a banquet in honour of the visiting black American scholar, W. E. B. Du Bois – the highlight of the social calendar. On 3 May 1915, the *Gleaner* printed the roll call of the country's representative men invited to the banquet to pay tribute to the distinguished guest who certainly 'belonged to the aristocracy of intellect in America'. The name Marcus Garvey did not appear on the abridged list (the young UNIA leader had not yet achieved sufficient national prominence), but in subsequent years the noble-headed and neatly trimmed Du Bois would recount that he was especially pleased, after the garden reception, to receive a polite and deferential note from his future rival: 'Mr Marcus Garvey presents his compliment to Dr W. E. B. Du Bois and begs to tender to him, on behalf of the Universal Negro Improvement Association, a hearty welcome to Jamaica, and trusts that he has enjoyed the brief stay in the sunny isle.'[23]

While Du Bois returned to New York secure in his position as an established champion of black civil rights, the thus far underappreciated Marcus Garvey was just at the beginning of his master plan to become a race leader. As far as the mulattos, quadroons and octoroons who filled the ranks of the respectable middle class were concerned, it was galling enough that this pretentious social climber who'd emerged tainted by the squalor of Smith Village had the temerity to challenge their claim to being the true representatives of the race; what particularly stuck in the craw was his supposed alignment with the 'cultured class'.

The hotchpotch of fuming letter-writers did not yet constitute a threat but were soon joined by one who would: the noted political heavyweight Alexander Dixon professed to be shocked and outraged by what he interpreted as Garvey's disdain for the masses. A cofounder of the National Club, and the first black man to be elected to the Legislative Council in Jamaica, Dixon snootily claimed to have no recollection of the club's former secretary. Now in his sixties and in poor health, the patrician elder-statesman had looked on imperiously, if also impotently, as Garvey's fledgling movement had taken root.

By appealing directly to white patrons, Garvey had circumvented the brown elite and established a credible, if small, base. The detour, though, could not be followed indefinitely. He needed the middle classes if the organisation was to expand, but he had no appetite for criticism. Consequently, there was little sign of conciliation. Garvey judged his critics as hypocrites. If he had transgressed it was only because he was saying in public that which was privately espoused in the parlours of new Kingston and in the well-meaning analysis of friends of the Negro like W. P. Livingstone. In his study of the evolution of black Jamaicans, the English anthropologist considered that 'too much is expected of the Negro', and added with impunity that, 'bearing in mind how near [he] is to the savage it is to his credit that he so seldom descends to the level to which he is more habituated'.[24]

No doubt fear and jealousy played their part in the enmity directed towards Garvey, but it doesn't seem to have occurred to him that one consequence of constantly drawing attention to himself might be greater scrutiny. A glowing self-assessment of the UNIA's first year prompted sceptics to complain further about the lack of financial transparency and to voice thinly veiled accusations of impropriety. Where had all the money gone?

Under Garvey's guidance, the donations which dribbled into the UNIA coffers were not, according to critical coverage in the *Daily Gleaner*, sufficiently returned to the poor and needy Kingstonians (as stipulated by their manifesto), but squandered on expensive and fawning telegrams to the King on his birthday. Worse still were the unsubstantiated allegations that monies solicited for other worthy causes, such as the industrial farm, were temporarily diverted into the bank account of the UNIA president to subsidise his living expenses, and that the IOUs – the promissory notes that built up – were never honoured. The bad-tempered spat that followed – played out in rival newspapers – was considered most ungentlemanly, and caused wavering supporters to reconsider their position vis-à-vis the Negro Society. Garvey was forced to call an emergency meeting to protest his innocence and defend his integrity but by then it was too late: several high-profile sympathisers had already begun to distance themselves from the man and his movement.

The vituperative onslaught threatened to undermine all the good works and advances thus far, and this fear and embarrassment was most acutely expressed in a letter of damage limitation to Booker T. Washington. The malicious attacks, Garvey believed, were motivated by revenge; the editor of the *Daily Gleaner*, Herbert George De Lisser, took a pique against the UNIA for patronising the advertising pages of rival newspapers – the *Jamaica Times* and *Daily Chronicle*. Garvey assured Washington that he would 'be able to furnish you and the American public with the best proofs of my integrity'.

Having done all he could to dislodge any notion of impropriety, it was time to get on the road and to take the message further afield. And what better place to return to, when feeling under attack, than home? Garvey actually settled on the idea of delivering his first major speech at St Ann's Bay, wrote Amy Ashwood, primarily because he was 'anxious about being ridiculed by Kingston sophisticates' and calculated that his home town was more likely to be sympathetic.[25]

Setting out for the north coast, Garvey later recounted how the organisation's first foray beyond Kingston was clouded by suspicions of sabotage. 'We left Kingston in an old Ford car, a "tin Lizzy",' recalled Ashwood, 'which sprang a leak on the way.' When the car, carrying Garvey, Ashwood and her brother (acting as chaperone) broke down at Spanish Town, just a few miles out of the capital, the driver left to find help, never to return. Late into the night, Garvey's party finally crawled into St Ann's Bay expecting a hero's welcome for the town's near-famous, native son: instead, he was greeted by a half-empty hall as many townsfolk had given up waiting and gone to their beds. Invited by his son, 'Garvey Snr sat stonily in silence'. The remaining crowd, though warm and approving at first, were increasingly bemused by the formality of the proceedings, and the ribald wags in the provincial audience somewhat punctured the grandiosity of the occasion. Amy Ashwood complained that 'not one soul in St Ann's Bay helped us with a penny'. But in the town's defence, Ashwood had skirted round the most likely explanation: that, in the mayhem, the treasurer forgot to call for a collection. Ashwood later conceded that Garvey had indeed written a speech for the treasurer that was 'intended as a stirring appeal for funds', but when the treasurer rose to speak 'alas his memory took leave of absence'.[26]

When they returned to Spanish Town, they had not one penny to pay for the car and driver they'd hired. Amy recounted her embarrassment in being pushed forward to seek out a clergyman who agreed to stand security for them. In subsequent months, a stream of other fundraising schemes also flopped. On 13 November 1915, a UNIA announcement in the *Jamaica Times* trumpeted the next week's big event: 'Buy A Rose Day'. The scale of that particular failure could be measured by the stench from the mountain of rotting roses blocking the doorway of 30 Charles Street. The expected beneficiaries, the poor of Kingston, would have to dine out on the memory of the big Christmas dinner from the previous year; and the untrained and unemployed would need to wait some time yet before enrolling at the proposed Industrial Farm and Institute. The early progress of the movement had stalled.

The sudden shards of gloom were arrested, at least temporarily, by the splendour of the first 500 respectable volunteers who, having met the brigadier's criteria of being able to clothe and feed themselves up until embarkation, now qualified to take the King's shilling. That same night, the society bid them farewell, with hearty good wishes, on their journey to England to assist in the war.

The end of the month brought yet another setback with the news of Booker T. Washington's death. Ever since reading Washington's autobiography, *Up From Slavery*, Garvey had nurtured a plan to travel to America to learn first-hand from the 'wizard' and chief engineer of the mighty, black-American political movement known as the 'Tuskegee machine'.[27] Washington had towered above all other black leaders with his domination of the Negro press, an intricate network of patrons both black and white, and the ambitious black industrial college he'd founded in Tuskegee, Alabama. Born a slave, Booker Talioferro Washington had risen from a humble start on the dirt floor of a backwoods cabin to become the spokesman of his race. Washington was the acceptable face of black America – but his smiling eyes disguised a ruthless determination to retain power. By the accounts of his many admirers, he was an unpretentious man who'd never forgotten his previous diet of grits and chitterlings, even when answering invitations to dine at the White House. Famously, he'd forged an unthreatening accommodation with white folks – characterised by his disarming Atlanta Compromise address of 1895 when, according to the *New York World*, 'The Negro Moses' advanced his homespun philosophy of how the two races might lead an economically harmonious but separate existence: 'In all things that are purely social we can be as separate as the fingers,' he'd argued, 'yet one as the hand in all things essential to mutual progress.' Towards the end of his life, however, Washington had had to fend off growing challenges from the likes of W. E. B. Du Bois who criticised his scheme for racial uplift with its emphasis on vocational courses rather than intellectual excellence.

For now, Garvey's approach was closer to the successful model of conventional Washingtonian wisdom, of lifting up the race through practical and achievable economic means.

As early as September 1914, soon after returning to Jamaica, Garvey had absorbed the lesson of Washington's appeal, and tailored his language similarly in courting favour with potential benefactors; he'd even, for good measure, extended an invitation to Washington to 'be good enough to help us with a small donation to carry out our work'.

Though Booker T.'s response was prompt and encouraging, to any student of diplomacy it was clear that his words were those of a man who daily received such requests for help. His sincere apology for 'not [being] able now to make a contribution toward your work',[28] while rather more than perfunctory, was actually only a grade or two above a standard reply. The subtlety seemed lost on his young admirer. When, in that same correspondence, Booker T. suggested, noncommittally, that the UNIA president should 'come to Tuskegee and see for yourself what we are striving to do for the coloured young men and women of the South', an ebullient Garvey wrote back with overbearing enthusiasm, thanking Washington for 'inviting me to see your great institution' and indicated that he had already packed his bags so that between 'May and June . . . I shall be calling on you'.[29] Correspondence was limited subsequently to a handful of letters but each one was deemed worthy of a public airing at UNIA meetings. With white-gloved reverence, the letter was removed from its envelope, unfolded and read out, or rather declaimed, by a most satisfied UNIA president so that members might vicariously share in the honour.

The significance of Booker T. Washington's letters lay in the weight Marcus Garvey attached to them. Short and to the point, they might seem no more substantial than the greeting and condolence cards he peddled on the streets of Kingston, but to an aspiring race leader and his fellow travellers, they demarked just how far he'd come: let critics sneer, here was validation of his endeavours from arguably the most outstanding black man of his time.

Now Washington was dead. Garvey genuinely mourned his loss and equally rued the missed opportunity to capitalise on their correspondence. He still had an unambiguous invitation to visit Tuskegee, of course, and with Washington's passing that dream was resurrected.

He wrote in a hurry to the former principal's private secretary, friend
and political agent Emmett J. Scott. Aware of the need to strike the
right note in paying tribute to the deceased whilst simultaneously
reminding him of his duty to honour the pledge made by his boss, he
implored Scott 'to do your best for me in that portion of the South . . .
If you were to turn [to] his files for April of last year you will see
where he [Washington] promised to help me whilst there.'[30]

Scott had greater concerns to address than the special pleading of
a distant stranger. His own designs on the vacant leadership of
Tuskegee were thwarted by the appointment panel. And when he did
get round to replying to Garvey the response was polite but not
encouraging.

Scott was not to know that the UNIA leader was of the school of
thought that translated 'no' as 'maybe' and 'maybe' as 'yes'. Apart
from a whiff of undiplomatic directness, there was certainly no crisis
of confidence on Garvey's part. After all, he'd moved quickly; he'd
embraced large ideas and formulated a plan for the salvation of the
race. By the age of twenty-nine, he'd travelled widely, educated himself
in the ways of the world and woken up to the realisation that he
possessed a talent to captivate an audience. But now, after two years
back home – having spent all he owned on the UNIA, along the way
being calumnied by many and praised by few – even for a man whose
naive but determined personality was daily hardening into one that
was built to transmit and not receive, the uncomfortable message
seemed to be getting through: not enough Jamaicans were prepared to
listen to what he had to say.

Good news was long overdue by the end of 1915. It arrived at the
beginning of the following year with the announcement from Tuskegee
that Washington's successor, Robert Moton, would be visiting Jamaica
in February. The report reignited Garvey's enthusiasm. Unfortunately
for him it also had the same effect on his enemies – some of whom
had longer-standing relations with the Tuskegee Institute – and one in
particular, Percival Murray, who was commissioned to act as Moton's
agent locally. Garvey's attempt to organise a reception for Moton drew
guffaws from a hostile press and was thwarted by Murray's intervention. In the excited jockeying for position to gain an audience with a
man of such influence, Garvey found himself at the wrong end of the
queue of supplicants: he was skilfully and quietly outmanoeuvred and
left on the margins, fuming and frustrated. It was difficult to salvage

a sense of dignity after being excluded from Murray's list of the 'representative men', the best of the island to whom such an esteemed visitor should be presented. On reflection, the ungentlemanly squabbling was confirmation of the impossibility of any reconciliation between Garvey and the political sharks who patrolled Jamaica's stagnant backwaters. With nothing much to lose now, he vented his spleen in a letter to the man from Tuskegee: 'I would not advise you to give yourself too much away to the people who are around you for they are mostly hypocrites,' he wrote, and in a version of the old rallying call of 'colour for colour' for allegiance to the Negro race, went on to warn, 'They mean to deceive you on the conditions here because we can never blend under the existing state of affairs.' Garvey had tried to blend with the brown elite and had been rejected.[31]

The Honourable Marcus Mosiah Garvey resigned himself to withdrawing his invitation to host a reception that in all probability had not yet been received. But he signalled that his thoughts were moving on beyond the island when he continued in a confidential whisper, 'I have many large schemes that I cannot expose to the public at present as my enemies are so many. I have been planning a tour of America. If by accident I am unable to meet you here I hope to in America.'[32]

This latest humiliation had thrown into ever sharper relief the degree to which Garvey's nascent movement had failed to thrive in Jamaica and introduced a sour note into his prognosis for the island. The fledgling organisation fought amongst itself. 'The advisory board was repeatedly disbanded and was reconstituted with new members.' Time and again his dismissed colleagues 'left [the organisation] with the chairs that Garvey requested them to bring to the meetings'.[33] Frustrated by the lack of progress, Garvey would complain that his downtrodden black compatriots were as narcoleptic as Rip Van Winkle and as apathetic as sodden leather. He had failed to build to a critical mass. In the final analysis, the moneyed class were not, he calculated, so much hostile as indifferent to his movement.

Having made the firm decision to leave the island, he had little time to settle his affairs. Even though his secret engagement to Amy Ashwood remained undiscovered, in recent weeks her parents had enforced a separation: they planned to have her return with them to Panama. There would be no lovers' farewell with his eighteen-year-old fiancée, and on her part, no opportunity to remind him of his romantic courtship of 'the star of his destiny' and of their pledge of loyalty to each other and to the movement. On 7 March 1916, Marcus Garvey packed his bags, put his precious books in storage, and signed up with the crew of the SS *Tallac* with a view to working his passage to America.

4

AN EBONY ORATOR IN HARLEM

Melting pot Harlem – Harlem of honey
And chocolate and caramel and rum
And vinegar and lemon and lime and gall
          Langston Hughes, *Harlem: A Community in Transition*

MARCUS Garvey disembarked from the SS *Tallac* at the port of New
York on a crisp spring morning on 24 March 1916 and headed straight
for Harlem. In the north of Manhattan, from 8th Avenue to the Hudson
River, there was hardly a black face to be seen. But Garvey had another
Harlem in mind. Like so many West Indians and African-Americans
before him, he was drawn to a Mecca east of 8th Avenue, where
between the Harlem River and row after row of streets from 130th to
145th, lay black Harlem. It was grand, brash, suffocating and thrilling.
As the Jamaican novelist Claude McKay was to write, nothing came
close to 'the hot syncopated fascination of Harlem'.[1]

No one knew exactly how many black people occupied the district.
Estimates ranged from 100,000 to 150,000 and each month hundreds
more newcomers from the southern states and from the Caribbean
swelled their ranks. These new migrants bumped up against each other
in the overcrowded tenement blocks. The airshafts that connected all
of the apartments, carrying all the discordant notes and musicality of
their lives, were to inspire Duke Ellington's signature 'Harlem Airshaft':
the roiling arguments, the cloying odours of fried chicken and overheated bodies, and the ragtime of tin-pan pianos made the airshaft an
unstoppable channel of communication.[2] Harlem's exuberance and
vitality was announced in every facet of life: the midnight blondes who

serviced rent parties; the 'numbers runners' and their big-bellied unofficial bankers who'd grown fat on commissions from lottery tickets;
the patron-hungry poets; the manicured barber's shop politicians; and
the ecstatic believers who thronged the mighty Baptist churches – all
were incontrovertible evidence that Harlem was fast becoming the Negro
capital of the world. It was a bewildering and exhilarating other world
for a youngish Jamaican migrant just off the boat from the sleepy
outpost of British colonial civilisation.

Garvey was twenty-nine, unheralded and unestablished. Yet again,
he'd have to start from scratch. He quickly found lodgings with an
expatriate Jamaican family: there were plenty to choose from. Of
Harlem's black population only a fifth had been born there. Its distinctly
Southern flavour came courtesy of the majority who had joined the
Great Migration, trekking north from states such as Georgia, Mississippi
and Alabama. British West Indians mostly made up the remaining one
in five Harlemites.

The trickle of West Indians to Harlem had begun in the early 1900s
when the USA took over the construction of the Panama Canal. The
energetic Colón men, who had accumulated wealth and an appetite
for travel, began making their way to Harlem with their families. As
the canal approached completion in 1914, the more resourceful of their
number also judged it the best time to move on: once the canal was
opened for business, the great army of Caribbean workers – labourers,
engineers, cooks and domestic servants – would be surplus to requirements. There was significant direct migration from virtually all parts
of the Caribbean, from Jamaica to Trinidad in the lesser Antilles,
boarding fast steamers that would reach New York in four or five
days. Though the majority went in search of work, the chance to further
their education was also a factor. In 1912 for instance, Claude McKay
had taken leave from his creative life to enrol on an agricultural course
at the Tuskegee Institute in the Southern state of Alabama, and only
later trekked up north to the Negro conurbation in Harlem.

Harlem exerted a romantic and magical hold on the imagination of
black people in the Americas. Marcus Garvey's and the UNIA's favourite
poet, Paul Dunbar, captured that sense of wonder in 'The Sport of the
Gods' when he wrote of black people who 'had heard of New York
as a vague place and a far away city that, like Heaven, to them had
existed by faith alone'. The first tentative steps to Harlem were taken
by black residents already living in lower Manhattan. They weren't

just moving because they aspired to better living conditions; in 1900 fear was also the spur. On 15 August that year racial tensions exploded and rioting broke out in the rough 'Hell's Kitchen' following the death of a policeman killed in a tussle with an African-American whose wife the patrolman was trying to arrest for soliciting, having mistaken her for a prostitute. Vengeful policemen reached an understanding with an angry white mob that descended on the district beating and bludgeoning any black man who was unfortunate enough to be on the streets. A similar riot a few years later (in 1905) convinced unsettled and unprotected Blacks to pack up and move out to the safe, if expensive, haven of Harlem.[3]

Families doubled up or took in lodgers to meet the rent on the solid, overpriced brownstones. Garvey was doing his Jamaican landlord a favour in occupying 'a little hall-bedroom, hardly heated or well ventilated', remembered Edgar Grey, an early acquaintance. Decades later, Grey was still quoting from his vivid recollection of 'a poorly clad asthmatic Negro', whom he saw 'in Rose Dairy room, day after day, eating portions of corn beef hash at the small cost of fifteen cents . . . I visited his lodgings and saw there dozens of empty sardine [tins], beans and cooked or prepared soup cans from which he had eaten morsels so rude and meagre as to draw forth the pity of any who saw him.'[4] Garvey's rationing was an absolute necessity, as early on, his asthma limited his ability to work. Even with this self-sacrifice and careful budgeting, he could barely meet the cost of his rent – much to his landlord's dismay.

As was often said at the time, the black man in Harlem was like a poor relation who'd inherited a limousine he could ill afford to maintain.[5] Designed in the 1880s for the Jewish and Scandinavian middle-income class, the apartment blocks had shot up in just over two decades, but the developers had miscalculated and too many had been built. The building boom had anticipated the extension of the subway to Harlem. There were fantastic profits to be made; speculators bought and sold contracts for properties that they never even took possession of. But the overheated market had suddenly cooled. By 1900, empty apartments were beginning to eat away at the nerves of investors and the future returns expected from the thousands of dollars ploughed into their construction. Something had to be done. Anxious white landlords who noisily professed their reluctance to trade their consciences for a profit, did so quietly nonetheless. Black entrepreneurs such as the real-estate agent, Phillip A. Payton, were increasingly taken up on their offer to fill the unrented apartments with aspiring black tenants willing to pay over the odds. Realtors who knew the market believed that prices were so high that blacks would never be able to sustain a presence there. The *Harlem Home News* saw things differently. 'We now warn owners of property,' the paper proclaimed in July 1911, 'the invaders are clamouring for admission right at their doors and that they must wake up and get busy before it is too late to repel the black hordes.' Complacent white residents, who were still holding out in the spring of 1914, might have been advised to pay closer attention to the news that the black St James Presbyterian church intended to head north from midtown to Harlem. Church leaders were finely tuned to the temper of their congregations. Once churches like St James's had decided to move then any semblance of temporariness, of a possible, eventual return from whence the new migrants had come, disappeared. The consequences were not unexpected: a trickle of white tenants fleeing from the area in panic turned into a stampede. There was a concurrent rush of African-Americans moving up, socially, economically and literally to take their place.[6]

Dreams of a better life, afforded by their arrival in Harlem, were capped by the reality of work opportunities – most often limited to menial and manual labour. The lucky 50 per cent found employment in familiar roles: for men it meant donning the uniforms of lift attendants, janitors, Pullman porters and longshoremen; the bulk of women's work was as domestic servants in the middle-class homes of white New Yorkers beyond Harlem's borders. Though the workforce might have been defined by the same titles and job descriptions available to them in the Southern black belt, they rejoiced in having freed themselves from the acquiescence and subordination that had tethered them in Atlanta or Charleston. Typical of such sentiments was the Southern migrant who wrote back home: 'I am fixed now and living well ... Don't have to mister every little boy comes along ... I can ride in the street or steam car anywhere I can get a seat.'[7]

The predominance of such revelations ran counter to the experiences of Marcus Garvey and his compatriots for whom doffing your cap to the Massa was a tradition long since passed with emancipation, preceding their entry into the land of the free. Foreign-born black immigrants to the district, wrote Wilfred Domingo, 'find it impossible to segregate themselves into colonies; too dark of complexion to pose as

Cubans or some other Negroid but alien-tongued foreginers, they are inevitably swallowed up in black Harlem'. Garvey's fellow member from the Jamaican National Club days, Wilfred Domingo, had been in New York since 1912. Though they might appear indistinguishable, Domingo delineated early on certain tensions and frictions between West Indians and African-Americans. This was partly cultural. Their differences were obvious, for example, in their ways of worship. 'While large sections of [African-Americans] are inclined to indulge in displays of emotionalism that border on hysteria,' observed Domingo, West Indian Negroes exhibited 'all the punctilious emotional restraint characteristic of their English background'. It was their attitude towards employment that was most marked. Significant numbers of skilled West Indian workers had migrated to New York and were not about to trade their artisan crafts for menial work without a fight. They applied for 'positions that the average African-American has been schooled to regard as restricted to white men only'. The dream would not be deferred.[8]

In 1915, before leaving Jamaica, Marcus Garvey had corresponded with Domingo. Soon after his arrival, Garvey solicited his help, and Domingo had generously steered him towards useful contacts and job opportunities. Brandishing his credentials as a master printer and the much-exploited endorsement from Alfred Burrowes, under whom he'd originally served his apprenticeship in St Ann's Bay, Garvey landed intermittent printing jobs.

The idea of securing funds for the 'Industrial Farm' back in Jamaica seems to have been Garvey's primary concern at this point. Establishing himself on the unofficial lecture circuit in church halls, libraries and other municipal centres, drawing on the tradition of the late nineteenth-century Chatauqua Literary and Scientific Circle, was the means to do so. The philosophy of the Chatauqua circuit (with its emphasis on self-help and education), chimed with Garvey's UNIA programme; he'd already been practising it in Jamaica, without realising there was a name and tradition. Although his compatriots had not been receptive to his ideas, by the time he'd set sail for America, Garvey considered himself a public lecturer. He never wavered from the idea, which though enunciated in 1937, clearly applied to 1916:

> I am a public lecturer, but I am President-General of the Universal Negro Improvement Association . . . There is always a charge for admission, in that I feel that if the public is thoughtful it will be benefited by the things

I say. I do not speak carelessly or recklessly but with a definite object of helping the people, especially those of my race, to know, to understand, to realise themselves.[9]

Garvey's confidence was high but he would need to hone his skills to attract an audience who, through the power of his oration, might be motivated to donate to such a worthy cause. By April, a month after his arrival, he'd saved enough to place a down payment on renting St Mark's Hall, 57 West 138th Street for an evening, to serve as the venue for his American debut.

Garvey printed his own handbills and distributed tickets around the streets of Harlem. The minor recognition he'd achieved in Jamaica, notwithstanding the last two months of demoralising stagnation, could not be built on. He was unknown. Shrewdly, he calculated the need for someone special to introduce him to a Harlem audience. On the morning of 25 April 1916, Garvey pocketed a few of the tickets and set off for the Lenox Avenue subway. He brushed past the pushcart pedlars – including the likes of 'Pigfoot Mary', 'Hot Dawg Dan' and 'Pickled Patsy', famed for her pickled watermelon rinds – all vying for pitches outside the recently opened station, and wended his way downtown. There, with startling chutzpah, the unknown race leader with a following of zero hurried on through the doors of 69 5th Avenue and into the offices of the National Association for the Advancement of Colored People (NAACP). He had come to seek out the biggest name in black American life: W. E. B. Du Bois, the solitary black board member of the NAACP and editor of its magazine, the *Crisis*, a monthly tome which solemnly billed itself responsible for providing 'A Record of the Darker Races'.

W. E. B. Du Bois had been catapulted into lead position as *the* voice of black America, following Booker T. Washington's death. An opponent of Washington, the Harvard-educated scholar advocated a policy of liberal humanistic education which could compete with anything the Ivy League colleges had to offer. 'I believed in the higher education of a Talented Tenth,' Du Bois explained, 'who through their knowledge of modern culture could guide the American Negro into a higher civilisation.' His position was unashamedly elitist, arguing that it was both desirable and necessary to show that black intellectuals, the 'Talented Tenth' of the general Negro population, were the equal of their white counterparts – in literature, classical music, composition and art, but especially literature – and by so doing this 10 per cent would act as a vanguard, forcing mainstream American society to integration – a process that the historian, David Levering Lewis, summarised as 'civil rights by copyright'.[10]

Garvey straightened his jacket, pulled back his shoulders and courteously asked to see the editor. Unfortunately, Du Bois was out of town, and the Jamaican caller had to settle for leaving a short, deferential note inviting the celebrated editor 'to be so kind as to take the "chair" at my first public lecture to be delivered on Tuesday 9th May at 8 o'clock. My subject will be Jamaica.' More in hope than expectation, he also left behind a couple of complimentary tickets and a request that Dr Du Bois distribute his circular among prospective patrons. Later, Garvey would recall how his disappointment was offset by the peculiarity of what he had witnessed in the NAACP offices: the stark absence of coloured staff among the officers of a supposedly coloured organisation. He claimed to have been perplexed and 'unable to tell whether I was in a white office or that of the NAACP'. Marcus Garvey returned that night to the decidedly black Harlem neighbourhood and busied himself with polishing his speech and ironing out any first-night nerves that a less confident speaker might have admitted to himself on the eve of his debut.

In the event, Du Bois declined the invitation so graciously extended to him. It was a wise choice if the account of that evening by Wilfred Domingo, who was in the audience, is to be believed. According to Domingo (who wrote up his account years after the two men had acrimoniously fallen out), the evening of entertainment on 9 May 1916 was a mixture of tragedy and farce. From the outset things boded ill. The replacement 'chair' did not show on time, and the impatient orator, after nervously pacing the floor for half an hour, mounted the platform shaking like a leaf and, after struggling to make himself heard above the heckles and whistles, fell off the stage – in a pitiable stage-managed attempt, Domingo concluded, to garner some sympathy and draw the proceedings to a close. Amy Jacques offered a more charitable interpretation: deprived of sleep and so hungry that his belly was knocking on his backbone, Garvey had inevitably swayed and tumbled from the podium after a dizzy spell. No matter who was correct, it was an inauspicious beginning to his campaign to win over Harlem's masses – all thirty-six of them.[11]

There was little sign of Garvey descending into a pit of despair.

Rather the opposite. Three days later, in a letter back home to Thaddeus McCormack in Kingston, he modestly announced plans for a major tour of the USA, 'a big programme which I feel sure will put us in a good position'. The money he would garner from this improvised lecture tour would be ploughed back into the organisation once he returned to Jamaica. Though upbeat, Garvey was anxious about the safekeep of his few possessions which had furnished the UNIA reading room in Kingston: 'I am at a loss to know what has become of my things. There was a table . . . and a case . . . also books, papers, desk, chairs, pictures, etc.' He suspected that the fourteen chairs and table (loaned from a local restaurant) might have been confiscated by bailiffs in lieu of rent, and he promised to send McCormack enough money so that they might be redeemed. Boston was to be the first city on his tour, and he signed off grandly by advising his old friend, 'all my letters can be addressed to me here at my headquarters'. There would have been little room for filing correspondence in the tiny lodge room at 53 West 140th Street.

The route of Marcus Garvey's lecture, fact-finding and fundraising tour would eventually take him to the South where powerful black pastors exerted immense influence over their congregations. Before turning south, Garvey took a curious but symbolic pit-stop at the Tabernacle Church of Billy Sunday – a huge wooden structure temporarily erected at Broadway and 168th Street with a seating capacity of 18,000. Reverend Sunday was *the* great white evangelist, famed for the full-bodied dynamism of his sermons, delivered to massive congregations at revivalist meetings with no need for loudspeakers or any other form of amplification. To witness William Ashley Sunday in full flow was to be in the presence of a man possessed with the spirit of light that the Spanish call *duende*: the ability to transmit a supreme and powerfully felt emotion. Billy Sunday had it, but, judging by his efforts at St Mark's Hall, Garvey still had a long way to go.

He was, however, headed in the right direction, hastening to the Tuskegee Institute, to the shrine of Booker T. Washington to pay his homage. Laying the foundations of a Jamaican Farm and Industrial Institute, based along the lines of Tuskegee, had been the dream that had fuelled Garvey's passage to America in the first instance. At last he'd be able to see at close range the likelihood of that particular and Southern conceit serving as a useful model in the Caribbean. Countless others had made the pilgrimage before him. His compatriot, the poet

Claude McKay, had beaten him to Tuskegee by a couple of years and had even enrolled on a course offering a diploma in scientific farming.

Fairly early on McKay realised he'd made a mistake. With hindsight, a writer reputed for his sharp and violently subversive poetry was bound to find the conservatism of the institution oppressive. Worse still, its formal and functional architecture – following the blueprint of a modern industrial machine – was replicated in the souls of the students. After much agonising, McKay (like Ralph Ellison, another dropout who was to satirise Tuskegee in his famous novel *Invisible Man*) had reached the conclusion that the academy imposed a rigid and prescriptive way of thinking on formerly fertile undergraduate minds. Such an assessment would have found no favour with Marcus Garvey. Tuskegee was a marvel of black endeavour. There was nothing in Jamaica to match its physical splendour and high-minded ideals. One hundred acres had been given over to a spacious and aesthetically pleasing complex built on rich red Southern soil. Loving care and consideration had gone into its creation, with lawns so neat one imagined them trimmed with nail scissors. Everything underscored its principal purpose to turn out graduates schooled in the latest understanding of modern agriculture. In so doing, Tuskegee proved its attachment to the spirit of the founding father. In his famous Atlanta address of 1895, Washington had outlined how self-reliance might be achieved by a people waking up to the resources that were much closer to hand than assumed. The plight of Negroes was akin to a vessel which had strayed dangerously off route and given up hope of rescue. From the platform at Atlanta, Washington enlarged on this theme:

A ship lost at sea for many days suddenly sighted a friendly vessel. From the mast of the unfortunate vessel was seen a signal: 'Water, water. We die of thirst.' The answer from the friendly vessel at once came back: 'Cast down your bucket where you are.' The captain of the distressed vessel, at last heeding the injunction, cast down his bucket and it came up full of fresh, sparkling water from the mouth of the Amazon River.

In the summer of 1916, the maritime analogy was not so secure. Though established only thirty years previously, to the thinking of its critics like Du Bois, Tuskegee was already out of date – strangely unsuited to the new world that was a-coming. Far from heeding Booker T. and casting down his bucket in Southern waters, the Negro was disengaging from the strictures of the agrarian South, packing up his family and possessions, and venturing to the great conurbations in the North. In the next three years alone, more than half a million black families were on the move, getting out as best they could on horse-drawn carts, vans and segregated 'Jim Crow' trains. Theirs was an emotional and symbolic uprooting, witnessed time and again by men like Alonzo Whittaker, a veteran porter of the Louisville and Nashville Railroad Company. As his train prepared to cross the Mason-Dixon line (the psychic and symbolic boundary demarcating the Northern states from the Southern), Alonzo Whittaker removed the 'Jim Crow' signs from the carriage, and took it upon himself to counsel the tearful migrants:

> Some of you thought there was a big white line here, but there is not; there is just a plain river, the Ohio River by name. Some of you have never been up here before and some of you are not going back South again, and I can hardly blame you. [But] whatever you do, do not go into the North to take revenge on the other race there . . . for the beatings and killings we received in the South.[12]

Garvey was heading in the opposite direction to see for himself what conditions were like. After all, the vast majority of black people, fully 10 million, still laboured in the South. Almost a million were farmers – though a distinction needed to be made between farmers who owned their plots and those who rented them. The black man was most likely to be a tenant farmer who rented not just his farm but also the tools and the mule from a landlord whose greed (little attention was paid to an accurate keeping of accounts) left the desperate tenant in a state best summarised by the popular refrain:

> Nought's a nought,
> figger's a figger.
> All for the white man,
> and none for the nigger.

Few records are available of Garvey's odyssey in the South. From the snatches available, it's clear that, despite his pride, he had no option other than to sit in the segregated 'Jim Crow' railway carriages assigned to black passengers once they'd crossed the Mason-Dixon Line. His criss-crossing of the country again mirrored the poet Claude McKay. But even if by some happy coincidence they'd found themselves aboard the same train, it's unlikely that the aspiring orator would ever have encountered the verse-writing vagabond: McKay, the man destined to kick-start the Harlem Renaissance in a few years' time, was a waiter on railroad dining cars. Sleeping compartments and dining cars were off-limits to black passengers in the South – no matter their hunger or tiredness. Not that Marcus Garvey had much time for either. In six months, he would sweep across thirty-eight states, conducting his one-man survey of African-American life.

At each stopover Garvey listened to and learnt from the elders of the African Methodist Episcopal and black Baptist churches. Dipping in and out of their places of worship, the secular young man was Johnny-on-the-spot, rising early to answer the call to prayer and taking his place in the pews to observe the profound influence of the ministry in the South: hymns and sermons comforted the African-American in his belief that this world was not his resting place, that he was only passing through. Yet still, the black man craved some sense of the race's success. Such was the racially alert state in the early days of the twentieth century that significant black achievements were often elevated beyond merit. Roundly celebrated was the vigour of the dock worker Charles Knight who brought the world record to America, driving 4,875 rivets in one day, outstripping the former champion by 400; and then there was the Georgia farmer who, in beating off all challengers (including white farmers) to be the first to take his bales of cotton to market on seven consecutive years, was proclaimed 'King Cotton'.[13]

The African-American's suffering, or at least his standing, had, in part, been ameliorated through the civilising agencies of Booker T. Washington's academy. Its graduates were at the head of the queue when it came to the handing out of jobs dependent on technical ability and applied learning. But if Garvey hoped to get some sense of the direction the Tuskegee leadership might now take in its founder's passing, he was to be disappointed. The prized meeting that he'd sought and obtained with Robert Moton (Washington's successor) was not the high-water mark of collaboration he'd hoped for. Marcus Mosiah Garvey must have wondered why he'd bothered to put himself through the hundreds of miles of hardship and 'Jim Crow' humiliation only to be greeted in a half-hearted 'we salute you in your efforts to uplift the race' manner, disguised by soothing language, laced in the sugary, overly

polite Southern tradition. Where he might reasonably have expected –
once the socialising was out of the way – serious attention and the
meat of concrete advice to be served, as it were, alongside the after-
dinner coffee and cigars, in fact scant consideration or encouragement
was given to his ideas for a Tuskegee-style institute in Jamaica. Instead,
Garvey endured a painfully formal meeting in which Moton merely
mouthed platitudes.[14] Short-changed and mightily perplexed, he set off
once again across state lines in the South.

The one constant, from as far as Louisiana to Tennessee, was the
clanking chorus of the cotton 'gin' machines drawn by mules across
sharecropping land. Rather like the Caribbean peasant's association
with sugar plantations, the so-called 'American Negro romance with
cotton' was a limitation borne of necessity – an uncomfortable reminder
of the not-too-distant slave past. Those with enough grit, determination and good fortune weaned themselves off the dependency. One such
was the fabulously wealthy Madam C. J. Walker. On the strength of
her black hair and beauty empire, she'd succeeded in freeing herself
from unpromising beginnings in the pestilent swamplands of Delta,
Louisiana. 'I gave myself a start,' she famously quipped, 'by giving
myself a start.' Her businesses certainly gave plenty of young black
women an opportunity. She'd started with 'two dollars and a dream'
and had gone on to pioneer a unique way of selling. Long before the
advent of 'Avon Ladies', the well-groomed door-to-door sales agents
attending a Madam Walker class would be grilled on the primacy of
hygiene, safety and deportment. These neatly dressed, transparently
hygienic and manicured precursors of Avon Ladies toured the country
expanding Walker's beauty empire. Her only child, A'Lelia, would
inherit a fortune and a highly successful business. Enrolling at the
Walker College of Hair Culture, beauticians would qualify for 'a passport to prosperity' once they graduated. But the secret of Madam
Walker's success was in selling not only beauty, but also pride. The
Baptist churches that Garvey attended thronged with congregations
who held firmly to two fundamental beliefs: that their abuse in the
South was temporary, and that they no longer needed to live with the
curse of the Negro hair that they were born with. Everywhere he went
that was evidently so – thousands of black women of all classes softened and straightened their unwieldy, frizzy hair with Madam Walker's
preparations.[15]

C. J. Walker was just the kind of philanthropic black entrepreneur whom Garvey hoped to court. Unfortunately, whilst he was riding the Jim Crow railways in the South, she had climbed into her splendid seven-seater open Cole touring car and bid her chauffeur drive north; Garvey would later catch up with Walker in Harlem and launch an unremitting but subtle campaign to solicit her help.

The pep and snap of this first black millionaire was to inspire his assessment in the *Champion* magazine. Garvey had stopped off in Chicago and stepping into the offices of *Champion* had impressed the editors with his energy and wide-awake ambition. Garvey returned the compliment, writing that 'the American Negro is the peer of all Negroes, the most progressive and the foremost unit in the expansive chain of scattered Ethiopia . . . the acme of American enterprise is not yet reached. You have still a far way to go. You want more stores, more banks and bigger enterprises.'[16] Garvey could not yet hope to garner the enthusiasm of audiences for a woman who – born uneventfully as Sarah Breedlove and transformed into Madam C. J. Walker thirty-five years later – could now blaze into town after town like a visiting royal: Garvey and Garveyism was not yet a brand. But his turn in the South and contact with black communities in the North was giving rise to an evanescent Garvey: the nervous and humiliated speaker on his debut in Harlem had disappeared, and a newly confident visionary emerged in his place.

The visit to the Southern black belt was daily opening his eyes to an unexpected vista of possibilities. Towards the end of March 1917, Marcus Garvey wound up his tour with his signature humility, advertising 'a call for all colored citizens of Atlanta' to attend a 'Big Mass Meeting' to hear the great West Indian Negro leader, 'Professor Garvey, an orator of exceptional force [who] has spoken to packed audiences in New York, Washington, Philadelphia, Louisville, Nashville . . .' and so on, and so on.

He spoke with abundant pleasure about the unexpected sight of Negro banks, theatres and real-estate agencies, and saluted the active part played by certain industrious blacks in commerce, who put their sleepy Jamaican cousins to shame. Such positivism had to be offset against the intermittent blight on the American landscape: firstly, the boll-weevil infestation in the cotton, and secondly, the burning crosses erected by hooded stalwarts of a resentful and resurgent Ku Klux Klan.

Perhaps it was naivety that carried Marcus Garvey so fearlessly into the heart of danger, when so many terrorised black people were heading in the opposite direction. A daily diet of humiliation and abuse was the lot of Southern African-Americans. Worse still, lynching was common south of the Mason-Dixon Line – thirty-seven were recorded in 1917 and their numbers would almost double the following year. Lynching was not just the murder of black men and women by a mob. It was preceded, in the case of black men, by their mutilation ('surgery below the waist'), after which they were doused with petrol, set on fire and burnt until all of their blood vessels, veins and arteries, exploded. Bits of their bodies were routinely chopped off as souvenirs before the mob was sufficiently satiated to leave what was left of them dangling from a tree. As a five-year-old, Charles William Brown remembered the sight of the big cross where 'they burned a Negro at the stake', at Jacksonville, Florida. Years later, Brown could still recall the 'smell [of] his burning flesh five miles away . . . after the flames were over, and he was burnt to a crisp, [they went] around and cut things off of him – off the fingers and toes . . . and they'd take them home, the white women and put them in glass jars and set them on the mantelpiece'.¹⁷ The anti-lynching campaigner, Ida B. Wells, related to Garvey her first-hand accounts of such barbarities when he visited her in Chicago. Wells had been chased out of the South (following voluble death threats) after she'd published details of the southern custom of lynching.

Such atrocities were not known in the Caribbean. The idea that a man could not travel just where he wished, without fear of assault or abuse, was anathema to Marcus Garvey. Besides, as Amy Ashwood testified, he possessed a great store of personal courage. Even so, it was not a propitious moment for a foreign black man to be travelling alone through Oklahoma, Mississippi and Alabama, equipped only with an uppity tongue. Unaccustomed as he was to the vagaries of the South, Garvey couldn't have read the warnings, foretold in the Negro spiritual:

> Boll weevil in de cotton
> Cut worm in de cotton,
> Debil in de white man,
> Wah's going on?

Unscathed and unmolested, Garvey returned to Manhattan after more than six months on the road. Between his departure and return, a roster of pastors had virtually set up camp outside Penn station touting for newly arrived Southern worshippers to join their congregations uptown. Black Harlem was still expanding, creeping down towards 125th Street, much to the chagrin of certain members of the elite who, in drawing the desirable distinction of living on or south of 125th Street, could no longer amuse themselves with the enquiry: 'How are the folks up in Harlem?' They *were* in Harlem, whether they liked it or not. The border was continually being redrawn. Further south in mid- and lower Manhattan, encouragement to move on up to the Negro capital was increasingly the sermon delivered by the preachers of Baptist and African Methodist Episcopal churches who guided their flocks towards home ownership as if it were a vital appendix to the Ten Commandments. If the congregation was heading home to Harlem, the clergy correctly deduced they too would have to move on up with them. Collection plates were passed round, like hands in a poker game, with the stakes continually raised until the pot was sufficient for handsome churches to change hands from white to black. A smaller number of Moravian and Anglican churches (often little more than shopfronts) were established to serve the Caribbean believers. Even so, the growth of churches could not keep pace with the expanding population. The combined ministries were so popular that they belched out Sunday worshippers who had shouldered their way into the temples and still struggled to find a place to kneel, despite the extra services that were laid on throughout the day to accommodate them.

Lord-loving Harlemites at St Mark's church hall would be privy to the second coming of Marcus Garvey – provided they could spare the dollar for the ticket. At the same venue where he'd made his debut the previous year, the leader of the Universal Negro Improvement Association was guaranteed an audience of at least twelve – made up of the newly joined members of the New York branch of the organisation, which he'd founded in May. He was also magnanimous or thick-skinned enough to extend an invitation to Robert Moton who had rebuffed his advances in Tuskegee. But topping Garvey's wish-list of guests to the high-class benefit evening was the former American president, Theodore Roosevelt. The VIP tickets may have been returned by Roosevelt but Marcus Garvey took vicarious pleasure in the fact that at least they were acknowledged. At 8 o'clock on 26 June 1917, the attendance and acknowledgement were modest. The competition would have been stiff in any case, for the congregation of the church was shepherded each day of the week by charismatic pastors. And further, Garvey needed only to step outside St Mark's church hall to gain some understanding of what else might have gone wrong.

As well as the church, the social events at the church hall, the speakeasy and the cabaret, there was now another new game in town, free, competitive and outdoors. The unseasonably warm weather of 1916 cued the birth of a new form of street entertainment: the stepladder orators. These ebony sages set up their stepladders and soapboxes at agreed points along Harlem's main drag; the most favoured assembly spot was on the corner of 135th Street and Lenox Avenue where the expansive pavement was wide enough to accommodate several hundred people. The stepladders would be hauled through the shopfronts of sympathetic tailors or cigar-store keepers; a topic was agreed on and the battle of ideas would ensue. By taking to the streets the zealous orators circumvented the old-school local leadership – the representative men who practised a form of benign patronage. The Young Turks eschewed the niceties of conventional politics: any subject or any person was likely to be criticised with faint regard for reputation. With great daring and fearlessness, they aired popular grievances about the violence meted out to migrants in the North; the denial of jobs based on colour; and the high rents tenants were often forced to pay for slum apartments – on this latter point, the extortionate landlords (no matter their creed or colour) were named and shamed.

The granddaddy of all the speakers (even though he was only thirty-four at the time) was Hubert Henry Harrison. An intellectual lightning conductor, he drew the highly charged masses to his street seminars on topics that ranged from Darwin's theory of evolution, through to the Marxist philosophy of the development of capitalism. Depending on whether you read reports in the *Harlem Home News* or *New York News*, speakers such as Harrison were either harbingers of a golden period when Harlem would 'eclipse the age of Pericles and Socrates', or self-appointed bores spouting their prejudices at 'bug house corner'.[18] On one essential point both journals agreed: Caribbean men and women were much over-represented among these rabble-rousers or activists; the job specification – eloquent, overeducated and underemployed – suited them perfectly.

It was a game that suddenly all of his unofficial schooling – the elocution lessons, the debating societies and the tour of black churches in the South – seemed to have been carefully leading Garvey towards. He had found a voice, a strange and eclectic one – part evangelical (borrowed from Billy Sunday), part formal King's English, and part lilting Caribbean speechifying. He was on-song, just needing a receptive audience which, in the spring of 1917, seemed to be tantalisingly close. But still the Jamaican migrant had no ready entrée to the masses. There'd been a false start the previous year, but then, graciously, the young electric socialist A. Philip Randolph had entered the scene. Randolph was a gifted speaker and one of the 'most notorious street radicals in Harlem'. Rival soapboxers paid him the compliment of rarely encroaching on his territory. According to his biographer, 'if other soapboxers wanted to hold on to their audience, they had to be careful not to hold their meeting too close to where Randolph was preaching'.[19] A. Philip Randolph proudly recalled his pivotal role in launching Garvey's subsequent career; how he'd sportingly stepped down from his ladder and offered it to the penniless Jamaican: 'Garvey got up on the platform and you could hear him from 135th to 125th Street. He had a tremendous voice.'[20]

His health and voice, though, were troubled by a bout of the pneumonia that was to recur throughout the most stressful times of his adult life. He was also emotionally wrought by the bleakness of his prospects. Months after his sojourn through black America, he had returned to his Harlem lodge room, exhilarated but broke, to a stack of pitiful, heart-rending letters from Amy Ashwood back in Panama. She was desperate for money. Her father's business ventures in Panama had evidently failed. Michael Ashwood had gone on alone to Florida and had not yet met with financial success. 'One year now since my father has not given me a cent,' Ashwood complained though she sympathised with him, realising he was not in a position to help. Her distress was compounded by the family home going up in flames: 'I have been burnt out twice since my father's absence and for one to be burnt out and penniless is hell.' Ashwood spared her fiancé no details. Her poverty had badly affected her health. She was not mindful of accusations of exaggeration or special pleading because her troubles were so great. She insisted that she had lost more than fifteen teeth in the last year. 'They are extracted now,' she wrote, 'and only waiting on the money to put them in.' $200 would suffice to pay for the dental work to restore the smile to her youthful face and go some way to restoring her faith in him. She scolded Garvey for not replying to her letters, whilst simultaneously pleading for financial assistance for her passage to America. In the plan Amy outlined how he might – pretending to be her uncle – act as guarantor. For good measure, she attached a shopping list of fine clothes. She may have been burnt out but she was determined, when they met, to look her best. Her travelling colours were black or navy blue. Garvey was requested to purchase 'one black suit, I like silk – stiff silk, a black hat like this with a white feather behind. One pair of high heel boots, bronze. One corset, straps over shoulder and a pair of stockings.' The clothing would need to be shipped over prior to her arrival.[21]

But Ashwood's secret fiancé was in no position to help. Not yet vagrant but most definitely out of work, Garvey now regularly joined the ranks of street scholars with stepladders at Speakers' Corner on 135th Street. Unexpectedly, he found the Harlemites, especially the West Indians, twitching with pride and excitement as he spoke. Though the immigrant West Indians and native black Americans shared a much-prized possession in the shape of Harlem, a current of suspicion and competition lingered just beneath the surface. The Caribbean migrants' boldness stemmed from the fact that they did not recognise the lesson, learnt by every African-American in the cradle, that the more distinguished jobs were off limits. After all they'd come from islands where social standing was based more on class than race. They constituted the most adventurous islanders; many had made a good living in Panama up until the completion of the canal in 1914, when their services were no longer required. In Harlem, they cleaved to each other, endured the monikers of 'monkey chaser', 'ring tail', 'cockney' and 'King George's niggers' and the snide lampooning song:

> When a monkey chaser dies
> Don't need no undertaker
> Just throw him in de Harlem River
> He'll float back to Jamaica.

The 'monkey chasers' formed fraternal organisations and social clubs and pooled their savings into unofficial, collective banking systems that offered each 'partner', after regular monthly deposits, a yearly draw from the rotating credit lines and emergency interest-free loans. Nonetheless, Caribbean immigrants were said to be aggressive in business and local politics, and – even when naturalised citizens – pledged allegiance, not to Uncle Sam, but to the superior King George V. As Claude McKay put it, 'West Indians [were] incredibly addicted to the waving of the Union Jack in the face of their American cousins.'²² At times, he acknowledged, it could be prudent for his countrymen to accentuate the difference between themselves and black Americans. McKay often told the anecdote of having once been swept up inadvertently in a police dragnet. When he was brought before the court the following morning, the judge dealt summarily with the rest of the defendants but his stance softened on hearing McKay's voice. He peered over his glasses and began reminiscing with the poet about a recent vacation in Jamaica and chastised the police for having made a false arrest. Henceforth, McKay had resolved 'to cultivate more my native accent'.²³

To the discerning ear it would have been easy to recognise Marcus Mosiah Garvey's own Jamaican accent but, as he declaimed from the top of a Harlem soapbox, it was masked by a style of speech that reminded Southern migrants of the forceful preachers in their 'shouting churches' back home. The genius of Garvey lay in his early ability to reach out to both native and foreign-born groups. The popular journalist, John E. Bruce, was among those who marvelled at the 'little sawed-off, hammered-down black man, with determination written all over his face, and an engaging smile that caught you and compelled you to listen to his story'.²⁴

That summer, it seemed the Jamaicans, Trinidadians and Virgin Islanders had brought the tropics to Harlem. Green bananas ripened on their window sills, pots of pimento flowered, and the trilling sound of their stepladder compatriots drifted in through open doors and windows. They turned out in their hundreds; the men uniformly in their straw boaters, and women carrying parasols, spilling off the pavement and onto Lenox Avenue, blocking traffic to hear Garvey's doctrine of self-help. Their numbers would soon be swollen by curious, impoverished African-Americans: the bellboys, janitors and maids who'd made the great trek from the South.

Garvey's big break amongst these harassed but slow-to-anger Southern Negroes came through the intervention of the radical Hubert Harrison. The American Dream had turned sour for Harrison. He'd arrived ten years earlier from the Virgin Islands and, like so many migrants, must have thought himself blessed with luck on his appointment as a clerk in the New York Post Office. All had gone reasonably well until he'd made the unforgivable mistake (in the eyes of certain powerful men) of criticising Booker T. Washington – an act akin to writing his own dismissal note. Though Booker T.'s agent in New York (a close friend of the postmaster) publicly declared no part in it, it quickly came to pass. By the time Garvey met Harrison, the former post-office clerk had already undergone a transformation into a class warrior. He'd been courted as the great black hope of the Socialists, and managed to eke out a living on a small stipend from the party which was keen to exploit his contacts and standing amongst black Harlemites, and have him serve as a recruiting agent. But after a few unproductive years (in which, for instance, trade unions still barred black membership and Southern Socialists continued to warn against the races blending 'at the present time') a chill of disenchantment had set in. Harrison had renounced his attachment to the party: instead the 'Black Scorates' – a reference to his formidable intellect and bespectacled, potato-shaped head – was promoting a philosophy of separation and black self-reliance. The *Voice*, the black paper that Harrison edited, made explicit his creed that the road to unity between blacks – of all description – would be through appealing to their hearts as well as their heads. And in the 'poetry for the people' section of that paper, he perfectly articulated his belief that there was no 'Negro problem' to solve; rather, there was a Caucasian one. His own poem 'The Black Man's Burden' summed it up. Rudyard Kipling had spelt out patronisingly in 'The White Man's Burden' that it was the Englishman's duty to regulate the affairs of backward and underdeveloped peoples of colour. In his sharp parody of Kipling, Harrison laid bare raw feelings of abuse and rank hypocrisy:

> Take up the black man's burden
> Send forth the worst ye breed
> And bind our sons in shackles
> To serve your selfish greed.

Where two years previously Hubert Harrison had taken the Socialist propaganda south of Harlem into the very belly of capitalism, setting up a soapbox on Wall Street, he now gave up on white people altogether. He devoted himself exclusively to lecturing among his own people and to the propagation of a New Negro Movement. Garvey was both alarmed and intrigued by the depths of Harrison's bitterness; certainly he was darkened by the shadow cast by the Black Socrates. But overriding any hesitation about following Harrison into the furnace of hate was the knowledge that through the Virgin Islander Garvey himself would gain an entrée to an even larger audience.

On 12 June 1917, Hubert Harrison had invited Garvey to share the stage at the inaugural meeting of his 'Liberty League of Negro-Americans' in front of some 2,000 Harlemites at the Bethel African Methodist Episcopal church. Harrison was a polished orator but, even so, he was no match for Marcus Garvey. 'This was Harlem's first real sight of Garvey,' and when he took the floor, 'his magnetic personality, torrential eloquence, and intuitive knowledge of crowd psychology were all brought into play,' reported James Weldon Johnson. 'He swept the audience along with him.'[25]

Garvey was a sensation that night, and more so at subsequent meetings. He began as a warm-up act to the Black Socrates but soon Harrison would find the roles of master and pupil reversed. There was no coup. Garvey simply wooed Harrison's supporters with the seductive sound of his beautiful voice and the simplicity of his compelling arguments. He was also fortunate that vanity does not appear to have played too great a part in Harrison's make-up. Hubert Harrison, like Garvey, was a man forever on the move. But he had a large family (of five children) to feed, and consequently could not be as single-minded in his pursuit of their shared ideals. He saw in Garvey an ally and man with the same amount of, if not greater, prodigious energy. The loquacious Jamaican spoke far longer than any other, and held, entertained and drew audiences away from his bemused, rival stepladder sages. Garvey's success was attributed to his profound empathy with the crowds. 'His words were compassionate,' recalled Virginia Collins, 'he spoke from his soul, and you had this feeling that you were there, that you [were] he, too, that you felt the same thing he was speaking of.'[26] Such sentiments were equally apparent to Harrison. They spoke the same language, in large part, he later mused, because Garvey had helped himself to some of his better ideas. But Garvey's latest mentor was a generous and patient intellectual who watched with little rancour as his followers turned towards his protégé.

The pitiful plight of the Caribbean black man's blood relations in the USA had stirred Marcus Garvey's imagination. He was starting to detach himself from an outlook formed through the prism of a Jamaican colonial world, governed firstly through class privilege and secondly by racial prejudices. On American soil that order was reversed: race came first. 'The American Negro,' he stated ironically, 'occupies the best position among all Negroes up to the present time,' and for that 'he has the white man to thank.' Garvey had found, perversely, in his travels throughout black America that 'the honest prejudice of the South was sufficiently evident to give the Negro the start with a race consciousness responsible for the state of development already reached by the race'.[27]

5

NO FLAG BUT THE STARS AND STRIPES – AND POSSIBLY THE UNION JACK

Come lay your kinkey head on Mammy's shoulder
Don't you cry you're Mammy's chocolate soldier.
And a soldier can't be crying, even though he's dying
Though your skin is dark at night,
I know your little pickaninny heart is white.

Sidney D. Mitchell and Archie Gottler,
'Mammy's Chocolate Soldier' (1918)

BESIEGED by rent collectors, debts he couldn't pay and a fiancée who showed no let-up in goading him to alleviate her own desperate circumstances, Garvey had been on the point of returning to Jamaica before he met Harrison. Yet with Harrison's tutelage, he now exploded each night onto the stage. So successful were these speeches that Harrison would later tell all who would listen that it was he who had brought the greatest orator ever seen to the Negro world's attention. Thoughts of returning home were put on hold as Garvey considered his options. Back on the tiny island of Jamaica he'd be working once again in miniature. The USA offered a much more exciting theatre of operation, a much grander canvas to match the scale of his unbound ambition. Garvey was the coming man, as far as sections of black America were concerned.

By 1917, American newspapers – not noted for their international coverage – were filled with dispatches from the ongoing carnage in Europe. On 2 June, President Woodrow Wilson answered the Allies' prayers and took America into the war under the slogan: 'Make the

World Safe for Democracy'. It was a declaration that presented a conundrum for African-American leaders, clearly the standard definition of democracy was not something that its black citizens benefited from at home. Woodrow Wilson had declared for America, but could he count on the African-American? Anecdotally, James Weldon Johnson, the editor of the conservative black newspaper, the *New York Age*, had evidence of ambivalence – at least from the snatches of conversations he overheard in a Harlem barber's shop. When its resident philosopher was asked if he'd join the army and take up arms against the Germans, he is said to have replied, 'The Germans ain't done nothin' to me, and if they have, I forgive 'em.'[1] A conclusive verdict had yet to be reached.

Garvey's future rival, W. E. B. Du Bois, seemed to have caught the prevailing patriotic mood when he advocated in the pages of the *Crisis* that the Negro should put to one side his 'special grievances' for now, and 'close ranks, shoulder to shoulder' with his fellow Americans.[2] The majority needed little encouragement. The recent Mexican border dispute had already whetted appetites. Young men eager for honour and glory were spellbound by the romantic headlines in the *New York Age* of the ambush of black soldiers, the 'Gallant Tenth Cavalry . . . [who] faced almost certain death at Carrizal with smiles and songs on their Lips'. And if the jubilant scenes which greeted reports in 1916 of the formation of a new, all-black regiment, the 369th, in Harlem proved anything, then it was that the black man, when it came to pass, would be just as prepared to smile and sing his way to the next world fighting for Uncle Sam on the battlefields of Europe.[3]

The Governor of New York, Charles Whitman, had been cheered at a casino in Harlem for his endorsement of the 369th. In recognition of their fearlessness in battle, the French would later dub them 'The Harlem Hell Fighters'. One of the district's leading clergymen, Adam Clayton Powell Snr, who was also on the platform that day, seemed to have anticipated Du Bois's hunch: 'We do not know any flag but the Stars and Stripes,' Powell told the Governor. 'We have always stood ready as Boston Common, Bunker Hill, Fort Pillow and San Juan Heights will testify, and we now stand ready to give our blood in the defence of the sacred principles enunciated in the Declaration of Independence.'[4]

Whether they shared that view or not, more than half a million African-Americans registered in the first week of July 1917, at the start of enrolment under the new Selective Service Act. Among the potential recruits was a twenty-nine-year-old asthmatic Jamaican who was speedily exempted on the grounds that he was physically unfit.[5] Garvey's registration card was completed more out of legal necessity than conviction. In the three years since the war began, his enthusiastic endorsement of the Allies' moral supremacy and that of His Majesty's forces to 'smite the common foe' had curdled. A certain cynicism had begun to set in. On 16 March 1916, over a thousand Jamaican recruits had boarded the *Verdala* bound for England. Fearing enemy warships on the north coast of Europe, the ship was diverted to Halifax, Nova Scotia. But before it could reach safe shores the *Verdala* sailed into a blizzard. The Jamaican volunteers were only kitted out in lightweight tropical khaki uniforms. Denied the heavier uniforms which were on board, more than half the soldiers suffered from frostbite; there were also substantial casualties. Thereafter, the War Office, perhaps not surprisingly, struggled in its recruitment drive.

Arguably, military ineptitude was not colour-coded. The British High Command, and General Haig in particular, only paused momentarily, if at all, before ordering thousands of his compatriots out of the trenches and over the top into no man's land, on suicidal missions. Similarly, when African-American troops of the 368th Regiment later advanced towards the enemy, they would complain, for instance, that the field officers' callous disregard for their survival left them battling with enemy wires without the provision of wire cutters, and exposed to German mortars and Gattling guns.[6] Hubert Harrison and Marcus Garvey reacted angrily to the often exaggerated accounts of black soldiers being assigned the most perilous tasks with their lives needlessly squandered.

Conversely, W. E. B. Du Bois raged against the insult to the vast majority of African-American soldiers in being relegated to supporting roles: more likely to be issued with a broom or shovel than rifle and bayonet. Better the news of the unprecedented and unbroken 191 days that the 'Harlem Hell Fighters' endured under enemy fire. The 'no ordinary sacrifice', of African-American men fighting in the First World War, Du Bois considered a 'deposit in the bank towards full citizenship' which would be drawn on at the conflict's end. But Garvey was not alone in doubting the wisdom of the *Crisis*'s, jingoism. In an ironic inversion of the usual state of affairs, no sooner was the ink dry on Du Bois's editorial than the conservative black press were taking issue with the militant editor's conservatism. When one considered Dr Du Bois's distaste for compromise, and factored into the equation the raft of injustices (lynching topping the list) that the black man could daily expect

in America, then his editorial was indefensible. For Hubert Harrison –
and by extension Garvey – it bore all the hallmarks of, at the very least,
questionable self-justification. 'All the more significant because of his
former services to the race', which, Harrison argued, were 'of a high
and courageous sort'.[7] William Du Bois should have known better.
Though the editor fudged the dates of his supportive article, its publication in the *Crisis* appeared shortly after he was offered a head-turning
captain's commission into Military Intelligence. The two events were
not unconnected. It was a rare miscalculation on Du Bois's part, notwithstanding that he eventually declined the offer of a commission.

Riding in on the coat-tails of Hubert Harrison, Garvey became a
vocal opponent of participation in the 'white man's war' in which the
lot of black soldiers mirrored their civilian counterparts: relegated to
segregated quarters, cooking, cleaning, transporting and burying their
fallen white compatriots. By the war's end he would openly proclaim:
'Why go over to Europe and fight for the whites and lose an arm or
leg when you can fight for a just cause?'[8] Why should black people
fight for democracy abroad when they didn't have the vote at home?
Or as A. Philip Randolph's the *Messenger* put it, 'We would rather
make Georgia safe for the Negro.'[9] In black churches, rented halls and
on street corners, Garvey and his fellow orators argued the point: that
there should be no conscription without representation. In the midst
of such conflagration, the War Department held out the hope that a
conciliatory tone in a militant organ such as the *Crisis* might neutralise
the volcano of African-American resentment that spluttered and then
exploded after the events of 2 July 1917.

Barely a month after signing up for the war, America had witnessed
its worst racial riot in decades – and not in the bigoted South but the
smug industrial North, in East St Louis. The Midwestern city had seen
a recent influx of southern blacks recruited by labour agents to work
in its factories. In the face of official discouragement from Mayor
Mollman of East St Louis (Mollman had requested an order advising
all Louisiana Negroes to stay away from the city), large numbers of
blacks had arrived in the last year. East St Louis had been gripped by
strikes, and while the white workforce remained locked out, rumours
abounded that non-unionised black labourers had been recruited as
strike-breakers, and were, in any event, undercutting their white counterparts. Resentment had rumbled on during the course of the year
and built, inevitably, towards an explosive peak. The spark for that

long-anticipated eruption of violence in East St Louis came on 1 July 1917, when a car filled with plainclothes policemen sped through the black part of town and was fired on by nervous local people who feared its occupants were intent on driving by and shooting. The next morning mobs of heavily armed white men, lugging cans of petrol, descended on the black district and started firing at will at any black person in sight; and setting fire to the district. Local papers reported 'boot-black Negroes' pathetically trying to outrun white mobs, and how Negroes were eventually shot down like rabbits, strung up to telegraph poles, and burnt out of their homes.

Armed men positioned themselves along the railroad tracks with their guns poised to shoot any escaping blacks. The reporter for the *St Louis Republic* described how, 'a crazed Negro would dash from his burning home, sometimes with a revolver in his hand. Immediately revolvers by the score would be fired. He would zig-zag through the spaces between buildings. Then a well-directed shot would strike him. He would leap into the air. There were deep shouts, intermingled with shrill feminine ones. The flames would creep to the body. The Negro would writhe, attempt to get up, more shots would be fired.'

Women also were guilty of the most vile abuses. Carlos F. Hurd, a reporter for the *Post-Dispatch*, was an eyewitness to the fury of white prostitutes who rounded on black women: 'I saw Negro women begging for mercy and pleading that they had harmed no one, set upon by white women of the baser sort . . . [who] beat the Negresses . . . with fists, stones and sticks.' Hurd was disgusted by the sight of 'one of these furies fling[ing] herself at a militiaman who was trying to protect a Negress, and wrestle with him for his bayonetted gun.'

The worst of the violence culminated in lynchings. In the *Post-Dispatch*, Hurd, who seems to have decided that the best way to communicate the full horror to readers was to focus on individual events, went on to report, 'the most sickening incident of the evening when they got stronger rope. To put the rope around the Negro's neck, one of the lynchers stuck his fingers inside the gaping scalp and lifted the Negro's head by it, literally bathing his hand in the man's blood. "Get hold, and pull for East St Louis," called the man as he seized the other end of the rope. The Negro was lifted to a height of about seven feet and the body left hanging there for hours.'

Once the mob's thirst for blood had abated, and men returned home for their evening meals, thousands of black people crept back under the untrustworthy protection of the National Guard to collect essential belongings before fleeing the city. Officially, the death toll was said to be thirty-nine blacks and nine whites. Unofficially, the final figure of black deaths was rumoured to be in the hundreds. On the index of previous civilian horrors, East St Louis was off the scale. Compounding the sense of African-American despair was that these brutal violations occurred while black servicemen trained in military camps and prepared to fight for their country – now at war – and set sail for Europe.

Du Bois and the NAACP responded by leading 10,000 protestors on a silent march (save for a muffled drum roll) down 5th Avenue in New York. Behind the drummers, women and children carried placards reading 'MR PRESIDENT, WHY NOT MAKE AMERICA SAFE FOR DEMOCRACY' and 'MOTHER, DO LYNCHERS GO TO HEAVEN?'. And in front of the lone dignitary carrying the Stars and Stripes was a banner stretching half across the street bearing the inscription, 'YOUR HANDS ARE FULL OF BLOOD'.

East St Louis had shown that black people could not count on the white National Guard to protect them. And if such murder could happen in the Midwest, then it could happen anywhere in the Union. New York may never have witnessed a stranger or more impressive sight than the silent march but Garvey's reaction was far more visceral. By temperament he was never given to quiet dignified diplomacy: he was much more inclined to make as much noise as he could, and was among the 'rabble-rousers' calling for armed self-defence.

At 3 p.m. on Sunday 8 July, six days after the disastrous destruction of lives and livelihood in East St Louis, Marcus Garvey took to the podium at the Lafayette Hall, New York. Quivering in every fibre, he launched into a step-by-step analysis of the roots of the violence that in some measure would tally with the verdict of the coroner's later inquest. For more than an hour he held the hushed crowd in a speech that was a prolonged howl of outrage. Pulling together newspaper reports and eyewitness accounts, Garvey addressed an incredulous and emotional audience which groaned, gasped, and cried out in shame as he catalogued the grim details. There'd been a dress rehearsal the month before when black passengers had been pulled from vehicles and beaten; then on 2 July the mob had run amok, burning, maiming and lynching while the National Guard who'd been dispatched hurriedly to the town – but, crucially, without ammunition – stood helplessly to the side.

Marcus Garvey laid the blame squarely at the feet of Mayor Mollman who 'fostered a well arranged conspiracy to prevent black men migrating from the South much to the loss of Southern farmers who for months have been moving heaven itself to prevent the exodus of [their] labour serfs . . . into the North'. Mollman, he believed, had created an atmosphere of hate, a 'Roman holiday' where 'the mob [had] feasted on the blood of the Negro'. To long and pronounced cheers Garvey raged that 'this [was] no time for fine words, but a time to lift one's voice against the savagery of a people who claim to be the dispensers of democracy'. East St Louis was called a race riot, but really it was a white riot. In his speech that evening, 'The Conspiracy of the East St Louis Riots', before several thousand outraged black people, Garvey catalogued the grievous ways in which the Negro had been betrayed:

> The black man has always trusted the white man. He has always clung to him as a brother man . . . When there was no white man in Africa to help the sickly and dying Livingstone, the black man, ever true, even as Simon of Cyrenia was true, in bearing the cross of the despised Jesus, came to the rescue of the suffering Englishman, and when he was dead, faithful as they were, they bore his body for hundreds of miles across the desert and plains of Africa . . . The Negro in American history from the time of Crispus Attucks at Boston, the 10th Cavalry at San Juan Hill, which saved the day for Roosevelt, up to the time when they stuck to Boyd at Carrizal, has demonstrated to the American Nation that he is as true as steel. Yet for all his services he receives the reward of lynching, burning and wholesale slaughter.[10]

Such horrors were not supposed to happen in America – in Tsarist Russia, perhaps, where Jewish communities cowered in constant fear of pogroms, but even there, the recent Bolshevik revolution spelt the end of such practices. How could a Negro pogrom occur in the land of the free, fifty years on from the Civil War that had ended slavery? The clock had been wound back to the dark days of antebellum life. Nothing good could come of East St Louis. It was a blight on the American landscape: a terrible line had been crossed and the great fear was of explosive repetitions up and down the country.

East St Louis also signalled a turning point in the life of Marcus Garvey. Henceforth, the improvement of Negro life in America would be his focus. His speech, 'The Conspiracy of the East St Louis Riots', announced as much. It was rushed to the printers, made up into a pamphlet and distributed widely throughout black America. The nascent UNIA would distribute the proceeds from the sale of the pamphlets to those who had suffered in Illinois. And importantly for Garvey, if, as seemed likely, hundreds of copies turned up in the black belts up and down America, his name and his message would became more firmly established in the churches, barbers' shops and social clubs of his new constituency. Garvey had concluded that another East St Louis was possible because 'white people are taking advantage of black men today because black men all over the world are disunited'. In particular, it was the Old Testament violence of Garvey's language – mixed with the spirit of defiance of the new Negro – that thrilled and disturbed.

Over the coming months, Garvey electrified audiences with speeches in which he exhorted his docile fellow blacks to stand up and fight back. He tapped into a deepening ground swell of fear and resentment. And if Garvey was sounding the alarm bells, as he surely was, then Americans (black and white) would soon be shaken by a frightening reveille on the streets of Houston.

NON-COMMISSIONED OFFICERS WANTED

WHITE MEN

Married or Single

EXPERIENCED IN THE HANDLING

OF COLORED MEN

For Enlistment as Non-Commissioned Officers in the Service,

Battalions, Engineer Corps

NATIONAL ARMY

So read a typical circular, distributed in connection with the army recruitment stations at Jacksonville, Tampa, Miami, Pensacola and Tallahassee. That was one of the biggest singular problems in the War Department's approach to the management of its black soldiers. As James Weldon Johnson pointed out, the experience of handling coloured men generally meant having 'the qualification of a slave driver, of a chain-gang guard, or of an overseer of the roughest kind of labour'.[11] The problem was compounded by the military high command's determination to confine Northern black recruits to camps located in the South. These recruits had, largely, not been exposed to the daily humiliations that their black brothers had come to expect in places like Jacksonville, Tallahassee – and especially Houston, Texas. And on the night of 23 August 1917, a battalion of the 24th Infantry – one of the Negro regiments, stationed at Fort Sam Houston – fed up with the 'Jim Crow' goading, brutality and beatings meted out to them by the Houston police, had had enough. They broke into the ammunition storerooms, loaded rifles and cut through downtown Houston in military formation, shooting as they went. By the end of their murderous spree nineteen people lay dead, five of them Houston policemen. In the subsequent courts martial, thirteen soldiers would be executed, and more than fifty sentenced to life imprisonment. James Weldon Johnson's appeal for Woodrow Wilson to show leniency towards the condemned men largely fell on the President's closed ears.[12] This was not totally unexpected from a man who had brought a Southern oligarchy to Washington; a president who, in the teeth of black protest over the racist assertions of the recently released *The Birth of a Nation*, had arranged for a private screening of the film at the White House. He rubber-stamped its interpretation of post-Civil War reconstruction in which the honourable Ku Klux Klan fought back against the excesses of Northern carpetbaggers and freed slaves. Wilson had said allegedly, 'It is like writing history with lightning. And my only regret is that it is all so terribly true.'[13] After East St Louis and the Fort Sam incident, the USA was like an old tree struck by lightning, more fragile as a result, but still standing. And it was about to learn the painful lesson that would recur in future internal conflagrations – race riots and lynchings – that Negroes would not consent to the role of victim.

Marcus Garvey instinctively understood this desire for retribution. But the majority of the established African-American leaders thought violence – other than the abstract and intellectual kind – was repugnant. Violence was the path traditionally abjured for practical and moral reasons. In the past, at similar forks in the road, the disarming sacrifice of Uncle Tom was mostly favoured over Nat Turner's apocalyptic destruction. After all, the slaves and their descendants were in a minority in the USA. They were always going to be outnumbered, and, more importantly, outgunned.

Events like East St Louis also proved that there was no guarantee of unity amongst the black population. The small number of upper-crust blacks who belonged to elite fraternities like the Society of Sons of New York, certainly didn't want to be lumped together with their less fortunate brothers. Given the history of America, one could imagine them arguing that it was surprising that there weren't more East St Louises, more murders and lynching. Amongst these well-to-do blacks, long settled in New York before the arrival of Southern and Caribbean migrants, it was considered almost bad manners to draw too much attention to such outrages. Mary White Ovington, one of the white founders of the NAACP, wrote, 'The taint of slavery was far removed from these people, who looked with scorn upon arrivals from the South . . . These old New York colored families, sometimes bearing historic Dutch and English names, have diminished in size and importance . . . [in relation to] the ambitious men and women, full of the energy and determination of the immigrant.'[14] Miss Ovington was one of the first non-blacks to recognise the appeal of Marcus Garvey.

For the first time, Garvey's ascension also came to the attention of the newly-formed Bureau of Investigation (BOI) which would soon fuel the growing paranoia of J. Edgar Hoover. Agents had begun to infiltrate street and church-hall meetings in Harlem, bringing back reports that Garvey had advocated, for instance, that 'for every Negro lynched by whites in the South, Negroes should lynch a white in the North'. Such violent rhetoric wasn't out of place in Harlem where some intemperate ministers were suggesting that their congregations forgo the uncertainty of prayer and invest in the surety of dynamite.

The associates of Harrison's Liberty League, with whom Garvey increasingly aligned himself, were equally militant – even more unguardedly so. Following an earlier violent conflagration, the veteran journalist John E. Bruce had written of the need for resistance and the application of force: 'If they burn your house, burn theirs. If they kill your wives and children, kill theirs . . . By a vigorous adherence to this course, the shedding of human blood by white men will soon become a thing of the past.'[15] If Garvey hoped to gain a following among those who listened to these men, then he gambled on the need to be just as zealous. He was careful to target his words to his audiences – secret servicemen excepted: such inflammatory invocations were not for the general public's consumption, and were never included in printed versions of his speeches. As in Jamaica, Marcus Garvey recognised that the custodians of conventional power were invariably white, and he was careful not to ostracise potentially influential and sympathetic patrons.

If he had harboured doubts before about making an impact in the USA, they were now dispelled: the Jamaican immigrant was on his way. Confirmation could be found in the pages of *Home News* – 'For the People of Harlem and the Heights' – which regularly carried reports on meetings held by 'Professor Marcus Garvey, late of London University'. In the euphoria of his rise, erroneous details were conveniently left uncorrected. Besides, the title more or less came with the territory. Scholarly black men in Harlem, denied conventional routes to those achievements (that is, being unable to afford the fees that might one day lead to a university degree), tended to write their own narratives. As the Reverend Charles Martin, a migrant from St Kitts, who through diligence and perseverance had established a ministry in Harlem, wryly recorded, among the preachers who elevated themselves to doctors of divinity without the paper qualifications, there was 'no spot like Harlem for conferring titles'.[16] Even the erudite Hubert Harrison – recognised scholar that he was – felt the need to invent a degree from Holland for which he was later roundly reproved. All through his life, Garvey seemed to be drawn to, and to attract, such self-educated men – mirror images of himself.

By the close of 1917, Garvey had succeeded in luring away most of the key associates of Harrison's Liberty League and welcomed them into the fold of the nascent Harlem branch of the UNIA. Men such as Samuel Augustus Duncan from St Kitts and the Barbadian, Isaac B. Allen, already held claim to some standing amongst Caribbean migrants. Allen, a former longshoreman turned real-estate agent, had scores of West Indian tenants and prospective property owners on his books, and Duncan, as leader of the West Indian Protective Society, offered a trusting hand to newcomers stepping off the banana boats into an uncharted future. Both understood the machinations of the city and of Harlem in particular; both saw in Garvey a spectacular crowd puller, an ambitious and intuitive promoter, and finally, an incomparable egotist. Garvey attracted and repulsed in equal measure. Attraction ultimately won over though, when the cynical but curious journalist John E. Bruce agreed to act as conduit for the UNIA.

Singularly admired by all the young radicals, John Edward Bruce had integrity and longevity on his side. Born into slavery, he'd followed Union soldiers north to freedom in the 1860s. From the age of eighteen, Bruce had steadfastly developed into an outstanding and campaigning journalist. He adopted the nom de plume 'Bruce Grit' in recognition of the grit he put into his pungent prose. In forty years, Bruce Grit had plotted his own race movements, agitated and cajoled through

reams of captivating journalistic writings, he made readers laugh at
the same time. It was quite an achievement and he was fêted for it,
particularly because, as a freelance writer with no secure berth, hunger
had continually snapped at his heels. At over six feet tall, with stiff
bearing and walrus-like moustache, he could unnerve strangers but his
manner belied a kind and generous spirit from which venom only occasionally escaped. Garvey's path to Bruce could be traced back to London
and Dusé Mohamed Ali. Yet another self-educated man, and amateur
African archivist, John Edward Bruce had, almost single-handedly,
pioneered a unique form of black journalism, connecting the three
corners of the former Atlantic slave trade; his journalistic writings
reached out to the diaspora, and were included, for example, in the
pages of Dusé Mohamed's *African Times and Orient Review*.

Bruce had monitored the trajectory of many young race leaders who
had flashed across the Harlem landscape. Twenty years earlier, he'd
have counted himself among them. As 1917 drew to a close, Bruce
still had plenty of grit and a few good years remaining. Garvey and
the movement that grew around him would act as a final spur, but
that was more than a year away. For now, John Bruce was content to
accept the UNIA post of chairman of the advisory board and to lend
his support – but not unreservedly so.

Garvey needed Bruce's seal of approval if the other Young Turks
were going to put aside their own ideas and fledgling societies to
embrace *his* UNIA. Without Bruce's endorsement, no matter how tepid,
Marcus Garvey would remain at the helm of an empty vessel, tacking
in violent waters, bereft of an experienced crew.

In November 1917, that crew consisted largely of conservative
figures such as Samuel Duncan and Isaac Allen. In an uncharacteristic
gesture of humility, Marcus Garvey relinquished the presidency of the
UNIA to Duncan, and limited himself – in theory at least – to the role
of international organiser. But even before the fundamental building
blocks were put in place, the ideological stress lines were beginning
to show. Marcus Garvey wanted to pick up and move on from where
he'd left off in Kingston, Jamaica – replicating a society with Negro
self-improvement from the peel to the core. But should the organisation be a social or political one? And if meetings were to culminate
in rousing renditions of the national anthem, should it be 'God Save
the King' or 'The Star Spangled Banner'?

Since arriving in Harlem, Garvey had steadily steered a course away from his old colonial self (defined through an allegiance to Great Britain and the Caribbean) and towards his newly adopted republican homeland – notwithstanding his unprocessed application for naturalisation and citizenship. How far the same could be said to be true of his new allies was uncertain. Samuel Augustus Duncan's stewardship of the West Indian Protective Society suggested otherwise. Its annual dinner was held on Empire Day, and it drew support from the kind of member who, on his first brush with racial prejudice in the USA, is reported to have blurted out, 'But I am a British subject. I will report this to my consulate!'[17]

The transfer of their allegiance constituted more of a seismic shift amongst his fellow islanders than Garvey had anticipated. Either he was far ahead in his thinking or they were far behind. Not to be outflanked by these primary West Indians who were, ironically, much more established in Harlem, Garvey brought in his boyhood friend, Wilfred Domingo, a fast-thinking chameleon with an equally fast-twitching smile, to help smooth over some of the teething difficulties with board members.

Garvey recognised the need to further justify his worth in their eyes. Setting out to win the sympathy of influential friends of the Negro, he drew up a list of the most likely candidates amongst Manhattan's glitterati. Pretty soon some significant figures were showing up for his massed meetings at the Palace Casino in Harlem. As in Jamaica, Garvey defaulted to the tried and trusted scheme of a popular elocution contest to generate widespread interest. He would signal the serious and civilising nature of the UNIA by the respectful company it kept. To that end, he set out to charm one of the most erudite men in New York, Nicholas Murray Butler, the autocratic and influential president of Columbia University. Out of curiosity or simple voyeurism, Butler astonished all but Garvey when he accepted the invitation to grace the organisation with his presence in judging the State Elocution Contest among the Negro people of New York. 'My compliments upon the admirable competition,' he later wrote to Garvey. 'I left the Hall with a new feeling of pride and satisfaction at what the members of the Association and their friends are accomplishing.'

Nicholas Butler's attendance was a coup and steadied the hand of wavering board members. Thereafter, Garvey doggedly pursued Butler like the punter who, having struck gold with his first set of lottery numbers, rigorously sticks to the winning formula. He ignored the diminishing signs of Butler's ever returning on subsequent invitations, until the polite excuses of his unavailability 'at this time' hardened into an unequivocal 'no!'.

If Nicholas Butler wasn't, ultimately, predisposed towards Garvey then neither, on closer inspection, was the movement's senior adviser. The courtship of John E. Bruce proved a boomerang that returned to strike Garvey. A cautious Bruce, seeking to establish the character of the man he was now aligning himself with, had contacted Garvey's former associate in London, Dusé Mohamed Ali. Towards the end of 1917, Ali's response arrived. And as Claude McKay would recall, when the unflattering letter was read out at an open UNIA meeting, 'it exploded like a well-timed bomb and broke up the organisation'.[18] For John Bruce had asked Dusé's appraisal of Marcus Garvey, 'the Oxford graduate'. A rather cantankerous Ali had written back disparaging Garvey, pointedly referring to him as a messenger – a not very good one – who'd been discharged, after three months, due to his unsatisfactory conduct. Mohamed Ali went on to surmise that Garvey's sole pretext for starting the UNIA in America was for collecting money for his own purposes.[19] The humiliation didn't end there. Over the next few weeks, Bruce piled it on ever higher. Believing himself to have been duped, he wrote angrily to the *New Negro* with a list of questions for Garvey, the 'wandering alien with a grudge against toil', to answer. He began by asking, 'Have you any means of support?' and ended with, 'Who are you anyway and what is your game?'[20]

Sensing his time was up with the organisation, at least as it was presently configured, Marcus Garvey resigned. But any suggestion that the UNIA could dispense with the services of its inspirational founder were quickly corrected. Far from the resignation being the final honourable act of a man disgraced, Garvey characterised what had happened as a putsch against him, engineered by Samuel Duncan and his supporters. They had sought, Garvey believed, to exploit the organisation for their own political designs. In the short term, the spurned UNIA leader relocated to the Old Fellows Temple and held rival meetings, whilst preparing for an increasingly favoured pastime: litigation. 'To throw off the political influence [of the rivals] I was even forced into court,' Garvey later recalled, with his tongue firmly in his cheek, 'for I had to somewhat beat up Duncan in detaching him from the presidency.' It was no contest. Garvey successfully wrestled the name back from his enemies, along with the majority of its members whom he now estimated to be 600. And one of the first acts of the newly reconstituted UNIA was to restore its Jamaican founding father to the presidency. The experiment of sharing the top honours with others would not be repeated.

The UNIA at war with itself was, in 1917, a microcosm of a nation that could similarly be so described. Since its entry into the World War, the internal conflicts within America had sharpened with dark warnings of the wisdom of arming black soldiers. Southern white students of the Negro mind pointed to the 'extreme emotional temperament of the African ... which is easily exalted to passionate partisanships'.[21] Put bluntly, could the Negro be trusted? Bureau of Investigation agents fanned out over America, particularly the black conurbations, looking for signs of disloyalty.

Harlem was riven with rumours of German spies, disguised as cigar-storekeepers and real-estate agents, who were said to be fomenting insurrection in the minds of an increasingly belligerent Negro population. In the weeks and months after black soldiers had run amok in Houston, paranoid doubts began to be voiced in parts of the US administration about the liability to disloyalty of the Negro. One rumour whispered through the district was that, in the aftermath of war and German success, the Negro would receive a fairer deal at the hands of the Kaiser, as well as the promise of 'social equality' – that eventuality, dreaded by much of mainstream America, was a code for black men's desire for sexual relations with white women. In the fevered climate of war such fanciful ideas were not discounted. One only had to look to the German propaganda which sought to undermine Great Britain, by encouraging disunity amongst her colonies; holding up the prospect, for example, of Indian independence, following a German victory.

A deterrent was needed. The Espionage Act was quickly followed by the Sedition Act in its passage through Congress – both were designed to quash sedition; to penalise those who 'wilfully utter, print, write or publish any disloyal, profane, scurrilous or abusive language about the form of government of the United States'; and to caution against any other actions that might undermine the war effort. It quickly snared A. Philip Randolph and Chandler Owen, the editors of the largely unread Socialist *Messenger* magazine (though the Bureau of Investigation took out a subscription) and authors of 'Pro-Germanism among the Negroes'. A. Philip Randolph, the young radical who'd introduced

Garvey to Harlem crowds, had to thank the prejudice of the judge in avoiding a jail sentence. Discounting the possibility that the two young African-Americans were intellectually capable of composing such a treacherous document, he concluded that they must be patsies for sinister white Socialists.[22]

Rumours of espionage were further offset by another of even greater potential damage – that of Negro life being callously squandered on the European battlefield. There were many variants of this rumour, but in essence they were the same: Negro soldiers were being used as shock troops, first out of the trenches and last back in, sacrificed as cannon fodder, and suffering terrifying casualties and ghastly injuries. Bureau of Investigation agents in Harlem traced one source of these rumours back to a small, portly street orator, who was gaining some notoriety as a Negro agitator. Marcus Garvey didn't dampen those suspicions by his tendency to clam up whenever a policeman edged closer to his audience. He would stand down from his soapbox and hurriedly set up on another street corner, away from the patrolman's gaze.

East St Louis and subsequent riots had put the authorities on edge. The year before, writing in the *New York Age*, James Weldon Johnson had reported on the 'splendid showing' put on by the new recruits of Pullman porters and railroad redcaps – the soon-to-be Hell Fighters – in a glittering military parade through Harlem. Crowds, including police officers and shopkeepers, cheered and laughed along with the regiment, headed that day by the great black vaudevillian, Bert Williams, sitting astride a magnificent white stallion.[23] Complete with an unfamiliar, ramrod military bearing, the droll, sad-eyed minstrel had thrown off his shuffling 'darky' impersonation for the day. But no one, it seems, had bothered to inform the horse. Performing from some other script, the horse bolted and headed for the subway. Williams recalled, as if in the midst of a floodlit routine, 'I talked to [my horse] when it left the parade and I talked to it down there in the subway, but I never did find out why it wanted to go there or why it didn't want to come out.'[24]

Now, one year on, uniformed members of the 369th Regiment caught 'assembling' on a Harlem street corner were cause more for suspicion than for laughter – at least to a passing patrolman, who ordered them to disperse. The soldiers stood their ground. The patrolman drew his nightstick, and attempted to arrest the most truculent member of the group. In the ensuing mayhem, police reinforcements quickly arrived and battled with the troopers and several hundred irate Harlemites who armed themselves with bricks and knives and rushed into the mêlée. The *New York Times* blamed Hubert Harrison and his radical friends who had 'Urge[d] Negroes to Get Arms' for inciting Blacks with their invocations of armed resistance.[25]

The formation of the 369th Regiment, due imminently to embark for Europe, was an exercise in good race relations that could not afford to fail. And after much lobbying of newspaper editors by the regiment's white backers, the riot was downgraded in subsequent reports to an unfortunate disturbance. The Harlem Hell Fighters would have the honour of being among the first troops of the entire American Expeditionary Force to be baptised in the bloody battlefields of Europe. But the fact that the 'unfortunate disturbance' had happened at all – and in the North – pointed to nationwide tensions that seemed to have been exacerbated by the sight of black men donning military uniforms; it also highlighted the authorities' growing unease over the influence of relatively unknown Negro agitators such as Marcus Garvey on excitable and febrile minds.

A. Philip Randolph had noted in his first encounter with Garvey that after his triumphant address, the orator sat down by the podium, composed himself and immediately started organising notes for his next outing; he'd even had the foresight to prepare circulars which were to be distributed amongst the crowd. The Jamaican, Randolph concluded, was a supreme opportunistic propagandist. Now that the USA and its black doughboys were committed to war, it, too, offered up opportunities for propaganda.

One such opportunity arrived in the diminutive shape of Sergeant Henry Johnson and his teenage compadre, Needham Roberts – members of the Harlem Hell Fighters who had sailed to France and were now enduring an unremitting German onslaught in the Allied trenches. 'Two Black Yanks Smear 24 Huns' trumpeted the *Stars and Stripes* on 24 May 1918. The army's internal newspaper revealed how the 'two strapping Negroes, a station porter and elevator boy' – when in civilian life – had been awarded the Croix de Guerre for valour in France after 'repelling a raiding party of 24 Germans'. Marvelling at the wounded Johnson, the subsequent headline in the *New York World*, 'The Battle of Henry Johnson', bore testimony to the fearful damage he inflicted with a broken rifle and 9-inch bolo knife in hand-to-hand combat in the trenches.

Johnson's heroics validated Negro participation in the conflict, ridiculed Southern doubts over African-American manhood and, for good measure, helped boost the sale of war bonds: 'Sgt Johnson licked a dozen Germans,' ran the Liberty Loans campaign. 'How many Victory Stamps have you licked today?'[26] The exploits of Johnson (thereafter dubbed 'Black Death') certainly knocked Marcus Garvey off the front pages of *Harlem Home News*. But now that battle was enjoined, the maturing race leader was prepared to concede that it was going to take 'the black man to whip the Kaiser's soldiers'. Despite his stated reservations about the wisdom of black involvement in the war, he revelled in, and drank from, the cup of their success, for surely there was 'not a more glorious record in the history of the war than the record of those two boys from the New York 15th'.

Johnson and his fellow Harlem Hell Fighters returned to a heroes' welcome the following year. The *New York Age* gathered itself to its full stature before launching into a reverential tribute to the Buffalo soldiers marching up 5th Avenue, passing close to the magnificent victory arch which was just nearing completion: 'Lieutenant Jim Europe walked sedately ahead, and [the] bandmaster had the great band alternate between two noble French military marches.' With studied pride the *Age* continued, 'On the part of the men, there was no prancing, no showing of teeth, no swank; they marched with a steady stride, and from under their battered tin hats eyes that had looked straight at death were kept to the front.'[27]

Marcus Garvey was buried in the midst of the jubilant, flag-waving crowds, straining to get a good look at the returning Hell Fighters on 12 February 1919. He is said to have wept salt tears at the sight of the splendid 369th, knowing full well that the bargain of full civil rights that they had bled and signed up for would not be honoured once the smoke of battle cleared. His suspicion that the old order would swiftly re-establish itself, was borne out by the changing fortunes of Sergeant Henry Johnson.

The wounded, wiry porter had been inundated with offers of lucrative lecture tours on his return. For the fantastic sum of $1,500 he'd dragged himself along to a first speaking engagement at St Louis. Over the previous months he'd been preened and paraded by officers as if he were a beloved military mascot. His commanding officer noted how the head of the regiment 'expressed the affectionate feeling of many of us when he said . . . the least we could do for [Johnson], after all he had done for us, was to treat him as the old 7th Cavalry had treated Custer's horse – let him nibble grass around Headquarters, and when company came, call him in and show him off'.

In St Louis, his patrons had reasonably expected a rousing and celebratory tale of how shared privation in the trenches had forged a unique respect between the races. But in front of an audience primed for adoration, Johnson unleashed a tirade of pent-up frustration over the abuse he and his black troopers had suffered to date. The burghers of St Louis were scandalised when the 'Black Death' veered wildly from the script and exposed the special grievances black soldiers felt towards their white comrades-in-arms. They were no band of brothers, he revealed, and the unpalatable truth was that Uncle Sam's white soldiers had refused to share the same trenches with them. Black members of the audience erupted in applause; the white audience was equally vociferous in its indignation. Johnson had to scuttle out of town. Soon afterwards a warrant for his arrest was issued for wearing his uniform beyond the prescribed date of his commission (even though he was still one month within the limit of his discharge). Thereafter, further speaking engagements did not materialise; overnight, Johnson went from the head of the celebrity list of after-dinner speakers to the top of the military intelligence list of Negro Subversives. A later retraction proved futile. Johnson had been undone by his candour, and Negro agitators like Marcus Garvey were put on note that the victory for democracy abroad had ushered in a new era of intolerance at home.[28]

6

IF WE MUST DIE

I'm not sure whether I'd prefer
to be gently lynched in Mississippi
Or beaten to death by cops in New York.

'Mr Dooley's Philosophy', 1902

WITHOUT doubt the bravery of black soldiers in the trenches did lead to a transformation in the way some white Americans viewed their darker compatriots. The Southern humourist, Irvin Cobb, was one of them. Cobb was famous for genial comedies which drew on a plentiful supply of stereotypical black characters with 'complexions like the bottom of a coal mine, and smiles like the sudden lift of a piano lid'. The unthreatening black world that Cobb wrote about was populated with flamboyant hucksters in ill-fitting suits, and simplistic coons, dozing under the shade of trees. But his journalistic accreditation with the American Expeditionary Force in 1918, and his subsequent contact with the Harlem Hell Fighters on the front line, complicated his perception of the Negro. At first, he'd described his visit amongst black troops in France as 'two days of a superior variety of continuous blackface vaudeville'. His account of an exchange between a white officer and Private Cooksey (a former Harlem lift attendant who grandly referred to himself as an 'internal chauffeur') reads suspiciously like a well-rehearsed vaudeville routine: The commanding officer asks Cooksey what he'd do if enemy mortars started landing close by. 'Kurnel, ain't going to tell you no lie,' says Cooksey, 'I fest nacthelly be obliged to go away from here. Fest put it in de books as "absent without leave" 'cause I'll be back jest ez soon as I kin get my brakes to work.' The colonel then asks Cooksey what he'd do should the enemy advance without warning. Cooksey answers again that he'd be forced to flee, but rest assured 'we'll spread de word all over France dat de Germans is comin'.' Come crunch time though, when the theory was put into practice and the mortars began to fall, Cobb reported admiringly that neither 'Cooksey nor any of his black mates showed the white feather or yellow streak or turned back'.[1]

Irvin Cobb underwent a Pauline conversion in France, observing the black sons of Mississippi and Alabama marching towards the Rhine. The normal, prejudicial, assumptions that came with their casual description would no longer hold: 'Hereafter,' he declared, '"n-i-g-g-e-r" will merely be another way of spelling "American".'[2] At the war's cessation, that new lexicography did not appear to have made its way south of the 49th parallel. There a military uniform would not necessarily spare the black man the wrath of the mob. In some quarters, it was deemed an impertinence – not quite the equal of the heinous crime of rape (the usual excuse given for a lynching) – but a provocation, nonetheless. By the year's end, at least ten black veterans, some still proudly clad in their khaki uniforms, would be lynched. In the bitter words of the campaigner, Ida B. Wells, when cornered by the lynch mob 'neither character nor standing avails the Negro'.[3]

If black people thought things might be different, now that the world had been made safe for democracy, then, Garvey advised, they'd better think again. Blacks kept their eyes and ears peeled for any sign of the impromptu gathering – of white men, women and children, with picnic baskets of cucumber sandwiches and ginger beer, accompanied by the shrill, rebel yell – that heralded the onset of a lynching. Even in progressive South Carolina seething hatreds were near impossible to contain. When a wealthy black merchant, Anthony Crawford, got into an argument with a group of white competitors, the sheriff placed him under arrest and locked him in the local jail for his own safety, only for the jail to be stormed by the mob. Mr Crawford was captured, strung up on a tree and his body shot though with hundreds of bullets. The *Charleston News and Courier* reported that he was 'the type of Negro who is most offensive to certain white people', and whilst in no way condoning the actions of the murderers, the paper noted that Crawford was 'getting rich for a Negro, and he was insolent along with it'.[4] The *Courier*'s pitiful apologia barely disguised the embarrassment and realisation that a culture which tolerated such acts of brutality degraded the white perpetrators as much as it destroyed black lives. The mob needed saving from itself. Fair-skinned blacks like the NAACP's Walter White who, at great risk to his own safety, infiltrated lynch parties and chronicled their murderous intent, reached the same conclusion: the poor white trash had sunk to such low levels of esteem and ignorance, that if they didn't have blacks to demonise, then they'd have no recourse other than to despise themselves.[5]

It wasn't safe to be black in South Carolina, nor in Illinois, Mississippi or Washington – the list was endless. Just walking in the wrong part of town, at the wrong time of day, death could take you away. Mothers counselled their adolescent sons in the fine art of deference, of keeping their insolent eyes to the ground and, as Ellison's *Invisible Man* is advised, 'to overcome 'em with yeses, undermine 'em with grins'.[6] That lynchings were carried out with impunity only exacerbated the fear that any black man (or sometimes woman) might unwittingly become the next victim of a random act of group violence. Self-preservation now underpinned Garvey's doctrine of self-respect. He sombrely warned that there was a grave danger that the Negro would soon be 'dying out'; that it was only a matter of time before the 'Negro will be as completely and complacently dead as the North American Indian, or the Australian Bushman'.[7]

If Garvey's prediction of extermination sounds preposterous and fanciful today, it was not, to petrified black folk, beyond the bounds of reason in that hateful red summer of 1919. It was a period of great unrest, of disillusionment and despair; a time when fevered apparitions of an apocalypse obscured any sighting of the Promised Land; and an age, the *New York Bee* believed, that cried out for a Negro Moses.[8] Garvey showed all the signs of potentially fitting the bill, of a Moses in the making. As a character in Ralph Ellison's *Invisible Man* says, 'Garvey must have had something. He *must* have had something to move all those people! Our people are *hell* to move! He must have had plenty!'[9] On the fringes of the Garvey fan club, all except a handful – including one unforgiving critic – shared that assessment: John E. Bruce still showed a preference for derision over praise for 'The Moses that was to have been, the Judas that is'. By his own standards, Marcus Garvey took an unusually phlegmatic approach to Bruce's continued sniping. He would bide his time in the hope that eventually he'd be able to turn the sceptic into a believer. However, Bruce Grit was not the kind of man to switch camps mid-race. But there were signs of desperation among the leaders of the splinter group. The constant tweaking of the name of their organisation – Universal Negro Protective Association (UNPA) and Universal Improvement and Cooperative Association (UICA) – resembling ever more closely the original UNIA, did little to arrest their diminishing numbers and the drift back to Garvey.

During the course of 1918, the membership of the UNIA grew at an extraordinary rate. The net was cast wide. Anyone 'of Negro blood and African ancestry' with sufficient disposable income to hand over 25 cents a month into the UNIA treasury, could apply. Since its incorporation on 17 June 1918, the organisation had issued thousands of membership certificates – neatly embossed and stamped with a greeting, 'To the Beloved and Scattered Millions of the Negro Race' – that promised to extend 'the principles of Benevolence' towards the physical and cultural development of each member. In six months, their numbers had outgrown the capacity of the rented Lafayette Hall, and Garvey now proposed a fund to raise $200,000 for a permanent home for the organisation. Once again, Theodore Roosevelt topped the list of VIPs invited to get things rolling. A donation from Roosevelt, no matter how small, would attract the attention of other potential benefactors.

The trading arm of the organisation, the African Communities' League, was filed for incorporation a month later. Garvey envisaged (among other things) an import-and-export business, the running of a restaurant and a steam launderette. As well as employing members of the parent UNIA, the businesses would benefit from those members as customers. This example of synergy was an early indication of Marcus Garvey's interlocking ambitions. Much would depend on the enthusiasm he could garner from his growing audience. The chance to consolidate brought out the showman in Garvey, who was increasingly seeking to build on the possibility for pageantry that his mass-meetings held – most notably, the outdoor, late-night gatherings that were said to have been illuminated by the sparks of scores of tap dancers.[10]

Very few Harlemites who came into contact with the UNIA could now resist the swell of excitement that accompanied such spectacular growth. The renegade Isaac B. Allen was certainly not immune. Garvey's rival, who'd helped to split the organisation the year before, had seen which way the wind was blowing, and pleaded for readmission to the governing body. When Allen climbed back on board, his commitment dazzled; he reappeared, washed in the detergent of zealotry that was guaranteed to remove the stains of his previous betrayal. Allen would have endorsed the sentiments of the recently joined Southern member – quoted in UNIA pamphlets – who asserted that 'Garvey gave my people backbones where they [only] had wishbones.'[11]

Marcus Garvey was still intoxicated by his own dream, and nightly summoned the memory of that lucid exaltation on board the SS *Trent,* from four years ago. To date, in the fulfilment of that vision to build a mass movement of black people, Garvey had overlooked the structural specifications required. The template he'd worked on up until this point (a nucleus of six directors and a subscription membership) hadn't allowed for the fantastic numbers that multiplied each week. A new style of thinking and a grander design was called for: Garvey would have to scale up the structure of the UNIA, from the equivalent of a modest church to a cathedral. Self-doubt was not an option. Even so, in those rare, quiet moments, when the hurricane of applause – that followed him everywhere now – died down, Garvey could just make out the faint but distinctive slow handclap of John E. Bruce: 'We like to listen to the music of his mouth,' Bruce Grit taunted, '[but] Mr Garvey will find that the Negro race is not so easily organised as he imagines . . . wise statesmen always conceal more than they reveal . . . You won't do Mr Garvey too *muchee talkee.*' The eloquent Jamaican could 'talk the talk' but could anything he said be substantiated? Bruce Grit didn't think so. 'He is a glib phrase maker,' Bruce concluded, '[who] will find that the Negro race . . . is a pretty good meal ticket until the period of disillusionment wanes.'[12] There was little room for any rapprochement between those lines. Bruce's skewering of Garvey was an about-turn from his previous generosity; back then in 1916, he'd offered his moral support, opened his contacts' book and 'given him a list of names of our leading men in New York who . . . would encourage and assist him'. But it was in their first encounters, before Garvey had fallen foul of Bruce's cynicism, that the sharp-shooting journalist and committed Freemason had given him an idea that would now prove invaluable.

When Garvey sat down to compose the constitution of the brave new UNIA he drew heavily on the charters of other fraternal benevolent organisations, like the black Freemasons. A life-insurance policy formed one of the central planks of the UNIA *Book of Laws*, providing death benefits to members. This was in line with other fraternities, and was particularly attractive to black people who were frequently denied such coverage by insurance companies. The UNIA promise of a final lump sum of $75 towards every member's funeral removed the spectre of the pauper's grave (soon to be Garvey Senior's destiny) that overshadowed their lives. Peace in death then, but the accent of the organisation was most definitely on prosperity in life. Mutual improvement associations were nothing new. Garvey's innovation was to attempt to weld commercial and cultural aspirations onto the body of the soon-to-be-improved Negro.

The source of the numerous titles enshrined in the UNIA handbook – including high chancellor, chaplain general, potentate and supreme commissioner – could also be traced back to African Freemasonry. Garvey borrowed some of the nomenclature along with aspects of its philosophy. The anachronistic-sounding 'potentate' was an abbreviation of the 'imperial potentate' of the Ancient Egyptian Order of the Nobles of the Mystic Shrine (or black shriners) made famous by the peerless black Mason, Prince Hall. In a prevailing climate of political impotence and disenfranchisement, only the Masons and parallel fraternities provided opportunities for black collective organisation – outside the church. The cautious and clever Prince Hall was just the kind of figure whom Bruce believed should serve as a model of shrewd leadership.

Prince Hall was born in Barbados in 1735 and was subsequently enslaved in North America. He won his freedom during the American War of Independence, and through persistence, guile and courage, he managed to establish the first black lodge in Boston – with the blessing of the parent Masonic body in England – much to the chagrin of white American counterparts.[13]

John E. Bruce was a fervent Prince Hall Mason (an active member of Lodge number 38), and though he declined to pin his colours to the Garvey mast-head, some of the other 'odd fellows' were not so circumspect. Besides, the UNIA seemed to share the same language: the titles came first, the costumes would follow. There were, however, fundamental differences. Garvey eschewed the secrecy of the society, and imposed no stringent selection procedures: the doors of the UNIA were open to all Negroes from all walks of life. Equally, there was one central tenet (shared with the black shriners) that was sacrosanct: in the shrine of the UNIA, the potentate would retain absolute power. And if Garvey was ever to play the role of casting director, he had only to look in the mirror to discover the most suitable (and bankable) candidate for the role. The job description stipulated that the potentate be compelled to 'marry only a lady of Negro blood'; retain the power to 'confer titles and orders of merit'; and from time to time issue 'articles' and 'messages' to the entire body of members. Marcus Garvey envisaged that those messages would be transmitted in a forthcoming journalistic organ, to be called the *Negro World*. Garvey's missives aside, the weekly journal would need wordsmiths as talented as the potentate-in-waiting to fill its pages with sparkling propaganda.

Among his compatriots in Harlem, the Socialist-leaning Claude McKay would have been an obvious candidate for inclusion on the pages of the *Negro World* but he kept his distance. McKay favoured the rambunctious rent party or salacious speakeasy over the Sunday-school theatrics animating Garvey's growing followers up at Lafayette Hall. The UNIA leader's regular sermon on self-defence did, however, resonate. After all, Pullman porters travelling in small numbers through hostile backwaters of bigotry were especially vulnerable. Trains risked pulling into towns on the verge of the racial conflagrations that had sharply increased after the war. In the 'Red Summer' of 1919, the nation ignited, turned vigilantes loose against the Reds in its midst, and boiled over with rage against the impertinent Negro. As McKay recalled, 'Our Negro newspapers were morbid . . . full of details of murderous shootings and hangings. Travelling from city to city, we Negro railroad men were nervous . . . less light-hearted. We did not separate from one another gaily to spend ourselves in speakeasies and gambling joints.' Instead, McKay's fellow Pullman porters cleaved together, some of them armed with pistols, 'and stayed in our quarters through the dreary ominous nights, for we never knew what was going to happen'.[14] It was from this terrible sense of dread and foreboding that McKay's great sonnet, 'If We Must Die', exploded out of him.

> If we must die, let it not be like hogs
> Hunted and penned in an inglorious spot,

While round us bark the mad and hungry dogs,
Making their mock at our accursed lot.
If we must die, O let us nobly die,
So that our precious blood may not be shed
In vain; then even the monsters we defy
Shall be constrained to honour us though dead!
O kinsmen! We must meet the common foe!
Though far outnumbered let us show us brave,
And for their thousand blows deal one deathblow!
What though before us lies the open grave?
Like men we'll face the murderous, cowardly pack,
Pressed to the wall, dying, but fighting back![15]

That one poem, published in the *Liberator* in 1919, encapsulated all the fear, frustrations and defiance of black people in America. It also tapped into the unstated terror of white America, for the price that had yet to be paid for its subjugation of the black man. From the slave insurrections of Nat Turner in 1831 to the murderous escapades of John Brown twenty-eight years later, America had been forewarned of an apocalyptic settling of the score that was to come. Claude McKay would have them believe that time had arrived. Although intended for the liberal white readership of the Socialist *Liberator* magazine, the scorching and heart-rending call to arms of 'If We Must Die' found its mark most keenly in the bosom of black folk: it wasn't poetry, it was unfettered truth. News of its potency spread throughout black America. It was quickly reprinted by the *Messenger* and *Crusader* in Harlem, and space was found for it in almost every significant black journal.

'If We Must Die' was mightier than any poem Marcus Garvey would ever write, and the UNIA leader recognised in it his long-held belief in the unification of art and propaganda as the keenest instrument of protest. Though McKay would baulk at a description of his work as protest poetry, it was the only poem he ever felt comfortable about reading aloud to his fellow dining-car waiters: 'They were all agitated. Even the fourth waiter – who was the giddiest and most irresponsible of the lot – even he actually cried,' McKay confided, 'and one, who was a believer in the Marcus Garvey movement, suggested that I should go to the headquarters of the organisation, and read the poem. As I was not yet uplifted with his enthusiasm for the Garvey Movement, yet did not like to say so, I told him truthfully that I had no ambition to harangue a crowd.'[16]

Now the war was over, old resentments resurfaced. There was continued anger: over the exodus of blacks in the South, resulting in a shortage of labour that hamstrung industry there; over the jobs in the North lost to non-unionised blacks that rightfully belonged to whites; and over the new Negroes who did not seem to know their place, neither north nor south of the Mason-Dixon Line. It was the same old tune. The difference now was the greater willingness of black people to answer violence with violence.

Men who'd survived the hell's fire of the trenches, who'd scrambled over the corpses of their comrades, been trapped on the barbed wire in no man's land, were unlikely to be cowed into submission back home or to embrace a return to the subservience of the past. Rather, as Dr Du Bois intoned in the pages of the *Crisis*, they would return fighting for equal rights:

> We *return*
> We *return from fighting*
> We *return fighting*
> Make Way for Democracy! We saved it in France, and by the Great Jehovah, we will save it in the United States of America, or know the reason why.[17]

Du Bois's feisty rhetoric was an echo of the militancy that ex-combatants like Henry Johnson had shown; the black soldier had acquired a new sense of dignity that he was reluctant to relinquish. Du Bois had been sent to France by the NAACP to determine for himself the new mood amongst the black combatants. And though the Harvard scholar's survey, *The Black Man in the Great War*, was tightly drawn around the achievements and frustrations of black Americans, it could equally apply to the black colonial forces of France and Great Britain. Taranto, in Italy, witnessed an early flare-up. Troops of the British West Indies Regiment became disgruntled when they were denied the pay rises and bonuses granted to the British Expeditionary Force on Armistice. In the weeks after the end of hostilities a worse insult was to come. On being ordered to put down their rifles and pick up mops and buckets to slop out the latrines of their white colleagues, the Caribbean soldiers had mutinied. That rebellion had been quelled by Colonel Maxwell Smith who, in his account of the mutiny, drew attention to the ominous dissemination of the *Negro World* among members of the battalion.[18]

The *Negro World* was not alone in reporting the rebellious impulses that had lain dormant for so long. In the face of McKay's 'murderous, cowardly pack', black Americans had fought back, and for six months in 1919 the violent confrontations between the races were splattered across the front pages of America's tabloids and broadsheets. This time whites, in increasing numbers, joined blacks in death, as race riots exploded on more than twenty occasions. A great ball of hate rolled through large swathes of the country that summer, knocking over cities – caught up in the conflagration – like ninepins.

The 90 degrees heat arguably contributed to the factors that tipped Chicago over the brink. On one of the hottest days of the year, tempers flared when blacks, carrying towels and swimwear, were deemed to have broken an unwritten law by invading a beach designated for 'whites only' on the banks of Lake Michigan. A rock thrown at a young black bather, Eugene Williams, hit him on the head and he subsequently drowned. Blacks retaliated. The police intervened. Guns were drawn, and a week of murderous reprisals followed. The police were overrun and, in a series of beatings, stabbings and drive-by shootings, more than fifty people were killed and hundreds were injured before the arrival of torrential rains and five regiments of heavily armed National Guard settled the matter.[19]

Fewer deaths were recorded in the capital, Washington, DC, on 21 July but the animosity was just as intense. Calm and sobering words, that were desperately needed, would not be found in the pages of the *Washington Post*. It too showed symptoms of succumbing to the race-riot excitement. Rather than counselling restraint and conciliation, the *Post* was spoiling for a fight. In language that was more usually found in bigoted local Southern journals advertising an evening's entertainment of lynching, the nation's premier newspaper announced that the 'mobilisation of every available serviceman has been ordered for tomorrow evening near the Knights of Columbus Hut'. And for readers who didn't get the hint, the *Washington Post* spelled it out in bold print: 'The hour of assembly is 9 o'clock, and the purpose is a clean-up that will cause the events of the last two evenings to pale into insignificance.'[20] The spur had been the 'alleged assault by race men upon white women'. And in the following days the *Cleveland Advocate* reported how a mob of 400 white men 'composed of soldiers, sailors, marines and civilians, armed with every kind of weapon' gathered at the appointed hour 'and proceeded on its avowed mission of cleaning up south-west Washington'.[21]

The expression of such violence at the very heart of American civilisation proved the need for continual vigilance throughout the Union. Whenever Marcus Garvey spoke of Washington or Chicago, he warned his audience that the mob would make no distinction between black Americans and Caribbeans. He had in mind those of his fellow islanders who complacently wrapped themselves in the Union Jack (spurning the Stars and Stripes) and consoled themselves with the thought that such things could happen 'only in America'. They would soon be disheartened and disillusioned by the reports reaching them about the scandalous treatment of their compatriots in Great Britain. One of the worst examples concerned wounded West Indian servicemen – some of whom had lost limbs – recuperating on hospital wards full of war veterans. Trouble flared when some of the white amputees, outraged at the suggestion of sharing recreational facilities with the black soldiers, sought to bar them from the pool room and canteen. Newspaper accounts reported the pitiful sight of amputees unhitching their false legs to use as batons to bludgeon each other. That year Cardiff, London and Liverpool (each with small but significant migrant populations) were convulsed by racial hatred. The ex-servicemen and their families who were burnt out of their homes were offered remuneration towards their repatriation and free passage on ships back to the Caribbean.[22]

At least there could be no repatriation of black Americans. The special grievances that W. E. B. Du Bois had once urged blacks to put to one side, he now argued should be at the top of the president's in-tray. The black population had fulfilled its end of the bargain, shoulder to shoulder with their white compatriots in the fight against a common enemy; it was time for some reciprocation.

Stripped of its poetry, Du Bois's open appeal to the fighting spirit of returning black soldiers was considered a menacing development by the White House. Before the war, such rhetoric would hardly have caused any fluctuation in the rhythm of the presidential heart. In 1917, Wilson was confident of the black doughboys' support for their commander-in-chief. A paranoid President had just declared war on Germany. 'These were the days,' recalled James Weldon Johnson, 'when the nation was in a panic over the rumours of pro-Germans and spies in their midst, troops were thrown around [government] buildings for their protection . . . and as I passed the White House, I saw a sight which gave me food for thought . . . Every man of the troops guarding the home of the President was a black man.'[23] Fearing for the security of the White House, Woodrow Wilson had settled on an all-black guard as being the most impenetrable and reliable.

Aside from the undetected German propaganda at work on the Negro population, Wilson had reasoned on the uncomplicated allegiance of the unhyphenated American who happened to be black. The same could not be said of so many recent immigrants he had in mind, for instance, the 500,000 German-Americans, potential reservists for the Kaiser's army whose loyalty was called to question. 'The Afro-American is the only hyphenate, we believe, who has not been suspected of a divided allegiance.' So said the Baltimore Sun, but it could equally have been speaking for the President. The Woodrow Wilson of 1917 had anticipated Cobb's conversion to the uniqueness of black patriotism (America was their home and Promised Land; there was nowhere else to go), but the President's thinking had evidently evolved since then. The war had unleashed a revolutionary fervour throughout Europe, and, en route to France to sign the Armistice, Woodrow Wilson was now quietly alarmed about the exposure of the likes of Private Cooksey to such un-American ideals. He worried in particular that they, the returning black combatants, would be 'the greatest medium in conveying bolshevism to America'.[24] The Attorney General, A. Mitchell Palmer, put it more succinctly: there was a great danger, he warned, that 'the Negro' was not just a carrier but had already contracted the deadly virus of revolution and 'was seeing Red'.

Marcus Garvey had been forewarned of the country's latent paranoia about the possibility of subversives in its midst when summoned by the fastidious and humourless Emmett J. Scott, special adviser to the Secretary of State for War on 'Negro matters'. The UNIA leader hadn't helped his cause by speculating in the pages of the Negro World that the next war would be between the white and darker races, aided by the Japanese. It was the kind of loose language which would have led to a prosecution during war-time, and still might, as the terms of peace had yet to be ratified.

Garvey received Scott's invitation with a mixture of apprehension and excitement. Whatever the outcome, the recognition of importance it conferred on him was a measure of his success. It didn't matter that the 'invitation' was more of an instruction; he would still have been reluctant to refuse. Garvey hurriedly boarded a train to Washington, adjusted his posture to one of unaccustomed deference, and presented himself at the offices of the special adviser, intent on disarming Scott and disabusing him of any suspicions. Scott was gratified. To his superiors in the military intelligence division, Emmett Scott reported how the West Indian representing the 'agitator type' virtually prostrated himself and 'thanked me most profusely for sending for him'. For close to two decades, Emmett Scott had served as personal secretary to Booker T. Washington, preening himself on his proximity to the man whose voice had governed a people. Yet, in his assessment of Garvey, the special adviser revealed the extent to which he had his finger less than adroitly placed on the pulse of Negro life; he concluded that 'while he can cause a certain amount of mischief, [Marcus Garvey] is not a man around whom any serious movements can be prompted'.

Luckily for Garvey, he was caught at the beginning of a wave of repression that had yet to harden its grip and orthodoxy; when there was still room for discretion, for a quiet word to suspects to mend their ways. Scott's memorandum noted satisfactorily that Garvey 'promised to change the general policy of his publication [the *Negro World*]' and that his 'activities . . . should not be seriously regarded'.[25] In his role as special adviser, Scott was meant to act as the eyes and ears of the administration, keeping tabs on the Negro temper and morale. Whilst not an invisible man, Garvey clearly benefited from the myopia of the conventional black American leadership who continued to underestimate his appeal, despite all evidence of his small but growing challenge to their hegemony over the black population.

Garvey emerged relatively unscathed from his audience with Scott, but the matter would not rest there. He was no longer operating below the radar: from now on he would be watched more closely, becoming the subject of at least two competing investigations. In the first instance, Scott's preliminary notes on Garvey were dispatched to Major Walter Howard Loving. A charming and sophisticated man, Major Loving, whose first passion was music, had led a military band in the Philippines until his retirement in 1916. When America entered the Great War, Major Loving was brought out of retirement, dusted down and pressed into the service of military intelligence; given a brief to tease out the seriousness of the German propaganda and other elements of subversion responsible for the unrest amongst his fellow Negroes. Loving was a canny negotiator and natural diplomat who'd successfully steered defiant black publications, like the *Chicago Defender* and the *Crisis*, towards a more moderate course.

The major had expected, once the war was over, to slip back into Civvy Street, but towards the end of 1918, he received news that his services were further required. Colonel John Dunn requested an audience with him, and handed over Garvey's slender file, with orders to thoroughly investigate the practices of the Negro agitator and his associates. Loving went to work the very next day. Attending a highly charged UNIA mass meeting, he brought along a stenographer, and coolly took a seat as speakers on the platform glared at him, warning the congregation to keep a vigil for any spies in the hall.[26]

Walter Loving turned out precise and relevant synopses, and shrewd assessments of Garvey and his movement. These were in marked contrast to the rambling, flustered, exaggerated and amateurish reports of the BOI agents who had infiltrated the UNIA and were providing their paymasters with breathless memorandums which, once deciphered, might best be summarised as 'nothing to report'.

Having secured a strong foothold in Harlem, Garvey was increasingly inclined to road-test his message and its popularity in other cities with sizeable black populations. The conservative audiences in Baltimore and Washington were not accustomed to the kind of peppery polemic that Marcus Garvey and the street orators delivered daily in Harlem, and at first they sat in 'awed silence'. Loving kept a record of all attempts to explain or defend Bolshevism to these audiences, and fretted that they were 'not only growing accustomed [to the radical style of thought] but were applauding it'.[27] But it wasn't Bolshevism, Marxism or Socialism, in any form, that captivated Garvey at the beginning of 1919. He was much more exercised by the window of opportunity that the forthcoming peace conference in Paris offered the Negro race. President Wilson had unveiled a fourteen-point plan for future world peace. There would be no material gain for America. It was an act of enlightened self-interest that propelled Wilson towards his God-given destiny of establishing a new and more equitable world order. The plan enshrined the principle of self-determination for small nations such as Romania and Montenegro, whose people had been the subjects of larger empires. In Paris, President Wilson, 'Wilson *le Juste*', was hailed as a conquering hero by jubilant crowds who showered him and his wife with cascades of flowers. But Garvey complained bitterly that Negroes were ignored in Wilson's master plan: 'We never heard one syllable from the lips of Woodrow Wilson or Balfour in England as touching anything relative to the destinies of the Negroes of America or England or of the world.'[28] Was not the Negro as deserving as the Montenegrin? This was the message that Garvey expounded, almost as a mantra. For he was not like previous Negro leaders, 'a prophet of the hereafter', but a promoter of the thrilling idea that the despised Negro need no longer wait for heaven: he could have his share of the pie here and now.

Prominent black figures also shared the idea that the time was ripe to prosecute the claims of the race. Among them was the millionaire empress of beauty products, Madam C. J. Walker. She opened the doors of her splendid Villa Lewaro on the banks of the Hudson to a coalition of willing Negro leaders. Garvey and significant others strutted in. They assembled under the umbrella of a new, hastily arranged organisation, the International League of Darker Peoples. The group passed important motions and proposed key amendments and additions to Wilson's plan. Two delegates, A. Philip Randolph and Ida B. Wells (sponsored by the UNIA), were selected as emissaries to the peace conference to put their case. Specifically they were to insist on a fifteenth point being added to Wilson's fourteen – the 'elimination of civil, political, and judicial distinctions based on race or color in all nations for the new era of freedom everywhere'. The outcome of this great whirl of activity would, of course, depend on the willingness of the authorities to pay even the slightest bit of attention. To the intellectual, Hubert Harrison's, way of thinking, the grand gestures and important-sounding resolutions constituted nothing more than the escape of hot air. It was all 'sublimely silly' because 'only the President has power to designate the American delegates to the Peace Congress'. Garvey and his fellow plaintiffs were largely mimicking the postures of statesmen without any real leverage or chance of success. Rather than waste money on a fool's errand, Harrison suggested they just 'send to France for copies of *Le Temps* or *Le Matin*'.[29]

Marcus Garvey had little time for Harrison's mocking. Still a rung or two below the major black players, he could now at least hold his own, and on occasion share a platform, with renowned race leaders like Ida B. Wells. The ebullient fifty-five-going-on-twenty-five-year-old woman was, in Loving's estimation, a far more volatile and dangerous character than the UNIA leader. Loving had monitored the comings and goings at Villa Lewaro and recommended that if Wells attempted to obtain a passport, the US State Department should immediately be alerted to the fact that the harmless-looking, four-foot-six mother of four was a 'known race agitator' – a description not intended as a compliment.

At the age of twenty-one, Ida B. Wells had become tethered to her own legend after she sued the Tennessee railroad company when one of their employees had sought to evict her from an expensive first-class seat. In refusing to budge from a seat reserved for white travellers, Ida B. Wells anticipated by some sixty years Rosa Parks's famous act of civil disobedience. The Memphis schoolteacher had dug her heels in and bitten the hand of the conductor who'd tried to accost her. Remarkably she won her court case. From personal indignation it was but a short step to vexation over the abuses suffered by the race; her subsequent devotion to full-time advocacy and anti-lynching campaigns had brought her to the locked gates of the White House. Ida B. Wells's credentials as a one-woman crusader – never travelling without a loaded pistol in her handbag – were unsurpassed. She'd fearlessly spoken out against mob law in Memphis and, consequently forced to flee the South, was always one step ahead of the crackers who dreamed of fashioning a noose for her neck. By her own admission Wells was 'tempestuous, rebellious and wilfully hard-headed'.[30] Walter Loving considered her lost to the virtues of dignified diplomacy and sworn to a lifetime of noisy opposition. Little more could be expected of her, but, to his dismay, several other respected figures were also said to be aligned to Garvey.

When he challenged John E. Bruce on his dealings with the suspect, Bruce wrote back sharply, as if he'd been slapped in the face, 'Please do not insult me by linking my name with any movement, plan, scheme or enterprise with which Marcus Garvey is identified.' Bruce Grit had been around long enough to have experienced an earlier example of America's periodic pandemic of political hysteria in the 1880s[31]: he correctly sensed the sinister implications behind Loving's investigation and with undisguised sarcasm and irony concluded, 'Put me down as 100% 'Merican, red-hot republican, and a shouting Methodist. If you can manufacture a traitor out of these "ingredients", send me the formula.'[32] It was a portentous comment, as the blood-letting was about to begin in another spasm of political scapegoating and the search for the enemy within.

7

HOW TO MANUFACTURE A TRAITOR

Shall an instrument of oppression
drawn from the repertory of the star chamber,
assailed by our colonial forebears as destructive of liberty,
and condemned by the Supreme Court as 'abhorrent' . . .
shall such an instrument be revived in the twentieth century?
                              The New Republic, 9 July 1919

THE Negro agitators posed only one of a myriad problems to unsettle
America in its transition from war to peace. The country had to
brace itself for the unexpectedly early return of 4 million soldiers,
at a time when the economy was spiralling towards recession. The
speed of the German army's collapse, following America's entry to
the war, had caught military planners off guard. Industries that had
been cranked up for war were suddenly no longer required; their
contracts cancelled with little thought given to how their productivity might be converted to peace-time use. The black workforce was
particularly vulnerable. As always, the Negro was last to be hired
and first to be fired. But this time round, poor white families were
only marginally better off than their black neighbours. Empty bellies
and no prospect of work were bad enough, but worse was in store.
Amongst the returning heroes were carriers of a deadly virus.

God-fearing Americans were not spared the worldwide influenza
pandemic that settled on the land towards the end of 1918. Turning
to the Bible for an explanation they pictured themselves cast in a re-
enactment of the plague that had befallen the Egyptians in the time of
Pharaoh. But neither prayers, nor holy water, nor lintels crossed in

blood offered protection from the virulent angel of destruction that brought fevers, heartache, anxious bedside vigils and finally death to hundreds of thousands of households.¹ Within the space of a few months bodies began to pile up at the mortuaries, and undertakers struggled to keep up with the demand for their services. All day long funeral processions crossed paths. These were the lucky ones. Many more corpses remained unburied through lack of funds, their coffins stacked up at cemeteries or awaiting collection from porches up and down the country – no part of the Union was exempt.

The state of Kentucky exemplified the scale of America's woes. There the coal mines had to close their gates for lack of both healthy and willing men. The flu epidemic stripped the mines down to a core of key workers and the subsequent wave of strikes depleted the work-force to the point where the coal pits became inoperable. It was a question of priority; and wavering strikers who were still strong enough to wield a shovel found their services in greater demand at cemeteries, putting their tools to use digging graves.

Millions of disgruntled labourers joined the miners in working to rule. On an average month in 1919, the country was paralysed by up to fifty independent strikes – the most potent and damaging was wrought in the steelworks. From Pittsburgh to Seattle, 350,000 steel men walked out on strike, threatening a seismic shift in the balance of power between workers and bosses. Steelworkers formed the back-bone of America's industry. They were, at once, both superhuman and subhuman, performing dirty, dangerous and vital work for a pittance. Steel had made America: steel ringed its railroads, sharpened bayonets and held up its skyscrapers. The men who descended daily into the furnaces of the steel mills exercised a fascination over Americans. In the midst of the strike, the country's leading playwright, Eugene O'Neill, turned his sympathetic socialist pen to the plight of the workers. In his bruising tragedy, *The Hairy Ape*, a transatlantic ocean liner owned by a steel magnate serves as metaphor for American society. Below deck, in the stokehole, the ship's brutish Neanderthal men shovelled the coals that kept the engines turning; they were the same industrial slaves who fed the furnaces of the steel mills. 'I'm what makes iron into steel!' screams the semi-literate antagonist, Yank. 'Steel, dat stands for de whole ting! And I'm steel-steel-steel! I'm de muscles in steel, de punch behind it.'² The refined and pampered passengers considered Yank and his foreign-born fellow workers barely

human, if they considered them at all. The play turns on this realisation when, on a tour of the ship, the desirable, lily-white young
lady recoils in horror at the sight of the 'filthy beast', the coal-
blackened, sweating and semi-naked Yank. He *is* the hairy ape made
suddenly and sharply aware of his lowly state; and, beginning to think
for the first time, is undermined by unflattering thoughts. Yank's eventual rage mirrored the rising tide of resentment expressed by the nation's
steelworkers over their primitive working conditions.

Twelve-hour shifts – half of that time spent shovelling, throwing
and carrying bricks and cinder out of the furnaces – would no longer
be tolerated. Over four bitter and hungry months on a diet of grave-
yard stew (hot milk and bread) the workers clung desperately to their
demands with naive conviction. But the steel companies were determined to preserve a non-unionised system and offered no alternatives.
The bosses' intransigence eventually won out through violent intimidation, the propaganda of a sympathetic press and the use of strike
breakers – the Negroes who arrived in sealed carloads shipped into
plant-yards. The shareholders' fantastic profits remained intact. That
victory, though, had been tempered by the glimpse into a terrifying
future. And when angry and confused Americans looked through the
smoke and mirrors for the root causes of the turmoil, they could
clearly discern an ominous red flag. The young social anthropologist
Charles Rumford Walker was among the first to record his compatriots' overwhelming sense of bewilderment. On the ferry returning
the demobbed first lieutenant and his men home from the war, Walker
asked the civilian pilot about the state of the nation. 'It's a mess over
here,' said the pilot 'There ain't any jobs, and labor is raising hell.
Everybody that hez a job strikes.' Pressed further the sailor offered
the most favoured explanation of the time: 'I don't know what we're
comin' out at. Russia, maybe.'[3]

American readers of the Harvard-educated Communist, John Reed,
had had ample opportunity to understand the meaning of 'the Russians
are coming'. Published in March 1919, and by July reproduced in its
fourth edition, his *Ten Days that Shook the World* was a first-hand
account of the tumultuous first few days of the Bolshevik revolution
of October 1917. In it, Reed pieced together the capture of Petrograd
and the old Winter Palace where 'servants in their blue and red and
gold uniforms stood nervously about'. Penetrating the 'malachite
chamber with crimson brocade hangings where the Ministers had been

in session all that day and night', Reed found 'the long table covered with green baize [and] before each empty seat was pen and ink and paper . . . scribbled over with beginnings of plans of action, rough drafts of proclamations . . . scratched out, as their futility became evident'. The provisional government had, inevitably, fallen to Lenin and the Bolsheviks in ten memorable days.[4] Even the least subtle American mind could make the connection: Winter Palace today, White House tomorrow.

It took a further two years for the aftershock of the revolution to reach the shores of the USA. What had inspired workers around the world – the Soviet decrees which proclaimed the abolition of all private ownership of land, and the establishment of a workers' and peasants' government – were viewed in Washington as dark and satanic, as well as being just plain wrong. They stood in opposition to every tenet of the American way of life. And, lest anyone should be swayed by the romance of a final levelling of society, there were plenty of commentators on hand to warn decent Americans, such as the hard-working farmers with a small amount of savings, that, come the revolution, they had just as much to lose as the shipping magnate or coal baron.[5] Newspapers encouraged the population to be vigilant. Surely it was true of any disease – the *New York Times*, the *Washington Post* and *Salt Lake Tribune* all argued – that early detection was essential for a favourable prognosis. Of particular concern was the fear that undeclared Bolshevik sympathisers were already at large in the schools' system. Brooklyn's Commercial high school provided an early warning in January 1919. During a class debate on the Great War one of the teachers became suspicious when pupils unexpectedly offered up a defence of the Bolshevik revolution. His report prompted an urgent inquiry by the school's governors; the leading, and only, suspect, an inspiring but provocative history teacher, Benjamin Glassberg, was quickly identified. The children were summoned and, when invited to, one by one lined up to denounce their teacher. Glassberg was suspended indefinitely, and when he was brought before the city's education board, his defence was further undermined by revelations that he was also a director of the Socialist weekly, the *New York Call*, and a part-time lecturer at the Rand School of Social Science: both were cited as evidence of his guilt.[6] Benjamin Glassberg's prosecution foreshadowed the widescale introduction of loyalty oaths for public-school teachers and other government employees. It was an indication of the first shoots of intolerance springing up throughout the country. Legislators on Capitol Hill even proposed a law that would lead to the imprisonment of any person displaying the red flag (warning flags raised by railroad or public-highways employees were to be exempted). That Marcus Garvey found himself caught up in this conflagration was no reflection of the inflammatory rhetoric of his speeches, heard at massed meetings and reported assiduously by excited BOI agents. Rather, the combination of the suspect radicals that his movement appeared to be associated with, as well as the overall tone of his recently launched publication, the *Negro World*, caused most alarm.

Marcus Garvey celebrated his thirty-first birthday with the launch of the *Negro World*. On 17 August 1918, admittedly four years after he'd first promised to send Booker T. Washington a copy, the official organ of the UNIA rolled off the printing press. Six sheets of news reports – especially national stories told from a black perspective, and world events that might impact on Negro people – together with essays, poems and uplifting editorials, would set readers back a mere 5 cents. On the front page, the proprietor's own contributions reflected the cadences and rhythms of his voice – he wrote as he spoke, in a simple, forceful and rhetorical manner – and pledges, promises and proclamations were laid before the reader much as they'd previously been laid before the King. In an editorial on 27 March 1919, he greeted readers, the 'Fellowmen of the Negro Race', with the news that, 'The Russian people have issued a proclamation of sympathy . . . towards the labouring people of the world . . . We are not concerned as partakers in these revolutions, but we are concerned in the destruction that will come out of the bloody conflict between capital and labour, which will give us a breathing space to declare our freedom from the tyrannical rule of oppressive overlords.'

Marcus Garvey reserved a Victorian formality for these earnest and respectful addresses to the members. The formality added water to the wine of an otherwise explosive content. Everything was for the greater good of the race. Only occasionally did vanity seep out from the edges of his prose when the strain of wanting to be taken seriously was all but exposed. The UNIA president was actually far more thrilled by the publication's solidifying of the movement. 17 August was a great day for the UNIA, for Garvey and the race. From the outset, Marcus Garvey announced the paper's intention to agitate and propagandise.

In early issues – written under the title in bold type – three simple words were reproduced: 'Negroes Get Ready'.[7]

Four years of dress rehearsals and dreaming up headlines weren't necessarily to the paper's advantage. The Negro World would have to take its place in a lively and competitive market, clamouring for attention alongside the more than 400 newspapers and magazines now published by African-Americans. Most of these were local journals full of tinsel and piffling gossip. The sensationalist yellow journalism practised by the Chicago Defender – with its unsparing, explicit depiction of the vile acts heaped upon the Negro, published alongside hair-straightening adverts like 'Kink-No-More' – was the most widely circulated black paper in the USA.[8] The Negro World struck a much more sober note. It positioned itself somewhere between the national newsletter of a high church and a political review with literary and international ambitions. There was nothing quite like it available to Negro readers, either north or south of the Mason-Dixon Line. But in New York, Garvey's weekly had to find its way amongst a number of established and robust publications such as the New York Age and Crisis, as well as fearless, lacerating left-wing upstarts typified by the Messenger. All race leaders recognised the importance of newspapers in disseminating their ideas beyond the immediate sphere of influence. Marcus Garvey was no exception. The New York Age had been a subtle vehicle for Booker T. Washington's Tuskegee Machine. W. E. B. Du Bois and the Crisis enjoyed the financial and spiritual backing of the NAACP: soon after its inception in 1910, the monthly magazine had become synonymous with its editor. The Crisis was W. E. B. Du Bois. The Negro World would serve as a platform for Garvey and an organisation now more often referred to as the Garvey Movement.

Garvey's paper emerged at the third stage of a tradition of African-American journals stretching back to 1827. The first phase had been characterised by campaigning newspapers, such as Freedom's Journal (founded by another remarkable Jamaican, John B. Russworm) that argued politely but cogently for the abolition of slavery. In its very first edition, Freedom's Journal begged to plead the Negroes' cause, 'too long have others spoke for us [such that] our vices and our degradation are ever arrayed against us, but our virtues are passed unnoticed'. Russworm nibbled at the conscience of white liberals for a few years before he answered a greater calling and emigrated to the newly colonised Liberia.[9] The disillusionment which followed the American

Civil War gave way to a second phase of African-American journalism in which black papers largely fell in line with Booker T. Washington's conciliatory, unthreatening approach to white dominance. After Washington's death and the Great War, a third phase had emerged with a return to protest journalism, with its gentlemanly velvet glove removed.

On the front page of every edition, the *Negro World* proudly proclaimed itself to be 'Devoted to the Interests of the Negro Race without the Hope of Profit as a Business Investment'. Profit margins were indeed tight. Six months after its launch the paper carried a special appeal. Without an immediate injection of $3,000 cash, it would be dead in two weeks. An emergency editorial called upon all Negroes interested in the salvation of the race (and in particular the salvation of the paper) to make a dollar donation. The core of UNIA supporters – casual workers, earning 50 cents an hour on ten-hour shifts – was unlikely to heed the call. Given his experience in launching papers in Panama, Costa Rica and Jamaica, it's surprising that Marcus Garvey hadn't foreseen such a likely outcome. But then this was an altogether more ambitious project, on a much grander scale; a less impetuous man might have proceeded more cautiously and not jumped straight in with a print run of several thousand. Of course a more cautious man might not have proceeded at all.

Garvey had spurned lucrative advertising contracts, and in honouring the UNIA mission of linking all the scattered people of the race, the paper was given away for free in certain sections of the world, without hope of return – never mind hope of profit. Financial fragility was the perennial problem that every black journal faced. It would have been difficult for any newcomer to stay afloat without some form of subsidy. But with patronage came the threat of unwanted interference and accusations of partial, if not wholesale, surrender of editorial independence. Few would contest that assessment. The previous generation of black journals, including *Colored American Magazine* and *Voice of the Negro*, had been subject to ugly struggles for control. It was often (privately) alleged that the then primary race leader, Booker T. Washington, had ruthlessly preserved his influence and stifled dissenting voices simply by buying shares in troublesome papers or lending them money. Such was Washington's unmistakable command over black papers that when, for instance, the African scholar Edward Wilmot Blyden wrote a personal letter to him endorsing his tactical, subordinate stance towards white authority, Washington wrote back, 'What you say is so entirely in keeping with my own views, that I have taken the liberty of asking Mr Thomas Fortune, editor of the *New York Age*, to let it appear.' A Washington request to an African-American editor was synonymous with an instruction.[10]

Despite the signs of a paper in distress, Marcus Garvey maintained confidence in the *Negro World*'s eventual pre-eminence in becoming the most important international black journal. In the interim, any shortfall in the donations necessary for the paper's survival would have to be met by the association's slender resources. None of the directors, including Garvey, as yet drew a salary, and judging by the trickle of disgruntled journalists who took him to court, Garvey expected the same sacrifice from the paper's employees. Such embarrassing beginnings were picked up gleefully by rival black newspapers. The *Chicago Defender*, which perhaps had most to lose from any encroachment on its readership, gave undue prominence to reports that the 'editor of a little weekly is being sued for [unpaid] wages'.[11] The Virgin Islander, Anselmo Jackson, was first on the witness stand in September, just a month after the launch of Garvey's paper; and the *Defender* was further pained to report in November that 'Marcus M. Garvey, who is still getting out a little two-page paper in Harlem' was again sued by a disgruntled reporter, Dorothy Hensen. The speed with which both freelance journalists pre-empted the usual explanation of 'the cheque is in the post' and sought redress in the courts confirmed a peculiar Caribbean tendency (from which Garvey was not immune) of viewing litigation as a first resort. Judgement, in each case, against Garvey dramatically depleted the organisation's meagre funds. Nonetheless, his gamble seemed to pay off as the *Negro World* weathered the storm of its early financial losses; circulation figures steadily climbed towards 10,000 by the end of its first year.[12]

The birth of the *Negro World* had only been made possible by the generosity of patrons at each end of America's political spectrum. Garvey's championing of the principle of putting the race first had loosened the purse strings of Madam C. J. Walker. In what was to be the last year of her life, Madam Walker was also keen to identify other good causes and recipients worthy of her largesse. She held court at her luxurious 34-room mansion on the Hudson and a procession of suitors came to call. Garvey performed a delicate balancing act with the philanthropic Walker whose clinging, invisible, complexion-enhancing face powder came in four shades: White, Rose-flesh, Brown and Egyptian Brown. The ink-black Garvey lauded her services to the race whilst criticising cosmetics manufacturers who traded on the pathology of self-loathing Negroes.

Marcus Garvey well understood the culture amongst black people of coveting fair skin and 'good' as opposed to 'bad' hair. 'Good' hair meant soft and manageable. The owner of good hair was in all likelihood the beneficiary of white input into the gene pool through the generations (shorthand for the rape of an ancestor by her slave-owning master), diluting one's despised Negritude. 'Bad' hair was dry and unwieldy, as coarse as the poor class of unmixed Negroes who sported it. Bad hair damned one to the lower orders. But women (and occasionally men) could disguise their origins by investing in black beauty preparations. Once your hair had been treated, attention might then be turned to your face, applying ointments ('Dr Fred's Skin Whitener' was a popular choice) that claimed 'in just three minutes [to] lighten the darkest skin giving it a feminine exquisiteness'. For the two or three weeks that these preparations lasted – before the hair and skin stubbornly reverted to type – black disaffection with their 'natural' look was replaced with an artificially induced fantasy of being classified a mulatto or octoroon. But, in keeping with its philosophy of race pride, the *Negro World* refused to carry adverts for hair-straightening and skin-lightening products, or any other 'advertisement that would in any way libel the race' – Madam Walker's included.[13] It was a costly policy. Most black newspapers depended largely on the advertising revenue brought in by selling space to manufacturers of bleaching products like 'Black No More' and straightening preparations like 'Dr Lee's Bobbed Hair' to keep in business. But Garvey equated the black desire for a Caucasian look with mental slavery. Now was the time, he argued, to 'take the kinks out of your mind, instead of out of your hair'.[14]

At the embryonic stages of the *Negro World*, other inconvenient principles had deferred to insurmountable practicalities. Even with a generous donation from Madam Walker, the cost of putting together a weekly publication was still beyond Garvey's pocket. Once more, he turned to his boyhood friend, Wilfred Domingo, for help. Since his arrival from Jamaica in 1910, Domingo had consistently made it his business to build up a network of influential acquaintances. Starting out as a medical student, Domingo flitted between a host of unsatisfactory jobs – from butcher to postal clerk – before careering towards a lifetime of activism. A. Philip Randolph credited him with 'a penetrating and logical mind

and a thorough grasp of Marxism', coupled with an unfortunate entrepreneurial fascination with the various ways of becoming rich.[15] Domingo
was a true believer in Marxism but not always a practising one. At the
time Garvey first ran into him, Domingo was churning out imagin-
ative business schemes on a weekly basis. At one point, he dreamed up
the idea of roasting and selling potatoes on the neighbourhood's street
corners, emulating the local celebrity 'Pig Foot Mary', who made a
fortune from hungry Harlemites who stopped at her stall for cooked
trotters. Domingo saw himself as part of a 'dusky tribe of destiny seekers'
and the West Indians in Harlem as bringing a precious vibrancy to the
host culture; the Caribbeans were 'a sort of leaven in the [African]
American loaf', possessing the same passion as the Jew for education
and business. According to Wilfred Domingo, the men and women from
the 'palm fringed sea shores and murmuring streams . . . fortified by a
graceful insouciance' had become trend setters virtually overnight. Nattily
dressed, strolling along Lenox Avenue in their light-coloured cotton suits
and white shoes, the West Indians, he noted, had at first been 'the butt
of many a jest from their American brothers'. Yet shortly afterwards
those same Americans had quietly 'adopted the styles that they formerly
derided'.[16] In two key areas the dapper Domingo was in absolute agreement with Marcus Garvey: that whenever possible one tried to dress to
distinction (in this he trailed behind the UNIA leader whose wardrobe
grew with his stature) and that the small businesses – jewellery, tailoring
and grocery stores – started by pioneering Jamaicans and other West
Indians were ventures that should be praised to the rafters. Primarily
though, it was the expiation of wealth as outlined in Karl Marx's *Das
Kapital* that most excited Domingo intellectually. He was an enthusiast
who cultivated political alliances without fully signing up to any one
group.

From 1918 onwards, Domingo was associated with the New Crowd
Negroes whose motto, 'The Negro need no longer fear the face of day',
each claimed credit for. They were graduates of the Harlem soapbox,
an iconoclastic group who were articulating 'an attitude of cynicism
that was a characteristic' hitherto 'foreign to the Negro'.[17] Their radicalism was 'motivated by a fierce race consciousness', and gradually
after the war those same sentiments were finding an audience amongst
disaffected black people. Increasingly, but slowly, the New Crowd leaders
waded through a molasses of nervous black resistance. They would need
to overcome a culture of stultifying caution that had evolved over decades

and centuries of bowed-head, hat-in-the-hand subservient strategies of survival. As one of the most astute chroniclers of these times, the black intellectual Alain Locke later observed, 'the Negro [was] radical on race matters and conservative on others, in other words, a "forced radical", a social protestant rather than a genuine radical'.[18]

The New Crowd, a younger generation of genuine left-leaning radicals led by A. Philip Randolph and Chandler Owen, were mostly associated with the Socialist Party. Domingo charmed the party's printer, Henry Rogowski, into extending a line of credit to Garvey that enabled the weekly *Negro World* to follow the socialist *New York Call* straight off the printing presses at 444 Pearl Street. In his eagerness to launch the paper, Marcus Garvey was not going to let the detail of questionable political persuasions prove an impediment. He convinced himself that if he hurried along inconspicuously then perhaps he would not be seen. But in the paranoid America of 1919 it was almost impossible for someone like Marcus Garvey to go unobserved and not to be judged by the company he kept.

Unnerving reports of UNIA meetings where Bolshevism was not unreservedly denounced were seized on by informants and inverted, so that the UNIA position that 'the Negro has no cause against Bolshevism' was translated into 'the Negro is pro-Bolshevism'. Whilst there is no evidence that the UNIA president ever showed any inclination or sympathy towards Socialism or Communism, that didn't stop the administration casting a suspicious eye at the goings-on at the fringes of his organisation. Socialists were increasingly sniffing around the Garvey movement; they'd both admired and envied his success in signing up huge numbers of working-class black people to the UNIA – an organisation that was still expanding. Garvey seemed an extraordinarily able propagandist; in the two years since his arrival, he'd built up a substantial following that dwarfed the black membership of the Socialist Party. Most left-leaning black workers were inclined towards the colour-blind Industrial Workers of the World (IWW, also known as the Wobblies), though their solidarity foundered on the IWW's propensity to call for industrial action at the slightest provocation. The old slogan, 'Every strike is a little revolution and a dress rehearsal for the big one,' froze on the lips of recruiters as potential black members backed away.[19]

In over a decade of striving, the Socialists had made even less headway than the IWW amongst the black proletariat. Perhaps Garvey might serve as a conduit to the masses? Activists certainly saw his huge potential and were beginning to explore ways of forging common cause with the UNIA. And if Garvey was increasingly seen as the lightning conductor of black aspiration and unrest, then the Socialists had flown a kite into that electrical storm in the shape of Claude McKay, the acclaimed author of 'If We Must Die'.

For a black poet to be published in a respected journal like the *Liberator* was considered, in 1919, a remarkable achievement, in and out of literary circles. Among the cognoscenti, the Jamaican poet's admirers ranged from the doggerel-loving Garvey to the erudite Harvard man, William Braithwaite, whose own anaemic poems were studiously colour-blind. But the sentiments at the back of 'If We Must Die' were as likely to be discussed in the barber's shop as they were in the literary parlour. It was commonly held that 'If We Must Die' had propelled McKay into a position of spokesman for the race. It also earned him a BOI file. As the first celebrator of a looming Harlem Renaissance, McKay was subsequently pulled in literary and political directions that weren't always compatible. Braithwaite cautioned him that compositions that revealed his racial identity would not be prudent, 'because of the insurmountable prejudice against all things Negro', and offered his own bleached verse as a model for McKay to best advance in the world of poetry.[20] Max Eastman at the *Liberator*, while conceding the ugliness of naked Red-soaked verse, urged him to continue proselytising with works of mass appeal. Further contradictory advice came on a trip to London, where McKay met his literary hero, George Bernard Shaw. The celebrated writer (aligned to the liberal Fabian movement) had oozed sympathy for a sensitive Negro soul who, regrettably, should expect few outlets for his poems. Shaw counselled the poet that he might have had more luck turning his skills towards pugilism and the ring. 'You might have developed into a successful boxer with training,' said Shaw. 'Poets remain poor unless they have an empire to glorify and popularise like Kipling.'[21]

Back in America, the management of the *Liberator* had seen things differently; in a vote of confidence in McKay's skills it had offered to make him an assistant editor. For a Negro poet to be appointed to such a position was beyond black dreams and expectations. A small circle of like-minded radicals cheered McKay's elevation to the editorial board. His graduation was a good omen and fuelled their own sense of a new day a-coming, when they'd no longer be toiling amongst the largely indifferent, unpromising and conservative Old Crowd Negroes, but harnessing a growing revolutionary spirit amongst the New Crowd. If handled correctly, Garvey's role might prove crucial in achieving their ends.

Once Claude McKay had settled into the job, Hubert Harrison and others were calling for him to exploit his new authority (courtesy of the impeccable leftist credentials of the *Liberator* offices) and convene a 'little meeting with the rest of the black Reds'. Aside from the opportunity for back-slapping and mutual appreciation, McKay recalled that 'the real object of the meeting was . . . to discuss the possibility of making the UNIA more class-conscious.'[22] The gathering of co-conspirators read like a *Who's Who* of former stepladder scholars, now editors of small but pioneering radical journals; among them was Wilfred Domingo (whose friendship with Garvey had become strained in the course of 1919). The black Reds' focus on Garvey was not simply an act of expediency. There seemed much to praise in a UNIA president-general who had predicted the expansive growth of Bolshevism 'until it finds a haven in the breasts of all oppressed peoples' of the world, culminating in 'a universal rule of the masses'.[23]

In his negotiations with the printer of the socialist *New York Call*, Domingo had acted as a kind of political guarantor for the Garvey movement. And though Domingo never embraced membership of the UNIA, partly as a reward for securing the arrangement with the printer, Garvey had appointed him to write the leaders of the new paper. It had proven an expensive mistake. In his editorship of the *Negro World* Domingo gave free rein to his own personal views. Under Domingo's watch, the editorials were a close match for the polemical and near-subversive writings published in the *Liberator* and the *Messenger*. At least that was what the intelligence operatives now continually monitoring the *Negro World* believed. The Bureau of Investigation and Military Intelligence reports had evolved over the months. The typical early entry by Major Loving on 5 January 1919 under the heading 'Negro Activities' had undergone a gradual transformation by April 1919 into 'Negro Agitation' before finally mutating into '*Negro World*: Probable Bolshevik Propaganda'.[24]

It wasn't the best of times to attract such a label. America's entry into the Great War had ensured that the world was made safe for democracy. But Russia's Bolshevik revolution, and the subsequent spread of its militant ideals, threatened to undo much of President Wilson's patient and persistent brokering of a just and lasting peace. In the chaos following the armistice, Europe flared up with a revolutionary fervour. Like the great influenza epidemic that went on to claim half a million American lives, virulent Bolshevik propaganda had not been checked in time and was now abroad in the USA, tolerated and freely disseminated in undesirable left-wing publications, most notably in the *Liberator* and *New York Call*. Right-wing papers, for whom Bolshevik thought was equally as dangerous as Bolshevik deed, fulminated at the government's inactivity. The *Philadelphia Inquirer* summed up their frustration when it observed, 'We may as well invite Lenin and Trotsky to come here and set up business at once.'[25]

In the view of the administration, some radicalised sections of the black population were the sleeping, junior partners in a cabal of Communists, anarchists, militant trade unionists and the Industrial Workers of the World in desiring the destruction of capitalist America and the creation of a Bolshevik state. The Attorney General, Mitchell Palmer, was a recent Red-baiting convert. When he'd first entered office, Palmer, a devout Quaker, had revealed his pristine, liberal instincts and angered the hawks in Washington by opening the jails and setting free thousands of enemy aliens and other prisoners who'd been arrested under draconian war-time Acts of Espionage and Sedition. Initially, he wasn't as convinced of the post-war dangers. Were there thousands of members of a secret enemy within the shores of the USA who had cunningly crossed through its porous borders disguised as economic migrants? If so, those were the very people he'd let out of the jails.

Critics like Senator Clayton R. Lusk of New York State aired the commonly held suspicion that the propagandists had by 'devious methods' infiltrated legitimate labour organisations and had especially taken root among the 'large and entirely unassimilated foreign-born, non-English-speaking industrial class'.[26] The Attorney General now argued that the state could at least curb the propagation of un-American ideals by censoring radical publications and disrupting their distribution through the mail. In the eyes of subordinates, such as J. Edgar Hoover, black publications including the rabid *Messenger* and the *Negro World* should also be scrutinised. Hoover was especially incensed when shown a copy of 'Socialism, the Negroes' Hope', written by Domingo for the *Messenger*, with a byline that identified the author as editor of the *Negro World*.

Voluntary self-censorship was the first line of defence but individual editors clearly couldn't always be trusted to gauge what limits they should place on personal freedom. The Censorship Board had yet to wind down after the war and Hoover lobbied but barely convinced sceptical civil servants that Garvey, along with the boyish editors of the *Messenger*, should be added to the list of suspects compiled for the Postal Censorship Book. There was a certain amount of exaggeration of the Negro problem and it's doubtful that Garvey would have been aware of the extent of the intelligence gathering.

Right at the start of its publication the *Negro World* had also found its way to the British colonies. If called upon, a certain twenty-one-year-old Jamaican living with her family in Panama City would have willingly introduced it to the other Caribbean migrants who'd decided to remain in Panama after the completion of the canal. Amy Ashwood's own bags had been figuratively, if not actually, packed for several months. But a year after she'd tracked down her fiancé – after the initial angry outbursts, chastising him over his neglect, and the gradual rekindling of their romance with a trail of perfumed letters and excited talk of a reunion – Amy Ashwood had still not booked her passage to New York to join her Napoleon. (Garvey was more inclined at this time to draw a comparison with Napoleon's nemesis, the black general Toussaint L'Ouverture, who'd led a successful slave revolt against the French in Haiti.[27] Back in 1914, it was Garvey's account of Touissaint's terrible bravery that had inspired Amy's own quickening sense of African identity.)

Ashwood's fondness for Garvey had not diminished but, through his frequent changes of address and peripatetic lifestyle, she'd lost contact with him for the second time. On top of which, she claimed, mutual acquaintances had informed her that Garvey had become mentally deranged in America.

Psychiatric illness was the seldom-discussed 'other side' to the myth of instant financial success expected of immigrant populations in the USA, especially the Scandinavians and Irish. However, there is no record of Garvey having succumbed to schizophrenia or any other kind of mental ill-health. He was prone to lung infection and had, on more than one occasion, been admitted to hospital suffering from pneumonia. It's also true that he was under enormous stress, was constantly over-reaching himself and possessed a single-mindedness of purpose that left no room for the kind of spectacular failure that was always a possibility. Ashwood is unlikely to have sincerely believed rumours

that Garvey had tipped over into some kind of mental illness.[28] Clearly
Garvey took his additional title of 'travelling commissioner' seriously
and communication between them had broken down once more. But
this only partially explained Amy Ashwood's delay.

Of far greater significance was the increasing attention paid her by
a family friend and mature gentleman caller almost double her age.
Allen Cumberbatch, a Trinidadian bachelor with a successful tailoring
business, was a popular figure in her family's circle. On several occasions, he'd been spotted escorting Amy on the ex-patriot social circuit.
Still, whether or not Garvey was on the horizon, the energetic Amy
Ashwood was one of those whom Domingo had described as 'dusky
destiny seekers' who could only resist the lure of New York, and Harlem
in particular, for so long. By the beginning of September 1918, she'd
finally purchased a ticket on a Royal Mail vessel bound for New York.
But when she set off for the wharf with her luggage, her plans were
not greatly developed: she had only a ticket and a prayer. Just before
embarking, Ashwood chanced upon a teacher from Colón called Parker
known to both her and Garvey. Parker had been in recent communication with the UNIA leader who, in his last letter, had been enquiring
about Amy Ashwood. It was an extraordinary piece of good fortune
as the teacher was able to give her details of Garvey's address in Harlem
just before the ship set sail.[29]

In her navy-blue travelling colours, with matching hat, Ashwood
was finally on her way; her love of Garvey and of the limelight had
been revived by the amazing tales of his success coming out of Harlem.
She pulled into port on 6 October 1918, charmed her way through
the clearing halls of Ellis Island and hurried to Garvey's headquarters.
The records of that encounter, based on later affidavits which are therefore qualified by the prejudiced but necessary justifications of plaintiff
and defendant, tell of a tempestuous and combustible reunion. For two
heart-rending years they'd been apart; and the romantic pledges so
sincerely made when last together, had been broken. Ashwood had
thought Garvey lost to her. In the interim, Marcus Garvey had devoted
his whole being to the founding of the organisation and was prepared
to sacrifice himself and his professed love for Amy Ashwood until such
time as he had met success. After two spectacular years, now at the
head of a much larger movement than had ever been realised in Jamaica,
he'd reached that point. But just as he was about to send for her
and her parents so that they might be married, he was informed that

Amy Ashwood was dead. That account was no more fanciful than her story of his derangement. Both believed themselves released from the pledges made in Jamaica. Both cards had been blotted, so there was no call for recrimination; the score was settled – almost. There was an addendum: Allen Cumberbatch. Back in Panama, there had, it transpired, been a tacit agreement between Amy and Cumberbatch that they would be married. It was devastating news. Yet Marcus Garvey, though initially agitated and provoked to the point of apoplexy by the revelation, remained, in the end, remarkably sanguine. At the very moment when the organisation needed to build on the momentum of its evolution, the dynamic Amy Ashwood had reappeared. Garvey found himself calmed by Ashwood's honesty and the soothing reassurance of her love for him. He 'asked permission' to contact Cumberbatch to inform him of her earlier pledge; Amy promised that she would write to the Trinidadian tailor breaking off the engagement.

Amy Ashwood had been busy in Panama promoting her own ideas of a confraternity amongst the local West Indian population: she joined the 'Democratic Club', which served as a social and political forum for the British West Indians in Panama; she organised charity events for various war works; most memorably, with the blessing of the British Consul, she started a 'Red Cross Fund' for Caribbean soldiers fighting in the trenches of Europe. Ashwood had an attractiveness and ability to flatter that was extremely persuasive. Even though now removed to Harlem, she maintained and developed her contacts in Panama (Allen Cumberbatch excepted). Her skills at recruitment and her organising panache were talents which were speedily put to use once she became an official of the UNIA; Ashwood was appointed the general secretary of the organisation a month after her arrival in November 1918. One task that Garvey assigned to her was the careful handling of Wilfred Domingo. Garvey had found that Domingo was stubborn and wilful; not at this stage in his political views, but over the matter of his remuneration for his work on the *Negro World*. Domingo had 'a habit of demanding prompt payment upon production of his article for the *Negro World*,' recalled Amy Ashwood. 'If the agreed $5 was not forthcoming on printing day, no power on earth could persuade him to leave the article in the office.'[30] The dissemination of his Socialist ideals was desirable but Domingo drew the line at personal and financial sacrifice. He was constantly exercised by the need for money to fund his various capitalist projects, particularly his import/export business with the Caribbean. He imported the ingredients for pepper sauces from the West Indies, wrote a radical contemporary, Ras Makonen, 'and in his own little factory in Harlem, he would chop them and produce various chutneys and sauces . . . Woolworths took his products and they don't play ball with anybody who doesn't deliver on good time. This economic basis put him on a level to meet the Socialist Jew boys of the period who also combined business and radicalism.'[31]

The traffic between Harlem and the Caribbean and the West Indian enclaves in Costa Rica and Panama was non-stop. It was through the advocacy of men such as the Panamanian-based teacher Mr Parker that word of Garvey's movement spread to the Caribbean, Central and South America. They were part of the great wave of migrants to the USA, sowing the seeds of an essential remittance culture that has continued till this day. As well as these regular returnees, Garvey relied on the willingness of merchant seamen to act as informal agents for the *Negro World*, carrying bundles of the paper from port to port. By such means the *Negro World* had been successfully distributed throughout the Panama Canal zone. Over in neighbouring British Honduras (now Belize), however, the paper was not given such a free run. British Intelligence officers deemed its circulation to be undesirable. But by the middle of 1919, Governor Eyre Hutson, whose predecessor had taken steps to suppress the journal, became alarmed when the ban seemed to result in many more copies being 'regularly introduced surreptitiously, and . . . largely circulated'. He also conceded that the restrictions were 'one of the grievances that led to a riot' later in the year. A proto-Garveyite, Samuel Haynes, was among the leaders of the demonstrators, made up of ex-servicemen and impoverished mahogany log-wood cutters, protesting the low wages of the mostly seasonal work on offer. Nonetheless, the British authorities, mindful of the scores of white-owned businesses destroyed in the riots, defended their actions against the paper on the grounds that the *Negro World* appeared 'to incite racial hatred and . . . was [probably] supported by German or Bolsheviki money'. It was more likely that this was simply a warming up of the same tepid, uncritiqued and unsourced intelligence in continuous circulation between Washington and London.[32]

Taken alone, the unlevelled American charge of sedition against the *Negro World* was impossible to substantiate. But standing alongside the fierce prose of an editor, Wilfred Domingo, who nightly spoke on a range of contentious subjects from Negro discontent to Irish autonomy, and who moonlighted on the radical *Messenger*, Garvey's paper's culpability was aggregated. Even though Garvey's fellow Jamaican was increasingly distracted by capitalist exploits, in Domingo, the paranoid investigators thought they had their man. Such was the heretical and farcical climate that mere mutterings of dissent could land one in deep trouble. One of the most bizarre and instructive examples of this occurred in a clothes shop in Waterbury, Connecticut, where Joseph Yenowsky, an unashamed Socialist, was employed as a salesman. Yenowsky slid into a discursive and injurious conversation with a customer about the elusiveness of the American Dream and corrupt industrial barons. The patriotic customer didn't appreciate the turn in the conversation and was further aggrieved when Yenowsky allegedly flicked through an openly displayed copy of the *Liberator*, pointed at a picture of Vladimir Lenin and remarked, 'There is what I consider one of the brainiest men in the world.' The enraged customer rushed out of the shop, and returned with a policeman who promptly arrested him. His unguarded remarks were enough to secure the unfortunate Yenowsky a six-month jail sentence for sedition. Its comic proportions were lost on the humourless Red-baiters ascendant in Connecticut at the time.[33]

There was equally nothing funny about spice-loving Negro agitators stirring up the resentments of the formerly loyal black population in Harlem. The whispers of rebellion evoked the kind of terror last seen during plantation days of slave insurrections. Even white friends and acquaintances of the Negro, like the anti-lynching campaigner Bolton Smith, noted the pernicious change that had come across the black man. Travelling on a segregated streetcar in Memphis, Tennessee, Smith had been alarmed by the sight of an elderly Negro couple brushing past him to take a seat in the section of the carriage reserved for white people. It was the kind of insolent behaviour that might lead to violence. Smith had offered to change seats with the Negroes to prevent (and save them from) any trouble. That example, and other mumblings of defiance, half-detected on the lips of sullen black men, had led Bolton Smith to conclude that 'the Negro is not as jolly, and as good natured as he once was'. He too pointed a finger of blame at the black press for 'shaming the Negro into this new attitude'.[34] Bureau of Investigation agents on the front line were equally convinced of the sinister implications behind the new Negro attitude, and were returning with more and more disturbing accounts: 'I have something to report to you in a few days that will give you a jolt,' one agent wrote tantalisingly. 'There is more in the wind than we think.'

A welter of memoranda (from BOI informants who infiltrated black radical organisations and toured barber shops in Harlem) landed on Hoover's desk in the Justice Department, yet no matter how quickly he rushed communiqués to his superiors there was actually little evidence that was actionable, certainly not enough to implement his recommendation that 'something should be done to the editors of these publications as they are beyond doubt exciting the Negro elements of this country to riot and to the committing of outrages'.

There were other not-so-hot heads who further doubted the quality of the intelligence that such sentiments were predicated on. In his tribute to black war veterans (for a proposed Negro memorial in Washington) the Supreme Court Associate Justice Wendell Phillips Stafford declared, 'Cite me a Negro traitor . . . Show me a Negro anarchist . . . Let me see a Negro Bolshevist . . . The only red flag the Negro ever carried was when his shirt was stained crimson by the sacrificial blood he gave to America.'[35]

Stafford's opinion, though, wasn't the received wisdom of the day. Such noble sentiments were a luxury the guardians of the liberty-loving country could ill afford. Or as the *Washington Post* put it, 'There is no time to waste on hair-splitting over infringement of liberty.'

The fear of the enemy within was a characteristic that had come to define the tension between the public and private domains of American life; at times of stress that fear tempered its celebration of individuality and cast a shadow over its Eden-like innocence. When researching *The Crucible*, (which drew parallels between the Salem witch-hunt and 1950s McCarthyism) the playwright Arthur Miller had reached the conclusion that there was some pathology at large in American society that required, every thirty years or so, these periodic scares and subsequent purges.[36]

Arthur Miller's theory was borne out by the events of 1919 – thirty years prior to McCarthyism – when fear of radicals was running to a pitch of seething paranoia; and also thirty-odd years previously, in 1886, when the USA had been convulsed by another Red scare. Then anarchists, who defiantly published their motto, 'A pound of dynamite is better than a bushel of ballots,' had terrified the authorities when a bomb exploded at a demonstration in Haymarket, Chicago, killing a number of police officers.[37] When Americans passed news-stands on 20 April 1919, they learnt that the Mayor of Seattle – one of the country's noisiest opponents of radical groups – had been the target of a bomb, delivered through the US mail. Subsequent attacks were only foiled by luck and the keen eyes of a scrupulous post-office clerk. Charles Kaplan's suspicions had been aroused by sixteen similarly labelled brown packages (all with insufficient postage) addressed to prominent members of the establishment. They included the Attorney General, A. Mitchell Palmer and millionaire businessman, R. D. Rockefeller. The blame for the failed bombing campaign naturally fell on the usual suspects – anarchists, Industrial Workers of the World and hardcore Socialists – but other lesser known organisations also found themselves drawn into the investigation. Marcus Garvey was understandably perplexed when police officers turned up at UNIA head-quarters with a search warrant, after an anonymous, malicious tip-off that the bombs had been posted from the offices of the *Negro World*.[38] Though the police were quickly disabused of the notion, their will-ingness to investigate such an obvious hoax presaged a future in which the paranoid authorities were unlikely to draw distinctions between radical organisations.

The better informed and more widely briefed insiders – Senator Lusk included – were adamant that Bolsheviks were at the back of the radical movement. Lusk clamoured for the authorities to flush out the parlour Bolsheviks and sewer Socialists. They had stealthily propagandised among factory workers, particularly the alien workforce, and were said to have infiltrated the American Federation of Labor (AFL). A. Mitchell Palmer, the Attorney General, catching up with the mood of the country, warned that, 'like a prairie fire, the blaze of revolution was sweeping over every American institution'. Palmer said he'd watched in agonising disbelief as the Red menace began 'eating its way into the homes of the American workmen . . . licking the altars of the churches, leaping into the belfry of the school'.[39] The evidence was there and the coming events of 1 May 1919 signalled that the threat of revolution would be met by an indignant population, stamped with 100 per cent Americanism. No further proof of conspiracy was needed for the uniformed veterans who commandeered a tank in Cleveland amidst the May Day red flag parade and drove it headlong into the radical crowd. A similar collective response took shape in New York where veterans and patriots – bricks in hand – marched on Russia House, a social club for Russian migrants, and set fire to books, magazines and Russian-language papers whilst forcing the onlooking émigrés to sing 'The Star Spangled Banner'. Further downtown, another angry mob, fortified by victory cabbage and liberty dogs (formerly sauerkraut and frankfurters), descended on the Rand School of Social Science and smashed their way through the Socialist institution, and 'liberated' the building (previously the home of the Young Women's Christian Association) by pinning the Stars and Stripes to a makeshift pole on the roof.

Americans vented a measure of their anger during the May Day riots of 1919 but public hysteria continued unabated; it erupted beyond all previous recorded levels the following month. A reflux of panic welled up in people's throats on 1 June, when news spread of a series of coordinated explosions that ripped through several cities. They were followed, even more ominously, by a detonation in front of the Attorney General's residence in Washington DC. Luckily for Palmer, who'd been reading in the library upstairs, the bomb-carrier had tripped on the steps outside. When the police assembled the human remains on Palmer's lawn, they also claimed to have discovered partially intact but legible copies of *Plain Words*, an anarchist pamphlet that threatened, 'There will have to be bloodshed; we will not dodge; there will have to be murder; there will have to be destruction; we are ready to do anything and everything to suppress the capitalist class.'

The newspapers screamed for revenge, for tough sanctions to be taken against both the terrorists and those who could be shown to be their supporters. 'I was preached upon from every pulpit,' Palmer complained, and 'urged to do something and do it now.' His immediate response was to enforce aspects of the war-time immigration code whereby any alien who simply read or received anarchist publications could be apprehended and possibly deported.[40]

Senator Lusk – by now the chairman of the committee appointed to examine the perilous conditions of Alien Anarchy in America – put all Socialist organisations on note that they would be investigated. He particularly had in mind those guilty of 'the changeless habit of dissatisfaction, and [guilty of] bringing it with them to our shores [where] it was not justified'. True to his word, Lusk ordered state troopers into the offices of the IWW and Rand School – a raid which swept up 'tons of radical propaganda', according to the *New York Times*, as well as 'forged stationery and a plan to deceive postal authorities similar to that used by the failed bombers'. During the public hearing into what had been unearthed amidst this radical bounty, Senator Lusk also revealed the discovery of a plan to foment revolution amongst Negroes that would bring down the US government. The press in the gallery strained forward to see the evidence in support of such an alarming hypothesis: Lusk held up a neatly typed essay entitled 'Socialism Imperilled, or the Negro – a Potential menace to American Radicalism'. The article was written by Wilfred Domingo – editor of the *Negro World*.[41]

When Marcus Garvey opened the newspapers the next day and his unsuspecting eye lighted on Domingo's name alongside the raid of the Rand School, he scoured the article with a precipitous dread and fury. He had tolerated his friend's Socialist transgressions up until now, as a loving father might the high-jinks of a reprobate son. Since their earliest encounter – serving a kind of political apprenticeship together at the National Club in the Jamaican capital – the two had maintained a nurturing and sympathetic relationship. But in the current repressive and paranoid climate, Domingo had exposed not just himself but the organisation to danger. After all, Marcus Garvey was not a citizen of the USA. He was an alien and was extremely concerned about the possibility of infringing any convention that might lead to his deportation. Expulsion would have meant the end of Garvey, and the end of the magnificent dream that he was well on the way to realising. His alarm over the perilous position that Domingo had inadvertently placed him in was of the same order as the directors of the Rand School of Social Science. The principal of the Rand School had sought to play down the charge of providing an outlet for sedition by drawing the investigators' attention to an envelope, stamped and addressed to Domingo, that was found alongside his 'Socialism Imperilled' essay, together with a letter of rejection: the Rand School had never intended its publication. The school's ignominious attempt to wriggle out of any association impressed none of the parties – certainly not an embarrassed Wilfred Domingo but, equally, neither the investigators nor Garvey. The caveat was a technicality, not mitigation for the Socialist content. And in Garvey's eyes, Domingo was further damned when his 'scientific editorials' in the *Negro World* were praised on the pages of the Socialist *Messenger* as the work of a Negro scholar 'who has the courage to say just what he thinks'.[42] That was the very gist of the problem as far as the UNIA leader was concerned; fury won over friendship as he summoned his old political soulmate to be 'tried' by the UNIA's nine-person executive committee. The seizure by the Lusk Committee had proven the final spur, but Domingo later conceded that Garvey had, in recent months, grown mightily dissatisfied with an editorial approach that had failed to boost the UNIA leader's ideas. Garvey had even gone to the lengths of taking out an advert in the *Negro World*, setting forth his personal propaganda in a signed article.

At the trial, Domingo was accused of straying way off-message from the UNIA position and of 'writing editorials not in keeping with the programme [Garvey] had outlined'. Wilfred Domingo survived the trial, but the trust between the two men was irreconcilably broken. Garvey readily accepted his old friend's resignation when it was proffered a few weeks later. The sacrifice of Domingo was one of the first demonstrable signs that in Marcus Garvey's ascent and development as a leader, once serious disagreements arose, past friendships and loyalties would be discounted. But in moving against Domingo, not only had Garvey lost a close and vital associate, he'd gained a life-long, vengeful enemy who, in years to come, would continue to probe for weaknesses and to inflict maximum damage.[43]

In the short term, the loss of Domingo would be offset by Amy Ashwood's ability to continue to charm the printer, Henry Rogowski, when funds were not available to pay him on time. Ashwood was Garvey's secret weapon, wheeled out to negotiate seemingly intractable difficulties. In the case of Rogowski, her delicate mission was to both 'obtain an extension of credit as well as the promise to print the next week's edition [of the *Negro World*]'. Garvey also depended on general secretary Ashwood to scout and secure properties for their meetings on favourable terms. She had neither Domingo's knowledge nor contacts, but her energy, flirtatiousness, chutzpah and inventiveness would prove a boon in the critical months ahead.[44]

Domingo's departure did not throw investigators off the trail of the UNIA and Garvey undoubtedly felt it politic to distance himself and the organisation further from his former ally. In a statement published in the *Negro World*, under the headline 'Extraordinary Announcement for Everybody, All Politicians Should Take Notice', Garvey attempted to clarify the position that 'this organisation has no association with any political party', and furthermore, 'Republicans, Democrats and Socialists are the same to us – and that persons who endeavour to use the name of the *Negro World* for enhancing their political fortunes do so without [our] approval.' As an exercise in damage limitation this was a spectacular failure. The following month Garvey held a mass meeting at Carnegie Hall and amongst the uninvited guests were agents of the Lusk Committee accompanied by a bomb squad.[45]

Meanwhile, the covert investigation of Garvey and his fellow black radical newspapermen continued apace. Hoover called for even closer scrutiny of the Harlem headquarters of both the *Negro World* and the *Messenger* which the BOI man believed to be the powerhouse 'of the Russian organ of Bolsheviki' in New York.[46] Actually, the editors were bashing away on one battered old Underwood typewriter, in a tiny room of a converted brownstone. Worryingly for the UNIA, Hoover seemed reluctant to relinquish the notion that 'there appears to be an intense feeling existing between Garvey and the group supporting the *Messenger*'.[47]

On 11 October, Hoover composed a memorandum to special agent Ridgely in which he spelt out his frustrations:

'He [Garvey] has . . . been particularly active among radical elements in New York City in agitating the Negro movement. Unfortunately, however, he has not yet violated any federal law whereby he could be proceeded against on the grounds of being an undesirable alien.'[48]

Garvey may have been a radically inclined alien whose speeches and writings occasionally veered towards sedition, but he certainly didn't fit the newspaper cartoon identikit of a scruffy, wild-eyed Bolshevik, with radical literature stuffed in his jacket pockets and a bomb in his beard.[49]

The attempt to pin a Bolshevik/Socialist label on him appears all the more perverse as Garvey was, at the time, busy establishing his capitalist credentials with a number of high-profile ventures. The coloured population of Harlem could now dine at the UNIA's lunch room, restaurant, tea room and ice-cream parlour at 56 West 135th Street. At the same address, Harlemites would also shortly be able to drop in and buy shares in an ambitious-sounding project, a steamship corporation called the Black Star Line. Soon Garvey was promising his followers a new business launched every month. Adverts placed in the *Negro World* reached far beyond Harlem, disseminating news of each achievement to black populations wherever they were so configured. Garvey was always the greatest advert for any enterprise linked to the UNIA. He was an extraordinary salesman who'd developed a philosophy where punters weren't just buying into a business but were placing a down payment on future black redemption. Garvey sold stock but fundamentally, in the words of Samuel A. Haynes, 'Garvey sold the Negro to himself.'[50] Garveyism would always remain a secular movement with a strong under-tow of religion. Doubters in a Garvey audience were more often drowned out by the collective din of those bewitched by the musicality of his speech. His language was biblical, the meetings were laced with hymns and Negro spirituals, and his end-of-service stock-selling appeals induced the kind of frenzy more familiarly found in the pews of black American churches.

When Marcus Garvey, accompanied by Amy Ashwood, took to the road on a mission to spread his message and sign up new members, the churches were usually their first port of call. Some church elders viewed Garvey's inroads into their congregations with apprehension – especially because, as his confidence grew, he became less guarded in his criticism of their greed and avarice. The welcome he received was not always warm. No matter how speedily the UNIA grew, Garvey's income was still largely dependent on monies gathered from speaking engagements; and he was to find that the opportunities to address church congregations stopped short of permitting him to call for an offering afterwards. Such was the proviso laid down by the pastor of a local African Methodist Church in Virginia. That restriction, however, had not taken Amy Ashwood into account. In her presence, Garvey's daring was doubled. When they discovered that the pastor had a mistress, Ashwood devised a ruse to send an urgent telegram to the man of cloth, pretending it was from his lover. With the pastor called away on a pressing business matter, Garvey delivered a rousing sermon and was free to call for a silver collection which apparently pocketed the couple several hundred dollars.[51]

The clergy's objections, though, were more often political than financial. Arriving in Detroit at the back end of June 1919, Garvey had taken up a longstanding invitation from Bishop Charles Spencer Smith of the African Methodist Episcopal church to call upon him for an inquisition dressed up as afternoon tea. No sooner had he bid his visitor farewell than the Bishop was feverishly writing to the Attorney General, denouncing the alien 'native of Jamaica' as 'in every respect a "Red",' a promulgator of a vicious propaganda that was 'calculated to breed racial and international strife'.[52] That assessment, scorched in fire and damnation, certainly chimed with the Attorney General's newly promoted special assistant at the Justice Department.

In the wake of the bomb scares, J. Edgar Hoover had been appointed to identify the extent of the threat posed by those disparaged as 'race pimps', peddlers of 'Socialist bilge' and 'Bolshevik twaddle'.[53] In a few months, Hoover and his zealous team had collated and cross-referenced the worst of the crop, and hatched a plan to round them up, in what became known as the Palmer Raids. Before the year's end, the files of tens of thousands of potential enemies of the state would be stamped in readiness for their expulsion from the USA. Widescale arrests began on the long night of 7 November 1919, the second anniversary of the Bolshevik revolution. The first wave of 249, including the infamous anarchist writer, Emma Goldman, and young Russian émigrés unfortunate enough to be attending night classes at Russia House that evening, were swept up in the raids, denied the privilege of a lawyer, bundled aboard the USS *Buford* (popularly known as the *Soviet Ark*) and deported to Russia.[54] In all, close to 10,000 suspects were arrested. Garvey escaped the first cull of alien anarchists but nonetheless his name was put forward to Louis F. Post at the Labor Department to ratify the case for his deportation. As with the vast majority of suspects, Marcus Garvey was spared deportation through the intervention of this seventy-year-old civil servant who insisted, much to the fury of the Attorney General, on going through the cases on an individual basis. There was insufficient evidence to proceed and Post's department concluded that the case against Marcus Garvey was not proven. The matter would have to rest there for now, but it was far from settled in Hoover's eyes.

The young attorney's gut feelings about the UNIA leader were backed up by the final report into the 'Radicalism and Sedition Among the Negroes as Reflected in Their Publications'. That report was certainly no hanging indictment but did suggest, to the earnest men who commissioned it, that steps needed to be taken now to forestall an even bigger problem in the future; before the welcome sound of Negro 'yessums' and the sight of happy Negro grins became a fable of yesteryear. The erstwhile reliable Major Loving signed off his investigation with a memorandum which was much more measured. He would be drawn only as far as the evidence warranted; after nine months of diligent intelligence gathering, Loving had concluded that there was no need yet to sound the alarm. The UNIA was, for instance, 'too young as yet to give it any special significance'. He agreed with white superiors who believed that coloured folk would be 'far better off without these self-styled race leaders who are springing up'. Nonetheless, he wrote flatteringly of Garvey as a 'very able young man', the promulgator of a 'clever propaganda'. But for the blackness of his own skin, Loving might have been suspected – after perhaps straying too close to his subject – of having gone native. The Director of Military Intelligence was quick to defend Loving as 'one of the best types of white man's Negro' who had grown a little uncomfortable about the direction taken when investigating the black Red Scare. Evidently, the major's enthusiasm for the project had cooled. He asked to be relieved of his duties and transferred back to the more harmonious world of his regimental band in the Philippines. The Red Scare had yet to run its course and Loving's assessment ultimately lost out to strident critics in the administration who viewed Garvey and the rest of the Negro editors with menace. The slave insurrections of the past paled next to the 'dangerous influences [presently] at work upon the Negro'. The final report concluded solemnly that 'to ignore all this as the ante-bellum characteristics of the plantation Negro preacher is . . . to go very far astray of the mark.'[55] The message was clear: Marcus Garvey and his ilk had killed Uncle Tom and resurrected Nat Turner.

Uncle Tom had served his purpose. According to the myth, the saintly protagonist of *Uncle Tom's Cabin* had shamed the North into issuing an ultimatum to the South: the stain of slavery must be washed from American society. When President Lincoln eventually met Harriet Beecher Stowe, the author of *Uncle Tom's Cabin*, he is said to have remarked, 'So you're the little lady whose book started this big war.'[56] In the abolitionist novel, the stoical and Christ-like Uncle Tom dies willingly at the hands of his master. Through his sacrifice others might redeem their humanity. *Uncle Tom's Cabin* was a best-seller several times over, found in the homes of enlightened white Americans (especially in the North). African-Americans, though, had become increasingly ambivalent about the character, Tom, even more so when he was transformed into a figure of fun in minstrel shows, portrayed as an unprincipled coon who would abase himself to please the white man. Black people had tried the Uncle Tom approach but it had gone on for too long with very little gain. In 1919, at the back of the unequivocal evidence that black military sacrifice in the Great War had been to little or no avail, at

this crucial and psychic moment in African-American lives, Marcus
Garvey was electrifying disenchanted black audiences with the simple
but militant message, 'The time for cowardice is past. The old-time
Negro has gone – buried with Uncle Tom.'[57]

8

HARLEM SPEAKS FOR SCATTERED ETHIOPIA

What is Africa to me:
Copper sun or scarlet sea,
Jungle star or jungle track,
Strong bronzed men, or regal black
Women from whose loins I sprang
when the birds of Eden sang?
One three centuries removed
From the scenes his fathers loved,
Spicy grove, cinnamon tree,
What is Africa to me? . . .

Countee Cullen, 'Heritage'

A tall, angular man stood at the back of the crowds on a street corner in the heart of Harlem. He wasn't one of the spies that Marcus Garvey constantly warned his followers to beware. He wasn't employed by the BOI or Military Intelligence. He had attended Garvey rallies before. Then, as now, he'd remained aloof and sceptical. But on the evening of 13 October 1919, as the autumn leaves began to fall from the towering poplars that lined 135th Street, so too did John E. Bruce's suspicions about the spectacular Jamaican start to recede. For, as Bruce wrote in his memoirs, he had listened to the Ciceronian orator at numerous events in church halls and at Harlem's Speakers' Corner, but on this occasion he 'heard' Garvey perhaps for the first time – and it was as if the whole of Harlem was speaking with one voice.

He'd listened and listened until he'd got a line on Garvey – ultimately on his honesty and tremendous earnestness – that would not break. Thereafter, John E. Bruce was a convert to Garveyism, immune to doubt, and would remain loyal to the man and the cause until his last breath, five years later. It was an extraordinary volte-face. Up until then Bruce had rarely passed up an opportunity to ridicule Garvey and his schemes, which seemed 'wild, chimerical [and] impossible of accomplishment'. Sixty-three-year-old John E. Bruce prided himself on an old-fashioned steadfastness, no matter how detrimental to himself: he might ultimately break under superior force or argument but, in the meantime, he would not bend. Prior to October, he suspected the UNIA leader of being nothing more than a 'four-flusher' or 'grafter'. By some miracle, the brother on the edge of the crowd now found himself uncharacteristically moved by the sound of Garvey's voice booming out over the chill night air.

In front of hundreds of devotees, Marcus Garvey built towards the evening's resounding, emotional conclusion; and John E. Bruce experienced what many had testified: that the Jamaican seemed to speak to him individually, as if he were inside his own head, speaking his own thoughts. That night, in his haunting and melodious voice, Marcus Garvey reiterated for his audience, as he had done hundreds of times before, the aims of the UNIA. But on this occasion he had managed to turn the cast-iron journalist away from his usual default position of cynicism. 'I said to myself, "Let him try out his plan; since no one else has submitted a better one, why oppose him."' John E. Bruce was surprised by how easy it was to let go of his prejudice; and further made a vow to himself. 'From that cold night in October,' Bruce recalled, 'I ceased writing and talking against Garvey.' What ultimately united the two men was Africa. Bruce was an amateur archivist of all things African, and over a number of decades had forged impressive links with African scholars such as Liberia's Edward Wilmot Blyden. With no funding, but with a passionate commitment, he'd also started the Negro Society for Historical Research with a fellow Afrophile, Arthur Schomburg. His bookshelves, staircase and even bathroom were brimming with scholarly texts and rare African books. But John E. Bruce, Garvey and a small band of self-taught historians, collectors and scholars were – in their unbridled enthusiasm for Africa – the exceptions.

To a majority of black people, scattered across America and around the globe at the turn of the twentieth century, Africa was just as dirty a word as Uncle Tom; a source of embarrassment, the skeleton in the ancestral cupboard which, if they stopped to think about it, was an uncomfortable reminder of their slave past. Africans were depicted in cartoons as a comical, conquered, barely civilised people with bones through their noses, riding semi-naked on the backs of alligators down the Zambezi. Many in a Garvey audience would have heard for the first time 'Africa' spoken of as the motherland. For the migrants who thronged to UNIA massed meetings, 'the old country' meant Louisiana or Alabama. Their connections had been severed from Africa generations previously; maybe, after 200 years, they were still aware of one or two words and mutated customs that had survived but beyond that there was no history; beyond that was only darkness. 'Every man,' says Arthur Schopenhauer, 'mistakes the limits of his mind for the limits of the world.' The truth of that statement, as far as black Americans in 1919 were concerned, lay in their inability to even frame the question, 'What is Africa to me?' Into that void walked Marcus Garvey and what he had to say had hardly ever been heard before.

Garvey appealed to the African-American who had previously known only the dimensions of his farm, the perimeter of his town or the outer limits of the district, from which no generation before him had ever moved. That migrant – wedded to the South – had made a massive psychic jump to Harlem's Negro metropolis; from an agrarian life to industrialisation. An even greater leap of the imagination was required to encompass Africa. Except in biblical terms, and even then only when the collection bowl came round on a Sunday service, African-Americans could hardly conceive of Africa. As the old Negro spiritual told it they'd 'Been in the Storm So Long' that they'd lost sight of the African shoreline and home. And yet, whether articulated or not, there remained in the recesses of black American minds, a longing to reach beyond the boundaries of a memory that stopped at slavery; a feeling that the lonesome young poet, Langston Hughes, looking out the window of the Pullman train that crossed the Mason-Dixon Line on a starless Southern night, dredged up in his bluesy 'The Negro Speaks of Rivers'.[1]

I've known rivers:
I've known rivers ancient as the world and older than the flow of human
    blood in human veins.

My soul has grown deep like the rivers.

I bathed in the Euphrates when dawns were young.

I built my hut near the Congo and it lulled me to sleep.

I looked upon the Nile and raised the pyramids above it.

I heard the singing of the Mississippi when Abe Lincoln went down to
    New Orleans, and I've seen its muddy bosom turn all golden in the
    sunset.

I've known rivers:

Ancient, dusky rivers.

My soul has grown deep like the rivers.[2]

In his yearning for a history, Langston Hughes dug up a past – and
made a spiritual, if not actual, connection between America and Africa
– where the Euphrates ran into the Mississippi, and the Nile into New
Orleans. But the break with the past had never been permanent; it
had only ever been a blip.

There'd been two widescale attempts to return former slaves to
Africa. The first unfolded throughout 1787 when, primarily through
the exegesis of the English abolitionist, Granville Sharp, some 300
black Britons – after suffering violent storms, much privation and a
one-in-five loss of life – established a settlement in Sierra Leone. News
of their daring experiment in black self-government (first as a British
protectorate and then a colony) later inspired the redoubtable black
Quaker, Captain Paul Cuffe (a free-born black man and one of the
richest merchants in America), to make two perilous expeditions to
Sierra Leone. Cuffe and his all-black crew of nine must have cut quite
a sight as his vessel, the *Traveler*, sailed into the mouth of the Sierra
Leone River. Cuffe was pleased to note that he was greeted cordially
by Governor Columbine, but, elsewhere, the captain was not impressed
by the indolence he saw all around him. The ascetic teetotaller believed
he knew the reason. The entry for his logbook on 1 March 1811 reads,
'Peopel of the colony are very fond of spiritual liquors . . . [and] of
haveing a number of servents about them.' Cuffe was particularly
perturbed by the state of their neglected farms. Even so he predicted
a brighter future for the colony, seeing no reason why it wouldn't one
day be numbered among the great trading nations of the world.

Cuffe was the bridge to another generation of former slaves (this
time from the USA) who founded an African-American colony (alongside their Afro-Saxon cousins) on the Grain Coast of the continent

in neighbouring Liberia thirty years later.³ That scheme was formally initiated in 1822 and supported by members of the American Colonization Society – comprised conscientious liberals who desired to atone for the sins of chattel slavery by engineering a voluntary return to continental Africa; and also slave-holders who sought to get rid of freed slaves whom they perceived as a threat to the smooth running of the chattel system, as well as their embarrassing illegitimate mulatto offspring with slave women.

No matter the motivations of those advocating recolonisation, the uptake amongst black Americans was always tiny and inversely proportional to their well-being in the USA: the exodus had been greatest when things were rotten and the devil was in the white man. But now, 100 years after those first settlers had taken a punt on their futures and laid down roots in a proxy, if not actual homeland, Liberia betrayed all the signs of its origins as a hastily conceived, bastard child of a state that failed to thrive: Americo-Liberians presided over a country that was free but broke, and desperately hoped to negotiate a loan from the USA. Despite all the vagaries of their existence, the sons and daughters of Afric were perhaps better off in America. And the lesson from life in the New World was that one's African-ness was a disadvantage – best not reflected on. Marcus Garvey would have his followers reconsider.

Tens of thousands of supporters seemed prepared to listen. In just over 18 months the UNIA had grown from its initial 13 members to an organisation that now boasted 5,500 members in Harlem, branches throughout 25 states of the Union, and additional divisions in the West Indies, Central America and West Africa. Garvey calculated that, by June 1919, his organisation had built up 2 million followers; William Du Bois made the conservative estimate of under 300,000 paying members.⁴ Throughout his career the great promoter in Garvey suffered from a tendency (often unnecessarily) to inflate figures. Du Bois's low estimate is also unlikely to have been accurate. The truth is no one really knew but, even allowing for both leaders' bias in inflating or deflating the figures, the growth of the UNIA was impressive. It was still dwarfed by the NAACP which at the close of 1919 registered 310 branches, but the NAACP had been aggressively campaigning for members since its inception 10 years previously, and benefited from the backing of wealthy white philanthropists (a group later characterised by Langston Hughes as the 'old entente cordiale of Jewish notables, Negrotarian publishers and civil rights grandees')[5]. If Garvey's organisation continued to expand at the same rate that it had thus far shown, then it would easily outpace its competitor within the next year or two.

There were aesthetic and philosophical differences between the two groups. The NAACP was an interracial organisation with a significant number of sympathetic white members; in fact the majority of readers of its journal, the *Crisis*, were white; integration was its endgame. The talented tenth of African-Americans to whom it made a naked appeal – the doctors, lawyers and public-school teachers – led a 'top down' movement that would eventually, in some distant future, cascade to the rest of the black folk. The UNIA was by contrast a uniquely black organisation that grew from the bottom up. A UNIA supporter might hold a joint membership card with the NAACP but she or he was generally closer to the bottom of the social and economic ladder; members aspired to greater personal social mobility and the elevation of the group. A large number, if not the majority, of UNIA adherents were said to be West Indian immigrants. Critics sneered that Garvey's organisation comprised pretentious Negroes, typified by its leadership of lawyers without a brief and professors without paper qualifications. Though the NAACP leadership might quietly scoff at its junior rival, the UNIA's end-of-year progress report for 1919 was extremely encouraging.[6] The dues paid contributed to the executive officers' small salaries and Garvey continued to supplement his income through his own lectures whether in a civic or church hall. As befitting the leader of a growing mass movement, the UNIA president general now betrayed signs of greater personal comfort – though not extravagantly so; he'd moved from a draughty hall room to a furnished room at 238 West 131st Street, a few blocks down from Amy Ashwood who'd moved into a flat rented by her father. Romance was relegated to several divisions below the UNIA. There was no talk of marriage or of Garvey and Ashwood living together; and no relaxing of moral propriety even when the two were alone on fundraising jaunts around the country. As Mrs Mary Johnstone, the landlady at 4458 Prairie Avenue, told BOI investigators, when Garvey and Ashwood visited Chicago later in the year, they pointedly took separate rooms. Their energies went into the organisation. To the BOI agent C-C who infiltrated the organisation at around the same time, Ashwood seemed 'to be Marcus Garvey's chief assistant, a kind of managing boss'.[7]

Garvey and Ashwood were as one in their celebration and elevation of black culture; Ashwood was lured towards the theatre, to reviews and cabaret in the company of performers such as Florence Mills and the all-black Lafayette players, whilst Garvey was more inclined to retire to his furnished room in Harlem with a copy of Blyden's work or something loaned to him by John E. Bruce or the amateur biblio-phile and collector Arthur Schomburg (a friend of Bruce whom he described as a 'mulatto who thought black'); both of whom were keen excavators of the Negro's past.

In articulating examples of Negro achievement in history, Garvey employed a range of methods which he believed would inculcate an idea of black pride amongst audiences at UNIA meetings. Recitations of Negro poetry were a favoured technique. In this Amy Ashwood proved a willing ally, and was a regular on the programme billing for the evening's entertainment. The irrepressible twenty-one-year-old could be relied on to rouse the masses with her hearty rendition of Paul Laurence Dunbar's 'The Colored Soldiers' – a celebration of African-American military endeavour. More often, though, Ashwood deferred to the regal Henrietta Vinton Davis who was the star attraction at these assemblies. Davis was a renowned elocutionist and dramatic actor – a pioneer who'd performed Shakespeare in front of integrated audi-ences. At a time when black performers were expected to 'black up' in caricatured minstrel roles, when coon songs like Ernest Hogan's 'All Coons Look Alike to Me' were the most popular form of entertain-ment, the idea of a classical black tragedienne was deemed laughable. There were significant numbers in the audience at Ford's Opera House in Washington on 7 May 1884 who found it difficult to accept Henrietta Davis in the role of Lady MacBeth, alongside a fellow black performer, Powhaton Beaty. The *Washington Bee* reported that 'there were many white people in the house who seemed disposed to turn to comedy the tragic efforts of the actors'.[8]

Inevitably, Davis's talents had been stymied by the dearth of serious roles for black actors. Long periods of inactivity were punctuated by a handful of tours of major cities in the Northern states, as well as Central America and the Caribbean, including a stint in Garvey's Jamaica in 1912. There is no record of Marcus Garvey having met Davis in Jamaica but she was given a sharp introduction to the pecu-liarities of the island's caste system that so maddened him. The future race leader had not yet made his mark on the island. That year far greater attention was given to the budding poet, Claude McKay, who recalled excitedly going backstage at the end of Henrietta Davis's recitation. The brown elite had turned out in full for the distinguished African-American visitor and had applauded her enthusiastically. But McKay also remembered how Davis had unwittingly transgressed by allowing herself to be represented on the island by a very black manager, much to the consternation of her lighter skinned hosts; and it was suggested that her fortunes might improve if she switched to a mulatto manager. 'This incident must have opened Miss Davis's eyes,' McKay noted, 'to the subtlety of the colour problem in Jamaica, which is never brutal like a fist in the face, as it is in America, but nevertheless it is always there.'[9] Later on, Davis returned to the USA and formed her own drama company in Chicago; she appeared resigned to her destiny, to trundle along with only a smattering of the recognition she deserved. But then Davis's life took an unexpected turn when, one evening in 1919, she received an invitation from Marcus Garvey to address a UNIA gathering at the Palace Casino. 'This woman [Henrietta Davis] commanded an audience, [she] could just hold you,' Maida Springer, then a young Garveyite, recalled. 'I would sit there in attention and with awe.'[10] Henrietta Davis was, likewise, entranced by her encounter with Garveyism and his ecstatic audiences; she was overcome by the emotional and intellectual charge of the meetings.

At the age of fifty-nine, she had found her true calling – one that would bind her love of drama to a celebration of African heritage. After that evening at the Palace Casino, she never returned to the stage (to the ridicule of some white audiences) but brought her theatrical skills and dramatic persona to the UNIA. Her repertoire included 'Cleopatra's Dying Speech' and 'How Tom Sawyer Got His Fence Whitewashed' by Mark Twain. But the woman who'd become the organisation's domestic and international organiser, reserved her most compelling performances for renditions of works by black writers. The Negro dialect verse of Paul Dunbar was the primary poetry of choice at UNIA gatherings. Dunbar was a poet for all seasons and for all ages. Henrietta Davis demonstrated as much when, in the middle of June 1919, she addressed his 'Little Brown Baby with Sparkling Eyes' to the children with satin ribbons in their hair and tweed bowties pinching their collars, who, whether willing or not, were required to accompany their parents to the Palace Casino. Besides, it was never too early in the life of a Negro to instil a sense of race pride. And, on that occasion, whilst reciting the poem for 'God's chillun', Davis balanced a black doll on her knee (kindly loaned by Ross and Berry, a Negro enterprise manufacturing black dolls in Harlem) for greater dramatic effect. If Henrietta Vinton Davis was demonstrably Negrophilic, then she, along with the UNIA inner circle, would always stress that this was underpinned by a love of Africa.

In later life, when Amy Ashwood attempted a biography of Marcus Garvey, she would stress his kinship with the Maroons of Jamaica, the escaped slaves of African descent who had fled, soon after their capture and transportation to the pearl of the Antilles, deep into the Jamaican interior where they waged an unremitting guerrilla war against the British. Decades of fierce resistance forced the weary colonial masters of the island to sue for peace and offer the Maroons a degree of autonomy in the malaria-infested Cockpit country. Their ferocity had, more ambiguously, been exploited by the British when, after a breakdown of the truce and renewed fighting on the island, 500 captives were deported to Africa, under the expectation (not guaranteed) that in gratitude for their spared lives, they would, in turn, help to put down a rebellion organised by freed slaves in the new settlement of Sierra Leone.[11]

Garvey's Maroon heritage was apocryphal. His father had been apprenticed to a former slave-owner; his grandfather was born into slavery and his great-grandfather before him. The parish records only showed a break in this pattern following the slaves' emancipation in 1834. Garvey, therefore, was not the descendant of proud and fierce Maroons but he was, nonetheless, well named. As was the custom, slave-holders branded their property after themselves, and the Gaelic 'Garvey' means warlike, though this is information that is unlikely to have been transmitted to a young boy growing up in the Jamaican hinterland: neither Irish nor African history was on the curriculum.

Colonial education on the island stressed the achievements of empire – the British Empire, that is, and not any ancient African equivalent. In his youth, Marcus Garvey had been a proud son of empire, who'd memorised, uncritically, wondrous poems and speeches from the panoply of British history; particular favourites were Glassford Bell's 'Mary, Queen of Scots' and Tennyson's 'In Memoriam'. It wasn't until his arrival in London in 1912, and his exposure to the writings of Edward Wilmot Blyden and Joseph Ephraim Casely Hayford in the book-lined offices of the *African Times and Orient*

Review, that the young Jamaican had begun to grasp an alternative history of Africa that placed it at the very centre of civilisation. Reading Blyden, Garvey felt himself let into an amazing secret; given a privileged glimpse back to the dawn of Ethiopia, through amber dusk and pastoral twilight, when Africa was the 'gateway of all the loftiest and noblest traditions of the human race'. From the offices of the *African Times and Orient Review*, Garvey had followed an African literary trail to the reading rooms of the British Museum where he'd immersed himself in *Christianity, Islam and the Negro Race*. So impressed was he with the expansive and scholarly outlook of its fiercely black author who had 'done so much to retrieve the lost prestige of the race', that Marcus Garvey took to quoting stirring extracts from Blyden's work: they would prove the bedrock of the UNIA president general's own concept of race, the 'problem of the color line' and the 'aristocracy of color'.

Blyden laid waste the then current racial hypotheses of African inferiority. He was a welcome counterpoint to English and American critical thinkers. Men such as the naval officer Commander Andrew H. Foote, whose zeal in policing the end of the trade in slavery did not moderate his jaundiced view of the black man. 'If all that the Negroes of all generations have ever done were to be obliterated from recollection forever,' Foote wrote, 'the whole world would lose no great truth, no profitable arts, no exemplary form of life. The loss of all that is African would offer no memorable deduction from anything but the black catalogue of crime.'[12] This ahistorical view of Africa was much in vogue in the modernist sport of extending Darwin's theory of evolution to the races. So that it came as no surprise to Meredith Townsend (the saviour of the *Spectator*) that Africans had 'never founded a stone city, never built a ship, and never produced a literature'.[13] Such a lowly estimation of the black race had not advanced much by 1919. Even, H. L. Mencken, a coruscating critic of cant and arrogance, ventured the opinion that 'the educated Negro of today is a failure, not because he meets insuperable difficulties in life, but because he is a Negro'. Mencken believed his African ancestry was the root of the black man's problem and that it would take him another fifty generations to be brought to acceptable standards of efficiency and purposefulness that came with civilisation. Even then, the superior white man would still be running the show as he was fifty generations ahead of the Negro.[14]

These were failings which had conveniently disqualified the African from self-governance and justified Europeans' civilising intervention. Such outward altruism disguised the initial self-serving economic reasons; in the case of Germany, for example, the colonisation of parts of Africa was propelled by the pressure to find free 'empty' territories for its impoverished and landless peasant communities.[15] That impulse was soon overtaken by the rush to extract precious minerals and other resources from the continent: 'I have the honour to inform you that from 1 January 1899, you must succeed in furnishing four thousand kilos of rubber every month' wrote a Belgian civil servant to a sponsored agent in the Congo. 'To effect this I give you *carte blanche*. You have therefore two months in which to work your people. Employ gentleness first, and if they persist in not accepting the imposition of the state, employ force of arms.' Those who refused to bend to the will of King Leopold's agents in the rubber groves risked having their hands cut off[16] – an unsavoury episode witnessed by the African-American soldier and journalist George Washington Williams in his open letter to King Leopold II of Belgium. Williams politely informed His Majesty that Belgium's representatives were stealthily 'engaged in the slave trade, wholesale and retail . . . giving £3 per head for able-bodied slaves for military service'.

At Cape Palmas, Williams struggled to contain his disgust as he observed how 'a vessel approached and began to transfer recruited workers . . . each boat brought 35 or 40 Kroomen packed as closely as chocolates in a box . . . [with] anxious and inquiring glances.' Williams concluded, 'Here was a scene, then, equal to anything in the slave trade, with but one element unsupplied – no chains about their necks.'[17] No one, least of all Leopold II, paid much attention to Williams's complaint. But lovers of literature would read of European excesses in the Congo a few years later when they were rendered, almost as a fable and with such polished revulsion, in the melancholic thoughts of Joseph Conrad, in his novella *Heart of Darkness*. 'They grabbed what they could get for the sake of what was to be got,' Conrad's narrator observes. 'It was just robbery with violence, aggravated murder on a great scale, and men going at it blind . . . not a pretty thing when you look into it too much.' Europeans did not flinch much at the excesses and barbarities committed on their behalf but, rather, in an absence of individual restraint, decided on a course of regulation.

The Berlin Conference of 1884–85 was an attempt by the German

Chancellor, Otto Von Bismarck, to referee the great carve-up of the continent, but his blueprint had never fully satisfied the rapacious instincts of the rival European powers. At the height of the Great War, in 1917, Sir Harry Johnston, a former diplomat and stranger to discretion, bluntly stated his estimation that the conflict 'was really fought over African questions', with Germany seeking to enlarge its influence on the continent by wresting Morocco from the French, and the Congo from the French and Portuguese. In the pages of the *London Sphere*, Johnston went on to elaborate on the achievable outcomes for the war, speculating that, 'Rightly governed, Africa will . . . repay the cost of our struggle with Germany'.[18] Johnston's prophecy would be tested two years later at the Paris Peace Conference, where, following Germany's defeat in the Great War, the fate of its possessions in Africa – German East Africa, as well as German South-West Africa (Namibia), Cameroon and Togo – was to be decided. With France especially in a vengeful mood, it was a safe bet that Germany would be forced to forfeit her African territories. In Marcus Garvey's conception, there was no better time for Negroes to stake a claim on the ancestral homelands that were about to come on the market.

To broadcast to the thousands whom he could now confidently expect to throng the UNIA meetings, Marcus Garvey once again booked the one venue in Harlem that was both large enough and just about affordable (costing $50 an hour), to meet his needs. The payment would be met by the UNIA president calling for a silver collection at the end of the evening. Each booking was now followed up by a visit from the authorities, and the proprietor, whose antipathy towards the movement deepened with each engagement, was hesitant. But Garvey found the businessman's feelings of guilt could be assuaged by agreeing to a price hike of another $10.

The Palace Casino, built in 1914 as a barn-shaped hall with an enormous floorspace (170 feet long) on 135th Street and Madison Avenue, was popular with Harlem's revellers, especially the risqué dancers of the turkey trot and black bottom. The sight of these sinners emulating crazed turkeys caused Reverend Adam Clayton Powell Snr to lament that 'the Negro race is dancing itself to death . . . [and] grace and modesty are becoming rare virtues'.[19] When it wasn't scandalising pastors with its modern dance craze, the Palace Casino also doubled up, some evenings, as a basketball gymnasium. But for much of 1918 and 1919, the casino was the preferred venue of choice for Marcus Garvey's rather more virtuous massed meetings – open to all, but turkey trotters and black bottomers were advised to leave their dancing shoes at home. The entire front page of the 1 December 1918 edition of the *Negro World* was given over to the forthcoming Paris Peace Conference and a request for the upstanding men and women of the Negro race to attend the Palace Casino theatre.

Air whirred round the pipes of the theatre's organ, as if yet undecided about how and when to turn itself into music. It settled into the half-familiar tune, not convincingly so, that did the job of passing time before the main event. Even though it was midwinter, many in the audience had brought along fans. In ones and twos, now, they began to flap, as more and more people streamed through the doors and the temperature rose from the body heat of several thousand excited souls. They'd come in answer to Marcus Garvey's call to assemble on the eve of the international conference. There was serious business to attend to: the membership that night was charged with the solemn responsibility of electing delegates to travel to Versailles to press the claim for Negro nation status.

Elizier Cadet sat in the front row. He looked unusually apprehensive. The young Haitian immigrant, with untroubled eyes and a face in which a smile seemed permanently trapped, had travelled up from West Virginia for the meeting. Cadet could be forgiven for being anxious. He'd been nominated by Garvey and was about to hear the outcome of the vote. But in reality, it was a foregone conclusion. Once caught up in Garvey's whirlwind, proximity to the man marked for greatness – at a time when the race was crying out for a leader who could get things done – brought swift rewards. Even so, Cadet marvelled at the speed of his own ascendancy within the movement. One moment he was an occasional reader of the *Negro World*; then he'd plucked up courage and written a letter to the paper denouncing the mendacity of the US military occupation of Haiti.[20] The letter had caught the editor's eye, and the next moment Cadet had been nominated as an interpreter to the prospective delegates, articulating the aspirations of 12 million black Americans at the great palace of Versailles – and all this before his twenty-first birthday. As was then said jokingly, Marcus Garvey was the kind of man whom his followers 'would bend over blackwards' to support, and the youngster was determined to live up to the faith Garvey had placed in him. If he could pull it off, it'd be an extraordinary feat. Cadet would be relying on his fluent French, limitless enthusiasm and boyish charm to aid the delegates; he'd not yet be able to draw on the influence of Damballah (the serpent god) or the psychic and mystical skills that he would, in later life, become famous for as a *vodun* high priest.

Immediately Garvey was sighted in the wings of the auditorium the 100-strong choir took up the strains of 'From Greenland's Icy Mountain' – the curious missionary hymn of deliverance adopted and adapted by the UNIA:

> From Greenland's icy mountains
> From India's coral strand,
> Where Afric's sunny fountains
> Roll down their golden sand;
> From many a palmy plain,
> They call us to deliver
> Their land from error's chain[21]

There was faint chance of African land being delivered back to the sons and daughters of Afric at the peace conference. Yet Garvey spoke as might a founding father of a new African nation. In doing so, he enlisted the support of several dead white men: America's revolutionary founding fathers. For was it not Patrick Henry who'd defiantly declared to the British, 'Give me freedom, or give me death'? Why then should anyone expect such sentiments to be absent amongst black people? Why then should anyone shudder to hear a black man invoke the spirit of America's violent but honourable beginnings? If it was appropriate for Patrick Henry and George Washington, was it not good enough for the UNIA leader? Garvey also sounded, at least for the benefit of his members, as if he fully expected the Allied forces to hand over Germany's confiscated African territories to him and the UNIA. But more than America's founding fathers, Marcus Garvey had the Irish cause and the blood sacrifice of the Easter Rising to thank for his rapidly developing ideology of Black Nationalism.

Irish Nationalists, under the banner of the 'Irish race at home and abroad', had long clamoured for an independent homeland. Sinn Feiners would be among those lobbyists raising their voices for the recognition of 'Ireland for the Irish', 'Palestine for the Jews' and 'India for the Indians' at the Peace Conference. At such a pivotal moment the black man was in danger of being left behind. But for months now,

Marcus Garvey had taken his cue from the Irish. He'd invested in a megaphone and secured the use of a car and driver. Almost daily, sweeping through Harlem perched on the running-board of an open-topped Cadillac, with a megaphone to his mouth, he could be heard beseeching his fellow Harlemites, bellowing into the megaphone the slogan that, in the days ahead, would serve as shorthand for his dream: 'Africa for the Africans: those at home and those abroad.'

Given that the world's leaders were converging on Paris, and that Versailles was shaping up to be one of the most momentous events in history, it is surprising that Marcus Garvey didn't suggest himself as a delegate. Perhaps he sensed that such a venture would ultimately prove a fool's errand. Perhaps the UNIA leader recognised that the claim to the German colonies was only ever a bluff, that once exposed could only end in humiliation. A more compelling explanation for his reticence can be gleaned from totting up the number of UNIA branches that had come into existence by 1919. According to Henrietta Vinton Davis, by September that year there were 7,500 members in New York alone and branches established in 25 states of the Union – so it was beginning to mount a serious challenge to the authority of the rival and older NAACP organisation. With the UNIA still expanding at an extraordinary rate – in need, once more, of a review of its structure – now was not perhaps the best time to relinquish grip of the reins to set up camp in Europe. It seems Garvey decided it was better to let others take their rightful place in Paris; and hopefully to share in some measure of their success.

The ebullient Ida B. Wells jumped up on stage at the Palace Casino and pronounced herself 'ready to serve the race'. As the applause rang out, Marcus Garvey announced that he was fully behind the people's choice and was content to endorse her nomination, as well as that of A. Philip Randolph, the impressive editor of the *Messenger*. The youthful Elizier Cadet was chosen to act as the emissaries' translator.[22]

The UNIA was only one of several black welfare groups agitating for a place at the Paris Peace Conference. Marcus Garvey, along with the Reverend Adam Clayton Powell Snr and Madam C. J. Walker came together under the umbrella of the International League for Darker People. They would put to one side their small differences and not-so-small egos and pool their resources for the good of the race. The choice of Wells and Randolph as delegates was ratified along with Monroe Trotter and a handful of others. Madam Walker offered to meet the cost of their expedition. In the following days, the elected officials rushed around, excitedly making their preparations. However, the journey to France was dependent on their ability to secure passports and visas, and the authorities were not favourably disposed towards either Wells or Randolph. As each day passed with no sign of the relevant documentation, their anxiety over the soul-sapping bureaucratic delay was eventually replaced by the gloomy realisation that their reputations ensured that the visas would most likely not be granted. Ultimately, the American administration preferred to do business with Negro representatives whom it considered less problematic. Whilst the UNIA delegates, Wells and Randolph, were left clutching their unstamped passports, rival representative Negroes of the calibre of W. E. B. Du Bois of the NAACP and Tuskegee's Robert Moton were already on the high seas, having secured berths on the same ship, the *Orizaba*, steaming towards Europe.

The youthful Cadet, who was travelling on a Haitian passport, escaped the restrictions placed on his colleagues. And, as far as Garvey was concerned, the great hope of the Negro race now rested on his shoulders. Within a month, Cadet went from interpreter to primary negotiator – an elevation reflected in his eventual title as the UNIA's new 'High Commissioner' to the Peace Conference. Commissioner Cadet was soon showing his skills of ventriloquism. On the eve of his departure, flushed with excitement, he wrote to Henec Dorsinville, a compatriot in Port-au-Prince, with Garveyite flashes of brilliance about the great projects, such as the establishment of a line of ships between the West Indies, America and Africa, that would soon implement the mobilising of all the 400 million Negroes of the world. There were great prospects for both spiritual and material reward, and, with patience, he would earn a share of it. In a letter intercepted by the US Postal Censor, Cadet wrote with premature generosity, offering Dorsinville, not just the position of UNIA representative in Haiti and Panama, 'but also you shall be our commercial and industrial agent'. The New Negro meant business and former critics were forced to pay attention. The *New York Times* reported uncritically, 'The UNIA passed resolutions [which] suggested that the German colonies be turned over to Negroes under the rule of Negroes educated in this country and Europe.' British Military Intelligence continued to monitor Garvey's organisation. In a report that it shared with the United States Military Intelligence Division the following year, the British transcribed a speech in which Garvey had rallied his supporters with dreams of Africa: 'I want you to realise that this is the psychological moment for the organisation . . . It was the dream of William II for Germany to rule the world from Potsdam or from Berlin. In his dream he saw a great Central Empire . . . But [as he] declared war, so did he lose the war; and as he lost the war, he lost the vision of a great Central Africa. In his defeat of 1918, the renewed Negro has caught the vision not only of a great Central Africa for the Africans, but a United Africa for the Africans of the World.'²³

The details of such a fantastical dream were yet to be worked out. It was the kind of rhetoric that Garvey used to bolster his supporters when there was little sign of social and political equality for the descendants of Africans abroad or self-determination for the majority of Africans on the Continent. The rhetoric did not unduly alarm the British Secret Service at this stage. It succeeded only in irritating prominent Africans such as Senegal's Blaise Diagne, who considered it risible and an 'idée insensée'.

Cadet finally set sail towards the end of February, clutching the shopping list of demands, his optimism undiminished by the sad sobering voices, such as Hubert Harrison's cautioning that he was likely to be reduced to window shopping.

The representatives of thirty-two nations converged on Paris at the start of 1919. 'Not simply England, Italy and the Great Powers,' William Du Bois observed, 'but all the little nations . . . not only groups, but races – Jews, Indians, Arabs and all Asia' took up their invitations to secure a place at Versailles, at an event that, if President Wilson was held true to his word, would mark the beginning of a new world order. There could be no lasting peace, Wilson had said in the midst of war, unless it was a peace amongst equals. His statement left little room for caveats or exemptions. The time, therefore, was ripe for equal rights, and especially for racial equality – not just in the view of Du Bois, but also of his looming adversary, Marcus Garvey: it would have been a calamity to have had no Negro representation at this 'clearing house of Fates, where the accounts of a whole epoch, the deeds and misdeeds of an exhausted civilisation, were to be balanced and squared'. But weeks after the official opening of the Peace Conference (it would stagger on for more than six months) there was no welcoming committee to greet Garvey's representative as Cadet stepped off the train at Gare du Nord. The red carpet had already been rolled out for more deserving, visiting dignitaries on

numerous occasions in recent months, most spectacularly on the day
in January when the US President, Wilson *Le Juste*, had come to town
at the start of the conference. Since then hundreds of delegates from
around the world had descended on the French capital, together with
an army of reporters, monocled diplomats, degraded viziers of defunct
principalities, wiry currency speculators, hustlers and hangers-on of
every description. Much of Paris was still decked out in bunting, now
fraying and weather-worn. An American delegate, James T. Shotwell,
recorded in his diary the abundant signs of the war that had just
ended; martial law was still in place, gangs of khaki-clad soldiers
spilled off the boulevards, captured German cannon lined the Champs-
Elysées and a visitor who happened to drop into the Théâtre Fursy
would probably have been shocked by the acidity of the political
satires, *Les Chansonniers de Paris*, in which 'Americans were not
spared, but it was too funny to be malicious.'[24]

But despite the welcome signs of the return of a lusty, zestful spirit
to post-war Paris, there was sombre work in store for the delegates.
After so many millions had died in the war, there was an enormous
moral responsibility to realise the great ideals of the Treaty of Versailles.
In the months ahead, two fundamental principles would be argued over
and voted on: first was the creation of a League of Nations which its
architects believed would not govern the fractured world but 'act as a
symbol of . . . human conscience, however imperfect, to which real
governments of existing states can be made answerable for facts which
concern the world at large'; and secondly there was the need to establish mandates for the confiscated territories and colonies of the defeated
enemy (especially in German Africa) 'inhabited by peoples not yet able
to stand by themselves under the strenuous conditions'. The draft clause
concluded – and herein lay the rub for Cadet and Garvey – that 'the
tutelage of such people should be instructed by advanced nations'.

Those nations in the forefront were, necessarily, the successful
belligerents of the Great War – the USA, Great Britain, Italy and France
– the so-called Big Four. Readers of the *Negro World* might be forgiven
for thinking that the Garvey movement was to play a key role. On 13
March 1919 the faithful members of the UNIA gathered at the recently
inaugurated Universal Restaurant in Harlem at a meeting presided over
by Marcus Garvey to hear the wireless cable of his young emissary's
first dramatic reports from Paris read out. Cadet did not disappoint,
and Garvey revelled in the young man's early achievements as a proud

father does in his son's first tentative steps. In the High Commissioner's
account, he had marched to the great chateau of Versailles, ascended
the grand staircase and delivered the UNIA resolutions directly to the
President (the French PM Georges Clemenceau) and the Secretary of
the Peace Conference. Cadet wrote that he had returned the next day
for an answer. Pleas for hush whispered round the Harlem restaurant
while the reader scanned the rest of the cabled telegram for the answer.
'They promised,' confided Cadet, 'to get it for me as soon as possible.'[25]
The UNIA celebrants who moved on to the Palace Casino that night
included confidential sources in the pay of British Military Intelligence
who relayed the minutiae of Garvey's meeting. But far from being
perturbed, British officials appeared rather drily amused, having detected
elements of fiction in the young commissioner's account. 'I imagine the
part played by Mr Cadet,' one official concluded, 'is less prominent
than Garvey would wish his readers to believe.'[26]

Elizier Cadet had been given an unenviable task. Without official
accreditation it was nearly impossible to wade through French bureaucracy which had been significantly increased for the conference: slipping
a guard a couple of cigarettes was no guarantee of admission to any
of the venues or debates. It proved difficult enough for Cadet to attract
the attention of those delegates who should have been sympathetic.
Partly, he suffered bad luck. Calling on the Cuban delegate, he found
him bedridden, suffering from influenza.[27] An audience with the tetchy
Liberian delegate, Secretary of State and President elect, C. D. B. King,
got off to a bad start. King was chaperoned by an American-appointed
financial adviser, Henry Worley, and so perhaps was playing to the
solitary member of the gallery. Worley reported that when presented
with copies of the *Negro World*, the Liberian scoffed at the inflammatory headlines: 'If the American Negroes were so thoroughly
dissatisfied with the social and political conditions in America,' Secretary
King is said to have asked, 'why [then] did they not go to Liberia . . .
and become citizens there?' King's plain-speaking contrasted with the
politeness and importance shown towards W. E. B. Du Bois who
reported back to the NAACP board that 'the Liberian delegates to the
Peace Conference are with us!' Actually, for all his political leverage,
Du Bois fared not much better than the inexperienced Cadet in setting
out an agenda for the delicate subject of the inequality of the races to
be discussed at Versailles. Before leaving for Paris, Du Bois had written
to President Wilson, but the subtle hints from the editor of *Crisis* that

he be offered an official role at the Peace Conference were ignored by the President. Being a senior member of the NAACP, Du Bois had been able to exploit the connections of the wealthy white liberals who backed the organisation, and call in the necessary favours that allowed him to scramble aboard the *Orizaba*, carrying fellow newspapermen to the conference. But once in Paris, like Cadet, he had no official role. In decades of campaigning on behalf of black citizens of the world, though, he'd also built up a healthy book of international contacts. In Paris, Du Bois solicited the help of the decorated Senegalese deputy to the French National Assembly, Blaise Diagne, to secure permission for a Pan-African Congress to be held in Paris. Diagne was highly regarded, especially after his efforts in the Great War in helping to recruit Africans (280,000 volunteers from Senegal alone) into the depleted French army, and he successfully lobbied Prime Minister Clemenceau on Du Bois's behalf. A Pan-African Congress was some consolation but even then there were restrictions. The gathering would inevitably draw attention to the plight and grievances of Negroes throughout the world, including the USA, and the American delegation suspected that Clemenceau had only granted permission for the congress in order to irritate President Wilson. Tempers had already begun to fray between the national delegations. On one occasion, in the French Assembly, Clemenceau had called Wilson a man of noble '*candeur*' which translates not as candour but as 'simple-mindedness'. In the uproar that followed, '*candeur*' was quietly changed to 'grandeur' for the official records. The French, nervous of further upsetting American racial mores, stipulated that the Pan-African Congress could only proceed on the understanding that there would be no publicity. Race appeared then as the embarrassing older relative (at Versailles), one who had to be hidden away lest he spoil the party.[28]

Arrangements were made for the African Congress, composed hurriedly of fifty-seven representative men who came together after Du Bois had mounted a trawl through Paris of congruent West Indians, Africans and black Americans who had either escaped the censure of their respective governments and obtained passports, or who happened conveniently to be in the capital at the time. They crunched through the crisp February snows and met discreetly at the Grand Hotel where resolutions were passed without fanfare. Principally, the Allies were asked to administer the former German territories in Africa on behalf of the Africans who 'should only exercise self-government as fast as their development permits'. Though borne of the real fear of rejection in Paris, the overall tone of muted reasonable requests contrasted with the thunderous rhetoric of Marcus Garvey and others (even Du Bois before leaving America) who demanded African home rule as the black man's right.

The convening of an African Congress had preceded the arrival of Garvey's man in the French capital. Unknown and unheralded, it is unlikely that Cadet would have found his name on Du Bois's list. Equally, it is uncertain whether Cadet would have agitated for a place even if he had arrived in time. For, although the congress has come to be noted as an important landmark in the development of Pan-African thought, at the time those fifty-seven pioneers were largely talking to themselves. To circumvent the official opposition to the event being given any publicity, William Du Bois quietly printed hundreds of copies of the resolution passed by the congress. He hoped their discreet distribution, to the delegates of the Peace Conference and other influential outlets, might work subliminally in their favour.

Cadet's approach was far more direct. Armed with letters of introduction from Garvey, the High Commissioner camped outside the offices of the major Parisian newspapers, firstly the liberal Le Matin. There, he reported, the editor listened sympathetically and was 'deeply touched to hear my statement concerning the atrocities committed against our brethren in the Southern States of the USA'. But Cadet left that liberal institution with nothing more than saccharine bon mots ringing in his ears. Doorstepping the editors of La Presse and L'Intransigeant proved more profitable. He was encouraged to leave behind articles upon which, he assured the UNIA leader, he had secured promises of publication. Actually, Cadet's reports back to Harlem were a strange mix of the fiction of startling progress coupled to undisguised frustrations and humiliations. A cursory inspection even at the margins of the breathless and exciting news dispatches reveals early doubts creeping in; there lingers the fear, for example, that no sooner has Cadet left the offices of the small Parisian publications than the unsolicited articles will most probably end up on the copy-editor's spike. And then, in the same breath, he is charging off, with not a second to spare, to press for an audience with other eminent men.[29]

Whilst Cadet outlined a catalogue of disappointments, the readers of the Crisis could follow every small triumph of its editor, Du Bois, who revelled in the respect accorded him in France: 'The Mayor of

Domfort [for example] apologised gravely: if he had known of my coming,' Du Bois wrote, 'he would have received me formally at the Hotel de Ville – me whom most of my fellow-countrymen receive at naught but back doors, save with apology.'[30] The chair of the African Congress could also count on the quiet but committed support of a small group of influential French sympathisers, brought together in a salon of Madam Calman-Levy, widow of the esteemed Parisian publisher. His time in France had been stirring and revelatory. As Du Bois steamed back to America, Cadet was forced to admit that his own hoped-for success had mostly eluded him. Finally, he could not discount his disappointments and impotence in Paris. *La Presse* and *L'Intransigeant* did not keep their word to publish his articles. Low on funds and with little to show for his Herculean efforts, Cadet cabled Garvey for help and hinted strongly that Du Bois's secrecy and success had worked to his (Cadet's) disadvantage. Cadet claimed to have made explicit – through published articles – the conditions of lynching and other injustices endured by the Negro in America but that Du Bois had repudiated his statements by defeating his articles in the French newspapers.

On 22 March 1919, Cadet's cablegram was delivered to UNIA head-quarters, and Marcus Garvey was apoplectic when he read it. He called for an emergency mass convention 24 hours later and 3,000 near-hysterical supporters crowded into the Mother Zion AME Church in Harlem and heard their furious leader howling with indignation at Du Bois's perceived treachery. In front of the baying crowd, erstwhile admirers of the *Crisis*'s editor leapt to the stage and denounced the Harvard graduate as a traitor to the race and a 'good nigger' who'd been granted a passport to France because he 'positively would not discuss lynching, peonage, disfranchisement and discrimination'. A resolution was passed and cabled to the French press that repudiated Dr Du Bois for 'placing obstacles in the way of the elected representative efficiently discharging his already difficult duties on behalf of the Negro race'. A collection of more than $200 was raised to help Cadet combat Du Bois's negative propaganda and to enable his return to the USA.[31]

W. E. B. Du Bois, the scholar whose important work *The Souls of Black Folk* was placed alongside the Bible in the households of educated African-Americans, did not have to rely on informants to learn of this violent, sudden backlash and challenge to his authority and integrity: he had only to purchase a copy of the *Negro World*. There in unsparing detail his alleged treachery was laid before the reader. The man who many (including himself) saw as the rightful heir to Booker T. Washington's leadership of black America was vilified as a 'reactionary under [the] pay of white men' and therefore more than happy to act as a 'mouthpiece of the government'.

Du Bois was stung into answering back. In a wary defence that barely masked his dismay, he claimed ignorance of the young Haitian's existence: 'The truth was that Mr Du Bois never saw or heard of his [Garvey's] High Commissioner,' the editor wrote snootily in the *Crisis*, 'never denied his nor anyone's statements of the wretched American conditions, did everything possible to arouse rather than quiet the French press and would have been delighted to welcome and co-operate with any colored fellow-worker.'³²

Four months after he had set sail for France, William Du Bois returned to New York to find the black political landscape much changed. Back in December, if he considered Marcus Garvey at all, then it was as no more than a minor irritant. After all, Du Bois's expedition to France, his convening of a Pan-African Congress and forthcoming history of black involvement in the Great War should, not unreasonably, have rehabilitated and endeared him towards black doubters whose eyes had rolled on the publication of his controversial 'Close Ranks' essay, that supported the USA administration's war effort. Instead, in the spring of 1919, Dr Du Bois found himself the easy target of a foreign-born Negro leader whose own momentum seemed unstoppable.

As foretold, black expectations were not met at Paris. The Peace Conference eventually determined the mandates for the confiscated German African colonies, mostly in favour of her European adversaries. Mandates for Togoland and the Cameroons (both partitioned) were awarded to France and Great Britain; the greater portion of German East Africa (known as Tanganyika) also went to Great Britain; the remainder of German East Africa (now known as Urundi-Burundi) was awarded to Belgium; and finally the conference awarded a mandate for South-West Africa (Namibia) to South Africa.³³ Garvey angrily dubbed the events in Paris 'the "Pieces Conference" because its unholy intent in depriving men of their liberty has made no headway for the restoration of peace'. Versailles had initially proved a welcome diversion. It had temporarily stopped the Negro from practising disappointment. Finally, though, it had delivered the black man from his delusion, cured him of the fantasy of inclusion proffered by the Peace Conference when it had seemed to hold his destiny in the balance. It was potentially a debilitating blow from which he might take years to recover. But the obvious setback, at least to the aims of the Garvey movement, would be offset by an announcement soon trumpeted in the *Negro World* and picked up by other curious newspapers. The *New York Call* led the way on 27 April 1919 with its headline, 'Negroes Plan to Found Ship Line'.

9

FLYIN' HOME ON THE BLACK STAR LINE

Brothers, sisters, countrymen,
You'd better get on board.
Six steamships want to sail away,
Loaded with a heavy load.
It's gwina take us all back home,
Yes, every native child.
And when we get there,
What a time . . .
Flying home on the Black Star Line

'Black Star Line,' 1924

IF Harlemites looked for grandeur amongst the overcrowded tenements in 1919 they would not find it. To see grandeur they would have to close their eyes and imagine themselves transported to the tantalisingly close but unobtainable lavish homes of the ebony aristocrats up in Harlem's exclusive enclaves, Sugar Hill and Strivers Row. Apart from the magnificent churches, there was no entrée to grandeur in Negro life. But when Marcus Garvey closed his eyes in the middle of the year, he did not imagine the saccharine luxury of a Sugar Hill penthouse with a chauffeured Cadillac parked outside and a Scandinavian maid to open the front door. No, what he saw were ships, not one or two but a whole line of Negro-owned steamships sailing across the Atlantic. It was an impossible idea. There had been no hint of anything like it ever being achieved in recent history.

The beginning of the twentieth century marked the romantic peak of the great maritime age, of hulking steamships of enormous tonnage and passenger ships of comfort and splendour. But those vessels belonged to powerful nation states, trading on decades and centuries of experience: the Negro had experience of being a commodity, not as a captain of industry or magnate of a shipping line. Aside from that, Garvey's improbable, grandiose scheme was also counter-intuitive. The usual narrative of the rags-to-riches Horatio Alger-type myth was to start small, with 25 cents and an idea worked out on your kitchen table; to go from door to door, as in the case of Madam Walker, selling your wonderful new hair product and steadily, over years and decades of thrift and hard work build up an empire. Garvey's track record included the launching of a newspaper, a restaurant and a laundry. To then go on, almost overnight, to establish a shipping company could not be said to be a natural progression. But the great dreamer became increasingly emboldened by the fantastic growth in numbers and the euphoria of black people who signed up to his organisation. They were dazzled by his certainty and by his unrivalled eloquence. Garvey came to embody the movement and where another man might have fretted and been overwhelmed by the transference of his supporters' dreams and emotions, Garvey thrived on it. Claude McKay accurately captured the excitement of his audience when he later wrote, 'Garvey shouted words, words spinning like bullets, words falling like bombs, sharp words like poisoned daggers, thundering words and phrases lit with all the hues of the rainbow to match the wild approving roar of his people.'[1]

The audience at a Garvey meeting were just as susceptible as the rest of the population to the ideals of the American Dream. In Harlem the dream was just one roll of the dice away, or a lucky combination of numbers for 'policy' or increasingly in the purchase of shares. The Great War had immediately been followed by the period of wild speculation, of 'fatuous optimism' and its near cousin intractable pessimism. It had led to a more radical mindset amongst the black population, the cause of which the Nevis-born Marxist Cyril Briggs rather prosaically attributed to high rents. 'Landlords and real-estate agents in Harlem are doing their level best to increase the converts of Bolshevism in the district,' wrote Briggs. In such a climate, when economic hardships had put the 'bite on' black people, they were desperate for some kind of relief. Historically the church had provided spiritual comfort in the absence of financial health.

On 16 October 1919, in the pages of the *Negro World*, Garvey gave voice to the popular sentiments of his supporters when he expressed their discontent with the present state of affairs: 'We have been very spiritual in the past; we are going to take part of a material now and will give others the opportunity to practise the spiritual side of life.'[2]

Garvey's supporters looked upon his success, at his momentum, and felt, perhaps for the first time, that they had signed on with the winning side. Early on, Marcus Garvey had championed the idea that real emancipation would come through economic independence; the mighty dollar was the great leveller in American society. And yet when he'd arrived in 1917 the great Negro capital of the world could boast not one decent restaurant owned or operated by black people. Harlem's two popular cafeterias were similarly white-owned. Garvey's Universal Restaurant challenged them with its 'down-home' Southern cuisine. There *were* black businesses in Harlem but for the majority of them the black man or woman who greeted the customers was just a front. In 1917, the *New York Age* reported that there were 145 black businesses in Harlem, and less than a quarter of them were owned and operated by Blacks. Claude McKay conducted his own survey and found that 'the saloons were run by the Irish, the restaurants by the Greeks, the ice and fruit stands by the Italians, and the grocery and haberdashery stores by the Jews. The only Negro businesses, excepting barber shops, were the churches and the cabarets.'[3] Even when black businesses were established there was a problem with patronage. Because of the lack of precedents, most African-Americans had grown accustomed to dealing with white businesses; and, even when presented with a black alternative, continued to patronise their white counterparts, no matter how shabbily they were treated by them.[4]

The most imposing building in the neighbourhood, the Hotel Theresa, refused to admit black guests. The ivory-white mannequins on window display in Harlem's department stores taunted and mocked the population; there was not one large department store where black folk could comfortably try on clothes, shoes or hats. Garvey countered by opening the movement's Universal Millinery Store where toques, fedoras, panama hats – almost every fashion of headwear – decorated its double-fronted windows, and African-American assistants fussed over African-American customers. By contrast, Blumstein's, the big department store on 125th Street, did not, and would not, employ a single black clerk or shop assistant. Not until 1926 would signs of improvement emerge, when the National Urban League was able to run ads in its newspaper *Opportunity* such as, 'Wanted: A very good shipping clerk (light colored only – West Indian preferred)'.

In the same edition, *Opportunity* proudly announced that 'a Harlem department store has employed three colored sales ladies. A national chain grocery has employed its first colored clerk.'[5] But that was seven years away. Garvey was far ahead of the game. The UNIA planned to open shops and factories that would employ thousands, and establishments that would cater for their comforts. Any black person could make a reservation at the Phyllis Wheatley Hotel. The hopeful young journalist, George Schulyer, who rented a room there and who was already fine-tuning a discerning and cynical style, remembered that 'the place was spick and span'. Schulyer did not believe in a separate African-American identity. In his conception, an African-American was merely a lamp-blacked Anglo-Saxon. Yet even Schulyer reflected admiringly on the centrepiece of African-American culture that greeted guests as they stepped off the street and into the entrance hall of the Phyllis Wheatley Hotel, with its 'large striking painting of the famed Negro poetess of Revolutionary days gazing down benignly from the wall'.[6]

The new, black-owned, shipping line promised a high-class service for black passengers. No longer would the Negro traveller have to settle for the privations and humiliations of steerage class. He would be welcome to a first-class cabin (at three-quarters of the usual price) on the proposed Black Star Line. Quite simply, the Black Star Line was, in Garvey's conception, the black equivalent of the White Star Line whose transatlantic steamships, famed for their emphasis on comfort, elegance and safety (notwithstanding the unfortunate *Titanic*), had made their owners a fortune. Its black cousin would be owned by black men, its crew would be singularly black and its passengers also. For Garvey's dream to be fulfilled the Black Star Line would operate between American ports and those of Africa, the West Indies, and Central and South America, and, along the way, it would serve as a further tool towards Negro improvement, both spiritual and financial.

The *Negro World* notified Harlem's black population that plans would be unveiled at a monster convention of the race to be held at the Palace Casino. And to those critics who, from the start, thought the scheme fanciful (where after all was the money to come from?)

Garvey had a simple answer: black people themselves would provide the $2 million needed to inaugurate the Black Star Line. $1,250,000 would be raised from the Negroes in the USA each donating a dollar. Similar donations from the West Indies would contribute a further $250,000; 50-cent donations from Central and South America would net $300,000; and the African continent would have the honour of reaching the final amount by making 25-cent donations totalling $200,000.

Such a breakdown seemed further proof, in the eyes of doubters, that the idea was not serious but ill-conceived and shot through with whimsy. Even admirers urged caution – Ida B. Wells amongst them. Ahead of the last mass meeting, Garvey had greeted her off the train at Grand Central station, and swept her into a car that flashed though Harlem on a tour of the latest UNIA acquisitions. A horse-drawn cart that collected the dirty clothes for the UNIA laundrette had been upgraded to a truck. Premises had been obtained for a second restaurant. Though Ida B. Wells was a great talker, there was little chance to interrupt the stream of Garvey's bountiful thoughts that raced to the summit of his most grand idea thus far – the nascent Black Star Line and the fantastic opportunities that it would bring. The car pulled up at the Universal Restaurant; the engine idled, and Garvey awaited the verdict of his guest. Ida B. Wells argued that the scheme was too large but, she continued as he waved aside her reservations, if Garvey was determined to push ahead then might it not be wiser to wait, at least until the organisation was on a sounder financial footing. After all, the *Negro World* was still struggling to make a profit and the first restaurant – though enthusiastically patron-ised by Harlemites – had yet to offer a return on its investment. Garvey had hoped and expected Ida B. Wells to endorse his plans but, when she got up on the podium, she voiced the kind of scep-ticism and straight-talking for which natives from Missouri were proudly famous: 'He [Marcus Garvey] says you Negroes are organ-ised but I'm from Missouri, you'll have to show me.' Wells wanted to see and hear concrete and realisable plans but all she heard sounded fanciful and impractical and she kept up the mantra: 'I'm from Missouri; you've got to show me.' Wells's words were not part of the script; 'they sowed doubt amongst the audience', wrote Amy Ashwood, and Garvey was so furious that he 'refused point blank to pay her the $150 fee and travelling expenses'. Ashwood quietly ushered her out of the hall and accompanied her to the station with the assurance that Garvey would send on the appearance fee once he'd calmed down.[7]

Marcus Garvey did not pause too long to reflect on Ida B. Wells's warning. He was like a novice driver who had a destination in mind but had forgotten the road map, and rather than lose time by turning and going back for it, decided to drive on, through diversions, down blind alleys and even off the beaten track until arriving at the place he'd been heading for: much energy would be expended along the way, and it would prove a sometimes frustrating but ultimately thrilling ride. Amy Jacques saw this impetuous and impatient side of his character close at hand. 'He turned the pages of his past life as an avid reader turns the pages of an adventure story, and loses interest in the early chapters after reading them. Those who get hurt in these tense moments of the adventure are only regarded as necessary props to the build-up of the hero. He was quite as impersonal in this regard as any reader.'[8] The UNIA leader could not delay or defer his plans. What Wells mistook for arrogance was simply Garvey's profound belief that he was mystically tuned to the mood of the people. At the large convention on Sunday 27 April 1919, he called for donations to the Black Star Line and the people unhesitatingly responded, cramming envelopes with cash, pledges and promissory notes. Garvey had expected no less. His ambition and popularity multiplied each day. The two were reciprocal: his popularity grew with his ambition and the greater his popularity the more ambitious he became. Black Harlem was especially in love with him. Hugh Mulzac, a prospective UNIA recruit, was stunned by what he saw as he approached the UNIA offices at 56 West 135th Street: 'As I made my way toward the headquarters – or to within a block of it – I discovered a line more than one hundred yards long waiting to enter. There were job seekers and supplicants . . . and a few hero worshippers who simply wanted to tell Mr Garvey how proud they were of him for what he was doing for the race.'[9] That appreciation was daily turning into ready cash. The BOI informants who now regularly attended UNIA meetings were pained to report his success. They questioned Garvey's sincerity and speculated that he was only able to maintain enthusiasm for this latest project through a series of novel and cynical initiatives.

The weekly meetings were indeed, unashamedly, turned over

specifically to the task of raising funds for the shipping company. Donations leapt considerably when Edgar Grey, the general secretary of the movement whom Garvey trusted to deputise in his absence, introduced a visiting Liberian speaker, Mr Cooper who, the *Negro World* reported, endorsed the forthcoming shipping line and 'thrilled audiences with picturesque phraseology [as] he graphically told . . . of some of the latent powers of the Negro race in its native habitat'. That evening the envelope method of collecting donations for the Black Star Line 'was largely omitted because of a direct appeal made by the chair, which resulted in a mass collection to the table'. As a mountain of cash built up over the next few weeks, Garvey was quick to stress that in this, and all other business ventures, the UNIA was acting as guardian of the people, and that there would be 'no speculation in "the Black Star Line"'. The UNIA would hold the properties for the benefit of every man and woman of colour, and hence 'there would be no private dividends', as the money would come from voluntary contributions – in the same manner in which church congregations might top up their pledge of tithes to the church with ad-hoc contributions.

On 14 June 1919, the long list of subscribers who'd made donations ranging from 10 cents to 5 dollars could run their fingers down the columns of the *Negro World* to see their names and contributions honoured in print. This one stroke of publicity served both to encourage others and to silence cynics who were beginning to make rumblings about a lack of financial transparency.

A special account with the Corn Exchange Bank was set up to receive lodgement of Black Star Line donations. More money was passing through the UNIA office than ever before but the thrill of the ringing till brought unexpected consequences. Cash was coming in on such a scale that it embarrassed the organisation into undertaking the long-overdue audit of the UNIA accounts. A three-man auditing committee was appointed. But when the auditors, including the Jamaican UNIA secretary, Uriah T. Mitchell, began work in earnest, it was soon apparent why the exercise had been deferred for so long: the accounts were in a mess, the records had only been kept in a half-hearted manner, and no matter how great the latitude of creativity the auditors gave themselves the books refused to balance. At one of the meetings, reported Amy Ashwood, reasoned arguments gave way to fists. 'Garvey accused officers, including the treasurer

[James] Linton, of dishonesty. Linton sprang to his feet. Garvey . . .
hit out.' Resignations and dismissals immediately followed but the
violent arguments continued. Ashwood noted that the genial first
vice-president, Jeremiah Certain, was often called upon to mediate.
'Jeremiah Certain was slightly deaf in one ear and when things got
rough at our meetings, he would be called upon to verify one fact
or another.' Ashwood was amused by the skill with which 'he avoided
taking sides by . . . saying he had never heard'.[10] Certain's tactics
failed, however, to take the sting out of arguments which were increasingly personal and belligerent. Three weeks later, Uriah Mitchell
resigned and, along with the other appointed auditors, fearing a
scandal and the threat to their professional reputations, hurried to
the District Attorney's office with the unbalanced books under their
arms. Garvey had been on the road (leaving Grey in charge) visiting
Michigan, Virginia and Toronto, garnering even more interest and
dollars for the Black Star Line, and was particularly aggrieved to
return to find a summons from the assistant District Attorney Edwin
Kilroe on his mantelpiece.

The auditing committee had lodged a complaint, not only about
the poorly kept accounts but about the unremitting drive to collect
monies for a paper organisation (the Black Star Line) with no surety
of it ever being realised. Marcus Garvey rushed to the District
Attorney's office. Accompanied by Amy Ashwood he sat face to face
with his accusers, bristling with resentment at the ignominy of being
hauled before the law officer who asked to examine all the paperwork, documents and records of the association. After several hours
of scrutiny, the lawyer drew the proceedings to a close; the case against
Garvey was not proven but Edwin Kilroe threatened him with prosecution should he continue to solicit funds in such an improper
manner; investors would need to be offered at least the possibility of
dividends if the proposed Black Star Line became a financial success.
Whilst promising to heed the Assistant District Attorney's advice,
Garvey spat defiantly in the *Negro World* that just as 'there is a White
Star Line owned by white men, there will be a Black Star Line owned
by black men'. Edwin Kilroe got off relatively lightly. Garvey reserved
his greatest venom for the former allies, the 'stool-pigeons' who had
sought to damage the organisation under the camouflage of legal
propriety. No matter the veracity of the auditing gang of three's
concerns – in a climate where the lynching of black men and women

continued unabated, and where Negroes were burnt out of their homes in the all-American version of Russian pogroms and where black pleas for equality were spurned at Versailles – the 'pedantic quibbles' over well-intentioned efforts to uplift the race were viewed as nothing less than spineless treachery. From the pulpit of the *Negro World*, Marcus Garvey howled at the perfidious 'white man's niggers' and vowed to publish the names of the traitors, in bold black type, in subsequent editions of the paper, and to exhibit them in man-sized banners throughout the Palace Casino at the next meeting. No sooner had he fired off his rebuke in the *Negro World*, than Marcus Garvey quietly began planning to incorporate the shipping company.

It was too late to deter the unfavourable headlines that were bound to appear in the next few days. The *World News* was first off the printing press with: 'DISTRICT ATTORNEY SINKS "THE BLACK STAR LINE". HEAD OF NEGRO STEAMSHIP PROJECT PROMISES NOT TO COLLECT ANY MORE FUNDS'.

The head of the Negro steamship project reacted angrily. The news, which alleged a shortfall of over $1,000 between amounts taken in by the new shipping line and the figure recorded in UNIA accounts, was more than sufficient grounds for Garvey to default to litigation. He would immediately institute a $100,000 libel suit against the *New York World* for its malicious misrepresentation. That newspaper would be pursued no matter the law's delay, but Garvey had a more speedy revenge in mind for his critics who, with the arrival of warm weather, had invaded Lenox Avenue with their soapboxes and stepladders. Marcus may have graduated from the soapbox but, in attitude and outlook, he was never far from the street, and for one night only, he decided to go back and test himself against the enemy. The UNIA president had his followers spread the word all over Harlem that on 14 June, he would challenge the most vociferous of the street orators, William Bridges, to a debate at Speakers' Corner. Notice was served on his adversary at noon that day. Bridges was given nine hours to gather all his evidence (and wit) and would be allotted half an hour to address the crowd. Sportingly, Bridges mounted the platform at the appointed hour. The *Negro World* journalists were on hand to record the expected mismatch between a heavyweight and a featherweight: 'Bridges was visibly nervous all through his rambling talk' accompanied by hoots, jeers and a battery of heckles, so much so that Garvey intervened to 'ask the people to give the man a fair chance to speak'. Eventually Bridges shuffled off the platform to give way to the world-famed orator who, amid the wild applause, cheers and laughter, dispatched his critic as a 'beast in the image of God' who'd swallowed whole the white man's propaganda that the Negro was devoid of initiative, had never built any government, constructed roads or steamships, was dependent on the white man and 'was capable of doing anything only when [harnessed] and put to work like the mule'. The Negro was no beast, Marcus Garvey would have the crowd know, but if there were such a thing then William Bridges was its personification. The thousands roared their approval. Amy Ashwood mounted the platform and asked the crowd for three cheers for the UNIA, and the people cheered wildly for several minutes. A friend of Bridges who ventured to say a few words of support on his behalf was only just saved from injury, the *Negro World* reported, by the speedy intervention of officers of the association 'when they saw the crowd was bent on mobbing him'.[11]

Evidently Marcus Garvey took an holistic approach to his association with the UNIA. He lived a very public life and everything, including the bloodsport of pegging out an adversary, was done in the service of the UNIA. He had no purchasing power in the mainstream press, he couldn't go down to the gentlemen's club and steer a newspaper proprietor away from an unflattering and perhaps unfair portrayal. He couldn't ring up the editors and say, 'Listen old man, don't you think I deserve a right to reply?' He simply had the *Negro World* and the power of word of mouth. And those thousands who turned out on the warm summer night of 14 June witnessed not just the flaying of an inferior adversary but the sight and sound of Garvey at his most masterful as an orator. They also guaranteed that the news of Garvey's corrective to the lies, cynical gossip and libellous press reports would spread far quicker than through the vendors hawking their hostile papers at news-stands.

Within another week Garvey had incorporated the Black Star Line with four other directors, including the UNIA's general secretary, Edgar Grey, purchasing forty shares each at a cost of $5 per share. With his trademark exuberance and impatience for success, Garvey set himself and the organisation the near-impossible task of obtaining its first ship by 31 October, just four months later. He enlisted a small army of sales agents to promote the stock buying, and a brazen but simple propaganda. Every Negro worthy of the name would be impelled to purchase stock in this fabulous enterprise. Failure was not an option, for 'the Black Star Line would be floated, if necessary, in a sea of blood'.[12]

Certificates for the Black Star Line Steamship Corporation were printed on pale eggshell-coloured paper with an ornate green border featuring a vignette of a globe turned on its axis to reveal the African continent with the inscription 'Africa, the Land of Opportunity' emblazoned across it, and a steamship with a welcoming African on either side. These shares certificates, with their direct appeal to race pride, were marketed aggressively from the start. But a hard sell wasn't actually necessary. Garvey and his salesmen found themselves pushing at a half-opened door. Black men and women were dazzled by the idea and snapped up shares overnight.

Mariamne Samad's father was an enthusiastic member of the movement and one of the first to purchase shares. She remembers how he used to infuriate his wife by returning home, laden not with vital groceries but rather with certificates in the Black Star Line. Certificates would be piled high on a shelf and every so often brought down and proudly displayed on the kitchen table. He had no intention of ever trading them in, no matter how hard the times.[13] That sentiment, of making a difference in some small way, of investing in a great, unprecedented ideal, was reflected in the hundreds of letters and requests for certificates that poured into UNIA headquarters from black people around the world. From Panama, one eager prospective shareholder wrote, 'I have sent twice to buy shares amounting to $125 ... Now I am sending $35 for seven more. You might think I have money. I do not ... but if I am to die of hunger it'll be all right because I'm determined to do all it's in my power to better the conditions of the race.'

Garvey spoke in a way of the promise that had hardly been heard since the revolutionary preacher Henry McNeal Turner roused the masses in the first flush of optimism following the emancipation of slaves fifty years earlier. Slavery had not been the best preparation for industrial, commercial and intellectual endeavour: it induced a moral torpor, and though the spell had been broken it might take generations before the curse was lifted. Garvey understood this and the near-unrealisable desire to be just as good as the white man that risked rendering the black man a mere mimic of the real thing. Sentiments that the *Semi-Weekly Louisianan*, a black newspaper, had articulated in the first blooms of emancipation: 'Because we had to put up with a home-spun suit before emancipation we are determined to wear a silk one now . . . We are a poor . . . ignorant . . . inexperienced people as every day's transactions will prove, and yet . . . we will spend more time and money to appear what we are not, than it would cost to be what we pretend to be.'[14]

Altruism wasn't the only motive; prospective black stockholders were seduced by the petit-bourgeois ideals of participating in the American Dream, formerly the preserve of their white compatriots, that had been denied them up until now, as well as the lip-smacking promise of fantastic returns on their investment. The early signs of uptake were so encouraging that Garvey was eager to push on and expand into the South where, despite the Great Migration, the vast majority of black people were still to be found. It was then that the first signs of differences and a tussle between the directors began to emerge. Garvey was all for moving swiftly and capitalising on the excitement amongst the black population in Harlem and the Northern states that he was certain would be repeated in the South. Edgar Grey, the general secretary, along with Richard Warner, another director (a former associate of Grey's whom he'd vouched for and brought into the movement) promoted a more cautious approach, or rather one in which they had greater say. The speed with which the Black Star Line (BSL) was catching on with black Americans meant that, invariably, it came ever closer to achieving its objective. This in itself, conversely, brought with it anxiety and conflagration as the dream was being realised.

Only weeks after the company's incorporation, the boardroom of BSL began to splinter into opposing camps. Garvey's overbearing manner, his idiosyncratic and overconfident business sense (unsupported by any significant experience), irritated the relative newcomers Grey and Warner. They also complained that the UNIA leader's approach to collective decision-making was simply to cajole and bully the board into agreeing with him – a task which was made easier once stalwarts Henrietta Vinton Davis and the cigar manufacturer Jeremiah Certain were elected as directors. The leader's greatest talents were as a propagandist and promoter, and Virginia would be the target of his next conquest. He set out, accompanied by the treasurer, Ashwood and Davis on an ambitious stock-selling drive in the South, overriding the minority boardroom objections about the fledgling company's lack of established procedures. Important matters such as how to keep account of the sale of shares, where to bank the money, and when and how to settle demands for salaries remained unresolved. Garvey left the rival camp to tend the shop, as it were, disregarding his own diminishing confidence in their abilities and allegiance. The stock-selling campaign in Virginia was a big success and the UNIA leader telegraphed hundreds of dollars (via Western Union) back to Harlem. But celebrations were tempered by the antipathy of each camp towards the other which continued to harden as did suspicions over the handling of the large sums of money coming into the Black Star Line coffers – some of which temporarily found its way into individual bank accounts whilst Garvey was out of town.

The breakdown of trust was as alarming as it was sudden. By the beginning of July, Richard Warner was proffering his resignation (which was rejected) but even as he was doing so he and Grey had voluntarily gone to the District Attorney's office and dictated statements to the stenographer that criticised Garvey for diverting and dispersing some of the BSL monies to pay for bills incurred by the loss-making Universal Restaurant and for liquidating other debts. Garvey, in turn, was planning to prosecute Grey and Warner for misappropriation of funds, when he was once more summoned by the District Attorney.

Birth pains are expected at the beginning of most fledgling enterprises but the spectacular fallouts between Marcus Garvey and former colleagues, and the ensuing unbridled acrimony, became a regular pattern. This pattern is only partially explained by those allies, in businesses launched by Garvey, who felt aggrieved when the salaries that he'd promised, predicated on a future income of those enterprises, were not immediately realised. 'Garvey expected the employees to endure this [temporary] lack of pay stoically,' noted one contemporary, and 'to their demand for payment, [he] frequently countered with accusations, from inefficiency and delinquency to outright misappropriation of funds.'[15]

Garvey's movement attracted leaders who seemed quite prepared to make 'no ordinary sacrifice' when there was little to gain or lose. Their expectations were not, in the beginning, much greater than those for the numerous other mutual-aid and friendly societies to which they had previously belonged. These were intelligent young men and women forced through the vagaries of American society to

After the Earthquake. Harbour Street in Kingston, Jamaica, 14 January 1907.

Small-holding tenant farmers in the Jamaican countryside, c. 1909.

Jamaican construction workers on the Panama Canal, 1913.

Marcus Garvey on his wedding day, 25 December 1919.

(*Above left*) Edward Wilmot Blyden (1894), African scholar, Liberian politician and author of *Christianity, Islam and the Negro Race*.
(*Above right*) Joseph Robert Love was born in the Bahamas and migrated to Jamaica in 1884. He was the editor of the *Jamaican Advocate* and an early mentor of Garvey.

(*Above left*) Duse Mohamed Ali, theatrical impresario, proprietor of the *African Times and Orient Review*. Ali later worked for Garvey in the UNIA as Head of African Affairs.
(*Above right*) Asa Philip Randolph, Harlem street orator and co-editor of the *Messenger*. He was credited with stepping down from his soap-box and inviting Garvey to speak to the Harlem masses for the very first time in 1917.

Amy Ashwood, c. 1920.

Hubert Henry Harrison (*c.* 1920),
Virgin Island-born scholar and 'grandfather'
of the Harlem street orators. He was
affectionately known as the 'Black Socrates'.

"TO THE NORTH"

SOUTHERN NEGRO

A cartoon in the *Crisis*,
March 1920, depicting the
Great Migration of Southern
African-Americans to Northern
conurbations, a move fuelled in
part by fear of the Ku Klux Klan,
lynchings and other brutalities.

An African-American family just arrived in Chicago from the rural South, 1922. One of the hundreds of thousands of families who moved to the North.

Marcus Garvey as president of the Black Star Line, 1920.

A regular drill of the UNIA Women's Brigade, 1924.

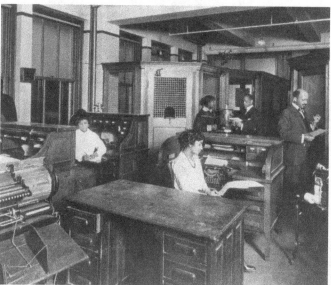

Office of the monthly magazine, the *Crisis* ('A Record of the Darker Races'). W. E. B. Du Bois, the editor and rival of Marcus Garvey, stands at the back on the right.

Booker T. Washington, founder of the Tuskegee Institute and premier African-American leader known as the 'Wizard' because of his rare ability to disarm the authorities and secure patronage from white benefactors.

A film still from D. W. Griffith's *Birth of a Nation*, depicting the Ku Klux Klan. The film was held to be responsible for the massive surge in the membership of the KKK after its release in 1915.

Children at the head of the silent march of 10,000 demonstrators down 5th
Avenue. The NAACP organised the procession to protest against the murder of
African-Americans during the East St Louis riots of July 1917.

Liberty Hall, site of the first month-long Convention of the Negro Peoples of the World,
August 1920.

accept jobs and positions below their intelligence; as post-office clerks, Pullman porters and hotel waiters. That the officers of the UNIA were idealists is beyond doubt, but they were also practical men and women; they were consummate joiners of organisations who hopped about from one group to another, according to their outlook and ambitions. Success when it had come in the past had invariably been on a small scale. But as the UNIA expanded, so too did their expectations for personal and political advancement; there was much more to gain and much more to lose.

Marcus Garvey was quick to find fault, and yet he believed that at the back of the adverse reactions to him lay an age-old problem: a black version of *schadenfreude*, the African-American and African-Caribbean's tendency to despise, rather than celebrate, the aspirations and achievements of his brother. 'The Negro's greatest enemy,' he would later lament, 'is himself.' The Black Star Line's initial difficulties betrayed all the signs of the race 'doing itself down', of a group that lacked self-belief. In the view of Garvey, this was the familiar and tragic characteristic of a people only recently (a couple of generations) up from slavery. He often drew the analogy between emancipated black people and crabs in a barrel. A crab that was capable of rising up and crawling out of the barrel would be impeded from doing so by the other crabs who dragged it down and cut its claws off to prevent further escape.[16]

In negotiating these jealousies and animosities around the fledgling Black Star Line, a modicum of restraint and level-headedness was called for. At the earliest opportunity, Garvey discharged Warner and Grey and publicly humiliated them at the next big UNIA meeting – for the first time held in a long, half-finished empty brick building that had previously been designed as a church for Baptists but abandoned. This was the organisation's new, permanent home; a rough-looking dwelling that had been renovated and roofed over in zinc. In the capacious and romantic imagination of Marcus Garvey it was transformed into Liberty Hall. Thereafter, the hall would serve as the spiritual mainspring of the movement and seek to emulate its namesake in Dublin which had been the site from where the Easter Rising had been launched in 1916.

Garvey had long held a fascination for the Irish cause. He aligned Irish subjugation and peonage under the British with the suffering of black people worldwide: 'As the Irishman is struggling and fighting for the fatherland of Ireland, so must the new Negro of the world fight for the fatherland of Africa.' The Irish had been kicked around by the English for centuries but it seemed that their dreadful past would soon reach its apogee. For Garvey, 'Irish' was virtually another name for Negro. Just like the Irish, Garvey believed that 'today the Negro seems to be the footstool of the other races and nations of the world; tomorrow the Negro may occupy the highest rung on the great human ladder'.[17] As the UNIA moved away from being just a friendly society to a political organisation, Garvey turned towards Irish Republicanism for inspiration. Sinn Feiners' agitation for home rule served as a blueprint for Garvey's evolving philosophy of Black Nationalism. He much admired the 'relentless propaganda in the interest of Irish Republicanism' that had been especially successful on American soil. On 11 June, the Irish revolutionary leader, Eamon de Valera, embarked on a much-publicised mission to the USA. On 23 February 1919, 6,000 Irish-Americans attended the Third Irish Race Convention in Philadelphia during which an Irish Victory Fund was launched that eventually peaked at $1,500,000. A week later, Marcus Garvey and the UNIA announced plans to hold an 'International Convention of the Negro Peoples of the World' for the following year. The symbols and stages of the quest for Irish independence were regularly alluded to by Garvey; he identified strongly with de Valera who in the summer of 1920 was declared by his adherents Provisional President of Ireland.

Garvey recognised that de Valera's mission was much more advanced than the UNIA's. He aimed to court Irish Republicans and invite them to address UNIA members; that eventuality was still a little way off, but on the night of Sunday 27 July 1919, Garvey's identification with the Irish cause peaked with the dedication of Liberty Hall. Henrietta Vinton Davis opened the ceremony with an ode and prayers before giving way to an impassioned UNIA leader. Garvey's voice crackled with an unusual hint of apprehension as he confided to the audience his foreboding. He had been instructed to present himself to the District Attorney's office the next morning, for the sixth time in as many weeks. Perhaps this speech 'would be the last one in many years as . . . certain sinister forces . . . were trying to have him removed from the scene'. Summoning the spirit of the blood sacrifice of past Irish Nationalists from Robert Emmet to Roger Casement, he vowed that he too was ready to be offered up as martyr. Enemies might yet succeed in 'striking the shepherd in order to scatter the sheep'. But as he neared the end Garvey asked those in the audience who were willing to sacrifice their lives for the race to stand up. As one, the vast gathering rose to its feet.[18]

The published vignettes of the extraordinary evening, of his defiant farewell, dripped with drama. But in the next edition of the *Negro World*, Garvey went even further.

Under the heading, 'Two Negro Crooks Use Office of the Deputy District Attorney to Save Themselves From Jail', in a diatribe which bore his fingerprints, Garvey alleged that Kilroe had offered the former BSL officers immunity from prosecution should they help 'frame [him] up' for breaking corporate law. As an experienced newspaper man, Garvey understood the perils of slander and libel. The courts were still processing the merits of the litigation he'd launched against the *New York World* and *Harlem Home News*. Yet on the front page of his own paper, he'd now penned an article that recklessly invited the charge of libel. An incensed Edwin Kilroe duly obliged. Within forty-eight hours, Garvey had gone from a position of uncertain judicious scrutiny to the certainty of his legal liability. If you wanted to libel someone you couldn't make a worse choice than upsetting a lawyer. Later in the month police officers turned up at UNIA headquarters to arrest Garvey on a charge of criminal libel. He was shocked and deeply humiliated, recalled Amy Ashwood, even though he managed to extract a concession from the police that he would not be handcuffed. President-general Garvey suffered the ignominy of being temporarily incarcerated at Tomb's prison and was only released once he'd met the terms of the $3,000 bail – a huge sum, the equivalent of five years' wages for the average worker. 'In a highly charged and apprehensive state', Garvey returned to UNIA offices with his fiancée where they waited in dread 'impatiently for the morning newspapers'.[19]

The potential libel was undoubtedly an expensive, self-inflicted injury but there was at least one boon from his reported troubles with the district's lawyers. A forty-three-year-old Bahamian, Joshua Cockburn, was amongst the West Indian migrants who continued to pour into Harlem. For almost a year now, he'd been casting about with little success for employment suitable to his skills. But reading about the difficulties of the embryonic Black Star Line gladdened his heart. The Negro Steamship Corporation would be his salvation.

For Captain Joshua Cockburn was one of the few black men in America
to hold a maritime master's certificate. He'd been at sea since he was
nineteen, and had worked his way from galley boy to second and
first mate on a series of British naval vessels before obtaining his
captain's licence. Captain Cockburn's cocksure confidence was softened by an engaging, flashing smile and beguiling deep-set eyes that
would have served him well in any game of poker.

Joshua Cockburn hurried to 135th Street and joined the long line
of supplicants – now including scores of prospective BSL stockholders
– and waited his turn to be presented to the UNIA and Black Star
Line president. Cockburn introduced himself as not just an experienced captain but a savvy businessman who could help convert
Garvey's dream into reality by negotiating the purchase of the
company's all-important first ship. Garvey was immediately impressed
with the smooth-talking, shiny-skinned black man in his sharp, white
captain's uniform. Even so, at this stage, it was not the conduct of
his character but the colour of the skin that was of greater importance. Though there was not yet a Negro steamship to command,
Garvey recognised the enormous propaganda value in having a black
man ready to take the helm. With Cockburn in tow, accompanying
the UNIA leader on promotional tours, the Garvey bandwagon rolled
on throughout August, steadily selling stock in the shipping line. The
25th of that month marked yet another stage in the project's maturity. That evening the organisation rented the 2,804 seats of Carnegie
Hall to accommodate potential new recruits and investors. Henrietta
Vinton Davis was greeted with polite applause at the start of the
meeting but it was the appearance on stage, shortly after 8.30 p.m.,
of the provisional first commander of the Black Star Line that truly
electrified the audience.[20] The widely advertised 'biggest ever reunion
of Negroes' from the diaspora certainly needed the extra seats. Despite
months of intelligence gathering, the authorities still didn't quite know
what to make of it all and, as earlier noted, Archibald Stephenson,
the anti-Red crusader from the Lusk Committee, decided to take a
look for himself. He made a clumsy and ostentatious entry to Carnegie
Hall along with detectives from the bomb squad and stenographers
who tapped away with quiet menace throughout all the speeches.
Mindful of their presence, the UNIA president reiterated that he led
a movement whose members were 'neither Democrats nor Republicans
nor Socialists nor Bolshevists nor IWWs', and, much to the amuse-

ment of the crowd, Garvey reminded them that 'when they were robbing us from Africa, they robbed us with all parties'. In that same speech, he implied that he had been vindicated and revelled in the fact that he would increasingly become a towering force and one to be reckoned with. Because, especially in that Red summer, when innocent Negro blood spilled so freely in America – when Mary Turner, a pregnant black woman, could be lynched, hung upside down, her belly slit open and her unborn baby trampled underfoot – Marcus Garvey would no longer hold his furious tongue, no matter who was present. He warned that in future, 'when they lynch a Negro below the Mason-Dixon Line . . . since it is not safe to lynch a white man in any part of America, we shall press the button and lynch him in the great continent of Africa.'[21]

On 25 August 1919, Marcus Garvey – harassed and harried by the authorities who would save the Negro from an alleged black swindler but not from the noose of the confirmed Southern white cracker – was not alone in spouting his defiance. Of all the new faces accompanying him on the platform that evening, even more so than Cockburn, the Reverend James Eason was perhaps the most significant. The flamboyant Eason was a prominent black American clergyman with a loyal following in Philadelphia. Eason was temperamentally inclined towards Garvey, much more so than towards the subservient old-school pastors, the 'prophets of the hereafter' whom Garvey grew to despise. Following the Philadelphia riots the previous summer, Eason had taken the practical position that the spiritual protection of the New Testament was not as comprehensive as that offered by the six cartridges of the Smith & Wesson. Reverend Eason had been linked with Du Bois's NAACP but now, in switching allegiance, he made public his disillusion with that relatively conservative organisation and signalled his faith in the UNIA as the best bet for the Negro. On a good night (and there were many of them) the 'silver-tongued Eason' (as he was commonly known) was a match for Garvey. He would prove instrumental in delivering hundreds, perhaps thousands more recruits to the UNIA – opening up fronts all along the east coast. By embracing the organisation, he also complicated the picture of its anonymous rank and file, overturning the simplistic notions of some critics that the Garvey movement was, essentially, made up of foreign-born black people. That largely untested assertion, amounting to no more than wishful thinking, was consistently the line taken by the BOI agents who reluctantly conceded that perhaps a 'few ignorant Afro-Americans' might also make up the numbers of the movement's sympathisers. The prospect of homegrown radicals was always much more frightening and incomprehensible than aliens or immigrants without the correct papers who might conceivably be deported.

Reverend Eason, who had broken away from the official AME church to form an independent People's Church of his own, would of course have eyed, in an arrangement with Garvey, reciprocal benefits – the chance to enlarge his own congregation from the ranks of the UNIA. For Garvey, the dangers of entering into a union with this radical preacher were outweighed by the opportunities for racial solidarity. Eason was black and transparent. The same could not be said of the other Methodist preacher, the Reverend D. Jonas, who seemed bent on insinuating himself into the organisation. Jonas was pale and opaque – an itinerant, Welsh-born pastor in search of a flock. One couldn't guarantee – he probably didn't know himself – where he would show up next. Reverend Jonas, late of Indianapolis, Chicago and Philadelphia, revelled in the Old Testament moniker 'Prophet Jonas' by which he was known throughout black districts. He'd been arrested several times during the Great War on suspicion of being a German spy and spreading subversive propaganda amongst the black population. The sins of Nineveh had become those of America, and Prophet Jonas had foresworn the comforts of his race (his Celtic roots were traced to Tredegar in south Wales) to dwell, most recently, in the belly of black Harlem. In his trademark crumpled white suit and straw boater, the prophet had become a familiar sight on the corner of 135th Street, taking to the stepladders vacated by Marcus Garvey and the other black orators, to preach singularly to the cursed Negroes, the sons and daughters of Ham. He'd swept into town along with the warm weather and the latest crop of hopeful street orators whom Garvey, without a shred of irony, labelled 'vulgar rabble rousers'.

As far as Garvey was concerned, a casual audit of the times Jonas frequented the UNIA's headquarters made for suspicious reading: it clearly revealed an upsurge in the Welshman's attendance when Garvey himself was out of town. 'That fellow,' Garvey once complained, 'always takes advantage of my absence and comes to the [Liberty] hall.' But to what end?

Garvey was almost instinctively wary of Minister Jonas. The reverend's credentials – a tireless advocate of the put-upon black man as manifest in his role as secretary of the International League of Darker Peoples – gave him an outward appearance of sincerity but it was his actual appearance that was most problematic. Though rare, there were, of course, interracial organisations like the NAACP and many conscientious white people who made the plight of black folk their business. But looked at less sympathetically, Jonas was in the vanguard of another trend. Adventurous white people were increasingly drawn uptown to the daring and rapture of Harlem. In some aspects the Negro capital was on the verge of becoming a novelty cultural centre for thrill-seeking voyeurs. On Saturday nights, they'd be spied in the slow-moving cars that cruised up Lenox Avenue and back down 7th Avenue, taking in the vibe, their noses pressed to the glass and their eyes dilated by the spectacle of black lives lived in the open. Getting out of the cab was sometimes a risk though; as Claude McKay found when he brought a white friend, Max Eastman of the *Liberator*, up to the small cabaret operated by Ned on 5th Avenue. 'We arrived at the door . . . from where Max could get a glimpse inside. He was highly excited by the scene and eager to enter.' McKay called over to Ned but 'his jovial black face turned ugly as an aardvark's . . . He waved his fist in my face and roared "Ride back [downtown]! Ride back or I'll sick mah bouncers on y'all!"'[22]

Garvey too felt he'd detected in Reverend Jonas something of the 'slummer' and the soul of the tourist – one had only to scratch and it would come through. For just over a decade, Jonas had attempted to carve out a niche for himself as an intermediary between the races, and also to act as an unofficial and unsolicited chaperone for visiting African dignitaries to America. Though wary of him as an interloper, and considering him guilty of encroaching on his organisation, Garvey saw the reverend's usefulness, especially in his African agency. In July of that year, Jonas had exploited all his contacts and leverage to broker a series of meetings for an official Abyssinian delegation to the USA. Hot from their audience with the President at the White House, some of the delegates had been lured by Reverend Jonas to Harlem. The idea of Abyssinia (Ethiopia), its place in the Old Testament Bible and the romance of its imperial past, exerted a great hold on the imaginations of African-Americans, even among those with sparse knowledge of Africa. Garvey was thrilled to be able to make the announcement in large black type in the *Negro World*, 'PRINCE RENDIVA GERBAU OF THE ABYSSINIAN COMMISSION TO SPEAK AT THE PALACE CASINO', that confirmed the UNIA amongst those sponsoring the most prestigious and unprecedented engagement.

When the large and expectant crowd assembled that night for the talk from the Abyssinian nobleman they found themselves locked out from the venue. Nothing that Marcus Garvey said could induce the casino's owner to relent. The nervous authorities had ordered him not to open the doors.

If the authorities aimed to interrupt and curtail investment in the shipping scheme, they were too late. The idea had taken hold to a degree that not even Marcus Garvey had expected. The proposed line was *the story* in black circles and even rivals such as William Du Bois were fielding enquiries about it from friends and relatives out of town. Uncle James Burghardt wrote from Great Barrington on 21 August asking whether his nephew considered an investment in the Black Star Line to be safe. Du Bois fired off an immediate response, urging him not to 'under any circumstances invest any money on the BSL. The District Attorney . . . has pronounced its methods fraudulent.'[23] Others were not so easily dissuaded. By September, the Black Star Line had accumulated over $50,000 – more than enough for the deposit on a ship. Following the end of the Great War and the decommissioning of scores of vessels the corporation should have been spoilt for choice. The directors, though, were short on experience. The most established businessman in the group, Jeremiah Certain's area of expertise was confined to cigar manufacturing. The complicated regulations around the chartering, purchasing and sailing of vessels were bewildering, and it was with some relief and great expectation that the directors turned gratefully to Captain Joshua Cockburn. His teeth flashing with confidence, the captain professed to be honoured to act on the company's behalf – for a small remuneration. Within a few weeks he had some exciting news to report: he'd found an affordable vessel of suitable tonnage to meet their needs. The SS *Yarmouth* was a thirty-year-old tramp ship that had more than paid back the cost to its owners by ferrying cotton and coal during the Great War. It was a compact (squat would be too unkind) freighter with a cargo capacity of a modest 1,400 tons, and a disproportionately tall funnel that further disturbed its aesthetic appeal. She was not, Hugh Mulzac later recalled, 'a vessel to set a sailor's heart aflame'.[24] Nonetheless, in his report at a highly charged midnight meeting of an excitable board of directors, the captain judged her seaworthy and the asking price of $165,000 to be fair. The *Yarmouth*'s owners would accept a deposit of 10 per cent. In the meantime he advised that the company negotiate a charter for her at $2,000 per month. To the inexperienced directors such a figure might seem alarming, but their resolve was stiffened by Cockburn's calculations. The cost of chartering, he assured them, would be offset by the fantastic possibility for profits. The likelihood of deficits need not be entertained as Cockburn went on to explain: 'Even if the corporation did not make money on her charter, the psychological effect on the people would be so great that the chartering of the ship alone would boost sales of stock.' The boardroom hummed with unanimity and the motion was passed. Captain Cockburn had particular reason to be pleased. Not only had he negotiated a handsome fee that would take effect once he assumed command of the first Black Star Line ship, but he'd also made a covert arrangement (which he neglected to mention to the board) for a finder's fee and a share of the profits with the vendor. It was not in Cockburn's interests, therefore, to strike too hard a bargain for the BSL, rather the opposite: it had served his purposes to inflate the price. For now, though, everybody was happy. The deposit was paid and though the contract would only be complete and a bill of sale agreed once another $80,000 was handed over, the owners consented to Garvey's wishes for a mass UNIA inspection of the hoped-for flagship.

Several thousand UNIA members and BSL stockholders swarmed across the decks of the *SS Yarmouth* on Sunday 14 September. No amount of rust or sound of spluttering engines could dampen their ardour. The mood of veiled excitement, hope and superstition among the investors was akin to that of the betrothed on the eve of his wedding catching one last steadying glimpse of the bride-to-be.

With the corporation now committed to the *Yarmouth* and the self-imposed 31 October deadline looming for its launch, Garvey needed to beat the drum louder and faster for the issuance of stock. But over the next few weeks, the chief spirit of the association found himself subject to unwarranted and unwelcome interventions that threatened to set back the project or even to scupper it entirely. The principal culprit was the pugnacious proprietor of the *Chicago Defender*, Robert Abbott. Those who knew both men vouched for their similarity, that both might have been poured from the same bottle. Both were portly but ascetic men with conservative tastes (notwithstanding Garvey's ceremonial dress sense and love of parades, and Abbott's Dusenberg convertible and Rolls-Royce limousine – neither of which he could drive). Both had studied law – though Abbott had obtained a degree and Garvey only the gowns. Both had abundant energy and took a heavy hands-on approach to the running of their businesses. They also shared a fierce hatred of the injustice meted out to black people – views which they espoused in their journals – and it seemed both, very quickly, were convinced that the other was the very worst type of Negro.

Casting a cold eye over Garvey's plans for a shipping company and then back through the newspaper's archives, Robert Abbott found the corollary that he felt sure would diminish enthusiasm for the Black Star Line – the fiasco of the Alfred Charles Sam affair. Lest they forget, the *Chicago Defender* warned its readers that Garvey's Black Star Line proposition was 'similar to the [bogus scheme] tried on the American public a few years ago by Chief Sam, a notorious confidence man'. Back in 1914, Alfred Sam, the son of a Gold Coast chief of the Akyem Abuakwa district, had led a cult-like movement among black folk from Texas, Oklahoma and the West Indies, enjoining them to buy shares in his steamship *Liberia* which had ultimately failed – not least through the intrigues and intervention of American and British officials who viewed the scheme as fraudulent and its investors 'foredoomed to disappointment'. The *Defender* was perhaps harsh in its criticism as there is a strong body of evidence that Chief Sam's intentions (in breaking the West African trading monopoly of British firms like the Elder Dempster Line) were sincere. In the intervening years, however, there'd been scores of other schemes that proved insincere. Fraudulent Nigerian businessmen were perhaps the most inventive and cunning in inducing black Americans to hand over cash for bogus shipping companies. Robert Abbott would have readers believe that Garvey was the last in the line. Such aspersions cast by one of the proprietors of the country's leading black newspaper were potentially damaging. Garvey was lucky to have in his camp the recent convert, John E. Bruce. He called in a favour now, and Bruce, who thought the *Defender*'s attempt to compare Garvey with Nigerian con-men odious and ill-founded, showed himself equal to the task. Even the briefest glance at Bruce's resumé quickly revealed his impeccable African connections (business and literary). In the pages of the *Negro World* he suggested that the Black Star Line had also caught the imagination of West Africans, and in so doing, he quietly refuted the *Defender*'s allegations: 'My correspondents in Africa ... hail it [the BSL] as the harbinger of a new day for our oppressed people here and there.' Bruce too had caught the spirit and optimistically foresaw that 'hundreds of well-to-do merchants and traders along these African coasts ... will gladly avail themselves of the opportunity to ship their goods on [BSL] ships'.[25]

John E. Bruce's quiet and gracious endorsement was hugely beneficial but Garvey's own response to Abbott's jibes was to embark on an ambitious stock-selling tour of Chicago, right under the *Defender*'s nose. The Illinois capital was second only to Harlem as a refuge and hub for aspiring black people. The *Chicago Defender* and Robert Abbott had played a pivotal role in encouraging Southerners to migrate to the North. Helping to set up migration clubs, the paper even went so far as to publish train timetables, advertise job vacancies and suggest places where migrants might find affordable and acceptable accommodation. Letters of those desperate to escape the South, alongside those from the successful workmen who had 'left the South with trembling and fear', peppered its pages. The Great Migration marked the beginning of a second emancipation after the false dawn of the Civil War. The anxious new arrivals sent unimaginable reports back home. At first they'd searched nervously for the familiar strictures of 'whites only' and 'for colored' facilities, but before long were testing the boundaries of their new-found freedom, taking up seats beside white passengers who did not flinch.

The *Defender*'s campaign had proved successful, perhaps too successful for some of the older settlers in Chicago, who worried that the arrival of tens of thousands of their unsophisticated brethren might discredit the race; that the dominant white culture might not be able to distinguish between them and these raggedy-headed country bumpkins who wore their slippers to the grocery store and their overalls to church. It was these new settlers that Garvey's movement would appeal to and embrace, but it was also these new Chicagoans, and new readers of the city's black papers, that had caused the *Chicago Defender*'s influence to grow along with its expanding distribution (now edging towards 200,000 nationwide). Abbott was confident (he'd have preferred 'conscientious') enough to publish a list of

commandments for the newcomers to the black metropolis which
included:

> Don't use vile language in public
> Don't allow yourself to be drawn into street brawls
> Don't use liberty as a license to do as you please . . . and
> Don't be a beer can crusher

At the head of the aptly and ambitiously named *Defender*, Robert
Abbott considered himself an uplifting guardian and the city's black
population, especially the migrants, his wards. Marcus Garvey threatened to trample all over his neat back yard. Before setting out from
Harlem, the prospective president of the Black Star Line gave some
indication of what he had in store for Abbott; he lambasted him in
the *Negro World* as a man who encouraged self-loathing in Negroes
through his heavy reliance on the advertising revenue from hair-
straightening and skin-bleaching products. Abbott was a buffoon reliant
on cheap sensationalism, a man who was 'so ignorant and incapable
of fulfilling the position of an editor that his "frothy utterances . . .
have caused the entire race to be most seriously embarrassed"'. Garvey's
description was at variance with much of the industry's view of Abbott
as a black mini-version of the monstrous newspaper baron, William
Hearst. 'The *Chicago Defender* is a paper that so closely resembles,
in certain particulars, Hearst's well-known rags,' the *American Mercury*
magazine wrote admiringly, 'that its zealous contemporaries still hint
that Hearst is its real owner.'[26] Marcus Garvey was spoiling for a fight
with a formidable opponent who was wealthy, avaricious, courageous
and, at times, extremely vindictive.

The UNIA leader and his entourage of seven, including Reverend
Eason, Amy Ashwood and Henrietta Davis, rolled into Illinois Central
Terminal on 28 September 1919. They immediately made their way to
the black district on the south side of the city – a teeming centre of
Negro life where the recently arrived young poet, Langston Hughes,
recalled that 'excitement reigned from noon till noon'. The group
pushed on past the vice-riddled pool rooms and cabarets of State Street,
heading for the 8th Regiment armoury (the home of the local all-Negro
infantry) for a series of extraordinary mass meetings. The streets were
still being cleared up a month after one of the country's bloodiest race
riots, and black people were still in a defiant and indignant mood.

Despite the heavy rains, several hundred curious Chicagoans showed up at the armoury to get sight of the now famous Negro orator. Garvey's stated purpose was 'to offset the libellous impression created upon the minds of the people by the *Chicago Defender*' that the Black Star Line was a fraudulent enterprise. He had set aside a week to do so and would remain in Chicago until he felt secure in having achieved that purpose. The selling of further stock in Chicago, then, was secondary to shoring up the reputation of the UNIA and the Black Star Line.

There were few sales on the first night but, in a clear sign that business would pick up, the following morning Marcus Garvey was accosted by an enthusiast called Sheridan Brusseaux. He explained that his wife had been at the meeting but had missed the opportunity to purchase shares. Garvey did not have a stock book to hand but, struck by the man's insistence, asked his secretary to direct Brusseaux to the address of one of the stock salesmen. Though Brusseaux only bought two shares, his keenness surely indicated that the *Defender*'s negative publicity had been reversed.[27]

As the evening approached, the president of the Black Star Line set out once more through the drizzle for the armoury and was heartened by the sight of the large turn-out, equal to the night before. In fact their numbers had been swollen by a pack of local reporters. Closest to the platform, the *Defender*'s correspondent was best placed to record the drama that was about to unfold: 'Garvey stood up to address the crowd,' and according to the reporter, 'was on the verge of telling the people of the glories of the proposed Black Star Line, when Detective George Friend (of the Chicago Constabulary) stepped out to the aisle, calmly walked to the stage and "demobilised" the project.' Garvey was to be arrested for violation of the Blue Sky Law – an obscure offence which required salesmen to obtain an Illinois licence before selling stock in the state. The Blue Sky Law had been brought in a few years earlier to counter the confidence swindlers issuing worthless securities that had about as much value as the blue sky. Garvey protested his innocence and ignorance of the law to no avail. The policeman moved to escort him to the waiting wagon, and as he did so Garvey noticed a half-familiar figure at his side – the man who had approached him in the morning. Sheridan Brusseaux now identified himself as a private detective of the Keystone Detective Agency. Later in court it would be revealed that Brusseaux had been hired by Robert Abbott, the editor of the *Chicago Defender*. Garvey had been trapped by his enemy into breaking the law and, though the fine was paltry, the Chicago paper felt free to mock the UNIA and the Black Star Line which 'instead of sailing the Atlantic Ocean en route to some foreign port had anchored at the Harrison Police Station'.

Over the next couple of days the *Defender* went even further in inflammatory and satirical headlines reporting that Garvey had fallen foul of Edward Brundage, the Attorney General of Illinois: 'Brundage "Sinks" Black Star Line – Air Castle Steamship Sails into Illinois' was, without doubt, the most disturbing. The news brought consternation on the streets of Harlem, forcing Garvey to call an emergency meeting at Liberty Hall. Anxious investors crowded into the congested hall. Some had taken the *Defender*'s headline literally and feared that the Black Star Line had been sunk (even though the first ship was not yet in their possession) somewhere between Lake Michigan and the Atlantic Ocean. So jammed was the hall that people pressed to the steps leading up to the platform, ending up at the feet of the speakers, and still hundreds of others could not get in. Chicago had been an intermezzo, precipitating this next stage with Garvey now surrounded by members anxious to learn the extent of the damage; the leader whom guest speakers lauded as a latter-day Solomon was about to be judged by the people. Garvey rose to his feet and before he could say one word the clapping began: instantly the hall filled with a great wall of applause which did not abate for fully five minutes. The honourable Marcus Garvey turned in another mercurial performance castigating the 'bad niggers' full of malign intent who were trying to sabotage the Black Star Line. Garvey's voice boomed out over the hall, ostensibly speaking directly to his supporters but actually answering absent critics: 'You have brought this movement to the stage where your success is next door. All that you have to do is stick and stay.'[28]

There were now just three weeks to go before the 31 October deadline, by which time 'any Negro not a stock-holder in the BSL,' Garvey had warned, 'will be worse than a traitor to the cause of struggling Ethiopia.' Cheques and cash continued to pour in through the post at a rate not matched by the ability of the skeleton staff to keep up. Reams of paperwork remained unprocessed.

Into this chaotic climate walked a twenty-two-year-old middle-class Jamaican immigrant (a graduate of the elite Wolmers Girls' School) who could well have been forgiven for believing her arrival at UNIA headquarters that summer to be preordained. Her gentle almond eyes and comely demeanour were much remarked on but Amy Euphemia Jacques was also a bold, determined and resourceful young woman. Her great-great-grandfather, John Jacques, had been the first mayor of the Jamaican capital, Kingston. Her father, George, who owned several properties and land in Kingston, had been a manager of the Paloma cigar factory. The Jacques family, then, were of comfortable middle-class stock. But when her father had died unexpectedly in 1913, Amy had assumed the role of head of the household. She was seventeen. The family's suddenly reduced finances thwarted her career prospects. Where she had once dreamt of becoming the island's first female barrister, she now accepted a position as a clerk in legal chambers – sublimating her former ambition with reveries of escaping Jamaica.[29] After four stultifying years, Amy Jacques could delay no further. As soon as part of her inheritance matured on her twenty-first birthday, she paid over the $65 that secured her passage to America and, making a pledge to her anxious mother to return 'if conditions were unbearable', she set off for Harlem.

Amy Jacques had a character built to endure. Although she was a fair-skinned woman of Jamaica's brown elite, her relatives in New York had declined to sponsor and accommodate her because 'they all passed for white', moving freely in mainstream society with the benefits of Caucasian life and none of the deficits that were attached to black skin; associating with a dark cousin would have exposed their true racial identity. Jacques had consequently had to invent another relative in order to obtain the necessary documents to travel to the USA.

Amy Jacques had been slow to appreciate the attraction of Marcus Garvey. But eventually, curiosity over the conflicting accounts of the UNIA had drawn her to one of his Sunday meetings, and like so many others, she'd left mesmerised by the president's powers of oratory. A follow-up tour of the headquarters soon metamorphosed into an unofficial job interview, after her frank remarks as to the disarray of the office. 'I am placed in a very awkward position,' Garvey confided to her. 'I have to employ all-coloured staff, many of whom have never had the advantages of working in business offices.' The UNIA leader showed her into his office and opened a large cupboard crammed full with stacks of unopened letters. They had built up during his absence on a speaking tour. 'I haven't time to teach someone to open, sort and put notations on them before handing the moneys enclosed to a treasurer,' he lamented. 'You see the awful predicament I am in for lack of qualified honest people.'[30]

In her retrospective account decades later, Jacques wrote that Garvey persuaded her to lend a hand a few evenings a week, and quickly appraising her efficiency, pleaded with her to accept a full-time position. There is no mention in her narrative of the involvement of her close friend Amy Ashwood. Yet in Ashwood's account, she had invited Jacques to stay with her in Harlem and had recommended her for the secretary's job. Amy Jacques's studied oversight was grounded in their later spectacular fallout over the amorous intentions of Marcus Garvey – a man whom they were both to marry.

Whether engineered by herself, by Ashwood or by happy accident, Amy Jacques's introduction to the UNIA proved most fortunate for employer and employee: Garvey was pleased with the way she overhauled the office and put it on a more efficient footing, and Jacques revelled in the role of his personal secretary and unofficial office manager, the kind of position which, despite her obvious abilities, she would have had trouble finding elsewhere. The federal census of 1915 in New York (which showed clerical workers and salespersons constituting 2.7 per cent of the Caribbean workforce) pointed to the negative disparity between what skilled West Indians searching for employment thought commensurate with their island experience, and what they were actually offered.[31] Though they suffered less than indigenous black workers in this respect, West Indians still came up against a rigid colour line that was difficult to breach. There was no colour bar at the UNIA, of course: one of the great attractions of the organisation was its openness. The UNIA was home to Harlem; it was for and of the people, and there would be no exclusion; the door was always, seemingly, open.

Just before noon on Tuesday 14 October, George Tyler, a part-time vendor of the *Negro World*, walked through the door of the brownstone UNIA offices on 135th Street. He had no appointment but that, in itself, was not unusual: people showed up all the time, occasionally still clutching the coupon they'd perhaps cut out of the *Negro World*, and now intended to redeem for a share certificate in the Black Star Line. Especially if the Garveyites were coming from out of town or from abroad they'd want to memorialise the day, Amy Jacques recalled: '[They'd] want to see Garvey personally after transacting business and inspecting various departments; they just wanted to shake his hand, so that they could tell the folks back home that they had held his hand and that he sent greetings and good wishes.' George Tyler had purchased $25 worth of bonds in the Universal Restaurant. But he hadn't brought along the stubs to check on his investment, and he wasn't lugging along a bundle of unsold copies of the paper; George Tyler was holding a gun. Before the receptionist even had time to look up, he'd brushed past her, shouldering and kicking open doors in the downstairs offices and all the while calling out in a strident and insistent voice demanding to see the UNIA leader. Garvey was working with Amy Ashwood and another secretary on the floor above. He came to the top of the stairs to investigate the commotion and did not, at first, notice that the man causing all the fuss held a .38-calibre pistol in his hand. George Tyler took aim and fired. The first shot went wild and Garvey ducked instinctively. The second bullet grazed his temple; the next two slammed into his legs and Garvey crumpled to the ground. Ashwood rushed to tend to Garvey; the other officer, Mrs Mary Clarke Roach, thrust herself in front of the fallen leader, standing between Garvey and the gunman; together the two women shielded him from further gunshots. In the slowed-down 'no-time' of the attack, the switchboard operator managed to grab Tyler and tried to wrestle the gun away from him but the would-be assassin broke free and fled the building, chased by other UNIA members. Halfway up the street, Tyler was speedily apprehended by a passing patrolman, handcuffed and taken to the local police station. Minutes later an ambulance arrived to rush Garvey to casualty for an emergency operation.

Almost immediately speculation began as to the assassin's motives. Newspapers the next day stated that Garvey had owed Tyler $25 from money he'd lent to start up the Universal Restaurant. The shooting, they claimed, was the culmination of several rows. When, in the past, he'd asked for his money back, the disenchanted investor had been continually rebuffed and had become incensed when, rather than a refund, he was offered the equivalent of $25 in shares in the Black Star Line instead. The theory did not seem probable, but neither did the rumour circling Harlem that Tyler had confessed to his cellmates that he'd been sent by the District Attorney 'to get Garvey'.

The morning after the assassination attempt, Tyler was to be taken

from Harlem police station to the courts. Two guards were escorting
him back to his cell 'for his coat and hat when he suddenly wheeled
about and leaped over the edge of the third floor'. Landing face down
thirty feet below, Tyler fractured his skull. In a bid to escape he'd
leapt to his death.[32]

Garvey lay recuperating in his hospital bed from the bullet wounds
when the news of his assailant's accident (later updated to suicide)
came through. Garvey had survived with injuries that were not life-
threatening, but the *New York Times* was among those papers who'd
flashed confusing reports that the UNIA leader had been shot in the
head, just over the right eye, and was said to be critically injured.
Before the attack, Marcus Garvey had planned to give a talk in
Philadelphia and, defying his doctors, he set off for the People's Church
just five days later. When, at the appointed hour, their president
mounted the stage, limping on the cane that would always accompany him thereafter, the congregation erupted in boundless jubilation
and ecstasy. After the reports of his demise, some believed they were
witnessing a miracle. It was a hugely transformative moment. From
then on, according to Professor Robert Hill, the curator of Garvey's
papers, the career of the UNIA leader took on quasi-religious proportions. He'd been shot in the head and survived: the faithful thought
him immortal.[33] Overnight the purchase of shares in the Black Star
Line shot up. Marcus Garvey seemed to anticipate the response when
he assured the audience that 'if the shots caused the organisation to
advance 2,000 per cent, then I am satisfied to die'. Days before the
31 October deadline, thousands of dollars poured into the UNIA's
recently reorganised offices. A poorly paid longshoreman named
Cornelius Martis became one of the biggest investors. As recently as
2005, documents discovered by Rachel, the great-granddaughter of
Martis, included two certificates issued in 1919 with Marcus Garvey's
signature that showed Cornelius Martis had purchased 80 shares
amounting to $400 (equivalent to $5,000 today) – an extraordinary
testament of faith in Garvey and the BSL.[34]

On 30 October 1919, the UNIA rented one of the biggest venues
in Manhattan, Madison Square Garden, to mount one final push
towards reaching the level of funds needed to secure the release of the
Yarmouth over to the Black Star Line. A Lusk Committee Intelligence
Report estimated 6,000 people at the meeting, most wearing 'the colors
of the new UNIA flag, red, green and black' – red for the red blood

spilt, green for the green pastures of Africa and black for its chosen people. The Lusk Committee's Doris Henry conjured up a frightening mélée of passion and fanaticism, of wild singing interrupted when Captain Cockburn and 'the crew of the new Black Star Liner [all in uniform] came in and the howling and yowling of the mad mob drowned all the music'. The pale face of Doris Henry quivered when she recalled how Garvey raged: 'We Negroes are now whetting up the swords to fight for freedom and if the white people treat us right we will combine, otherwise the Negroes will join Japan and the East.'[35] Pamphlets and handbills scattered around the Garden emphasised the redemptive power of the Black Star Line. One advert stood out from the rest. It pictured a black woman kneeling with her arms outstretched, her desperate children clinging to her side, and a burning cross towering over the flames from her ruined home. The caption above read, 'Negroes Awake! The hour has come to save your Race from the burning stake. Invest in the Black Star Line.'

An evangelical fever matched the enthusiasm of the eleventh-hour stock-buying, marking a subtle and psychic shift in the transferral of emotions away from the abstract Garvey movement and towards its personification. Even amongst lapsed Christians and agnostics, Marcus Garvey's near-death and resurrection appeared God-given. The Lord had delivered unto black people a latter-day Moses, who through the purchase of ships, was going to lead them to the Promised Land. Professor Buck typified the sentiment of the speakers that night when his voice thundered over the auditorium: 'God is saying I have heard the call of Ethiopia and 400 million strong they are coming out and they are going to march under the leadership of the one man I have selected in the person of Marcus Garvey.'[36]

The next day, on 31 October at noon, just as Marcus Garvey promised, the Yarmouth weighed anchor at 135th Street pier on the Hudson River. A crowd of several thousand jubilant supporters had marched to the pier to witness the launch of the ship; one of the greatest moments in Negro history. The UNIA band struck up, hundreds jostled up the gangways, having paid the dollar to take part on its maiden voyage, and a cloud of flying boaters and hats of every description pierced the cold October air. The Yarmouth moved off and the vestiges of scepticism around the UNIA leader and mockery of him disappeared overnight.

'The Eternal has happened,' Marcus Garvey proclaimed from the pages of the *Negro World*. 'For centuries the black man has been taught by his ancient overlords that he was "nothing" is "nothing" and never shall be "anything" . . . Five years ago the Negro . . . was sleeping upon his bale of cotton in the South of America; he was steeped in mud in the banana fields of the West Indies and Central America, seeing no possible way of extricating himself from the environments; he smarted under the lash of the new taskmaster in Africa; but alas! Today he is the new man.'[37]

A STAR IN THE STORM

What we need is another Emancipator who will tell the Negro youth,
'You can succeed in big business just as you succeed along other lines
of intellectual and mechanical endeavour. [Once you] learn the detail
necessary to success, you can even sail the high seas and run a steamship
line . . .'

William Ferris, *Negro World*
11 October 1919

'WHEN the Garvey organisation purchased two trucks the people were exuberantly enthusiastic,' wrote Claude McKay. 'When it acquired an old boat and manned it with a Negro crew, they went delirious.'[1] The delirium continued throughout the day of the *Yarmouth*'s maiden voyage. Unknown to the jubilant crowd, their celebrations were in real danger of being spoilt by a mix-up over the transferral of the insurance for the vessel. Leo Healy, the representative of the anxious vendor, had hurried to the pier with orders to stop the *Yarmouth* sailing. But with a wary eye on the crowd, whose excitement was at fever-pitch, Healy reached a compromise with the ship's new crew. Along with his port captain, Leo Healey would chaperone the *Yarmouth* which would be allowed to sail out of sight of the crowds further down the Hudson but only as far as 23rd Street.

A couple of days afterwards, the insurance was placed on the boat and with the crew and fifty passengers, including Henrietta Davis, on board, the *Yarmouth* was made ready to sail for Cuba. But it had been an inauspicious start, an omen which taxed the limits of the sailors' superstition. Captain Cockburn, who now commanded a salary of $400 per month, at the head of the *Yarmouth* slipped her out to sea under the cover of darkness because, he informed his boss, 'I felt there was some trick or scheme [a]foot to prevent my sailing.'[2]

An air of heightened suspicion had crept over the movement following the attack on their leader. Members generally concurred with Garvey's assertion that the shooting had been part of a sinister plot to get rid of him. It was a strange coincidence that in the forthcoming criminal libel charge against the UNIA leader, the only witness whom the district attorney aimed to call was the assailant, George Tyler; it struck some as even more of a coincidence that Tyler had, twenty-four hours later, committed suicide – apparently.

Marcus Garvey's most fervent admirers, the type of West Indian whom Hubert Harrison characterised as the 'hoe-handle and cow-tail brigade' might well have considered their countryman immortal but it was not a view likely to have been held by the subject of their idolatry.[3] After all, to be shot and wounded is to be undermined and stripped of any delusions of invincibility. Though his appetites for power, dignity and recognition were not diminished by the gunshot injuries, one of the first things Marcus Garvey did after the attack was to solicit the services of a bodyguard. A committee of members had impressed upon Garvey the need for him to arm himself. He'd turned down that suggestion but agreed to a bodyguard. The appropriately named Marcellus Strong unplugged himself from his former job as switchboard operator and took up a gun; he would remain faithfully at Garvey's side throughout his time in Harlem.[4]

Later in the year the BOI informant whose dispatches were signed P-138 seemed to be under the impression that Marcellus Strong had multiplied. P-138 wrote that he had detected at least five bodyguards in the UNIA's secret-service squad. Following at a distance as Garvey walked down Lenox Avenue, the agent observed 'two of the guards some distance in front of [Garvey], one a little nearer to him in front, forming a triangle, the other two men came behind about thirty feet apart . . . When anyone passed near Garvey these men closed ranks.' P-138's reports always contained more heat and drama than those of the other two informants, and, on this occasion, he was particularly agitated and eager to report that 'one of the fellows put his hands behind his back, clasping them together thereby lifting his coat tail, exposing the shining butt of a revolver'.

Whether aware of it or not, the BOI agent was pandering to his paymaster's dark and foreboding fantasies of armed Negro men running amok on America's main streets. The appearance of black men with rifles on their shoulders, snapped to attention, in dark blue military uniforms parading through the streets of Harlem, had already begun to cause alarm in Hoover's circles. These were the men of Garvey's newly formed African Legion, a ceremonial outfit whose future presence at UNIA parades would enhance the spectacle and boost the drama of the occasion. The men in uniform looked fabulous, remembered Mariamne Samad, whose father was in the legion and later a key figure in the secret service which evolved as an offshoot. The African Legion appealed to Garvey's romantic side, the crystallising sense of the uniqueness of his role in instilling pride and creating a parallel world equal to that of the white man. The former Jamaican Prime Minister, Edward Seaga would later applaud his intentions not to rely on the white man, 'not to knock on gates where they were not wanted but to build their own castles; not to respect uniforms for which they were not given the opportunities to play a role in the hierarchy of whatever uniform system but to create their own uniform regimes'.[6] Ex-combatants from the Great War formed the backbone and cadre of the African Legion but it also drew in raw recruits seduced by the glamour. This was yet another manifestation of Garvey's shrewd understanding of psychology. 'To most white people, Garvey seemed a figure out of vaudeville,' observed the social worker and NAACP founding member, Mary White Ovington. But she quite clearly saw the effect Garvey had on black working lives, in his own semi-military attire and in the uniforms for the Legion: '[He] appealed to the love of beauty and colour so keen in the African, and aroused his self-respect and pride. The sweeper in the subway, the elevator boy, eternally carrying fat office men and perky girls up and down a shaft, knew that when night came he might march with the African army and bear a wonderful banner to be raised some day in a distant and beautiful land.'[7] Reports of these African storm troops in Harlem and other divisions in Newport News and elsewhere caused brows to furrow in the corridors of the BOI. Furthermore, British Military Intelligence had received disturbing anonymous communications. British Cabinet Office files for April named D. Shirley, a partner of the S. G. Kpakpa Quartey, a merchant of the Gold Coast, as the commander of the Universal African Legion. Shirley was alleged to have hatched a plan to smuggle these men (the battle-ready amongst them) into Africa and the West Indies as Black Star Line passengers –

though to what end it is hard to imagine.[8] Whilst the British didn't take the tip-off too seriously, the BOI decided, on 13 February, to investigate more thoroughly. Agent 800, James Wormley Jones, a former captain in the US army, was the first black man to be appointed as a full-time agent of the bureau. He'd served in the disgraced 368th Infantry of the 92nd division during the Great War, and was one of the few black officers to escape censure after the disastrous retreat from the Argonne forest offensive on the French front. The division's commander, General Ballou, had vented his spleen in a briefing to the accredited war correspondent: 'I regard the colored officer as a distinct failure,' the general raged. 'He is cowardly and has none of the traits to make a successful officer.' That vitriolic newspaper copy and its uncontested conclusions had been wired round the world and had been scorched into America's collective memory.'[9]

Partly motivated by this opportunity to redeem himself, if not the regiment, through important work, Jones was also driven by a sincere belief that Marcus Garvey was sowing pernicious seeds of discontent between the races in America. Jones's reputation in Newport News (a stronghold of the Garvey Movement) grew at lightning speed and he quickly managed to infiltrate the UNIA. Despite, initially, having to address suspicions aroused by his very light complexion, Jones would soon be privileged to address a full house at Liberty Hall. The *Negro World* reported how Mr Jones, 'mistaken by the audience for a white man', spoke passionately about his racial identity and seemed to embrace the so-called 'one drop rule' whereby having literally one drop of black blood meant you were considered a Negro. 'I have no more privileges than the blackest man in the eyes of the white man. He considers me a Negro just as any Negro,' Jones assured. Moreover, in his speech he went on to condemn the race's own colour and class distinctions.

Within weeks, brother Jones had gained the confidence of his superiors to such a degree that he was instructed to help train the paramilitary UNIA legionnaires.[10] They drilled every Thursday night at Newport News, and Captain Jones reported ominously that they had appropriated the oath of allegiance that every US soldier takes, and altered it so that they no longer pledged their loyalty to the President of the United States, but to the Honourable Marcus Garvey instead. The potential threat from these 200 volunteers was largely overstated. As Mariamne Samad recalls, 'the rifles were ceremonial – the pins had been removed so that they couldn't fire – the men were fabulous to look at, drew a lot of admiring attention from the ladies and would not have wanted to get those creased and starched uniforms dirty.'[11] However, there were others, such as the rough-house war veteran of the British West Indies Regiment, Sergeant William Wellington Wellwood Grant, for whom the veneer of a smart uniform could not disguise the sheer brutality of the man within. Grant – later, in charge of the local Harlem African Legion known as the Tiger Division – had a propensity to crack heads rather than attempt persuasive argument, which eventually led Garvey to expel him from the UNIA ranks.[12]

From hereon in the BOI kept a detailed and open file on Garvey and his movement; the records gave Hoover and his superiors a comprehensive account of the daily inner workings of the UNIA. Captain Jones was one of three black BOI agents to infiltrate the UNIA. He was preceded by Special Agent C-C and later overlapped with P-138. All three were able to provide intimate details of the day-to-day running of the organisation. C-C was the code-name given to Dr Arthur Ulysses Craig, an accomplished teacher who came to prominence in the parlours of the African-American educated elite when he qualified as the country's first black electrical engineer. C-C had no difficulty convincing Captain Cockburn to take him on as a technical assistant. From that close vantage point, he chronicled the negotiations for the SS *Yarmouth* – a vessel he considered in very poor condition – and Cockburn specifically requested his help in testing the boilers of the tired old tramp steamer. There was no place for pathos in his reports. But though Dr Craig was a patriot, he was also black. He would not have been immune to the conundrum of black life which W. E. B. Du Bois memorably labelled as 'double consciousness' – one couldn't just be an American; one was conspicuously, for ever, black *and* American.[13] Craig well understood the burdens of being a 'first black' in whatever chosen field, and he would have taken no joy from observing Garvey's inexperienced black directors being so mercilessly exploited as they tried to establish a footing in a hostile white business world.[14] Though Cockburn had pronounced the *Yarmouth* seaworthy, it was soon apparent that it needed extensive repairs. In Hugh Mulzac's estimation 'her boiler crowns were in need of repair and her hull was practically worn out. She could not have been worth a penny over $25,000 when the Black Star Line acquired her for $165,000.'[15]

Captain Cockburn was presented with a final bill amounting to a whopping $5,000 just to get the ship out to sea; he baulked at the extortionate cost but the repairers held the ship to ransom, threatening it with an order of attachment if the bill was not met. This was news he deferred in relaying to Garvey because as he later confessed, 'I did not care to disturb your feelings before sailing.'

The $5,000 trick was, Cockburn gradually gleaned, the prelude to a plot to sabotage the *Yarmouth*. The firemen shovelling coal into the furnace could not raise more than 65 pounds of steam, so that the ship trundled along at a mere 7 knots per hour. A watchful eye was kept for ships on the seas that the *Yarmouth* would not have the speed to avoid crashing into should they get too close. Some members of the crew were also proving difficult to control. Though trumpeted as having an all-black crew, the *Yarmouth* had trouble filling the most senior posts with able seamen, and two white men had been recruited – the chief engineer and the chief officer. These two resentful sailors now began to show a distinct lack of respect for the chain of command. In the blackest night, whilst Cockburn took a nap, the chief officer somehow managed to steer the *Yarmouth* onto the Cay Sal bank, sent out an SOS and gave the order to abandon ship. Cockburn woke to find the passengers issued with lifebelts and the lifeboats being swung out from the davits. Overriding his fellow officers, he had to threaten to shoot in order to restore command, and eventually managed to refloat the ship.[16] The captain suspected the accident to have been deliberately engineered by the two white men and prayed daily 'to keep my temper and patience until I can be rid of them'.

Marcus Garvey had already been through sufficient intrigues and reversals not to discount his captain's theory, but Cockburn's rumblings of treachery were out of sync with his employer's joyous telegrams of near-complete vindication – save from an expected core of residual resentment. The much-heralded launch had silenced all but the most pathological critics who were soon spreading malicious rumours; that of the fifty passengers on the *Yarmouth* only a handful were paying; the majority were stock-salesmen; and finally, that the ship was only ever a clever inducement for the gullible to buy even more shares.[17] A scan of the passenger list casts doubt on such a cynical claim: only three of those who boarded the *Yarmouth* had any involvement with the Black Star Line, and the success its president was counting on was one of expansion. Garvey envisioned a future with not one or two ships but a whole fleet put into service for the benefit of the race. The news from Cuba was far more encouraging when the *Yarmouth* docked

at Sagua, La Grande. 'People here are just crazy about the organisation,' Joshua Cockburn enthused. 'The stevedore's gang containing just
a handful of men brought up two hundred and fifty dollars' worth of
shares in just a twinkle.' On a more sober note, Cockburn hinted that
he planned to discharge the chief engineer and pleaded with Garvey
to find him a replacement from Cardiff (home to many black seamen
awaiting berths on tramp ships). If all went to plan, the Black Star
Line would need to recruit another crew as well. For Garvey now
promised the faithful that the company would launch its next ship by
the end of February 1920.

Marcus Garvey was in a hurry to make amends for his forebears'
narcolepsy. 'The Negro who slept and wallowed in the mire for centuries
has just begun to turn and he has now placed his hope in God and
himself and he is going forward to achieve.'[18] He didn't quite say it
but this was a version of that old Negro expectation from emancipation: 'Massa day done, it's our turn now.' The launching of a Negro
steamship was such a spectacular achievement that he had plenty of
reason to crow – even former adversaries agreed. John Banton's heart-
felt and contrite apology printed in the Negro World was typical of
the violent swing towards Garvey: 'When you first launched [your]
ideas, I had the misfortune of butting up with men of your own race . . .
and criticising you to the detriment of your character, and even
expressing their opinions in regards to the soundness of your mental
facilities, but in the shortness of time they have confounded themselves,
and, like the dog, they have returned to their own vomit.'[19]

Even the frosty W. E. B. Du Bois was forced to admit his qualified
admiration of the man. William Du Bois kept his distance from Garvey,
and at first simply tried to ignore him, hoping that the man, and his
movement, would fade away. But Garvey was impinging on African-
American life in a way that was impossible to ignore, though Du Bois
still refused to accept the UNIA as anything more than a foreign/largely
West Indian movement. In his magazine Crisis, the editor conceded
that 'Garvey was an extraordinary leader of men . . . [who] with singular
success [has] capitalised and made vocal the great and long-suffering
grievances and spirit of protest among the West Indian peasantry'.[20]

Du Bois wasn't yet ready to surrender to the Jamaican immigrant
the mantle of the leader of the black people in America. His logic and
intellectual tidiness would not permit such a notion to take root, but
on an emotional level he must have realised that he was losing ground

to the Jamaican. Though he'd never heard Garvey the orator in full flow, he would have been aware of the endorsements from high-profile African-Americans such as Henrietta Vinton Davis and William Ferris (whose judgement couldn't be ignored) that Garvey was the 'real thing'. The problem for Du Bois was that although he spoke clearly and passionately in his prose, he was not, in person, an inspirational or magnetic character. 'Meeting Du Bois was something of a personal disappointment,' Claude McKay observed. 'He seemed possessed of a cold, acid hauteur of spirit, which is not lessened even when he vouchsafes a smile.'[21] Physical distance was also a factor. Garvey had established himself in the heart of the pulsating, vibrating, dirt and detritus of Harlem. Du Bois and the talented tenth were enshrined in fastidious offices downtown. And decry as he might the Garvey theatrics up in Harlem, up in Harlem was where, in 1920, the head Negro-in-charge needed to be.

When Marcus Garvey and Amy Ashwood were reunited in 1918, he explained that he'd failed to contact her in the first years of his arrival in the USA partly because he wanted to make something of himself before sending for her. By most standards of excellence, he'd certainly made something of himself now. Still, the character of their relationship from the reunion in 1918 until late 1919 was awkward, businesslike and subservient to the growth of the organisation. That all changed at 11 a.m. on 14 October. Ashwood's disregard for her own safety in preventing the assassin from further firing on Garvey had a profound effect on her former paramour. Whilst he was in the Harlem hospital, Ashwood collected up all his possessions from his furnished room and removed them to the apartment at 522 Lenox Avenue which she shared with her father. She subsequently devoted herself to nursing the wounded leader back to recovery. Soon afterwards, Garvey proposed marriage to her; the date was set for Christmas Day.[22] It promised to be a hectic couple of months in both their private and professional lives, with the couple planning for an elaborate wedding at Liberty Hall, and Garvey and Cockburn negotiating for the Black Star Line's first major contract. Ashwood invited her close friend Amy Jacques to be her maid of honour and to help with the wedding preparations. In a sense, the forthcoming marriage was UNIA business, and Ashwood believed she was grooming Jacques to take on a more substantial role in the organisation. Her confidence in the other Amy was matched by Garvey who on 12 December sent a note to the New York Postmaster revoking all previous orders and henceforth arranging for Jacques to be specially authorised to sign for all registered letters delivered to him or the Black Star Line.

The *Yarmouth* was now steaming between Cuba and Jamaica where excited crowds daily lined the pier at Kingston harbour anticipating her arrival. Once she docked, the *Yarmouth* would pick up additional passengers for the return leg of the journey back to New York. The Black Star Line expected a full complement of passengers to take advantage of its widely advertised offer: 'We Will Take You 25% Cheaper Than You Can Go On Any Other Line'. The directors were also hoping to extend that promise to the Green River Distillery Company in securing what they imagined to be a lucrative contract to ferry $5,000,000 worth of whisky, champagne and wine from the USA by 17 January. The date was critical, for on 16 January 1920 the 'noble experiment' of Prohibition would come into force in America.

Once the contract was agreed, Garvey could concentrate on fulfilling the pledge he'd made to Amy Ashwood at the start of their courtship five years earlier. In recognition of their public and private personae, two ceremonies were planned for the wedding, and for Garvey, at least, two separate dress codes. A commemorative photograph of the groom on Christmas Day shows him in a traditional morning suit with a perfectly pinched cravat, ornate cane and silk gloves in one hand and a top hat in the other; in the top right-hand corner of the photo is a graphic inset of the African continent. That morning, Amy Ashwood, in a trailing silk gown, joined him at the altar for the private Catholic church wedding. It was followed by an extraordinarily elaborate affair at the organisation's headquarters at Liberty Hall.

The 3,000 celebrants who squeezed into the hall were treated to a carnival of colour and pageantry, presided over by five church ministers. The 100-strong choir was at the couple's disposal as well as the African Legion's guard of honour. 500 guests from around the world were invited (Ashwood's Panamanian friend, Allen Cumberbatch, though notified, was not on the list). Thereafter, the limited but open invitation to UNIA members came with but one request, for them to wear their buttons as proof of membership. Hundreds of curious onlookers, on the pavement outside Liberty Hall, strained with one eye to get a view of the proceedings, and, with the other eye, ogled at the mountain of wedding gifts valued at $3,500.[23] The wedding allowed Garvey to indulge in his heightened feeling for the nuances and gravitas of public drama. He could change from morning suit to tunic and plumed helmet. More importantly, he could turn to the UNIA's constitution and book of laws (that underscored the formal incorporation of the UNIA in July 1918) and, for one spectacular night, transform Liberty Hall into 'the "Court Reception" at which the Potentate [Garvey] and his Consort [Ashwood] shall receive in presentation those distinguished ladies and gentlemen of the race and their ... children whose character, morally and socially, stands above question in their respective communities'.[24]

For an unashamedly romantic man, Marcus Garvey had a decidedly odd idea of the place of mystery, allure and indulgence in the immediate aftermath of a newly-wed's life. On their two-week honeymoon to Canada, he had decided to invite along a small retinue of UNIA staff, including his personal secretary, Amy Jacques. The leisure of sightseeing would be punctuated by three mass meetings in Toronto and two in Montreal. Garvey had paused to be married but the honeymoon period would not extend to the actual honeymoon. Mrs Garvey had been forewarned and had had some little time to acclimatise to the expectation of work and pleasure in Canada. When they reached the border, however, it was Garvey who was caught off guard by an unwelcome surprise: a customs officer carried out a routine search of his wife's luggage and found a concealed bottle of liquor. Garvey was teetotal – Amy had stashed away the bottle without him realising – and though he knew that his new wife liked a drink, his embarrassment at the border was acute. The disclosure for a middle-class woman was most unladylike; for the Consort of a potential Potentate it was even more unbecoming. Garvey was persuaded by the arguments of the Temperance Society that consumption of alcohol was morally reprehensible. Its transportation was, of course, another matter.[25]

Edward D. Smith-Green, the secretary of the Black Star Line, had the good fortune of having been scouted by Garvey. He was, in the president's estimation, 'a clever, well-trained accountant from British Guiana, who could not be eclipsed for competency anywhere'. He'd been one of the founding members of the UNIA in Harlem but, doubting its longevity, had drifted away. When, in the middle of 1919, Garvey came to cast for talented individuals to help float the Black Star Line, he remembered the Guianese accountant. By then, Smith-Green was working in an ammunitions factory in Trenton, New Jersey – rather down on his luck with but three or four suits to his name. Garvey paid for his train fare and brought him back to Harlem. Within a few months, he had gone from counting and recounting his slender wages each week to handling hundreds, sometimes thousands of Black Star Line dollars coming into his office each day. Garvey noticed he'd also become something of a fashion plate, changing his suit each day; his changed demeanour – one of self-satisfaction – was expressed through the snap of his colourful bow-ties.

In December 1919, Edward Smith-Green's luck had turned. At the beginning of the month Smith-Green was shot in a bungled robbery by an unknown assailant. Though the injury was not serious, the shock had obviously had a deleterious effect on his pregnant wife. She died a few days later, and was given a public funeral in New York.[26] It was not the best preparation for what was to come. Now he was to be the Black Star Line's principal negotiator in agreeing terms to ship a large consignment of whisky out of the country. Between them Garvey and Green (without seeking advice from the captain) chartered the *Yarmouth* for a fee of $11,000. In the event, this would not even meet the transportation costs; but worse still, in their naivety, they neglected to write a limited-indemnity clause into the contract. If anything went wrong the Black Star Line's liability would be unlimited.

The task was made doubly difficult by the unmovable deadline of 17 January and by the fact that the *Yarmouth* hadn't yet returned from her maiden voyage when the deal was being struck. She would need extensive repairs before going out to sea again. The company's naivety was further exposed when the final bill for repairs was presented: at $11,000 it was ten times the estimate. If Garvey didn't pay, the *Yarmouth* wouldn't sail, and if the *Yarmouth* didn't sail it would be liable to substantial damages to the whisky company. Garvey paid. By the time the ship was ready to take on the cargo, there were only a few days remaining till the start of Prohibition. Garvey and his captain set to each other in violent, roiling arguments over the terms of the contract which Cockburn considered derisory. The Black Star Line would only receive $11,000 when the going rate on such a valued freight should have been closer to $100,000.[27] Unknown to Garvey, his captain was also in negotiations with the client. It was one thing for the distillery to threaten a fledgling company like the Black Star Line with breach of contract; it was another to collect damages. If the whisky wasn't out of the country before the Prohibition deadline it would be confiscated, and Cockburn was refusing to sail, claiming the ship wasn't ready. The directors of the distillery were frantic and, in a secret deal, offered Cockburn a $2,000 incentive. He immediately ordered the crew to start loading the 20,000 cases of whisky, 500 cases of champagne and 350 barrels of wine. The *Yarmouth* just managed to clear port in time before the midnight deadline and set sail for Havana. Then 100 miles out to sea, off the coast of Cape May, she was caught in a storm. The valuable cargo had been loaded in such haste that it shifted in the hull, giving the vessel a heavy starboard list. Cockburn ordered the men to throw 500 cases of whisky overboard to steady the ship and prevent her from capsizing. (It was later rumoured that a number of tugboats had followed the *Yarmouth*, lain in wait for just such an eventuality and picked up the discarded bounty.)[28]

Captain Cockburn still struggled to control the ship which rolled and yawed in the heavy weather, and eventually he radioed an urgent signal to the coastguard for help. The Black Star Line's flagship suffered the indignity of being towed back to New York harbour for further repairs, and was laid to anchor off the Statue of Liberty.

At the regular Liberty Hall meeting on 25 January, Garvey told the audience, with unintended irony, that the past week had been somewhat trying, that the plotters who hoped to crush the organisation had not relented. It had been 'a week of brain against brain and the Black Star Line [has] survived'. The debacle was not over yet.

On the afternoon of 3 February, Prohibition officers stormed the *Yarmouth* after being alerted that some cases of whisky were being taken off the boat and sold on to bootleggers in Brooklyn. British Military Intelligence reports, which were increasingly shared with their American counterparts, noted the brouhaha surrounding the misfortunes of the *Yarmouth*. Garvey and a team of Black Star Line officials immediately besieged the offices of the Prohibition Agency and 'after much burning of long-distance wires and a conference in the US Attorney's office' managed to free the impounded cargo.[29]

What should have been a straightforward business transaction turned into a minor comic opera (the last act was still to be performed) and illustrated the kind of difficulties that were to continue to plague the organisation's inexperienced team. Garvey had not been able to send to Cardiff for a black officer to replace the *Yarmouth*'s recalcitrant chief officer but in Hugh Mulzac he found an African-American sailor whose commitment to his craft was matched by his enthusiasm for the UNIA. During Mulzac's job interview, Garvey did most of the talking and took off 'every few moments in a flash of oratory, his black eyes flashed and his quick fingers drove home each point . . . wildly castigating white men for their cruelty and extolling the greatness of ancient African civilisations . . . "You are going to help man a vast fleet of speedy ships," he said . . . Before I left I had purchased five shares.'

Mulzac was piped aboard the *Yarmouth* and was soon perturbed by what he found. The boat was partly waterlogged. The passengers were in a pitiful condition. 'They had to sleep in cold, wet, filthy rooms and were partly frozen. For a moment he wavered, for he 'had just given up a decent position for the sake of race pride'. However, the new chief officer decided to make a fist of it and almost immediately 'called for a gang of stevedores and made the crew snap to'.[30]

Hugh Mulzac recalled first-hand the degree to which Garvey's ideas had infected black people beyond the USA with the *Yarmouth*'s arrival at Havana. Hundreds of sympathisers had camped out to greet them 'showering us with flowers and fruit'. In the evening, President Menocal gave a banquet in their honour at his palace and promised his government's support for future BSL ventures. The one unfortunate note was the *Yarmouth*'s bad timing. She had arrived in the middle of a long-shoremen's strike during which her cargo of liquor could not be unloaded. Because of her lack of protection from a demurrage clause, the unlimited liability meant the delay (a penalty of several thousands a day) ate into any profits the line hoped to make, swallowed them up entirely after a week and pushed on into a massive deficit after a month. Thirty-two days on from their arrival in port the crew was able to unload the cargo.[31]

There was some consolation. Secretary Smith-Green had accompanied the *Yarmouth* and took with him two stock books of the Black Star Line which were completely sold out. Scores of Cuban businessmen had also pledged their cooperation and a substantial landowner had vowed to switch the shipping of his sugar from the all-powerful United Fruit Company to the Black Star Line – 'if we could promise him seaworthy vessels and good service'. When Garvey addressed the audience of stock-holders at Liberty Hall and read out the secretary's cable from Havana, though, the largest cheers came with the unexpected news of the crew's royal welcome at the presidential palace. The UNIA leader chose not to itemise the daily financial losses that the expedition had thus far incurred. If he had been pressed to do so, he would have undoubtedly set that 'regrettable deficit' alongside the incalculable benefits of the presidential endorsement. A worldwide network of Negroes trading between themselves had been Garvey's eternal dream, and Cuba heralded the first tentative signs of its real possibility.[32] The response in Cuba emboldened him in the pursuit of other business ideas and ideals. Why settle for a millinery store when you could cut out the middle man and manufacture the hats yourself in your own millinery factory? That was the kind of thinking behind the Negro Factories League which Garvey incorporated in January 1920. He would need figures such as the redoubtable Hugh Mulzac to stand a chance in establishing such businesses. The call had already gone out for 10,000 intelligent young Negro men and women of ambition to take advantage of the leadership possibilities that were opening up. As Hugh Mulzac noted, the hopeful supplicants who queued round the block at 135th Street occasionally included sharks and charlatans but a significant number of promising candidates also came through, not always with the correct paper qualifications, but with energy and enthusiasm and transferable skills.

The young J. Raymond Jones typified this group. He started work on the organisation's unprofitable wet-wash laundry. Plying for trade with a leased horse and wagon on a single route, the laundry served only one apartment building, and had struggled to break into this competitive market. Jones's innovation was simply to get rid of the horse and wagon, invest in a second-hand Model T truck and offer an incomparable service to the customer with the promise, 'We Return Everything but the Dirt'. Further routes quickly developed. The popularity of hot-roasted sweet yams sold on the sidewalks sparked another idea: the UNIA was perfectly placed to secure deals between the small black farmers in Oklahoma and Tennessee and street vendors who catered to the Southern palate of the new migrants in New York. The UNIA also cultivated an interest in small traders, especially amongst Harlem's Caribbean population, of whom it was often said that once they were 10 cents above a beggar they'd start a business.[33]

Although Garvey soon appointed a firm of respected accountants to monitor the UNIA books, and Amy Jacques's discipline and office efficiencies started to bite, the leadership continued to move monies between its businesses – with the Black Star Line taking the lion's share. Raymond Jones recalled that early on the shipping corporation became a financial furnace that needed to be fed, no matter its diminishing returns. On one occasion he brokered the sale of two tank-car-loads of cane molasses direct to a firm on Wall Street for a tidy profit. With some pride, he rushed to Garvey's office on an impulse to share the good news, 'I suppose to impress the great man,' and made the mistake of leaving the cheque with the president, 'for later I had a devil of a time retrieving the money to pay the [vendor] in Georgia.' There was no dishonest intention on Garvey's behalf, Raymond Jones concluded, just a deficiency of business acumen and a belief that 'all proceeds from the business ventures should go to the UNIA. When I suggested 20 per cent to the Association, in order to have money for expansion and a cash reserve, his answer was an emphatic, "No!"'[34]

Despite his frustrations, Jones never reached the crossroads of disbelief. Faith sustained him in his efforts to make a contribution and to excel. In the presence of Garvey's 'powerful personality . . . nothing could compare to the primal feelings of pride in race and strength in unity and the hope for posterity'. Garvey must have sent forth his spirit along with the *Yarmouth* also. It was something of that feeling of fellowship and exaltation that excited the black populations of Costa Rica and Panama when they learnt that the flagship was headed their way.

Sixty years later, Simon Clarke still remembered the occasion when, together with his older brother, he was given a packed lunch and 'set off on foot for Christ Church by-the-sea . . . and waited from nine in the morning till nine at night without catching a glimpse of the ship on its way through the Panama Canal'. Over the coming months that extraordinary desire to celebrate the simple existence of the Black Star Line was replicated throughout the Negro world. The idea of a black-run shipping line and its visionary leader had captured the collective black imagination.[35]

The *Yarmouth* eventually reached Colón, and Hugh Mulzac (a precise man not given to exaggeration) was amazed by the 'thousands of Panamanians who swarmed over the docks with baskets of fruit, vegetables and other gifts'. Exaltation mingled with relief. Thousands of Caribbean labourers had been driven to desperation by conditions in the zone, following the downscaling of their work and rights since the opening of the canal. They were enormously anxious to leave. To them, the *Yarmouth* had become a rescue ship. It had appeared on the horizon when they had all but given up hope. The crew improvised and made up accommodation for 500 of the lucky ones whom they agreed to carry as far as Cuba.

Stopping off, on Garvey's orders, at Bocas del Toro in Costa Rica, the crew were greeted by similarly ecstatic crowds, the peasants coming down from the hills on donkeys and makeshift carts. 'When we threw our heaving lines ashore,' Mulzac confided to his diary, 'the peasants seized the hawsers as they came out of the water and literally breasted us alongside the dock.' Whilst he could not fail but to be flattered by all the praise and adoration of the celebrants, Hugh Mulzac worried that the ship was in danger of becoming a trophy, and the crew part of an elaborate exhibit. It was a view reinforced by the fact that there was no cargo to pick up in Costa Rica.

Every time the *Yarmouth* weighed anchor and set a course for home, a message would be relayed ordering another detour and change of destination. Garvey seemed determined that as many UNIA celebrants and prospective UNIA members as possible should get to see her. There was a piece of unexpected good fortune in Kingston, Jamaica. The *Yarmouth* picked up a bonus shipment of 700 tons of coconuts, and Captain Cockburn was relieved that the vessel was being returned to more conventional use. By now, she'd been away for several months and when the ship received yet another change to the itinerary, ordering her to Boston, Cockburn objected. It made no sense because he 'would be passing New York to go to Boston'. Garvey would not demur. 'Do the best you can,' he pleaded, 'because those people there want to see the ship, and the arrangements are made for your coming.' Cockburn did as he was told. When the *Yarmouth* finally returned to New York and a hero's welcome, 'the coconuts, of course, were rotten'.

At times, Garvey sounded like an overadoring parent and the *Yarmouth* his first-born but, in the absence of more orders for cargo to be picked up and delivered, he was anxious to capitalise on her propaganda value. Given the magnitude of the task to rouse the people from their slumber, it was not only tempting but absolutely vital to exploit the *Yarmouth* for all her worth. 'Prior to the establishment of the UNIA, it was difficult to get black people to raise capital for entrepreneurial pursuits,' wrote Raymond Jones. 'Somewhere between slavery and the twentieth century the system of capital formation, called *esusu*, characteristic of West African societies and always extant in West Indian societies, something was lost among Negroes in the United States.'[36]

Garvey's ability to loosen their purse strings should not be under-estimated. However, he was enormously helped by his good timing. The post-war downturn in the economy was followed in 1919 and

1920 by an economic boom. President Warren Harding was soon to come to power on a ticket promising a return to normality. Harding unashamedly embraced the spirit of the age, of easy credit and get-rich-quick business deals. It was a time of extravagance, of reckless speculation on the stock market that led to a sharp boom and a share-buying craze amongst the population. Shares and commodities were passing hands at a furious rate. Black people were just as infected by the speculation fever and Garvey offered them a timely outlet. He preached a new gospel of success which tied an individual's financial and spiritual improvement to the elevation of the race: a Garveyite could get rich buying stocks and shares in the Black Star Line, *and* feel good about it.

Negotiations for two more ships were well underway by the spring of 1920. $10,000 was placed as a down payment on the $35,000 steam paddle-ship, SS *Shadyside*. 'Hot, isn't it?' teased an advert in the *Negro World* for the steam paddle-ship. New Yorkers need swelter no more intoned the *Black Star Line*. Its family excursions promised beautiful scenery, cool breezes and entertainment courtesy of the corporation's brass band, once its latest acquisition started paddling down the Hudson. The fantasy fleet started to feel even more concrete by April, when Garvey was able to report what 'to the ordinary optimist would seem a miracle', that the board had also agreed to pay $60,000 for the SS *Kanawha* – a pleasure yacht which they hoped to convert to commercial use, and which would be launched in a few days.

By June the readers of the *Negro World* had become familiar with yet another looming landmark in the UNIA's short history – the greatest convention held by the race that would span the whole of August. A convention fund was naturally launched under the heading, 'How Much Will You Give to Help Redeem Africa and Thereby Your Own Race?'

BOI agent 800, James Wormley Jones, who'd been promoted to the publicity committee, was so alarmed by the welter of response, he advised his handlers to do all they could to ensure that Garvey was denied a permit for the convention. Sifting through letters, mostly coming from the South, the agent inadvertently highlighted the depth of the emotions Garvey had unleashed, especially among 'the writers [who] speak of going back home to Africa'. One woman wrote to say she was 'going to sell her cow and send money to the convention'; another woman travelled all the way up from Oklahoma, 'seeking news

about it so she could travel back and inform people'; a prominent
Panamanian businessman 'arrived [in town] carrying $50 in gold for
the convention'. The nervous BOI man cited all three examples as indi-
cating the effectiveness of Garvey's dangerous propaganda in equating
the Black Star Line with Africa.[37]

Marcus Garvey didn't have to rely solely on his abilities of promotion. The fierce enthusiasm that his movement generated was
increasingly being picked up by mainstream newspapers. The *World*
magazine sent Herbert Seligman, one of its star correspondents, up to
Harlem to capture the flavour of excitement emanating from Liberty
Hall. Mr Garvey operated 'at the juncture of mysticism and share-
selling', according to Seligman. 'To walk into those offices is to enter
a fantastic realm in which cash shares and the imminence of destiny
strangely commingle.' The growing cult of Garvey's personality was
impossible to miss: 'At the centre of those dreams, spinning them like
so many webs, writing, travelling across the city to Liberty Hall to
exhort huge crowds, and centring himself in the uncertain complexi-
ties of the business ventures, is Marcus Garvey, West Indian Negro.'[38]
Seligman likened his hold over his followers to that of Billy Sunday,
the great white evangelist. Hundreds of thousands (Garvey amongst
them) flocked to Sunday's travelling wooden tabernacle and been swayed
by his sermons. And, just as during the Great War, the believers heeded
Sunday's invocations to buy war bonds to help defeat the enemy and
restore democracy, then so too were Garveyites investing in a new and
worthy crusade to restore the fortunes of the despised Negro. The
trenchant and amusing insights of the *World*'s correspondent into the
character of the UNIA president ultimately fell short of grasping Garvey's
true appeal. At this stage, at least, Garvey was not proposing a black
Zion or a black Socialist utopia. He was making a straight pitch to
the petit-bourgeois capitalist instincts of the majority of black folk,
who had little to lose, to take a punt on a likely winner.

The small investors who thronged the offices of the UNIA on 135th
Street were not so far removed from the punters who daily gave themselves over to the craze of 'policy' or 'the numbers' – the illegal,
semi-underground lottery that had a firm hold over the population of
the Negro Metropolis. Playing the numbers was, according to Claude
McKay, 'the most flourishing clandestine industry in Harlem'.[39] Anyone
could play. It required only nickels and dimes to score a fabulous 'hit'.
Placing a bet for less than the price of a packet of cigarettes might win

a smoker the equivalent of a week's wages. Over the ten years since the policy's introduction (in 1910) the numbers racket had evolved into a smooth-running gambling system involving scores of operators who criss-crossed Harlem. The winning number was generated from the totals of foreign and domestic sales on the stock market, published daily in the *Wall Street Journal* (which, judging by the number of Harlemites scouring its pages, appeared to be as popular as the *Negro World*, *New York Age* and *New York Amsterdam News*). A punter might perhaps venture to the local candy or cigar store (fronts for 'policy'), decide on a number (a date of birth, prison or psalm number) and buy a ticket from the runner who would run to the unofficial bankers (kings and queens) who would pay out to the lucky winner (and collect far more from the losers). Everyone seemed to be playing the numbers in Harlem: the watermelon man, the barber, the pastor and the Garveyite. The bankers, especially if they paid on time and in full, became local celebrities, benevolent 'kings' and 'queens'. Marcus Garvey never played the numbers but the most revered banker, the 'king of kings' was the Virgin Islander, Casper Holstein, famed for his patronage of the arts, charities and other good causes, including the UNIA.

Holstein was one of a handful of black notables who helped in the 1920s to kick-start the Harlem Renaissance – an artistic flowering that saw such dazzling writers and performers as Langston Hughes, Zora Neale Hurston and Paul Robeson drawn to the Negro Metropolis. Holstein's money was welcome; the man was not. He was never invited into the respectable parlours of the patrons of the talented tenth who either bank-rolled the Harlem Renaissance themselves or introduced the artistes to willing Negrophilic benefactors such as Charlotte Osgood Mason.

A fondness for artistic endeavour did not excuse the 'policy' kingpin's degrading influence on Negro life: to the midwives of the Renaissance, Casper Holstein was ultimately an unsavoury gangster – more notorious than notable. Marcus Garvey was not so judgemental. Whilst Holstein's pecuniary contributions might have caused some discomfort amongst the organisation's inner circle – even though his dollars did not figure in the official UNIA accounts – he remained, as far as its president was concerned, a valued supporter of the movement. Garvey even invited him to write an occasional column for the *Negro World* in which he lambasted the USA over its stewardship of his native Virgin Islands. If, as Eric Walrond wrote, 'amongst [the Virgin Islanders]

Holstein was considered a messiah', then it was mostly as a result of his largesse. Marcus Garvey spoke to the same demographic constituency. Both he and Holstein were of the street: there was a correlation between the rise of each – though comparatively Garvey's trajectory was far more spectacular. Walrond may have been right about Holstein's standing amongst the common people. But for every admirer of 'Holstein the Messiah', there were a hundred candidates who'd propose that in Marcus Garvey the Negro had finally found the true Moses after so many false and failed impersonators.

Amy Ashwood was coming to believe that the extraordinary dedication of Garvey and the degree of devotion he inspired was beginning to unbalance her new husband. 'In the full glare of the limelight the Marcus Garvey I knew receded into the shadows,' she later wrote in her memoir. 'The public figure Garvey took his place.' Neither man nor wife had much privacy. They continued to live amongst the debris of wedding gifts in Amy Ashwood's cramped apartment. Her father had moved out and was almost straight away replaced by her brother, Claudius, along with a friend. Somehow the newly-weds still found space to provide a room for the maid of honour and Garvey's personal secretary, Amy Jacques. Though crowded, the apartment was still big enough to accommodate them all, and in any case, the extra source of income would help with the expense of the rent. But Ashwood soon began to complain that her husband seemed to pay more attention to his secretary than his wife. Their intimacy was 'open and manifest and almost brazenly flaunted'.[40] When disputes arose in the household, wrote Ashwood, Garvey invariably sided with his secretary. Her husband seemed to spend more and more time away from the apartment, and would often not return until two o'clock in the morning and sometimes not at all. Marcus Garvey had kept his bachelor's furnished room, and in the early hours, when there was still no sign of him, Amy Ashwood would hail a taxi and rush over to it, only to discover he hadn't slept there either. Frequently now, after many an embarrassing and frustrating hunt of all the rooming houses and boarding houses in Harlem, she still wouldn't be able to find her husband.[41]

The first months of marriage had been a return to the tempestuous and fractious tenor of their New York reunion two years previously. Garvey's grievances against his wife stemmed from her refusal to mould her behaviour in a manner befitting the wife of a leader of the masses. Ashwood saw no reason to curb her drinking: it was not to excess.

Neither did she consider it inappropriate to spend time in the company of male friends. The UNIA leader was not amused by the irony of the contrast between his strong-armed control of an organisation, now estimated (by him) in the hundreds of thousands, and his inability to exert any reasonable influence over his wife.

The apartment was a crucible of disaffection. Garvey, who now went for days without speaking to his wife, sought counsel from his secretary who, when pressed, told her boss that Ashwood had confided that she was still in written communication with Cumberbatch, her paramour from Panama. Amy Ashwood came to believe that her husband had a rigid understanding of the expectations of a wife; he had transplanted that conservative idea from Jamaica to America where the modern concept of marriage allowed for greater latitude: within reason a wife might lead a life that was not wholeheartedly dependent on her husband for fulfilment. The very qualities that had attracted Marcus Garvey to his wife seemed suddenly and peculiarly to repel him. In *Miss Sarah Jack, Of Spanish Town, Jamaica*, the English novelist Anthony Trollope painted a wry account of Jamaican social mores: 'Flirting is an institution in the West Indies,' mused Trollope, 'practised by all young ladies, and laid aside by them when they marry.' Ashwood's crime, in her husband's eyes, was that she continued to flirt, even if harmlessly. Garvey would later complain that Ashwood was 'trying to return to the life [he] sought to reclaim her from'. His unease coincided with a certain wariness about the smart-suited 'fashion plates' that were increasingly coming into the organisation and securing the kind of well-paid position previously unimaginable to them. One of these fellows, Garvey later recalled, 'had all the women around and [to] my surprise after a while, he also had under his influence my wife'.[42]

Garvey summoned his secretary and Henrietta Vinton Davis, ostensibly to ask for their guidance and advice about his wife's behaviour. But essentially he had already come to an unflattering conclusion about her merits as a wife, and was edging towards a final, irreversible decision. Of that period, Jacques wrote that Garvey weighed in the balance the two poles of life with Ashwood which could either be 'wrecked because of her conduct or embellished by her deportment'.[43] Amy Ashwood had the kind of infectious personality that drew people towards her, but, as Garvey reflected, instead of doubt and suspicions being allayed, his spirit darkened – culminating in a late winter evening when he thought he'd caught his wife in compromising circumstances.

Garvey burst into the apartment and found her taking tea with a gentleman caller who was perched on the arm of the sofa. Amy Ashwood protested her innocence. As she remarked to Mariamne Samad decades later, 'with china cup in one hand and a sandwich in the other, I can't imagine what I was supposed to have been guilty of'.[44] Nonetheless, the descent of their marriage accelerated thereafter. Garvey continued to rage over her drinking which, though consisting of a physician's prescription for light wine and eggs, she failed to convince him was medicinal. Ashwood was pregnant – news that she prudently kept to herself. As Garvey had withdrawn his 'husband's favours' in January, if the pregnancy went to full term and she delivered a child, it is most unlikely that Garvey would have proven to be the father. The anxiety over her semi-detached spouse was compounded by his lack of regard for her feelings of nervousness and nausea. The private Garvey had no time for domesticity. Rare occasions of intimacy soon boiled over into arguments that seemed to continue, in his absence, with her former maid of honour. When Amy Jacques had had her fill of quarrelling she moved out of the apartment; Garvey immediately packed up and did the same. Amy Ashwood did not stay brooding in the apartment; she searched for Amy Jacques and pleaded with her, eventually persuading her to move back in. That seemed to act as the catalyst to Garvey's own return a few days later. Return did not lead to rehabilitation. After a brief respite, their rancour rose and fell repeatedly with the sun and moon, leading, inexorably, to a final reprise of abandonment. Later, Amy Ashwood was to suffer a miscarriage but Garvey's stance towards her was not softened sufficiently for him to draw back from the decision to start proceedings for an annulment. Their marriage had lasted a little over three months. The UNIA president took both Amy Jacques and Henrietta Vinton Davis into his confidence before making his decision known in public. He was concerned about the negative publicity that would ensue and perhaps how Ashwood's exclusion might impact on the smooth running of the UNIA. But, in the final analysis, Garvey considered his young bride a liability and she had to go. One of the key officers of the UNIA at this time was Reverend Weston and he recalled that when the separation occurred, it was a huge blow to the entire movement. Ashwood had been a fantastic galvanising force within the UNIA, so the breach was not just a marital separation: 'People loved, loved Amy Ashwood. They were entranced by her manner and personality, and her departure was the first great split in the movement.'⁴⁵ Garvey's rejection of his wife would not be reversed. Thereafter he refrained from communicating with her, save for instructions to his lawyers. He first requested an annulment, claiming that Ashwood had used 'fraud and concealment' to induce him to marry her and that she was guilty of adultery. Though no 'correspondent' was named at this stage, Garvey furnished the court with evidence of Ashwood's previous sexual indiscretions. Ashwood herself provided him with the ammunition. In a tearful letter, pleading for their marriage to be saved she had written:

'I would have given up long ago, but you gave me hope and caused me to live, when I nearly fell in the estimation of the whole world. I have not forgotten Marcus, but you said to me then, and these were your exact words: "Amy, I will marry you if the baby is not even mine."'

Amy Ashwood launched a counter-claim that she was blameless and that her husband had abandoned her, leaving her destitute and without means even to provide shelter for herself. Amy Ashwood asked the court to award her $75 per week alimony but Garvey told the bench that he only earned $25 per week; that he worked sixteen hours a day and was on the road practically all the time raising funds. He paid $96 per month for his rent, was saddled with debts of several thousand dollars to the Harlem Furniture Company and $700 to the Bloomingdale company for the purchase of a grand piano. It was galling that whilst he lived frugally on cheese and crackers, Amy Ashwood 'attended upon the theatres two or three times per week, and goes in expensive style as though she had the income of a millionaire'. The court eventually settled on alimony of $12 per week but whilst Garvey might have considered that he'd won a moral victory, his desire for a divorce had not been granted – for now. Court proceedings between the two would rumble on for another two years before Garvey, having satisfied legal requirements by establishing a temporary residence in Missouri, secured a contentious divorce in Jackson County (later legally challenged by Ashwood) in the summer of 1922. Amy Ashwood would always maintain (right up to her death in 1969) that she was *still* married to Marcus Garvey.

The young, now separated, wife blamed her maid of honour, Amy Jacques, in part for the gulf between her and her husband. Though there was no hint of impropriety between the UNIA leader and his personal secretary, Garvey's subsequent dealings introduced an element of doubt, at least in the mind of his spurned wife; Amy Ashwood believed she had been manoeuvred out of the way to make room for Amy Jacques.

As spring blossomed in Harlem, Garvey was determined to order his personal life to blend even more seamlessly with the needs of the organisation. To that end, he summoned Henrietta Vinton Davis and Amy Jacques once again to discuss an unusual proposition. Garvey had moved into another apartment on 129th Street and now invited both women to share the accommodation with him. Such an arrangement would run counter to the current social conventions – not quite rising to the red-heat that might tip it into a scandal, but tepid enough to set tongues loose. Garvey was prepared to take the risk. Embarking on this next important phase of the organisation's development, he made a clear-eyed calculation of the need for the loyalty, comradeship and proximity of Jacques and Davis in his life. The women accepted. As well as holding important positions that were integral to the operations of the UNIA, Jacques and Davis were content to keep house for their leader. Neither appeared to agonise over the decision. Jacques gave the disarmingly simple explanation that by walking home together, they 'would be better protected at nights coming from meetings'.

By the middle of June, not only had Garvey banished his wife, he had also rid himself of any residue of sentimental thoughts of his father. Garvey Senior died on 9 April 1920. The old man had spent the last few years of his life in a poor people's almshouse in St Ann's Bay, Jamaica. The son's resentment of his father still ran high in his veins. He would meet the minimum requirement and pay for his father's funeral but he stubbornly refused to foot the bill (when a summons was taken out on him) from the almshouse because 'his father had done nothing for him'.[46]

The purging continued in Garvey's professional life. Despite the fanfare of the returning *Yarmouth*, the stock-holders' annual report showed the company operating under great financial distress. The secretary, Smith-Green, was severely criticised for the disarray in the accounts of the *Yarmouth*'s expedition but the bigger culprit appeared to be its captain.[47] There were so many unreliable sources that it was difficult to unravel the cause of the misfortunes that had befallen the organisation's first ship. Conspiracy theories and other speculations swirled around the Harlem offices of the UNIA and Black Star Line. The dark excitement drove the BOI informant, Herbert Boulin, to even greater heights of melodrama, reporting to his paymasters that, on learning of the *Yarmouth*'s first tragic running aground, Garvey had confessed to him that he had contemplated suicide. P-138's memoranda always erred on the side of hyperbole, especially when he strained to deliver news of UNIA conflagrations and self-inflicted injuries. A more cynical man than Garvey would have been alert to Boulin's sycophancy and ingratiating attempts to make himself indispensable. But cynicism was not a quality that Garvey possessed in great store; for all of his worldliness, Marcus Garvey was prone to the kinds of fits of surprise that are the preserve of the optimist; and, in his isolation, he reached out and innocently confided in undercover BOI agent P-138.[48]

As well as Captain Cockburn's incompetence, ugly rumours had now reached Garvey about the captain's graft. It was an unsavoury catalogue of corruption. Cockburn had received a secret commission from the *Yarmouth*'s vendors; from the Green River Distillery Company he had accepted $2,000 reward, a 'consideration, as a present for the extra amount of energy that I put into getting the cargo off the dock';[49] he had also colluded with the ship's repairers and pocketed a percentage of their exorbitant fees; and finally, the near-ruinous running aground of the *Yarmouth* on its maiden voyage was less likely due to sabotage than to the fact that the captain was drunk. On 31 July 1920, the *Negro World* notified UNIA members and stock-holders in the Black Star Line that both Cockburn and Smith-Green had been sacked, having failed to give satisfaction as to their 'honest integrity'.

Several seething directors at the earlier board meeting wanted to pursue the corrupt captain through the courts, but others were 'against antagonising [him] as he was in a position to cause much harm and embarrassment in consequence of their delicate situation'. Put bluntly, the annual report showed incomings of $763,124.14 and outgoings of $763,124.14. Dividends would have to be deferred (indefinitely) because the Black Star Line had not made one red cent.

HE WHO PLAYS THE KING

The Talented Tenth of the Negro race must be made leaders of thought and missionaries of culture among their people. No others can do this work. The Negro race, like all other races, is going to be saved by its exceptional men.

W. E. B. Du Bois, *The Negro Problem*, 1903

'ALL Negroes who are interested in themselves, in their race, and in the future generations,' the *Negro World* trumpeted, 'will wend their way to New York City to form part of this great convention assembled.' The first international conference of the Negro peoples of the world, organised by Garvey to begin on 1 August – the anniversary of the slaves' emancipation in the Caribbean – was the apotheosis of everything he stood for. After months of planning, the last nail had been hammered into the new improved Liberty Hall – expanded to three times is original size to accommodate the thousands of expected delegates. Though dark skies rimmed Manhattan, the thunder came from within the hall. Marcus Garvey stretched forth his arms and spoke: 'For over three hundred years we who are denizens of this Western Hemisphere have been held in slavery. For that period of time we have been separated from our brothers and sisters in the great continent of Africa, but this Sunday morning brings . . . Negroes from every country together.' His greeting was the prelude to a great opening procession to be staged the next day.[1]

At precisely 2 o'clock, the parade set off from the UNIA offices on 135th Street. All along 7th Avenue, crowds jostled for the best view of the spectacular procession weaving through Harlem. Four mounted policemen led the way. Marcus Mosiah Garvey, resplendent in his majestic robes and plumed bicornate helmet, followed in an open-topped sedan with the Honourable Gabriel Johnson, Mayor of the Liberian capital, Monrovia. The sun caught the glint of brass of the UNIA marching bands; 100-strong choirs accompanied them. And then the Black Cross nurses in their stiff white tunics and flowing caps; sabres clanked on the thighs of uniformed legions. Next came the UNIA divisions, identified by their state or country banners; still others bore inscriptions such as: 'Down With Lynching'; 'The Negro Has No Fear'; 'Toussaint L'Ouverture Was an Abler Soldier than Napoleon'; and 'Garvey, the Man of the Day'. A great roar went up with the sighting of the all-black crew of the *Yarmouth* (minus its captain) in their gold-braided jackets; and about 500 automobiles brought up the rear. It was an amazing display that jolted New Yorkers out of their complacency, seasoned as they were to all of the hulla-baloo of grand parades and the climax of political elections. Hugh Mulzac, whom Garvey had appointed master of the SS *Phyllis Wheatley* (even though it had not yet been acquired), marvelled at the crowds: 'As far as I am aware it was the greatest demonstration of coloured solidarity in American history, before or since.'

In part, Garvey had conceived of the event as a version of the coron-ations so beloved of the British and her sons and daughters of empire, with all the stage props of a royal court. Though this would be no formal inauguration of a hereditary succession, the UNIA-sponsored international convention would culminate in the crowning of a provi-sional president of Africa. His Majesty would be elected by the delegates, and would be charged with governing an as yet undelin-eated African Empire constituting the 400 million Negroes of the world. The system of honours that Garvey proposed and the confer-ring of titles on an imagined African government-in-exile was the one aspect of the convention that would receive the most unflattering rebukes from Garvey's critics. He thought his proposal no more absurd than Eamon de Valera's appointment that year as the provisional pres-ident of Ireland.

The UNIA leader should have been alert to the fun that newspapers would make of his assumption, given that, as he later noted, when English journalists printed de Valera's new title alongside his name they enclosed it 'in inverted commas, to try to show those who were his enemies that his claim to that title was ridiculous'.[2]

The possibility of a provisional president of Africa seemed a lot further away in 1920. There was the small matter that there were only two independent states in Africa (Liberia and Ethiopia), and the inconvenient fact that European colonial powers had not shown any signs of tiring of their possessions. The lack of consultation with the people and (perhaps more importantly) the chiefs and local rulers on the African continent was also problematic. Finally, Garvey would have to reckon with prominent African politicians, such as Blaise Diagne, whose elevation to the French Chamber of Deputies was seen by the urban African elite in Senegal as a triumph of accommodation. Garvey, though, was not so naive as to assume their endorsement but he recognised the validation that the inclusion of indigenous Africans would give the movement. On the podium beside him was George O. Marke, the official representative of the Freetown division of the UNIA in Sierra Leone; next to Marke was the man who would be elected Potentate Leader of the Negro Peoples of the World, otherwise known as Gabriel Johnson. Described by the stenographer of the convention as 'haughty and aristocratic', Johnson had every reason to be pleased with himself; he was a member of one of the powerful Americo-Liberian families and ruling elite in Liberia. His father, Hilary Johnson, had been elected president of Liberia in 1884; the latest president, C. D. King, was married to his niece; his brother was the attorney general; for his part, Gabriel Johnson had been a brigadier general in the army and was the current Mayor of Monrovia. Once the convention was over, Johnson would, presumably, put away the gowns of the potentate and return to Liberia in his more humble capacity as mayor of the capital. As with many of Garvey's earlier promotions the idea of African titles, unrolled at the convention, was meant more in gesture, albeit a grand gesture intended to inspire and unify the Negro world.

The possibility for black unity had been extended to all potential friends and established enemies alike. Aside from the election of the continent's provisional president and potentate, a number of other equally grand-sounding appointments would be made. In the spirit of solidarity and democracy, Marcus Garvey had written to enemy headquarters at the NAACP, specifically to W. E. B. Du Bois to inform him that, at the convention, the leader of the American Negro people would be elected by popular vote. Du Bois was an obvious candidate, and Garvey wondered whether he would be 'good enough to

allow us to place your name in nomination for the post'. The suggestion had caused the noble Du Bois nostrils to flare. 'I beg to say that
I thank you for the suggestion,' Du Bois wrote back tersely, 'but under
no circumstances can I allow my name to be presented.'[3]

Since the beginning of the century, Du Bois had carefully plotted a
course towards a Pan-African goal. Through cunning and diplomacy
he'd overcome the enormous resistance of the post-war powers and
engineered the African conference in Paris. Du Bois hoped to build on
that success and host another conference in 1921. Even at this early
stage there were rumblings of opposition from the Europeans and then,
as Du Bois later reflected, 'there came, too, a second difficulty which
had elements of comedy and curious social frustration, but nevertheless was real and in a sense tragic. Marcus Garvey walked into the
scene.' As he saw it, William Du Bois now had to contend with a noisy
and insouciant Marcus Garvey making absurd claims to an African
empire. The clumsiness and weakness of its conception 'lay in its intemperate propaganda, and the natural fear which it threw into the colonial
powers'.[4] On a purely aesthetic level, the NAACP leader believed
Garvey's convention to be something of a circus; also that it undermined his carefully orchestrated attempts to uncouple the negative
imagery of the black man widely promulgated in the mainstream culture.
The Brahmin in Du Bois was especially sensitive to vulgarity. Depictions
of black life which played into the hands of white-held stereotypes
particularly irked. Years later, Du Bois would famously comment on
reading Claude McKay's highly peppered tale of fecund Negro life,
Home to Harlem, that it left him feeling as though he needed to take
a bath. As to Garvey's 'pranc[ing] down Broadway in a green shirt' it
was equally distasteful and he would have no part of it.[5]

The thousands who lined the route of the parade were, however,
enthralled. Harlem hadn't seen such sights since the ticker-tape celebrations that marked the return of the Harlem Hell Fighters. Now
that famous regiment's band struck out together with the bands of
the UNIA and the Black Star Line, swinging along Lenox Avenue,
breaking out from military marches and wowing the crowds with
popular jazz scores and finishing with 'Onward, Christian Soldiers'
as they marched into the great hall of Madison Square Garden.

An estimated 25,000 Negro participants filed into the stadium. A
podium, specially constructed to accommodate more than 200 dignitaries, towered above the masses. It was festooned with flowers and

ringed by the Star-Spangled Banner, intertwined with the red, black and green flags of the UNIA. At 8.45 p.m. the president-general of the UNIA, the honourable Marcus Garvey, led the high officials and distinguished guests towards the speakers' stand; the audience rose en masse and a great wall of applause reverberated round the building. Gazing down magnanimously from the platform the UNIA leader saw himself reflected in all the glory of the occasion.

An intense but gentle-seeming man, with eyebrows forked in a semi-permanent frown, was the first to speak. The Reverend George Alexander McGuire (the first black man to be appointed an archdeacon of the Protestant Episcopal Church), set a tone of dignified gravitas in his opening invocation. Finally, Garvey stood. He removed a scented handkerchief from his breast pocket, cupped it over his nose and inhaled (a ritual he now performed before major speeches). At length he hushed the audience. 'I have in my hand two telegrams,' he bellowed. The first from Louis Michael, a prominent Zionist in California, congratulated the movement and drew parallels with the Zionist cause. 'I join heartily and unflinchingly in your historical movement for the reclamation of Africa,' Michael wrote. 'There is no justice and no peace in this world until the Jew and the Negro both control side by side Palestine and Africa.' Pushing on through the rising applause, Garvey proceeded to read out the other telegram that *he* had sent to the Irish Republican leader, Eamon de Valera: 'We believe Ireland should be free even as Africa shall be free for the Negroes of the world.' The crowd roared its approval – Garvey had been saying much the same with uninterrupted vigour for the last year, but in August 1920 it echoed with even greater resonance.

'We are assembled here tonight as the descendants of a suffering people and we are determined to suffer no longer,' Garvey trembled. His powerful voice called out and the people responded with 'amen's and 'praise the Lord's. 'Wheresoever I go, whether it is England, France or Germany, I am told, "This is a white man's country." Wheresoever I travel throughout the United States of America, I am made to understand that I am a "nigger". If the Englishman claims England as his native habitat, and the Frenchman claims France, the time has come for 400 million Negroes to claim Africa as their native land.' And on now through the great thunderclap of tears, screams and applause, Garvey asked, 'If you believe that the Negro should have a place in the sun; if you believe that Africa should be one vast empire, controlled by the Negro, then arise.' The gigantic assembly rose and sang the National Anthem of the UNIA. They had no trouble singing in unison; after all the crowd was mostly made up of members of UNIA branches that had been established throughout the USA, Sub-Saharan Africa, Central America and the Caribbean. Marcus Garvey's determination to convey the impression of a global conference meant that occasionally long-term residents of New York found themselves corralled into representative roles other than their Harlem addresses would suggest. Hubert Harrison recorded the 'opening fanfaronade' in his diary and noted wryly that 'Garvey insisted on recognising me when I rose to speak as 'the gentleman from the Virgin Islands' – which sent no delegates, although Virgin Islanders among the Liberty Hall entourage had brought a banner and marched behind it in the parade.'[6] For the most part though, there was no reason for exaggeration or marshalling of the facts: official estimates were of a crowd of up to 25,000 inside the Garden.

Though the name 'Marcus Garvey' had not yet penetrated the African continent in any significant way, by the conference's end, largely through its worldwide newspaper coverage (including the *Negro World*), the UNIA's stock would begin to rise throughout Sub-Saharan Africa. Such that in less than a year, Belgian officials would be expressing disquiet about unrest among American Negroes in Belgian Congo and would launch an investigation to 'discover how the *Negro World* found its way into our colony and possibly to look for the troublemaking agents whose influence might spread from this country throughout Africa'.[7]

Dotted around the enormous auditorium of Madison Square Garden, in ones and twos, a small number of sceptics remained firmly planted in their seats as Garvey towered above them on the podium. Despite his disavowal of the movement, W. E. B. Du Bois is said to have snuck in at the back. The *Negro World*'s new editor, William Ferris, claimed to have spotted the familiar noble head of the patrician leader amongst the assembled crowds.[8] His curiosity had been sufficiently aroused to include a questionnaire along with his rejection of Garvey's recent offer. The full name of the organisation, number of members, kinds of property held, and other seemingly candid questions were requested simply so that readers might glean something of Garvey's life and organisation from an article Du Bois intended to write in the *Crisis*.

Garvey had, quite rightly, considered the request anything but guile-
less and had refrained from answering.

Du Bois had kept his distance and arrived at a policy of wilful
ignorance. He now set himself the task of discovering all there was
to know about the Garvey Movement. Infiltration was, of course, out
of the question. Instead he'd solicited details (with the offer to pay)
from a range of organisations including the US Shipping board, Lloyd's
Register and educated Jamaican correspondents to help him get a fix
on his formidable adversary. The material they provided might, in the
short term, seem to complicate the puzzle of Marcus Garvey but, in
any case, inside information was no guarantee of greater compre-
hension. Two BOI agents mingled with the adoring masses. Both
Agents 800 and P-138 remained bewildered by Garvey's success.
Another agent, WW, who'd earlier claimed to be able to discern a
West Indian from an African-American just from their features, now
wasn't so sure in his conviction of it being a largely Caribbean organisation. And bizarrely, 'So far as I can see,' wrote P-138, 'the movement
has ceased to be simply a nationalistic movement but among the
followers it is like a religion.'[9] As far as one delegate, Reverend Brooks,
was concerned there were but two great things in his life: two Gs.
There was God and following close behind there was Garvey.[10] This
adoration had a particularly Caribbean essence; the yearning for black
success. Growing up in Trinidad a generation later, the writer V. S.
Naipaul observed how the first black leaders answered a need that
almost seemed visceral. 'In colonial days in the British West Indies
the black people had no heroes,' wrote Naipaul, 'for the early leaders
who were their very own, West Indian blacks had more than adulation. They wished their leaders (who had started as poor as everybody
else) to be rich (by whatever means) and powerful and glorious . . .
The leader lived (or lived it up) on behalf of his people; and the people
lived through their leader.'[11] The BOI agents witnessed how Garvey
had become a vessel for the emotional needs of the people, but they
didn't understand what was going on. The attraction of Marcus Garvey
seemed beyond reason.

Closer scrutiny of the president-general's personal life yielded more
confident interpretations. Mrs Garvey was nowhere to be seen. 'On
leaving the hall,' P-138 reported, 'Mr Garvey was accompanied by
his girl [Amy Jacques], known as his secretary, without whom he
never walks.' Other agents went further in their conjecture, reporting

rumours of improper relations between Garvey and his secretary. Allegedly on some trips made from Philadelphia to New York, they'd both travelled in a Pullman sleeper. The source of the rumours was the disgraced former official of the Black Star Line, Edward Smith-Green, whose own confidential informant was Amy Ashwood.[12] But none of the agents questioned the motives of a man smarting from the humiliation of his recent dismissal. Rather, they licked their lips over the details that would surely emerge from a more thorough investigation. If true, in travelling across state borders with a woman (who was not his wife), Marcus Garvey might well have violated the Mann White-Slave Traffic Act. That legislation was originally designed to impede prostitution; to prosecute men who transported women and girls across state lines for immoral purposes. It had been on the statute books for ten years and rarely enforced except in a few celebrity cases; the irreverent black heavyweight boxing champion, Jack Johnson, had been the first to be prosecuted for sending his future wife, Belle Schreiber (then a prostitute), a railroad ticket from Pittsburgh to Chicago. Though the allegation against Garvey was little more than spurious hearsay, over the next few months BOI agents were encouraged to elicit whatever information they could to justify a prosecution.

August proved a fallow period for the BOI snoops. Marcus Garvey hardly ventured outside Harlem. When he wasn't presiding over the conference, the UNIA leader was answering a stream of journalistic bids for interviews. With the spectacular parade and gathering in Madison Square Garden, the mainstream press had woken up to Garvey's rich potential for dramatic copy – much of it gently mocking. The *Literary Digest*'s headline on 4 September, 'The Purple-robed Champion of "Africa for Africans"', was fairly typical. Ironically, the sharpest criticism came from within his own camp from the pen of the *Negro World*'s literary editor, Hubert Harrison. The Black Socrates who had given Garvey his entrée to the masses back in 1917 had stood to one side and watched the movement take-off from the runway he had inadvertently provided. Claude McKay was amongst those artists and intellectuals who enjoyed Hubert Harrison's company. He wrote that when Harrison laughed 'he exploded in his large sugary black African way, which sounded like the rustling of dry bamboo leaves agitated by the wind.'[13] Hubert Harrison bumped into his former protégé just before Garvey's wedding in December: 'After a hearty handshake, [he] told me that he had been looking for me for several

weeks . . . he made me the offer of the principalship of the new college
which he had projected as one of the main institutions of the UNIA.
His office was a curious shambles. The work of the UNIA, of the
Black Star Line and of the newspaper, were all jumbled together in
one room. We went out onto the landing. There it turned out he
wanted to associate me with Professor Ferris in editing the paper and
later to assume headship of the college when it was organised.'[14]
Harrison had gone to work on the paper and stripped it of 'all the
wasteful glory'. He carefully 'tethered the literary effusions in which
Ferris and his friends were prolific', and cut right back on the endless
editorials. There was not much that could be done with the chief's
lugubrious weekly missives which went in unchallenged. Nonetheless,
everyone was pleased with the results, including the readers whose
numbers swelled to 50,000 per week. Harrison was sufficiently content
to add his initials to his contributions. His regular income of $30 per
week was enough to assuage his wife's 'termagant temper'. After nine
months of Harrison's diligent and effective stewardship, old resentments were beginning to re-emerge as Harrison believed himself
drowning in the 'insane collection of bombastic rantings . . . delivered
by pin-headed preachers and other ignorant howlers [in Liberty Hall]'.
By the opening of the convention in August Harrison had become a
hostile witness to the goings-on in Garvey's organisation. 'The man
has a perfect mania for flamboyant publicity. And this, I think, will
wind a rope around his neck later.'[15] Such was his assessment but,
luckily for Garvey, the editor of the Negro World considered it prudent,
at this time, to confine his views to his diary.

As the convention unfolded over the month, the playwright Eugene
O'Neill was putting the finishing touches to Emperor Jones – billed
as a drama depicting the rise of a black man 'from stowaway to
Emperor in two years'. The protagonist, Brutus Jones, is a successful
faker lording it over a group of his people in the style of an emperor.
He is only able to do so because his people are 'a mass of Negroes
in a primitive state of intellect'. Harrison viewed the play as a fine
picture of the Garvey Movement and believed it held the ashes of a
prophecy. Brutus Jones is 'an inflated mountebank with a ballast of
shrewd'. If Harrison was thinking more of Garvey when he penned
those words, it was a long way from their optimistic reunion nine
months before.

Harrison's previous magnanimity towards Garvey seems to have deserted him at this point – at least in private. Like so many talented people who flirted with the movement, what ultimately seemed to stick in his craw was the fact that the fates had bequeathed this wonderful opportunity and adoration to Garvey when there were others, less colourful but perhaps more deserving of the honours – such as Hubert Henry Harrison.

Such sentiments, though veiled, seemed to be at the back of the *Crusader* magazine's approach to the convention. The *Crusader*'s incendiary journalism was the brainchild of the talented journalist (and by 1919, committed Marxist) Cyril Valentine Briggs. He'd sounded the chords of his leftward leaning earlier that year when the magazine posted an advert announcing the formation of a Communistic semi-secret society. There were no dues or fees to enlist in the African Blood Brotherhood, but there was one strict require-ment: 'Those only need apply who are willing to go to the limit.' The satisfaction of taking a stance of uncompromising militancy paled when the Brotherhood proved too successful in its quest for exclu-sivity: too few candidates, it seemed, had sufficient daring to volunteer. From its inception in 1918, the *Crusader* had made overtures towards the UNIA. First published by the Hamitic League of the World, an outfit with a pristine racial orientation, the *Crusader* was in sympathy with the broad aims of the Garvey Movement and admiring of its popularity.

Cyril Briggs also envied Garvey's commanding voice. But for his stutter, Briggs might have made a great orator; he was passionate in his commitment to the race, clear-eyed, persuasive and principled (he'd resigned from a well-paid post on the *New York Amsterdam News* when his anti-establishment editorials were censored by the propri-etor). Subtle subversion was his literary forte. He was born in the British Leeward Island of Nevis, in the same year as Garvey, yet he adopted a headmasterly approach to the UNIA leader, upbraiding him for occasionally going awry and squandering his talent. A few blem-ishes on his report card but otherwise Garvey showed great promise, especially with his excitedly anticipated all-Negro Harlem conference. A *Crusader* article which previewed that event under the caption 'A Paramount Chief for the Negro Race' so pleased Garvey with its 'most intelligent explanation of the real purpose of our Convention', that he commended it to readers of the *Negro World*. It appeared to Briggs though that Marcus Garvey had paid sole attention to the headline, for a closer reading of the text revealed its author's anxiety over the conference's presumption in electing high officials for a future African empire, to be drawn inevitably from the ranks of the UNIA. As a friend, the *Crusader* gently chastised Garvey for his oversight; he surely recognised the wisdom, if not necessity, of 'a public invitation extended to all Negro bodies'? That was the *Crusader*'s view in April. By July (on the eve of the conference) the magazine was raising its voice. Whilst it praised the UNIA leader for heeding its advice and at last extending an 'open invitation', its editor was absolutely dismayed by the suggestion that only UNIA delegates would be allowed to vote for the candidate who 'will occupy the place of world leader of all Negroes'. Briggs and the *Crusader* were under no illusions as to who was earmarked for the role. They feared that the rapture of his audience was beginning to intoxicate the UNIA leader. 'Our advice is to take the race and his associates more into his confidence as befits a democratic era. His mind had been imperialistic and arbitrary in the past.'[16] Even if Marcus Garvey had been inclined to listen, he would have struggled to hear that whisper urging humility amidst the din of drum rolls and hosannas that swelled around him in the headlong march towards Madison Square Garden. Disillusioned, the *Crusader* concluded that 'thus does a noble concept suffer from selfishness and smallness of mind', thereby spoiling what should be 'the greatest event in modern Negro history'. Hubert Harrison put it more tersely when he wrote towards the conclusion of the convention, 'Thus ends the most colossal joke in Negrodom, engineered and staged by its chief mountebank.'[17]

British readers were apprised of the scale of Garvey's ambitions for the first time in 1920 when the *Daily Telegraph*'s correspondent wrote of the goings-on at Madison Square Garden. Contrary to Du Bois's estimate of colonial wrath, the *Telegraph*'s man was more amused than alarmed by what he found. The smirking newshound lampooned the 'modest aims' of the convention that could only be satiated 'if all the white nations with colonial possessions in Africa [would] kindly clear out of the continent'. The logic which now said the time was ripe for Ethiopia for the Ethiopians was preposterous because it was undeniably the case that 'the Negro race, with its many amiable qualities and fine physique, has never proved capable of self-dependence and self-government, except in the primitive tribal form'. The *Telegraph* also revelled in pointing out to its readers what it saw as Garvey's laughable revisionism of the Negro's place in civilisation: 'History has never been able to find a time,' the paper loftily proclaimed, 'when the Negroid races were the real masters of Africa, unless it was in the Palaeolithic age'.

The *Daily Telegraph*'s correspondent didn't envisage a return to the Palaeolithic age, though without Europe's tutelage and protective civilisation the Negro race would succumb to the most base and aggressive stocks of the Bantu and Fulani, and go back to the bush.[18]

The benefits of the British civilising influence were keenly felt in the bosom of Samuel Duncan. Garvey's former ally had been bitterly brooding in his impoverished camp (the West Indian Protective Society of Africa) whilst the ranks of the Garvey Movement swelled. Duncan was not generally disposed towards generosity. He did not consider Garvey harmless, nor was he inclined to treat the convention in the light of a joke. Earlier in the year, Duncan had worked himself up into such a frenzy that he'd fired off a letter to the British Secretary of State for the Colonies. In it he warned Earl Curzon of Kedleston and His Majesty of the dangerous propaganda peddled by the UNIA which if 'not effectively checked by proper official action . . . will stealthily work among the natives and stir up strife and discontent among them'. In particular, Duncan hinted that a recent violent strike in Trinidad among the Workingmen's Association and the subsequent disruption of colonial rule on the island could be traced back to UNIA involvement. Duncan's message, stated plainly, was that Garvey's ideas were souring the good work of 'those of us who are endeavouring by every lawful and legitimate means to bring the two races together'. He ended his letter with a call for the governors on the British-ruled islands to 'take energetic action to suppress this pernicious foreign agitation'.[19]

When news of Duncan's treachery was leaked to Garvey, he reacted furiously and immediately sent out circulars to a number of Caribbean governors designed to limit the damage of a former friend whose poisonous pen was wielded through 'jealousy of [my] success'. It's unlikely that Duncan's puerile missive achieved much more than antagonising Garvey. Embassy officials who sat in on some of the meetings of Duncan's organisation took the view that he himself 'appears to be something of an agitator' and that as far as his complaints went 'it is a case of the pot and kettle as between the two Societies'.[20] In any event, Duncan was advocating a policy that the British had already largely enforced. A report from the British Cabinet Office on 10 November cited the disturbing propaganda of the *Negro World* and its editor who had proclaimed that '400 million black men are beginning to sharpen their swords for the war of the races'.[21] Copies of the *Negro World* had already been seized in British Guiana and Honduras. In Jamaica, the Postmaster had instructed that copies be opened and retained; legislation had been tabled in the Windward Islands for executive powers to exclude the weekly paper; the St Vincent Government *Gazette* reported (in October 1919) that any person who knowingly brought into the colony any copy of the *Negro World* could, on conviction, serve a prison term (possibly with hard labour) of six months'[22]; both Antigua and Dominica had recently passed decrees against seditious publications like the *Negro World*; and Trinidad was soon to pass amendments that would prohibit its importation.

Negro World circulation was also being disrupted in Panama and Costa Rica, where agents for the paper complained 5,000 copies were seized on orders from the Governor, and, insultingly, were then being sold on to stall owners for use as wrapping paper at 40 cents per pound. Far more sinister than official harassment by Governors in Central America and the British censors' response was the recommendation by one of the BOI infiltrators that the agency compile a list of all the agents and subscribers to the *Negro World*. Agent 800, who was now working in reception at UNIA headquarters, was pleased to be able to post the paper's mailing list to his superior: 'Most of these people are more or less radical and I thought it would be best to have their names and addresses in case anything may happen in their towns or cities.'

As yet there were no moves by the state against Garvey. The BOI's J. Edgar Hoover, his appetite whetted by suggestions of violation of the Mann White Slave Act, merely advised that agents continue their investigations 'but that no definite action should be taken towards the prosecution of Garvey at this time until all evidence is collected'.[23]

A more immediate threat came from the courts. Garvey's trial for criminal libel against the District Attorney, Kilroe, and the two former UNIA colleagues, Warner and Grey, whom he'd libelled as crooks, was heard in the middle of the UNIA convention. P-138 warned his handlers that thousands of Garvey's followers would descend on the court-house and were sure 'to start trouble so as to make Garvey a martyr', and that he had heard many alarming threats from the crowd to kill the traitors Warner and Grey. Tempers were running high but on the day, a public apology and the offer of a printed retraction proved acceptable to Kilroe and the court case was concluded. A subsequent civil suit from Warner was settled out of court for a modest $200. Garvey's contrition was not interpreted by his supporters as a defeat, rather the opposite. 'His followers were very jubilant and termed it a victory over the District Attorney and the law,' reported the agent, and conversely Garvey was now 'held in higher esteem than ever before'. Garvey wisely did not crow over the decision. The convention had stalled in his absence, showing up the fact that no important decisions could be made without guidance from its spiritual leader. Garvey possessed the supreme confidence and certainty that is the preserve of genius; and it was one of his many paradoxes that whilst he inspired those around him with 'new thoughts', his domination of the organisation robbed even the most able colleagues of initiative.

In the first week of the convention, fifteen minutes were given over for individual delegates to air the particular complaints of their representative group. By the end of the week, it was hoped that 'every Negro [would] understand the universal situation of the race'. At the back of that desire was the question of representation and the presumption that the delegates represented anybody (especially in Africa) other than themselves. Garvey would argue that his convention with 25,000 attending was far more representative than the 57 delegates of African descent who would be invited to Du Bois's Pan-African Congress in European capitals the following year. The need for a collective African voice (at home and abroad) was beyond dispute. Only then might they raise their voices in such a powerful and disturbing way that they would be heard by the colonial masters of Africa and the Caribbean, and their equivalents in Washington. The founder of the Society of Peoples of African Origin, J. Eldred Taylor, recognised as much when, in the pages of the West Africa Mail and Trade Gazette, he reflected tartly on the failure of African leadership: 'What have we done to merit recognition? . . . Here and there the voice of a leader has sounded in South Africa, in the West Indies, in West Africa, but we ought to follow the example of our people in America (not Garvey's group) who have for years been toiling and agitating . . . to secure the redress of grievances and the adjustments of wrongs.'[24]

On the question of the value of the UNIA many delegates at the

August Convention would have parted company with Taylor but there were also conflicting accounts of the benefits of belonging to the UNIA. In Guatemala, a UNIA-sponsored strike amongst United Fruit Company workers had led to the company capitulating to their demands to a 100 per cent increase on their $1.50 per day wages. However, in Panama, striking labourers on the canal had been greeted by soldiers with fixed bayonets and ousted from their homes, and were now stuck. 'You cannot get a boat to leave there,' complained the delegate. 'If you go to the United Fruit Company and ask for passage, they say, "No, we have no passage for you; wait for the Black Star Line."'[25] The *Yarmouth* had indeed come to the rescue on that occasion. The delegate's tale had also served to emphasise the dependency of a people, especially an island people, who might have to wait for months for one of the major shipping companies to dock at local ports. Furthermore, passage on the steamships was so expensive that it acted as an impediment to travel, even between islands that were only tens of miles away.

The first days of the conference confirmed how such constraints had isolated black people from each other, such that there was little commonality of feeling, and debunked the myth, for example, that Caribbean people were a homogenous group: the man from Kingston in Jamaica knew about as much of conditions in St George's, Grenada as did the migrant from Memphis, Tennessee. The UNIA forum would effect a change in their relations; delegates would come to recognise themselves in one another. And it was from the soundings of their collective grievances that Garvey would begin to frame a Declaration of Rights for the Negro people of the world. Conceived as a bill of inalienable rights, modelled on the United States constitution, it would put right the wrongs of 300 years – all approved and signed off in less than a month.

All through August urgent discussions swirled around Liberty Hall, throughout the day and long into the night. In between the sessions, the UNIA band struck up with mood-mellowing numbers that offered some relief from the intense debates. Garvey allowed himself little time to pursue interests outside the event, other than perhaps reading in the specially upholstered chair that grateful members had presented to him. 'He had no recreation, as it was dangerous to go to theatres,' Amy Jacques recalled. There were numerous rumours of what seemed like credible threats to abduct Garvey. The theatre was ruled out of bounds, in any event, for the UNIA leader because of the kind of shows that were on offer in Harlem. As pointed out by Hubert Harrison, the *Negro World*'s chief critic, even at the Lafayette theatre the sensitive punter would struggle to find a show that 'pleases without dirt and tickles, without the usual contemptible "niggerisms" which so many of our actors insistently obtrude even into a Broadway show'.[26] 1921, though, marked a turning point in the history of black theatre in New York with the opening of a novelty revue show, *Shuffle Along*. Not only did that show make a star of the singing and dancing comedienne, Florence Mills; but *Shuffle Along* boasted a cast that included the then unknown performers Josephine Baker and Paul Robeson. It heralded a great outpouring of black artistic talent that came to be labelled the Harlem Renaissance. Black performers, writers and visual artists headed for Harlem, and white cultural tourists followed hard on their tails – not just in search of illicit Prohibition-busting entertainment. Now, as well as the unedifying but good-time swinging hi-de-ho cabarets, audiences might savour the energy, exuberance and unrivalled talent of performers such as Florence Mills, Bessie Smith and Ethel Walters who teetered on the edge of being risqué but were never vulgar; and theatres, too, opened their doors to a crop of dramatists, singers, songwriters and composers who would eventually count Amy Ashwood amongst their number. In the years after her expulsion from the UNIA, as well as taking an active role in Pan-African movements, Amy Ashwood transformed herself into a lyricist and musical director of shows like *Brown Sugar* and *Hey Hey*, produced, at the Lafayette theatre, in collaboration with her business partner and chaperone, the Calypsonian musician, Sam Manning.

Even though there was scant possibility of bumping into Amy Ashwood at this stage of her musical career, Marcus Garvey absented himself from public performances other than his own. One relaxing hobby that he enjoyed with Amy Jacques was the amateur collector's search for fine pottery. His idea of relaxation was for him and his secretary (accompanied by his secret security shadows) to wander round antique shops and flea markets purchasing old ceramics. 'When he brought them home,' Jacques wrote admiringly, 'he would spend time and patience placing them in the right setting, colour scheme and the most effective lighting . . . He enjoyed sitting in an easy chair and contemplating the beauty of the setting he had created, or the exquisite workmanship of a Satsuma piece from Japan, a Delft vase

from Holland, or the delicacy of an eggshell goblet.'[27] Garvey started
to build up a collection of antique vases and other objets d'art that
gradually took over his home on 129th Street. A *New York Herald*
reporter noted hundreds of vases 'in his luxuriously furnished apartment. Large palm plants were all about the room, which was virtually
filled to over-flowing by vases and bric-a-brac of every possible description and period design.'[28]

The journalist from the *Herald* may have intended to mock Garvey's
'court' but the UNIA leader was quietly thrilled by the portrayal.
Starting from a standpoint of assumed inferiority, Marcus Garvey had
promised (in the build-up to the convention) that the events of August
would reveal to the world the true face of the race's leaders – the 'big
Negroes', who would be honoured for their services to the race. Du
Bois might recoil at the idea of a black leader prancing down main
street in a gauche outfit, but Garvey would argue that Du Bois was
the kind of 'lost' figure whose sense of worth was only given validity
once it was bestowed by the white man. In 1919 Du Bois shared with
readers of *Crisis* a Negro triumph in Paris. 'My eyes have seen and
they were filled with tears. The mighty audience filled the Trocadero,
and in the centre of the stage stood a black man, lithe, tall and
straight; on his breast were orders (crimson badge of the Legion) . . .
A general of France stepped forward, touched him on either shoulder
with his naked sword and said, "I nominate you Bkhone Diop, cheva-
lier of the Legion of Honour." The great audience arose and roared.'
So Du Bois could write frothily with moist eyes about the honouring
of a black soldier by the French, but Garvey, embracing similar ideas
of dignity, honour and recognition was somehow distasteful. Marcus
Garvey saw himself as a model for a whole group of despised people
who aspired to a greater idea of themselves; dressed in his Victorian
military regalia he was the embodiment of that idea. His supporters
luxuriated in his success and took vicarious pleasure in it. Garvey's
transformation, on another level, was a Negro version of the American
Dream that Ralph Ellison was to capture in *Invisible Man*: 'You could
actually make yourself anew . . . All boundaries down, freedom was
not only the recognition of necessity, it was the recognition of possibility.' Garvey made things possible and the people responded in kind.
There was no tradition in their culture that black people could return
to, no chevaliers of the Legion of Honour, no Victoria Crosses. Garvey
was working in the dark and his imagination led him to established

models; he borrowed from royal Anglo-Saxon pageantry, from the Prince Hall freemasons and from Caribbean carnival, and he fashioned something new. The newspapers might scoff at their efforts as a risible circus show or pathetic imitation but amid all the pomp and ceremony the convention was underpinned by serious intent. As far as Garvey and his delegates were concerned, they were participating in a parliament of Negroes.

If the UNIA president was guilty of making too much of their equal status, defining their worth by a white man's yardstick, then this was largely explained by the great weight of negativity saddled to the black man. Even as late as 1920, mainstream American publishers such as William Randolph Hearst could make reference to black people as the missing evolutionary link between man and ape without fear of censure. As the conference entered its second week and the framers of the Declaration of Rights sharpened their thoughts for the task ahead, Marcus Garvey couldn't resist taking a swipe at the dilettante Social Darwinists in the press. 'The newspapers have been speculating. Hearst a few days ago told us that [the pugilist] Jack Johnson, being a Negro, was only a few degrees removed from the gorilla . . . [But] apes never wrote books. Apes never wrote a bill of rights.'

But who should be the authors of the Declaration of Rights and what of the wording? The wrangling over the terms began straight away. The committee comprised a majority of UNIA delegates and a handful of independent associates including the radical young editor of the *Messenger*, A. Philip Randolph, and the 'Black Socrates', Hubert Harrison. Since his appointment as associate editor, Hubert Harrison had been the writer most responsible for injecting pith and pungent prose into the columns of the *Negro World*. He now attempted the same at the convention: to breathe fire into the resolutions and to stiffen the backbone of the Bill of Rights, or as agent P-138 put it, 'Harrison insisted that the majority of the bills were not strong and outspoken enough; the white man must be denounced in the strongest language in the Bill of Rights. On his suggestion, a number of them were sent back to the framers (he offering his help), to put the necessary "kick" in them.' Hubert Harrison's militant position was the same as the one he'd been advocating for years, that 'we cannot abdicate our right to shape more radical policies for ourselves'.[29] Hubert Harrison may have provided much of the intellectual rigour at the heart of the conference but he was all too aware of the limits of his influence over Garvey. Harrison wrote publicly with fiery optimism, but, in his diaries, he chafed at his own impotence and straitened circumstances. He had made a necessary compromise in accepting the $30 weekly salary for the editorship of the *Negro World*. The movement gained much kudos from its association with a man of such gravitas. But ultimately Garvey treated Harrison as a trophy – to be displayed rather than deployed.

'Today, most Negroes in and out of the UNIA . . . assume that the men of abilities like Ferris and myself who are with Mr Garvey, are, somehow, permitted to lend the aid of their knowledge and abilities to the work in hand,' he sighed, 'but it isn't so at all.'[30] The *Negro World* lauded Harrison as 'the most scholarly and learned member of the convention' but as even the BOI informant could see, despite all Garvey's assertions that his will was sublimated to the common purpose of this parliament of Negroes, it was 'Garvey [who] still rule[d] with an iron hand'. By way of example, agent P-138 cited the angry discussions around resolution 47. 'No Negro shall engage himself in battle for an alien race,' the bill declared, 'without first obtaining the consent of the leader of the Negro people of the world, except in a matter of self defence.' Several nervous delegates immediately saw the danger in what was being proposed and opposed it on the grounds that if implemented, its adherents might stand accused of breaking the law. The opponents, led by Reverend McGuire, wanted the wording softened so that instead of 'refusing' Negroes might 'protest' conscription. When reason did not prevail the arguments turned personal. Delegates wanted to know whether Garvey would take a moral stance in any future military conflict, and suffer himself to be jailed just as the Socialist leader, Eugene Debs, had been during the Great War. Debs was still serving a ten-year sentence in the Atlanta Penitentiary for interfering with the draft. Following America's entry into the Great War, he had told a crowd at Canton, Ohio, 'You need at this time especially to know that you are fit for something better than slavery and cannon fodder' – words which could so easily have come from the pen of Marcus Garvey. But the UNIA leader sidestepped the question, and merely reiterated that the Negro's future allegiance was to himself; the time had long passed when the Negro would be prepared to die for the white man. The resolution was adopted, with thirty-six voting in favour and twenty-four against. The final count highlighted the extent to which Garvey had blurred the distinction between delegates and attendees – for propaganda purposes. Though thousands attended the convention, the majority were, of necessity, excluded from the final debates and voting. Eventually, the committee of just over one hundred delegates would actually decide on the Bill of Rights and the subsequent election of officials.[31]

In all, fifty-four resolutions were passed, and the Declaration of Rights, when it came to be written included:

'We deprecate the use of the term "nigger" as applied to Negroes and demand that word "Negro" will be written with a capital "N".'

'We declare the League of Nations null and void as far as the Negro is concerned, in that it seeks to deprive Negroes of their liberty.'

'We strongly condemn the cupidity of those nations of the world who, by open aggression or secret schemes, have seized the territories and inexhaustible natural wealth of Africa, and we place on record our most solemn determination to reclaim the treasures and possession of the vast continent of our forefathers.'

On the evening of Sunday 15 August, the UNIA president general strode onto the platform with the declaration in his hand. The Legion of Honour stood to attention beneath him, holding aloft the flags from each member nation. As Garvey read out article by article of the declaration, 'the audience broke out into uproarious applause, cheering, shouting, whistling and waving handkerchiefs'. And as he reached the conclusion, the audience sprang to its feet and sang most fervently the new anthem of the association, 'Ethiopia, Thou Land of Our Fathers'. Garvey announced the distribution of 100,000 copies of the document which, he stated, 'had received the signatures of every official of the UNIA and of every accredited delegate. Every coloured man, woman and child should possess a copy of it and have it in their homes.'

More than one hundred delegates on the committee had put their signatures to the declaration. They included physicians, Booker T. Washington's former lawyer, pastors, Socialists and Freemasons. But there had been a couple of high-profile abstentions. Hubert Harrison refused to sign because the Bill of Rights wasn't strong enough, and William Ferris declined because the Declaration had gone too far. The declarations were bound to reflect predilections of the committee members. The physicians' concerns, for example, found their way into the body of at least one of the bills.[32]

Few would have denied Garvey's impressive achievement to have marshalled such competing forces so quickly and to have pressed them into agreement. Without Garvey's 'iron hand' there was the real danger that the convention might just have acted as a vent for Negro frustrations, as similar smaller events had done in the past, and led to the interminable meditations on the intractable problems that the Negro faced and the special grievances that were his lot. There were inevitable mumblings and grumblings over the UNIA leader's alleged autocratic stance but Garvey seems to have acted more like an impassioned foreman of the jury pressing for unanimity rather than a majority vote. Along the way he dispatched other more naked challenges to his authority – the most explicit coming from a Nigerian delegate, Prince Madarikan Deniyi. The prince (later denounced as an impostor in the *Negro World*) and the small West African contingent were most incensed by the suggestion that no native-born African should be elected provisional president of the continent. Garvey argued that such an appointment would serve to antagonise the colonial powers who would soon engineer a way of getting rid of him. The African prince smarted at the impertinence, and even more so when, at precisely 1 p.m. on 31 August 1920, Marcus Garvey, in flowing robes of scarlet and a gold-tasselled turban (denoting the insignia of office) stepped onto the podium at Liberty Hall and was greeted with loud cheering on his inauguration into office. There may have been some element of self-aggrandisement in Marcus Garvey donning the robes of emperor but, in a selfless way, the new African president was also advancing himself as a model, one in who, as he rose, black people could take vicarious pleasure. As reported in the *Crisis*, Garvey graciously accepted the signal honour of being provisional president of Africa and the responsibilities that went along with it: 'It is a political job; it is a political calling for me to redeem Africa. It is like asking Napoleon to take the world. He took a certain portion of the world in his time. He failed and died in St Helena. But may I not say that the lessons of Napoleon are but stepping stones by which we shall guide ourselves to African Liberation.'[33] Towards that end Garvey would eventually launch an Africa Redemption Fund. He'd already set his sights on a new headquarters for the UNIA in Monrovia and had even sent out a UNIA official, Elie Garcia, to conduct a report on the country.

On Garvey's enthronement, Prince Deniyi's sarcastic mutterings, hitherto confined to the corridors of Liberty Hall, now exploded into print in a letter to the *New York Tribune*. 'The descendant of slaves like Marcus Garvey' had no mandate from the chiefs or princes of Africa to start an African Redemption Fund. Deniyi raged that 'the so-called Negro Moses is using his fraudulent schemes to catch suckers easily as molasses always catch[es] the flies without any molestation'.[34] Garvey's supporters were becoming increasingly familiar with the angry and intemperate outbursts of former allies directed at their chief. Criticism, from a haloed African delegate, was particularly embarrassing. But if the ire of the new provisional president of Africa was piqued then he resisted the temptation to descend into an undignified squabble. The president left it to others to reveal the real motives actuating such baseless claims. John E. Bruce, the journalist with a sharp eye for hypocrisy, sprang into attack. Bruce reminded readers that Deniyi had appealed to the convention for funds for his passage back to Nigeria to carry out the organisation's work. Prince Deniyi's sincerity was now in doubt for had he not 'appeared in a gorgeous robe and turban . . . resplendent in his African royal pompery and marched with the marchers with heaving breast and the pride born of fiction'. Even so, Deniyi's vituperative criticism was always going to find a willing home at a number of newspapers who considered Garvey's coronation absurd and only made possible through the patronage of gullible fantasists. The African president-in-waiting's claim to 3 million supporters was to be applauded, in the opinion of the sardonic editor of the *Baltimore Observer*, and due recognition given to the labouring ranks from which they were drawn: 'Marcus should have on the official seal of empire, a washtub, a frying pan, a bail hook and a mop.'[35]

The more success Garvey gained, the more opinion of him polarised. The conservative black paper, the *New York Age*, noted for its gentlemanly criticism of the anti-Negro policies of Woodrow Wilson, was not so assiduous in its treatment of the race leader of the hour and the ambitious convention that he'd presided over. Away from the elaborate robes of office and impassioned oratory, the *Age* suspected that the real intention of the mass convention was to be gleaned from the insistent demand for support for the Black Star Line and the various enterprises promoted by the leaders 'which gives the whole meeting the appearance of a gigantic stock jobbing scheme, put forth under the guise of racial improvement'. The *Age*'s editor, Frederick Moore, went even further in an interview with the young historian, Charles

Mowbray White. In an astonishingly unguarded attack Moore predicted that the funds collected by Garvey to fuel his African dream republic would quickly dry up. 'He won't hold that money long enough after landing as the natives will pounce on him and sack his treasury so clean that he won't have enough to finance a meal for himself in a quick lunch counter.'[36] Moore's unfortunate comments highlighted the extent to which the established African-American middle class were perplexed and embarrassed by Garvey. His tightening grip on a constituency of the black labouring and artisan class, which should, by rights, have been their own. To the same historian W. E. B. Du Bois added rather forlornly, 'It may be that Garvey's movement will succeed. I shan't raise a hand to stop it.'[37] To the impartial observer, it looked as if Marcus Garvey had already seized the ground once complacently occupied by Du Bois's Talented Tenth. His critics seemed churlish and to have been subject, of late, to a diet of sour grapes. Even if Du Bois had raised a hand, he would have had little chance of stopping the Garvey juggernaut that was pushing on towards its programme for Africa.

The widespread reporting on the convention had done more than anything else to internationalise the movement, and popularise the idea of Africa as the motherland. Garvey expanded on his doctrine of 'Africa for the Africans, those at home and those abroad'. He was not suggesting for 'all the Negroes of Harlem and the United States to pack up their trunks and leave for Africa'. Marcus Garvey was enough of a realist to recognise that African-Americans would not forgo the comforts and benefits of living in places like New York unless the essentials of life there could be replicated in Africa – until Harlem was, as it were, reproduced in Liberia. There'd be no great black American exodus to Africa until the UNIA had established cities with the equivalent of Lenox and 7th Avenues, apartments and bellhops shouting 'Going up!' Nonetheless, Garvey was arguing for a kind of vocational talented tenth to volunteer as vanguards in the development of Africa. 'The majority of us may remain here,' Garvey argued, 'but we must send our scientists, our mechanics and our artisans and let them build railroads, let them build the great educational and other institutions necessary, and when they are constructed the time will come for the command to be given, "Come home" to Lenox Avenue, to 7th Avenue.'[38]

That vanguard would be travelling home on a Black Star Line ship.

By the end of September the provisional president promised the faithful an ocean liner, to be christened the *Phyllis Wheatley* (after the pioneering black poet), that would run regularly between New York and Monrovia.

The euphoria that followed the closing days of the convention, of the dreams of an African empire, contrasted with the parlous state of the Black Star Line coffers. When Hugh Mulzac presented an invoice for unpaid wages, the vice-president wrote back embarrassingly that the company was 'practically in financial suspense'. Mulzac had been nominated to captain the future SS *Phyllis Wheatley*. The vice-president hoped to send a cheque in the near future but in the meantime, he advised Mulzac to 'make a voyage on somebody [else's] ship and be available in December [for the Black Star Line]'.

As well as meeting the salaries of more than a hundred staff, repaying loans and servicing other debts, much more money would be needed to redeem Africa. Garvey, once again, reached for the successful model of liberty bonds which the USA government had successfully rolled out during the Great War. Black people had shown their patriotism and bought hundreds of thousands of these bonds. Instead of America first, the provisional president would now ask them to put their race first. 'In a world of wolves one should go armed,' argued an editorial in the *Negro World*, 'and one of the most powerful defensive weapons within reach of Negroes is the practice of Race First in all parts of the world.'[39] Adverts would soon appear in the *Negro World* posing the simple question, 'Will Negroes Allow the Whites to Take Africa?' If readers answered, 'No,' then they could demonstrate their conviction by sending in $5 to help the cause of liberty. Their forebears had been violently wrenched from their homes during the 300 years of the Atlantic Slave Trade; further sacrifices would be necessary to reverse that passage and carry Garvey's programme through, perhaps even a blood sacrifice.

Claude McKay believed that Garvey and his inner circle had an idealised view of the continent that could only be maintained in ignorance. 'He talks of Africa as if it were a little island in the Caribbean Sea,' complained McKay. He sensed that Garvey at least understood that Africa was not simply a large homogenous nation struggling for freedom; McKay doubted that the UNIA could be so naive, and yet 'ignoring all geographical and political divisions, he [Garvey] gives his followers the idea that that vast continent of diverse tribes . . . [is]

waiting for the Western Negroes to come and help them drive out the European exploiters'.[40] But that is exactly what Garvey believed. What he planned was a wholesale rewriting of the old order. The Negro race was as scattered as the Germanic people had been before the appearance of Bismarck. And what had it cost to weld the scattered Prussian states into one great German empire? Blood and iron. 'It cost the blood and manhood of the Teutonic race.' And, vowed Garvey, 'As of theirs, so will it be of ours.'[41]

It wasn't Bismarck but Napoleon that Garvey had in mind when it came, at the conclusion of the conference, to electing the men and women who would serve as an African government in exile. They included Reverend James Eason as the leader of the Negroes in America to reside in the 'Black House' in Washington DC; as expected, the Mayor of Monrovia Gabriel Johnson was appointed potentate, leader of the Negro Peoples of the World, and the Reverend George McGuire was named the chaplain general of the UNIA. Their generous salaries of up to $10,000, approved at the convention, reflected their dignity and responsibility – notwithstanding that there was presently no money to honour such a commitment. With munificence worthy of le petit general, Garvey would later shower his loyal inner circle and deserving members of the race with titles like 'Duke of the Nile' and 'Baron of the Zambezi'. The veteran journalist Bruce Grit would be knighted 'Duke of Uganda'.

Marcus Garvey knew that he was a man of history, carrying the weight of black expectation. He had moved at great speed in the course of three years, from a penniless migrant to provisional president of Africa. He had a superabundance of confidence and yet Van der Zee's photographic portraits of him at this time reveal a tender, sad-eyed, vulnerable man looking into a future reflected back into history. There is no consort at his side; the black Napoleon was in the throes of formally severing ties with his former Josephine, Amy Ashwood, and the inconvenience of a less-than-Godly domestic life. She had done much to boost him but had also anchored him, however briefly, to the social structures of marriage. Finally, her demands on him as a man were at odds with the self-sacrificing role he sought to inhabit as a symbol.

Garvey embraced many traditions as he entered the triumphant years ahead. What he lacked after the spectacular August convention was the Roman tradition of the central importance of humility. At the height of empire, when the victorious general was honoured with a procession through Rome, he was required to include a slave in his chariot; when the praise from the adoring masses crested, the slave's job was to whisper in his ear, 'Remember you are only human.' After 31 August 1920, to the hundreds of thousands of admirers who sang his name, the provisional president of Africa was no longer a mere mortal.

LAST STOP LIBERIA

It is certainly better for American Negroes to die of African fever in the efforts to contribute to Africa's development, than to be riddled by the bullets of the white mob who control the local government of the United States.

Orishatuke Faduma (American Negro Academy, 1915)

WHEN the card was posted through her door telling Josie Gatlin to get out of town before 1 June, she knew just what to do: she packed. The 3,000 black residents of Okmulgee, Oklahoma, had received similar threats, and a local white newspaper had published a warning on its front page: the entire 'colored' population was ordered not just out of the town of Okmulgee but out of the state of Oklahoma 'or suffer the consequences'.

A few days later, Josie Gatlin's party of four gathered together their most precious belongings and set off from Oklahoma. Mrs Gatlin was convinced that if she got as far as the water then her great trek would be almost over. By the water she meant Manhattan. Once they reached New York, there was only ever one destination in mind for Josie Gatlin and the members of her impromptu emigration club – the headquarters of the UNIA in Harlem. All she'd need to do thereafter would be to make her way to the pier at 135th Street, and walk up the gangway of the Black Star liner that would carry her to Liberia.

There was one major snag: Garvey's clever propagandists hadn't anticipated their arrival. The BOI informant in their midst reported how perplexed UNIA staff were at the sight of these natives of Oklahoma, laden with trunks and suitcases, besieging their offices. The vanguard from Okmulgee were proof not just of the fear of violence at the hands of a white mob, but also that the Black Star Line propaganda had been successful – perhaps a little too much so, because the UNIA's prospective ocean liner, the SS *Phyllis Wheatley*, was not yet in their possession.[1]

Oklahoma had itself been the centre of an earlier migration of black families from the deeper South, lured by the prospect of open land and affordable homesteads; the discovery of oil had fuelled a mini-boom that peaked at the start of the twentieth century. Thousands of African-American households had followed the unpromisingly named 'trail of tears' and escaped the vagaries of their disenfranchised, dirt-poor existence in Mississippi and Louisiana. Many found the claims made for Oklahoma had been exaggerated and their lot only marginally improved; and further that with black elevation came white resentment. Josie Gatlin got out just before the start of a terrifying riot in Tulsa, Oklahoma just 30 miles from Okmulgee.

It had all begun innocuously. A young black delivery boy, Dick Rowland, had been charged with attempting to assault a seventeen-year-old white elevator girl in the Drexel building. In fact, Rowland had merely tripped on entering the elevator and brushed alongside the girl. He was arrested nonetheless and a wild storm of rumours quickly spread. An angry, armed white mob converged on the jail. They were met by a group of young rifle-wielding black men determined to prevent Rowland from being lynched. Shots were exchanged and the mob chased the black men towards Greenwood, the part of town commonly referred to as 'little Africa'. In the ensuing days, Tulsa erupted in flames of seething hatred, sections of the black population were rounded up and marshalled into makeshift detention centres, scores of people (mostly black) were murdered and the prosperous black quarter (including more than 1,000 properties) burnt to the ground.[2]

Mrs Gatlin was lucky. The *New York Times* carried 'many pitiful tales' of the misery and suffering of the Negro refugees. Some survivors had ventured into the burned district 'to come away with small bandana handkerchief bundles filled with their entire salvage from once excellent homes'.[3]

Josie Gatlin had seen the trouble coming and escaped just in time. She needed no further proof that black people were not wanted, not just in Oklahoma but America. Arriving in Harlem, Mrs Gatlin and her group of refugees had a terrible tale to tell. In the pages of the

Crisis, they poured out their grief: 'The practice of peonage was common, colored farmers were kept always in debt, the planters taking their crops and giving them only a bare subsistence in return.' The fear for one's life was the only additional incentive they needed to quit the territory.[4]

The exodus (proposed by Garvey's movement) to Africa, and Liberia in particular, was an extension of that same impulse for sanctuary; for black people like Josie Gatlin to find their own place in the sun, and to shelter under their own vine and fig tree, as foretold in the Old Testament.

Liberia was a gallant experiment. On the West Coast of Africa, 30 or 40 square kilometres of land bordering Sierra Leone had been sought by the American Colonization Society as the site for the return of free African-Americans. On 5 February 1820, Reverend Daniel Coker, 'a descendant of Africa' set sail on the *Elizabeth* with 90 migrants, Reverend Samuel Bacon and two other agents of the society, with whom Coker professed to be 'fully satisfied, [especially with] their piety'. Indeed, the colonisation society was comprised of humanitarians such as the pious Samuel Bacon but the majority of its members were slave-holders, acting more perhaps out of enlightened self-interest.

The first settlers, carried by the *Elizabeth*, were unsuccessful in their bid for land and took refuge in the British colony of Sierra Leone. It was not until the following year that Reverend Bacon, after patiently negotiating with the native 'children of the forest' and King Jack Ben of Grand Bassa, secured a tract of land around the mouth of Cape Mesurado. That settlement eventually became Monrovia – named in honour of the then United States President, James Monroe.[5] Within the space of a few decades the African-American returnees had extended their control over tens of kilometres of the interior. By 1847 Liberia was recognised as an independent state, presided over by a small self-perpetuating elite. During the latter half of the nineteenth century their numbers were swollen by up to 20,000 pilgrims who made their peace with America and their God and braved the passage to Liberia.

Crossing the Atlantic was always perilous. Of the dozens of voyages, that of the *Azor*, sponsored by Martin Delaney, was perhaps the most memorable. Delaney, a black doctor, galvanised a group of African-American businessmen into forming the Liberian Exodus Joint Steamship Company. Investors ploughed $10,000 into shares to buy the 400-ton vessel which was expected to complete a number of trips to West Africa. The story of the *Azor*'s first (and only) journey was captured movingly in the account of the journalist, A. B. Williams, who accompanied the ship. In the spring of 1878, 206 passengers sailed from Charleston on board the *Azor* sounding the chords to 'The Gospel Ship is Sailin''. The headings from A. B. Williams's letters, charting their journey, make for sobering reading: 'Out on the Deep, Deep Sea; No Medical Stores or Stimulants; The First Death and First Birth; Deception Practised by the Exodus Association; Measles Aboard; A Sudden Death; and Yet Another; Sixth Death; Two More; Ship Fever Certainly Aboard; Water Running Short; More and More Deaths; a Terrible Tornado; Fresh Provisions All Gone.' By the time the *Azor* reached Monrovia more than 20 emigrants had died.[6]

The bravery of these early pioneers to Liberia was matched by the conviction that they were forsaken in America. The committed needed little encouragement. Nonetheless, the Colonisation Society waged a subtly aggressive campaign highlighting the benefits of migration. In 1858, James Hall the Society's agent in Maryland courted the state's free people of colour in a speech which spelt out what all in the audience knew to be true: 'You are disfranchised; you are liable to insult at every step, and even your private dwellings are not sacred from intrusion and violence of lawless ruffianism; legal redress you have none; what greater absurdity could be imagined than for a black man to present himself at polls; although born on the soil you must be considered aliens.' The alternative, as Hall saw it, was to flee to Liberia: 'Go and live, the saviour of yourselves, your families and your people, or stay and enjoy a living death.'

Sixty years on, a living death was all that Josie Gatlin had to look forward to in Oklahoma. Distressed, dejected and demoralised, she had been persuaded by the logic of flight, of lighting out for the African territory. But she travelled under a deception, arguably self-inflicted. Along with her fellow travellers, Mrs Gatlin had convinced herself that transportation to Liberia would be free. After all, the gang of four were paid-up members of the UNIA, and at least one had a handful of shares in the Black Star Line. Their testimonies were reported in the New York papers and evidently prompted closer scrutiny from the BOI whose agents traced the trail of confusion back to the Okmulgee branch of the UNIA. An unidentified African 'with pop eyes, and a double fold to his lip [who] spoke with a brogue' was said to have gone among the UNIA membership propagandising. Investigators found that the 'pop-eyed African' had spread the news that a special train was being sent to take the willing to New York, all for a modest $15; they should be prepared to leave for Liberia soon after. Mrs Gatlin and Co. had packed for the future, pinned their UNIA buttons to their chests and hurried to the station.

Had Marcus Garvey's back-to-Africa idea been a novel venture then perhaps the would-be pilgrims might have been more cautious. But the programme enunciated by the provisional president of Africa was the latest of perhaps half a dozen previous attempts by black people themselves to establish large-scale African-American migration to Liberia – Martin Delaney was just one among them. Oklahomans with reasonable memories could recall the seductive power of Alfred Chief Sam's emigration scheme of 1913. At its peak almost 200 Chief Sam emigration clubs had been formed throughout Oklahoma and the South-west – with shareholders entitled to free transportation to the Gold Coast.[7] That scheme had eventually foundered but not before 60 club members had been successfully transported to the continent.

Marcus Garvey saw himself as following in a tradition that stretched back even further to the indomitable black Quaker, Captain Paul Cuffe. In February 1816, after a terrifying voyage of 56 days during which 'the ship and crew seemingly were in jeopardy', Cuffe sailed into Freetown in the British colony of Sierra Leone. The captain landed 'nine [African-American] families, eighteen heads of families and twenty children [who] were well received both by the Governor and Friendly Society'. At the end of his perilous venture Cuffe was 'not permitted' by pedantic officials, 'to land tobacco, soap, candels nor navel', the trade of which would have gone some way to meet his expenses. But his obvious disappointment was offset by the promising prospects for his passengers whom 'the Governor saith shall be intitled and have grants to them the same quantities of land as the former settlers had'.[8]

A conspicuous 'munificent philanthropy' had also marked the approach of the American Colonization Society less than a decade after Paul Cuffe's trail-blazing: free transportation to Liberia was offered, along with a generous grant. The only significant drawback enumerated by the society was the peculiar African coast fever that every non-native was subject to, and though it was admitted that 'in some cases it proves fatal', the prospective settlers were assured that 'after becoming acclimated, coloured people do not suffer from this disease'.[9]

By the end of the nineteenth century, out of several million black candidates, fewer than 16,000 took up the offer of the American Colonisation Society and boarded ships to Liberia. Whilst this suggests that the society struggled to sell the idea of Africa to America's black population, in practice they had more trouble selling the idea of themselves as 'white friends' of the Negro. Black Americans were sceptical, if not cynical, about the organisation's aims. The arguments over their intentions still had not abated decades after the society had become defunct. The UNIA offices were packed with sceptics – not least among them was Hubert Harrison. The literary editor of the *Negro World* articulated the popularly held view that benign 'white friends' were then, as now, actually malignant and detrimental to Negro advance – whether it be the interracial NAACP of 1921 or its predecessor, the American Colonization Society. 'Wide awake Negroes were able to show that its real purpose was to get rid of free Negroes because, so long as they continued to live here, their freedom was an inducement to the slaves to run away, and their accomplishments demonstrated to all white people that the Negro was capable of a higher human destiny than that of being chattels.'[10]

Black Americans, then, held a concomitant ambivalence towards Africa. After three centuries on the continent, African-Americans considered themselves as American as any other hyphenate – and in many cases (compared to Eastern European migrants) even more so. In the euphoria that followed on from the end of the Civil War and the emancipation of the enslaved, the number of emigrants to Liberia trailed off considerably. The post-bellum years threw up formidable black leaders who saw the chance for black folk to stake their equal claim on America. Henry McNeal Turner, the chaplain of the 1st Regiment, United States Colored Troops, was one such man; he became the kind of national figure for which there had been no precedent. Turner bore striking similarities to Marcus Garvey. The *Crisis* was to write of him: 'Turner was the last of his clan: mighty physically and mentally who started at the bottom and hammered their way to the top by sheer brute strength, they were the spiritual progeny of African chieftains and they built the African church in America.' At the war's end, Reverend Turner criss-crossed the country, imploring the black population to expand on its new-found freedom. In the period known as Reconstruction, Northern administrators travelled to the South and worked with these black leaders to establish an equitable new order. Within a few years, though, that enthusiasm began to wilt under the

strain of a resurgent white oligarchy in the South, and the implemen-
tation of local 'Jim Crow' laws which ushered in legal segregation.
Black euphoria turned to despair and Henry McNeal Turner was one
of a number of senior figures who thought it prudent to reconsider the
merits of a return to Africa. So ardent a proponent did Turner become
that at one stage he accepted the vice-presidency of the American
Colonisation Society. From the 1880s onwards he grew even more strident in his belief in the urgency of exodus: 'There is no manhood future
in the United States for the Negro,' was Turner's prognosis. 'He may
eke out an existence for generations to come, but he can never be a
man – fully symmetrical and undwarfed.' His prescription was repatriation: 'I believe two or three million of us should return to the land
of our ancestors and establish our own nation.' Bishop Turner was
convinced that a debilitating culture of complaint was evolving in black
life. By embracing repatriation blacks would 'cease to be grumblers
and a menace to the white man's country, or the country he claims
and is bound to dominate'.[11] Turner was thrilled on his arrival in
Liberia, 'one of the most paradisaical portions of earth my eyes ever
beheld'.

Turner, like Garvey, would be accused of mistaking propaganda for
reality. Surgeon James Africanus Horton, also a champion of African
sovereignty, did not offer such a misty-eyed view. In January 1866, he
wrote with soldierly precision, 'The entrance to Monrovia reminds one
of the entrance to a purely native town, where the light of civilisation
has never reached . . . it gives the idea of the existence of great inertia.'[12]
The inertia was unforgivable and Horton invoked the spirit of another
champion, Hilary Teage, in reminding Liberians of their special responsibility: 'Upon you . . . depends, in a measure you can hardly conceive,
the future destiny of the race. You are to give the answer whether the
African race is doomed to interminable degradation – a hideous blot
on the fair face of creation, a libel upon the dignity of human nature;
or whether they are capable to take an honourable rank amongst the
great family of nations.'[13]

But who were these migrants? In the first instance they were true
believers. The idea of Liberia consistently fired the imagination of frustrated and ambitious intellectuals. In spite of the advocacy of its white
supporters, the young colony attracted racially alert young men and
women from North America and the Caribbean for whom it offered
exciting possibilities of self-expression (stymied in their place of birth)

and an outlet for their zeal. Early on, Liberia was to benefit from the altruism and pioneering spirit of men such as the Jamaican, John Russworm, and Edward Wilmot Blyden from the Virgin Islands. Russworm, who'd published *Freedom's Journal*, the first black newspaper in America, emigrated to Liberia in 1829 and quickly established the *Liberia Herald*. The young scholar Edward Blyden would eventually assume the editorship of the *Herald* when he arrived in Liberia in the 1850s.

Blyden developed a volatile and complex relationship with his adopted country. In his long life he would serve as a professor of classics at Liberia College, as Liberian Secretary of State and as a constant critic of political corruption, culminating in an unsuccessful presidential bid.[14] Black readers in Africa and throughout the diaspora took vicarious pleasure in the prominence given to Blyden's scholarship – even, or especially, when attached to some disquiet. Reviewing Blyden's *Christianity, Islam and the Negro Race*, John X. Merriman, prime minister of Cape Colony wrote, 'If one thought that the cultivated writer represented any aspirations or ideas of a considerable section of black people, it would give one an uncomfortable feeling, but he is as much a "rara avis" [rarity] in his way as Toussaint L'Ouverture was. Blyden is successful in pointing out the failure of European enterprise to touch more than a fringe of the Continent and showing how climate enforces his demand of "Africa for the Africans".'[15]

In anticipating Garvey, Blyden clearly enunciated the need for Africans at home and abroad to reclaim the continent. And the Jamaican 'Negro of unmixed stock' must have thought himself the subject of Blyden's prophetic black Moses when the Liberian scholar wrote, 'The Negro leader of the exodus, who will succeed, will be a Negro of the Negroes, like Moses was a Hebrew of the Hebrews – even if brought up in Pharaoh's palace – no half-Hebrew and half-Egyptian will do the work.'[16]

Marcus Garvey was inspired by Blyden when he first discovered his work in the reading room of the British Museum in 1913. Now he looked to the nineteenth-century scholar when framing his own ideas, not just of a return to Africa but also of the importance of being alert to enemies within the race. If Blyden was a vindicator of the race, he was also a stern critic of what he saw as the treachery born of miscegenation. Blyden despised the brown Americo-Liberian elite that ran the country and was not averse to spelling out their failings. His tendency towards frankness sometimes got the better of learnt prudence. On one occasion, when commenting in a publication of the undesirability of mixed races, Blyden, who described himself as 'pure Negro', expressed the view that 'decadent mulattoes in important positions accounted in part for Liberia's want of enterprise and progress'. The critical response to his article eschewed journalistic repartee. A mulatto-inspired crowd of 'forty poverty-stricken and ignorant blacks' set upon Blyden, tied a rope around his neck and dragged him through the streets of Monrovia. The scholar's desperate pleas for mercy were drowned out by the baying mob; his life was only spared through the intervention of his highly regarded friend, D. B. Warner. Thereafter, Blyden temporarily fled to neighbouring Sierra Leone. His virulent antipathy towards the light-skinned rulers of Liberia remained with him throughout his life. In old age, as he prepared for the end, he is said to have remarked, 'When I am dead – write nothing on my tombstone but . . . "He hated mulattoes."'[17]

Garvey hadn't yet reached such a conclusion. At the start of 1921, he was busy courting the light-skinned members of the Liberian regime and offering up the tantalising prospect of a loan from the UNIA. The Liberian treasury was empty and the government had been locked into interminable negotiations with the Americans for a $5 million loan. Whilst arms were not yet outstretched towards the alternative offered by Garvey, the early indications were that the authorities in Monrovia were favourably disposed towards the UNIA. The organisation felt enthused enough to beat the drum for Liberia, to chastise Washington over its vacillation and to launch its own drive to collect $2 million towards a Liberian Construction Loan – replacing the earlier Liberian Liberty bonds promotion.

Garvey was now working intensely on three fronts: negotiating to secure the transatlantic ocean liner; securing land for the UNIA repatriation project in Liberia, and the all-consuming fundraising drives. Movement on the latter was slow. As one insider put it, 'the stock-selling scheme seems to have been worked to death'. In addition, the organisation suffered from stock-sales agents who developed a hitherto unknown condition – the 'loss-of-stock-certificate-book' syndrome or the 'loss-of-briefcase-containing-stock-books' syndrome. When not presenting with these unhealthy signs and symptoms, too many agents returned empty-handed with padded expenses for accommodation, road and rail travel that ate into profits.

A range of novel ideas were dreamed up to further boost the UNIA coffers. One of the more colourful was the gold, silver and bronze Crosses of African Redemption. Garvey conceived of these medals as the Negro equivalent to the English Victoria Cross and the German Iron Cross. But they were not the reward for conspicuous courage; rather for extraordinary generosity. For a subscriber to qualify for such an honour he or she would need to pledge a loan: $50 for a Bronze Cross, $100 for a Silver Cross and $500 for a Gold Cross. The casting of these tributes never exceeded their initial run and made little dint in the organisation's financial difficulties. Neither did the more modest subscriptions of $25 which would guarantee lenders that their names and photographs were published in the *Negro World* and *Universal African Volume*. Much, much more money was needed to keep the dream afloat.

Garvey does not seem to have entertained nostalgia for his simpler earlier life. His anxiety over the monetary machinations necessary to manage his increasingly unwieldy organisation was overridden by a titanic confidence that is bestowed on few men, and the recognition that he himself was the movement's greatest asset. With this in mind, he started putting together a plan to embark on yet another round of mass selling of BSL stock: this time he'd have to travel further afield to induce black folk in the untapped regions of Central America and the Caribbean to buy into his dream. For though the Black Star Line expected Negroes the world over to trade with one another, it had a larger purpose than transporting coconuts, whisky and figs: steaming between Africa, America and the Caribbean Garvey's ships also aimed to ferry the likes of Josie Gatlin, daughters and sons of former slaves, back to Mother Africa.

Stock selling was always going to be difficult during the economic depression that followed the post-war boom. That the movement managed to keep the tills ringing during these straitened times was in large part the result of the huge surge of interest that followed the August convention. In 1921 the UNIA secretary general recorded a four-fold increase in the number of divisions, rising from 95 to 418, with a similar number waiting on the New York branch to process their applications for charters.

Nonetheless, the black workforce in America was hit particularly hard by the downturn in the economy. Garvey, much to the growing irritation of his Socialist allies, had very little time for the sentimental notions of class solidarity. He advised members to keep a wary eye out for the competition 'because a Pole is just packing up his baggage in Poland coming over here after that job. An Irish girl is just packing her grip to come for that job you have now; and I am advising you to hold out until we can tell you from the platform of Liberty Hall we have better jobs for you in Liberia.'[18]

It was neither an Irish girl nor a Pole who, after her ship docked at New York and once she'd cleared Ellis Island, made her way uptown to 129th Street in Harlem to enquire about a position as housemaid. Thirty-seven years old and recently married, Indiana Peart had last seen her brother Marcus four years ago. President-General Garvey, the provisional president of Africa, opened the door. He was heavier now; a little thicker around the jaw and waist. His jet-black, ackee eyes still twinkled and a warm easy smile broke out over his face. The familiar, commanding voice and manner was more studied than before; and his slight limp might have gone undetected but for his use of a walking stick.

Back in Jamaica, though unfeignedly proud of him, Indiana had not foreseen that her brother, who then scratched out a living selling greeting and condolence cards, could have been capable of such mighty deeds. The scale of his fame she now saw reflected even in the decoration of his over-elaborate apartment. Indiana was petite and timid, and was dwarfed by the surroundings, the vases that lined all the walls, the large portrait of her brother in the parlour and the polished grand piano. Garvey offered Indiana and her husband, Alfred Uriah Peart, a room in the apartment. He put her in charge of its upkeep on a salary of $35 and found a place for Alfred in the organisation's steam laundry. Garvey's sister and brother-in-law would remain in the apartment at 129th Street for two years. The joy of reunion with her brother soon passed; gradually depression and despondency set in. Amy Jacques, who also had a room, recorded Indiana's dismay at the exacting duties and misery brought upon her brother by his fame. 'She grieved silently. After a time she tried to shut it out of her vision by withdrawing to her room when her brother was home; she persuaded [Alfred] to do the same.'

Marcus Garvey had neither the time nor inclination to reflect on his sister's pitying gaze, trained on him from the shadow of her bedroom door. Very little of Garvey's personal correspondence from this time has been found. The many reported speeches, though, record the degree to which he was consumed by the vision of an African empire. He was a consummate dreamer; and the eternal longing for the African mother-land was at the back of every thought. At the start of 1921 he continued to divine a plan for the continent on a scale that, to many, was unimaginable and unrealisable. Even Du Bois conceded that 'the new cry of Africa for the Africans strikes with a startling surprise upon America's darker millions', and that Garvey was at the head of a move-ment that is 'as yet inchoate and indefinite but tremendously human [and] piteously sincere'.[19] It was not beyond possibility that the dream of Africa might yet be realised, perhaps not on the level he imagined but at least at some lower frequency.

Marcus Garvey was not so naive as to proceed without sounding the depths of the problems the movement might encounter in Liberia – without testing the assurance of the Secretary of State, Edwin Barclay, that Liberia stood ready to 'afford the Association every facility legally possible in effectuating industry, agriculture and business projects'.[20] He had taken the precaution of commissioning a report from the organ-isation's auditor-general, Elie Garcia, months before the August convention. Garcia, a neat and nimble, puckish Haitian, had approached the task with forensic gusto. He had actually produced two reports; one for public consumption which was detailed at the convention, and the other confidential report for the eyes of Garvey only. The public document was a jaunty run through the honours bestowed upon him by enthusiastic audiences. Garcia was amused to report that two dele-gations from rival UNIA branches had greeted him upon arrival in Monrovia with both literally picking up his bags and pulling him in different directions; both beseeching him to endorse the one and repulse the other. Garcia neatly mediated and resolved the problem with some tactic to endorse the one group who had a substantial number of members and to encourage the other – which seemed to exist only on paper – to perhaps consider setting up a branch elsewhere.

When it came to the real purpose of his confidential investigation in Liberia, Garcia was brutally frank about the Americo-Liberians' shortcomings. They were the ruling class and 'although educated, constitute the most despicable element in Liberia . . . To any man who can write and read there is but one goal: a government office, *where he can graft.*' Above all, Garcia deplored the caste system that he observed. The love of liberty may have brought the African-Americans to Liberia but they had not extended those rights to the local indigenous population. The African-Americans had fled a slave system and trans-planted much of the master/servant ethos to their new-found land; the iniquities and inequalities were pronounced. Garcia related an anecdote of a shopping expedition to Monrovia by way of example: 'As I was stepping out of the store my companion [an Americo-Liberian] told me: "Why, I don't suppose you are going to carry this bundle yourself?" "Why not?" said I. "It is a very small parcel." He answered that it was not the custom in Liberia for any gentleman to carry parcels; therefore [defeating] the usefulness of having slaves.' Garcia was also affronted by the obvious large-scale misappropria-tion of funds. Forty years on from James Horton's description, Garcia observed that the infrastructure of the republic was not much changed: 'There is not a mile of road in all Liberia and in Monrovia not a street worthy of the name. Bush grows in front and around the exec-utive mansion. Yet the average Liberian is as proud as a peacock and boasts that [at least] he 'never sang in a cornfield'.

For all of his criticisms, Elie Garcia was optimistic about UNIA involvement. In stating his belief that 'our work is bound to be successful along all lines', he added one caveat – the need for greater diplomacy: 'The article [of the UNIA] Constitution dealing with powers of the Potentate and some references in the *Negro World* in regard to the election of a ruler for all black people have been a troublesome night-mare to them.'

Diplomacy wasn't the provisional president of Africa's strongest card. Neither does discretion appear to have been inserted into the *Negro World*'s style book. Long before any formal contracts with Monrovia had been exchanged the organisation was calling for craftsmen to volun-teer their services for the soon-to-be-established settlement.

'Wanted Immediately,' a UNIA advert blazed across the pages of the *Negro World*, 'Architects and Contracting Builders to go to Liberia. Must be willing to sail between January 25 and February 20, 1921'.

Adverts in the *Negro World* depicted Africa as the land of oppor-tunity. And in truth, Liberia *was* rich in minerals and had vast tracts, millions of acres, of uncultivated fertile land, but it was nearly bank-rupt. Garcia reckoned the Liberians were weighted down by debts of $1,700,000 which they could barely service. The terms of credit, so far proffered by the United States administration, had been too humiliating even for cash-strapped Liberians to accept. Garcia had read the American proposals which he considered 'from beginning to end the most insulting and humiliating document ever presented to a free people'.

Liberia hesitated to ratify the loan agreement with the USA and Garvey saw an opportunity to exploit the stalemate. In his eyes, a UNIA offer 'to help the Government of Liberia out of its economic plights and to raise subscriptions all over the world to help the country to liquidate its debts to foreign countries' would be an irresistible inducement. At first, with Pavlovian expectancy, the Liberian oligarchy (as represented by Gabriel Johnson) quietly salivated at the thought of an alternative source of funds coming its way.[21]

The likelihood of the UNIA deal eventually being realised rested in part on the glad-handling Johnson, Mayor of Monrovia, whom Garvey had in his pocket, or at least on the payroll at $12,000 per year. With Johnson's enthusiastic endorsement, Marcus Garvey sent the fastidious accountant and stenographer Cyril A. Crichlow, along with George Marke, to Monrovia to secure land and property on favourable terms and to put in place the foundations for the imminent recolonisation of Africa.

If all went to plan, Liberia would serve as a vital beachhead from where the UNIA could extend its tentacles over the whole of Africa. Initially a six-man team of commissioners would be sent out to Liberia, including an agriculturist, a building engineer, a surveyor and a chemist. On 18 January 1921, Garvey wrote excitedly to Gabriel Johnson about the practical steps for 'carrying out their construction plan for Liberia'. Johnson, the Supreme Potentate and Crichlow, the Resident Commissar (Garvey excelled in his use of their recently bestowed titles) were to be co-signatories on any large-scale expenditure: when Johnson was unavailable then His Highness the Supreme Deputy Potentate, George Marke, would sign on his behalf.[22]

This business of titles was the cause of some initial anguish. On the voyage over to Liberia, Crichlow took possession of the $2,000 travelling expenses and had to assuage Marke (several ranks his senior) who was affronted at having to travel second class – just like Crichlow. At a reception in honour of Gabriel Johnson, it was made clear that the Liberian authorities were disturbed by their high-faluting, international titles which suggested an authority over the entire Negro race, in excess of the local remit of their hosts. When called upon to make the toast to his uncle-in-law, Gabriel Johnson (the UNIA's supreme potentate), President King pointedly raised a glass 'to the Mayor of Monrovia'.[23]

Marcus Garvey was counting on Mayor Johnson to use his good offices with the president to secure a concession on 1,000 acres of arable land in order that they could 'start immediately planting the earliest crop, so as to be able to take care of the other workmen, and also to enable [the building engineer] Mr Jermott to start putting up buildings to accommodate the men'.[24] Johnson was happy to oblige. He would have Garvey understand, though, that finding property in or around the capital was out of the question. However, he proposed a 'township near Monrovia which may be about 30 or 40 miles away, has some roads, partly built', as the best available solution, and that a cheap workforce should be employed locally rather than sending to the USA for their expensive African-American counterparts. Johnson secured terms on the land, a farm owned by local Liberian Mrs Moort. The crops planted in the land, leased largely at Johnson's say-so, failed to thrive. The UNIA's agriculturist was suspicious, and Crichlow reported his complaints that 'the land is poor and worn-out, and there is a feeling that the property was palmed off on the Association as a personal favour by His Highness to Mrs Moort'.[25]

The immediate strains on the commissioners would soon become apparent. Lines of authority, clear on paper, were not so in practice on the ground in Monrovia. Crichlow, Marke and Gabriel Johnson all thought they were in charge. Crichlow quickly developed distaste for Liberian intrigue and nepotism. He had inadvertently been given a description of it when the commissioners met Edwin Barclay, Liberia's secretary of state. Barclay warned them that Britain and France (with neighbouring colonies of Sierra Leone and Ivory Coast) had already expressed an unhealthy interest in the UNIA's plans beyond Liberia and the bellicose propaganda and talk of 'driving Europe out' of Africa. Barclay advised the UNIA to learn from the Liberian approach, namely that 'it is not always advisable nor politic to openly expose our secret intentions . . . our secret thoughts. That is the way we do . . . or rather don't do in Liberia. We don't tell them what we think; we only tell them what we like them to hear . . . what in fact, they like to hear.' Crichlow, though, had come away with an unsettling thought: if Barclay had articulated Liberia's sly and duplicitous approach to the French and British, why would it not be so for the UNIA?[26]

Setting out his instructions for the mission, Marcus Garvey had encouraged Crichlow to keep a tight grip on expenditure and to ensure that everyone, including the potentate, gave value for money. The UNIA headquarters would cable over the funds for salaries for Crichlow to disburse each month. Marcus Garvey hadn't built in any leeway for the local penchant for graft. The first sign of real trouble came with the appointment of the potentate's son, Hilary Johnson, as a clerk in the office. It was Crichlow's suggestion, calculated as a gesture of good faith to the potentate, and besides he was of 'higher intelligence and ability than the average Liberian young men'. The move soon backfired. The son's work ethic was second-rate: time sheets were an alien concept, and most often he would wander in late in the afternoon and occasionally not at all. Reluctantly Crichlow brought the son's tardiness to the potentate's attention and in doing so, 'committed the unpardonable sin and have been persona non grata ever since with both father and son'. Soon after, Johnson's son was signing correspondence as if he, and not Crichlow, was the resident commissar – an attitude encouraged by the potentate. As Crichlow's perception became more selective, he started to glean the extent to which the potentate himself hardly carried out any duties in support of his $12,000 UNIA salary; instead his energies were given over to a number of money-making schemes that relied on the exploitation of the organisation. One was an 'old leaky bui[l]ding on Broad St, that had funds come as requested, he would have repaired and sold or leased to the Association'. Crichlow seemed at a loss to know what to do other than 'simply allow matters to take their course'. Even after several exhausting months, he was disinclined to break ranks.[27]

Whilst Crichlow agonised over the little progress that was being made and the money squandered, Gabriel Johnson was sending cables to New York for the funds needed for keeping the good work going. On 24 March 1921 Johnson wrote, 'have received favourable new concessions', and added tantalisingly, 'we cannot give you any information by cable or letter. Remit by telegraph immediately $5,000 . . . Complete sawmill equipment needed immediately. Ship by an early steamer, the first if possible.' Without the thousands of dollars asked for, Johnson later warned, work would be compelled to stop.[28]

There was a strong case for monies to be directed to Liberia but the same could be said for the purchase of the next Black Star Line ship, the salaries of the crew of the *Kanawha*, and the maintenance of the headquarters. The organisation was haemorrhaging money.

Notwithstanding the dramas swirling all around him, Marcus Garvey was not averse to even more self-dramatisation. Earlier in the year, he had whispered to a hushed Liberty Hall audience, 'Two weeks from this I shall suddenly disappear from you for six weeks. You won't hear from me during that time, but don't be alarmed because we Negroes will have to adopt the system of underground workings like de Valera and other white leaders.' BOI informants had already passed on the details of the secret manoeuvrings to which he was referring, namely that he was preparing for a fundraising tour of the Caribbean. The amateur sleuth need not rely on subterfuge to come to the same conclusion; all he had to do was pick up a copy of the *Negro World* on 18 January, read the announcement that the Black Star liner *Antonio Maceo* (*Kanawha*) was due to leave New York shortly for Bermuda, Cuba, Haiti, Jamaica and Panama, and make the not unreasonable deduction that one Marcus Garvey might be on board. Sir James Willcocks, the governor-general of Bermuda, certainly thought so. He wrote to the newly appointed British Secretary of State for the Colonies, Winston Churchill, proposing 'to prohibit their landing . . . since the association is openly revolutionary'.[29]

Garvey was determined to embark on the tour despite the protestations of some of his anxious inner circle who feared that once he'd left the shores of the United States the authorities would make it difficult for him to return. Their assumptions were correct; Hoover and the BOI especially anticipated his departure; telephone wires burned, and reams of telegrams were dispatched as speculation mounted that this most unwelcome guest would be sailing from Key West. There was a danger though that Hoover would be disappointed. In the weeks before he hoped to travel, Garvey appeared to do everything in his power to ensure that he was denied a British passport. On the podium at Liberty Hall, he delivered a series of spectacularly anti-British speeches, singling out Winston Churchill as 'the greatest Negro hater in the British Empire' whose appointment was due to his willingness 'to carry out that savagery and brutality among the darker and weaker races of the world through a system of exploitation that will bring bankrupt Britain the solvency she so much desires'.[30] Luckily for Garvey the official who interviewed him for a passport adopted a conciliatory line. Having pointed out 'the benefits which have accrued to the Negro race under British administration', the consul general stamped his passport and waved Garvey on, modestly pleased to have had the good sense to initiate a policy, 'that will eventually have the effect of causing him to be less radical in his attacks on constituted authority'.[31]

On 22 February Marcus Garvey bid farewell to his loyal supporters; they'd be able to follow the dramas of their leader's progress through the Caribbean in the pages of the *Negro World*, and in six weeks he'd return in triumph amongst them. The UNIA leader's mission was clear. The association's fortunes rested on his ability somehow to raise extra funds in the Caribbean and Central America. Once more he'd have to roll out the old Garvey magic and through his powers of oration, rouse and inspire the poor black populations of Kingston, Havana, Colón and Limón to give over their tithes and widows' mites in the hope of restoring the UNIA coffers. As well as Black Star Line stock, he'd be encouraging subscriptions to the Liberian Construction Loan.

Garvey's itinerary had been amended after the delays brought about by yet more repairs to the *Kanawha*'s boilers. The ship still wasn't ready towards the end of February and, as the president of Liberia was due shortly on a state visit, Garvey was tempted to put back his date of departure from 28 February. In the event, financial urgency took precedence. There was also the anxiety on the part of the president's advisers not to reveal his true, amicable feelings towards Garvey and UNIA lest it unsettle his American hosts.

A number of BOI agents were drafted into raising the level of surveillance on Garvey. Hoover alerted the immigration authorities in Florida of the imminent arrival of the notorious Negro agitator 'in order that should [he] actually depart from our midst the Labor Department may have their ports of entry scrutinised for his return'.[32] The immigration officers were far less coy in their response, requesting that Hoover furnish 'whatever facts you may have which might be used as a basis for excluding Garvey should he attempt to again enter the United States'.[33] Marcus Garvey, accompanied by his secretary Amy Jacques and her younger brother Cleveland, duly arrived in Florida, having boarded a train for Key West, and took up berths on the USS *Governor Cobb* which slipped anchor on 28 February bound for Havana. A few days later the USS *Panhandle* pulled into New York harbour with the Liberian president, Charles D. B. King, among its passengers. An overly deferential but low-key delegation from the UNIA hurried to the Waldorf-Astoria Hotel on 7 March 1921 to welcome the president and to wish him success in his negotiations. The *New York Times* seemed as much concerned about President King's elaborate regalia, especially 'his hat, decorated with bird of paradise plumes', as it was about the purpose of his visit. There was little journalistic excitement over the story of a president at the head of a mission still clinging to the belief that it might conclude negotiations begun in 1918 for the $5 million loan.

Also on board the *Panhandle* was Roscoe Mitchell, returning from a six-month survey for the US Shipping Board. As reported in the *New York Times*, Mitchell had bleak news for the Black Star Line and other American-registered steamship corporations. But he reminded those 'who feel doleful over conditions to keep in mind that England has more than 2,000,000 tons of shipping idle at present'. It was of little consolation to the Black Star Line. Marcus Garvey and his board hadn't finished paying for the *Yarmouth* and yet it had probably sailed for the last time; the *Kanawha* looked impressive but it was still being fitted out with expensive repairs; and the directors' board was urgently trying to acquire a much larger vessel to run from America to the West Coast of Africa. The BSL was, in effect, endeavouring to establish a shipping line in an overcrowded market in the midst of a slump in world trade. 'The rates are so low,' said Mitchell, 'that if the ships are operated it would be at a loss, and the British ships do not pay their expenses.'[34] Considering the US Shipping Board had so many unprofitable vessels on its books, it should have proved reasonably straightforward for the Black Star Line to acquire one.

As far back as the convention in August 1920, the Black Star Line had promised its investors a transatlantic vessel that, once purchased, would be rechristened the *Phyllis Wheatley*. By March 1921 there was still no sign of the vessel. The dates announced in the *Negro World* for the launch were constantly being revised. After the disgraced Captain Cockburn's services were dispensed with, the Black Star Line lacked a black entrée into the complicated world of the United States Shipping Board – the regulatory board overseeing all maritime acquisitions and charters. During the Great War America had built and acquired an enormous tonnage of ships. After the war, as part of its reparations, Germany was stripped of its merchant fleet, and the United States, not to be outdone by its European allies, had gained a share of the confiscated vessels. By 1921, America did not know what to do with all the ships it had acquired. As Edward Hurley recalled, 'the war-built ships were "white elephants". We had too many of them. Nobody wanted them.'[35] Bidders were, therefore, in a strong position, but, even after acquiring three previous ships, the board of the Black Star Line were still largely naive in their grasp of the way things worked. Marcus Garvey had delegated Orlando Thompson, in his absence, to oversee any purchase, and Thompson approached the broker Anton Silverstone (who headed his own brokerage firm) to represent the company. His complexion (Silverstone was white) was unfortunate but where ideology rubbed up against practical concerns in UNIA circles, practicality won. There was no alternative; the idea of racial purity would be diluted as and when necessary.

Silverstone's style was breezy and direct – no-nonsense. Serious negotiations began in earnest in March. He first proposed to purchase a ship himself, the *Hong Kheng*, for $200,000 and then sell it on to the BSL, accepting instalments, and netting himself a healthy profit of over 50 per cent. That deal quickly fell through. Over the next few months, in negotiation with the United States Shipping Board, Silverstone made bids for two other ships. At the same time as inviting offers, the board was also considering requests for charters on each of these ships. The US Shipping Board was a vast organisation that was determined to liquidate its $3 billion worth of investments, yet it was prone to procrastination and vacillation. Silverstone would be invited to tender bids that were invariably rejected as too low; increased offers were tentatively accepted and then rejected in favour of the chartering firms whose interest in the ship fluctuated. That opposition would once more withdraw from negotiations, the Black Star Line offer would be approved, and a cheque for the deposit sent, but then further obstacles would drive negotiations into the sands. After several months of Black Star Line offers passing like shuttlecocks between the various departments (Sales/Operation/Construction and Repair) Silverstone rolled up his sleeves and exploded into print. The Black Star Line 'cannot afford to do any more "Pusseyfooting"', he complained to the chairman of the Shipping Board, Albert D. Lasker. 'We have complied with all the requirements but it seems as if I am "bucking-up" against the "color line" or some other "underground" wires.' Silverstone appealed to the fair-minded chairman that, 'this is a business proposition and "parlour-politics" should be cut out'. He was also aware that his client was growing impatient with him. Elie Garcia went to Washington to check on the reliability of Silverstone's version of events. At an emergency meeting a vote of no confidence in the broker was passed but then came the last-minute news that the papers had been signed and the vessel secured. The joyous directors of the Black Star Line paused only briefly to congratulate themselves. Stock-selling circulars were dispatched with photographs of the ship, with the original name, the *Orion*, scratched out and replaced with the *Phyllis Wheatley*. Preparations were quickly made for the *Phyllis Wheatley* to stop at Philadelphia and Norfolk to be shown to the faithful. A number of prominent men of the race were also sent a special invitation to lunch on board the ship on 4 July. A meal would unlock their enthusiasm, suggested Orlando Thompson, and thereafter 'the high standard of the ship cannot fail to impress their minds to our benefit'. Plans were also made for prospective stock-holders to inspect the ship, but at a price: 30,000 tickets would be printed, charging each bearer $1.00 for admission. But the end of June passed without any sighting of the ship; 4 July slipped past also. The registration of the *Phyllis Wheatley* to the Black Star Line was thrown into abeyance as there were still some clauses in the contract that needed to be agreed. The transaction had not gone through. The BSL hierarchy was mightily disappointed but not disheartened. At this stage it was not yet clear that the transaction would never be completed.

Marcus Garvey's fortunes fared much better in the Caribbean. The memories of minor humiliations, of being laughed off the stage, sporting khaki shorts and spouting the King's English to an audience in St Ann's Bay that mocked his pretensions, were, mostly, long behind him. Dressed now in a brown Palm Beach suit and Panama hat, with the insignia of office pinned to his vest, the UNIA president, commander-in-chief of the Universal African Legion, president of the Black Star Line and provisional president of Africa, stepped off the gangway at Kingston, Jamaica, returning to his homeland after an absence of five years. An eager newspaperman from the *Gleaner* hurried aboard the vessel even before it had been made safe. The journalist's respectful account read as if he'd been permanently bowed and on one knee; he assured readers that his first impression was that Mr Garvey had not much changed except in girth. In the nine short days of his visit, Garvey planned to shake up Jamaica with a series of big meetings and concerts, beginning with an appearance at the island's premiere venue, the Ward Theatre. Marcus Garvey declared he had returned with new thoughts that might be alien to the people of Jamaica; he brought with him the spirit of the New Negro manhood movement; and also the end of sycophancy. The thirty-three-year-old also brought with him the news that even the Negro could, and was entitled to, climb the ladder of success. To friends such as Adrian Daley who'd been associated with him from 1914, Garvey had undergone a most remarkable transformation. He appeared an 'invincible democrat' and 'human encyclopaedia'.[36] Daley was brimming with admiration. How else could one consider a man who'd started life with such limited expectations, barely a degree or two above the peasant. Garvey had not accepted his lot in life but he was no fainthearted sympathetic liberal; he was scathing of members of the race who lacked self-worth. 'You Negro women,' he told an audience on the first leg of his Caribbean tour, 'you don't appreciate yourselves; if so you would not be scrubbing the white women's floors.' On another occasion, he bemoaned the fact that 'Negroes are the most lazy, the most careless and indifferent people in the world and it simply sickens one to feel that he is identified with [such] a people.' It was Jamaican indifference, so crushing in its banality, which had caused him to leave. Only once he'd travelled to the United States and made a name for himself had he subsequently been appreciated by his own people. Validation could only be gained beyond the 'Isle of Springs'. Jamaica, he cursed, was the most backward nation on earth. He was not minded to spare anyone's feelings, now that he had temporarily returned, especially the undeserving ruling elite: 'Jamaica, as I can see, is controlled by a few inexperienced "imported strangers", whose positions in Jamaica as officials and heads of departments have come to them as "godsends" ... Through the system of any white being better than a native, these imported gentlemen are continuously being sent out to the colonies,' which are viewed by Britain as 'dumping ground[s]'.[37]

The provisional president of Africa had meant to ride above all the old hurts. Instead he busied himself making new enemies in Jamaica, crossing swords with petty adversaries and settling old scores. Reverend Gordon Somers who reminded him that he'd been slow to expedite a £7.00 bill when last on the island was a 'spineless, cringing hypocrite'. Reverend Ernest Price, who lamented Garvey's failure to start a Tuskegee type institute in Jamaica, was an imported white gentleman 'who would much prefer to see ... Negroes ... taught to plough, hoe, wash plates and clean pots than to have Negroes ... running big steamships across the ocean'.[38] Garvey was able to deflect much of the flak directed at him as the vacuous and sanctimonious rumblings of envious inferiors whose privilege of birth falsely gave them a standing in colonial life of which they were unworthy; they'd never known poverty and never had to leave the island to find their way in the world. The criticism over Garvey's neglect of his father, who'd died the year before, was more difficult to shift. Garvey Senior had spent the last eighteen months in and out of a charitable almshouse that catered for the elderly poor and destitute back in his hometown of St Ann's Bay. To end his days in such a manner in Jamaica was a disgrace, not just on the dying man but on the family that was supposed to care for him. One critic wrote to the *Gleaner* that the elder Garvey had 'languished in [St Ann's] almshouse whilst you [Garvey] were masquerading as "Honourable" in a foreign land'.

With this verbal volley, critics, who up till now had been shelling the outlying forest and missing the citadel, appeared to have found their range. An indignant Garvey was stung into response. 'My father gave me at the age of fifteen the care of my mother and elder sister when he himself was in a position to care for his family. He squandered his money and made ill use of his properties.' The honourable UNIA leader believed himself beyond reproach, for in cabling money for his father's burial, Garvey had done 'more for him than he did for me'. Garvey's old mentor, the printer Alfred 'Cap' Burrowes waded into the debate with a defence of his former apprentice who 'might not have been in the position at some time of his life to support his father', but at least 'the [elder's] death – was not permitted to be that of a pauper'.[39]

But now that the old man was in the ground, other damaging details emerged. Particularly the rumour that when Marcus Garvey returned to Jamaica, and was presented with the outstanding bill for his father's upkeep in the almshouse (£46.00), that he flatly refused to 'pay a farthing as his father had done nothing for him'. The local parish board had decided to close the case but when the authorities in Kingston were alerted it was deemed too good an opportunity to miss. The colonial secretary suggested that 'it should be arranged that he [Garvey] shall be questioned as to the fact [of the rumour] . . . at some public meeting'. The scheme to shame him in public did not succeed. Garvey paid up instantly when served with a warrant.[40]

The arguments between Garvey and his detractors raged back and forth in the letters' pages and editorials of the *Gleaner* over the course of April. The UNIA leader's transformation and return to his homeland was a major story, but it was knocked off the front pages and eclipsed by news of the strange, visionary revivalist preacher with whom Garvey was unflatteringly compared. Alexander Bedward had been seeing visions all of his adult life. Cataracts coated the eyes of the mystical preacher whose popularity had been sparked when he divined the healing powers of a river on the edge of Kingston. Over two decades, thousands of supplicants had sought him out, attending his weekly mass baptisms at the perfectly named Hope River. 'Every consideration for decency was lost,' growled the *Gleaner*, as they waded into the water (some fully naked), into the arms of the preacher – their ecstasy voiced in song:

> Dip dem Bedward dip dem
> Dip dem in the healing stream
> Dip dem sweet but not too deep
> Dip dem fe cure bad feelin'.[41]

Bedward dipped the lame and they threw away their crutches; he dipped the lovesick and their lovers returned; he dipped lepers covered in unsightly sores and they emerged from the water with smooth shiny skin – or so his followers believed. At one meeting, 10,000 sinners and sufferers turned over themselves, and their souls, to Alexander Bedward.

Marcus Garvey's return to Jamaica had coincided with a resurgence of Bedwardism. The prophet (Bedward) had dreamt of a manifestation; he'd foreseen that on Friday 31 December 1920 at 10 o'clock precisely, he would ascend to heaven. On that day, his followers had gathered in his compound to make the ascent with him. They sold their worldly possessions, put on white gowns, climbed to the tops of trees, and at the appointed hour, jumped, fully expecting to fly to heaven. Bedward's vision was not made manifest. 'Bedward Stick to the Earth' scoffed the *Gleaner*. Now, just a few months later, on 28 April 1921, 600 of his followers (undeterred by the previous failure, and some now on crutches) answered his call and marched to Kingston to take part in another manifestation. The authorities were sufficiently alarmed to call out troops of the West India Regiment. Bedward was arrested and put on trial for disturbing the peace. He was acquitted on the grounds of insanity and carted off to Bellvue Asylum (where he would remain until his death nine years later).[42]

As with Bedward, so too with Garvey. When critics chided Garvey with the comparison, they suggested that flying home to Africa on the Black Star Line was as fantastic and fanciful as the idea believed by Bedward's followers that on 31 December they'd be flying home to heaven. But Garvey's dream was not the product of a neuropath's imagination. They may have sent poor Bedward to the asylum, but, Garvey smilingly reassured his followers, 'They'll have a hard time to send me there.' All jesting aside, Marcus Garvey resented the inference that his supporters were somehow being duped or, as Reverend Price maintained, those 'mistaken enough to follow him' were being led 'into a very dirty ditch'.[43]

Marcus Garvey endured the insults, for he remained on the island longer than intended. He had arranged to move on to Panama and Costa Rica but found his plans frustrated by Charles Latham, the American consul in Jamaica. Latham was overly accommodating of Hoover and US immigration officials' desire to thwart Garvey's return to America. Fearing that he might attempt an indirect approach through the back door of the American-controlled zone of the Panama Canal, Latham was instructed to refuse him a visa to the zone as well as to the United States. Pictures of the subject, over the caption 'Hon. Marcus Garvey, DSOE (Distinguished Service Order of Ethiopia)' were circulated to customs services. American ports were alerted to keep a watchful eye out for Garvey amongst immigrants. When Garvey fetched up at the American consulate in Kingston, requesting a visa for Panama, he was informed that an immediate decision could not be made on his application. Subsequent visits were equally frustrating. Though his travelling companions, Amy and Cleveland Jacques, were issued visas, Garvey was not. Garvey's plans were also upset by further delays to the *Kanawha* on which he was expected to travel. No sooner had the repairs to its boilers been completed than the *Kanawha*, pulling out of the harbour, crashed into the government pier in Norfolk, Virginia. The president of the Black Star Line was forced to book a passage on another ship, sailing first to Costa Rica.

After weeks of frustrating setbacks, Garvey's visit to Costa Rica was, from the outset, a spectacular triumph. Thousands of West Indians worked on the banana plantations owned, or controlled, by the mighty United Fruit Company. The UNIA had especially established itself amongst these migrant workers. Press reports in Costa Rica estimated that 'nearly 10,000 people showed up to hear Garvey speak in Limón'. Approaching the port Garvey saw 'miles of cars stretched on the railroad track . . . the people came down from all sections; they hung outside of the coaches at the doors and windows, and they sat on top of the coaches; they did not have enough coaches to bring them down from different parts of the line'. Garvey sparkled in such a wonderful setting and the people were so moved by his oratory and by the carnival atmosphere of the occasion that they showered him with money. At one stage, the local United Fruit Company manager, G. P. Chittenden, reported an amazing spectacle: 'I know that at one meeting two scrap baskets and one suitcase full of United States gold notes were collected [Garvey announced that he would receive nothing but US currency in contributions]; I know that at another meeting he stood beside a pile of gold notes which reached above his knees. It is impossible to estimate the amount collected but it might easily be as much as $50,000, all of which he took away with him in cash.'[44]

Amy Jacques struggled to count whilst her brother, Cleveland, 'was occupied all day and all night writing out shares in the Black Star Line and selling bonds of the Liberian Construction Loan.'[45]

The managers of United Fruit, anxious about the effect Garvey might have on the productivity and compliance of their workforce, took a sophisticated and pragmatic approach to the UNIA leader: they welcomed him as a man they could do business with. 'If you play up to his vanity a little,' wrote Chittenden, 'and talk to him the way you talk to one of your own laborers with whom you are on extra good terms, you will have no trouble with him.'[46] Chittenden was as good as his word. He made an arrangement with Garvey so that the great orator's public talks would not coincide with the precious time set aside for loading the banana boats. In exchange the United Fruit Company laid on a special train and coaches (previously reserved for white passengers) to transport Garvey around the country. Company managers also arranged for him to be introduced to President Julio Acosta in the capital. Such reverence on behalf of the company and adulation on the part of the people would have swelled the heads of most men. The provisional president of Africa 'as representative of the Negro peoples of the world', graciously let it be known that he was especially 'pleased at the satisfaction it gave to the people of Costa Rica'.[47] The pleasure was not all one way. Company files show that the vicarious delight taken by UNIA members in their leader's success was translated into a monthly remittance of $2,000 well beyond Garvey's departure.[48]

Marcus Garvey's next stop was to be Panama. He entered Panama under a visa granted by the Panamanian consul at Boston. Costa Rica's neighbour was also the site of United Fruit Company farms and a considerable Caribbean workforce. The Bocas del Toro plantation, for example, employed 6,000 day labourers. The company was so gratified by the way Garvey's visit had turned out, and his moderating effect on the workforce, that they provided a launch to take him to Panama. Chittenden wrote ahead to his counterpart in Bocas del Toro, in a bid to allay any fears that he might have had anticipating Garvey's arrival, because 'he [Garvey] states that he too is an employer of labor, understands our position, is against labor unions, and is using his best endeavour to get the Negro race to work and better themselves'.[49]

The response was not so welcoming in Panama. In Bocas del Toro and Almirante, where the crowds, instead of crowning Garvey with eulogies, wanted hard questions answered about the state of their investment in the Black Star Line. American military intelligence reported that 'the Negroes [also] became incensed over the fact that Garvey raised the price of admission to his lectures, from fifty cents, the advertised price, to one dollar'. Hecklers in the crowd berated Garvey and hurled abuse at him. Finally he brought the meeting to an end, imperiously stating, 'I cannot come all the way from New York to speak to you for fifty cents.' Amid the uproar he continued, 'You are a bunch of ignorant and impertinent Negroes. No wonder you are where you are, and for my part you can stay where you are.'[50]

Marcus Garvey left the recalcitrant crowds where they were in Almirante and Bocas del Toro and headed for Colón, where he knew he ran the risk of being refused entry by the American administration that controlled the canal zone. Under the terms of the Hay–Bunau–Varilla Treaty, the United States had been granted extraordinary concessions, effectively giving them administrative control over a huge swathe of Panama that physically included the terminal cities of Colón and Panama City but over which the Panamanians retained sovereignty.[51]

Realising that the port authorities would have been alerted to be on the lookout for him, Garvey wrote that he resorted to a little subterfuge of his own: 'I was determined to get there from under the sea; so I took a submarine.' In Garvey's account, summoning a submarine is made to sound as easy as hailing a taxi. No matter the means of his arrival, he did set foot in Colón and by the time the authorities were alerted to his arrival, it was too late: the crowds around him were so dense that the officials could not get through. From Colón, he went on to Panama City where Garvey reported, 'I met the largest crowd of people I have ever seen at any one time.' In a scene of unrestrained enthusiasm the crowds smashed the windows of the carriage he was travelling in, lifted him out of the train and carried him to a car. But so many people were on top of the car that it couldn't move. The tyres were punctured and the car lifted onto the rim of the rail track and pushed all the way to the city.[52]

Despite the obvious affection for him, Garvey left Panama with only a tenth ($5,000) of the contributions he'd collected in Costa Rica. Without the vital visa to take him on to America, he had few options open to him other than to sail back to Kingston. Charles Latham speculated that Garvey would try to smuggle himself into the USA disguised as one of the crew of the *Kanawha* that had now finally made its way to Kingston – a suspicion that appeared to have been borne out by a curious headline that made the front page of the *Negro World* soon after: 'Garvey Sends Message of Appreciation to Members and Friends of Liberty Hall – Early Return Now Expected.' A flurry of cablegrams followed, sent out from Washington to its consuls in Central America, with instructions to deny visas to the entire crew should Garvey's name appear on the list. On 25 May, the *Kanawha* set sail for Panama. Although the president of the Black Star Line did persuade Captain Richardson to sign him on as purser, when Garvey boarded the *Kanawha* he found its boilers still spluttering and groaning, the crew nearly mutinous and the handful of passengers complaining about their foul language. Captain Richardson and Purser Garvey were soon embroiled in disputes as to who was in charge – the master with a decade of experience or the novice purser. After three days at sea the *Kanawha* limped back to Kingston in some distress.

When Marcus Garvey had set out from New York in February, he had scheduled a trip of no more than six weeks. But now, four months later, he was still languishing in Jamaica, repeatedly denied a re-entry visa to America every time he applied. Rumours were rife on the streets of Harlem that Garvey would never be allowed re-entry and the UNIA executive council was beginning to panic: members' loss of faith would have disastrous consequences. Garvey's generals voted to send the counsellor general, William Matthews, to Washington to lobby the state department on the paramount importance of their chief's return. Without Garvey's galvanising influence, their business ventures (already in a parlous state) might tip over and fail completely. Matthews also made discreet overtures towards staff at the visa control section but the days passed without progress, and the longer his courtship of officialdom went on, the more his client's chances seemed to recede. Garvey was approaching desperation. Then suddenly, one morning, there was a hint of good news. Armed with a new set of instructions from the lawyer, Garvey once more visited the American consul, but this time to ask them to send a cable to the state department (at his own expense) requesting a visa. It was not standard practice but two days later, the state department wrote back, 'Visa authorised Marcus Garvey. Cable name of steamer and date of sailing.' When Hoover was alerted to this unexpected development, 'in case you may wish to give Garvey a thorough overhauling upon arrival', he ordered an immediate investigation into how this extraordinary volte-face could have come about. Whether or not there was any truth behind the rumour that a $2,000 bribe had been paid, by the end of June there was now no way to stop Marcus Garvey heading back to New York.[53]

The UNIA high command gave a collective sigh of relief. They had explored all possible angles to secure the return of their leader. Garvey's iron hand would be welcomed to strengthen the stalled negotiations on the elusive *Phyllis Wheatley* and to exert some discipline (albeit long-distance) over the representatives in Liberia. Relations between the appointed secretary, Cyril Crichlow, on the one hand and the elected deputy and supreme potentates, Marke and Johnson, on the other, were, as far as could be gleaned from cryptic cablegrams, deteriorating at an alarming rate. The trouble between the three centred on the control of funds (sent out monthly from the UNIA HQ in Harlem). Crichlow, with a commendable accountant's diligence, would not relinquish his hold on monies sent to him without being clear with regard to the purpose for which the money had been sent. Events took a decidedly dark turn when the potentate stopped talking to Crichlow and instructed a solicitor to communicate with him instead. Crichlow had grown alarmed by his seniors' calculated policy of sidelining and undermining him.

Crichlow sadly reached the conclusion that headquarters had all but abandoned him. He festered in Monrovia, visited by malarial fevers and a declining bank balance and the alarming prospect that he would not even be able to afford his passage back to America.

In his increasingly alarming reports to his political master, then stranded thousands of miles away in the West Indies, the loyal Crichlow mapped out a landscape of staggering Liberian corruption: a scientific expedition, ostensibly to research the mineral wealth of the interior, metamorphosed into a luxurious and cripplingly expensive safari. Crichlow catalogued an inventory of financial mismanagement, painting a bleak scenario on the prospects of a reasonable return for UNIA investment. He was desperate to return to Harlem to give his side of the events of what had befallen the movement in Liberia, and he was rewarded with Garvey's stinging criticism of his accountant's pedantry. In attacking the messenger, the UNIA leader ignored the crux of his message.

For all of the UNIA president's careful wooing of the Liberian administration, it was, maddeningly, Garvey's rival, W. E. B. Du Bois, who seemed at this crucial point to have the ear of the authorities. With some gentle prodding from Du Bois, President King had taken up his offer to clarify in the pages of his *Crisis* magazine, the Liberian government's position vis-à-vis the UNIA. The president duly obliged with an open letter, overturning 'some wrong impressions [that] seem to exist about the present conditions in Liberia'. Whilst acknowledging that his country could not accommodate 'large, miscellaneous numbers of immigrants', the president welcomed 'strong young men trained as artisans . . . [and] engineers'. But finally, with Garvey's movement unmistakably its target, he warned, 'Under no circumstances will Liberia allow her territory to be made a centre of aggression or conspiracy against other sovereign states.' It was not quite the knockout blow to the UNIA's ambitions that Du Bois was hoping for, but the organisation, along with Garvey, was left reeling.[54]

NOT TO MENTION HIS COLOUR

A little fat black man, ugly but with intelligent eyes and big head, was seated on a pink platform beside a throne.
W. E. B Du Bois, 'Back to Africa', *Century Magazine*, 1923

ON his way to breakfast at 10.00 at the Sheraton Hotel in Cincinnati, on 19 May 1924, W. E. B. Du Bois, the foremost scholarly black man of his day and exemplary critic of Garvey, stood waiting with his host, Professor Wendell Phillips Dabney, by the elevator that would take them to the restaurant. With a ping, the doors suddenly opened and out stepped a group of splendidly costumed black ladies, who formed a guard of honour, a phalanx around a 'stout dark gentleman, gorgeously apparelled in military costume'. 'Ye Gods,' exclaimed Dabney in a later account, ''twas Garvey. He saw me, a smile of recognition, then a glance at Du Bois. His eyes flew wide open. Stepping aside, he stared; turning around, he stared, while Du Bois, looking straight forward, head uplifted, and nostrils quivering, marched into the elevator.' The two men never spoke. The doors closed comfortably and the editor of the *Crisis* (having pretended not to see his rival) ascended. 'Du Bois and Garvey Meet!' screamed the headlines of the *Cincinnati Union* (a weekly black paper) the next day. 'No Blood Is Shed!'[1]

The 'no exchange of blows' report of that meeting alluded to the fierce, almost visceral hatred, 'a hate that only kin can feel for kin',[2] that Du Bois and Garvey felt towards each other by the middle of 1924. Of his enforced, but temporary, exile in the Caribbean, Garvey had become convinced that the influential editor of the *Crisis* had somehow played a part. Neither was forensic dust-powder needed to detect Du Bois's handprint on the damaging open letter of the Liberian president published in April's edition of the *Crisis*. Battle had clearly been enjoined by 1921. At stake was nothing less than the future determination and direction of 14 million African-Americans and countless other black people in Africa and the Caribbean.

Dual membership of the UNIA and NAACP was not yet being discouraged but Du Bois was increasingly perplexed to witness that, in spite of his obvious faults and mistakes, Garvey's influence over black people continued to grow, not just amongst his natural constituency (the so-called cow-tail and hoe-handle brigade) but also as a result of defections from the margins of the NAACP. Educated African-American integrationists shook their heads along with Du Bois. Samuel Redding, whose father was a stalwart of the NAACP, recalled his bewilderment when a Garvey rally came to Wilmington Delaware in the early 1920s: 'They came with much shouting and blare of bugles and a forest of flags . . . Among the marchers my father spotted "black yeomen" – dependable attendants at meetings promising Negro uplift, and loyal though somewhat awed members of the NAACP. Some of them my father had personally recruited, and low groans of dismay escaped him when he saw them in the line of the march.'[3]

Garvey communicated on a level that 'black yeomen' could understand, and touched on the emotional intelligence of his audience in a way that Du Bois never could. In Harlem he was in the mix, at the very centre of black America. He understood the temper of black people and wove himself and his movement into the tapestry of their lives. Harlem made Marcus Garvey; it energised him, fed him with ideas, and kept him on his mettle. And although by temperament and inclination the upper mid-town gentility of the NAACP suited William Du Bois, even he proposed moving its offices up to Harlem, to be closer to the people.

It might also have made for better relations with Marcus Garvey. The lack of contact between America's two black leaders only exacerbated their problems. Du Bois kept a studied distance in his comfortable offices on 7th Avenue. Garvey was just as cocooned up in Harlem. As the UNIA leader's status and paranoia grew, he surrounded himself with an ever-thicker wall of armed bodyguards. It was left to each other's publications to do the talking. Du Bois's high-church official tone in the *Crisis* was more than matched by Garvey's *Negro World*: punchy, street-level sarcasm from editors who had honed their skills atop soapboxes at Harlem's Speakers' Corner.

According to Hubert Harrison, as well as his magnificent skills of oratory, Marcus Garvey had one other significant advantage over Du Bois: his colour. 'Every Negro who has respect for himself and for his race will feel, when contemplating such examples as Toussaint L'Ouverture, Phyllis Wheatley . . . and Marcus Garvey the thrill of pride that differs in quality and intensity from the feeling which he experiences when contemplating other examples of great Negroes who are not entirely black.'[4]

William Edward Burghardt Du Bois was, by his own admission, not *entirely* black. He revelled in his mixed heritage: Dutch, French Huguenot, 'a flood of Negro blood' but 'thank God! No "Anglo-Saxon".' Marcus Mosiah Garvey was, by contrast, determinedly 100 per cent black. This was at a time when African-Americans were prone to fabricate hereditary lines that accentuated their differences from the common Negro stock – a sentiment satirised wickedly by Zora Neale Hurston when she wrote of her origins, 'I am colored but I offer nothing in the way of extenuating circumstances except that I am the only Negro in the United States whose grandfather on the mother's side was *not* an Indian chief.'[5]

Garvey was unique in that he 'sold the idea of the black man to himself', recalled S. A. Haynes, 'with the same zeal and enthusiasm that white Americans, Englishmen [and] Frenchmen use[d] preserving their racial identities'. It was this idea of solidarity that first drew the young, fair-skinned Amy Jacques to Garvey. In their first meeting he 'stressed the fact that the skin-colour class system did not exist in America, as all strata of the race were treated as one'.[6] A concept of racial purity evolved into a fundamental belief during his time in America. Garvey never exhibited the kind of racial antipathy towards mulattos articulated by his spiritual mentor Edward Blyden. He did, though, hold reservations about Du Bois that, stripped bare of his unease over the professor's complex character, came down to his suspicion of the mulatto Harvard man's inequitable diffusion of blood. Educated in his formative years in Jamaica, Garvey was not inoculated against the prevailing racial theories of the time, expounded by amateur anthropologists such as W. P. Livingstone. 'The root stock [Negro] possesses all the fundamental virtue of virgin races,' Livingstone scribbled in *Black Jamaica*, whereas 'the [mulatto] hybrid is a compound of both; the intelligence of one [white parent] meets and amalgamates with the animalism of the other, producing a strange nature.'[7]

In his personal life, Marcus Garvey stepped back from such certainties, especially when they began to complicate a blossoming romance. By the prevailing standards of the day, Amy Jacques, his secretary and travelling companion over the last year, was considered a mulatto. When, in a rare unbuttoned moment, Jacques wrote of their growing intimacy, it was clear that her boss and paramour was, in part, attracted to her mulatto comeliness: 'My hair, let down, thrilled him. It was long and naturally wavy; he asked me never to cut it. The first time he saw it down, curiously he felt some strands and said, "Why, it is so soft." As I tossed my head, he exclaimed, "Oh, but it is so alive!"'[8] In the racial orientation of Jamaica, 'good hair' (wavy hair was good) accompanied a 'good colour' (anything but black, and the fairer the better). Jamaica, and the British West Indies at large, had evolved a system of ascending miscegenation, that is, blacks rose through 'genetic association' with whites.

Over decades the practice had left a psychic scar on Jamaican society. Pondering what he'd observed when he'd previously visited the Antilles, W. E. B. Du Bois concluded that islands like Jamaica had 'become disgusted with their old leadership. These are largely mulattos and it was British policy to induce them by carefully distributed honours and preferment, to identify their interests completely with whites.' America by contrast was not so plagued by disunity between the different shades of black people, largely because a system of descending miscegenation had evolved, where the progeny of any amount of mixing (even if only the recipient of one drop of black blood) descended to the Negro race. As Gilbert Thomas Stevenson pointed out in *Race Distinction in American Law*, 'miscegenation has never been a bridge upon which one might cross from the Negro race to the Caucasian'. Keen students of racial distinction had developed their own idiosyncratic tests to unearth blacks posing as whites where no documentary evidence was immediately available. The NAACP field operator Walter White was so fair-skinned that the organisation would send him undercover to the South to investigate lynchings. Walter White would recount stories of being petrified by bigots on trains who were convinced that a close inspection of the cuticles of his fingernails would flush out the 'yaller niggers who look white' and determine their true race. The 'cracker' (Southern gentleman) took Walter White's hand and said, 'Now if you had nigger blood, it would show here on your half-moons.'[9]

There was a black aristocracy in America. They were numbered primarily amongst the blue-veined families of Washington whose skin was so light their veins could be made out underneath. This group, sometimes called the 'upper tens' or the 'pink tea set', had emerged in the midst of the opportunities opened up by post-bellum reconstruction. They were said to comprise 400 old families (an earlier incarnation of Du Bois's Talented Tenth) whose self-regard caused Garvey's ally John E. Bruce to lampoon them as 'a species of African humanity which is forever and ever informing the uninitiated what a narrow escape they had from being born white . . . [who] wouldn't be caught dead with an ordinary Negro'.[10]

As the conflict between Garvey and Du Bois began to take shape, the African-American leader would accuse the Jamaican immigrant of misconstruing the relations between the light-skinned high yallers (yellows), cinnamon-coloured and coal-black Negroes in America. Garvey was guilty, charged his rival, of importing a Jamaican concept of racial orientation which overstated the real but minimal tensions between the social classes of black Americans. There was a 'kernel of truth' in Garvey's observation but, as far as the black aristocrats were concerned, it was not only ill-mannered to advertise it but naive and politically damaging, playing right into the hands of the race's delighted white enemies.

Du Bois's criticisms of him in the *Crisis* had stung Garvey into answering back in kind (actually with interest) at Liberty Hall in an especially advertised evening for Sunday 2 January 1921 in which the UNIA president devoted over an hour to 'W. E. B. Du Bois and His Escapades'. A packed house assembled to witness the tirade. To rolling applause, Du Bois was dismissed as 'the white-man Negro who has never done anything yet to benefit Negroes'. Du Bois was a friend of the 'upper tens' whilst he, Marcus Garvey, was 'along with the working class Negroes'.[11]

In saying so, Garvey reiterated the kind of aspersions that Du Bois viewed as intolerable. He conceded that 'the ties between our privileged and exploited, our educated and ignorant' were not as strong as they should be. Nonetheless Du Bois warned Garvey, 'American Negroes recognise no color line in or out of the race, and they will in the end punish the man who attempts to establish it.'[12]

There was still the slight possibility in 1921 of an accommodation between the two men. Garvey reached out to his nemesis on several occasions, inviting him to attend UNIA conventions and in December to pen a Christmas message for the edification of the *Negro World*'s readers. Each time he was politely but firmly rebuffed, and Garvey's overtures were not reciprocated. On the contrary, Du Bois seemed determined to put as much distance between the two associations as possible. Garvey's second International Conference for the Negro Peoples of the World, planned for August, would overlap with his rival's Pan-African Congress, and Du Bois was horrified when uninformed critics confused both approaches to Africa as one and the same: the work of 'delusionists and dreamers'. Not only was Marcus Garvey excluded from the guest list of the Pan-African Congress but an alarmed Du Bois hurried to correct 'some public misapprehension of our aims and purposes'. On the eve of the congress, he wrote to the Secretary of State, Charles Hughes, to assure him that 'it has nothing to do with the so-called Garvey movement and contemplates neither force nor revolution in its program'.[13]

The language was critical but still, at this point, restrained. Du Bois might quietly congratulate himself that he had managed to quieten fears and garner some sympathy from the US government and colonial powers, but he was highly annoyed by the distraction caused by his noisy adversary. Years later he was still fuming over 'the unfortunate debacle of his [Garvey's] over-advertised schemes [which] naturally hurt and made difficult further effective development of the Pan-African Congress idea'.[14]

Garvey would also be accused of stymieing the slow but steady shift towards integration that the interracial NAACP and Du Bois were so cleverly and stealthily promulgating. One of its founders, Mary White Ovington, celebrated those ideals of racial interactivity in her memoir *When Black and White Sat Down Together*. But the optimism sounded in her title caused a shudder in mainstream America, especially in the South, with its allusion to social equality. Everyone knew that social equality was the code for an unspeakable and dreadful taboo: that if today the races were sitting down together, tomorrow they would be lying down together. Garvey rightly calculated that his conservatism would be comforting to the dominant culture.

During his tenure President Lincoln himself had at once broached the subject and put it out of bounds when addressing one of the latent fears of emancipation when he asserted, 'Because I do not want a colored woman to be my slave, it does not follow that I want her to be my wife.' The present incumbent, Warren Harding, on the election campaign trail in Birmingham, Alabama, to the delight of its Southern gentlemen, had recently put it more tersely: 'Race amalgamation, there can never be.'[15]

Prior to June 1921 there had not been much talk, on Garvey's part, of racial purity. His anger over the perceived mulatto assault, and conspiracy to keep him out of the United States, uncoupled reason and attached a freight of antipathy towards mulattos that had until now lain dormant. In a country infected with racial pathology, the promotion of a policy preserving separate races was not going to lose him many votes and it cast him in direct opposition to Du Bois and the NAACP. Du Bois had recovered some of the ground lost by his despised 'Close Ranks' editorial. Curiously lyrical essays once again mingled happily with sharp and forensic analyses and militant editorials. On the question of colour and commingling of the races, though, he was cautious and not so sure-footed. Setting out his views on social equality, 'The *Crisis* [Du Bois] advised strongly against interracial marriage in the United States today because of social conditions and prejudice and not for physical reasons; at the same time it maintains the absolute legal right of such marriage.'[16]

Not until 1924 would such a possibility be rendered in fiction. Even then, Eugene O'Neill's drama, *All God's Chillun Got Wings*, managed to upset both black and white audiences. Black people felt the playwright had cowardly loaded the dice somewhat by engineering that soon after marrying the black protagonist, the white woman goes mad; and white people abhorred the very idea of a white woman in wedlock with a black man. In her critique of the play, Mrs W. J. Arnold spoke for every self-respecting daughter of the Confederacy when she said, 'The scene where Miss Blair is called upon to fondle a Negro's hand is going too far, even for the stage.'[17]

As if in response to Du Bois, President Harding had argued the same, that 'men of both races may well stand uncompromisingly against every suggestion of Social Equality'. Marcus Garvey devoted an evening of analysis at Liberty Hall to the president's speech which he considered a well-aimed slap in the face of William Du Bois. Members rolled with laughter in the aisles as Garvey ridiculed Du Bois for having received 'the unkindest cut of all', when the president had implored that 'the Black man should be encouraged to be the best possible black man, and not the best possible imitation of the white man'. The president, Garvey concluded, was, in fact, advancing a plank of the UNIA's programme. Marcus Garvey had returned from exile with a determination to assuage the white power structure, and typical of the man who always favoured bold gestures, he was going to make it incontrovertibly clear that America had nothing to fear from the UNIA. At the same time the dangerous and hidden ideals of his black adversaries would be illuminated. The leadership of his organisation differed from that of the NAACP, Marcus Garvey spelled out, in maintaining that 'not all black men are willing to commit race suicide and to abhor their race for the companionship of another'.[18]

Marcus Garvey was feeling his way towards an ideal of racial purity where 'instead of encouraging a wholesale bastardy in the race, we feel that we should now set out to create a race type and standard of our own'.[19] At the same time as this fine-tuning of a new black aesthetic, he was also sharing his apartment in Harlem with two fair-skinned (brown) women, one of whom – Amy Jacques – he now proposed to marry. In Jamaica, such a move would have been interpreted as the aspiration of an ambitious black man keen to marry out of his class and colour; there were few precedents. From Jacques's perspective, it was not the kind of offer that a young lady, brought up in the milieu of middle-class life, would have come to expect. Since her arrival in Harlem and involvement in the UNIA, Jacques had travelled a long way from the society of debutantes, high teas and winter balls. The petite twenty-six-year-old Jamaican wasn't the first choice. Garvey, she claimed, would have preferred to find an African-American wife to please the members. He had considered proposing to the elocutionist Henrietta Vinton Davis but she, at sixty-two, was far too old, and Garvey wanted a son.

Despite the ugly rumours of infidelity, there had been no hint of a romance between the secretary and her boss. When Jacques weighed the pros and cons of marriage, neither love nor desire figured in the equation. 'I did not marry for love,'[20] she confided to Robert Hill many years later, 'I did not love Garvey. I married because I thought it was the right thing to do; in order to protect him and to be close enough to help him in the difficulties that lay ahead.'

In Jacques's own account in *Garvey and Garveyism*, her future husband's proposal reads like the minutes of a dutiful business proposition: 'He turned to me, and very adroitly put the onus on me, stating that it was in my power to help the organisation in this crisis.' Both parties understood from the outset that their marriage would be subservient to the needs of the movement. On the morning of 26 July

1922, Marcus Garvey sat at his desk and composed a careful request for an audience with the President of the USA. In the afternoon, he hosted a celebratory lunch for UNIA dignitaries on the anniversary of Liberian independence; and in the evening he and his bride-to-be slipped away to Baltimore for their wedding the next morning. Thereafter, it was down to UNIA business as usual. In fact, one of Mrs Garvey's first marital duties was to lend her new husband $400 to meet an emergency for the organisation: a field officer of the rival NAACP was eager to defect to the UNIA and needed the $400 to relocate from St Louis to Cleveland, Ohio.

Tantalisingly, the NAACP's William Pickens had also been on the brink of going over to the Garvey movement. For him to do so would have been something of a coup. Pickens had distinguished himself at Yale. The black Ivy League graduate had naturally gravitated towards the NAACP but had found neither the pay nor the position commensurate with his intelligence. Pickens was a professor of foreign languages and Dean at Morgan State University. He submitted his resignation (from the NAACP) in the summer of 1921. But what William Pickens did next is disputed. According to Jacques and Garvey he approached the UNIA for a job. According to Pickens, *they* approached him. What is beyond dispute is that the UNIA's interest worked to the Yale man's good fortune, prompting an improved offer from the rival NAACP to remain with them.[21]

The wavering of William Pickens was indicative of how unsure black activists were in the 1920s about the primacy of the role played by the NAACP relative to the UNIA. Many of the activists of black organisations were 'itinerant joiners', shuttling between camps as their philosophies or programmes developed. Loyalty was not a given. The future was a lottery, and it took a brave man to throw in his lot unreservedly with one group to the exclusion of all others.

This, though, is just what Garvey demanded of his officers. Memorising the words of the new doctrine would take a little while. The old (pre-Caribbean tour) mantra of paying allegiance solely to the flag of the UNIA was returned to the think tank, to the vault of ideas that needed a little bit more work. In the meantime, pledging allegiance to the flag of the country in which members resided (most notably the USA), rather than a future African state, was just about OK – for now. The first signs of their leader's new-found deference to authority and retreat from radicalism were evident even prior to his re-entry to the

United States. On the way back, his ship had stopped off at Belize, and Garvey, eager to display the reformation of his character, requested an audience with Governor Eyre Hutson at Government House. Hutson considered the meeting of such importance that he commissioned a shorthand writer to record the interview. On 5 July, Governor Hutson sent a transcript of his interview with Garvey to the Secretary for the Colonies, Winston Churchill. It was soon apparent that Garvey had voluntarily walked into an interrogation. Early on, the Governor opened a file of newspaper cuttings which he considered 'offensive to me as it is to every other loyal subject of His Majesty the King', and slid them across the table for the subject's perusal. Garvey's eyes quickly alighted on the phrase, 'Let us pray for the downfall of England', that was attributed to him. There was worse to come with the prediction, 'As the Tsar lost his throne some years ago, so I fear George of England may have to run for his life.' The transcript of the interview did not note the degree of Garvey's discomfort as the Governor continued to read from the 'certified copy', but it is apparent that the UNIA leader was embarrassed and shocked. He paused to compose himself before mounting a recovery. 'Your Excellency will realise that we are seldom reported correctly in the press,' Garvey replied blithely, waving away the cutting. It was an argument that the Governor would perhaps have found persuasive, 'if the article had appeared in any other paper than the *Negro World*'.[22]

The files, of course, were never likely to disappear. Retrospectively, Marcus Garvey had to accept that he was always going to be considered of doubtful loyalty. But he hoped for a probation, so that, with time, the semi-dormant authorities (with one baleful eye on him) would go back to sleep. As soon as he touched down on American soil, Garvey set about ensuring that the high officers of the movement understood that a new course had been set – with immediate effect. 'For some unknown reason,' the slow-witted BOI informant was soon reporting, 'all the officials of the Black Star Line are very patriotic in their speeches.' P-138 was even more perplexed to hear Garvey 'dictating a speech loudly to his stenographer [in which] he spoke of the kind treatment the government had accorded him . . . pledging his support to the USA always.'

Loyalty and betrayal were the qualities most keenly felt in the Garvey movement at this time. Delegates to the forthcoming UNIA conference were encouraged to identify and renounce the traitors in their midst – no matter their rank or how trivial the nature of their treachery. 'If at any time you have met a representative of the council who was dishonest, immoral, who was untrue to this cause,' Garvey advised delegates, 'it is for you, let him be High Potentate [or] President-General, [to] bring your charge against him at the bar of this convention.' There could be no confusion, in the minds of the salaried officers, over the requirement for absolute allegiance to the organisation. Even so, a number of senior officials had exploited Garvey's absence in the Caribbean to pursue their own agendas – with differing degrees of legitimacy. And so the blood-letting began. The accused were now put on trial by the UNIA, charged with duality.

The chaplain-general, Bishop Alexander McGuire, known for the 'vim and force' of his oratory, was first among the defendants. Bishop McGuire had bided his time, waiting until Garvey was out of the country before stepping up his evangelism among UNIA members. He'd sifted through the records of the UNIA, obtaining members' addresses, and planned to propagandise the idea of an independent black Episcopal movement as a seed-bed for his own fledgling African Orthodox Church. McGuire had taken it upon himself to draft the Universal Negro Catechism, providing a course of instruction in religious and historical knowledge pertaining to the race. He aimed to offer some relief for black worshippers whose entrée to the Old Testament was predicated on their association with the murderous Cain. Once Cain had killed his brother, Abel, and was for ever 'marked' (blackened) by it, there was nothing on offer for the black reader (whose skin bore the mark of Cain) but guilt and shame, and a cast of biblical characters who seemed to reinforce the myth that the Negro was cursed. The Universal Negro Catechism would break the spell – in subtle ways. So, for example, the passage in the Bible when Shulamith, the daughter of Pharaoh who was betrothed to Solomon, describes herself as 'dark but comely' was retranslated by McGuire as 'dark and comely'. McGuire explained his belief that 'white translators use "but" in preference to "and" to create the impression that one who is dark is not expected to be comely'. In part, the Catechism would also illuminate the virtuous black presence in the Bible or, as Garvey put it, 'cut out all in the Bible that doesn't suit us'.[23]

McGuire's work was as quietly impressive as the man. Although moderate in the exercise of his authority, the bishop was a patrician whom Garvey suspected harboured larger ambitions to the detriment

Marcus Garvey in full regalia during the UNIA parade of 1924.

J. Edgar Hoover, director of the Bureau of Investigation, 1935.

Parade of the UNIA convention. The placard in the car bears the inscription 'The Negro Has No Fear', 1920.

Claude McKay, Jamaican novelist, poet and leading light of the Harlem Renaissance. His defiant poem, 'If We Must Die', was written in response to the lynching and murder of African-Americans during the 'Red Summer' of 1919.

Garvey and officials on the review stand of UNIA parade, 1922.

The aftermath of the Tulsa Race Riot, 1921. The photograph shows the burning of the African-American section of the town.

W. E. B. Du Bois, at his desk
in the offices of the monthly
magazine, the *Crisis*.

UNIA legionnaire and his family.

Amy Jacques Garvey, March 1923.

Stock certificate for the Black Star Line.

Inspection of the SS Yarmouth by UNIA members in 1919.

Offices of the Black Star Line. The giant-sized measuring stick gives a running total of the money received from shares sold in the Black Star Line.

UNIA delegation to Liberia, 1924. The leader of the delegation, Henrietta Vinton Davis, sits in the front row in the middle.

Henry Y. Bonds and family, c. 1912, who attempted to immigrate to Liberia on several occasions between 1912 and 1919.

Mourners at the grave of John E. Bruce (an editor of the *Negro World* and close advisor to Garvey), 1924. Bruce's widow, Florence, stands beside Garvey (third from right). The men in white aprons are Free Masons from Bruce's African-American lodge.

RALEIGH'S STATE FAIR

GARVEY

YOU NIGGARS, HAVE'NT GOT A THING. IF I WERE DEPENDING ON YOU FOR MY TRANSPORTATION, I WOULD HAVE NEVER GOTTEN HERE, THE WHITE MEN ARE THE PEOPLE TO LOVE. THEY HAVE EVERY-THING. THROUGH THEIR LOCOMOTIVE I AM HERE. IF THEY TREAT YOU MEAN; LOVE THEM MORE. THEY ARE YOUR SUPERIOR-IF YOU WERE RICH, YOU WOULD'NT LIKE TO ASSOCIATE WITH PEOPLE LOWER THAN YOU ARE. OF COURSE NOT.

A WELL KNOWN JACK ASS AND HIS FAMOUS ANTI-NEGRO ORATION.

Satirical cartoon in the *Messenger*, March 1923, depicting Garvey as a jack-ass. The editors of the *Messenger* were at the fore-front of the 'Garvey Must Go' campaign.

Prison docket of
Marcus Garvey,
Prisoner 19359,
Atlanta Federal
Penitentiary,
February 1925.

UNIA member outside of
the Garvey club in Harlem.

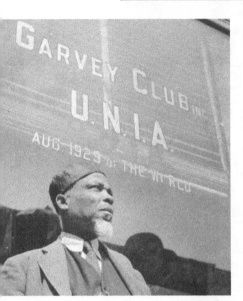

Garvey's sons, Marcus Jacques Garvey (right)
and Julius Jacques Garvey, Jamaica, 1940.

Marcus Garvey handcuffed to a marshal,
under escort to the Manhattan House of
Detention (Tombs Prison), New York,
February 1925.

Marcus Garvey, about to be deported from the USA, addresses his followers in a farewell speech from the deck of S.S. *Saramacca*, New Orleans, 2 December 1927.

Advertisement for Garvey's memorial service, a month after his death on 10 June 1940.

...ey's Memorial Procession

Founder and President General of the Universal Negro Improvement Association,
Died in London, England, on June 10, 1940

Sunday,
JULY 21, 1940
at 12:30 p. m.

LINE FORMS
Garvey Club, Inc.
169 West 133rd Street
New York City

We are Calling Every Race Loving Man, Woman and Child to Get in Line and Pay Honor to A GREAT CHARACTER of the NEGRO RACE

MEMORIAL SERVICE WILL BE HELD AT
St. Marks M. E. Church
BISHOP L. H. KING, Pastor
138 Street & St. Nicholas Avenue, N. Y. C. at 2:30 p. m.

We cordially invite the cooperation of Churches, Lodges, Civic Organizations and other Fraternal Bodies, as well as Individuals, to aid in this Tribute. Eulogy by Prominent Speakers. Special Musical Programme.

━━━━ AUSPICES: ━━━━
Special Memorial Service Committee
Consisting of all Divisions of the
U. N. I. A. Greater New York

Capt. A. .L KING, Chairman   JOHN MARSHAL, Secretary
Pres. Central Div. No. 100—A

Miss E M. COLLINS	THOMAS W. HARVEY	Capt. G. HARRIS
Secretary-General	High Chancellor	Pres. Garvey Club, Inc.
Lieut. R. LEWIS	CARLOS COOKS	C. JACOBS
Pres. New York Division No. 340	Pres. Advance Division	Pres. Brooklyn Div. No. 336
R. OSBORNE	A. JACOBS	G. HINDS
Pres. East Brooklyn Div. No. 252	Pres. Pan-African League	Pres. Fred Douglass Division

ALL ARE WELCOME : : : ADMISSION FREE

of the UNIA and of course its leader. When thus charged, McGuire proffered a dignified resignation which the executive council, after making a brief show of pained deliberation, speedily accepted. Allegations of dual service were also levelled at several other officers of the UNIA including Dr Ellegor, Reverend Tobitt and Dr John Gordon. A more obvious charge of embezzlement was laid at the absent feet of Reverend Brooks – a former UNIA executive who was accused of rendering unto himself $1,000 which rightly belonged to the organisation. Brooks hadn't been seen for a number of months and wasn't answering his mail or front door. When Amy Jacques later answered criticism over the high salaries paid to the executive officers she ventured that it was in part to withdraw the temptation that officers might have – aptly demonstrated by Brooks – to augment their salaries illegally. Nonetheless, it was an elementary mistake. The salaries that had been unanimously and self-righteously voted on and pledged after the first conference were an unsupportable drain on the organisation's finances. Again, the inflated salaries exposed the complex relationship between the leadership and its members. With some pride, Garvey would tell a colonial audience in Jamaica that though he was entitled to draw a combined salary of $27,000 for the three posts that he held, he had made a sacrifice for the good of the organisation, and would only accept $11,000. But even with this reduced amount Garvey would boast that he was 'getting more pay than the Colonial Secretary of Jamaica, and that's a job for life', knowing full well that the audience would dance a jig of joy and applaud this black success till their hands were red, as if the windfall was their very own.[24] But as the losses, especially from the Black Star Line, began to mount up, Garvey called for similar sacrifices from his unenthusiastic cabinet. One of the most controversial (and least popular) measures advocated by the president-general, at the second convention, was that henceforth wages should be cut in half.

Lawyers would later be instructed to begin proceedings against Brooks to recover some of the missing money. The reverend was in disgrace and no one mourned his loss. The departure of some of the other executives was more problematic, particularly Gordon and McGuire, both of whom would subsequently defect to Cyril Brigg's camp, the African Blood Brotherhood (ABB).

As in the previous year, the brotherhood had accepted the open invitation to attend the second International Convention of the Negro

Peoples of the World. This time they badgered and cajoled Garvey into permitting the Communist leader, the luminary Rose Pastor Stokes, to address the floor. Rose Stokes was a fabulously wealthy white Socialist, who'd earned her colours working in a cigar factory before marrying a millionaire and converting him to the cause. Her militant track record included a jail sentence for a seditious speech on the eve of America's entry into the Great War.[25] Apart from a delegation of Irish activists who had been welcomed by Garvey at the end of the very first convention, there was no precedent for extending invitations to white people. After all it was an international convention of Negroes. An exception was made for Rose Pastor Stokes. Garvey had graciously given way to her on the platform at Liberty Hall, but nervously prefaced her speech by a semi-jocular introduction, insisting that the press in the gallery fully understand that his organisation would take the good from all the political 'isms' and that by providing a platform for Stokes to expound on the plight of bleeding Russia, he was in no way aligning the UNIA with the Soviets.

Garvey gave the impression of being slightly amused by the clenched-fist, chest-thumping, well-mannered activist, as if she were an eccentric aunt whom one had to humour. Briggs had dotted members of the brotherhood around the auditorium to cheer her on, and Sister Rose positively revelled in her moment of manna among Harlem's workers.

Garvey's good humour did not extend much beyond Rose Pastor Stokes's address to the convention when her appearance at Liberty Hall was uncovered as part of a larger campaign to win over support from the UNIA membership. Stokes had approached Hubert Harrison who, when he wasn't penning editorials for the Negro World, tried sporadically to garner enthusiasm for the Liberty League, his own moribund organisation that had been first into the field well before Garvey's more spectacular UNIA. Stokes's offer of funds to help resurrect the League had been spurned. For Harrison to have acted otherwise, having written extensively on the dangers of accepting white patronage, would have been to lay himself open to a charge of hypocrisy. With that route closed off, the Communists hoped – through the ABB's Cyril Briggs and Claude McKay – to insinuate themselves into the UNIA's 'great army of awakened workers' who, with careful handling, might yet be led towards 'the finer system of Socialism'.[26] The catastrophic riot in Tulsa had given a fillip to the African Blood Brotherhood when the rumour began to spread throughout the black belts of America that the ABB had smuggled guns into Tulsa. Briggs was loath to disabuse the public of the idea. The ABB was 'essentially a secret organisation' he confided to Garvey midway through the convention. Statements put out by the Associated Press to the effect that the ABB 'fomented and directed the Tulsa riot'; e.g. agitated, supplied leaders, ammunition, etc., 'while not literally true can still give you an idea of the nature of our organisation'.[27] The misconception was too good an opportunity to pass up. Garvey, though, judged that the ABB had overstepped the mark in its political opportunism when some of its antics at the international convention (more sinister than mischievous) were brought to his attention.

In the absence of a regular convention bulletin, the ABB published its own subtle and subversive version, the *Negro Congress Bulletin and News Service* – its title and layout intentionally giving the impression that it was the official weekly account of the debates, meetings and resolutions at the convention. Sharp-eyed delegates began to grow suspicious when the organisers (especially through its news bulletin) seemed to demonstrate signs of a hitherto unseen streak of self-criticism, low-key at first but then taking a more strident turn – criticisms that were then reproduced in black newspapers. Most embarrassing was the unanswered question about what had happened to the long-heralded SS *Phyllis Wheatley*. Delegates and Black Star Line investors were eager to see whether the ship lived up to the UNIA adverts. It was billed as being capable of carrying 4,500 tons of freight, as well as 2,000 passengers in luxurious style; equipped with electric fans, music and smoking rooms and refrigerating machinery. Typical of the complaints taken up by the California *New Age* was that of delegate Noah Thompson who said he 'was in New York thirty-five days, and with others persisted in demanding to be shown the ships, but was told daily that they could see the ships "tomorrow", and "later", but "tomorrow" never came'.[28] If Marcus Garvey was understandably irritated by the constant sniping of the African Black Brotherhood, then the sight of its vendors hawking the (anti-Garvey) *Chicago Defender* on the steps of Liberty Hall was a provocation too far.

On the twenty-fifth day of the convention, Garvey was determined to call a halt to the distribution of the brotherhood's 'scurrilous pamphlet' and put Bolshevism to flight. From the floor of Liberty Hall the names of the ABB delegates were called out for them to answer the charge of attempting to discredit the UNIA. No one answered and then, just as the chairman called for an examination of all delegates' cards, 'a man was seen to rise hastily and scurry across the hall, plunge through the doorway, beating his way in precipitate flight towards Seventh Avenue'. When the laughter in the hall had subsided Garvey addressed the audience. Cyril Briggs of the brotherhood was, in reality, he warned, 'the paid servant of certain destructive white elements which aimed at exploiting Negroes for their own subservient ends'. The time for the masquerade was over. Communism was 'a white man's creation to solve his own political and economic problems'. The imbroglio engineered by the brotherhood would no longer be tolerated. Their delegates' cards were ripped up and they were immediately expelled from the convention.[29]

The ABB was routed. Briggs, now that his hand was revealed, evinced a sorrowful but righteous regret over this breach of unity. The spurned ally penned a political love letter to Garvey. There was still a chance for reconciliation. Despite their differences, which probably came down to style and temperament, 'the main aim of both organisations is identical'. Briggs could even forgive him for 'resurrecting medieval systems and titles and making the glorious UNIA movement into a tinsel show', for their dispute was a quarrel between brothers and he refused 'to engage in intra-racial strife that would weaken the race'.[30]

Garvey's response was swift and brutal. The UNIA 'can form no alliance with any organisation of Negroes working secretly to attain and enjoy rights and privileges which ought to be won in a manly open fight', the *Negro World* stated coldly. And with one eye on the Red-baiters in Washington concluded that 'it [the UNIA] is not going to be tainted by personal or official contact with such a body'. Further, ensuring that the fair-skinned Briggs was left with no doubt about the possible restoration of relations, Garvey warned readers in the *Negro World* that the founder of the African Blood Brotherhood, Cyril Briggs, was in actuality a WHITE MAN masquerading as a Negro for convenience.

In one hasty move, Garvey had severed contact with an organisation that had for over two years served to articulate the UNIA's ideals, and by attacking Briggs in such a base and shocking way, he had made a personal and bitter enemy of a man who would soon be sharpening his sword with one aim: thrusting it in between the ribs of the provisional president of Africa. Briggs, who another paper had once dubbed 'the angry blond Negro', was livid. He sued Garvey for criminal libel and brought his 'colored' mother to the court to prove his origins. Even after Briggs had had his day in court, Garvey's supporters continued to taunt the wretched man. On one occasion, recalled a fellow member of the brotherhood, Briggs marched to Liberty Hall and 'amid a group of threatening Garveyites . . . temporarily overcame his impediment of speech . . . and made a long and powerful speech', defending his position.[31]

Briggs won his suit against Garvey but the legal satisfaction was evidently not sufficient. Thereafter Cyril Briggs steered away from any kind of cordiality towards the defendant. Marcus Garvey became his preoccupation; he breathed, ate, drank and slept with pathological thoughts of revenge. In page after page of the *Crusader*, acres of copy – all negative – were given over to the irreversible valediction of his former ally. When Briggs put the UNIA leader, and those around him, on notice that 'the race will not forget nor lightly hold the fact that any Negro was too pro-Garvey to be really pro-Negro', Garvey could not have foreseen the depths Briggs would go to in order to undermine him; his sense of betrayal and rejection cut so deep that the militant Socialist was even prepared to approach the intelligence agencies of the despised capitalist state and offer to inform on Garvey.[32]

Extraordinary though Briggs's response was, it paled beside the onslaught to come from Garvey's primary ideological enemy, W. E. B. Du Bois. Hatred can perhaps thrive all the more thoroughly when applied in pure abstraction and at a distance. The icily silent encounter by the elevator at the hotel in Cincinnati in 1924 was the closest the two men ever came to meeting. In his first public pronouncement on his rival in December 1920, Du Bois had confided to readers of the *Crisis* that he had found Garvey 'a little difficult to characterise'. By the end of the year he would begin to feel the need to respond to what he perceived as Garvey's campaign against him, to the 'unremitting repetition of falsehoods and personal vituperations'. The paradox of Garvey's inconsistency towards him was never solved by Du Bois but scouring the pages of the *New York Call* on 1 August 1921 he might have found a clue. In an appeal for unity at the start of his conference, Garvey had written, 'This is not a time for personal difference, not a time to ask a man what college he graduated from.' That same month Garvey had felt confident enough to challenge Du Bois, with all of the Harvard man's academic and intellectual armoury, 'to meet me on the platform of Liberty Hall at midnight, at noon, at any time, and I will make you look like a bit of cotton'. Du Bois's scholarship and credentials were impressive. His first-rate degrees from Fisk and Harvard and decades of scholarly writing had earned him the prestigious Spingarn Medal awarded annually for 'the highest and noblest achievement by an American Negro'.[33] By contrast, as a young man, Garvey had only managed to snatch a few evening classes in law at Birkbeck when struggling in London. Nonetheless, Garvey was a man of much learning; he'd benefited from his contact with amateur scholars such as Bruce Grit and Hubert Harrison; he'd read widely, had an insatiable appetite for history and natural love of the classics – but he had no degree.

Critics and adherents of Sigmund Freud's dazzling new theories discerned elements of an inferiority complex in Garvey's unearned attribution of DLC (from the University of London) to his name and his stately costume, 'an academic cap and gown flounced in red and green'. Ostentation was a constant charge levelled at him and his movement but Garvey never tired of questioning why great European powers should have a monopoly on pomp and ceremony. His former ally, Dr Gordon, summed up the UNIA philosophy of lifting the people from their stupor when he admitted that 'if we had to hire a man and pay him a hundred dollars a week just to beat a drum and the beating of that drum created the proper impression, we would be glad to hire him'.[34] Such ostentation, on Garvey's part, was only ever for public consumption. Privately he was an extremely conservative man, Robert Hill believes, with manners best described as Victorian. Amy Ashwood had considered this to be the source of their marital difficulties when she later reflected, 'His psychosexual development and orientation while appropriate in a West Indian milieu of that period was outmoded in an American social climate where a wedding ring is not a symbol of total possession.'[35] His private persona was at variance with his public stance; there he appeared a supreme promoter and self-styled performer. On top of which there was the accretion of public expectation – a view that even James Weldon Johnson (in the enemy NAACP camp) would have had some sympathy for, as professional titles created a conundrum for black public speakers. In his biographical writings Johnson remembered the time when, just before he was due to address the congregation in a Southern church, the local pastor leaned over to him and whispered, '"What might be your entitlements?" I whispered, "Just Mister."' The preacher looked alarmed. In front of him the audience sat in worshipful silence. 'With deep sincerity he whispered back again,

"I can't introduce you to these people as *just* Mister."' And so Professor Johnson got up to speak.[36]

Unquestioning acceptance certainly had its attractions over Du Bois's jaundiced scepticism, which bordered on disdain. The Pan-African Congress was a vexed case in point. Through his lieutenants, Garvey would have Du Bois and the organisers of the congress believe that he was indifferent to the snub they'd delivered in declining to invite him. Rather, William Du Bois should be thanked for sparing him its 'poetic vapourings and plaintive wailings'. The prospective cast list was also unappealing. While the Garvey of 1918 would have been delighted to receive Colonial Office representation at one of his meetings, the Garvey of 1921 considered Du Bois's courtship of colonial officials 'who will explain frankly the present government's attitude towards Africa and its future', perverse and pathological.[37] Perverse because, as Garvey joked, it was akin to a congress of rats agreeing that a cat should oversee proceedings. Pathological, because it reinforced the suggestion that validation could only come from white colonial European powers.

Towards the end of his convention Garvey would show Du Bois, and anyone who cared to pay attention, that there was another way. On 27 August 1921, the provisional president of Africa did not just recreate, he instituted a brand new tradition of the Negro Court.[38]

The 500 guests began arriving at 7.30. They rolled up in limousines to the kerb outside Liberty Hall. A specially erected canopy extended from the lintel of the doorway over the pavement. Hundreds of onlookers pressed up against the African Legions who formed a guard of honour for the stiff-backed high officials, chaperoning their elaborately dressed ladies as they sashayed into the hall. Once through the doors, guests were admitted into an auditorium overflowing with ferns, daisies and bouquets of roses. The banquet would be served on two long rows of tables, decorated with fruit, viands and delicacies. The menu printed on gold-embossed card included, *Punch Africanos*, *Liberian chicken*, *Liberty special ice cream* and *Black Cross Macaroons*. Black, red and green streamers rimmed the hall which was illuminated by an enormous red lantern in the centre and smaller Japanese lanterns forming a chain from one end of the hall to the other. Up on the platform, overlooking this magnificent spectacle, the supreme potentate, Gabriel Johnson, with the president-general, Marcus Garvey, sat on mahogany parlour lounging chairs, generously loaned by the president-general for the occasion. President Garvey, sporting a new uniform,

looked uncharacteristically discomfited by his military hat tipped with
white feathers, black broadcloth trousers with a gold stripe down the
side, a Sam Browne belt across his chest, gold epaulettes, a gold sword
and white gloves. If he was anxious about how the event might be
covered, he needn't have worried. The press who'd scrambled for the
limited tickets would overreach themselves in descriptions of the revival
of these scenes from African antiquity, from the age of the Ethiopian
empire and the Queen of Sheba. Marcus Garvey had envisaged just
such an occasion when he'd sat down to write the UNIA's constitution three years previously. The supreme potentate, Gabriel Johnson,
was, nominally, the world leader but every dignitary who filed past
and bowed reverentially knew that the man who stood to his right,
fidgeting in his starched uniform, was really in charge. Several young
ladies, making their social debut, were also presented to His Highness
the potentate, but the primary object of the banquet was to honour a
handful of outstanding individuals for their contributions to the race.

All the while that the choir sang, it slowly built to a pitch of exaltation, and finally a bugle called the great mass to attention. The
chaplain-general signalled for the great congregation to rise. Beside him
were sealed envelopes containing certificates of knighthood. 'For 300
years we have been imitating the social standards of alien races; copying
their etiquette; bowing down to their grooves of society.' The chaplain
reached for the certificate. 'But the time has come when due to this
genius [Marcus Garvey] we see that for which we have long waited –
the first court held by Negroes under their own leaders.' The knights-
to-be were summoned to the stage and knelt before him. First the
Negro World's literary editor, William Ferris, and then the veteran journalist John E. Bruce – both received the Order of the Nile. George
Tobias was knighted with the Order of Ethiopia, and Lady Commander
of the Sublime Order of the Nile was bestowed upon Henrietta Vinton
Davis. They rose and bowed to the potentate and the hall exploded in
cheers and clapping such that all those honoured were virtually lifted
back to their seats on the crest of applause.

After the supper, the Grand Court Ball began. Lady Henrietta Vinton
Davis and the Supreme Potentate led the way with the first dignified
dance. Soon the revellers would be pushing onto the dancefloor, kicking
out their feet in one-steps, two-steps and waltzes. Harlem, after all,
was at the beginning of a Negro renaissance and the spirit of Garvey's
UNIA – perhaps not quite at the hedonistic, Bessie Smith end of the

spectrum – was part of it. 'Home, Sweet Home' playing out the evening on the stroke of midnight perhaps signalled the movement and Garvey's inherent conservatism. But all would leave Liberty Hall that night with the memory of the haunting and melodious voice of their leader heralding the birth of a new and glorious era – a sentiment felt by all and expressed by the chaplain: 'We [Negroes] are now about to set our own standards of society.' That phrase queerly anticipated the cultural call to arms issued by Langston Hughes, the very personification of the Harlem Renaissance, a few years later. Hughes was to write:

> We younger Negro artists who create now intend to express our individual dark-skinned selves without fear or shame. If white people are pleased we are glad. If they are not, it doesn't matter. We know we are beautiful. And ugly, too. The tom-tom cries, and the tom-tom laughs. If colored people are pleased we are glad. If they are not, their displeasure doesn't matter either. We build our temples for tomorrow . . .[39]

That expression of non-alignment, of setting out one's own standard of society, was to come. In 1921, Langston Hughes, with the blessing of W. E. B. Du Bois, reached out to white patronage and fertile, interracial relations, at a time when Marcus Garvey was more and more defining a world for himself and his followers that was universally black.

BEHOLD THE DEMAGOGUE OR
MISUNDERSTOOD MESSIAH

The mighty objects he beholds
act upon the mind by enlarging it
and he partakes of the greatness he contemplates
                    Thomas Paine, *Rights of Man*, 1792

AT the end of each year W. E. B. Du Bois published a progress report of the race as an inventory of debits and credits. In the debit column for 1921, below the list of 'fifty-nine Negroes lynched in Tulsa' and 'Harding's "racial amalgamation there cannot be" speech at Birmingham', Du Bois had typed in the name, 'Marcus Garvey'. Though he increasingly considered Garvey's contribution disastrous, it was a measure of the difficulties assailing Black America in 1921 that the president of the UNIA and moribund Black Star Line still ranked below the continued Ku Klux Klan-inspired atrocities meted out to the black population, particularly, but not exclusively, in the South.

In the autumn of 1921, the *New York World* had decided to send a team of reporters undercover to investigate the depth of national support for the Klan. For several weeks the *World* ran articles which exposed the great popularity and influence of the Ku Klux Klan in America. The paper professed to be shocked but Klan watchers had been charting the extraordinary rejuvenation of the organisation over the last few years. It was commonly agreed that there was at least one attributable source to that expansion: the epic silent film, *Birth of a Nation*, which premiered in cinemas around the country and at a private screening room in the White House in 1915.

Aside from its filmic novelties, and powerful and melodramatic script, *Birth of a Nation* succeeded largely because it pandered to a revisionist idea of the American Civil War in which the innocent South is beaten but unbowed. As the film opens, the war is over; the world of the defeated South is inverted. White Northern 'carpetbaggers' have snapped up business and plantations for a pittance. In league with the newly appointed black legislators, they keep the Southern white population in subjugation. In 1915 and beyond in cinemas across the country, white jaws dropped as the villainous Gus, a freed slave, appeared on the screen. He wears the uniform of the victorious Union army. Gus has been loitering ominously outside the home of the family who used to own him. He follows the lily-white virginal Southern belle, Marion, to the woods. There, in the words of the author, Thomas Dixon, 'the black brute, Gus, his yellow teeth grinning through thick lips', makes a preposterous proposal of marriage to Marion. 'Marion's delicate lips trembled with fear colder than death . . . Gus stepped closer with an ugly leer, his flat nose dilated, his sinister bead-eyes wide apart, gleaming ape-like.' The innocent maiden recoils in horror. She flees through the woods pursued by Gus and eventually scrambles onto a mountainous ridge. A soundless scream fills the screen, and rather than surrender to the rape that Gus surely intends, Marion leaps to her death. Towards the end of the film, the chivalric Ku Klux Klan night riders, in their terrifying white gowns, track down the monstrous Gus, and lynch him.[1]

Despite black protests, D. W. Griffiths's *Birth of a Nation* was screened in thousands of cinemas in the USA. In the months after the film's release thousands of recruits, fired by its perpetuation of the myth of the South's ante-bellum Eden, built on a benign system of slave-holding plantations so cruelly destroyed, signed up to the white supremacist secret society. The Klan had been in decline since its post-Civil War and Reconstruction heyday. Back in the 1860s and 1870s, according to legend, the avenging nighthawks of the Ku Klux Klan restored the old chivalric concepts to the South in the aftermath of her traumatic defeat; they saved white women from the lustful and rapacious instincts of the freed black man. The Klan was romanticised. Men who'd never even been on horseback claimed to have ridden with the Ku Klux Klan, and to have put an end to 'the Negro's pernicious domination'. In reality the Klan terrorised the black population, burning down black schools and churches, drumming out of town, maiming or executing 'highfalutin' niggers' who did not know their place.

Fifty years on from the Civil War, *Birth of a Nation* resurrected a Southern cultural romanticism, clustered around the idea of a Lost Cause, and a defeated but defiant South that still dreamed of recapturing the old glory. Membership of the Ku Klux Klan (open solely to white Protestants) soared: black people, along with Jews and Catholics were the degenerate enemy. The Klan was widely assumed to be at the back of many of the atrocities, beatings and barbaric lynchings perpetrated against African-Americans, who lived in fear of the midnight knock on the door, the burning cross on the lawn and the disappearances of neighbours of whom it was unwise to enquire.

The Klan was feared but it was also reviled. Black people were revolted by its activities; they raged at the violence and at their own impotence to do much about it. At the turn of the twentieth century, when W. E. B. Du Bois wielded his pen in the defence of a black labourer, Sam Hose, who had killed his landlord in self-defence, the Klan would reveal what little difference his intervention would make. Du Bois wrote out 'a careful and reasoned statement' and was on his way to the offices of the *Atlanta Constitution* when 'the news met me: Sam Hose had been lynched . . . they said his knuckles were on exhibition at a grocery store farther down on Mitchell Street, along which I was walking. I turned back to the University.' Thoughts of the murder of Sam Hose and the ghoulish display of his remains were too much for the young, idealistic Du Bois to bear. He wrote that something died in him that day. There was a sense of the futility of his scientific learning: 'I began to turn aside from my work.'[2]

The figures made for gruesome reading. From 1865 and the 'surrender' of the South until 1922, more than 3,000 black Americans, their bodies defiled and burnt, were lynched with the connivance – and often at the instigation – of the Ku Klux Klan. Such acts of barbaric mob rule were carried out with impunity: no one was ever arrested. By 1922, African-American leaders had settled on a plan they hoped and prayed would temper the murderous influence of the Klan. Organisations like the NAACP pumped all their energies into the promotion of an anti-lynching bill. But Marcus Garvey had a more direct approach in mind.

On 25 June 1922, Marcus Garvey stopped off at Atlanta and did what no black person in America had ever contemplated: he headed straight for the offices of the Ku Klux Klan. The UNIA chief had an arrangement to meet the Klan's Imperial Wizard which, when it was made known to the wider black public, would mark the most significant turning point in his popularity, as even his most ardent fans were confused as to what it all meant.

The turn towards Atlanta, Georgia and the South came out of a ratcheting up of the pressure on Garvey and the movement. The Black Star Line was perilously teetering on the edge of collapse; the first ship, SS *Yarmouth*, had been sold for scrap six months previously; the derelict crew of the *Kanawha* were stranded in Antilla, Cuba, without food or coal, aboard a vessel whose boilers were beyond repair; and the pleasure boat, the *Shadyside*, was last seen banked and rusting on the Hudson. The future of the Black Star Line rested on the *Orion* (*Phyllis Wheatley*). Although the corporation had dispensed with the services of its broker, it had not yet abandoned hope of eventually acquiring the ship. Garvey's unequal optimism, if not as infectious as in previous dark periods, was at least enough to sustain the fiction of an imminent revival in their fortunes. He was not to know that lawyers for the US Shipping Board were advising that 'the Black Star Line be given one more chance to comply with the contract'. Provided the BSL could meet and honour a performance bond, the sale might still go through; at the same time the council was adamant that if, however, 'a bond with satisfactory surety [is not] furnished promptly the sale will be cancelled'.

UNIA businesses had settled into a mode of operation, commonly known as 'kiting', where all income is channelled into one pool and moved from profitable enterprises to failing ones, simply so that the businesses are kept going. In an effort to rationalise the organisation's losses, Marcus Garvey had asked for and obtained (not without some resistance) greater executive powers over UNIA funds. Its headquarters had been inundated with demands for missing wages, fees and other payments. The entire crew of the SS *Kanawha*, the Liberian commissioner, Cyril Crichlow, and the Pan Union Company (seeking compensation for the failed delivery of its liquor) formed part of a long line of recalcitrant plaintiffs who were suing the UNIA. Garvey ordered a list to be drawn up, prioritising payment to the potentially most troublesome. Even if no one else was paid, staff were to ensure that 'Dusé Mohamed Ali [the UNIA's 'foreign secretary'] received his money promptly, every week'.[3] Hubert Harrison was also high up on the list. Bizarrely, Harrison, who held nightly meetings attacking Garvey (and had especially done so in his absence, during Garvey's extended Caribbean tour), was still being paid as an editorial writer on the *Negro*

World 'although', noted one Military Intelligence Officer, 'he does not send anything in for the paper'. The most likely conclusion believed the officer was that 'Garvey is afraid to dismiss him'.[4]

There was also trouble in the divisions. The parent body in Harlem was struggling to maintain its control over prosperous branches like those in California which sought greater autonomy, and threatened to opt out altogether if they didn't get it. Garvey sent the head of the African Legion, Captain Gaines, to Los Angeles to put down the rebellion. But the unsubtle Gaines, with military, ramrod bearing and accompanying unyielding manner, managed only to alienate his hosts and accelerate their secession.

Garvey found himself assailed on a bewildering myriad fronts; his enemies had an uncanny knack for finding each other – with a little help from the bureau's special agent 800. As well as infiltrating the UNIA, 800 had been sworn into Briggs's African Blood Brotherhood and had even taken their secret oath. In over two years working under-cover, 800 had become adept at manipulating Garvey and his opponents in a practice commonly known in Jamaica as 'carry go/ bring come'. 800 was passing on information, informing on both to each other and withholding just enough for rivals to feel indebted and dependent on him. In one memo he outlined how for several nights he'd been rummaging through files at the UNIA offices trying to find Cyril Crichlow's confidential report on the Liberian mission to Garvey. But now that Crichlow and Bishop McGuire had also aligned themselves with the Brotherhood, they might be induced to make public what they saw as the corruption at the heart of the UNIA. They'd also be step-ping out from underneath Garvey's shadow. After all, McGuire had joined the African Blood Brotherhood 'because it welcomes into service strong and intellectual men of the race without attempting to dwarf them before one giant mastermind'.

On 18 December 1921, they took their first tentative steps, taking over the Rush Memorial Church, to deliver their message to the people of Harlem. The church hall crackled with the kind of illicit excitement more readily found in the gambler's bear-pit. But the risk that the conspirators knew they were undertaking misfired. Crichlow, McGuire and their new associates had woefully underestimated the depth of Garvey's support and the great outpouring of antipathy that would be directed towards the traitors whom he had warned his followers to expect. In front of a noisy and expectant crowd, 'Dr McGuire rose to speak,' reported the *Negro World*, '[but] hardly had he begun than the audience laid a verbal barrage against him. Invective after invective was hurled like rapid fire at the bishop which even his stentorian voice could not withstand.' Subsequent speakers met with the same response.[5]

Garvey was loved by thousands of black people in a way that his critics consistently failed to understand, partly because it went beyond reason. They could see that he was loved, when there seemed every reason to despise him. It was not rational; it was emotional. Garvey was loved because he was persecuted, just as his followers were persecuted; and when he alluded to the stoical black man, as he often did, as a modern-day Simon of Cyrenia who had helped Christ bear his cross, then the thousands in the audience looked up to see in Garvey, a bleeding black Christ, with a shimmering crown of light over his head.

To many at the Rush Memorial Church, who had invested not only money but their hopes and dreams in the UNIA, the treachery of McGuire and Crichlow was akin to the officers abandoning ship while they, the loyal crew, remained below deck, bailing out the waters from a vessel that still stood a chance of staying afloat. Garvey's plight was their own; if he was brave enough to tie himself to the mast and weather the storm, then so too were they. Ordinary UNIA members were heartened by Garvey's fearlessness, and mistook the law's delay in prosecuting their leader, not only as an indication of the weakness of the case against him but also as a sign that perhaps Garvey had already defeated the unfair challenge. Besides, what else could they do but stick and stay? The alternative was far too dreadful to contemplate.

The UNIA's sense of triumph, though, of seeing off the enemy, was short-lived. 800's memoranda detailed the prevailing gloom that had settled over some of the more enlightened members of the inner circle, over the certainty that something bad was about to befall them: 'Tobias tells me that he can't sleep at night,' wrote 800, 'for he knows this thing can't go on for ever and he is afraid that he will have to pay.' The wretched Tobias's nightmares were filled with the insuperable tangle of the UNIA finances. They were made all the more real when reading the *Crusader*. In its pages, Cyril Briggs had let loose Garvey's erstwhile boyhood friend, Wilfred Domingo who, with the fastidiousness of an investigative journalist, set about uncovering the trail of money. His essay, 'Figures Never Lie but Liars Do Figure', charting the flow of credits and debits, was an unsparing audit of UNIA accounts that must have made for painful and deeply embarrassing reading by Tobias and the rest of Garvey's high command. Hubert Harrison also confided unwittingly to the undercover BOI agent that he was sure something shortly was going to happen to Garvey, 'and if Garvey wasn't such a fool, he would go to him and tell him about it and tell him how to make a getaway'.[6]

The leader could not remain unaffected indefinitely by the anxiety swirling around his camp. Curiously, at about this time, a statement was issued by the UNIA – without an obvious cause – which read as a defence of Garvey for having 'risked his future, his money, his reputation, his all to start the organisation when all other educated Negroes called him a fool for doing so'. It went on to chastise his invisible enemies, 'a congregation of dismissed, disgraced and so-called resigned employees of the UNIA, Negro World or Black Star Line'. Neither were the strains and stresses of the workplace relieved by the doom-laden atmosphere at home. One night Garvey returned to the apartment in the dark to find that his sister Indiana and her husband had 'packed their bags and sailed for Jamaica, without even leaving a note'. According to Amy Jacques, Garvey's dismay was overridden by a feeling of relief. 'At least,' Garvey is said to have told his wife, he would no longer have 'to feel her [Indiana's] pitying eyes' following him around the apartment.[7]

If only the Black Star Line could clinch the deal on the Orion (Phyllis Wheatley) then the organisation might yet begin trading almost immediately, and gain some kind of a reprieve. Remarkably, at the beginning of 1922, the Black Star Line appeared to be inching towards satisfying the demands of the US Shipping Board. But the panel's decision was to be irreversibly influenced by a newspaper headline its members sat down to read over breakfast on 13 January 1922: 'Garvey, Financier and "Sir President of Africa" Is Held'. The New York World went on to report that detectives had visited 'Harlem's wizard of the Black Star Line', at his apartment on 129th Street and arrested him on a federal charge of mail fraud. Garvey was bundled into a police car for the short ride to the Federal Building and later released on bail of $2,500. The World depicted the arraigned leader as an ungracious, 'portly figure wrapped in a fur-collared overcoat' who seemed 'irritated at the proceedings and refused to talk with reporters'. Specifically, Garvey was accused of sending circulars through the postal system, advertising the sale of stocks in a ship, the Orion, that his corporation did not yet own. The circular included a photograph of the ship, presumably the *Orion* but with its name scratched out and *Phyllis Wheatley* written in its place.

Marcus Garvey was deeply affronted by the ignominy of his arrest; particularly by the accusation that he stood to gain personally by duping naive stockholders into investing in a phantom ship. Newspapers were quick to sketch him as the equivalent of a fancy and flamboyant medicine man dispensing snake oil to ignorant black folk. Garvey winced at the headlines. In a hurriedly prepared statement, he wrote, trusting that 'no one from the people would believe that I could be so mean as to defraud a fellow Negro'. The allegation was a blow to his dignity even though he doubted whether anyone who knew him would question his sincerity: 'I have an ideal that is far above money,' said Garvey, 'and that is to see my people really free.' There was malice at the back of his arrest which was the unholy work of thieves, rogues and vagabonds whom he had kicked out of the movement and who were now bent on revenge; they had judged him, he wrote, from the corrupt standards of 'the thief who does not like to see another carry a long bag'. Garvey's protestations might have sounded convincing to his own ears but the test would come when he chose to reply not through a newspaper editorial but directly to the people, and brave an audience in Harlem.[8]

The night after his arrest, a tremulous but indignant Garvey appeared on the platform at Liberty Hall and, even before he'd said a word, reported the *New York World*, 'was hailed tumultuously as the "Prince of Men" . . . [by] more than 1,000 Negroes [who] cheered wildly for the Provisional President of Africa and booed the newspapers'. Similar scenes were repeated across the country when Garvey embarked on a tour to limit the damage done by his arrest and to promote further stock-buying. If anything, his popularity had increased as his followers proved sympathetic to his assertion that the plot had been laid long ago and that the Post Office department was merely being used 'to carry out the designs of enemies of the race who had opposed the UNIA over the last four years'. The 'sawn-off, hammered-down' little general had the overwhelming support of a membership who, though not inured, had grown used to attacks on him; they were more inclined to agree with Garvey that the Black Star Line's failure was the work of saboteurs, 'paid by certain Negro Advancement Associations . . . to dismantle our machinery and otherwise damage it so as to bring about the downfall of the movement'. Although the NAACP was not directly named, the inference was clear: the rival organisation was to blame, Du Bois in particular, possibly in league with government secret service agents, the French and British colonial authorities, and conservative black newspapers; all united in a conspiracy to destroy the UNIA leader.[9] Du Bois took his cue from the arrest to publish a salvo against a demagogue from whom, courtesy of the authorities' timely intervention, black people had been delivered. 'From now on in our new awakening, our self-criticism, our impatience and passion, we must expect the Demagogue among Negroes more and more.' Du Bois left readers in no doubt that Marcus Garvey was in his mind's eye when he described the demagogue as one who 'will come to lead, inflame, lie and steal. He will gather large followings and then burst and disappear.' It had been a near miss. Disaster had been averted but Du Bois's sigh of relief was accompanied by a further warning: 'Loss and despair will follow his fall until new false prophets arise.'[10] The political death notice that Dr Du Bois composed for his nemesis was premature. In fact, his note struck falsely; the reaction of many Harlemites showed that black people were far more likely, at this juncture, to judge that the nation's premier black leader was the victim of a conspiracy. From the pulpit at Liberty Hall, Marcus Garvey returned the faith the membership placed in him when he defiantly warned the authorities that the movement he had started would never be crushed: 'Put me in jail; put me in the gallows [or] put me in the electric chair . . . the [African] programme shall go over.' A thousand Garveys would spring up to take his place.[11]

The US Shipping Board were not so easily swayed by his rhetoric. On the contrary, the adverse publicity effectively killed off the negotiations for the SS *Orion* between them and the Black Star Line. The corporation continued on its inexorable slide towards insolvency. The UNIA leadership and BSL directors' board were showered with subpoenas and their unity – already under strain – began to fracture; three others, Thompson, Garcia and Tobias, would eventually be indicted along with their leader. The *Negro World*'s associate editor, Hubert Harrison, was also interviewed, but he volunteered his information without waiting for a summons to be issued. Harrison had given Garvey his first big break back in 1917, and although he'd been semi-detached from the *Negro World* for the past few months, he'd kept a dossier of – if not incriminating then at least embarrassing – documents on the inner workings of the movement. Harrison's diaries show that he'd become disenchanted and progressively embittered with Garvey from as far back as the momentous first convention at Madison Square Garden. His entry for 31 August 1920 ends with his description of that spectacular event as 'the most colossal joke in Negrodom, engineered and staged by its chief mountebank'. In 1920, the discreet Harrison, who did not contest any of the elected posts, made the quiet note to himself: 'Delegates are still asking why did I withdraw. Time will tell them: I won't.' Eighteen months later, with Garvey bloodied, Harrison judged the time had come to tell all. Not only that, Garvey's former mentor, who had disguised a long harboured resentment that 'Garvey appropriated [from me] every feature that was worthwhile in his movement', was suggesting potential witnesses for the prosecution, and even offering to coach the bureau's officers on the best line of questioning.[12]

A trickle of disgruntled stock-holders presented themselves voluntarily to the Bureau of Investigation. Thomas H. Cort was typical of the sensible but idealistic prospective investor who'd been prudent enough to travel from his home in Galveston, Texas to New York; he had sounded out and even interviewed executive officers of the UNIA and BSL; thrilled by what he had heard, Thomas Cort's caution had disappeared into the ether only to be replaced abruptly by a gambler's impetuousness based on a hunch. In a flush of enthusiasm, he'd bought $200 in BSL stock. He continued to check up on his investment in the course of a lengthy correspondence with UNIA headquarters, which he kept up for over a year, before reluctantly concluding that his money had gone the same way as his caution. But there might yet be some satisfaction to be gained from at least seeing Garvey prosecuted.[13]

Tens of thousands of small investors had bought shares totalling close to $1 million in the Black Star Line but there were never more than a handful of Thomas Corts who made formal complaints to the authorities. Investors largely spurned the overtures and inducements of bureau agents who penetrated the black belts in search of anti-Garvey litigants. The stock-holder Edward Orr was an exception. Orr had the temerity to sue Garvey and the Black Star Line for the $105 he had invested but was unlikely ever to see again. Finding in favour of the plaintiff, the Socialist judge, Jacob Panken, painted an unflattering portrait of the defendant: 'It seems to me that you have been preying on the gullibility of your own people, having kept no proper accounts of the money received for investment, being an organisation of high

finance in which the officers received outrageously high salaries . . .
You should have taken the $600,000 and built a hospital for colored
people in this city instead of purchasing a few old boats. There is a
form of paranoia which manifests itself in believing oneself to be a
great man.'[14]

Panken's advice, that the '"dupes" who have contributed to [the
Black Star Line]' seek recompense and apply to the courts for the
appointment of a receiver, went unheeded. Astonishingly, there was no
'run' on the organisation. On the contrary, Marcus Garvey's personal
stock held up remarkably well despite the judgment against him. The
heads of the rival NAACP were perplexed. 'Among the poor and
exploited,' wrote Mary White Ovington, with more of a hint of envy
than animosity, 'even among those whose money he misappropriated,
he is defended with an ardour that abashes the critic.'

There was no pandemonium at the venues where Garvey subsequently spoke; no clamouring for a return of funds. There was instead
an extraordinary willingness, amongst his followers, to close ranks and
rally round their persecuted leader; an acceptance of his assurances
that their money would be returned eventually and of his assertion
that this arrest was 'but a concoction decided upon by the unseen
forces operating . . . to find some criminal excuse by which the promoter
of the greatest movement among Negroes could be held up to world
scorn and ridicule'. Garvey mistook those unseen forces for his African-
American rivals. In none of his writing at this time does Garvey seem
to conceive the degree to which the campaign against him was actually being engineered by the state – or perhaps he chose not to. It was
abundantly clear to others. The Communist, Robert Minor, questioned
the solicitude of the authorities acting on behalf of the shareholders.
As Minor observed, investigators found it enormously difficult to break
down African-American cynicism over the motives of a government
which had not made a priority of black welfare in the past; he doubted
whether the 'lickspittles of Capitalism', the corrupt beneficiaries of the
Teapot Dome scandal, would 'have any objection to fleecing the Negro
masses'.[15]

Despite the talk of his preparedness for martyrdom, Marcus Garvey
underestimated the seriousness of the charge against him and the
determination of Hoover and the Bureau of Investigation to secure
a conviction. Hoover worried that Garvey might yet wriggle out of
the prosecution. His agents informed him that Garvey's lawyer was

confident that, for a $20,000 bribe parcelled out amongst certain influential individuals, the case against his client would be dropped. Agent 800 assured his bosses, though, that 'Garvey would not come across with the money'. Much to his lawyer's frustration, Garvey would wake up to the threat only after his first formal interview with the federal authorities and once he gleaned the extent of the evidence in their possession, but by then it would be too late.[16] Judging from the amount of time he devoted to talking about the prosecution, Garvey was undoubtedly concerned about it, but he had developed, especially in the last few years, an extraordinary capacity to compartmentalise his problems, to render them as if they were happening to some third party. Outwardly, after the initial shock of his arrest, Garvey appeared to recapture his natural exuberance. Captain Jones, the BOI informant, was amazed by his bullishness, reporting three months later that 'Garvey seems to have lost sight of the fact that he has ever been indicted or that he will ever be tried. To talk with him you would think that he has never been in court.'[17] Once more Garvey was brimming over with energy, rejecting the counsel of advisers who called for a period of retrenchment and making plans, excitedly, for a tour of the southern and western states. After all, Marcus Garvey was never one for brooding in his tent. He was much more inclined to strap on his armour, to go out and engage the enemy in battle. But it would also be a tour of distraction and diversion. For though he was thrilled by the chance to return to the campaign trail, it was not a propitious time to be striking out for the territory.

The news from the South was sobering. The Ku Klux Klan was ascendant; proselytising field workers of both the NAACP and UNIA, going into small towns with delusional doctrines of black equality, were an obvious target. The look and sound of these activists – bow-tied and suited with Northern twangs and Caribbean lilts – made them conspicuous, no matter how cautious or vigilant they were. At the beginning of May 1922, the UNIA commissioner Robert Moseley canvassed in and around Jacksonville, Texas, moving among the black sharecroppers of the Mountains and the Church Hill Old Farm region; he was invited to speak at local Baptist churches and found the congregations sympathetic. Moseley travelled between the towns buoyed by the warmth of their hospitality and his success in marketing the organisation, but when he finally arrived at Jacksonville, he was pulled off the train and locked in jail on a charge of vagrancy. UNIA HQ wired funds to him. He paid the fine and headed back towards the station. But, as he later wrote to Garvey, starting down the street Moseley was abducted by men in two cars and driven to woods on the edge of town. There 'they made me let down my trousers and threw me to the ground. One held my head, one on each arm and leg.' The ringleader proceeded to horsewhip him. Once his tormentors had finished with their fun, a terrified, bruised and bleeding Moseley fled the town on the very next train.[18] Marcus Garvey was due in the South the following month and would not be dissuaded by Moseley's experience. Presently, he and a party of officers were rounding up support in the West.

Garvey planned a show of strength in Los Angeles. He sent word in advance to the local divisions of details for a parade and the line of march to which the faithful were encouraged to join. Blaring trumpets from the UNIA announced the start of the parade of several thousands which included colour bearers, a float with the Goddess of Liberty and Feminine Deity of Africa, the local legions, officers and Black Cross Nurses of the Los Angeles and other divisions, and the honourable Marcus Garvey accompanied by his private secretary, Amy Jacques. Los Angeles was the most important staging post in Garvey's campaign throughout California to win back the defectors and solicit new members. From Oakland he sent a telegram back to Harlem's Liberty Hall, in the manner of a victorious general, assuring the membership that the mission was completed:

> Entire State recaptured for organisation; defeated enemies in Oakland and held enthusiastic meeting by enjoining Chief of Police, who was under influence of enemies of movement. Great triumph; splendid loyalty to cause from Frisco to Los Angeles. Entire North and Southwest rallying to colors of organisation.[19]

The account of Garvey's conversion of enemies, as his roadshow rolled on through California, was supported by military intelligence officers. Commander J. J. Hannigan reported the strange spectacle of detectives, who had infiltrated the audience at Oakland and who had readied themselves for the possible arrest of Garvey should he inflame racial hatred, only to find that they 'encored him along with the others when he commenced to speak'. Hannigan's memo to his superiors included the confounding assessment that in the San Francisco Chapter alone '400 [new] members have come into the organisation since Garvey's visit . . . the negroes seem to have a childish faith in him'. Many were undoubtedly bewitched by the leader's ability to chastise and inspire at the same time. Wherever Garvey ventured he secured the largest venue possible, and tirelessly recycled the same brutally frank message. It was dark and foreboding, and even, in parts, apocalyptic. 'Negroes [were] the most careless people in the world,' and African-Americans were mistaken in their belief that the white man, having built his railroads, his opera houses and other building blocks of civilisation, was going to yield that civilisation to the black man. But that bleak view was coupled to the promise of salvation that only a prophet with an almighty self-belief could uphold: 'If the Negro wants the comforts of modern civilisation . . . to ride in Pullman cars . . . and occupy orchestra seats,' Garvey advised that he should give up any expectation of being invited to the seat of government in the USA, and 'go out and create for himself a United States of Africa'. From California, he would take his message to the South: 'I may pass this way but once,' he told audiences in Oakland, 'if I come not again, remember that Marcus Garvey was here and in his humble way tried to convey to you the sign of the times.'[20]

His prophecy would be conveyed by the *Negro World* to the larger black world. Black people throughout the diaspora would be invited to join their African-American brethren and take shelter under Garvey's African vine and fig tree. Although he was impatient for his ideas to be adopted, Garvey also understood that for him to succeed black people would have to break with the past and recast their minds – a process that might take generations before it came to pass. He understood the basic psychology of the people: he was one of them and acknowledged the distance he had travelled in his own not so distant past, to divest himself of his former colonial self, a time when he had sung the British national anthem 'to the King with more fervour, more lustre than anyone else'.[21] He expected to be persecuted: it was the lot of any leader of a downtrodden people. What Marcus Garvey was now demanding for Great Britain's black citizens of Empire, Mahatma Gandhi was demanding for its Indian subjects. On 10 March, Gandhi was arrested and put on trial for a series of articles in *Young India* which were considered seditious. Gandhi pleaded guilty to preaching disaffection towards the [British] government established by law in India, and was subsequently sentenced to six years' imprisonment. The

Negro World followed closely the course of his trial, and Garvey aligned himself to the Mahatma, 'one of the noblest characters of the day', whose sacrifice, like the Irish Republican martyr, Terence MacSwiney, would 'ultimately pave the way for a free and independent India'. Africa should be free, just like India and Ireland. In order to concretise the idea of an African homeland, Garvey was prepared to act expediently and embrace even the most unlikely of allies. One such was the southern Senator, T. S. McCallum who, the month before, had proposed a bill for the United States 'to secure sufficient territory in Africa to make a suitable and final home for the American Negro'. The Mississippi senator's proposal, and archaic flapdoodle of ideas to 'colonise Africa with the surplus American colored population' struck Garvey as 'not far-fetched . . . but reasonable and feasible'[22] – a view strengthened when the resolution was passed by the state senate by a majority of almost three to one, and not diminished by its final rejection in the House of Representatives.

Garvey was gradually reversing the setbacks to the organisation. Even the disappointing announcement that sales in the Black Star Line had inevitably ceased, he advanced as a painful but a necessary learning stage. The UNIA leader felt strongly that the tide was slowly but inexorably turning in his favour once more, and that his movement was at the epicentre of a black zeitgeist. By 1922, Egypt had achieved a semblance of home rule; the American administration had approved the $5 million loan to Liberia; and French colonial rule was under attack, if only in the shape of a novel, *Batouala*, whose frank portrayal of the brutality of life in its African territories – earning René Maran the prestigious Prix Goncourt – shattered the much-trumpeted illusion of France's benign administration. All were supporting evidence, convincing Garvey of the rightness of his instinct.[23]

The UNIA convention was now instituted as an annual event. Following his arrest, Garvey and his officers recognised its magnified importance. Any significant dip in the numbers attending would reflect the distemper of the people and a cooling of enthusiasm for the UNIA programme. Having championed the convention as an all-black event in previous years, Garvey now opened it up to include white participation. European ministries of the colonies were invited to send representatives, along with sympathetic senators. From his old contacts' book a number of establishment figures, such as Nicholas Butler, who had been successfully courted in the early days of the fledgling organisation, were also invited.

The honours system was to be rolled out again during the convention. At the top of the list was William Pickens, the writer and aspiring executive of the NAACP who'd written with understanding and sensitivity about the UNIA. Garvey intended, with conference hall's blessing, a reshuffling of his cabinet. He first wrote to Pickens, reminding him that 'there is always a place for you . . . not at the foot, but at the very head [of the organisation]', and followed up with an offer of a cabinet position, notifying Pickens that his name had been put forward for one of the highest honours.[24]

Several months had passed since Garvey's arrest. The trial date had been postponed on at least three occasions, leading Garvey and his advisers to conclude that the case against him was weak since the government had failed subsequently 'to find any incriminating evidence'. But if those signs were correct, that in the near future he would ultimately escape the trap laid by the government, it would prove only a temporary reprieve. On 25 June 1922, he set himself a far bigger trap. From Atlanta – the centre of the revived Ku Klux Klan – Marcus Garvey sent what might have appeared on the surface to be yet another boosting, self-congratulatory telegram to Liberty Hall but which, on careful reading, contained news of an extraordinary meeting:

Have this day interviewed Edward Young Clarke, acting Imperial Wizard Knights of the Ku Klux Klan. In conference of two hours he outlined the aims and objects of the Klan. He denied any hostility towards the Negro Improvement Association. He believes America to be a white man's country, and also states that the Negro should have a country of his own in Africa. He denied that his organisation, since its reorganisation, ever officially attacked the Negro. He has been invited to speak at forthcoming convention to further assure the race of the stand of the Klan.[25]

Marcus Garvey believed that he had pulled off the most amazing coup. To have entered voluntarily the headquarters of an organisation that was morally, and at times directly, responsible for the most repulsive and heinous crimes against black people in America, required enormous personal courage. It also spoke of the kind of stupefying certainty that is the preserve of few; and of a colossal arrogance in disregarding how his actions might be perceived – even by well-wishers. In the immediate aftermath of the meeting, Garvey declined to broadcast any details, but his spokesman was quoted as divulging the bewildering news that 'Garvey intends to reorganise the Black Star Line shortly, and it is possible [the Imperial Wizard] Clarke may buy stock in the new company'.[26]

The machinations of a black leader convening with the Ku Klux Klan made the front pages of many black papers, with worrying signs that the meeting was not going to be portrayed in the victorious manner in which Garvey had conceived it. The *New Era* dismissed Garvey's intervention as the work of one who did not 'fully understand the heart and aspirations of the race', and a future, chosen leader would be 'a son of the soil and not a foreign-born would-be diplomat'. Further evidence of looming trouble came with William Pickens's rejection of the medieval 'dishonour' of becoming 'a Knight, or Duke or some other breed of Nobleman'. Reflecting on what he perceived as Garvey's new alliance, the honour might just have well been offered by the Ku Klux Klan, and Pickens 'would rather be damned or murdered by such an organisation than to be . . . rewarded by it'.[27]

Since its opening in 1919, Liberty Hall had become the ever-rejuvenating nerve centre of the movement and, on a personal level, a place of safety and sanctuary for its leader. It was to Liberty Hall that Garvey now returned. But amongst the cheering of 3,000 members who turned out to hear their leader was the previously unfamiliar sound of dissenting voices and murmurings of discontent. For gone was the raging general of previous years who had defiantly screamed for armed self-defence, to answer a black lynching with a white lynching. In his place was a much more sober pacifier who acknowledged the superior and destructive power of his white adversaries, whom black people were best not to aggravate. In Garvey's conception the Ku Klux Klan represented the invisible government of America that was determined to keep the country white. In his defence, Garvey expounded on the need to get up close and study one's enemy in order to be effective. Several months previously, in its exposé of the Klan, the *New York World* had ridiculed it as a money-making organisation in which the 'Klan itself owns the company manufacturing the regalia of cotton robe and hooded cap, which is sold to members for $6.50 and costs $1.25 to make. Its lucrative possibilities have recently been increased by the decision to admit women as well as men to membership. The sisters can now come on in with the brothers – at only $10 per come-on.'[28] Initially Garvey had praised the *New York World*'s journalistic investigation of the Klan as rendering 'a splendid service to this great Republic by its exposé of the underhand methods of this anti-American society'. Members of the Klan, he warned, 'seek to outrage and endanger the lives and property of others through their unlawful attacks'. Bizarrely, the *World*'s mocking of the 'invisible empire' had had the unexpected consequence of boosting membership ten-fold; even 'New York [had become] a stronghold of the Klan'. South of the Mason-Dixon Line, though, was where Klan activity mostly thrived, and Garvey, rethinking his position, was especially scathing about those brave African-Americans who spoke defiantly from a position of safety in the North, leaving their poor brethren in the South (neighbours of hateful white 'crackers') to pick up the bill for that defiance. He heaped scorn on the NAACP's attachment to an anti-lynching bill (sponsored by Senator Dyer) which he rightly predicted would never be approved by the Senate. The Klan, Garvey believed, was represented through all walks of white American life – the postman, the teacher, the policeman, the politician. And he concluded by pleading with his critics not to rush to judgement until the word-for-word account of his meeting with the Imperial Wizard was published in the *Negro World* and the Klan's *Searchlight*.

It was a vain hope. Schadenfreude slid from the lips of the gossips in the parlours of the Talented Tenth in black America where Garvey's coup was seen rather as a titanic blunder. Walter White was shown a memorandum of the Ku Klux Klan meeting which, he claimed, amounted to a Faustian pact 'whereby Garvey was to be allowed to come into the South to sell stock to Negroes in his various enterprises . . . and in return [would] seek to break up organisations among Negroes opposed to the Klan, particularly the NAACP'.[29] Acting as secretary to the NAACP, White had tried but failed to obtain the actual transcript of the meeting which was never published. Given the climate of hostility between the two rival organisations it's not surprising that Walter White was all too ready to portray Marcus Garvey as a latter-day Mephistopheles. White's assessment came after a significant hardening in the NAACP's public stance towards Garvey. But if the attitude was uncharitable, then the language was, at least, temperate. By contrast the radical journal, the *Messenger*, dispensed with any pretence towards civility. From its offices in Harlem, in the same building and the floor above the UNIA Publishing and Printing House, the *Messenger* published a vicious and vituperative editorial that signalled the start of an irreparable break with Garvey. On the front page of its July 1922 edition, above a headline noting 'Negro homebuyer's anxiety over falling rents', the *Messenger* made plain its disgust with the UNIA leader: 'Garvey, Black Eagle, Becomes Messenger Boy of Clarke, Ku Klux Kleagle.' The paper's co-editor Chandler Owen's loathing took a particularly nativist turn, lambasting him for the 'fool talk [that] emanates from a blustering West Indian demagogue who preys upon the ignorant'. The fearless editor put Garvey and his supporters on note that the *Messenger* was 'firing the opening gun in a campaign to drive Garvey and Garveyism in all its sinister viciousness from the American soil'.[30] True to his word, Chandler Owen and his co-editor, A. Philip Randolph (who'd sportingly introduced Garvey to the street audiences back in 1917), went on to spearhead a 'Marcus Garvey Must Go' campaign. They were joined by William Pickens (fresh from penning his rejection of a knighthood) and another NAACP man, the Detroit preacher, Robert Bagnall – forming a union of convenience (the editors of the *Messenger* had previously, contemptuously, labelled their new ally Pickens as a stalwart of 'the conservative Negro leadership'). Together they announced a series of public forums to be held every Sunday in August, in the Lafayette Building, just a few streets down from where Garvey was presiding over the UNIA's third convention. In their minds Garvey had sinned, not just in convening with the masked devils of the Ku Klux Klan, but in the implication of surrender, that black Americans should forfeit their rights to life and liberty in America. A statement to that end, that Garvey is alleged to have made in New Orleans, was also printed on the handbills advertising the meetings. It read:

> This is a white man's country. He found it, he conquered it, and we can't blame him if he wants to keep it. I am not vexed with the white man of the South for Jim Crowing me because I am black. I never built any street cars or railroads. The white man built them for his own convenience. And if I don't want to ride where he's willing to ride then I'd better walk.[31]

A boisterous crowd of 2,000 packed into the Shuffle Inn Music Hall in the Lafayette Building to hear Pickens deliver a sharp rebuke on 'what to do when Negro leaders league with Negro lynchers'. At least half the audience were made up of Garvey supporters who reacted indignantly when Pickens exaggeratedly claimed that his life had been threatened, but refused to name by whom. The local police department, fearing trouble, stationed patrolmen throughout the hall but, apart from a regular chorus of 'Garvey Must Go' from the most vociferous Garvey-baiters, the event was a relatively tame affair in which the worst abuse hurled at the absent UNIA president was that he was 'a little half-wit lil[l]iputian'.[32]

The playground name-calling would not have prepared Garvey-watchers for the farrago of shrieking malevolence that was to come. First out of the blocks was the NAACP heavyweight, Robert Bagnall, who published a piece of literary assassination in the *Messenger* which began and ended in bile. Garvey, he maintained, was 'a Negro of unmixed stock, squat, stocky, fat and sleek, with protruding jaws, and heavy jowls, small bright pig-like eyes and rather bull-dog-like face. Boastful, egotistic, tyrannical, intolerant, cunning, shifty, smooth and suave, avaricious . . .'

Bagnall's nauseating assault marked a new low in black solidarity. There had been fundamental disputes between rival groups before, most notably between the pro- and anti-Booker T. Washington camps, but never had there been such an open and public display of disdain and contempt by a black thinker towards one of his own. Bagnall crossed a line and made it possible and probable that others would follow. Though his admirers would rush to Garvey's defence and take issue with Bagnall, it was Pickens's attack that seemed more disturbing to Garvey; the sense of his desertion and betrayal was especially hurtful. Garvey would have rejoiced in Pickens's return to the fold more than he would over a hundred righteous new recruits to the movement.[33] As it was, Pickens, high on the NAACP-roasted hog, had chosen to sup with the devil: 'I wonder if anybody has patted Pickens on the shoulder,' mused Garvey, or 'taken [him] by the hand. I would not doubt [it] . . . because I have seen him recently very much in the company of white folks, and any time a Negro gets into the company of white folks he becomes a dangerous Negro.'[34] Garvey's critics could easily have roared back that especially dangerous was the Negro who sits down with men wearing white hoods. 'The bite, bitterness and fire in the belly of Marcus Garvey' was a return to a familiar theme of treacherous black brothers who only trusted in their validation through proximity to the white man. It seems that its very closeness to the truth is what so enraged Garvey's rivals. 'Now back of his exaggeration,' Dr Du Bois would admit, 'lies a "kernel of truth" that gains him his following; there are plenty of black folk who are bitterly ashamed of their color.' Though it was perhaps forgivable that they shrank 'with blind repulsion from the uglier aspects of their race's degradation'.[35]

The *Negro World* would charge that Du Bois was really writing about himself, that he who hailed from a Brahmin caste refused to accept the pre-eminence of someone deemed of the lower caste, such as Garvey. A *Negro World* essay entitled 'With Apologies to Shakespeare' likened the UNIA president to Julius Caesar, and Du Bois and the anti-Garvey cabal to Brutus and the unscrupulous and inferior plotters. In Act XCIX, Senator (James Weldon) Johnson echoed the dismay of the plotters:

> Why, man, he doth bestride the world of Negroes
> Like a Colossus; and we petty men
> Walk under his huge legs, and peep about
> To find ourselves dishonourable graves,
> Now, in the names of all the Gods at once,
> Upon what meat doth this our Garvey feed,
> That he is grown so great.[36]

J. Edgar Hoover was equally irritated by the continuing menace of the 'notorious Negro agitator' and frustrated over his stalled prosecution. On 10 August he wrote to the relevant department urging 'early action upon the prosecution . . . in order that he [Garvey] may be once and for all put where he can peruse his past activities behind the four walls of the Atlanta clime'.[37] Hoover's anxiety over Garvey's renewed activities stemmed from the spectacle of the opening of the latest international convention which on 1 August came with an added attraction.

A biplane swooped down over Liberty Hall, roaring back and forth over the heads of the delegates. At the controls sat the beaming twenty-five-year-old Trinidadian, 'Colonel' Hubert Fauntleroy Julian – the first black man in the western hemisphere to qualify as a pilot.[38] Even in a black metropolis bulging with eccentric characters, 'Colonel' Julian stood out in his plus fours, long woollen socks, two-tone brogues, striped silk tie and tight leather skullcap. Once removed, his aviator's goggles revealed a Hollywood matinee idol's good looks: a pencil-thin moustache lined lips that were always on the verge of breaking out into a smile. He was immodestly handsome, and at air displays did a brisk trade in autographed photos as well as kisses, sold at $5 a time and 'if the girls were young and pretty, they got their money's worth'.

In the spring of 1922, the 'colonel' had already achieved a measure of fame when he descended on Harlem, literally, parachuting from his plane, avoiding skyscrapers, radio masts and telephone wires, on a publicity stunt for a local optician. He'd quickly gravitated towards the UNIA, joined the African Legion, and been praised by Garvey as a credit to the race. Julian didn't have the field entirely to himself. 'Brave' Bessie Coleman, who'd learnt to fly in France, was also introduced to adoring audiences at the convention. She gave flying exhibitions to the Harlem crowds and, though she wasn't as spectacular as Julian, she surpassed him in competence. Nonetheless, it was the flamboyant Julian whom Garvey enlisted as an officer in the UNIA; thereafter, as a speaker, the aviator packed out Liberty Hall with his simple message: 'You can do anything anyone else can do. Just get up and try.' Try and try again were fitting words to describe the young and somewhat inconsistent pilot. His pioneering parachute jumps – yet to be perfected – were preceded by huge billboard advertisements on 139th Street that encouraged Harlemites to 'Watch the Clouds This Sunday – Julian is Arriving from the Sky Here'. Amateur bookies offered short odds on his survival, and local undertakers bid for the rights to bury him. On his maiden jump, dressed in a theatrical devil's costume, Julian leapt clear of the plane, opened his 'chute, struggled with the guidelines, missed his target and landed on top of the post office. Six months later, he jumped again, this time playing the saxophone, and crashed through the glass skylight of Harlem's police station – a performance that thereafter earned him the sobriquet 'The Black Eagle of Harlem'.

'Colonel' Julian was both a colourful distraction and a useful promoter of Garveyite ideals, none more so than when he planned a solo intercontinental flight from America to Liberia – a project which he envisaged would be funded by Negro donations. Early on, 'Colonel' Julian moved to scotch rumours that investors would be throwing away their money on an aeronautical equivalent of the phantom *Phyllis Wheatley*. He arranged for the plane to be brought to a vacant lot in Harlem where it was christened *Ethiopia 1* and the legend, 'Dedicated to the Advancement of the Race', was inscribed on its side. On 4 July, Julian arrived at the 139th Street Pier. The flight plans for *Ethiopia 1* had met with the same kind of scepticism that Garvey and the BSL had suffered before the launch of the *Yarmouth*. Critics wrote off the Black Eagle as a showman and opportunist. Raising funds had proved difficult, especially as the NAACP had refused his request to endorse the project. Nonetheless, at the appointed hour of 3.00 p.m., in front of a crowd of tens of thousands and a grandstand packed with UNIA dignitaries and the uniformed Legion, 'Colonel' Julian loaded his suit-cases, labelled 'Tropical', 'Arctic', and 'Stormy Weather', into *Ethiopia 1*. Julian reviewed the final preparations, and his patched-together Boeing hydroplane was blessed by the West Indian revivalist preacher, Reverend Theophilus Martin. But just before take-off, three men, fran-tically waving bits of paper, emerged from the crowd. They were Julian's creditors and they threatened to ground the plane until their demands for an outstanding payment of $1,500 were met. Into the mêlée marched the irrepressible Sergeant William Wellington Grant and a squad of African Legions. 'We'll raise that fifteen hundred in an hour,' prom-ised the sergeant. Two hours later the plane was cleared for take-off. *Ethiopia 1* bombed along the Harlem River, bouncing intermittently, and climbed to several thousand feet. After only a few minutes in the air, it appeared to be in trouble; it kept tilting heavily to starboard and couldn't get level. A pontoon had been damaged. During take-off the float had scooped up gallons of water, and approximately 3,000 miles from its destination of Monrovia, *Ethiopia 1* nosedived into Flushing Bay. 'While more or less on his course,' noted the *New York Times*, the bay 'had not been a scheduled stop'. The 'colonel' was dragged out of the water and ferried to the local hospital, vowing to make another attempt as soon as his dislocated shoulders, broken leg and pride had mended.[39]

During the 1922 convention it was proposed that the Black Eagle be appointed to head a new aeronautical department in the UNIA. That decision was one of the few areas of agreement in an otherwise fractious month-long gathering. It had all begun so promisingly. 'Harlem was in gala attire,' reported the *New York World*; 5,000 people joined in the march and to an impartial observer the parade 'did not suffer by comparison with that of 1921'. The respectable turn-out was a relief but even more exciting to Garvey was the news that his strenuous lobbying, for the movement to be assigned a place at the League of Nations, had paid off. At its inception, Garvey had declared the league 'null and void as far as the Negro is concerned'. He'd since had a change of heart, implementing a policy that strained a point or two beyond dignity, for recognition. League officials had conceded that the UNIA had 'a real case which we cannot totally ignore and should not greatly encourage'. They suggested rather haughtily that '[Reserved] seats for the Assembly would seem to be the least, and the most, we can do.'[40] Memos between European ministries also attested to the inexplicable but undeniable fact of a sustained UNIA influence in Africa. 'Although the outward appearances and the pompous parades . . . [were] expressions of the infantile psychology of the Negro race,' the Italian Ministry of the Colonies counselled against complacency for the showmanship did not diminish the importance of Garvey's 'back-to-Africa' principle – and further, he warned, 'An Africa which gives hospitality to Negroes who have the education, instruction, feelings and lifestyles of the Americans would be more difficult to colonise than the one before the war.'[41]

The nine candidates, proposed for the honour of representing the Negro race at the League of Nations, were whittled down to five. Garvey explained that he couldn't spare more than that number and calibre of men required for the task, when there was a pressing need for them in New York. A modest crowd turned out to send off George O. Marke and the other UNIA delegates to Geneva 'to petition the League for the granting of German territories in South-West Africa to the black peoples of the world'. At almost any other time the news would have elicited a crescendo of self-congratulation from the executive body, but as was evident right from the start of the convention, Garvey and his officers were suffering from a chronic fragility; were beset by seemingly intractable financial difficulties, and under siege from transparent and hidden adversaries. Even though the body of the *New York World* coverage of the opening parade was favourable, its headline, 'Garvey Reviews his Nobility Amid a Few Nosebleeds', alluded to dissension and scuffles on the fringes of the parade which for the first time was not just guarded by a cordon of police, but a battery of black private detectives and 'a score or more of uniformed men of the Association'. They shielded the UNIA president and the other dignitaries when they alighted from the vehicles and took their places on the reviewing stand in front of 2305 7th Avenue – the site of the Universal Publishing House. A key photograph of the reviewing stand that day accidentally illustrated the uncomfortable predicament that Garvey found himself in at the beginning of August 1922. Keen-eyed patrolmen stand to the side and in front of the UNIA leader, on the lookout for trouble, but sharing a casual conversation; on the makeshift stand, four rows back from Garvey, and enjoying the view as the sun bounces off their straw boaters, are Chandler Owen and A. Philip

Randolph, his rabid critics who were pumping out their 'Garvey Must Go' pamphlets from the same building on 7th Avenue which they shared with his publishing house. Indeed, Owen and Randolph had purposefully planned to hold their anti-Garvey Sunday meetings during the same month of the convention. With potential enemies in front and back and swirling all around him, Garvey had nowhere to hide; Harlem was his nerve centre but was now also home to a self-righteous and resourceful enemy; and further, Garvey was increasingly apprehensive about whom he could trust.

The *Negro World* reporter commissioned to record the daily workings of the month-long convention wrote, without irony, that Marcus Garvey was the one man who was capable of 'holding together and in harmony the various elements and forces composing the present convention'. Perhaps the writer had been tipped off about the unprecedented step the UNIA leader was about to take. For the first time ever, Garvey assumed the role of Speaker of the Convention, presiding over the hall in the place of the elected speaker, Adrian Johnson.

The morning session of 4 August began with singing and prayers before delegates settled down to business. Speaker Garvey startled the convention with the news that immediately set the tone for the month-long convention. The first item on the agenda would be the impeachment of the Hon. Adrian Johnson, charged by the president on three counts – neglecting to pay his dues to the movement, lacking in the intellectual rigour required to carry out his tasks in office, and disloyalty. Johnson was outraged and 'hastily left . . . in a disgruntled and ugly mood . . . shouting back at the chair', threatening to sue the organisation for his unpaid salary.

The incumbent surgeon-general, Dr J. D. Gibson, was also impeached for making false presentations about his qualifications as a physician, and for 'disloyalty'. Those who doubted Dr Gibson's guilt had their misperceptions corrected when witnesses later reported – after the recess – that Dr Gibson had made derogatory remarks about President-General Garvey. Gibson had allegedly grumbled from the back of the hall, 'If the people are going to sit still and let the "Tsar" rule the organisation, there will be no organisation; it will be smashed.' Dr Gibson was hurriedly impeached.

A happier note was struck by the delegate from Bocas del Toro in Costa Rica who enlivened proceedings with a rendition of a song that was the biggest hit at their meetings. It was called 'Garvey is the Leader in Whom We Trust'. But the first week of the convention ended with rumours of a private conference at the UNIA's Phyllis Wheatley Hotel, attended by Reverend Eason (the leader of the American Negroes). Allegedly the purpose of the meeting was 'to curtail the power of the president-general'. A motion expressing confidence in the president-general was passed unanimously by the convention without debate. But with the 'Garvey Must Go' campaigners mustering just a few blocks away from the UNIA convention, amid speculations, rumblings and carping 'off stage', a vote of confidence was cold comfort.

Halfway through the convention, the most bizarre rumour of all was reported in the *Negro World*. Under the headline, 'Enemies Plot to Do Away With Hon. Marcus Garvey', the paper detailed a plot to assassinate the president. A 'reliable source' had attended a secret meeting in Harlem where in the midst of a heated discussion 'an avalanche of cheers' greeted one of the conspirators who'd suggested 'the only way to get rid of him [Garvey] is to get him'. The paper assured concerned readers that though the UNIA leader was convinced that 'there wasn't any of the burlesque' in the threats to his life, when questioned about whether he was afraid he said calmly, 'They may assassinate me but the fight for Africa will not lessen.'

On 18 August, when Marcus Garvey mounted the podium to present his president-general's report for the year, all equilibrium seems to have deserted him. He lashed out at the 'incompetent, disloyal, dishonest and characterless individuals' who constituted the majority (eighteen out of twenty) of his executive council, who instead of performing their functions had 'carried out intrigues, plots and other evil designs' against him in the course of the year. He declined to name the culprits or elaborate further except to confirm that he had decided 'to work no longer with such individuals' and that, in the future, the cabinet should not be elected but appointed. Having detonated his unexpected bomb, Garvey sat down and pandemonium broke out over the convention centre. 'Many officers,' reported the *Negro World*, 'desired that Garvey exclude them from the general imputations contained in his remarks', but the UNIA leader declined to comment further.

The convention report for the next day carried a strange announcement: 'President-General Resigns!'

Marcus Garvey formally tendered his resignation as leader of the UNIA and provisional president of Africa. The news was accompanied by sarcastic cheers from some sections of the hall. Garvey gave as his reason for resigning that 'he refused to associate any longer with a body of men who were not honest enough to do things above board'. But he left the way open for his return with the explanation that 'when one resigns because of his conviction, he sometimes comes back a more dangerous fighter than ever before . . . Some say, "Garvey must go," but we shall see in a short while who must go . . . before the UNIA can indulge in a clean fight with those from without, now we have to clean from within.' Garvey appeared to be trying to force the wholesale resignation of the executive council, to flush out the enemy within. A 'copious influx of resignations' followed – but they were invariably those closely associated with Garvey, such as Henrietta Vinton Davis and William Ferris. The majority stubbornly held out, including the man on whom he had most firmly set his sights, the American Leader, J. H. Eason.

Trouble was certainly coming but in the interim a phoney war would reign with some delightful distractions that focused on Africa. The colourful and eccentric delegate Harry W. Kirby kept popping up with chimerical suggestions to be adopted by the convention. His recommendation that a secret society, 'The Order of Ethiopia', be established, whose members could be 'taught the mother language of the Negro, by which, in whatever part of the world he may be, he can converse with his fellow brother without anyone else being able to understand', introduced much mirth into the galleries and ultimately 'fell rather flat'. Perhaps alarmed that Kirby's ideas of Africa were indicative of the delegates' overall ignorance of the continent, Dusé Mohamed Ali offered a lecture that served as a 'rapid sketch or survey of political conditions existing in Africa at the present time'. But the highlight of the convention's entertainment was a grand fashion parade and pageant 'of women of African nobility . . . Escorted by the Universal guards, [they] walked in procession half the length of the hall to the platform, where they were seated on either side of "Her Royal Highness the Queen of Sheba", represented by Lady Henrietta Vinton Davis.' She was eventually joined by more than a dozen others. Mrs E. M. Barber caused a flutter of additional excitement as she displayed her costume representing 'Her Royal Highness Ato Herony, wearing an original Abyssinian dress woven and hand embroidered by African natives, and original ostrich plume'.

Once the gowns were put away, war was resumed. A rather innocuous report (which appeared in the convention bulletin) of a wrangle between

Garvey and Eason over salaries (Eason claimed to be owed more than $1,000) was the prelude to an outright attack on Eason. For as well as acknowledging the legitimacy of the reverend's salary claim, Garvey was able to inform the convention that inadvertently the investigation had thrown up examples of impropriety. Three days later Garvey provided a detailed list of Eason's transgressions and duly charged him with serious and impeachable wrongdoings.

It was a dangerous moment. The 'silver-tongued Eason' was a tough and resourceful orator – a much-admired lieutenant, especially by African-Americans, and effectively second only to Garvey in his influence within the movement. The case against Eason would have to be carefully framed and rock-solid. It was not. Instead, the pettiness of the charge, when it was articulated, was almost beyond belief. As outlined by Garvey, Eason had erred by selling pictures of himself and the president-general of the UNIA and of pocketing the proceeds; other questionable instances of financial dishonesty (borrowing money from UNIA members) were added to strengthen the case against him. The real unstated charge was that in the rancorous bear-pit of Liberty Hall, in the fevered atmosphere of betrayal that whispered from every wall, Eason could not be trusted. It was, in a sense, a reasonable assumption.

Eason had bristled at Garvey's encouragement of the cult of personality that had grown up around him. President-General Garvey had become, of late, far too imperial for Eason's republican tastes: the phonograph recordings of Garvey's famous speeches on sale at the convention; life-size portraits of the UNIA leader that graced the walls of HQ and the line of march on UNIA parades, might be excused as necessary propaganda rather than projecting the eminence of the leader. They were just about acceptable to Eason (after all his own souvenir medallion might also be purchased by the faithful); but, recently, the UNIA leader had all but abandoned any lingering pretence of collective decision-making. The debacle over the Ku Klux Klan was the clearest example. In October 1921 Eason told a Liberty Hall crowd, 'It is laughable to hear some people here in Harlem say they are ready for the Ku Klux Klan, when they have not even a pop gun with which to defend themselves.' The threat of violent self-defence, Eason maintained, was the watchword of the UNIA – an organisation that he was proud to be part of because it was 'trying to create a force, a power among Negroes, by getting them all lined up, that will enable them successfully to combat against the Ku Klux Klan or any other band or group of people whose purpose and object is to destroy or oppress Negroes'. He was proud also of the sign that had subsequently been erected at Liberty Hall which read, 'The New Negro is Ready for the Ku Klux Klan'. Now, less than a year later, came the galling and unforgivable news that Garvey had met the Imperial Wizard. In two hours of self-righteous diplomatic folly, Eason believed, Garvey had stripped the movement of its popular militancy and irreversibly tarnished its reputation with a despicable act of appeasement. Eason had held his silver tongue in the interests of unity but Garvey rightly anticipated that it would not be much longer before it would be let loose. By levelling a charge of malfeasance against the American leader, Garvey had pre-empted Eason's public attack on him that was bound to come.

Reverend Eason consented to being put on trial but only if he could state his counter-claims to the entire convention. Garvey agreed. But during Eason's trial the reverend was to find that the charge sheet against him had expanded. Witnesses were encouraged to come forward with other accounts of Reverend Eason's behaviour that was unbecoming of a man who held such a high office; in particular that he was a 'whisky-head' who, when on the road with female officers, had drunkenly barged into their hotel rooms, late at night, and tried to climb into bed with them – before passing out.

Predictably, Eason spelt out much graver accusations against Garvey on 22 August, though couched in generalisations – 'incompetence, forming an alliance with a discreditable organisation and creating an unfriendly feeling among American Negroes'. No one from inside the organisation had ever publicly spoken about its leader like that before. That such words were pronounced by one of its most revered members aggregated the offence; Eason's allegations struck Liberty Hall like an almighty thunderclap. 'An air of disgust and displeasure pervaded the entire audience,' noted the convention report, and when the American leader itemised his charges against Garvey, 'outward expressions of wrath were registered . . . [with] hisses and derisive remarks arising from all parts of the hall'.[42] In a lengthy, pedantic and angry exchange – with both men relying on the services of the organisation's attorneys – the outcome was not unexpected. Garvey was vindicated; judgment was found against his assistant. Eason was dismissed from his cabinet position and expelled from the UNIA for a lifetime (99 years). Reverend

Eason's subsequent attempts to take on the agreed role of plaintiff and have Garvey tried, foundered immediately on the technicality that the reverend was now no longer a member of the organisation; he was not privileged to level such an accusation.

With Eason out of the way, there was diminished resistance to Garvey's suggestions that the rest of the cabinet be requested to resign; they were given ten minutes to do so and duly obliged. At the end of the month when nominations for the vacant post of president-general and provisional president of Africa were called for 'the convention was literally stampeded . . . it seemed as though every delegate rose simultaneously and vied with one another to place the name of Hon. Marcus Garvey'. No count was needed for the unanimous re-election of Marcus Garvey, and following the revisions to the constitution, he was then free to make his own appointments.

The newly re-elected president-general had banked on the necessary but unpleasant business of purging the high command to bring an end to the infighting. 'No great movement,' he had said, 'can successfully lead itself on to victory against any opposition while having within its ranks those who give aid and comfort to the enemy'. But a pall of discontent settled, like a damp and persistently cloying fog, over the remaining days of the proceedings. Eason's allies struggled to rid themselves of the thoughts of the injustice meted out to their man; they consoled themselves with the spurious argument that the dastardly deed was not the fault of Garvey but the work of new confidants who'd inveigled themselves into positions where they were more than capable of 'putting devilment in the president's head'.[43] These Garvey boosters who justified, without irony, the need 'to weed out the figureheads who seem to think that we come to destroy all the Negroes who do not agree with us', had not bargained for the BOI informants who waited at the gates of Liberty Hall for the resigned and expelled former executive officers. They constituted a group who now more than ever was disinclined to be governed by the dictum, 'If you can't bring yourself to praise then at least "do no harm".'

At the conclusion of the convention, Garvey strove for an amicable separation from those officers who voluntarily retired or were forced to do so. Now that the deed was done, he spoke sympathetically about the sense of loss they might feel. Garvey bid them think beyond themselves for the good of the organisation. Their removal was purely business and the retiring officers should feel proud of their past contributions. In a gesture of magnanimity, Garvey invited them each to make a final farewell address to the hall.

The former high chancellor was the first to speak, followed by the commissioner-general and lastly the Honourable U. S. Poston, the ex-minister of labor. With a sweep of his arm, Poston turned to the new executives lined up alongside Garvey and offered a word of warning. Conjuring the spectre of Napoleon, years after his many glories, now exiled on St Helena, he bid Garvey to reflect on the wisdom of the *petit général*'s painful reminiscence: 'Had my council properly advised me, had they opposed me at times, France would have ruled supreme.'[44]

There were still powerful and forthright individuals on the fringes of Garvey's movement but after the purges of 1922, their numbers were severely depleted. Similarly, too, the voices of moderation in the 'Garvey Must Go' collective were drowned out by bellicose and belligerent opponents, girded to tell the most unflattering truths. As the convention drew to a close, and each side slid towards a modus operandi bereft of limiting rules of engagement, their internecine squabble was about to take a dark and sinister turn.

15

CAGING THE TIGER

To jail Marcus Garvey would dim romance; like jailing a rainbow.
New York Journal, 18 January 1922

ON the afternoon of 5 September 1922, A. Philip Randolph was working at his desk in the cramped offices of the *Messenger* at 2305 7th Avenue (two flights up from UNIA Publishing House), when a brown paper package was delivered, addressed to him. On the back, in place of the name and address of the sender, was simply written, 'From a Friend'. Randolph sized up the package, pondering its New Orleans postmark. As he began to rip open the paper he noticed some 'whitish powder' falling out. It stopped him in his tracks. Randolph, a smooth and elegant fellow, had a reputation for being unflappable, but the anonymity of the sender and the strange powder alarmed him, and aroused his suspicions. A. Philip Randolph telephoned the local police precinct and suggested they send over someone from the bomb squad. The police took the call seriously and dispatched detectives straight away. Arriving at the *Messenger*'s offices, the detectives took the precaution of lowering the package into a bucket of water. Doing so removed the chance of any explosion. Once everyone was satisfied, they could then inspect the content. Randolph later reported to readers of the magazine that 'to the utter amazement and horror of everyone, upon opening the package a human hand was found'.[1] The hand had been severed at the wrist. As 'the back [was] covered with red hair', reported the *New York Times*, it was 'evidently that of a white man'. The clue as to the identity and motive of the sender came with a letter that accompanied the package, signed KKK:

Listen Randolph: We have been watching your writings in all your papers for quite a while, but we want you to understand before we act. If you are not in favour with your own race movement, you can't be with ours. There is no space in our race for you and your crowd. We have sent you a sample of our good work, so watch your step or else . . .

Now let me see your name in your nigger improvement association as a member, paid up too, in about a week from now. Don't worry about lynching in the South. If you were here, you wouldn't talk about it. Now be careful how you publish this letter in your magazine or we may have to send your hand to someone else. Don't think we can't get you or your crowd. Although you are in New York City it is just as easy as if you were in Georgia.

The *Times* concluded that the threatening letter was 'thought to refer to a controversy between Randolph, in his publication, and Marcus Garvey, self-styled President of the Provisional Republic of Africa'. A. Philip Randolph certainly concurred but then he was also the likely source of the *Times*'s speculation. Randolph later voiced his suspicion in the *Messenger* that the 'Klan had come to the rescue of its Negro leader, Marcus Garvey'. Garvey was scandalised. But despite his protestations of innocence, others recalled a speech Garvey had made at the convention the month before, when he is said to have advised Owen and Randolph 'and others who disagreed with him' to 'get themselves another job', as he, Garvey, 'could not be responsible for anything that might happen to them because they might come up with a hand or a leg or a broken head'.

Still, no one was ever arrested over the incident, and the UNIA leader was adamant that he had nothing to do with it. In his view, the bizarre event amounted to little more than a 'publicity stunt'. It was to be expected, Garvey informed readers, because Randolph and his band of black Socialists 'have been trying to steal some of my own publicity for a long time'.[2]

Envy clearly had a part to play in their enmity. By 1922, the *Messenger*, the fearless agent of subversion, had lost much of its power and many of its black admirers. Given the choice, the journal-reading black proletariat opted for the *Negro World*. The rival Socialist magazine conceded that Garvey had 'inculcated into the minds of Negroes the need and value of organisation', but it was the wrong kind of organisation. It was this sense, the lost opportunity effectively to evangelise among the black masses, as much as Garvey's cosying up to the

Ku Klux Klan, that drove the otherwise cool Randolph to a pitch of fury. As he later admitted, 'Against the emotional power of Garveyism, what I was preaching didn't stand a chance.'[3]

The affair of the severed hand served only to exacerbate their differences and unnerve neutral observers about when and how this quickening conflict might end.

Apart from the long-term undercover agent 800, the BOI now employed at least three others – one of whom, the black special agent James E. Amos, seemed specially adept at tracking down potentially hostile witnesses to Garvey and 'bringing them in'. In a previous incarnation, James Amos had served as President Theodore Roosevelt's bodyguard and valet; his graceful efficiency and disarming manner equipped him for this new and delicate task. Amos had been assigned to the case at the outstart, from Garvey's arrest back in January 1922, and by the end of the year, he didn't even need to venture from the bureau's office to openly solicit information. All manner of associates of the UNIA presented themselves to him. Among those interviewed in September included the recently expelled Dr Gibson and Reverend Eason, who were willing to provide 'letters, papers and . . . anything else that will be of service . . . when Garvey is tried . . . and are willing to testify for the Government anytime they are called'.[4] Rumours of the scale and success of Amos's investigation were sufficiently worrisome to Garvey for him to send his attorneys to see whether it might yet be possible to broker a deal with the investigator. Amos dutifully reported back to his superiors 'a proposition to have the Department of Justice quash the indictment if Garvey would pay back dollar for dollar to all the stockholders. The funds for this compensation would be generated from a tax levied on each member of the UNIA – a suggestion which Amos laughingly dismissed as 'robbing Peter to pay Paul'.

No matter the difficulties that daily threatened to envelop him and the movement, Garvey was determined to push ahead with new ideas. Not for him the caution that might be expected from a frightening glimpse over the precipice. As even his enemies acknowledged, Garvey was a superb organiser and promoter. By its very nature, promotion is attached to risk; some promotions will succeed and others will fail. Garvey would answer his critics by asking them what they had done for the race; where were the hundreds of thousands of black people that they had inspired; where were the enterprises that they had launched to employ black people? He had given the black race new thoughts about itself and convinced a whole people that, contrary to what they were led to believe, they were not necessarily born to be hewers of wood and drawers of water. Success was not finite and might best be measured decades hence – in the achievements of subsequent generations. At one stage, when asked about the failure of the Black Star Line, Garvey snapped back, 'We have succeeded in the sense of our desire for success.'[5]

September brought further opportunities for a capacious imagination which was constantly running ahead. Barely a week after he had closed the convention, Garvey once again selected from his wardrobe the ceremonial garments of office, 'a flowing robe of crimson slashed with green' – replacing the traditional scarlet and blue, worn by an English honorary doctor of civil laws – complete with Oxford academic cap, in preparation for the unveiling of the Booker T. Washington University. The educational institution, housed in the UNIA-run Phyllis Wheatley Hotel at 3–13 West 136th Street, was planned as a memorial to Washington. Garvey conceived it as building on the ideas of the famous Tuskegee Institute, and more than 100 students (from around the world) were expected in the first intake. At its core was the principle that graduation from the Booker T. Washington University would be a requirement for each future representative of the UNIA.[6]

Education was also the credo of the UNIA's theatrical presentations. A racially edifying impetus underscored the midnight staging of the dramatic club's *Tallaboo* at Harlem's Lafayette Theatre. The play might not be able to compete with the glamour and pizzazz of *Shuffle Along*, the record-breaking Negro musical comedy, but then it had no intention to. *Tallaboo* was a corollary to *Shuffle Along* which, at its heart, was the 'burlesque of two ignorant Negroes going into "big business" and opening a grocery store [which] was a never-failing producer of side-shaking laughter'.[7] *Tallaboo*, with its equally impressive cast of thirty characters, never offered such comic diversions, but rather promised to interpret the ideals of the UNIA – perhaps not a winning formula for a sell-out show. Wavering prospective punters, though, would soon be able reach a decision by reading a review in the organisation's new daily newspaper, the *Negro Times*.

The *Daily Negro Times* came courtesy of a new printing press costing $12,000 which Garvey had installed in 2305 7th Avenue, and made ready for its launch in September. Aided by a regular United Press ticker (which ticked away with copy from all of the major news agencies) the *Daily Negro Times* aimed to cover world news from a black perspective. For the executive editorship of the paper, Garvey took the kind of bold and far-sighted decision that he was famed for, and which, perhaps, no other newspaper proprietor in the whole of America would have considered. He appointed a sixty-six-year-old man who, at various times in the past two decades, had been more commonly associated with hobos and other unfortunate destitute alcoholics. For more than twenty years, from 1880 onwards, Timothy Thomas Fortune had been the leading black journalist in America. He'd owned and edited the *Globe* which metamorphosed into the *Freeman* and finally the influential *New York Age*. A handsome and erudite man, great things had once been expected of T. Thomas Fortune in the last flush of the nineteenth century; he'd been an electrifying race leader of some import. But by 1907, he was well on his way to becoming a tragic and embarrassing figure. He'd succumbed to the ravages of alcohol and poor mental health, and sold his controlling interest in the *Age*. Thereafter, he had eked out a living as a freelance writer, during the lucid intervals that punctuated his addiction. Timothy Fortune was an old friend of Bruce Grit. Bruce vouched for him, and Garvey gave the old man a chance; perhaps his last chance to be reunited with his former splendid self. Other newspaper proprietors had averted their pitying gaze when the etiolated Fortune came knocking. But for a brief and exciting time, in his last years, Timothy Thomas Fortune would find a home on a Garvey newspaper, and be reacquainted with a consistent journalistic and literary life long forfeited.[8]

'Newspaper' would have been a generous description of the *Negro Times* as far as Garvey's critics were concerned; they considered it to have been conceived by Garvey primarily as a vehicle for propaganda. If true, then there was plenty of adverse propaganda to counter, particularly the allegations of Garvey's self-aggrandisement. The most fantastic claim, spouted by his old enemies at the *Chicago Defender*, was that Garvey was building a palatial dwelling for himself, rumoured to cost $45,000, in Larchmont, NY – one of the most exclusive and fashionable colonies. It was a claim which drew deep draughts of laughter from Garvey. Surely, it was, he said, akin to Moses building a mansion on the banks of the Nile 'while the people were passing in the wilderness'.

There were signs that Marcus Garvey was growing tired of the constant sniping from the black press and less able and inclined to shrug off the negative comments as the carping of inferior Lilliputians who were excited by no other sport as much as binding a Negro Gulliver. Increasingly, he saw the black press as simply instruments of 'a people who are enemies to themselves'. Everywhere he went now, he was called the Negro Moses – sometimes sarcastically. He was prepared to pay the cost of leading black people out of the wilderness but still he was surprised by their ingratitude. He shared such dark thoughts with an audience at Liberty Hall and reminded them that the Israelites – buoyant on setting out – had begun to propagandise against Moses 'when they had gone not even half the journey . . . [and] started to doubt his ability to lead them to the promised land'.⁹

Counter-propaganda was the impetus behind Garvey's first published book. It had been his young wife, Amy Jacques's, idea to put together a collection of his speeches and epigrams 'to educate the reading public . . . and to help to counteract many of the misquoted statements attributed to my husband'.¹⁰ That calm, unflustered statement of intent belied the urgency felt by Jacques to put out something that might act as a corrective to the degrading vitriol swirling around Garvey. The book *The Philosophy and Opinions of Marcus Garvey* was much needed as an unthreatening apologia to white America. Some of Garvey's intemperate, fiery and rebellious language would have to be smoothed over. Any suggestion of settling of scores, retaliatory lynching of white people, 'sharpening of swords' for the conflicts ahead and pushing forward through 'oceans of blood' would be excised.

The aim, therefore, was to present Garvey to the larger white world in the way that his followers saw him. To them, Garvey by his own example, by his learning and dignified bearing, was not only a symbol of the utmost humanity of the Negro but also of the overlooked and repressed talent of people of African descent. With dissertations that ranged from evolution to world disarmament, Garvey emerged from his *Philosophy and Opinions* as the embodiment of an idea: that the African was just as capable of erudition, scholarship, refinement and leadership as anybody else.

The problem, though, for the UNIA leader was that whenever he spoke now there were enemies (especially amongst African-American leaders) ready to pounce on every word so that a typical 'tough-love' speech was characterised as the twisted logic of a Negro-hater. At the state fair in Raleigh, North Carolina, he meditated on a favourite theme: Negro indolence. Robert Poston, a UNIA officer, stood by his side 'constantly chiming a string of approving "all rights"', as Garvey sought to inspire by berating the black audience for its laziness: 'If I waited for Negroes to convey me from New York to Raleigh,' he lamented, 'I would be walking for six month[s].' Curiously, reported *Greensboro Daily News*, even as Garvey 'took the hide off his hearers . . . they cheered'. The architects of the 'Garvey Must Go' campaign were condemnatory. Months later, the *Messenger* depicted Garvey in an editorial cartoon wearing his familiar academic cap, but with the body of a donkey, and a caption which referred to a previous editorial, branding Garvey, 'A Supreme Negro Jamaican Jackass'.[11]

In seizing on Garvey's West Indianness (and this was increasingly the case) his African-American critics defaulted to prejudices that had characterised much of the internal conflict in America's recent history. The Red Scare of 1919 was predicated on much the same assumptions; in that case on the un-American Bolshevist activities of recent migrants. But the nativism cost the editors of the *Messenger* little save for the wrath of their present Caribbean allies such as Wilfred Domingo, Garvey's former friend. Domingo detected a hypocritical willingness on their part to exaggerate the differences between black Americans and Caribbeans, in much the same way that they had accused Garvey of overstating the class differences between the various shades of black Americans. Supplicants to Garvey, who'd previously claimed the singular honour of being first to introduce him to the African-American masses, were now competing for the title of being the first to unmask the West Indian enemy within their midst – a man who ostensibly looked like any other African-American but who had subliminally and successfully introduced dangerous, foreign ideas, having cast a spell over their earlier impressionable selves.[12]

Reverend Eason's expulsion from the movement also opened up another potentially dangerous front against Garvey. The reverend was a powerful orator whose standing had not waned with his removal. Indeed, prior to his expulsion, he had voiced a popular sentiment that West Indians were looked on more favourably in the hierarchy of the movement than their African-American counterparts; that Jamaicans, Trinidadians and Barbadians, for example, were over-represented in the high command. The thirty-six-year-old Eason may have been discarded but he was not about to accept early retirement and to relinquish his ambitions and his own vision of the future of African-Americans. In September, much to Garvey's annoyance, James Eason announced the launch of the Universal Negro Alliance, and bragged of wrenching Garvey's followers away from him. Both men would be appealing to the same audiences. Though Eason would stress that once his programme was up and running, it would focus on the near and attainable, not the far and fanciful; there were ample concerns for the black man to address right on his doorstep in America, never mind chasing sunsets in a mythical African homeland or sending delegates on fool's errands to the League of Nations.[13] But if Eason stood any chance of making inroads into Garvey's substantial movement, he would have to tap into prime audiences, such as those in Pennsylvania and Louisiana, where he would often find himself trailing in Garvey's footsteps; his rival had been there well before him. Once the 'mouthagram' (as his wife Amy Jacques affectionately referred to him) got on the road, there was no stopping him; Garvey talked and talked and never stopped, although there were intermittent attempts by the authorities to muzzle him.

The staunch Garveyite, Queen Mother Audley Moore, recalled a UNIA delegation besieging the Mayor of New Orleans to permit Garvey to come into the city and speak in the middle of 1922. It was an extremely tense and volatile occasion. Garvey had received death threats, and a huge audience, protective of their leader, turned out to hear him: 'We all was armed. Everybody had bags of ammunition too.' Even Queen Mother Moore was packing a couple of pistols – little 38 specials – 'one in my bosom and one in my pocket'. There was the possibility that the authorities might ban the rally at the last minute. 'So when Garvey came in, we applauded, and the police were lined man to man along the line of each row.' Audley Moore's memory focused on the pivotal moment when Garvey began to criticise the mayor for being a stooge and the police chief interrupted and threatened to arrest Garvey. 'When he did this, everybody jumped up on benches and pulled out their guns and just held the guns in the air and said, 'Speak, Garvey, speak.' And Garvey said, 'As I was saying', and he went on and repeated what he had said before, and the police filed out of the hall like little puppy dogs with their tails behind them.'[14]

On his return to New York, Garvey would tell of the dramatic events slightly differently. He had indeed been prevented from holding a meeting on his first night in New Orleans but through his lawyers, Garvey obtained an injunction restraining the chief of police from interfering with his speech. The next night thousands of supporters turned up to hear him speak at Longshoreman's Hall in New Orleans. 'Several dozen Secret Service men and detectives lined up at the front of the platform,' said Garvey and 'things got so hot that the police chief rose' at one point and threatened to arrest him. Garvey told the man to 'Sit down there! Sit down!' The humbled police chief then marched his men down the aisle; lined them up outside the hall, brought up a patrol wagon and waited for the meeting to end, and unwittingly, concluded the UNIA leader, provided 'a guard of honour for me to march through'. A lynching party was said to have lain in wait for Garvey at the end of his speech in New Orleans and was only foiled by the presence of police who had lined his route from the Longshoreman's Hall to the place where he was to sleep that night.[15]

Garvey's telling of his time in New Orleans was not as colourful as Queen Mother's rendition but they shared the same sense of triumph that he would not be silenced.

'Speak, Garvey, speak' – the same cry was chanted wherever Garvey went on his tour. Speaking was his great gift and Garvey generated such excitement that no admirer would risk failing to catch a glimpse of him. It was this ability to articulate the 'submerged thoughts of an awakening people' that sustained Negro belief in Garvey and bemused and befuddled enemies such as Du Bois. The list of those who doubted Garvey was growing daily but then there was also a concomitant expansion in new recruits to Garveyism. Even now, and amongst African-Americans who should, Du Bois believed, have known better. William Sherrill, a successful businessman, a black freemason and comfortably insured for a lifetime, if not of the American dream, then its near elite African-American equivalent, was clearly NAACP material. But one night, as he later told it, on the way to the theatre, he saw a huge crowd outside a church and was drawn to enquire what was going on. 'A lady turned to me and said, "Man alive, don't you know that Marcus Garvey is there talking."' Sherrill purchased a ticket and squeezed in at the back of the church and 'heard a voice like thunder from Heaven'. Garvey was in full flow: 'Men and women, what are you here for? To live unto yourself, until your body manures the earth, or to live God's Purpose to the fullest?' After an hour Sherrill realised that he was going to miss the theatre. 'I stood there like one in a trance, every sentence ringing in my ears, finding an echo in my heart.'[16] William Sherrill was converted that night, and within a year, at the end of the international convention, he'd been made a key appointee in the UNIA, replacing Eason as leader of American Negroes.

If Sherrill gave testimony to Garvey's continued 'magnetism and persuasive eloquence as a speaker', there were other indications that the president-general and his movement might be forced to share the limelight in the near future. Months after his own visit to New Orleans, he was receiving reports that the local branch were flirting with the enemy, his former right-hand man, Eason. A bullish officer from HQ, Thomas Anderson, was charged with enforcing discipline, and with some relish he set about reminding the secretary of the New Orleans division that 'an enemy of the President General . . . is an enemy to the organisation'. Anderson expressed some sympathy with the secretary, whose long-standing association with Eason was perfectly acceptable during the two years when the American leader was still favourably regarded, but now that Eason had fallen from grace and was *persona non grata*, if by some oversight, 'Mr Eason is still in your community,' the secretary was cautioned, 'you know what attitude you should assume, and this is expected of you.' In case the New Orleans secretary should be in any doubt, Anderson underlined the point: 'At this time the Parent Body is not in attitude to tolerate the slightest suspicion of disloyalty.'[17]

A lower threshold of intolerance seemed to infect the movement generally. The *Norfolk Journal* (a black paper) bemoaned the fact that Garvey's supporters drew little distinction between news and editorials. 'We have become weary of trying to reason with them . . . they are going to fume and fuss and slander all who do not agree with them anyway.'[18] On 21 October, the fuss turned into a riot at the Sterling Hotel in Cincinnati when Samuel Saxon, a lecturer from New York, weighed into Garvey at the start of a meeting aimed at exposing the UNIA. Garveyites in the audience took exception; knives were brandished and, trying to flee the auditorium, Saxon was stabbed and hit over the head with upturned chairs.[19]

William Pickens also claimed Garveyites tried to intimidate him when he was about to give a talk at the AME church in Toronto. They barred his way at the entrance to the church and, 'fingering their hip-pockets', cautioned him against criticising the movement. Pickens allegedly answered back in kind that he would 'not be frightened for the millionth part of a second by any lily-livered, coconut-busting monkey chasers, even in Canada'.[20]

One clue to Garveyite hypersensitivity to criticism lay in the final line of Pickens's anecdote: 'coconut-busting monkey chasers' was shorthand on the streets of Harlem for West Indians. Foreign-born UNIA members especially resented the way that Garvey's nationality – his being Jamaican or West Indian – was highlighted, and instinctively closed ranks and rallied round their man. Poring over the volumes of abuse heaped upon Garvey, they could be forgiven for believing that the UNIA leader's most serious crime was not the content of his programme but his nationality. The xenophobic stench was fresh in the nostrils of Wilfred Domingo who resigned his commission from the ranks of the Garvey-baiters, his former allies on the editorial board of the *Messenger*, who led the 'Garvey Must Go' campaign. 'I will not point out,' wrote Domingo, deliberately pointing out in an open letter to the *Messenger* in March 1923, 'that it is incompatible with your professed Socialist faith for you to initiate an agitation for deportation or to emphasise the nationality of anyone as a subtle means of generating opposition against him.'

Such sentiments amongst West Indians were not so delicately expressed the month before. Then James Eason addressed an anti-Garvey meeting in Chicago which ended in mayhem when a policeman who sought to apprehend a disruptive Garveyite was shot and wounded.[21] But it wasn't just West Indians who were sensitised to perceived acts of betrayal; black America was steeped in a tradition of pathological in-fighting and a visceral hatred of duplicity that went back to the days of slavery when even the smallest act of rebellion might be foiled by informants. 'There was a terrible oath you had to take,' remembered Mariamne Samad. 'It was, "May my tongue cleave to the top of my mouth if I were to do anything to hurt my race."'

There is no evidence that any of these assaults by Garvey supporters were coordinated. But certainly anxiety about loss of control and over-sensitivity – if not paranoia – had crept into the organisation. HQ was particularly vexed by the perceived lack of compliance from the division in New Orleans. Something had to be done. Garvey fastened onto a more subtle approach. On 9 November, he dispatched Esau Ramus to New Orleans with a letter of introduction to William Phillips, the secretary of the local division. The letter requested that the secretary 'find some organising work for him [Ramus] to do for the Division in going around enlisting new members and helping generally'. Phillips wrote back that he was happy to oblige, that he was arranging for Ramus to visit members in their homes with items such as '[the] new constitution, buttons, anthems etc', with a view to 'selling such articles as he can get from the Parent Body'.

Two days later, Phillips wrote again. He had learnt that Ramus was

intent on offering an altogether different kind of service. Rather than
retailing UNIA memorabilia, 'Mr Ramus is endeavouring to organise
a police and secret service.' The secretary hoped to minimise any obstacles but Ramus's efforts, to date, had 'not met the approval of the
majority of the officers'.[22]

Esau Ramus (sometimes John Jeffries), it now transpired, was one
of the chiefs of the secret service for the Garvey organisation, which
had grown out of Garvey's ceremonial, uniformed African Legion,
following the attempt on his life in 1919. Operatives of the secret
service were secret in name only: the membership knew that it counted
amongst its number UNIA police and secret service agents who masquer-
aded as janitors and vendors of the *Negro World*. Ramus had formally
joined the UNIA in Philadelphia where he worked ostensibly as the
janitor at the local Liberty Hall. New Orleans had about thirty men
on the force and, with or without help from the secretary, Ramus was
determined to bind them together under his authority. Sometime in
November, Esau Ramus moved into the home of a forty-two-year-old
Jamaican longshoreman and local chief of the UNIA police, Constantine
(Fred) Dyer, and, as might be expected of a competent secret service
agent, quietly went about his work.

The trial date for Marcus Garvey and the other defendants in the
mail fraud case was set for 15 December, but, as had already happened
on several occasions, the proceedings had to be postponed (due to the
deferral court's crowded calendar) and a new date scheduled for the
first week in January. Garvey had made plans for a new European
fundraising and lecture tour, and whilst they were set aside, his rival
James Eason pushed off to the South once more to bolster his support
in New Orleans, assuring the BOI agents that he would be back in
New York on 2 January should he be called as a witness.

Reverend Eason had been invited by a committee of members of his
new Universal Negro Alliance to preach to the congregation of a local
Baptist church, St John's on 1st Street. The congregation was mostly
made up of African-Americans, but that night there were about half a
dozen Jamaicans in the church. The presence of one of the Jamaicans,
later identified as Constantine Dyer, struck some parishioners as odd
because they knew him but had never known him to set foot in the
church before. At the end of the service, at about 10.30 p.m., Eason
left St John's and was greeted on the steps by a number of old friends.
They were walking away from the church when there was a sudden

commotion behind. Three strangers had been following Reverend Eason's group; they ran up now and one of them pulled out a gun and fired. The first shots struck the pavement. The next bullet went into the back of Eason. He stumbled and half-turned to see his assailant fire another shot into his forehead. The reverend collapsed. Some of Eason's friends chased after the assailants but they fired back at the pursuers, leapt a fence and made their escape. The grievously wounded Eason was taken to the Charity Hospital. He survived long enough to give a description of the events. He told reporters that he was in no doubt as to the motive of the shooting. 'I am positive,' he asserted, 'that my assailants were acting on instructions to put me out of the way and prevent my appearing as a witness at the Garvey trial.' Eason was in a critical condition but, dipping in and out of consciousness, he appeared not to understand the seriousness of his injuries. He would, he said, be able to identify the gunmen. But in the early hours of 4 January 1923, Reverend James Eason died from his wounds.[23]

The parishioners of St John's were able to identify two of the assailants as Garveyites. Soon after, newspapers reported the arrest of William Shakespeare, Negro 'chief of police' of the UNIA and Constantine (Fred) Dyer, Negro member of the 'force'. Both men were charged with Eason's murder. Neither man claimed responsibility for the attack but they were quoted in the *New York Amsterdam News* as saying they were glad and that 'Eason richly deserved what he got'. Shakespeare and Dyer were indicted for his murder. But there was a third man. The BOI quickly dispatched its undercover agent 800 to New Orleans to investigate; Garvey had already sent Thomas Anderson, a UNIA official, from Harlem to New Orleans to liaise with the local New Orleans division. Anderson now wrote back to the secretary-general, Robert Poston in Harlem, of the unexpected arrival of Captain Jones: 'That stout bright fellow, formerly connected with the *Negro World*, is here and is making himself active, we are informed, as regards this Eason matter. We are convinced that he is in Federal employ.' Even though the local division suspected that Captain Jones was a federal agent, he was able to confirm the identity of the third man: Esau Ramus.[24]

Ramus had skipped town and was rumoured to be in Detroit. His 'mysterious trip to New Orleans', coinciding with Eason's murder, only confirmed J. Edgar Hoover's suspicions of a direct UNIA involvement; but, in their eagerness to support his hypothesis, junior BOI agents appear to have marshalled hearsay rather than facts. According to the investigating agent Amos, Marcus Garvey was informed of the assassination of Eason within minutes of the shooting. Amos alleged that a telegram had been sent to Garvey's wife simply stating that 'the work had been done'.[25] In an interview with the *New York Times* on 21 January, the UNIA leader stated vehemently, 'We have absolutely no connection with the murder of J. W. H. Eason, and the statement that Eason was a star witness against me is without foundation.' With the UNIA now under enormous pressure, it might have been expected to distance itself from Shakespeare and Dyer; instead Garvey called for a defence fund to be established for the two men, and put out an insipid obituary of Reverend Eason in the *Negro World* which suggested his death was the result of an unsavoury love tryst with a married woman.[26]

Esau Ramus was eventually apprehended by the BOI a couple of months later. He claimed (off the record) to have received instructions from Garvey that when Eason spoke in New Orleans 'his meeting must be broken up or he (Eason) must not return to New York alive'.[27] The word from UNIA HQ offered a far less sinister explanation for Ramus's visit to New Orleans; the secret service man had proved a nuisance in New York and he was simply sent south – out of a sense of exasperation – to get him out of the way. There was never any direct evidence, despite the rumours, to implicate Garvey in Eason's murder. Although Garvey could be violent in his language with talk of 'wading through oceans of blood' and 'sharpening swords', these were the words of rhetorical speech of a conservative man steeped in the 'fire and brimstone' of the Old Testament. It was the kind of language which the authorities always worried might incite excitable, less grounded individuals to violence, and perhaps on this occasion did so. Ramus's allegations were never put in court, as he was wanted, tried and sentenced for a previous armed robbery. By then the prosecution of Dyer and Shakespeare was well under way. In April, both men were tried and convicted of Eason's killing and sentenced to eighteen-to-twenty-year prison terms.

Black newspapers deplored the murder of Eason. They were, by turns, alarmed and deeply fearful; but mostly they were embarrassed by the odium it brought on the race. Perhaps the *New York Amsterdam News* expressed the sentiments of the majority when it issued a dire prediction for the UNIA following the reverend's fateful shooting: 'We are not willing to go so far as to say that Marcus Garvey was implicated directly or indirectly in the cowardly assassination of J. W. H. Eason . . . The men who actually shot Mr Eason may have thought they were doing the UNIA a service, but they are mistaken. What they actually did was to give it its first serious blow – a blow from which it will never, never recover.'

Events moved very quickly thereafter. The murder of Eason acted to release the 'Garvey Must Go' group from any trace of restraint. They were in constant communication with agent Amos of the BOI, and included him now in the coordination of the release of an open letter to be sent to the Attorney-General, Harry M. Daugherty, and copied to as many sympathetic newspaper editors as possible around the country, drawing his attention to 'a heretofore unconsidered menace to harmonious race relationships'. The letter, signed by eight of 'the most distinguished and responsible businessmen, educators and publicists among the colored people of the United States', was no less than an attempt to discredit and finally destroy the Garvey movement. It began, 'There is in our midst certain Negro criminals and potential murderers, both foreign and American born, who are actuated by intense hatred against the white race.' The UNIA was, according to the authors, 'composed in the main of Negro sharks and ignorant fanatics', led by a man who wasn't even a citizen of the United States but rather was 'an unscrupulous demagogue who has ceaselessly and assiduously sought to spread among Negroes distrust and hatred of all white people'. The letter went on to catalogue the incidents of thuggery, violence and intimidation that had culminated in the murder of Reverend Eason. The eight respectable authors called on the Attorney-General to 'use his full influence completely to disband and extirpate this vicious movement, and that he vigorously and speedily push the government's case against Marcus Garvey for using the mails to defraud'. The signers of this letter were:

William Pickens
Robert Bagnall
Chandler Owen
Robert Abbott
George Harris
John E. Neil
Julia P. Coleman
Harry H. Pace[28]

A. Philip Randolph and W. E. B. Du Bois declined to add their signatures to the letter. Though both men had done much to lay the ground work for it, they were more politically attuned to the possible fallout from such an overt act of aggression against a black organisation and, worse still, collusion with the government. Marcus Garvey was apoplectic when he eventually got sight of the letter. The NAACP members and the editor of the *Messenger* formed the core of the eight angry coloured plaintiffs; and Garvey seethed, lashing out at them as informants, as modern versions of the faithful house slaves who ran and alerted their beloved master whenever there was a hint of trouble brewing among the field slaves on the plantations: 'Like the good old darkey, they believe they have some news to tell and they are telling it for all it is worth'.[29] In prejudicing him and his organisation in the minds of white people, Garvey fumed, they had committed 'the greatest bit of treachery and wickedness that any group of Negroes could be capable of'. The letter to the Attorney-General was shocking and unprecedented and its authors, Garvey vowed, had 'written their names down everlastingly as enemies of the race'.[30]

It took another black man – distanced from the two rival groups (the NAACP and UNIA) – to unpick the crusts of malice and self-righteousness and to elucidate what was really going on. The name Perry W. Howard came attached with numerous epithets, including 'the highest paid Negro in government' and 'the smartest Negro in politics'. President Harding had appointed the shrewd Mississippi lawyer as special assistant to the Attorney-General, and when Howard reflected on the spat between the two black organisations ('a case of my being a Methodist and assailing the other fellow for being a Baptist'), although he confessed to having 'blood in my eyes for the NAACP', he worried about the public perception that the NAACP and Department of Justice were working hand-in-glove. Writing to Hoover's boss at the BOI, William Burns, he assured him that he held no brief for the UNIA leader, and yet believed that the attack on Garvey 'reduces itself to a cannibalistic scheme of one rival getting rid of the other by annihilation or otherwise'.[31] Perry W. Howard was a beneficiary of the patronage system, the political horse-trading between the Republican and Democrat parties through which they parcelled out key governmental positions. Nonetheless, he was primarily a 'race man' who lamented the gulf between the two black organisations.

Perry Howard believed there were more obvious candidates worthy of government investigations into allegations of malpractice. President Harding had only recently died. He had presided over one of the most corrupt governments in America's history, most manifestly so in the infamous Teapot Dome Scandal. The fallout from Harding's malad-ministration was only just beginning to be felt. Such was the depth of the corruption that the Attorney-General would soon be ensnared. By the prevailing standards of the day, even according to his more sympa-thetic critics, Garvey was guilty of no more than sincere but staggeringly incompetent management. However, stalwarts of the NAACP such as Samuel Redding's father and its leading light, W. E. B. Du Bois, feared wholeheartedly that the real danger was that if the UNIA failed then they would all fail; the reverberations would be felt throughout Black America. In its promotion of the core ideal of black economic inde-pendence, Du Bois conceded that the UNIA had stumbled upon an immensely worthy mission. Nonetheless, when he surveyed the dire circumstance of the UNIA business empire and the Black Star Line in particular, Du Bois saw lamentably 'the collapse of the only thing in the Garvey movement which was original and promising'.[32]

The feud between Garvey and his detractors continued well into the New Year. Garvey published a pamphlet responding to the composers of the letter to the Attorney-General in which he could not help but scratch at an old wound. Focusing on the complexion of the signator-ies, he noted that, 'nearly all [are] Octoroons and Quadroons. Two are black Negroes who have married Octoroons. One is a mulatto and Socialist, a self-styled Negro leader who expressed his intention of marrying a white woman but was subsequently prevented from doing so by the criticism of the UNIA. With this lone exception all of the others are married to Octoroons.'

Up until this point, Du Bois had maintained a dignified distance from the turmoil surrounding the death of Eason and the contentious letter to the Attorney-General. Now, as if in answer to Garvey's latest provo-cation, Du Bois devoted an essay to him and his spurious dream of 'Back to Africa', in the February edition of *Century* magazine. Du Bois once again wrote of his nemesis, more in hope than in actuality, in the past tense. He strived to be fair – within the limits of his prejudice – towards a confused, bombastic but sincere race leader. At this critical time in the nation's history, a West Indian demagogue had appeared, 'not the worst kind of demagogue but, on the contrary, a man who had much which was attractive and understandable in his personality and his programme'. Garvey was an implacable Moses who inspired 'orgies of response and generosity'. Nonetheless, Dr Du Bois lamented, as anyone with common sense would, the 'utter futility of his programme'. His essay was imbued with pathos, for Garvey, he felt, was leading the Negro to the very edge of despair, and his failure would be theirs too. Around the edges of Du Bois's assessment there leaked an uncontained disgust. Ultimately, his lowly educated adversary was 'a little fat black man, ugly, but with intelligent eyes and a big head', who 'screams his propaganda' from a serio-comic seat of empire, 'a low rambling basement of brick and stone . . . this squat and dirty Liberty Hall'. Set beside the patient striving of the American Negro, Garvey had achieved 'nothing in accomplishment . . . only waste'.

Marcus Garvey could not have been expected to let the matter rest there. The opportunity for any rapprochement, if it ever existed, had long since passed. Back and forth, thrust and parry, punch and roll. The two men squared up to each other like evenly matched pugilists; but there would be no sweaty embrace of camaraderie after the bout was over. To the pamphlet excoriating the 'Eight "Uncle Tom" Negroes . . . Who wrote the infamous letter to the Honourable Attorney-General' Marcus Garvey appended a supplementary chapter, 'W. E. Burghardt Du Bois, As a Hater of Dark People', written in a crucible of injustice which dribbled with hate. Booker T. Washington used to say, 'To keep a black man in the gutter a white man must stay in the gutter and hold him there.' On 13 February 1923, Marcus Garvey, the 'little, fat black man', descended into the gutter and waded through the excrement and thick slime to meet Du Bois the 'unfortunate mulatto who bewails every drop of Negro blood in his veins'.[33]

In his article Du Bois had characterised Garvey as the heir to Booker T. Washington but whereas the earlier man had merely put forward a programme of accommodation for African-Americans which eschewed politics, in his courting of the Ku Klux Klan, Garvey's greater evil was his advocacy of a policy for black Americans, amounting to wholesale, unilateral capitulation. It was a policy that said, 'Give Up! Surrender! The struggle is useless; go back to Africa and fight the white world.'

Garvey was neither pushed nor drawn to defend the untenable association with the Klan; he simply cared not a jot about the interpretation put on it by others, least of all Du Bois, the 'lazy dependent mulatto', and his cohorts at the NAACP. Equally, he claimed to have paid little attention to the legal charge against him and the upcoming trial. The evidence, however, suggests entirely the opposite. From the outset of their indictment, Marcus Garvey had shared no code of silence with the accused; on the contrary, he'd emphasised in speeches and in the columns of the *Negro World* that he'd been out of the country when the allegedly illegal practices of mail fraud had been carried out. In the intervening months, any vestige of trust he'd had in his co-defendants had been wiped out by an incremental, niggling anxiety. The vice-president, Orlando Thompson, had already been relieved of his power of attorney over Black Star Line affairs, and the secretary of the Line and auditor of the UNIA, Elie Garcia, was about to be made aware that, come the trial, it would be every man for himself. One night in early January, Garvey was going through the lodgement of takings at the end of the working day when he stumbled across a forged cheque for $47, ostensibly signed by Elie Garcia. The secretary was out of the building, and Garvey ordered immediately that Garcia's office be vacated and the door nailed up. The president-general later related how Garcia, who'd been tipped off, 'came back into the building in a crestfallen and crying attitude. I stared at him and he voluntarily confessed . . . He beseeched me to give him another hearing before I took steps to prosecute.'[34] Garvey would not relent. Garcia was arrested and tried for petty theft. On his conviction, the *Negro World* pointedly speculated – with a nod towards the pending mail-fraud trial – about further revelations of illegality: 'Mr Garcia has handled thousands of dollars of the Association's moneys, and it is understood that an examination of his books is being made to find out the extent of misappropriations.'[35]

On 18 May the year-long delay in the mail-fraud case came to an end. Each of the defendants, Garvey, Garcia, Tobias and Thompson, retained individual counsel. Garvey objected to the trial being presided over by Judge Julian Mack, who was rumoured to have connections with the NAACP. If true, there would be an obvious conflict of interest as the rival NAACP was resolutely opposed to Garvey. Mack was a prominent Zionist and social reformer with sympathies for the uplifting programme of the NAACP but he had no direct proven link with that organisation. He rejected the implication of bias. In his ruling – a kind of legal clearing of the throat – Mack conceded that 'the parties are entitled to understand the state of mind of the Judge in this case'. He assured Garvey that his attitude was 'one of extreme friendliness toward the colored people', and refused to step down.[36]

There was heightened security at the court-house amid rumours, reported by BOI agents, that UNIA divisions were stockpiling arms and ammunition, and that some of Garvey's supporters attending the trial would be carrying weapons. From the very beginning, the judge showed that he would take a severe line against any suggestion of interference or intimidation of government witnesses. A number of anonymous threats had been made, and the Black Star Line naval officer, Hugh Mulzac, who'd been subpoenaed by the government, claimed to have been warned by the UNIA legionnaire, Linous Charles, that 'if he testified against Garvey, he would get [him] if it took the rest of his life'. The judge sentenced Charles to six months in jail and set bail at $10,000.[37]

The night before the start of the trial, Garvey spoke to a rapt audience at Liberty Hall. He was on fine rhetorical form, assuring his followers that the coming events in New York's Southern District Court marked a new 'guide post for the race'. Personally, it would test his manhood like never before but he was prepared to 'face the arrows of hell for the principles of the UNIA'. He summoned the ancestors in whose name he'd first been drawn to serve the race, when ten years ago swept along in an epiphany, at the end of his time in England to Jamaica in a third-class cabin, he'd asked himself, 'Where is the black man's government? Where is his king and his kingdom?' Then, as now, he was motivated by the crying voice from the grave that said, 'Garvey, we have suffered for 250 years for your day and for your time; we expect something of you at this hour.' Having thus steeled himself for battle, Marcus Garvey was affronted, when on the first morning of his day in court, his African-American attorney, Cornelius McDougald, counselled surrender. McDougald advised him to enter a plea of guilty on a technical charge with the expectation that this would elicit a minimum sentence. Back in the apartment later that night, Amy Jacques recalled how the roiling argument exploded and caused a rift between the two men: 'Garvey felt that his attorney was being used innocently to trap him, and asked [McDougald] to withdraw from his court defence. In leaving, the lawyer warned, "It will go hard with you."'[38] McDougald was referring to the decision that Garvey now proposed to conduct his own defence.

Marcus Garvey would have been familiar with the maxim, 'The man who acts as his own lawyer has a fool for a client.' But Garvey had such confidence in his powers of persuasion that he considered himself the exception that proves the rule – a man of Ciceronian oratorical skills who could move an audience of tens of thousands must be able to hold sway over a dozen of his peers. But therein lay a potential booby-trap for Garvey: the question of scale. As the trial unfolded, Garvey would struggle to contain a style and voice tuned to the demands of the ecstatic massed meetings in huge venues, and adapt them to the quiet intimacy of the chamber room. Without the restraining influence of his own counsel, Garvey strutted across the courtroom floor, bellowing at the prosecution witnesses; growing hot and irritated by their evasions or unintelligence. Too often, Garvey was distracted by insignificant facts or inadmissible evidence, and taxed the judge and jury with his pedantry. For more than a month, the hot days of hair-splitting deliberation dragged on. Only occasionally did the judge betray signs of tetchiness at Garvey's ignorance of legal matters, reminding the novice attorney that he was a trial judge and was not meant to be 'conducting a law school'.[39]

Mostly, the latitude that Judge Mack granted him was generous, but Garvey was tripped up more by himself than by the prosecuting counsel. In one instance, he called a defence witness who, when asked to comment on Garvey's character, answered, 'Doubtful.' Worse still was to come when Garvey put the BOI agent Amos on the witness stand. When it became clear that Amos could not be prised away from answering in a manner that was damaging to him, Garvey pleaded that Amos's testimony be struck from the records but the judge, opening wide his hooded eyes, reminded him gently that Amos was a witness that the defence had called.

In order for Garvey to be found guilty of fraud, the prosecution would have to prove that the president-general had sent out adverts through the post, encouraging investors to buy shares in the Black Star Line knowing that those shares would be worthless. Strangely, the case turned on an empty envelope. The prosecution maintained that its witness, Benny Dancy, had been sent a BSL circular advertising shares in the SS *Phyllis Wheatley*, but Dancy's only proof was an empty envelope bearing a BSL stamp. Dancy had received envelopes previously that contained BSL letters, and assumed such was the case with this envelope now being put forward as evidence; it was just that the letter contained in the empty envelope had been mislaid. An experienced lawyer would have easily exposed the flaws in the prosecution witness's testimony but Garvey struggled to make his point.

His cross-examination of Dancy was torturous and, ultimately, revealed Garvey's lack of legal training.

Garvey: Can you remember what you saw in the letter positively?

Dancy: I just told you I couldn't remember all – do you understand it?

Garvey: I am not vexed with you.

Dancy: I am not vexed with you; you raised your voice to me; I raised mine to you.

Garvey: I am not vexed, I just want to hear what you say.

Dancy: Take your time.

Garvey: Would you really swear . . .

Dancy: I just told you I couldn't remember all the letter. Bring the letter up here.

Garvey: None of the letters that were shown you were the letters?

Dancy: What?

Garvey: The letters that the District-Attorney showed you, they weren't the letters?

Dancy: They weren't the letters?

Garvey: Yes.

Dancy: Yes, they were the letters.

Garvey: And you don't remember what was in them?

Dancy: I can't remember all of them; I got so many letters.[40]

As counsel for his own defence, Garvey was on surer ground with the former officers of the Black Star Line who formed the majority of the prosecution witnesses. Tellingly, though, as the trial progressed, it revealed the idiosyncratic and shoddy inner workings of the organisation, and the degree to which most of the important decisions were only ever taken with Garvey's cognisance or approval. Garvey was the big 'I am' of the movement, and each new piece of evidence that clicked into place only seemed to confirm that impression.

In Garvey's interminable three-hour-long closing address, he portrayed himself as an unfortunate and selfless leader, surrounded by incompetents and thieves. Edgar Grey was 'a reckless, irresponsible man, full of talk, representing nothing'. Richard Warner was 'a rubber-stamp man without character', Sidney de Bourg was 'the aged man . . . who has sent his soul to hell', and Captain Cockburn was simply 'the swindler'.

Garvey was belligerent where perhaps grace, humility and even humour were called for. He was preceded by Henry Lincoln Johnson, the attorney for another of the co-defendants, and might have been wiser to adopt Johnson's approach. Johnson likened the Black Star Line's difficulties to a nursery rhyme: 'For the want of a nail a shoe was lost, for the want of a shoe a hoof was lost, for the want of a hoof a horse was lost . . . all for the want of a horseshoe nail.' And the Black Star Line owed its ills to the want of a *Phyllis Wheatley*. 'But for the loss of the [SS] *Phyllis Wheatley*, Negroes would have been now captains of the sea. There would certainly have been no trouble between [Captain] Cockburn and Garvey. They would have been in faraway Africa enjoying the tropical breezes.' Reflecting on the gulf between the dream of the Black Star Line and the actuality, Johnson's witty, pungent and succinct summation left the jurors with a plea for compassion that was compelling and almost impossible to discount. 'The truth is there is no such thing as any conspiracy. [But] if the indictment had been framed against the defendants for discourtesy, mismanagement or display of bad judgement they would have pleaded guilty,' said Johnson. In paying close attention to testimonies, Johnson realised that of all the defendants, Garvey was the most vulnerable, and he implored the jury to consider that 'the innocence of one would affect the innocence of all and there was not one dime lost that could be traced back to Mr Garvey.'[41] That point had been made most emphatically by an emotional Marcus Garvey in his final exhortation to the jury: 'If you believe . . . that I would look upon the struggles of a people to rob them of a penny, I should die, and not only before man, but to be sent to the farthest depths of hell by my God.'[42]

The prosecuting attorney Maxwell Mattuck closed his delivery, honing in on Garvey, whom he believed to be the biggest and most dangerous culprit, with the simple but passionate appeal to the jurors: 'Gentlemen, will you let the tiger loose?'

After four gruelling weeks, just after 12.30 on 18 June, the jury rose and, closely guarded by US marshals, retired for deliberation. The anonymous threats had continued throughout the trial, and ranks of special patrolmen and members of the bomb squad decorated the corridors and courtroom. Garvey remained in the courtroom throughout the long wait, pacing the floor, occasionally fanning himself and mopping his face with a handkerchief. Ten hours later the jury returned. His co-defendants were found not guilty. The verdict on Marcus Garvey was, 'Guilty.' 'Mr Garvey immediately burst into a storm of rage,' reported the *Kansas City Call*. 'An undignified tirade of foul abuse and low language' followed, according to Hubert Harrison, in which 'both judge and district attorney [were described] as "damned dirty Jews".' And the *Call* painted a final pitiful picture of the convicted UNIA leader 'escorted to the elevator . . . by eighteen marshals through a crowd of sobbing sympathisers'. Garvey was led across the 'bridge of sighs' that connected the court-house to the Manhattan Detention Centre, commonly known as the 'Tombs prison'.

In a previous incarnation the Tombs had been designed in a style patterned on an Egyptian mausoleum. That building had been torn down in 1897 and in its place a granite prison had been constructed that, though now resembling a medieval castle, had retained its moniker, the Tombs. It was grim and forbidding, 'as depressing within as without', housing 400 inmates in cells that were designed 'on a none too liberal basis'.

Marcus Garvey's rage was still boiling over when the cell door closed on him at the Tombs. Fuming at the injustice, he divined a sinister plot which he scribbled feverishly to alert his followers about: 'The peculiar and outstanding feature of the whole case is that I am being punished for the crime of the Jew, Silverstone . . . who has caused the ruin of the company . . . I was prosecuted in this by Maxwell Mattuck, another Jew, and I am to be sentenced by Judge Julian Mack, the eminent Jewish Jurist. Truly I may say, "I was going to Jericho and fell among thieves."' Continuing with the biblical allusion, he concluded, 'Christ died to make men free; I shall die to give courage and inspiration to the race.'[43] Prior to the trial, Garvey had never displayed any anti-Semitic tendencies.[44] Rather he had celebrated Jewish thrift and group solidarity, and voiced common cause with the concept of Zionism. He escaped the kind of public censure that might have been expected from his ugly remarks, but numerous black commentators, such as the Jamaican historian and journalist Joel A. Rogers, believed it had some bearing on the eventual outcome when he was returned to court for sentencing.

With little deliberation on the part of Judge Mack, Marcus Garvey was sentenced to five years in jail and ordered to pay a fine of $1,000. Joel Rogers was amongst those who thought the sentence harsh and that the judge – predisposed to be especially fair to 'coloured' defendants – had been swayed at the end to impose the maximum penalty after Garvey's unseemly comments about a Jewish cabal. Several hundred weeping and wailing supporters gathered around the Black Maria outside the court-house and surged forward as their handcuffed leader was bundled into the van and taken back to the Tombs. The court had refused to fix bail but granted a stay of execution pending Garvey's appeal. If the appeal failed, then it was designated that he serve his sentence at the Federal Penitentiary at Atlanta, but then on 22 June 1923 the *New York Times* reported the rumour that ultimately, Garvey would be 'sent to Leavenworth, Kansas, because he objected to a Southern prison, fearing hostility'.

Garvey's conviction came towards the tail end of the Harding admin-istration – judged, as we've seen, to be one of the most corrupt governments in its nation's history. Although the jails weren't filled with corrupt politicians and businessmen who'd benefited from their associ-ation with them, there were a significant number of high-profile figures such as the former Governor of Indiana, Warren T. McCray, to keep Garvey company whilst incarcerated. Their sentences weren't always commensurate with the crime. The *Financial World*, for one, believed Garvey had good reason to feel aggrieved. 'Here we have Fuller and McGee, the plundering brokers, who succeeded in getting away with more than $6 million through their crooked bucket-shop, receiving a sentence of less than a year . . . Over in the Federal Court, Marcus Garvey, an intellectual Negro . . . was sentenced for five years . . . It would appear that the greater the loot the less severe the penalty upon conviction.'[45]

In the black American world, critical response to Garvey's sentence formed along expected lines. Hubert Harrison doubted Garvey's asser-tion that the trial had been a 'frame-up, to get him alone' and that the later inclusion of the three other defendants served as camouflage. Garvey's five-year sentence, Harrison believed, was entirely self-inflicted and could be traced back to the folly of Garvey discharging his lawyer.[46] Du Bois would go further, arguing that Garvey 'convicted himself by his own admissions, his swaggering monkey-shines in the courtroom with monocle and long-tailed coat and insults to the judge and pros-ecuting attorney'.[47] In his loathing of Garvey, Du Bois had some keen competition from Wilfred Domingo. The first editor of the *Negro World* would eventually send a congratulatory telegram to the district attorney which suggested that 'right-thinking Negroes everywhere will applaud you for having caged the tiger at last'.[48] But apart from Domingo, there was very little clucking or crowing over Garvey's demise.

Garvey's and the Black Star Line's failure was every aspiring black

American's failure. Months, sometimes years later, it produced a dull referred pain, whose source was not always immediately obvious, but was reminiscent of so many aches that had gone before. James Saunders Redding recalled how the collapse of the Brown and Stevens Bank – 'the richest and safest Negro bank in the world' – in which the Black Star Line had some deposits, brought his father to the verge of tears 'not because he lost money in that disastrous collapse – he didn't – but because that failure cast dark shadows over the prospects of a self-sustaining Negro culture'.[49]

In the mainstream press, there were some who were already mourning his loss; sorry that all the fun and sport Garvey had given would also be lost. Theirs was an echo of Arthur Brisbane's lament on Garvey's original arrest. Brisbane, a wry and sardonic business partner of the newspaper baron William Randolph Hearst, thought it was 'too bad [because] the Distinguished Son of Ethiopia makes the world more interesting than before he came . . . to jail Marcus Garvey would dim romance, like jailing a rainbow'.[50]

At least 2,000 protestors assembled at Liberty Hall the week after the sentencing of their UNIA leader. Many were angered by what they saw as a politically motivated plot to remove the head of the organisation, to strike the shepherd, as Garvey had always foretold, and thereby scatter the sheep. The most vocal called for the signing of a petition, asking the US President to free Garvey, but the petition was not uniformly taken up. The Bureau's special agent Andrew Battle attended the meeting and, to the relief of his paymasters, reported the divisions that he claimed had opened up, along national lines, between West Indian members – who approved the Negro World's denunciations of the governmental intrigue – and African-Americans, such as the international organiser, Henrietta Vinton Davis, who counselled against dissent that might be regarded as unpatriotic and work to the movement's detriment. From the prism of his cell, Garvey saw a kaleidoscope of conspiracies. If there was to be a coup, now, with the president-general locked up in Tombs prison, was the time to strike. During the trial, when friendly UNIA witnesses, called by the defence, were questioned by Garvey, they'd been nervous less they incriminate themselves, and their responses had been guarded. Ruminating on the failures of his court case, that caution was now cast in his mind, at best as 'inspired disloyalty' and at worse as treachery. Amy Jacques shuttled between UNIA headquarters and Tombs prison, briefing her husband on the machinations of the movement. Despite his incarceration, Marcus Garvey was still able to issue edicts to the governing body. Within days, he had instructed that senior officials, including Henrietta Vinton Davis and the head of the African Legion, Captain Gaines, be taken off the payroll – a decision that was made in anticipation of any challenge to his authority, but that was also one that would reduce the financial burden of meeting their salaries.

Gaines was, in any event, considering his resignation. He'd been made anxious by all the talk and rumours over arms and ammunition, even though a police raid on UNIA offices in Harlem had not discovered so much as a 'wooden pistol or grain of ammunition'.[51] Gaines was wary of any attempt to link him with some of the more volatile officers of the African Legion, men such as William Wellington Grant, known for his hair-trigger potential for violence. For her part, Henrietta Davis would be put on a kind of probation; she would draw no salary, but be sent out as a fieldworker, and allowed to claim a 15 per cent commission on funds collected for the organisation. The urgent task of accumulating sufficient funds for his own defence was entrusted by Garvey to a committee headed by his wife.

Garvey wrote his last will and testament, naming Amy Jacques as the sole beneficiary in the event of his death. Jacques's faithfulness and commitment to her husband were beyond question. She continued to make her regular pilgrimage to the gloomy prison, to the visitors' room and the tiny screened compartments. The middle-class, great-great-granddaughter of the first Mayor of Kingston struggled to keep the tears from her eyes and her sense of shame in check in surroundings that Bertram Reinitz of the *New York Times* described as 'a deafening chorus . . . carried out in many languages . . . [of] women heard pledging their loyalty in tones an octave higher than a Commanche yell'.[52]

Ostensibly, Garvey was not diminished in spirit by his incarceration but a flood of letters, articles and written denunciations spoke to his state of heightened anxiety and deep humiliation. Vernal J. Williams was an early target of his wrath. Garvey lashed out unsparingly at the 'ingratitude' of the UNIA lawyer, whom he had found work for in the organisation when Williams was a struggling law student. Imprisoned and without funds, Garvey was outraged at what he saw as the lawyer's betrayal, in withholding official UNIA papers until his salary had been paid. But Garvey's sharpest invective was reserved for the NAACP, for whom he now had nothing save contempt, nor they for him: 'The leaders of it hate Marcus Garvey because he has broken up the "Pink Tea Set",' wrote the UNIA leader. They had launched a conspiracy to do away with him after he had forced them to recognise 'black talent in the Association equally with the lighter element'. Venom and anxiety scratched at the back of his throat, and there was a previously unfamiliar sensation: panic over the unknown impact of his incarceration on the organisation.

Marcus Garvey's imprisonment did precipitate a significant drift of members from the organisation, although the sound of nervous feet heading for the exits did not yet suggest a stampede. There were those, too, who went to great lengths to disassociate themselves from Garvey. Dr Du Bois was among those who had printed the deliciously scandalous news that the eminent Emmet Scott, the former private secretary of Booker T. Washington, had accepted a knighthood from the UNIA in 1922. Scott denied the allegation and wished it known as widely as possible that he did not kneel, nor receive 'Garvey's foolish decoration'.[53] The Reverend Ethelred Brown, also, evidently felt tainted by his association with his compatriot. His embarrassment actuated a sermon that Brown delivered on unwarranted 'Garvey-istic Devotion' during which the reverend, nonetheless, counselled his congregation against jeering at his former employer, even though Garvey had exposed the race to the 'humiliation of hearing the funeral march played once again over one more pretentious Negro reform movement ended in dismal failure'.[54]

Garvey wrote that he was treated kindly by the warden and prison officials, but the months rolled on interminably, as each application for bail was rejected. Whilst Garvey languished in Tombs prison he had ample time to reflect on the cause of his organisation's dismal failure. He sat down and tried to order his amazing story in a long essay, later published in pamphlet form, which charted his journey from the pearl of the Antilles to his oppressive cell in Tombs prison. The essay was understandably self-serving. Firstly, it aimed to neutralise his enemies. As he explained, 'Being black, I have committed an unpardonable offence against the very light-coloured Negroes in America and the West Indies by making myself famous as a Negro leader of millions.' Secondly, the essay presented a palatable picture of himself to white America. Who could argue with his desire to head off the approaching apocalyptic collision between the races by 'pointing the Negro to a home of his own'? If Garvey had a deep sense of foreboding about the race, then he also hinted at his fears for his own future, whether intentionally or not. The description of his father – 'a man of brilliant intellect and dashing courage. He was unafraid of consequences. He took human chances in the course of life, as most bold men do, and he failed at the close of his career' – might so easily fit a word picture of Garvey himself.

Garvey gave his essay the title 'The Negro's Greatest Enemy'. That idea, and favourite theme, that the black man was his own greatest enemy, was one that he held all his life. It was also a belief which curiously sustained him now in his darkest hour, in the grey gloomy surroundings of the prison. It helped explain the failure of the Black Star Line.

On starting the Black Star Line, Garvey would later write, he had 'the greatest confidence in every Negro at first'. It had been his dream to have every position from pantry boy to captain filled by black people. He had done so, and appointed a black board of directors. Garvey had thought to himself that, 'every Negro felt like I did [and was] a great enthusiast to see the race go forward in success'. Now, after several months in a dark and cramped cell, the unbearable truth had crept up on him: 'I gave everyone a chance, and the story is that very nearly everyone that I placed in a responsible position fleeced the Black Star Line.'[55] It would be several years before Marcus Garvey would commit such thoughts to print. But, alone in the Tombs prison, in the summer of 1923, awaiting a decision on bail – which might never be granted – he clearly felt betrayed. The black man had no respect for another in a position of authority above himself. This explained the rationale behind the failure of the Black Star Line, but also too many of the other enterprises that the association had begun, that had now gone to the wall. The steam laundry on 142nd Street that employed fifty people had to close down after too much infighting; the printing plant followed soon after: 'Men who would work honestly and uprightly with white men started to work as they felt when they came to our [printing] plant,' Garvey complained.[56] It wasn't his theory alone. It explained why the black aristocrats up on Sugar Hill preferred Scandinavian maids to black ones.

When the gloom lifted and the morning sun rose again Garvey might forgive himself, and even congratulate himself for the chance he had given to thousands of black employees. After all, as he told the jury, he had taken 'girls who could only be washerwomen' in middle-class

white homes, and made them 'clerks and stenographers . . . in the Black
Star Line offices.'

After three months, doubt was even further banished when Judge
Martin Manton (standing in for the appeals judge who had gone on
holiday) answered Garvey's and the whole movement's prayers when
he announced that the UNIA leader would be set free, provided his
supporters could raise $15,000 for his bail. Amy Jacques embarked on
a feverish campaign to raise the money; through promissory notes
extracted from arm-twisting phone calls, wired cash and a round of
personal appeals to members, she managed to secure the full amount
by 10 September 1923.[57]

Liberty Hall was a riot of applause, 'Amens' and 'Hallelujahs' the
night their founder returned to them three days later. He was greeted
by another returnee, Bishop Alexander McGuire, who had pitched in
and rallied to Garvey's colours during the build-up to his prosecution.
McGuire had found himself once again smitten by 'the binding spell,
the indefinable charm which Mr Garvey exercises over us'. The bishop
drew the parallel, as so many had done before, between Garvey and
Moses. 'We have reason to believe that his enforced solitude has clar-
ified his vision,' and just as from Horeb and Mount Sinai, 'Moses came
back to Israel with new revelations,' then so too, 'Negroes everywhere
will be the beneficiaries of the NEW IDEAS . . . he has gained during
his vacation [in the Tombs].'[58]

Once the 'Tiger' was free of his cage, he was keen to take his new
ideas out on the road to test them on the people, and to savour the great
expanse of the country after his captivity. He had also promised his wife
a holiday that naturally would be combined with work. One of the high-
lights of the tour was a stopover at the Tuskegee Institute in Alabama.
Tuskegee was cemented in the nation's imagination as a beacon of virtue,
and a successful Southern example of African-Americans benefiting from
liberal white philanthropy. Garvey had clashed with the principal Dr
Moton in the past; he'd even ridiculed Moton as an old fuddy-duddy,
hat-in-hand Negro, genuflecting in front of the white man. The fact that
Robert Moton would now invite the convicted criminal, Marcus Garvey,
to address the students in the Chapel at Tuskegee, was a huge testament
of faith in him. The UNIA leader's guilt may have been proven in court,
but, for a large number of black people, his reputation as a sincere and
honest race leader remained intact – a point that was further underlined
when the institute accepted a small donation of $50 from Garvey.

Marcus Garvey was gratified by his reception at Tuskegee, but it was more like work than rest. During their two weeks in California Jacques was more successful in persuading her husband to take time off, particularly for a tour of the Hollywood studios in Los Angeles. Postcards of their vacation have not survived, but the tourist photograph of Amy propped up on a beach donkey with her unsmiling husband in a heavy overcoat does not suggest a man at ease with the concept of leisure.

Though he might look glum, Marcus Garvey carried no bitterness in his heart. It was an attitude that even surprised his wife. By temperament, he was and would always remain a 'romancer and poet'. Marcus Garvey's capacity to shrug off disappointments was remarkable, but the injuries he'd suffered at the hands of W. E. B. Du Bois, the 'Garvey Must Go' campaigners and the NAACP could not be dispelled; they were elusive sirens – tantalising and tormenting. They followed him throughout his two-month tour and vexed his spirit. They, in part, informed the new ideas that he'd conjured up in prison, which, stripped of the rhetoric of racial uplift, centred on withdrawal and flight. There was no long-term future for the black man in America. In all the speeches that he made, Garvey seemed increasingly convinced of that now. Arriving in Oakland, he spelt out his belief that 'America will always be a white man's country . . . 'Tis hard, 'tis woefully hard for a Du Bois or a Weldon Johnson to admit this, but how can one wisely "kick against the pricks"?' He was tired of those friendly whites who would make the Negro 'the wards of a mistaken philanthropy'.[59]

During his visit to St Louis, to the Negro section represented by the 'famous anti-lynching advocate', Congressman Dyer, he howled, 'I was not allowed to be served a chocolate sundae in a drugstore because I was black.[60] . . . I could not get a soda served even by a dirty Greek, who kept his so-called white soda fountain in a Negro section!' So much for social equality and the NAACP's foolish dream of integration, Garvey seemed to be saying. 'Between the Ku Klux Klan and the Morefield Storey NAACP, give me the Klan for their honesty of purpose towards the Negro.'[61] In Youngstown, Ohio, Garvey delivered an appeal to the 'liberal, philanthropic, liberty-loving' soul of white America, where he elaborated on his apocalyptic treatise on the doomed relationship of the races. 'So long as white labourers believe that black labourers are taking and holding their jobs . . . so long as white men and women believe that black men and women are filling positions that they covet; so long as white men believe that black men want to associate with and marry white women then we will have prejudice and not only prejudice, but riots, lynchings, burnings, and God to tell what next to follow!'

Garvey wasn't essentially voicing opinions markedly different from those he had held before. At Liberty Hall, in March, he'd held up a press report from Missouri and simply read out the disturbing bulletin: 'A carefully organised campaign of intimidation has driven more than 2,000 Negro workers from their jobs . . . Negro leaders charged that threats were sent by white labourers fearful of losing their jobs . . . Ambrose Young a Negro appealed for protection. Young said . . . "I found [a] note on my front porch. It said: 'Nigger, if you can't read, run. If you can't run, you're as good as dead.'"'[62] In that same Liberty Hall meeting, Garvey had concluded, 'What has happened in this Missouri town is going to happen all over America.'

Marcus Garvey's position hadn't changed in October. His new idea was simply an old idea that he was advocating more forcibly than ever before: that black people pack up their bags and go. He even devised a letter in the form of a questionnaire that was sent to the Attorney-General and a number of senators. The letter canvassed the opinions of senators as to whether they might assist in his call for the large-scale repatriation of black people to Africa. Garvey's enemies were bemused by this disturbing twist in his thinking, namely the open solicitation of white support beyond the Ku Klux Klan. Some settled on cynical explanations. The editor of the *Pittsburgh Courier* viewed the letter as Garvey pitching for a pardon and, worse still, nakedly 'selling his whole race for a pardon'.

Paradoxically, Garvey had emerged from prison advocating much more political engagement. In a speech the week after his release he implored the audience to 'get registered wherever you are. If you are citizens, for your own convenience and for the convenience of carrying on [our] programme you must get naturalised . . . because when the final time comes, we are not going to beg this question, we are going to force it.'[63]

Up until now Garvey had largely eschewed conventional politics in America. He'd always maintained that the UNIA should remain a social organisation. The sudden volte-face had an immediate effect on the political landscape – especially as far as the NAACP was concerned. Samuel Redding grew up in a NAACP stronghold and recalled how 'the coming of the Garveyites shattered the defensive bulwark around the protective community of Negroes'. In the district, with a large black population, black folk had enjoyed political control: 'The same men had been returned to office again and again. What they did there seemed not nearly as important as just being there. They had enormous prestige . . . and they had not had to fight to keep it.' But in the elections that year Garvey sent out agents from Harlem, and the local UNIA divisions put up their own candidates who split the black vote. The campaign, wrote Redding, 'smelled of pitch and brimstone and led to street brawls . . . and while Negroes fought one another, whites won the offices'.[64]

William Du Bois watched the resurgence of Marcus Garvey and this disturbing turn of events with dismay. The spring of the following year brought even more alarming news. Du Bois and his colleagues were stunned when, after the fiasco of the Black Star Line, Garvey announced in the pages of the *Negro World* that he had incorporated a new steamship line, to be called the Black Cross Navigation and Trading Company. 'No stock will be sold in this new company, but all interest will be held by the UNIA and its members,' and in a tone of high, seriousness but quiet triumph, Garvey continued, 'It is expected that this ship will sail on September 1, carrying the first organised group of colonists to Liberia.' Du Bois was dumbfounded. Hadn't he already dispatched his enemy? Hadn't Garvey been dragged through the courts and unmasked as nothing but a common criminal? Du Bois was amazed, as Amy Jacques put it, that after the successes of the 'Garvey Must Go' campaigners revealing to the nation the menace of the man, 'Garvey hadn't gone yet'.[65]

Du Bois could no longer abide the casual vituperation heaped on the race, and on its guardian and champion, W. E. B. Du Bois. In praising the honesty of the Ku Klux Klan, Garvey was 'not attacking white prejudice, [but] . . . grovelling before it and applauding it', argued the editor of the *Crisis*. And now he mustered all his energies for one last exterminating essay that would answer one simple question: Is Marcus Garvey 'a lunatic or a traitor'? By the article's close it was clear that Du Bois considered him both: 'The American Negro has endured this wretch too long with fine restraint and every effort of cooperation and understanding. But the end has come. Every man who apologises for or defends Marcus Garvey from this day forth writes himself down as unworthy of the countenance of decent Americans. As for Garvey himself, this open ally of the Ku Klux Klan should be locked up or sent home.'[66]

Du Bois was cursing into the wind as Marcus Garvey had already begun to roll out his plan for the re-colonisation of Africa. It had been three years since the first UNIA mission to Liberia. Three officials, the Princeton-educated Sir Robert Poston, Milton Van Lowe (the organisation's new attorney) and the indefatigable Lady Henrietta Vinton Davis, were chosen now as delegates to go to Monrovia. They were to finalise arrangements for the settlement of colonists on the land in Grand Bassa County that had been provisionally set aside for them. The delegates set sail for Liberia on board a Cunard vessel, the SS *Britannia*, on 11 December, full of excitement and expectation for their symbolic sojourn in the motherland and relishing the weight of their historic mission. They would arrive a month later, having stopped off first at Lisbon in Portugal, and would just miss out on all of the festivities surrounding the inauguration of President King of Liberia – not that they had been invited. It was with some nervousness that Garvey noted the announcement, also in December, that the US President, Calvin Coolidge, had appointed Du Bois as special minister plenipotentiary to represent him at the inauguration (a privileged appointment he'd lobbied hard for by calling in a favour from the official William H. Lewis). Du Bois would arrive ahead of the UNIA envoys, and the prospect of him interfering with their plans worried Garvey sufficiently to seek advice from John E. Bruce, who had strong contacts in Africa. Bruce thought of sending a cable to his old Ghanaian friend, J. E. Casely Hayford. He wrote to Garvey on 2 January:

> Dear Chief,
> If you think it worthwhile (I think it is), you may cable in my name the following to Hayford at once: Dubois – Crisis – on trip to Africa, bent on mischief, due to failure of his 'Pan African Congress'. Financed by Joel Spingarn, a Jew, and other interest (white) inimical to African independence. Watch him . . . Bruce Grit.

Garvey had entrusted his envoys with a letter to be hand delivered to the President of Liberia, which reminded him of the bitter internecine struggles, of the 'tremendous fight of the lighter element against the darker ones', namely the conflict between Garvey's camp and Du Bois whom Garvey imagined even now was strutting around the Liberian court like a pompous proconsul. Marcus Garvey wasn't fully aware of his rival's close relationship with leading members of Liberia's hierarchy; and he hadn't factored into the equation the NAACP leader's own detailed plans for how Liberia, through American aid and investment, might be freed from the quagmire of near bankruptcy. Those plans, detailed to both President King and Secretary of State Hughes, left no room for the spurious and fanciful option proposed by the UNIA. Nonetheless Garvey's envoys were treated cordially in Monrovia, and their plan for a first wave of 3,000 immigrants was put to the president when they met him on 11 February. President King gave assurances for three colonies at the Cavalla, Sino and Grand Bassa, and when Lady Henrietta spoke with admiration about the geographical layout of Cape Mount that had so impressed the visitors when the *Britannia* came into port, the president replied, with careless munificence, 'You can have land there also.' Robert Poston was so elated by the day's negotiations that he sent a telegram back to Garvey with one word: 'SUCCESS.' Robert Poston was not party to the press release composed by the commercial intelligence bureau which revealed that President King would only partake in an unofficial interview. The memo stipulated that 'any proposal suggesting location for 3,000 immigrants to Liberia must ultimately be denied'.[67] Meanwhile the envoys bashed out plans with the advisory board, including that preference should be given to emigrants from the USA under the age of fifty with strong physiques and determination to become citizens of Liberia; that all emigrants needed to possess at least $1,500 in cash, and that emigrants would not be sent out in groups of more than 500 at a time. Although Garvey worried over Du Bois's influence, President King, the internal memo pointed out, was 'keeping his mind on the obligation of Liberia to the great powers, and as much to the maintenance of the independence of the republic'. Liberia bordered French and British colonies and was keen not to provoke them. Indeed the British legation in Monrovia, monitoring the UNIA, was especially anxious about rumours of a plan to establish at least two settlements along the Liberia–Sierra Leone border which might lead 'native Africans to insurrection against the rule of the white man'.[68] The resurgence of Marcus Garvey was sufficient for a nervous High Commissioner of the Union of South Africa to remind British Passport Control that Marcus Garvey and his officers were to be denied entry to South Africa.[69]

Garvey's emigration scheme also sparked editorial debates in other parts of British Colonial Africa. Ahinnana (thought to be the pseudonym of J. E. Casely Hayford), writing in the *Gold Coast Leader*, asked cogently, 'At the present moment throughout the African colonies and settlements European enterprise of every description is encouraged and welcomed. Why, in the name of reason, should any obstacles be placed in the way of the enterprise of the African abroad?'[70] The African abroad should remain there according to the *Nigerian Pioneer*. Its editor placed his patriotism firmly in the eye of the reading public when it declared, '"Africa for the Africans" like other beautiful and hysterical political cries will end in smoke. West Africa has inseparably and indissolubly woven her destiny with that of Empire.'

The ardour of Garvey's emissaries would not be dampened, even with the tragic death of Robert Poston at sea, when the party was travelling back to New York. Poston had contracted a fever and eventually died from lobar pneumonia on board the SS *President Grant* on 16 March 1924. The chief steward, J. Milton Batson, later reported that he had met Poston shortly before his death when he was 'in the pink of health but obviously broken from despondency as a result of the failure of the [UNIA] delegation'. Robert Lincoln Poston had stuck by Garvey during the fallout from the purges of 1922. He had remained conspicuously loyal, cheering Garvey on from platforms up and down the country. Poston had stood at Garvey's shoulder offering the barely audible 'all right' and 'yessum' and 'tell 'em Marcus'; Poston, with a pronounced lisp, had sung his praise of Garvey from his own unique 'amen corner', encouragement that had raised the UNIA leader's power of oratory to ever greater heights. Now Poston was dead and would not, and could not, be replaced. Poston would be eulogised and posthumously appointed 'prince of Africa' but the future prince had told Batson that he was returning to the USA with bad news about the UNIA's prospects in Liberia. News that he was not sure how President-General Garvey would take because 'no one could tell what Marcus Garvey would do, as no one knew what Marcus Garvey would do until he did it'.[71]

Robert Poston's death meant Marcus Garvey was spared his emissary's message; Poston's fellow delegate to Liberia, Henrietta Davis, had a far more optimistic tale to tell. Davis spoke triumphantly to a hushed audience at Liberty Hall on 19 April, of the magical moment when she first touched Liberian soil, and Scott's 'Lay of the Last

Minstrel' shot into her mind: 'Breathes there a man with soul so dead, who never himself hath said, "This is my own, my native land."' President King, she recalled, had spoken with 'a zeal, enthusiasm and appreciation that could not have been excelled by the Hon. Marcus Garvey himself'. The proposed settlements would be located in the most fertile lands, and the first step should be to 'send material [and] artisans to lay out the land and build homes.'[72] Davis counted herself worldly enough to be able to distinguish between diplomacy and duplicity, and Garvey took her at her word. By that stage, of course, he was hardly prepared to countenance advice that differed from his views. After all, wasn't this the same President King who, when back in 1920 it was intimated that Garvey wanted to set up headquarters in Liberia, is reported to have said, 'Well, let them come!'[73]

A team of UNIA technicians – including a carpenter, builder and mechanical engineer – was hurriedly assembled to set sail for Liberia. Liberty Hall was filled to capacity on 4 June, to bid farewell to the men who would 'form the vanguard of African Redemption'. The mining engineer Wallace Strange, whom Garvey, with his usual measure of moderation, introduced as 'our Colonel Goethals' (the principal engineer of the Panama Canal) mesmerised the audience with his calm and earnest speech. Wallace Strange believed his whole life had been 'a special preparation for this moment'. His heart was filled with trepidation, with the responsibility of finding the technical solution to Marcus Garvey's fantastic dream. He, like everyone in the audience, belonged to Africa and he assured them, 'I am going to give all that is within me to start its development.' As he finished, the admiring crowd pressed close for a farewell handshake.

Two weeks later Garvey took out an advert in the *New York World* announcing plans to raise a fund of $2 million 'to bear the cost of constructing and establishing the first colony' to which more than seventy people had so far contributed just over $4,000. But the surge of optimism did not last.

The *New York World*, along with every other major paper in New York, as well as the major black papers, was the recipient of a strange press release from the Liberian Consul General in the US on 10 July. When that press release was published in the following days, it effectively put an end once and for all to Marcus Garvey's settlement schemes in Africa. The most damaging aspects of the release left no room for a mollifying reinterpretation: 'No person or persons leaving the US under the auspices of the Garvey movement in the US will be allowed to land in the republic of Liberia. All Liberian Consuls in the US are instructed and directed not to visa the passports of any persons leaving the US for Liberia under the direction of the movement.'

The contingent of UNIA engineers and planners, including Wallace Strange, were still on the high seas when the news came through. As soon as they arrived at Monrovia, they were immediately arrested and summarily deported. The thousands of dollars of UNIA equipment was impounded and later auctioned off to pay for the cost of storage.

Even by the standards of the troubles that had landed on Marcus Garvey's desk over the last few years, the Liberian rejection and the means of its presentation were shocking. Garvey was still reeling three weeks later. It called for a response but the news had induced a cata-tonia of disbelief. For once, Garvey faltered. The fourth international convention was about to open, and overnight the main plank of his programme had disappeared. His eventual letter to President King was sad and meek and clung desperately to the faintest possibility that the statement 'attributed' to King might yet be false; might prove to be a terrible mistake. For Garvey could not believe that the president 'could be responsible for doing anything that would tend to dampen the spirit of love' that the UNIA held for Liberia.

It was clear to him, though, once the smoke and fug of confusion had cleared, who was to blame. Not the good people of Liberia, nor their oleaginous head of state. His adversary, W. E. B. Du Bois, had bent the ear of President King at his inauguration and prevailed upon him to oppose the UNIA. Du Bois threw his hands up in all innocence at the suggestion. Though his protest that he had 'nothing at all to do with the relations between Garvey and the Republic of Liberia' was not entirely convincing,[74] Garvey had undoubtedly underestimated Liberian nervousness about how their association with his movement might be perceived by their potentially hostile neighbours. And then there was the Firestone Rubber Company. Marcus Garvey's envoys had been unaware of a bigger player in the field, courting the Liberian authorities for a favourable deal on land. The Firestone Rubber Plantation Company had its sights on 1 million acres of Liberian land, which they would eventually secure at 5 to 10 cents per acre.

There are divergent accounts surrounding the issues but it is suggested from communiqués between President King and his cabinet that, from the outset, the Liberian authorities had little intention of granting concessions to the UNIA. The two unflattering reports on Liberia (the first commissioned by Garvey from Elie Garcia and the second, unsolicited, account from the disenchanted Crichlow) that were eventually leaked to the Liberians certainly damaged the UNIA's chances. But circumstances had further conspired against the UNIA with the marginalisation of the UNIA potentate, Mayor Gabriel Johnson, once he'd accepted a highly attractive and lucrative government position in the Spanish-run, West African colony on the island of Fernando Po.

The trouble for Garvey was that the idea of an African escape route had moved from being a Utopian ideal, to a desperately sought practical alternative to life in the USA. There could be no turning back from this African place in the sun, and such was the degree of Garvey's self-delusion that for much of 1924 the *Negro World* was still advertising one-way fares to West Africa.

Despite years of negotiation, despite all the financial inducements and pilot projects, the Liberian deal was dead in the water. Back in the USA, Garvey's expensive lawyers would not be drawn on the likely outcome of the appeal against his conviction, and now his emergency exit doors to Liberia were locked and chained from the outside.

16

INTO THE FURNACE

Stand with us in our struggles for
The triumph of the right,
And spread confusion ever o'er
The advocates of might.
And let them know that righteousness
Is mightier than sin
That might is only selfishness
And cannot, ought not, win

UNIA prayer by John E. Bruce

THE photograph is a study of group reflection. Not one of the ten people – nine men in dark suits and a lone woman in black dress and veil – caught by the photographer, James Van Der Zee, looks at the camera. Most gaze into the distance, to the past and the future. Only two men, a priest and Marcus Garvey, stare into the grave. They have come to bury the grand old man of the movement and 'Harlem's first royalty', the journalist who put grit and verve into every thought, John E. Bruce ('Bruce Grit').

A couple of hours before the photo, 5,000 UNIA members, led by the African Legion in full regalia 'with sabres drawn', had accompanied the cortège, marching sombrely from the funeral parlour to Liberty Hall. There they recited the prayer of UNIA meetings that Bruce had written and dedicated to the movement back in 1919. At sixty-seven, Bruce Grit's passing was not unexpected; he'd been ill for the past two years but had grounded the movement on American soil like no other, and his loss created a vacuum which exposed the reduced state of the

UNIA, already impoverished by the tragic and premature death of the thirty-six-year-old Robert Poston on his route back from Liberia. Both men were devoted to the UNIA but in Bruce Grit, previously decorated as 'the Duke of Uganda', Garvey had found an Afro-centric writer (long before such a term existed) who championed the movement with the crusading ferocity of the convert that he'd become on a chilly autumn evening in 1919.

In the wake of Bruce's death, the movement seemed, in some part, to have lost its way. Just how far it had strayed might be gleaned from two opposing decisions it subsequently took. Bruce would have applauded the first on a bed of hosannas up to heaven; the second he'd have cast into the furnace of hell. Both were concerned with ideals of blackness. To understand the first, one needed to be reminded of the old African-American joke, which loosely went: If Jesus Christ was alive and looking for accommodation in New York, his dark appearance would have prevented him from living anywhere else but Harlem. During the August convention of 1924, Reverend George McGuire took that conceit one stage further with his 'canonisation of the Lord Jesus Christ as the Black Man of Sorrows'. Jesus, McGuire informed UNIA members, didn't just look like a black man; he was a black man – an idea that Garvey endorsed when he announced that 'since whites are seeing [H]im through the eyes of whiteness, we are going to see [H]im through the eyes of blackness'.[1] The second, opposing decision to this celebration of blackness, centred on the urgent need to generate funds. That pressure led the *Negro World* to renege on a sacred principle by flooding its pages with lucrative adverts for hair-straightening and skin-bleaching preparations. One didn't celebrate black beauty by applying Tan Off to one's skin. Pragmatism, then, dictated the un-Bruce-like compromise with ideals. But the week after his old friend's funeral, Garvey made a spectacular announcement that revealed just why he was prepared to risk John E. Bruce turning in his grave. A deposit of $30,000 had been placed on the SS *General G. W. Goethals*. The new shipping company had partly purchased its first vessel. To take full possession of the ship, they would need to find another $70,000 – a feat the UNIA had achieved three months later when Amy Jacques broke a bottle of champagne on the bow and rechristened the vessel SS *Booker T. Washington*. The 5,000-ton vessel was purchased on 20 October 1924. In addition to cargo, the ship could accommodate 75 first-class passengers and 100 second-class.

In the teeth of recession it was a remarkable achievement, as well as the perfect rebuff to the non-stop barrage of corrosive criticism from the likes of George Schuyler. A nasty odour had risen recently from the prose pages of Schuyler – a scholar of sarcasm who believed that Garvey's best ideas had not come to him after quiet meditation in a university library but rather 'one evening [when] absently thrusting the remainder of the pigfoot into his overall pocket, he sat in his favourite trash box'. Schuyler had joked mercilessly about looking forward to Garvey's re-education in 'his five-year semester' in a federal penitentiary.[2] But, at the beginning of 1925, Marcus Garvey walked out of the darkness that had threatened to engulf the movement and towards the light. He was illuminated by the hope that the Court of Appeal would be persuaded of the merits of his case and overturn the error of judgement of his conviction.

At its heart, Garvey's counsel argued, the fraud case rested on the simple question: On whose behalf was Garvey being prosecuted? The same investors, whom he was alleged to have swindled, had responded in their thousands, enabling Garvey to purchase the new ship. The stock was never offered to the public; only to Negroes who 'were more intent on the ultimate and uplifting salvation that was promised to the Negro race . . . than to the paltry profits that might be realised'. But where Garvey's lawyers saw sincerity, the Court of Appeal detected the cynicism of a race pimp who may have 'fancied himself a Moses, if not a Messiah . . . [but] stripped of its appeal to the ambitions, emotions or race consciousness of men of colour, [his scheme] was a simple and familiar device of which the object was to ascertain how "it could best unload upon the public its capital stock at the largest possible price"'. The Court of Appeal affirmed the judgment. There need be no further delay to Garvey's removal to the Atlanta Penitentiary.

When the news reached Garvey in Detroit, he wired back immediately, 'Coming On First Train Out'. His lawyers contacted the District Attorney who, recalled Amy Jacques, 'gave his personal undertaking that he would bring in his client the following morning'. But a warrant for Garvey's arrest had already been issued and some papers flashed the news that the UNIA leader was now a fugitive from justice. Special Agent James Amos hurried to Harlem, just as Garvey and his wife travelled back by train to New York. Amos, now accompanied by two US marshals, boarded the train at 125th Street and, moving quickly through the carriages, found and pounced on his prey. A stunned Marcus Garvey was handcuffed, taken back to the Tombs prison and locked up overnight.

By the following morning, Marcus Garvey had recovered some of his composure. 5 February 1925 was to be the most important day in the organisation's history. The unthinkable was about to happen, and the editors of the *Negro World* rose to the task, capturing the moment in fine cheery prose on its front page:

'Tell Mr [Clifford] Bourne to telegraph me at Atlanta word of the ship.' With these words to his secretary, one of a small group at the Pennsylvania Railroad station, Hon. Marcus Garvey, handcuffed to a deputy marshal, settled in his seat in a coach of the Washington Express, and was soon chatting unconcernedly with that stern-faced officer.

It was 12 o'clock Saturday. Mr Garvey had just been rushed from the Tombs prison to the Pennsylvania station to begin his trip to Atlanta penitentiary. He arrived with two Marshalls, the one . . . to whom he was handcuffed, and the other a six-footer, with the aspect and bearing of a retired prize-fighter, two pistols strapped to his side . . . walking along the station platform to the coach, casting uneasy glances behind and beyond. Mr Garvey sees his secretary hurrying past . . . 'Hello!' comes a cheery greeting, with a characteristic smile, 'everything O.K? Received my message?' 'Yes, Sir,' is the reply and, as if the command 'eyes right' was given to a military squad, Marshals and detective, ill-suppressed smiles on their faces, turn and stare. 'Sir!' they seem to say, 'What manner of man is this Garvey?'

Mr Garvey is now seated in the coach, and the crowd outside peering through the windows increases. A reverend gentleman, noticing the suppressed air of excitement among his fellow travellers, lowers his newspaper and takes in the scene. All the passengers are whispering to each other . . . On the other side of the coach a newspaper photographer is hard at work vainly signalling Mr Garvey to turn his head that he may be the better shot! 'Make way,' someone cries, and Mrs Amy Jacques Garvey enters the coach, a through ticket to Atlanta in her hand. The efforts to deceive as to the time of Mr Garvey's departure have been unavailing. A sympathetic reporter tipped off Mrs Garvey, a couple of officers of the UNIA and two lawyers, as they waited at the Tombs prison, of his impending departure. A taxi was pressed into service. At the station . . . practically the whole staff of 'Red Caps' . . . had constituted themselves into a committee to inform them of the moment of the great leader's arrival. As Mrs Garvey enters the coach and takes her seat, three seats in the rear of her husband, someone taps on the window and Mr Garvey turns and sees his wife. His smile is in evidence again . . . Mrs Garvey, brave little woman, sits calmly, looking at her husband, then at his custodians, then back at her husband. The coach door slams. The train moves. 'Damn,' says a burly 'Red Cap' his eyes filled with tears, 'What a shame!' The most-feared, greatest Negro in the world is on the way to a federal prison.

On the long journey South, Garvey was not so concerned about his impending incarceration than on leaving the organisation in good working order. Amy Jacques managed to secure some time alone with her husband but there was no possibility of indulging in these last moments of intimacy. Prudently, she had brought along a notebook and 'took instructions for the officers [of the UNIA]' and 'messages' for the *Negro World*.

The train arrived in Atlanta the following morning. Husband and wife were now separated. So anxious was she not to lose sight of Garvey that she hurtled off the carriage and rushed through the 'white' waiting room and leapt into a cab. The car had been idling but the ignition was now switched off, and Jacques was politely informed that 'down here, white men can't drive coloured people'. She didn't stop to consider how this Southern reception might be translated for her husband once he arrived at the penitentiary. She hurried to the 'coloured' section, found a cab and followed her husband to the jail, all the while encouraging the driver to toot the horn so that Garvey would realise she was still close by. Mrs Garvey was stopped at the gates by a guard who coolly, but without malice, informed her that she would not be able to see her husband for two weeks. Masking her tears as best she could, Amy Jacques watched her husband disappear into the belly of the prison.[3]

The number 19359 was the most popular choice of players of 'policy', the illegal lottery in Harlem, throughout the spring and summer of 1925. It became so after the Atlanta penitentiary assigned 19359 to the most famous black man – now most famous imprisoned black man – in the world. The federal prison at Atlanta was often said to resemble a university hall, built in the classical Italianate style that would become so beloved of Mussolini's Fascists. Visitors approached via a long curving driveway, lined by elegant art-deco lamp posts that guided them to the entrance at its cusp. A carefully tended lawn swept around the front and sides of the building. It was deceptive, designed purposefully so, wrote Eugene Debs, 'to relieve the grimness of grey wall and steel bars', and to give the impression that the state had 'provided [the criminals] a comfortable resort'. Prior to Garvey's arrival, Debs, the Socialist leader sentenced for sedition during the Great War, had been its most famous guest. Whilst still locked up, in 1920, Eugene Debs convinced close to a million Americans to vote for him as President, revealing that his presidential headquarters was the kind of 'holiday camp' where prisoners were compelled to 'submit to the iron discipline enforced there, eat nauseating food and feel themselves isolated, cramped [and] watched day and night'.[4] Prisoner 19359 would find that conditions had not changed in the three years since the release of Eugene Debs.

Garvey, who always had a clear idea of his worth, had set his face at defiance by the time he entered the Atlanta penitentiary. He would not, he said, be beaten by state-sponsored persecution and the indignities of his imprisonment; he would not be 'dwarfed and dulled by deadly routine'. Marcus Garvey was built to lead and, even from the confines of the Atlanta penitentiary, he would inspire. On the first night of his incarceration, when the malodour of defeat closed in on his darkening cell, Marcus Garvey sat down to write, and roused himself to a height of eloquence previously unsurpassed. In an open letter to the Negro people of the world, he asked his followers to pray for him, and entrusted his wife whom he had left 'penniless and helpless to face the world' into their care; and finally he imagined himself dead – his enemies satisfied – and he, like Macbeth's ghost, forever walking the earth: 'When I am dead wrap the mantle of the Red, Black and Green around me, for in the new life I shall rise with God's grace and blessings to lead the millions up the heights of triumph with the colours that you well know. Look for me in the whirlwind or the storm, look for me all around you, for, with God's grace, I shall come and bring with me countless millions of black slaves who have died in America and the West Indies and the millions in Africa to aid you in the fight for liberty, freedom and life.'[5]

A night of exaltation was greeted by a dawn of anxiety over intractable difficulties that, once sleep approached, tricked him into their ease of settlement. Waking, it started all over again. The morning post brought a pledge of allegiance from William Sherrill, the acting president-general, dipped in a vat of sycophancy that must have given Garvey pause for thought about the calibre of men whom he'd be relying on outside the prison walls. A month later, Sherrill was writing again to reassure Garvey that he was no Brutus intent on killing Caesar: 'I have not the genius or breadth of vision possessed by you.' William Sherrill protested to the nth degree his loyalty to the imprisoned leader, yet kept a distance from Atlanta, and rarely wrote to him save to reaffirm his loyalty.

Sherrill's perceived lack of respect for Garvey was as nothing compared to the disregard shown by his first wife, Amy Ashwood. With Garvey safely under guard and heading from Harlem to Atlanta, Ashwood hired a number of vans, enlisted a group of helpers and drove round to Garvey's apartment. Once there, she forced her way in and was intent on liberating various household items (including the grand piano) that she considered her own. Garvey's neighbours intervened. UNIA officers and the police were called. Ashwood stood down her furniture removers and left without any spoils. But having made an inventory of the furniture, she obtained a restraining order preventing Amy Jacques from doing anything with the contested items whilst Ashwood launched an appeal against the legality of the divorce that Garvey had secured from a court in Missouri.

Amy Ashwood's challenge to the imprisoned Garvey was a foretaste of what was to come. Though the force of his personality radiated out from the bars of his cell, President-General Garvey's ability to exert his authority was inevitably retarded. Regular letters and visits from his second wife as well as a procession of UNIA officials – excluding William Sherrill – kept feelings of isolation at bay. Amy Jacques managed to disguise the 'eloquent hurt in her eyes' that all admirers felt when calling on the great man in his new surroundings.

Garvey was steadfast, though the shock to his system was considerable. Even the judge, Julian Mack, who'd originally convicted him, was sympathetic to the suggestion that Garvey should be allowed to serve his sentence in the Northern city of Kansas, rather than Atlanta in the South where he now found himself, and where the black man was more likely to be given a raw deal. The first few months of incarceration were true to that expectation. Garvey related that the influence of his enemies had extended to the very heart of the prison. Word had been passed along, such that 'the deputy warden [Julian A. Schoen] made every effort to carry out [their] wishes . . . he gave me the hardest

and dirtiest tasks in the prison'.[6] Garvey, by his own admission, 'philo-
sophically accepted the duties' which he euphemistically labelled 'water
working'. Early on, though, he recorded a bruising encounter with a
guard who had shouted, 'Here, you coon.' Garvey pretended not to
hear him until the guard called him 'coon' a third time. Whereupon
the president-general of the UNIA turned round and asked, 'Are you
speaking to me?' Garvey's impertinence elicited a string of uncouth
invectives from the jailer who concluded his rant with the assessment,
'You are nothing but a nigger, a coon. You are not in New York; you
are not up above the Mason-Dixon Line, and you are a coon like all
the rest.'[7] Garvey endeavoured to extract a smattering of dignity from
that altercation but the prison record of it hints at the humiliating
adjustments that the prisoner would have been forced to make. The
prison records cite a violation on 11 May 1926 when Garvey was
charged with insolence. The guard is quoted as saying, 'I told this man
not to interfere with the cleaners when I had them on a job. He
commenced to argue, I told him to hush. Then he said no man was
able to make him hush talking, in a defying way. Even clenched his
fist like he was going to strike me.'

Prisoner 19359 was reprimanded and warned. Deputy warden Schoen
noted, matter-of-factly, that 'as head cleaner, this prisoner was over
anxious about work'.[8]

Writers and journalists were especially keen to be granted an audience with the humbled provisional president of Africa – mostly they
were refused. The considerate journalist and historian, Joel A. Rogers,
who would include Garvey in his incomparable *World's Great Men of
Color*, was one of the lucky few beyond Garvey's inner circle allowed
to pay his respects and act as guide for the thousands of readers of
his syndicated column. Once past the heavy iron-barred door, Rogers
was greeted by a stocky figure clad in ordinary workmen's clothes,
'nothing to indicate a prisoner in popular belief – but an unbelievable
contrast to the figure in the glittering uniform, gold epaulettes,
plumed hat, sword and spurs on the prancing steed, who as leader
of 400,000,000 Negroes of the World,' led his followers through the
streets of Harlem. Though Garvey had lost a lot of weight, Rogers
confirmed for the readers of the *New York Amsterdam News* that his
zest and imagination were unbounded. '"When I get out of here," he
[Garvey] said, with all that old fire that had held his great audiences
spellbound in Madison Square Garden, "I mean to do a thousand times

more."' When Rogers asked him about his current duties he was circumspect, simply stating that 'he was not permitted to name [them]'. Perhaps knowing his friend had been commissioned to write up the interview for a leading black journal, Garvey was embarrassed to register with readers that the provisional president of Africa's present job description was 'head cleaner'. Nonetheless, when Rogers's hour came to an end in the Atlanta penitentiary, he was consumed by one thought: 'The once humble peasant that had just disappeared behind the clanging gates had started something that, liked or hated, is destined to affect the future of humanity in no mean way.'[9]

That legacy was now transferred, temporarily, into the care of a small, bony man, spiked with ambition, who was soon caught up in a set of Machiavellian machinations all of his own making, borne of a determination to free himself from the constant threat of Garvey's overpowering influence – no matter that the chief was locked up more than 800 miles from Harlem.

The NAACP's Mary White Ovington strained to be fair when she visited Atlanta and interviewed Garvey for her book *Portraits in Color*. She found his enthusiasm for his race undimmed by the humiliations of his imprisonment. Ovington wrote of her interview with Garvey that though he saw 'no hope for the American Negro . . . [because] this is a white man's country, and he will be pushed harder than ever against the wall. In the British West Indies there is more hope. There, some day, by the force of his numbers, the Negro may dominate. But Africa is still the one land where it is possible to build a Negro state.' In taking her leave of the prisoner, Ovington was cheered to note that he was not ultimately dispirited: 'Garvey can talk to you upon this theme hour after hour. You feel it continually passing through his mind as he goes about his monotonous prison tasks, that it is his last waking thought.'[10]

The UNIA was a huge, unwieldy organisation and the stand-in president, Sherrill, suffered from too great a gulf between ambition and ability. He was clearly out of his depth, or so a significant number of UNIA veterans thought of this latecomer to the cause, especially after Sherrill remortgaged Liberty Hall to liquidate debts, but at the risk of creditors eventually foreclosing on the UNIA's hallowed headquarters. His vacillation over the management of the SS *Booker T. Washington* at one stage led to a near mutiny on board. Garvey was later informed that the 'crew, being dissatisfied, have refused to raise steam', and matters were further complicated by the fact that the 'Steamboat Inspection Department [would] not permit us to replace crew until paid'.[11] The intransigence over back-payment claims by the crew would eventually have to be brought to an end. If the crew sued and the case went to court there was a real danger of history repeating itself and the company being forced to sell the ship, invariably at a loss, to satisfy the crew's and other suits brought against it. Garvey saw it as yet another example of the black man's curse; of his reluctance or inability to take orders from a fellow black.

Marcus Garvey still entertained ideas of an early release from Atlanta to help the movement resolve some of its present difficulties. One of his biggest gripes against Sherrill was that the stand-in president expended too little effort in agitating against his imprisonment, in lobbying and launching petitions and appeals on Garvey's behalf. Sherrill, it seemed, was in no great hurry to see his boss released. The acting UNIA leader only visited Garvey after he had been in prison for three months, and even then it was to brief him against his rivals in the movement. Sherrill's opponents were, in turn, sending cables to Garvey informing him that 'membership [was] unitedly opposed to any attempt to Americanise the association and ignore you as active head', and requesting his endorsement, perhaps in the form of a 'helpful' statement from him, to ensure that such a desirable state of affairs was maintained.[12]

Whilst the men of various factions lined up against each other, Garvey could at least count on the devotion of a handful of women to put his needs and desires above all else. The exceptionally loyal Ethel Collins kept a watchful eye over excesses and shenanigans in the central UNIA office in Harlem. Henrietta Vinton Davis and Maymie De Mena – an odd pair, the former had undergone a matronly transformation during her service for the UNIA, the latter resembled nothing so much as an elegant flapper – were effective troubleshooters, willing to be dispatched to the regions whenever necessary. But Garvey leant most heavily on his stoical wife who made the trip to the penitentiary every three weeks. Occasionally, outside this routine, she later wrote, Garvey would summon her, and travelling down 'the suspense and anxiety until the express reached there was awful. If there were any manoeuvres going on that made him suspicious . . . then I had to spread joy, and plenty of it.'[13] During his imprisonment, Garvey suffered increasingly from ill health, from lung infections and chronic bronchitis, and Jacques ensured his supply of remedies and tonics, along with occasional food parcels to relieve him of the prison diet. In fact, apart from the first few months of humiliation and poor health, Garvey did not appear to suffer too greatly from the strictures of the new regime. The Bible was a source of refuge. He told E. B. Knox that he 'kept his hand in the hand of God'. But as well as spiritual comforts there were material ones; Garvey received considerable amounts of money during his time in jail – several hundred dollars a month. Garvey's prison records reveal that whilst most visitors left only a few dollars or cents, more substantial amounts were wired to him regularly (the identity of the sender was not recorded by the penitentiary officials) and his wife also brought in dollars – usually twenty or thirty each month. Jacques was also relieved when 'at times he telegraphed for more money, or special gifts . . . I was allowed to have [them] sent direct from big department stores such as Macy's or Gimbels.'[14]

Occasionally, the wardens took exception to the bounty Garvey was receiving when it seemed at too great a variance with prison food. He was isolated and put on a restricted diet when discovered, on 22 March 1927, to be in possession of contraband food – a steak.[15]

But more than food or medicine, it was books and newspapers that Garvey craved. He fired off telegrams to his wife whenever the subscription to the *Washington Post* dropped off; other major newspapers were regularly requested, along with a steady stream of books.

Marcus Garvey was extremely lucky to have wed such a hard-working and resourceful partner, whom he continued to think of as 'the bravest little woman' even as he added to her load. Jacques shouldered the major responsibility for activating petitions when they lapsed, and ventured deeper into the dangerous South, in search of support and untapped sources of revenue for his defence fund. On one such occasion, Amy Jacques arrived in Baton Rouge, and learnt that a black man had been butchered and lynched the night before. Fearing for her safety, the local townspeople advised her to take the very next train out of town; she was adamant that she would not be intimidated: she stayed and preached. After the service, the local doctor offered to put her up in his home for the night. But before setting off in his car, she recalled, 'he placed his shotgun in a contraption he had erected through the open windshield, took out a big pistol and placed that beside him; turning to me, he said, "Sister, get yours handy." I took out my "Colt". Now, said he, "We are ready to travel."'[16]

Fundraising wasn't always as memorable, but it was a constant – necessary to pay for the legal challenges to his sentence that Garvey continued to mount, and for the campaign to build up a critical mass of people who thought in a similar vein. Another book of the world according to Marcus Garvey, his 'philosophies and opinions' would be instrumental in such a scheme, and, at Garvey's behest, his twenty-nine-year-old wife swung into action. Once she'd compiled the book – itself a Herculean task – she was instructed, particularly, to make sure that as well as sympathisers such as Mahatma Gandhi, influential American politicians received complimentary copies; acknowledgements of receipt of the book were treated almost as favourable reviews. In the preface to *Philosophy and Opinions*, Amy Jacques spelt out that her motives were 'in order to give the public an opportunity of studying and forming an opinion of him, not from inflated and misleading newspaper and magazine articles'. Some of her husband's more violent speeches were (of necessity) sanitised; context was key. It was appropriate to arouse an angry black crowd in the aftermath of a lynching with calls for vengeance but white readers might have been alarmed by the heat and militancy of the same speech at several removes from the incident that sparked Garvey's violent eloquence.

Seeking to project a positive image of himself, prisoner 19359 faced constant and unexpected challenges. In the same month that he sent his wife the manuscripts for the second volume of *Philosophy and Opinions*, Marcus Garvey was forced to issue a warning notice in the *Negro World* for the public to spurn 'unscrupulous persons selling my picture handcuffed to two marshals'.

Amy Jacques kept up a constant stream of letters to the Attorney-General and US President, petitions and requests for interviews that might secure a commutation of his sentence. When she wavered, he implored her to 'keep sending out the letters in lots of one hundred at a time'. Oftentimes the correspondence between husband and wife was curiously businesslike and dispassionate, with Jacques working herself to the point of exhaustion whilst worrying over *his* state of mind and frequent silences. Occasionally, Garvey's letter betrayed a darkening, if petulant, depression:

No use writing when instructions are not carried out. When you were here I requested you to do certain things and they have not been done

except in the case of Washington. Why then should you expect me to
be writing without attention being paid? Love and happy [C]hristmas,
   Popsie

At such times Amy Jacques questioned her value to him. What did
he ever give in return? She imagined herself 'like a gold coin – expend-
able, to get what he wanted, and hard enough to withstand rough
usage in the process.'
   When hints of her loneliness and vulnerability seeped through, her
husband seemed genuinely surprised. 'Why didn't you turn on the radio
when you were alone?' he whispered tenderly on 9 June 1926. 'Have
you discarded it already?' And in the same letter sought to reassure
her that 'your editorials are all good[,] Miss Vanity, that's why I have
said nothing, otherwise you would have heard from me on the subject . . .
Be good to yourself and keep growing fat.' Amy Jacques had lost a
lot of weight. In her pursuit of justice for her husband, she had neglected
her health. But then, one year on from his imprisonment, came startling news. On 16 January, Amy Jacques was alerted to a story on the
front page of the *New York Times* printed in bold headlines that
suggested that Marcus Garvey had been pardoned. The news was quickly
picked up by black papers, including George Harris's *New York News*,
but as the day unfolded, it became clear that the story was a false
alarm, based on nothing but rumour. Jacques steeled herself to bring
the truth to her husband. The next morning she rushed to the post
office with a sobering telegram: 'George Harris published information
in big headlines incorrectly.'
   Two days later Garvey wrote back phlegmatically, 'I am not surprised.
I never expected it anyhow so I am not disappointed. The whole affair
is an amusement to me . . . Cheer up and be not dismayed . . . Tell
people pray for cause.'
   By the end of the month, the Attorney-General, John Sargent, was
briefing President Calvin Coolidge on the matter. Sargent admitted
that he'd received an enormous petition for Garvey to be freed, 'signed,
so I understand it is claimed, by over seventy-thousand Negroes'. In
addition, he had granted a lengthy interview to a delegation of 'prominent Negroes, who seemed to regard Garvey with great veneration'.
Sargent was mindful of Garvey's controlling influence but while 'his
further imprisonment will result in dissatisfaction' to many thousands
of black Americans, the Attorney-General feared that 'his release and

deportation would by no means eliminate him as a menace'. Garvey then, was still thought of as a threat, and the country's leading lawyer further discounted that the prisoner's chronic lung condition rendered him a candidate for compassion.

Prisoner 19359 had been in and out of the infirmary. Garvey's asthmatic attacks had increased during his prison term. He smoked Paiges, a popular brand of asthmatic cigarette that offered temporary relief. There was no tobacco in the cigarettes but a herbal remedy made up of anise, sage and thyme mixed with eucalyptus and atropine; inhaling the smoke dilated the bronchi in the short term, making it easier for Garvey to breathe. His condition was exacerbated by stress and judging by the repeated requests for the asthma cigarettes, the strain he felt under must have been considerable. Away from the bear-pit of intrigue that these days passed for UNIA HQ in Harlem, one might have imagined he'd surrender to the enforced tranquillity of Atlanta, but the truth was otherwise: Garvey's physical marginality and his frustrations at control by proxy only magnified his anxiety.

One consequence of this was his over-reliance or even dependence on the *Negro World* in setting the future agenda for the association. If prison produced paranoia, it also allowed for moments of intense lucidity. 'The time has come for the Negro to forget and cast behind him his hero worship and adoration of other races . . .' So began the editorial on 6 June that was later recast as an essay on 'African Fundamentalism' where Garvey laid out a creed that would guide black people through life, and reunite them with some fundamentals of their history that had been denied them for so long. As black folk, he wrote, 'we must inspire a literature and promulgate a doctrine of our own'. Black civilisation, he argued, 'had reached the noon-day of progress' in advance of the Caucasians: 'When we were embracing the arts and sciences on the banks of the Nile, their ancestors were still drinking human blood and eating out of the skulls of their conquered dead.' Finally, readers were reminded to work and pray for 'the founding of a racial empire whose only natural, spiritual and political aims shall be God and Africa, at home and abroad'. Subscribers to the *Negro World* who missed the relevant edition could spend 50 cents and buy a page-sized pamphlet that the paper helpfully suggested should have pride of place on the picture rail. 'Take down the white pictures from your walls!' ran the advert. 'Let them echo your racial aspirations.'[17] Earnest Sevier Cox was an unexpected purchaser for whom the text resonated. But it's unlikely that the Southern separatist and self-published author of such contentious tomes as *White America* and *Lincoln's Negro Policy* would have cleared space on his picture rail, mantelpiece or anywhere in his home for *African Fundamentalism*.

Earnest Cox had dedicated his adult life to solving the 'Negro question'. It had taken him to the African continent where he studied 'how other people control their Negroes' and, on the home front, had led him to devise schemes for 'the disposal of the Negro' in America, principally through 'repatriation to the African continent'. Cox and Garvey had found each other, much like the luckless unaccompanied seniors at the last dance of the prom. When the lights came on they were still together. Throughout his incarceration Garvey kept up a correspondence with both Cox's White American Society and John Powell's Anglo-Saxon Clubs. Powell visited him for 'cordial talks' in Atlanta and Garvey encouraged both men to address UNIA branches. Garvey even went so far as to repudiate Thomas T. Fortune, when the veteran journalist and now editor of the *Negro World* raised a literary eyebrow at this new alliance. Fortune had the temerity to protest that both white supremacists had 'no authority to use Mr Garvey and the UNIA to further their infamous propaganda of isolation and degradation of the Negro in American life'.

Ultimately, Garvey was perhaps less concerned with this abuse of new white friends than the elderly Fortune's fit of nostalgia for editorial independence, no matter that it was at variance with 'the policy of the organisation . . . defined by [the proprietor] more than a thousand times'. The absent proprietor couldn't afford though to alienate staff at the paper, as it was his one effective tool to maintain some order and authority over the organisation. Their complaints of non-payment of salaries were met by him with swift assurances. He viewed attacks on the staff as challenges to his authority, so that when UNIA officers tried to sack the managers of the paper, he responded angrily, 'No one has any power to dismiss [them] . . . If they are dismissed you shall dismiss me and remove forthwith my name from the paper,' he added petulantly. 'I am sick of the tricks.'[18]

By 19 February 1926 Garvey had lost confidence in William Sherrill, the acting president-general; he'd had more than enough of his scheming and malfeasance. It was time to act. Garvey sent a telegram to the *Negro World*, whose editors printed it verbatim on the front page of the paper: 'I endorse completely step taken by you and committee of presidents in exposing Sherrill. Weston who has encumbered Liberty Hall is equally guilty of deceiving people. The people should take immediate legal actions against them . . . They are unworthy men and no sympathy should be shown them.'

Garvey now enacted a plan to remove the acting president by calling an emergency convention – not at Liberty Hall in Harlem where Sherrill had now established a stronghold, but in Detroit. Garvey listed twenty-seven charges against Sherrill, each one a good reason to vote him out of office. The convention duly obliged and a tearful Sherrill, protesting his innocence, was deposed. Of all the charges, it was his handling of the doomed SS *Booker T. Washington* that had most aggrieved Garvey.

'As the ship was lost to Negroes on the stroke of the auctioneer's hammer,' the *Negro World* lamented on 3 April 1926, 'Sherrill . . . and officers of the Black Cross Navigation and Trading Company, exchanged sheepish glances with each other . . . What thoughts were theirs as they beheld the tragic climax to their mismanagement, God alone can tell.' The *Booker T. Washington* was sold for a paltry $25,000, well short of the $100,000 that the company had first paid for it. The new officers, headed by Garvey's appointee Fred A. Toote, also attended the auction but, reported the paper, 'No one would have thought any of the one group [was] acquainted with the other.' No record of what Marcus Garvey might have said on hearing the fateful news of the *Booker T. Washington* has been found; it is of course possible that his distress was so great that he could not speak.

With Garvey sidelined and the organisation still riven with the same financial reversals, former adversaries began to contemplate that they might have been too narrow and selective in their criticism; they started to take a softer, more sympathetic stance towards the man whom they'd previously demonised as a demagogue. Cyril Briggs, who even up to Garvey's incarceration had maintained an undiluted animosity towards him, now wrote chastising those who 'in a brazen effort to pass the buck', conveniently sought to make a scapegoat of the fallen leader. Over the debacle of the *Booker T. Washington*, he asked cogently, 'Will Marcus Garvey, in his prison cell at Atlanta, be blamed for this loss too?' The farce would not end there. The Sherrill and Weston group refused to accept the legality of the emergency convention. Although Sherrill and Co. had been deposed from their positions in the Parent Body of the UNIA, they still remained as leaders of the local New York division, and a dispute soon arose centring on Liberty

Hall. On 1 August the local New York leaders mounted their own rival convention.

Months earlier, an officer, whose loyalty to Garvey was intact, had alerted Garvey to looming trouble at Liberty Hall because Sherrill's allies had 'sowed the seed of doubt and misapprehension in the minds of the membership'. The loyal Garveyite was so disaffected that he had stopped attending as he couldn't abide 'to have to sit and listen to discrediting speeches of you and members of the Council'.[19]

On the first day of the rival convention, Garvey loyalists tried to prevent it opening by nailing shut the doors of Liberty Hall. In the resulting fracas, the Garveyites relented, the boards came down and the convention went ahead without them. By 3 August, there were signs that this truce was merely a lull, when the New York Times reported George Weston's speech from the podium of Liberty Hall: 'Although the schism in the association seemed to be widening, all members would be welcome in the hall.' However, Weston warned, 'Garvey's adherents could not speak from the floor unless they retracted accusations made against William Sherrill.' Weston was adamant, and if the pro-Garvey group refused to cooperate, he added ominously, 'we will have to travel along our own lines, for our own success and toward our own objective'.

There were no retractions. There was, conversely, a cementing of opinions on both sides, and an animosity aggravated by a determination to criminalise each other. Garveyites brought charges of burglary against their opponents after Sherrill's allies raided UNIA headquarters and removed confidential records, financial ledgers and even cheques from the offices on 135th Street. At the end of the two-week convention, the rival UNIA group issued a damning press release in which they lambasted their 'swollen headed' former leader for 'lavishly misappropriating [funds] in a grandiose effort to keep from paying the penalty of his crime in the same fashion as he had before appropriated them to advertise his name and grandeur'.[20] The claims and counter-claims against each group culminated in them both seeking resolution – particularly over the legal status of Liberty Hall – through the courts. By the time the lawyers were brought in, all possibility of rapprochement was lost. The courts ruled that the two distinct groups, the pro-Garvey UNIA parent body and the New York local division, should jointly share Liberty Hall for the month of October 1926, with each group occupying the building on alternate weeks. Thereafter, from November onwards the New York branch was granted full possession – although the parent body retained the mortgage.[21] It was a sad end to Garvey's tenure of the spiritual seat of the organisation, and it must have been hard for the lonely and dejected inmate of the Atlanta penitentiary to resist the thought that they were fighting over the dying coals of a once great movement.

Buoyed by their success, Garvey's rivals eyed other prizes and assets whose ownership might be contested. The UNIA leader was particularly vexed by ugly and underhand attempts to attack him by attacking his wife. Sensing danger, he sent an urgent telegram to Jacques on 29 July which simply stated: 'Keep out of all disputes. Love Popsie.'

In Garvey's reading, enemies within the UNIA were lending themselves to renewed efforts by the BOI to ensnare his wife in the financial difficulties over the organisation's acquisition of a failed school in Virginia. The BOI – fed malicious rumours by the rival UNIA – alleged that Garvey's wife was somehow working on instructions from her husband to fraudulently solicit funds for the school. Prisoner 19359 appealed to John Snook, the warden of Atlanta penitentiary, to intervene on his behalf. Snook was sympathetic. Whilst he might not have shared Garvey's outrage over the plot 'against a lonely woman who is to be hounded in the name of the government to please a group of real-estate sharks, crooked lawyers and other enemies of mine who think they can completely crush me through . . . injury to a loyal and loving wife', Snook discounted the theory that Garvey (whose correspondence was censored) could have been issuing instructions to his wife as alleged by the BOI.[22] Marcus Garvey's impotence even to protect his wife was dispiriting.

The very foundations of his marriage to Amy Jacques were also under attack throughout 1926. Lawyers acting on behalf of his first wife had applied to the Supreme Court to review the case. Amy Ashwood still maintained that Garvey's divorce from her had been hurried through a court in Missouri whilst she was out of the country, that Marcus Garvey was guilty of adultery prior to his marriage to Jacques and that in any case, that marriage was illegal.

Ashwood was back in Harlem, living at 666 St Nicholas Avenue. Garvey's lawyers, with their client's consent, decided now to launch a counter-offensive. They hired a black private detective, Herbert S. Boulin, to gather information on Ashwood's personal habits. Boulin was not too fussy about which briefs he accepted; as P-138, he had previously been in the employ of the BOI, spying on Marcus Garvey. Now, acting incognito, the private detective managed to secure a room as Amy Ashwood's lodger in Harlem. By 8 April 1926, Boulin was ready to strike. At 3.30 a.m. (with several witnesses/spectators, including Garvey's bodyguard Marcellus Strong, in tow) Boulin returned to the apartment. In the dark he crept into Amy Ashwood's bedroom, and claims to have discovered her undressed and lying in bed with a man, later identified as Joseph Fraser. Sparing its readers' blushes, the *Chicago Defender* rushed into print the next day with the headline, 'Detectives Surprise Pair in Bed: former imperial couch room had been turned into a love nest.' Amy Ashwood was reported to have launched into a bitter tirade against her former husband, before recovering her composure to condemn the American concept of moral turpitude. Her companion was merely keeping vigil while she was ill, she said, and 'the raid was a mere scheme of followers of the imprisoned leader of the UNIA to defame her character'. By the time the revisited divorce case came to court in New York, on 15 December, her stance as the blameless, virtuous and wronged woman had been severely undermined. The jury had seemed receptive to the suggestion that Marcus Garvey had committed adultery – a former lodger, Mrs O'Meally, testified that she had, on innumerable occasions, seen Garvey and Miss Jacques retire at night and come out of the same room in the morning. But then the trial suddenly swung against her when Hubert Harrison (father of five), who held no brief for Garvey (having previously offered his services to the prosecutors in the mail-fraud case) was called to the witness stand. Reaching into his briefcase, Harrison produced a bunch of letters written to him by Amy Ashwood. A letter dated 24 February 1925 proved most damaging when it was read out in court:

My dearest,

   You are a wonderful man and I could die in your arms. You are so fascinating and tender. I am going to remain in America for one year. If I may, and I know it is going to be a blissfully happy mental communion of souls – maybe I have it but perfect – the combining of one nature with tender impression, the meeting of their lips and then the climax. Oh the ecstasy of it is an art . . .

   Dearest love, as soon as I can I'm going to fix up a love nest . . . I know how you stand financially, don't think I ever cared about that. I love you for yourself.

Your love ADE[23]

Both Garvey and Ashwood were found guilty in the trial. 'Victory, if there is such a thing in this case,' wrote the *Gleaner*, 'has been scored by Garvey in that . . . Mrs Amy Jacques Garvey, wife N°. 2, is still the legal wife of Garvey until the court sets aside his Missouri divorce.' The report of the trial, with its salacious headlines and 'spicy' letters was an unsavoury episode in Marcus Garvey's life about which, from his cell in Atlanta, he did not much care to read.

Increasingly, towards the end of 1926 and the beginning of 1927, Garvey sought refuge in literature. *The Meditations of Marcus Aurelius* was a constant companion, and he now borrowed and built on his reading, composing poignant but consciously accessible verse, forged from the heat of his prison life. *The Meditations of Marcus Garvey* was perhaps the most transparent example of literary sources. But Garvey's theme always came back to Negro identity. He articulated the black man's lot – and his own – of being trapped in the white man's world and at his mercy in an epic poem he began in 1927 called 'The White Man's Game, His Vanity Fair'. Garvey's poem, inspired by John Bunyan's *Pilgrim's Progress*, was written he said, 'in [a] peculiar form . . . it is not verse, neither is it orthodox prose, but it is a kind of mean adopted for the purpose of conveying desired thought'.[24] The thought being that Marcus Garvey was innocent:

> In the vicious order of things to-day,
> The poor, suffering black man has no say:
> The plot is set for one 'gainst the other
> With organisation they mustn't bother.
> 'If one should show his head a leader,
> Whom we cannot use, the rest to pilfer,
> We shall discredit him before his own,
> And make of him a notorious clown.'

On the anniversary of his second year in jail, Garvey once again appealed to the President to free him. To strengthen his application for executive clemency, Garvey imaginatively enlisted the support of the original jury who had found him guilty. Nine of the ten members who could be contacted endorsed Garvey's plea in the belief that he had been 'sufficiently punished'. But the government was still nervous. Despite all the signs that his organisation was imploding, the selective perception of him remained intact. 'Owing to his great popularity with the colored race and their unbounded confidence in him and his failure to recognise that he has done anything wrong,' wrote James Finch, the Pardon Attorney, 'the chances are that if, or when, released he will again exploit these willing victims with the same result.'

Amazingly, the people's sympathy for Garvey multiplied the longer he remained in jail. When, two weeks later, news spread of a deterioration in his physical condition, they redoubled their efforts and renewed their call for Garvey's release. Following an acute flare-up of his old bronchitis, Garvey was admitted to the prison hospital suffering from influenza, 'with a temperature', reported the physician, 'somewhat in excess of 102 [degrees]'. UNIA members flooded the Department of Justice with letters and further appeals. Earl Little, the father of Malcolm X, led the way from Milwaukee, Wisconsin with a petition which suggested Garvey's release would be the President's 'priceless gift to the Negro . . . causing [his] name to be honoured with generations yet unborn'.[25]

J. A. Marshall wanted the Attorney-General to know that 'while the world is rejoicing over the new "Hero of the air, Lindbergh", the Negro is worrying over their leader, Marcus Garvey'. Even Amy Ashwood added her voice to the calls for her former husband's release. In writing to President Coolidge, Ashwood's consideration of the well-being of prisoner 19359 played only a walk-on part in her quickening emotions; self-interest was her primary motivation. With Garvey locked up, she would not be receiving any alimony. The followers of Prophet George Hurley were more exercised by the surety of Garvey's innocence; Hurley delivered a petition on behalf of 700 members of his Hagar Spiritual Church. The bid to free their leader was also on the agenda of the UNIA Chattanooga division, when they met in Steele orphanage, their local Liberty Hall, on 4 August. But their experience that evening highlighted the extent to which the authorities, in some parts of the country, still clung to the view of Garvey and his agents as 'belligerent negro radicals'. A police squad which attempted to raid the meeting was debarred from entering by an armed member of the African Legion on the door. Shots were fired, UNIA men joined in and when the gun battle was over, one policeman and two UNIA members lay fatally wounded.[26]

The adverse publicity from Chattanooga caused a blip, nothing more, in the momentum behind the campaign to secure the release of Marcus Garvey. Letter writers in Detroit took their plea to the streets when the local UNIA division staged a silent parade through the city. A huge picture of Marcus Garvey was balanced on the back seat of the open-topped high-powered vehicle that would ordinarily have been reserved for the president-general. Thousands of protestors turned out to cheer the marchers, led by three contingents of African legions who displayed banners including 'Free Garvey and Bring Joy to Negroes'. Black news-papers also joined in the accelerating campaign to free the UNIA leader. 'Why is Garvey in prison, anyway?' the *Detroit Independent* wanted to know, speculating that 'the same lamentable fate that befell Marcus Garvey, regardless of innocence or guilt, might probably befall any other Negro leader'. The *Chicago Whip* went even further, romanti-cising the tragedy of the fallen leader: 'Behind his sordid, sombre prison's walls this black man with Napoleonic vision sits crushed in body and mind.' The *Whip* willingly surrendered to sentimentality in its depic-tion, informing readers that 'the glint of steel that once burned in his eyes is fading out and he sits, thin and emaciated, gazing always forward with a far-away stare', and ended by urging black leaders to emerge from their shameful indolence and 'march to the front in behalf of Marcus Garvey'.[27]

Remarkably, William Pickens was one of those whose conscience whispered to him uncomfortably in the night. Pickens had been one of the most vociferous cheerleaders of the 'Garvey Must Go' campaign, and Garvey's memory of their last encounter was unpleasant: he'd observed how, on the announcement of his sentence, Pickens had rushed over to congratulate his prosecutors, patting them on the back. The same William Pickens now wrote in the pages of the *New Republic* that 'Garvey was not at heart a criminal . . . [but] believed, foolishly of course, that by taking in more money he would rescue the enter-prise and save everything'. The sad truth, Pickens concluded, was that Garvey was 'a visionary, a bold dreamer . . . who helped to jail himself by being braver than the others'.[28] Towards the end of 1927, the calls for Garvey's release were binding his supporters and sympathisers into a raucous mass that caused unease in government circles. But Garvey left his attorneys to press his case with the authorities; he was distracted by the impending loss of the Liberty Hall in Harlem. Though weak-ened by his chronic illness, he still had the will, if not the energy, to embark on a fevered, last-minute round of letters and cables to UNIA officers in a desperate bid to save the very cradle of the organisation from foreclosure. The new UNIA leader (more accurately described as the personal representative of the president-general), E. B. Knox, visited Garvey on 23 August 'to get detailed instructions'. But by then the end was almost in sight. Liberty Hall had been remortgaged on several occasions in order to satisfy other creditors. Several potential saviours had intervened along the way, most tantalisingly the numbers runner, Casper Holstein, who at the start of 1927 paid $36,000 to redeem all of the outstanding mortgages. Holstein assured a mass meeting of the faithful at Liberty Hall of the purity of his altruism and 'asked for nothing but the execration of Negroes throughout the world if he . . . attempted to do anything which would hurt the interest of the membership or imperil their property'. But a few months later, Holstein's natural business acumen had reasserted itself when the UNIA failed to meet its payments to the previously inexecrable Holstein. When Liberty Hall was put up for sale, Garvey, who had not wanted to enter into any arrangement with the 'policy king', wrote despairingly to Knox, 'I have no more advice to give,' and, his mood darkening as he conceded defeat, added, 'If the people are too ignorant to protect their interests I can do no more.'

Though E. B. Knox was prepared to carry out the president-general's bidding to the very letter, Garvey's effectiveness was undoubtedly limited by his imprisonment. It was too late for Liberty Hall, but there were hints now of the US administration beginning to buckle under the weight of support for Garvey. On 12 November, the Attorney-General John Sargent compiled a detailed brief for President Coolidge. Garvey's case was 'most unusual', Sargent opined, 'notwithstanding the fact that the prosecution was designed for the protection of colored people, whom it was charged Garvey had been defrauding . . . none of these people apparently believe that they have been defrauded, and manifestly retain their entire confidence in Garvey.' The great danger foreseen by Sargent was that 'instead of the prosecution and imprisonment of the applicant being an example and warning against a violation of law, it really stands and is regarded by them, as a class, as an act of oppression of the race in their efforts in the direction of race progress and discrimination against Garvey as a Negro. This is by no means a healthy condition of affairs.' There was but one conclusion for the President to draw: Garvey's sentence must be commuted to expire at once. On

18 November President Coolidge issued the instructions but the celebrations of their leader and his delighted supporters were to be muted by one all-important caveat: Garvey was to be set free on the understanding that he would be deported immediately.[29]

A few days later immigration officials arrived at the penitentiary in Atlanta and Garvey was discharged into their custody. Instead of a welcome return to the UNIA fraternity, the supreme leader was escorted onto a train bound for New Orleans where the SS *Saramacca* awaited his immediate deportation. There was still a faint possibility that he might escape expulsion. Under the law, aliens resident in the US for less than five years who had been convicted of mail fraud and given sentences of more than one year in prison were liable to expulsion. But Garvey had arrived in America six years prior to his conviction and so did not fall under the provisions of the Deportation Law. That argument, though, was weakened by the fact that Garvey's residence had not been continual. It had been broken by his fateful tour of the Caribbean back in 1921 when he'd been kept out of the country for five months; the years prior to his readmission in July 1921, government lawyers could argue, would count for naught.

On 3 December 1927, a snappily dressed Marcus Garvey, wearing a light brown checked suit and carrying his trademark silver-headed malacca cane, stepped out of the police car and into the rain. Several of his followers volunteered umbrellas and they huddled around him as he crossed the wharf and made his way up the gangway to the SS *Saramacca*. Garvey's name had travelled before him. Up to a thousand supporters assembled at the dock in the New Orleans drizzle to pay their respects to their leader before his forced departure into exile. 'A lot of people gathered very early so to make sure that they caught a glimpse,' remembered Virginia Collins. 'The people could stand on the levee close to the river . . . they were for miles and miles, a lot of people.' Their long coats and black umbrellas gave them the air of mourners, and from the deck, just before the ship pulled away, Garvey tried to rally the crowd, reminding them of how far the movement had come, and that there was still cause for celebration. Reporters from the *New York Times* were amongst scores of journalists there to record his farewell speech: 'I leave America fully as happy as when I came, in that my relationship with the Negro people was most pleasant and inspiring,' Garvey told the crowd. 'My entire life will be devoted to the support of the cause. I sincerely believe that it is only by nationalising the Negro and awakening him to the possibilities of himself that his universal problem can be solved.'[30] The UNIA president waved a handkerchief as the *Saramacca* started to steam down the Mississippi. 'The ship was high, way up,' remembered Collins. 'Those that were close enough could see him but people in general, they was just waving, waving, waving and crying and waving . . . because it was just like you was losing your own, or losing yourself . . . What are we gonna do now? That was uppermost in people's thoughts.' The straightforward answer was that Garvey's followers in America would have to continue without him. The *Saramacca* was charged with returning their leader to Jamaica. His grand ambition, in the USA at least, had come to an inglorious end.

SILENCE MR GARVEY

Gwine home, won't be long
Gwine home, sure's you born . . .
I'm gwine home, I can't wait
'Cause I've got the West Indies Blues
        'West Indies Blues', Dowell and Williams, 1923

FROM New Orleans to Kingston: from a funereal Mardi Gras to ecstatic Carnival. In the two-week passage Garvey's mood brightened as the *Saramacca* steamed towards his homeland. The Jamaican celebrants would be kept waiting a little while longer, for en route, the ship stopped at Cristobal in Panama. Down at the pier, supporters – their numbers swollen by West Indian dockworkers – gathered 'eager to see the martyr', reported the *Star and Herald*, and all the men lifted their hats simultaneously, 'in respect [of] the immortal hero'. The nervous authorities, though, would not allow Garvey to disembark. A committee of six UNIA officials were permitted aboard; they held a two-hour conference with their leader and presented him with a bouquet of flowers and a purse filled with cash donations, collected from its 2,000 members. The funds would be added to the $10,000 American UNIA members had bequeathed to their leader to help him settle in Jamaica. The next day Garvey was transferred to the SS *Santa Marta*, and set sail on his final passage to Kingston.[1]

'From early morning a seething mass crowded the thoroughfares where the procession was likely to pass,' reported the *Daily Gleaner*. In fact, so many people turned up outside the UNIA headquarters at Liberty Hall in the Jamaican capital that the authorities, fearing an accident, persuaded Garvey to postpone his address to the faithful until a larger venue could be found to accommodate them the next day. On 10 December 1927, Garvey's motorcade had spluttered haltingly through the overwhelming mass of well-wishers en route to his reception. 'No denser crowd,' the *Daily Gleaner* reported, 'has ever been witnessed in Kingston.' Garvey's estranged sister Indiana was amongst the dignitaries who greeted him. She brought along her daughter Ruth. Garvey lifted her up and embraced her in front of the crowd. The three-year-old did not understand all that was going on but years later she recalled, 'I knew that it was something of very great importance because there were thousands and thousands of people shouting, cheering and waving banners.'[2] Outside Liberty Hall, Garvey clambered up on to the roof of his car and gave a short electrifying speech, excoriating the American authorities who had maliciously imprisoned him. 'They dragged me through the streets of Harlem like a common thief,' he cried, 'but oh, thou God of Ethiopia, who when the Assyrians spat upon thee and Jews jeered thee, remember, it was Simon of Cyrenia, a Negro who helped you to bear your cross. Can you forget the Negro now?' Vivian Durham, who was in the crowds, remembered that at the end of his powerful oration, tears rolled down the cheeks of even the men; the crowd's applause crested and the brass band broke into a rousing rendition of the UNIA anthem. This, then, was no chastened prodigal son but a returning hero, still nominally the head Negro of the World.

But not everyone had been looking forward to his return. In an earlier editorial, entitled 'Trouble Coming', the *Gleaner* asserted that 'there can be no doubt that he [Garvey] will prove a dangerous element in Jamaica', and anticipated that on his release 'we may have a problem on our hands unless we act with a firmness and determination'.[3] The 'we' referred to the middle and upper classes for although the *Gleaner* was distributed and read widely throughout the island, contemporary critics argued that it primarily 'served the interests of the planting and business community'.

At the Ward Theatre, the nation's largest venue, Garvey formally addressed Jamaicans and set out his plans for his 'sojourn' on the island, during which he promised to 'do absolutely nothing to create any cleavage between the people living here'. But as a patriot and descendant of slaves he could not avert his gaze from 'the naked . . . dirty and diseased condition' of the people, and while they die in poverty 'let the Chinaman and Syrian sap the wealth of the country'. Garvey was echoing the populist sentiments of politicians from preceding decades who agonised over coolie immigration. The latest immigrants, the Chinese and Syrians, were easy targets. Garvey was too shrewd not to realise that the major subjugation of the black population came not from this tiny group but the long-established brown elite, but he was also savvy enough not to make that link – at least at this early stage, forty-eight hours after his return.[4]

It would be misleading to suggest that the supporters who helped Garvey to realise nearly £100 in collections in his first week back were only drawn from the working classes. His admirers, noted Governor Jelf, included middle-class men of 'undoubted ability' such as the former Mayor of Kingston, H. A. L. Simpson, but whom, alas, betrayed signs of 'few scruples'.[5]

The authorities immediately revealed their approach and interest in Garvey by assigning one of the most able detectives in the constabulary, Charles Patterson, to shadow the UNIA leader wherever he went on the island. Patterson was a careful and fastidious man with a curious, almost writerly eye for detail. Among the points of interest Patterson highlighted in his first report was that at the end of his speech, Garvey 'demonstrated how the people should shake hands in an orderly manner when greeting anyone in a large audience'. President-General Garvey had evidently not abandoned the core idea inherent in the title, Universal 'Negro Improvement' Association – a philosophy of personal development for black people. Garvey wandered down from the balcony, reported Patterson, to the ground floor of Liberty Hall 'and every person in the premises went and shook his hand'.[6]

It was apparent that Marcus Garvey had returned with a grandeur and majesty never before witnessed on the island. The colourful diversion would be temporary. President-General Garvey had no intention of establishing a permanent base on the island. The clue was to be found in his use of the word 'sojourn'. Once the glitter and fanfare of his homecoming ended and he reflected on his expulsion from America, having been forced to give up a dazzling international stage, Garvey anticipated that he would not be able to settle for the village hall. The island's Governor, A. S. Jelf, also tried to second-guess Garvey's next move. Writing to Sir Vernon Kell, the head of the British Security Service, Jelf observed that 'an island the size of Jamaica affords little scope for a man of his magnificent ideas'.[7] Garvey would have to make do with Jamaica in the short term.

In their haste to banish him from their shores, the US authorities had allowed Marcus Garvey no time to settle his professional or personal affairs. His wife had remained behind to organise the removals. Garvey had amassed a library of 18,000 books and hundreds of precious antiques.[8] With only passing reference to the magnitude of the task, Garvey wrote magisterially to his wife, 'I do not want you to leave even a piece of paper behind for I want all my books.' Jacques was instructed to include 500 volumes of his *Philosophy and Opinions* in the shipment as he planned to send a copy to each member of the British parliament.

That same afternoon, he wrote again in a spin of excitement, eager to start this new phase of his life. He was languishing in Kingston waiting for her arrival but would sail for a tour of Central America by 14 January. 'If you delay in America, you will have to look after yourself, because I will be gone,' he added brusquely. 'Have the packers pack the things and don[']t attempt to waste time doing that yourself.' That morning, Garvey had rushed down to the post office and discovered a registered letter from her, complaining about the packing. Jacques had called several firms but, given the delicacy of the antiques and the large number of precious items including a grand piano, only two firms would offer quotes. 'I could not leave until the furniture was on the freighter', 'and the bill of lading handed me by the packers', Jacques later grumbled, as anything could have happened to 'Garvey's things'. One month out of the Atlanta penitentiary, and the old obsessive Garvey, neglectful of domestic life, was reasserting itself. He had no thought 'or remembrance of the promised vacation together alone', said Jacques, overtaken with a sense of foreboding, for 'if the last three strenuous years didn't warrant it, then what more would?'[9]

Garvey did not pause to consider his wife's needs, but even if he had, then her tetchiness and disappointment would be offset by the exciting news that he had 'purchased on the 15th a nice little home for my Mopsie on the Lady Musgrave', costing $1,200. Garvey had set his sights on a reincarnation in Jamaica. The property which he named 'Somali Court', was close to the English Governor's mansion, in an exclusive residential area 'inhabited primarily by upper-class whites'. President-General Garvey swooned over the scale of the property, which included piazzas, outhouses, a flower garden and more than an acre of land. The black American newspapers described Somali Court as 'a lovely mansion with liveried servants' and dubbed it 'Garvey's Black House'. But Amy Jacques would eventually find a property bought from a lady 'whom contractors had deceived in the construction and cost. There was no tile work, and the finish was poor.'[10]

Amy Jacques arrived on 26 December, and her resentment over that period had not deserted her when she came to write her memoirs forty years later. 'When the furniture arrived, he arranged it just where he wanted it.' Any romantic ideas that she might have harboured, of a reunited couple blissfully setting up home together, were finally dispelled when Jacques realised that she was only allowed 'to sort and classify the books'. Neither wife nor husband's humour was much improved by an unwanted, early Christmas present from the *Daily Gleaner* which alerted Jamaicans to the news that Amy Ashwood planned to 'sue Marcus Garvey in our courts', as the first wife still 'contends she was never divorced'. The paper also maintained that Garvey had no passport; that the authorities were disinclined to issue him with one; and that he was, consequently, a virtual prisoner in Jamaica of the British Government. The allegations were enough to elicit from an unamused Garvey the first threat of litigation (should no retraction be promptly forthcoming) since his return to Jamaica. Though the *Gleaner*'s defence, that it was merely reproducing a story that had first appeared in the *Panama American*, was disingenuous, Garvey had been frustrated, and would continue to be so, by a mundane but deadly British Colonial bureaucracy, whose end result, whether official policy or not, was to confine the UNIA leader to his homeland.[11]

In Garvey's conceit, the headquarters of the organisation would be wherever its president-general happened to reside. Now that Liberty Hall in New York was virtually lost, he set about recreating a new Liberty Hall to serve as the cradle of the movement, at 76 King Street in Kingston, Jamaica. At the beginning of January, Detective Patterson noted work had begun remodelling the upper floor of the building which now housed 'six Royal Type-writing Machines, new fixtures of oak tables, chests of drawers [and a] new set of wicker chairs'.[12] Back in Jamaica, Garvey toured the districts, reaching out to the peasants so disparaged by Hubert Harrison as the 'hoe and cow tail brigade'. But his lectures and speeches at the Ward Theatre and the other large venues on the island were targeted at the petit-bourgeois middle classes, the artisans such as the former teacher and now farmer, Theo McKay (brother of the writer, Claude McKay), and the contractor and builder A. W. Henriques (rumoured to be one of the wealthiest black men in Jamaica) who did not baulk at the few shillings' admission charge on the door. To give the poor who couldn't afford the fee a chance to hear him, Garvey would regularly speak for free at Liberty Hall and later at Edelweiss Park. One Sunday morning, the railway worker Isaac Rose put on his best shirt and starched trousers and made a special trip to hear him speak at Edelweiss Park. Everybody was dressed as if they were attending church, and when Garvey appeared, Rose was stupefied. He had been a boyhood friend of Marcus Garvey, and couldn't believe the transformation. Six uniformed bodyguards made an arch with their swords under which Garvey walked to the stage. He was immaculate, remembered Rose. 'Garvey wore a black pants and a white sash with three different colours on it across his chest, and a regalia, a robe over him. It yellow. And he had something like a crown on his head. Not even the King of England dressed like him. So knowing him as I know him and never seeing him dressed like that I said, "Me Ass, look Marcus!" . . . People felt proud of him. Proud!' But like so many who were touched by Garvey, it was primarily what he had to say with his 'commanding voice' that so impressed Rose. 'He spoke ordinary, plain talk . . . but he wasn't no ordinary man. Anything he told you came to pass . . . Garvey was a prophet, a man that was sent from God.'[13]

In 1927, with the prophet on a leave of absence from America, other messianic figures emerged. During Garvey's incarceration, the organisation had been fractured and riven with doubt; it had passed through a succession of leaders, each one initially elevated as loyal and upstanding only to be discarded once the extent of their disloyalty was made plain. In E. B. Knox, the present incumbent in New York, Garvey believed he had found a true and honest disciple. In the last few months of his imprisonment, Garvey had turned to the Bible for wisdom and understanding. Whilst reading the letters of Paul to Timothy, the parable of the false imprisonment and persecution of Paul struck Garvey as a template of his own life; it had touched him to the core. On the eve of his deportation from New Orleans, it had been Knox who accompanied Garvey up the gangway, Knox into whose care he had delivered his followers and from whom he'd extracted the promise not to swerve from the course of Garveyism. Just as Paul had urged his disciple Timothy to stay behind and preach the word to the timid followers of Ephesus whilst he went on to Macedonia.

On 9 January 1928, E. B. Knox, acting in his capacity as the personal representative of the president-general, published a special message to the officers of the UNIA. Taking out a full page advert in the *Negro World*, Knox announced in bold, screaming headlines that 'The Parent Body is to Function as Before'.[14] That notice, suggesting more than a hint of desperation, could not conceal the cracks that had begun to appear in the organisation, and not just in New York.

In Florida, the young and mesmerising 'Princess' Laura Adorker Kofey, a former member of UNIA, had already lured members away from the organisation. The thirty-five-year-old preacher aroused the exaltation of poor urban black people, along the way inspiring a cultish devotion that flourished even more so in the absence of the organisation's president-general. In the spring of 1927, whilst Garvey was still locked up in Atlanta, Kofey had become a sensational field-worker for the movement; in a campaign through the South, excitedly followed each week by the *Negro World* which kept score of new members, she won over thousands of recruits for the organisation in the black belts of Miami, Tampa and Jacksonville. On 9 July, one correspondent enthused over the Gold Coast Princess who 'stormed St Petersburg when one thousand Negroes heard her upholding the principles of Africa for the Africans and its founder, Hon. Marcus Garvey'. She'd professed her admiration for Garvey when visiting him in the penitentiary in the autumn. But by October, the *Negro World* was issuing warnings to the divisions not to entertain 'Coffey, alias Princess Coffer and Lady Coffe who has been collecting funds from members . . . under the guise of sending them to Africa, etc. Should she make further appeals, members should have her arrested.'[15]

At a time when a flood of Africans, trading on their exoticism, claimed royal heritage, 'Princess Kofey's origins were disputed by the UNIA. They suspected she was actually born in Atlanta and was intent on exploiting the name of the movement to fraudulently obtain funds and build up a membership of her own. When Kofey was expelled from the organisation, she took hundreds of the new recruits with her to form the African Universal Church which not only had similar aims to the UNIA, but an identical motto, 'One God, One Aim, One Destiny', much to the irritation of local Garveyites. That irritation was said to have boiled over on 8 March, when Kofey opened her Bible to preach to 300 followers at a converted store-front in Miami. Eyewitnesses claimed that after Kofey was introduced by another preacher, he stepped back and gave a sign. Immediately a gunshot rang out from the back of the hall. Maxwell Cook, Kofey's former UNIA bodyguard, was immediately set upon by the enraged congregation who beat and stamped him to death. Two other Garveyites were later arrested and acquitted of her murder, and national newspapers rushed into print with unfounded allegations, implicating the UNIA leader. 'Deported "Liberator" is said to Have Sent Agents to Kill Woman Opposing Him' was actually the head-line in the *New York Times* but it could easily have been any of the major dailies who took the same line and tone in their reports.

Kofey's death did not much affect Garvey's standing amongst UNIA members in Central America and the Caribbean, but it certainly caused further ructions in the USA, where the invocation to the divisions and chapters for the parent body 'to function as before' sounded like gallows humour. In the final year of his imprisonment in Atlanta, Marcus Garvey had written the lyrics to a popular song called 'Keep Cool' but in 1928 and 1929 that record was not being played on phonograms of UNIA divisions. Bitter rivalries caused splits in numerous branches, most notably in New York where Sergeant William Wellington Grant once again captured the headlines of the *New York Times*: 'Sabers Used in Fight of Negro Factions.' The *Times* detailed a battle in the streets of Harlem when 'fifty members of the UNIA, resplendent in blue uniforms with gold braid and armed with unloaded Springfield rifles and with sabres . . . tried to force their way into Liberty Hall . . . where the Garvey Club, a rival Negro organ-isation similarly equipped, was holding a meeting.' In the ensuing mayhem, Grant found himself numbered among the wounded combat-ants who were subsequently hospitalised.[16] Such thuggish behaviour was a long way from the climate Marcus Garvey was cultivating in his Jamaican headquarters with the resurrection of elocution contests and music-appreciation evenings. Garvey certainly did not approve of the Sergeant Grant approach to conflict resolution.

Soon after Princess Kofey's death, Garvey summoned E. B. Knox, the titular head of the UNIA in America, to Jamaica, making it clear that it was not a request but an order. Notifying members back in the US of his safe arrival, Knox explained the purpose of his mission was to 'receive instructions over the future operation of our great organisation in America'. Though dry-eyed over the murder of Laura Kofey, the president-general was livid about the indiscipline, lack of cohesion and potentially disastrous consequences for the UNIA. Garvey had summoned his pliant appointee for a lightning refresher in the requirements of leadership. Knox wrote diplomatically that he was 'making the rounds with [Garvey] every night' in his hectic lecture schedule around the island and was 'being drilled in the work', before Garvey set sail for England in the middle of April.[17]

England wasn't the preferred destination for the resurrection of the UNIA. The first choice had been Central America and the Caribbean, but Garvey found himself blocked and stymied by the British and American authorities at every turn. The wording may have differed but the sentiment was the same: Garvey was to be denied. Meriweather Walker, the Governor of the Panama Canal, was inclined 'to refuse [Garvey] to land . . . on the ground that his presence would be disorganising to our West Indian employees'.[18] Costa Rica had been a plum source of support and revenue for Garvey in 1921, receiving monthly subscriptions of approximately $2,000. But at the beginning of March 1928, in a memo to Washington, the US minister to Costa Rica, Roy T. Davis, had the 'honor to report that Garvey recently has been denied admission to Costa Rica'.[19] The Governor of British Honduras, John Burdon, likewise informed the Secretary of State for the Colonies that he had prohibited Garvey from landing, adding drily that a recent call for a mass meeting of local UNIA members had been 'a complete fiasco', answered by just twenty-seven people. 'There [is] fair ground for hope', Burdon concluded, 'that it will break up before long.' Alerted about Garvey's intention to visit Trinidad, Governor Horace Byatt quickly convened a meeting of the governing executive council, at which it was decided vis-à-vis the 'undesirable immigrant', that an order should be issued 'prohibiting him from landing in Trinidad'.[20]

Though plans had been cemented to render the British West Indies out of bounds to Marcus Garvey, no such restrictions were put in place to deter his travelling to England. On the eve of Mr and Mrs Garvey's departure, the couple hosted a farewell reception. Accepting the presentation of a purse containing £50, Garvey confidently predicted that he would receive an equally hearty welcome in England, for he was going to a country 'where he would be heard by men, who knew the sympathy of humanity . . . men who were themselves reformers'.

The Garveys must have felt that confidence was misplaced when seeking hotel reservations. None of the first fifty establishments that they tried could accommodate them. 'The clerk generally [offered] the excuse that all rooms have been taken.' The Garveys lodged for the first two nights in the Cecil which Amy Jacques recorded approvingly was 'a swanky London Hotel where gartered flunkeys bowed us in'. Their budget would not stretch to a third night, and thereafter the couple rented a private house at 57 Castletown Road, West Kensington, where they remained for the next four months.[21] In order to make contact with the small but committed branch of the UNIA, the Garveys would have to travel to the other side of town. Black men in London – mostly former seamen from the Caribbean far outnumbered black women and 'somewhat destructive of [their] principle[s]' the London Garveyites had largely taken white English wives. 'These women,' wrote Joel Rogers, 'take great interest in their men's activities, and at the Marcus Garvey hall of the East End of London . . . shouted the "Back to Africa!" battle cry as enthusiastically as the men.' Their eagerness called for and elicited a generous response from Marcus Garvey. 'Only persons of African descent could become registered members of the organisation,' recalled Amy Jacques, but as the English wives were so very helpful and sincere, 'an Auxiliary was formed for them.'

Readers of the *Negro World* could follow Garvey's British adventure in regular updates sent in by the president-general. On 21 May, he quivered with excitement about his plan to take over the Royal Albert Hall, a vast Victorian structure with seating for 3,901 for a landmark speech on 6 June: 'All London already is talking about this meeting and we're hoping for a big time,' he clucked. A soprano accompanied by a pianist also featured on the bill that evening. Curious black Londoners, seamen, students and local members of the UNIA along with their English wives attended, and a smattering of liberal intellectuals.[22] President-General Garvey was introduced to the hall by Charles Garnett, a leading member of the liberal group called the English League of Universal Brotherhood and Native Races Association. Garnett had made shrewd suggestions to Garvey about the necessity of tweaking his speech towards the sensibilities of an English audience. But when the UNIA leader, who'd grown accustomed to addressing thousands in venues like Madison Square Garden, looked out to the masses in the Royal Albert Hall, he was confronted by row upon row of empty seats. There was no sudden loss of appetite on the speaker's part. He waded through the disappointment and gave a résumé of his life in the UNIA, presented with both a dignified earnestness and easy humour. His enemies had tried to label him a 'Socialist' and 'Bolshevist', he said but had reluctantly settled for 'crook'; he went to prison for an 'empty envelope'; and England could have South Africa but the Negro should have his slice of the African pie. And as Garvey neared the end of his speech, he directed his final words at the missing thousands: 'Any rebuff you give as touching the representation I make on behalf of the people will not only be an insult to me but to 280 million Negroes whom I represent.' On 23 June, underneath the headline, 'A Nightmare Negro: Black Rascal's Platform Ramp', the reporter for the weekly *John Bull* had evidently declined to heed the advice of Garvey, whom he considered 'one of the biggest scoundrels and impostors that ever blushed under the ebony hue of a Negro skin'. Garvey immediately lodged a libel suit against the paper. The British authorities, if not nearly as nakedly disdainful of the black leader, also treated him in an offhand manner. Garvey was aggrieved at being shut out from British territories in the Caribbean, and sought an interview with the Colonial Secretary, Leopold Amery, who simply and deftly sidestepped the request and was artfully perplexed as to why Garvey would think it had anything to do with the Colonial Office.

Later in the year, the couple travelled to Paris where they were more graciously received. It was a good time to be black in Paris. The city was gearing up to a sustained period of Negrophilia; in 1925, Josephine Baker had wowed audiences wearing nothing but a belt of bananas, and now, three years later, the Harlem Renaissance (or at least some of its luminaries) had transferred partially to the French capital. In a sense, Paris was better prepared for Marcus Garvey. It could even boast its very own French-African equivalent in Prince Kojo Tovalou Houenou. French African colonials in Paris found themselves in a delightful paradox: they were permitted to utter the near seditious sentiments about French Imperial rule for which they'd be locked up at home; but their metropolitan candour elicited little more than a serial Gallic shrug. After the very disagreeable and turgid dealings in London, Paris was a refreshing sorbet for the Garveys. Sounding more like the Francophile Du Bois on his mission to France after the Great War, Garvey eulogised the French who had admitted a Negro (Blaise Diagne) to the Senate, whilst America had no black representatives in the national governing body 'except, perhaps, a Negro doorman or janitor who might be seen in the House of Congress'. On the night of 6 October, Garvey was pleased to estimate his audience at the Club du Faubourg comprised 'about 1,500 white people, Frenchmen and women, and scattered Americans, as well as about 70 Negroes', including the Prix Goncourt winner, René Maran.[23] Amy Jacques noted wryly that her husband's appreciation of the interest shown in him cooled when it was also extended to his companion. Charmed by Amy Jacques and her halting schoolgirl French, a member of the Comité de Défense de la Race Negre sought Garvey's permission to meet his wife at a later date to continue their interesting conversation. Monsieur Garvey replied curtly, 'She is my wife!'[24]

In her black flaminga coat and elegant cuffs and scarves, Amy Jacques was the very picture of Parisian chic. Whilst Jacques wrote effusively of Paris and of their trips to the Louvre and Notre Dame, her husband worried over the possible perception that they were pampering themselves on a luxurious Grand Tour. His trip, he assured subscribers to the Negro World, bore no comparison to the way that his nemesis Dr Du Bois had previously cavorted round Europe, 'attempting to solve the most vexing problem of the age by attending garden parties of the near-great, then returning to America to write engaging travel stories and heavenly poems and to revel, in retrospect, in the exquisite delights of a tête-à-tête with H. G. Wells or Lady [Nancy] Astor.' One of the paradoxes of Marcus Garvey is that, at a fundamental level, the respect and recognition of such eminent folk is precisely what he sought: he craved the very thing that he professed to reject. But it was only personal gratification in the sense that he saw himself as the personification of the race.

At a fundamental level this is the role Garvey conceived for himself. Black people had lagged so far behind that they needed to catch up more speedily than a considered chronological development would allow. Therefore, the answer was to skip a few stages, so that what was lacking in substance could be made up by gesture alone. 'Gesture buoyed the Negro's self-respect,' wrote S. A. Haynes, one of the new intake of UNIA officials, 'and gave him a new hope and new vision.'

Gesture lay behind the UNIA leader's train journey to Switzerland. From the Hotel Victoria in Geneva, on 11 September, Marcus Garvey wrote to the Secretary-General of the league of Nations, Sir Eric Drummond, to renew the petition for a fairer deal for the black race, that his representatives had first put to the League in 1922. Adopting his most statesmanlike voice, Garvey assured Drummond that he and his international movement of black people were ready to comply 'in the observance of any reasonable suggestion made to them by the League for an adjustment of the grievous complaints they have made and the horrible conditions under which they live'.[25] The boldest point raised in the petition was that 'the entire region of West Africa could be brought together as one United Commonwealth of Black Nations, and placed under the government of black men'. The fifty-six other points raised included grievances over the continued American occupation of Haiti, and the infringement of black people's liberty to travel. By way of illustration, the petition rather coyly drew attention to the recent legislation and secret communications, between governors of British colonies, to impede the work of a 'certain influential black'.[26]

There would be no let-up in the unstated British policy of denying a platform to Marcus Garvey, as he was to find when attempting to speak in British Honduras, and even more poignantly so, when the Garveys travelled to Canada. Both passports were stamped without fuss when the couple landed in Montreal. They were detained only by reporters who wanted details of Garvey's speaking engagements. They took a taxi to the address where they were staying, but then no sooner had they unpacked their bags than policemen were knocking on the front door, and Garvey was arrested on a charge of 'illegal entry'. The next day the authorities conceded that they'd made a mistake, but not before Garvey had spent a night in jail, accompanied by sensational and unflattering news bulletins of his arrest. The Canadians had panicked and the *Montreal Gazette*'s report of the need to ensure that 'Canada shall not be used as a base for the purpose of the attack of neighbouring countries', gave a clear hint about the method behind the mistake.[27] He would be permitted to remain for a week in Canada provided he gave no public speeches. No such restrictions applied to his wife nor to her re-entry to the USA. They temporarily separated so that Amy could visit UNIA divisions in America to boost morale, as well as address the constant need for funds. Plans for him to speak in Toronto were also abandoned. En route back from Montreal, Garvey's ship docked at Hamilton (another UNIA stronghold) but supporters there, too, were denied an audience with their leader: Garvey was forced back up the gangway of the ship by armed soldiers and policemen guarding the pier.

The Garveys returned to Jamaica on 23 November 1928 and settled more comfortably into their home. Garvey's niece, Ruth, recalled this as a happy period, with Garvey acting as a surrogate father to her. Garvey's sister, Indiana, had been widowed and she and her daughter moved into a property close by. At that time Garvey did not have any children of his own and Ruth recalled him giving her free rein in his library with the instruction to 'Read, read, read.' As well as a library there was a music room with an 'auto piano [in which] one could insert music sheets on rolls in a special compartment and then pump out the tune which was played automatically'. But the young girl's strongest impression of her uncle was of his long walks 'around the lawns with his hands in his pockets as if he were studying something'.[28]

Garvey was never entirely relaxed, even on a seemingly leisurely stroll. One of the first announcements that he made on his return to Jamaica was his ambition to hold the next international convention in Kingston. If he couldn't speak to UNIA followers in North America, then the only solution was for them to come to him. He secured a new property, Edelweiss Park at Cross Roads in north Kingston, which would become the new HQ of the organisation, and the site of the forthcoming convention. Edelweiss Park ('the Wembley of Jamaica') would also function as a cultural centre for the edification and amusement of local people, with a moving picture theatre and other recreational activities. Vaudeville shows were put on, along with dramas written by local people, including the aspiring playwright Marcus Garvey. His *Coronation of an African King*, with a cast of over 100, was performed on 18 August 1930. With scenes from Senegal to Dahomey, the three-act play culminated in a violent final battle, and the coronation of Prince Cudjoe of Sudan – anticipating the crowning of Emperor Haile Selassie of Ethiopia, later that year in November. The same cast went on to stage several other plays including *Slavery from Hut to Mansion*. Unsolicited works from the country's most famous literary export, Claude McKay, were unlikely to be staged. McKay had recently provoked the ire of the president-general with the publication of a rich and bawdy tale of black life in the Negro metropolis of the world. *Home to Harlem*, populated by pimps, prostitutes, jazz men and demonic preachers, was dismissed by Garvey as a salacious tale, designed to expose the worst traits of the race and whet white readers' appetites about black fecundity and debauchery that was a 'damnable libel against the Negro'. *Home to Harlem* was at the other end of the spectrum from the stirring revues of black beauty that punters at Edelweiss Park might expect from the 'Glorious Glorias and Tropical Swains'. Garvey's attitude to culture was closer to the position advanced by his enemy W. E. B. Du Bois who celebrated the idea of Negro literature that aspired to the standards of the established Western canon, and in so doing undermined the subtle and unsubtle ranking of a culture and its people that put the Negro at the bottom. Fine writing acted by stealth to achieve a state memorably described by David Levering Lewis as 'civil rights by copyright'. Garvey thought along similar lines although his reasoning may not have been as subtle. He winced at the thought of black folk culture which retarded the race. Spirituals and jazz were created by black people, said Garvey, 'simply because we did not know better music'.[29] In Garvey's conception the Leider Songs rendered by the demure and comely Glorious Glorias were always to be preferred to Bessie Smith's 'Black Bottom'.

Had she been ten or twenty years younger, the Glorious Glorias was just the kind of tasteful show that the grand dame of the movement, Henrietta Vinton Davis, would have signed on for. But Davis had sacrificed her stage career to serve the UNIA. Now approaching her seventieth year, and after almost a decade of working for the organisation, she began to agonise over her itinerant life and unstable finances. Henrietta Davis had been almost alone among the senior American figures of the UNIA in muting her demands for unpaid salary. Rumours that she was considering a formal request for the missing $12,000 due her from years of underpayment reached Garvey on the first day of the international convention in Edelweiss Park, with predictable consequences. The opening of the convention had started magnificently with tens of thousands accompanying the UNIA parade through the streets of Kingston. Marcus Garvey was 'the most outstanding figure in the procession . . . and was cheered right along the way of the march'. The newspapers were especially struck by the glamour of M. L. T. De Mena, 'a striking figure, also in uniform', who strode towards Edelweiss Park, 'mounted on a grey charger with drawn sword'.[30] Garvey was joined on the platform by his wife, De Mena, Henrietta Vinton Davis and a host of other dignitaries including the Mayor and Custos of Kingston. 'The morning was a trifle hot,' the paper continued, 'but no one appeared bored . . . because of the splendid music and oratory of the speaker.' It should have been a triumphant day but Garvey was in a foul mood which could not be put down to the heat. Already irritated by innumerable financial niggles, the rumour of Davis's imminent betrayal (as he saw it) brought forth an angry public denunciation from the platform of the convention: 'I came here and started a new organisation, paid furniture bills out of my pocket, and now I learn that Miss Davis is demanding money on her back salary,' and with his voice trembling with incredulity Garvey brutally declared, 'I will not associate myself with any rascal that is dishonest.'[31]

Predictably, Henrietta Vinton Davis chose thereafter not to associate with Garvey's branch of the UNIA, but she never pursued him through the courts, as others were now doing for their unpaid back salaries. An old successful claim from the USA was now attached to Garvey in Jamaica with immediate repercussions for the future of the newly-acquired Edelweiss Park. The convention solidified the break between the two rival arms of the movement, but wrangles would continue for many more years, over the final breakdown between the division of the remaining UNIA assets.

Whilst Marcus Garvey was fighting familiar legal battles, he also returned from Europe to enter into Jamaican politics in a more conventional way. He put himself forward and was elected as a councillor for Kingston, and simultaneously announced the formation of Jamaica's first political party – the People's Political Party to contest the forthcoming elections for the fourteen seats of higher office on the legislative council. With one or two exceptions – including Garvey's first mentor, Dr Robert Love – the fourteen members of the legislative council had always been independent men, either white or 'not markedly coloured', usually of independent means, members of gentlemen's clubs, and the favoured sons of the plantocracy. Marcus Garvey's nomination marked a significant milestone in the nation's history. He recognised it as such and revelled in the moment. The euphoria was not long lasting. On 9 September 1929, Garvey received a tumultuous welcome as he addressed a crowd of 1,500 supporters, and unveiled the key points of the new party's manifesto. They included land reform, and here Garvey moved the crowd with a boyhood memory of his uncle, Joseph Richards, a hard-working Christian. 'Between his Bible and his hoe you could not separate him,' Garvey told the crowd, but the old man had been cruelly evicted from his farm on the whim of the landlord. Jamaica was populated by more than 100,000 tenant farmers, and Garvey's party would right the wrong inflicted on his uncle for the present and future generations of Joseph Richards.[32] Calls for a minimum wage would also be enshrined in the manifesto, as well as a pledge to build Jamaica's first university, a first national opera house, and a proposed law to impeach and imprison corrupt judges.

Scanning Garvey's manifesto, over breakfast the next day, caused no more than a ruffled brow on the foreheads of the king's representatives on the island, but the criticisms of the judiciary caused them to choke on their ackee and salt-fish, and sent them into spasms of apoplexy that would not abate until the culprit was brought before the courts and forced to account for his contempt. The policy was composed in haste, and had been framed by Garvey's belief about the injustice of the seizure of the Liberty Hall property in Jamaica. It seems naive, for the man who on his first return to Jamaica had written excitedly to his wife that 'everyone is scared of me', to expect such frightened adversaries to forgo the chance to do him damage, when such a splendid opportunity arose. In court, Garvey further compounded his mistake (in the ruling of Mr Justice Clark, the most sympathetic of the three judges) in seeking 'to defend himself with the aid of grammatical quibbles, of unimportant discrepancies of his speech, and even of mere printer's errors in his own newspapers'. For someone who was not long out of jail, the idea of returning so soon must have been particularly unnerving. But Garvey's belated acceptance of the charge and apology was too late for the other judges who found him guilty of demeaning the judiciary and undermining public confidence in them; they rigidly imposed a three-month custodial sentence (with Clark reassuring Garvey that 'there is no question of hard labour or anything of that sort') and £100 fine. After a pitiful exchange in which Garvey pleaded for time to sort out unfinished business, he was taken by motor car to the district jail in Spanish Town. It was perhaps the visible start of a very British approach to the removal of a threat: quiet, legal, merciless, slightly pompous but above reproach.

Amy Jacques arranged for the proprietor of a nearby lodging house to keep Garvey in clean laundry and ensure delivery of meals. Garvey's sentence was due to expire on Christmas Eve but the Governor thought it politic to bring his release forward, thereby reducing 'the risk of an ebullition of popular excitement'.[33]

Whilst in jail, Garvey had been unable to attend local council meetings; in the meantime, the other members convened a meeting to debate his absence, and passed a motion declaring his seat vacant. Garvey was livid and chose to express his ire most forcefully in the editorial pages of the *Blackman*, with the perhaps not unexpected consequence of another invitation to attend a court hearing. The editorial entitled 'The Vagabonds Again' was critical of the councillors who had voted to declare Garvey's seat vacant. Garvey was tried and found guilty of seditious libel and sentenced to six months in jail, but was freed on bond. He filed an appeal which he eventually won and the earlier court's decision was overturned.

Between his release on the first charge and his prosecution on the second, the leader of the People's Political Party managed to find time to campaign for the legislative council. In the Kingston parish of St Andrew, Garvey was up against the former representative of the council, George Seymour-Seymour, owner of the *Jamaica Mail*. Garvey accused his opponent of underhand methods of intimidation and bribery, of trying to buy votes through the rum shop. 'The people of my race, unfortunately, were fed on rum, sugar and water and sandwiches as a reward for their votes,' Garvey alleged.[34] But a snapshot of the clientele of such establishments would have found few men possessing either the necessary acreage of land or annual income that would enable them to vote. The majority of the peasant population was disenfranchised. In 1930, out of a population of just over 1 million, there were only 80,000 registered voters. On the eve of the election, Garvey's opponent wrote to Governor Stubbs recommending a heavy police presence at the polling stations to forestall any violence from Garvey's supporters: 'Hundreds of Garveyites pay taxes from 4/- up to 9/6. They think they are on the Voters List but [they] are not. Many of them will invade the Polls and demand that they register their votes. They will probably refuse to believe they are not on the list so block the booths. Can we have strong bodies of Police to move them on?'

Seymour-Seymour conceded that he might be exaggerating the

threat but argued that 'even if it might appear that I propose to use a 9.2 gun when a Webley might prove enough, one cannot be too careful at a time like this'.[35] Not only was it an exaggeration but it was based on an assumption about the aggression and violence of the lower orders from which Garvey drew his support. Garvey was always a staunch advocate of courteousness and respect and stamped out loutishness whenever it arose in the ranks of the UNIA. When Sergeant William Grant returned from New York, Garvey was appalled to learn of his well-earned reputation for indulging in bruising street-corner encounters. Grant's former loyalty could not shield him from what was to come. Garvey denounced him as ignorant, irresponsible and boisterous; he vetoed Grant's bizarre proposal for all members of the UNIA to be photographed and fingerprinted, and expelled him from the organisation.[36] The perception of the UNIA membership put out by opponents was at variance with the idea that Garvey held fast to; of building a self-respecting body of people who'd become known for being well-mannered and well-spoken.

Nonetheless, Seymour-Seymour's position on Garvey and Garveyism was, in line with much of the establishment, based on florid newspaper reports as well as memorandums from the continued police surveillance of the UNIA leader and now prospective legislative councillor.

When Garvey spoke at St Ann's parish, his undercover police shadow reported that though his meetings had ended with the singing of the national anthem, it was his opinion that Garvey's 'speeches are and will have a disturbing effect among people and if kept up will lead to riot and bloodshed'. Just as Garvey had been accused of exporting the invalid and foreign (Jamaican) concept of a colour line within the race (with light-skinned blacks dismissive of their darker brethren), he now stood guilty in the eyes of Inspector H. J. Dodd of St Ann's parish of importing a false and alien (American) concept of antagonism between the races. The inspector signed off his report with an ominous conclusion: 'His remarks tend to antagonise the Black Race against the White and create a feeling similar to that which exists between the two races in America.'[37]

In the event, Seymour-Seymour defeated Garvey by an almost two-to-one majority, receiving 1,677 votes whilst Garvey only managed to poll 915. It would have been a great surprise to the *Gleaner* if the wealthier citizens had done anything other than to 'support Mr Seymour down to the last man'. Having trembled at the prospect of a Garvey victory, the nation could now relax for, according to the *Gleaner*, the result showed that 'the vast influence that Mr Garvey was supposed to have exercised over the minds and actions of the majority of our people existed only in the imaginations of those who most dread his propaganda'.[38] The editorial writer on this occasion failed to mention that his paper had taken a leading role in the scaremongering.

Garvey was now stymied at home *and* abroad. Increasingly, he faced difficulties in maintaining contact with UNIA divisions in America and, more importantly, in ensuring financial support from them.

The operation of the UNIA had been enormously hampered when Garvey was censored by the American Postal Service for using the mails illegally to sell UNIA lottery tickets.[39] The Postmaster-General had immediately issued an order barring not just correspondence related to the lottery but all mail from the US to UNIA headquarters in Jamaica. One by one, Garvey was running out of financial options, and trying the patience of his wife. Amy Jacques only discovered that he had attempted to cash in life-insurance policies when the bank required his wife's signature as well, and she began to harbour dark thoughts that the organisation would always come before family life. By 1930, Jacques was expecting their first child and one evening, during the latter stages of her pregnancy, she recalled '[Garvey] brought home an acceptance for me to sign, so that he could pay pressing bills of the UNIA . . . I was lying down, too worn out and disgusted for words; I shook my head in disgust.'[40] The first child, Marcus Garvey Junior, was born on 17 September 1930 and his brother Julius three years later.

The pernicious effects of the Great Depression of the 1930s was magnified in already impoverished societies like Jamaica. Travelling round the country, Marcus Garvey was appalled by the conditions he met. It was a time prosaically recalled by Vivian Durham when 'poverty wore rags and rascality wore robes'. Garvey formed a delegation which asked for an audience with the Governor to state their findings and call for large-scale social intervention, instead of just continuing on the 'narrow policy of getting bridges built, a stretch of road repaired or a water tank erected'. There would be no New Deal policies instituted to alleviate hardship, partly because that suffering was not recognised. When Governor Jelf updated his file on 30 June 1930, he wrote to the head of the British Secret Service that Garvey had 'put forward the most grotesque proposals for the improvement of the human race and Jamaica in particular, which could not bear even looking into, still less encouraging'.[41]

In addressing his own poor personal finances Garvey attempted to diversify into small business, principally operating as an auctioneer from his office at Edelweiss Park. But he was continually under siege from creditors. The month after the birth of their second child, Amy Jacques was served a summons for non-payment of the year's taxes, and spoke of the shame and indignity of her court appearance. In her gloom she wondered about the comfortable life someone of her class would have expected to be living at this stage of their life relative to the discomfort she had chosen through an association with Garvey. The extent to which she had departed from the normal course expected of her was brought home forcefully shortly afterwards. Pushing the pram with her newborn on the main street of the capital one afternoon, Jacques was stopped by an old schoolfriend whom she hadn't seen in years. Years later Julius recalled his fair-skinned, middle-class mother's memory of that incident. Jacques's friend looked into the pram and asked in all innocence, 'What are you doing with this little black baby?'[42]

The Garveys struggled on through to 1935, drawing heavily on Jacques's savings but with diminishing returns as funds became depleted. When Garvey could obtain no more credit, out of desperation he steeled himself to compose a round of begging letters. Earnest Cox received an urgent letter dated 18 May 1933. Garvey had already remortgaged his house and personal properties, and now he wrote, 'I am about to lose my home and all I possess [unless] in the next thirty days at most I can pay off $10,000 of liabilities incurred to help the cause.'

That particular financial crisis was averted but soon after, he lost control of his own headquarters at Edelweiss Park when the mortgage on the property was foreclosed in 1934, and it was sold at public auction. The Depression roared on through the early 1930s.

Answering an inquiry from America as to the possibility of enforcing judgments against Garvey, the American Consul, Paul Squire, wrote back that it was impossible as Garvey was 'financially embarrassed, that even his water service has been shut off'. Garvey's periodical the *Black Man*, which only occasionally raised 'the fiery cross', Squire noted '[has] ceased to appear . . . and he is contemplating sailing for

England'. After conducting interviews with a range of informed individuals, the consul concluded that they all agreed that 'Garvey has
lost his local following'.[43]

The international convention held in 1934 was one last throw of
the dice, an attempt to rally the organisation and raise morale. It
failed to do so. It also failed to lift Garvey out of his sense of heavy
and oppressive gloom, and to shut out the echo from voices of past
officers of the movement who seemed to have foretold the passing
of his power. Men such as Ulysses Poston had warned him of the
danger, in the end, of being subject to the same fate as Napoleon –
broken and pitiful on the island of St Helena. Though Jamaica was
no St Helena, it was small and diminished him. 'From my observation,' Garvey wrote, 'I am forced to conclude that Jamaica is indeed
an ignorant community; it is limited in intelligence, narrow in its
intellectual concept, almost to the point where one can honestly say
that the country is ridiculous!'[44]

Worse still, though he still had the support of the poorest members
of society, those with the power of the vote through whom he might
have been able to effect change, had rejected him. On meeting Garvey
in 1924, Major Albert Newby Braithwaite had written in his assessment, 'If this man could be enlisted on the side of the authority . . .
his service might be invaluable.'[45] But ten years on, in Jamaica at
least, Garvey's services had been spurned. Jamaica he lamented had
become 'the place next to hell'.[46]

Garvey announced that he would leave the island and set up new
headquarters in London. In anticipation he agreed to an auction sale
of all the furniture in Somali Court. The day after, his wife recalled,
'we stood in an empty house, except for . . . the books, two large
pictures [of Garvey] and vases left unsold'. Two days later, he left
for England ('Gone to foreign' as Jamaicans say). Jacques was
instructed to rent out Somali Court, and find smaller accommodation until such time as he was able to send for her and the boys.[47]

Marcus Garvey sailed for England aboard the SS *Tilapa* on 16
March 1935, endeavouring to be upbeat about launching yet 'another
colossal programme aiming at stirring the Negro', from London.[48]
But Amy Bailey, an old friend whom he soon met up with in London,
recalled a tearful encounter with a saddened Garvey. She suspected
him to be homesick and was surprised by his answer to her question
about why he'd ever left Jamaica. 'Because I came to friends. I couldn't

trust Jamaica any more, and so I came to my friends in England, in London,' he confessed. 'I left Jamaica a broken man, broken in spirit, broken in health and broken in pocket . . . and I will never, never, never go back.'[49]

GONE TO FOREIGN

Sometimes I long for peace, but where could I find it?
Marcus Garvey, *Garvey and Garveyism*

ON Sunday afternoons, when he kicked apart the legs of his stepladder and it snapped into an inverted V, Marcus Garvey climbed to the top, opened his coat, flapped it behind him, shoved his hands into his pockets and began to speak. A crowd soon gathered around him; their numbers swelled as his voice boomed out over the traffic, the cooing pigeons and the ineffectual competitors who immediately jumped down from their soapboxes and tried their luck further away. It was as if Garvey had found his way back to the beginning, to the time when A. Philip Randolph had introduced him to the crowds on 135th Street in Harlem – except that this was a park and the audience mostly white, tourists and students assembled at the north-east corner of Hyde Park: Speakers' Corner. The opportunity to work on a crowd had always appealed to Garvey; to test himself against its volatility, to turn it, to take it over and harness its strength.

A visiting Grenadian politician, T. A. Marryshow, stood chuckling in the midst of the 'immense crowds' who pressed ever closer to the podium to hear the words and brilliant, rapier-like retorts to hecklers pour out of the new self-imposed Jamaican exile. 'Garvey's talk on "Abyssinia" on Sunday last, was magnificent,' Marryshow reported. 'He has a great stock of humour – I did not know it before – by which he ridiculed many an interrupter into embarrassing silence.'[1] Marryshow silently cheered on his clansman, and so too, at a remove of 3,000 miles, did the *Gleaner*; now that Garvey was gone, the paper had forgiven him his transgressions. In an earlier report, the *Gleaner* had written with giddy delight that, in Marcus Garvey's master plan, Speakers' Corner was but a stepping stone to the Houses of Parliament. He was well on the way, the paper effused, to receiving a Labour Party nomination to become an MP (the first of the Negro race) in the forthcoming general elections, although there was almost certainly only one source (the prospective MP himself), for that astonishing and unlikely story.

In the same article the paper registered a more concrete achievement of another compatriot in London. Amy Ashwood had opened a nightclub and restaurant, the 'Florence Mills' (named after the African-American performer) on New Oxford Street.[2] Amy Ashwood had never accepted the legality of Marcus Garvey's divorce from her. She had lived in the margins and shadow of his life. Now in 1935, she'd moved closer to the foreground. It was a jubilee year; London was teeming with the most energetic citizens of Empire, and the Florence Mills – with Ashwood's magnetism – had become, almost overnight, a hub for black intellectual life. Guests were attracted by the 'rice'n peas' West Indian cuisine. In the evenings they took to the dance floor as Ashwood's business partner, the Calypsonian Sam Manning, and his orchestra broke out into Caribbean melodies and the foxtrot. C. L. R. James, Jomo Kenyatta, George Padmore and Ras Makonen were amongst the glittering clientele.

Marcus Garvey did not patronise the establishment run by his former wife. His period in London would be marked by a vain attempt to reposition the UNIA at the forefront of black life. The organisation was fractured and diminished. In London it clamoured for attention in an already crowded field of small but dynamic black organisations, groups such as the LCP, League of Coloured People; WASU, the West African Students' Union; and IAFA, the International African Friends of Abyssinia. Nonetheless, Garvey attracted young and ambitious supplicants who wrote to him for advice and encouragement, from the outposts of empire, hoping for a head start at the beginning of their careers. Vivian Durham was typical. The twenty-five-year-old Jamaican journalist had served a kind of apprenticeship as Garvey's campaign manager for the Kingston councillorship. But whilst Garvey sympathised with the young UNIA idealist, recognising that opportunities were limited for a bright and sensitive working-class activist in the Caribbean, he could not offer him the position he so obviously sought. London, he wrote, was 'a bad place for you to come, except you have money'.[3] He would have given his younger self the same advice. President-General Garvey, at the head of an organisation which could still boast tens, perhaps hundreds of thousands worldwide, could barely afford to keep on a skeleton staff in London. A nucleus of never more than three or four employees attended to his needs.

From a small office that must, in his darkest hour, have reminded him of the cramped hotel room in Kingston where he'd started out in 1914, Garvey pumped out missives to the world. The letterhead of the UNIA headquarters at 2 Beaumont Crescent, West Kensington, with its London postcode offered some kudos, but nothing more. A new monthly magazine, a reincarnation of the *Black Man*, took its bow in 1935. The Guyana-born Eric Walrond, who'd worked on the *Negro World* during its peak Harlem period, joined Garvey in London, and was kept on a small retainer as reward for his contributions to the *Black Man*. Una Marson, who would eventually head the BBC's Caribbean Service, was grateful for her temporary position as his personal secretary, and augmented her salary with occasional pieces in the *Black Man*. The monthly journal offered Garvey's readers a snapshot of the black world, from the glamorous heart of the metropolis. The proprietor's column, 'The World as I See It', was an accurate index of his frustrations. The African-American actor and darling of left-wing circles, Paul Robeson, was a case in point. Robeson was the talk of the town in May 1935 when he took to the stage for the leading role in *Stevedore*. He played Lonnie, a dockworker, described by *Time* as 'a big taffy-coloured buck',[4] who is falsely accused of raping a white woman. Lonnie's rescue from the lynch mob by his fellow white workers hardly militated against the play's stereotypical depiction of the brutalised Noble Savage. The average Englishman would leave the theatre with 'contempt for the Negro'. It was no wonder, therefore, Garvey moaned, that 'cultured blacks and respectable people of colour find it difficult to secure courteous reception and accommodation in England at the present time'. Garvey reprised the same attack that he'd marshalled against Claude McKay. There was no doubt that Robeson was a good actor but, argued Garvey with a sigh, Robeson was unwittingly being 'used to dishonour and discredit his race'.[5] The error was exacerbated by his acceptance of the role of the subservient Bosambo in the film *Sanders of the River*. 'Paul Robeson has left London for Hollywood,' Garvey growled in 1935, 'to make another slanderous picture against the Negro.'[6] His disappointment over Paul Robeson was perhaps spiked by his own partial eclipse, and by the undisputable contention that the African-American actor was by then second only to Emperor Haile Selassie as the most internationally recognised black man.

Selassie was more deserving of sympathy. Haile Selassie was an embodiment of a Garvey prediction. For nearly two decades Marcus Garvey had steered his listeners towards the passage in the Bible which foretold that 'princes shall come out of Egypt'. In 1930, with Selassie's magnificent coronation, it had come to pass. A crop of international dignitaries had been treated to the splendour of an African coronation with ancient Abyssinian exoticism and first-world modernity, but without the aeronautical display of the emperor's favourite plane which his new instructor 'Colonel' Hubert Julian had managed to crash on the eve of festivities. Emperor Haile Selassie had been the beneficiary of Garvey's advocacy, and was now even more so when in 1935 the 'Beast of Rome' Mussolini started assembling his troops on the edge of Ethiopia. In editorials in the *Black Man*, Garvey championed the petit Ethiopian, Ras Tafari, as *the* messiah the black masses had been waiting for, who was now defying the might of a militarised European power, rendered most visibly so with news photographs of Selassie standing on an unexploded Italian bomb. Blacks from around the world were fired by the inspiration of Ethiopian resistance and outraged over the Italian aggression and its merciless use of mustard gas. 'Colonel' Hubert Julian, who'd been deported to America after the debacle of the emperor's mangled plane, had been amongst those blacks in the diaspora who had rallied to the cause and made their way to Ethiopia, joining ranks with the emperor's beleaguered forces.

Before Il Duce's assault on Ethiopia, Garvey had found much to admire in the rise of the Italian nationalist. When his old friend Joel Rogers came to interview him in Beaumont Crescent, Garvey told him excitedly that Garveyites had an earlier claim on Fascism: 'We were the first Fascists ... When we had 100,000 disciplined men, and were training children, Mussolini was still an unknown, [and] Mussolini copied our Fascism. But the Negroes sabotaged it.'[7] With his invasion of Ethiopia, Mussolini's rapacious imperial instincts had come to the fore. For any Negro worthy of the name, it was monstrous and galling. In July 1935, Garvey wrote to dispel some of the misleading statements in the English press like the *Saturday Review* which had printed a full-page photograph of the dictator under the caption, 'Mussolini – the World's Most Benevolent Ruler'.[8] Garvey countered that 'the real facts reveal Mussolini as a barbarian, compared to Haile Selassie, the Emperor of Abyssinia . . . the one man is a tyrant, a bully, an irresponsible upstart, whilst the other is a sober, courteous and courageous gentleman.'[9]

By October, Garvey was moderating and refining his position on the Italian–Ethiopian War, gradually shifting his gaze to the role Emperor Selassie continued to play. He began to think the unthinkable, that sadly Haile Selassie might well have brought on the disaster by his unpreparedness, which was 'characteristic of the Negro, [and] contrary to the doctrine of the UNIA preached even from the housetops for the last twenty years'.[10] The humiliation of Ethiopia, and by extension of the black race, could be traced to the rejection and betrayal of Garveyite principles, and the persecution of the man himself by sections of the race. At a time when black activists around the world were galvanising support and funds for Selassie and his countrymen, Garvey's intervention and criticism made for uncomfortable reading. But there was worse to come. In the spring of 1936, Haile Selassie's armies were in retreat. Heading south from Mai Chew, they were attacked by the Italian airforce, 'bombed, strafed and gassed along the entire route . . . until [the emperor's] army simply dissolved into nothingness'. Selassie escaped capture by fleeing first to Djibouti and then on to Jerusalem. In the *Black Man* Garvey lamented the emperor's negligence in surrendering 'the ancient sceptre wielded for ages by an historic line of black sovereigns'.[11]

From Jerusalem, the exiled emperor made his way to England. Crowds of supporters lined his route. George Steer, one of his advisers, had arranged for him to meet a party of British officials and dignitaries. Also awaiting Selassie at Waterloo station was Marcus Garvey and a coalition of black delegates who had assembled to welcome the monarch. But when they tried to address him, Selassie ignored them and carried on walking, and, reported Garvey later, 'the address that the delegates had to present to him had to be handed in by the holder, by running after one of the ordinary officials of the Ethiopian Embassy'.[12] Garvey said that he would not hold the emperor responsible for shunning his own race but thereafter the editor of the *Black Man* was more brutal in his assessment of Selassie. The emperor was a 'feudal Monarch who looks down upon his slaves and serfs with contempt',[13] Garvey noted. The UNIA leader failed to insert his own name among the serfs and slaves but he clearly felt slighted. He suddenly remembered now that when he'd organised his mass international convention in Madison Square Garden in 1920, a host of African delegates had attended but Selassie's government had returned the invitation unopened. In line with the Ethiopian ruling classes, believing themselves white, Selassie, Garvey maintained, had 'surrounded himself with white advisers, [and] taken the first step to the destruction of the country'. Garvey could not forgive him for being 'a great coward who ran away from his country to save his skin and left the millions of his countrymen to struggle through a terrible war'. The war was a lost cause and as far as Garvey could see, 'the emperor's term of usefulness is at an end for the present in Abyssinia'.[14]

To many of his admirers, Garvey's stance seemed bizarre and incomprehensible. If any cause would unite black nationalists then surely it was the Italian–Ethiopian War. As Claude McKay wrote, the Ethiopian World Federation was sustained by the same pool of supporters 'that gave power to the Garvey movement . . . Garvey's denunciation [of Selassie] did not swing his people.'[15] If anyone had transgressed it was not Selassie but Garvey. In America the UNIA leader's views appeared not just to be out of step but dangerous and damaging to the survival of the remnants of his organisation. The national organiser, Samuel A. Haynes, publicly criticised Garvey because 'reports from the field show that officers and members are deserting our divisions to join organisations and movements working to help Haile Selassie and Ethiopia . . . Disgrace stares us in the face. Mr Garvey is indifferent in the matter.'[16] There were signs also of Garvey's negative opinions on Selassie costing him friends and allies in London. When he mounted the steps of his ladder at Speakers' Corner he incurred the wrath of angry and volatile crowds. The Marxist Pan-Africanist, George Padmore, remembered that his stand 'made him very unpopular among the African university students, who attempted to break up his meetings'.[17] Padmore was on the side of the students. As Chairman of the International African Service Bureau, at rallies and debates in civic halls, Padmore regularly locked horns with Garvey. Ralph Bunche was in the audience during one of their debates on the Italian–Ethiopian War when the crowd started to turn on Garvey after he called the emperor a dumb trickster. Bunche wrote up the event in his diary on 30 May 1937.

Padmore had to protect Garvey from the white proletariat audience when 'Garvey attacked them as riff-raff, pointing out that the great empire would be lost if it weren't for the "great men" at the head of the govt.' Bunche noted that Garvey had particularly provoked the ire of the audience when he went on to attack 'Selassie for having white advisors'.[18]

Garvey had stumbled in his attack on Selassie. Where he might have been advised to pull back, he drove forward, hardening his criticisms. It was a huge blunder. The powerful Harlem preacher, Adam Clayton Powell Snr, believed, 'Garvey [had] signed his death warrant.' Powell summed up the danger for Garvey when he wrote, 'The halo around St Marcus's head is rapidly growing faint, and with it Negro nationalism. The figure of Emperor Haile Selassie, commanding the intense admiration and support of all racial groups, gives the Negro his first vision of internationalism.' Largely through his own devices, Garvey had been ostracised by former admirers. He'd also antagonised the key UNIA fundraiser in America, Captain L. A. King, by reprimanding him for collaborating with Socialists and enemies such as Du Bois on joint committees for the defence of Ethiopia. Once again Garvey was damaged and isolated. It was with exquisite timing, then, that Amy Jacques wrote to say that she was sailing with their sons to join him in England.

Amy Jacques, Marcus Junior and Julius arrived at Avonmouth in June 1937. The family had been separated for two years. Jacques recalled that 'in appearance, he [Garvey] had not changed much, though his hair was thinning out front'. It was a restrained but emotional reunion, and Jacques remembered, in her typically understated way, that 'he was pleased to see the children'.[19] Junior was six years old and Julius had just had his fourth birthday. Their father would have preferred to send them to a private school but he couldn't afford to, so they were enrolled in a free London County Council school in Kensington Gardens.

No sooner had Amy and the children settled into their new home and surroundings at Beaumont Crescent than Garvey announced that he'd be going away on business for three months. Amy Jacques was left in charge of the office whilst her husband set off on a lecture and fundraising tour of Canada and the Caribbean. He first went to Toronto for the annual UNIA conference. At the end of August, Garvey remained in Toronto to conduct lessons in a newly inaugurated course that he dubbed the School of African Philosophy. Over three intense weeks he gave tuition to a handful of select students in the history of the UNIA, as well as the art of diplomacy and other skills necessary for leadership. On his last night in Canada he gave a speech, determined to leave the delegates with one lasting thought: 'We are going to emancipate ourselves from mental slavery because whilst others might free the body, none but ourselves can free the mind.'[20] From Canada, Garvey continued to the Caribbean, where he charged himself with the task of reviving the movement and improving morale. He was so pleased with the outcome that he composed a little ditty:

> My trip to the West Indies has proven a boon,
> I hope to come this way again soon,
> I met there men, and women too,
> Whose hearts rang out with joys anew,
> I ne'er shall such joys forget
> As coming from those friends I met.

Garvey was lionised in the Caribbean. One might even imagine the poem accompanied by banjo and rendered as a calypso, but the idyll that the verse describes could not have applied to Garvey's experience in Trinidad. In 1937, there was a widespread strike amongst the island's oilfield workers. It was brutal and bloody, and Garvey arrived at the tail end of it. A small bearded preacher, Tubal Uriah Buzz Butler, had led the strike, inspiring the workers to a pitch of frenzy that bordered on insurrection. At one stage demonstrators had poured oil over a policeman and set him alight. The policeman had died. Bent on revenge, his colleagues armed themselves and took to the streets; riots ensued. By the time the strike was over, fourteen people had been killed, more than fifty wounded and hundreds arrested. Into this chaos walked Marcus Garvey and when the workers heard he was coming they naturally expected him to side with them. Garvey did not. Even before his arrival in Trinidad, he'd made clear his analysis that the strikers had been misguided, most probably by George Padmore's International African Service Bureau. 'Trinidad workers,' Garvey is reported to have said, should not 'risk their employment for the sake of these agitators in London who have nothing to lose.'[21]

Such views were unlikely to endear Garvey to the youngish Trinidadians, George Padmore and C. L. R. James. There was something 'magic' about George Padmore, believed his admirers; he'd relentlessly railed against colonialism and had little time for the petit-bourgeois sensibilities of Marcus Garvey. He'd been the Communists' 'point man' for the Caribbean but had resigned from the Communist Party in 1933. In his attack on Garvey, George Padmore formed a curious double act with his boyhood friend C. L. R. James, a Marxist intellectual who was just about to publish a book that would make him famous, a history of the slave revolution in St Domingue (Haiti), *The Black Jacobins*. James and Padmore were especially angered by Garvey's response to the labour disputes in the Caribbean; throughout 1937, the two men stalked him on Sunday mornings at Speakers' Corner, and ambushed him with inspired heckling whenever he rose to speak.[22]

On his return to London, Garvey rented a home for his family at 53 Talgarth Road, just a few streets away from his office. It was a tall building with four floors. Amy and the children were assigned to the rooms at the top. Garvey also moved in his secretary, who took a room next to his wife; Garvey occupied the second floor with his bedroom and library. For much of the time, Jacques complained that her husband was often distracted and took refuge in his library. 1938 was not a happy year for the Garvey family. Their anxiety mostly centred on the health of the eldest boy, Junior, who, after recovering from measles, contracted rheumatic fever, requiring months of medical care. It was a constant strain to keep the fire going in Junior's bedroom, and Jacques spent most of her time shuttling up and down the stairs, between the kitchen in the basement and the top floor, providing him with food and hot water. '[Garvey] came upstairs almost daily,' his wife later wrote. 'From the doorway he would ask how he [Junior] was, or come to the bedside and talk to him for a few minutes; but he was always too busy to stay any time.' The parents squabbled over the best course of treatment for their son until Garvey reluctantly relented and acceded to the wishes of his wife and the specialists that Junior be hospitalised.

In the summer of 1938, shortly after Junior had been discharged, Garvey made plans for another trip to Canada, for the annual conference in Toronto. Jacques, who had weathered a year of discomfort and anxiety, seemed to accept the news with her usual stoicism. She was only really concerned about the paltry sum of money that the departing head of the house deemed sufficient: 'Just before he was to leave, he handed me four sheets of type-written instructions, and told me I was again in charge of the office. Two pounds ten shillings ($10) was for house money and personal needs of the family . . . balancing the budget was taxing, to say the least of it.'[23]

A few weeks after Garvey's departure, his son's condition worsened. The rheumatism had affected the joints in his knees. One leg had been taken out of plaster and put in a hip-length woollen sock. The leg had become drawn and needed to be straightened again and replastered. But more than anything, the doctors advised he needed sunshine. The choice was either violet-ray treatment at an orthopaedic home in the south of England or the natural sunshine of the Caribbean. Jacques wrote that in the doctor's office she was asked, 'Where is the objector?' Garvey was in Toronto and so the burden rested with his wife as to whether their son would be 'allowed to grow up as a cripple'. Amy Jacques's emotionally charged memory reflects her agony over the decision that she knew instinctively that she was going to take. 'I sold a diamond ring, booked our passages, and cabled an SOS to my aunt for the balance. I told no one of my plans before sailing.' Jacques did not send a telegram to her husband. Instead, she left instructions with his secretary, Daisy Whyte. Her jewellery was to be put in a safe, together with the balance of any remaining money and two letters, 'one containing a statement on the office transactions, the other marked personal, explaining the urgency of Junior's case'. Daisy Whyte fretted. She was very upset, wrote Jacques, and her biggest concern was: 'How am I going to tell Mr Garvey?'[24]

At the beginning of September, Jacques and sons sailed from the Royal Albert Docks on board the SS *Casanare*. She would have been aware that she was returning to a country riven with strife. Like Trinidad, Jamaica had exploded in a violent labour dispute. Rioting first broke out amongst plantation workers on the Frome Estate of the West Indies Sugar Company on 29 April. Other workers soon joined the demonstrations, and within a few weeks the whole island seethed with rebellion, with the former UNIA Legionnaire, Sergeant William Grant, at the head of the protests. Grant and the union leader Alexander Bustamante were arrested. By the time Jacques docked in Kingston, British troops had been sent to put down the rebellion and a semblance of peace and order had returned to the island. Her husband was also rumoured to be on board the *Casanare* and despite the fact that newspapers published the passenger list, hundreds of cheering labourers and Garvey supporters had descended on the harbour to catch a glimpse of their hero. The rumours continued weeks after Jacques's return. The *Gleaner* spoke of unknown sources claiming that Garvey was steaming towards Jamaica on one of the CNS liners 'for the purpose of gathering first-hand data on the labour situation here'.[25]

Garvey was actually steaming back to London to discover, when he opened the front door of his home on Talgarth Road, that his family had left him. He was furious but his anger towards his wife was couched in silence. On 8 December, he wrote to his five-year-old son, Julius:

> My dear Chubbie:
> You will find enclosed the sum of One Pound (£1) as a Christmas Gift. You will also receive/two/suits of clothes and a set of books.
> I am surprised not to have found you at home when I returned from Canada, but I know as children you have nothing to do with what happened . . . If you can get your Grandmother to write to me for you, I shall be glad to keep in touch with you. Anything that you may want [,] write to me and I shall send it for you . . .
> I shall not be returning to Jamaica and . . . in case anything happens to me I want you to know that I have opened a Post Office Account at the West Kensington, North End Road W.14, Post Office in your name. On information of anything happening you must then communicate immediately to the Post Office . . .
> As stated, get your Grannie to write to me for you. Sincerely yours,
> Dad

Garvey communicated with his sons in this way over the next year, sending pocket money and gifts. His sons wrote back, updating him on their progress at school and, at their mother's prompting, requesting money for food, school, the movies, books and other essentials. On 11 January Junior asked for an ice-cream bucket and a new bed 'as Chubbie throws his foot all over my bad leg at night'.[26]

Regular correspondence followed and packages with gifts, such as fountain pens and essentials such as a pair of crutches for Junior. Through the boys' letters and occasional communication with his secretary, Amy Jacques chided her husband over the inconsistency of the payments and for his assumption that she would be cared for by her middle-class relatives.

On 25 September 1939 Garvey wrote to both of his sons:

> Dear Junior & Chubbie:
> The war has started and things are up-side-down. Hope you are well. I had not sent any money for three weeks. You will find enclosed $12.00 for two weeks money. I will send you balance next week. I received your letter about school. I will send the money next week. Keep good and

learn you[r] lessons O.K. I sent fo[ur] books and pen by Reggie also
Chubbie's bag.

Your Dad

Marcus Garvey cut a lonely figure in London, pining for his children and fuming over his wife who had abandoned him. He was more
isolated than ever before. The war made it doubly difficult for him to
keep in touch with the remaining UNIA divisions. But the dribble of
funds being sent into the headquarters at Beaumont Crescent could
not solely be explained by the war. The UNIA's membership in the US
had dwindled. In October 1939 Garvey's primary representative in
America, James Stewart, wrote a grim report to the chief that catalogued the state of the organisation's ill-health. In the town of Campbell,
Stewart's share of the proceeds of the divisional meeting was $1.50
with a cost of $3.00 for making the trip. The Hamilton division was
inactive as no competent person could be found to assume local responsibilities. The Cincinnati division was emblematic of all that was
presently wrong with the UNIA. Stewart wrote, 'They don't seem to
be able to separate themselves [from] magicians, candle burners, and
number givers and recently I was informed, the hall was closed on
Sunday and members went to church.'[27] The record of Garvey's reply
to Stewart has not been found.

'The collapse of the [UNIA] empire was sudden and tragic,' wrote
Adam Clayton Powell Snr in the New York Amsterdam News. From
the Harlem headquarters of his Abyssinian Baptist church, Reverend
Powell observed that no one had been able to galvanise the masses as
Garvey had. 'With Garvey's exile he became a black Trotsky to the
Negro masses. A sincere few tried to carry the UNIA along. [But] the
old fire that could only be instilled by Garvey himself was lacking.' In
an echo of W. E. B. Du Bois's 'Close Ranks' editorial from the Great
War, Powell argued that black nationalism should be set aside
temporarily as the greater and more urgent need was for 'the union
of all races against the common enemy of Fascism'. In any case, the
reverend concluded, 'Except for isolated chapters, the UNIA is finished.[28]

Even outside the USA, Garvey was virtually spent as a force. The
beginning of the war had, as Powell rightly predicted, thrown up more
pressing concerns than black redemption. The adoring crowds that had
greeted Garvey at Speakers' Corner had mostly melted away by the
end of 1939. They were replaced by jeering Socialists who ridiculed

him for his conservatism. A correspondent for the *Boston Guardian* wrote that 'his anti-labor bias caused him to be hissed off the platforms of Hyde Park'.

Amy Ashwood recalled a final chance meeting when, one Sunday morning, she saw Garvey out of the corner of her eye – as she had perhaps done before – but, rather than hurry past, on this occasion she decided to stop and approach him. As Ashwood later recalled she 'forgot all the bitterness of the years' that had passed, and walked with him to a nearby café for a cup of tea. Garvey had suffered from bouts of pneumonia and bronchitis during his time in London; he moved slowly but in his presence, she later wrote, 'I felt for a while the dynamic quality of Marcus . . . Those little black eyes were still twinkling but on this occasion filled with tears.' As they sat staring at each other, she imagined them transported to the past: 'There we were our special version of "Napoleon and Josephine", [and] I remember hearing Marcus utter in a low calm voice, lines of moving beauty and truth:

> The golden glory of love's light
> Has never dawned on my way
> My path has always led through night
> To some deserted by way
> But though life's greatest joy I miss
> There lies a greater strength than this
> I have been worthy of it.[29]

Later that afternoon, when Amy Ashwood walked through Hyde Park, she saw Garvey again 'stooping slightly, bending over his stick', as he took his place at Speakers' Corner. He caught sight of his former wife, and immediately 'drooping shoulders were straightened and he mounted the platform in the manner of the old Liberty Hall days. He tried hard to recapture the power of those days, but alas it was too late . . . He could no longer carry his listeners; even hecklers got the better of him. The Marcus I was listening to was no longer the "Tiger", the "Black Moses" . . . Tears were running from my eyes and I could stay in that place no longer . . . the old fire had gone.'[30]

On 20 January 1940, a sobering letter was circulated to all of the fellow officers and members of the UNIA informing them that their leader was dangerously ill. Marcus Garvey had suffered a stroke that left him paralysed down the right side of his body, impaired his ability to write and cruelly robbed him of his lovely voice. 'Immediate financial aid must be rushed to him,' Ethel Collins, the UNIA secretary-general, wrote in a panic from Harlem. 'We should see to it that Mrs Garvey reaches London as quickly as possible, if she desires to go.'[31]

Amy Jacques had no intention of travelling to London. His secretary, Daisy Whyte, offered to nurse Garvey back to health, and when he felt a little brighter, she even ventured to hire a driver who would ferry him through Hyde Park, with Garvey, disguising his disability, waving to members of the public who remembered his orations from Speakers' Corner. By March 1940, conversely, Garvey's eldest son, Junior, had made a full recovery. He was able now to walk without crutches and Jacques had his photo taken with Julius and sent it to their father. It had a profound effect on Garvey. His face was rendered passive by the stroke so that the tears when they rolled down his cheeks were all the more disturbing to Daisy Whyte. Garvey insisted on keeping the photo under his pillow and seemed to go into a decline and hardly eat. 'When the first money came in through the mails,' Miss Whyte remembered, 'he ordered me to send them [the boys] two pounds ten shillings which is ridiculous as there are bills to be paid.'[32]

On 6 April 1940, Garvey wrote to his eldest son: 'I am able to say a few words and am feeling a little better.'[33]

Not long after that, on Saturday 18 May, Daisy Whyte opened the post for Marcus Garvey. She placed the newspapers in front of him and he scanned the front pages. One in particular caught his eye. The top right-hand corner of the front page of the Chicago Defender carried the most extraordinary headline: 'Marcus Garvey Dies in London'. The Defender's London correspondent, George Padmore, had heard the rumour of his passing and had rushed into print with Garvey's death notice. The news report triggered a rash of further obituaries, telegrams and letters of condolence. Apprised of the falseness of her leader's premature death, Ethel Collins wrote to Amy Jacques that every paper, including the white papers, had picked up the story and 'were bur[y]ing him alive'. In the past, when Garvey had been the victim of inaccurate reports, he hadn't hesitated to sue the culprits, but now he had fallen silent, shocked at the news and the bilious and vitriolic obituaries that were printed. Believing in the reports' authenticity, UNIA members and admirers of Garvey held memorials in his honour. Daisy Whyte, tried to shield him from the worst obituaries but Garvey insisted on reading them. 'As he opened all his letters, and cables, he was faced with clippings of his obituary, pictures of himself with deep black borders,' wrote Daisy. 'He collapsed in his chair, and could hardly be understood after that.'[34]

Marcus Mosiah Garvey died on 10 June 1940. He was fifty-two. Amy Ashwood, along with Sergeant William Grant, had attended a wake held for Garvey at the Kingston division of the UNIA, when his passing was prematurely announced. She had told mourners that Garvey could not be dead because 'he would not die without contacting me'. The night after Garvey's actual death, Amy Ashwood had been disturbed by a dream. Garvey beckoned her to come out to the back of the house into the yard: 'There I saw him on the scaffold[ing] of a big ship driving rivets into its side. After he completed his task, he turned to me and cried out loud, "Build for Africa, work for Africa."'[35]

EPILOGUE

Alas, when will the happy period arrive that the sons of mortality may greet each other with the joyful news, that sin, pain, sorrow and death are no more . . . We will see the myriads descended from the Ark, the patriarchs, sages, prophets and heroes.
We will mingle with them and untwist the vast chain of blessed Providence.
Ignatius Sancho, *Letters of Ignatius Sancho* 1777

MARCUS Garvey was buried in a vault in the catacombs of St Mary's Catholic Church in Kensal Green, west London. But surely Garvey could not be dead – so believed his most ardent supporters. To them, the obituaries – for the most part unflattering – that appeared in newspapers throughout the world were the culmination of a concerted conspiracy to destroy the movement once and for all. The previous, erroneous reports of Garvey's passing had reinforced that perception. Even though a photograph was taken of Garvey in a lead-lined oak coffin, which was then distributed throughout UNIA divisions and other parts of the Negro world, it failed to convince some of Garvey's devotees.

The second round of wakes and memorials was staged in cities where support for Garvey was still strong; markedly so in Kingston and New Orleans. But perhaps the most elaborate ceremony took place in Harlem where members planned a procession through the streets to the memorial service, carrying a huge photograph of Garvey, escorted by uniformed members of the African Legion, and followed by the congregation and choirs.[1]

Later in the year, disbelief gave way to anger amongst friends and supporters of the dead leader, some of whom considered George Padmore's original obituary of Garvey to have been printed maliciously. On 18 August 1940, his widow, Amy Jacques's opening address to the UNIA conference was a mournful wail: 'Reporter! Newspaper Editors and Mud-slingers! You have killed him!' Ethel Collins recalled that indignant UNIA members had urged that they 'should not let [Padmore] the originator of this lie go free'. Marcus Garvey's death notices, they all concluded, had killed him.[2]

The UNIA leader had been spared a pauper's funeral but it had been an undignified end to such a momentous life. Garvey's secretary, Daisy Whyte, reported that it had been his 'last request to have his body brought back to Jamaica'. However, the turmoil caused by the Second World War effectively ruled out that possibility, and thereafter an ugly and unseemly spat developed between the two Mrs Garveys who fought over his corpse. On 16 February 1946, under the heading 'British Court Gets Contest Between Wives', the *Chicago Defender* sought to explain to its bemused readers that Ashwood was suing Jacques for the rights to the body.

At the heart of the dispute between the two Amys was the continuing legal wrangle over who was the 'real' Mrs Garvey. Both Amy Jacques and Amy Ashwood laid claim to the title 'widow of Marcus Garvey', and this, invariably, led to confusion, most memorably so at the fifth Pan-African Congress in Manchester in northern England in 1945. Amy Ashwood had helped to organise the international gathering, and she found it galling to note Jacques's presence at the official opening. For her part, Amy Jacques had stifled her objections at that meeting when George Padmore introduced W. E. B. Du Bois as the 'father of Pan-Africanism'. Such an honour should surely have been shared with her deceased husband, if only posthumously. By now seventy-eight years old, Du Bois was revered for his steadfast championing of Pan-African ideals as much as for his longevity, but the great lightning conductor of the temper of Africans and people of African descent had passed to younger men. A young Gold Coast Nationalist, Kwame Nkrumah, caught the mood of the 200 delegates with defiant Garveyite flashes, promising 'strong and vigorous action to eradicate [imperialism]'.

When, twelve years later, on Independence Day, as the first president of the Republic of Ghana, Nkrumah revelled in the fulfilment of his prediction, Du Bois was again a distinguished guest. But Ghana's new national flag, red, black and green (the UNIA colours), with a black star in the centre, suggested that the greater influence on the young president had been Du Bois's nemesis. In his autobiography, Nkrumah had paid tribute to Garvey, acknowledging the impact of the *Philosophy and Opinions of Marcus Garvey* on his own thinking. Nkrumah, said the Ghanaian historian, Adu Boahen, 'reached out for Du Bois out of reverence and because he was the lone survivor – but Garvey was the source'. In 1957, it wasn't yet clear, though, whether Marcus Garvey would be remembered more widely as the source of African and Caribbean agitation for independence.[3]

The centrality of Marcus Garvey to the UNIA and black people's perception of that organisation had been evident during his years of incarceration in Atlanta between 1925 and 1927. Then, in Garvey's absence, cultish characters such as the charismatic Father Divine and Laura Kofey had emerged, appealing to the unsatisfied expectations of a traumatised but still hopeful black population. Without Garvey at the helm, the UNIA shrivelled and along with it the collective memory of its leader.

After growing up in Jamaica in the 1950s, Robert Hill recalls that Marcus Garvey seemed all but forgotten; at the age of sixteen, Hill had not even heard of him. That Garvey's name retained some currency was largely down to the obscure religious sect, Rastafari. Overlooking his quarrel with the Emperor of Ethiopia, Marcus Garvey was revered by Rastafarians as the prophet who had foretold the coming of Haile Selassie. 'No one remember ol' Marcus Garvey,' chanted the renowned Reggae group, Burning Spear, but Rastafarians did, and, indeed, still do; they canonised him in their songs and adorned record covers with his iconic image.[4] In death, the enigmatic Garvey also became the subject of numerous myths, such as the belief that he was still alive somewhere in Africa. Forgotten was the sad fact that the great leader of the Back-to-Africa movement had always been denied access to the continent by the European colonial powers; he had never actually set foot on his beloved African soil.

By the early 1960s Garvey seemed such a distant and unimportant figure that when Amy Jacques trawled the publishing houses with a book proposal of her husband's life, she endured the humiliation of unending rejections; eventually Jacques privately published *Garvey and Garveyism* in 1963.

It wasn't until a little later, when the crisis hit the black world with the rise of the militant Black Power Movement in the USA in the 1960s, and the emergence of black leaders in Africa and the

Caribbean, seeking to forge new national identities, that people started to think again of Marcus Garvey. Nursing feelings of vindication, the old Garveyites stepped out of the cold, out of history, and proclaimed that, even in the darkest hours, they always held true to his ideals. Mariamne Samad went as far as moving from Harlem to Kingston in the 1960s to be closer to 'her man' as she affectionately referred to Garvey.[5]

In November 1964, more than two decades after his death, Marcus Garvey's last wishes were finally honoured when his remains were returned to the Jamaican capital. Garvey's body lay in state at the Roman Catholic cathedral whilst thousands of Kingstonians paid their respects, before his casket was taken by motorcade to King George VI Memorial Park and his body reinterred.

But there remains one last act of unfinished business: to this day, Marcus Garvey's many admirers still fume over his 1923 conviction for mail fraud, believing him to have been criminalised and stigmatised by a politically motivated prosecution.

For the last twenty years Garvey's sons, Julius and Marcus Junior, supported by Harlem Congressman Charles Rangel, have steered the group pressing for a United States presidential pardon for Garvey. In 2006, that call was taken up by Jamaica's first female prime minister, Portia Simpson-Miller, when she instructed one of the country's leading lawyers to take a fresh look at the proceedings around Garvey's original trial with a view to achieving a complete exoneration – as befitting Garvey, Jamaica's first national hero.

In the 1930s, the Marxist activist C. L. R. James had described Garvey's ideas as 'pitiable rubbish' but before his own death in 1989, James came to eulogise Marcus Garvey as one of the most important thinkers of the twentieth century.[6] Now Garvey's writings and papers are pored over in microscopic detail by scholars in the United States, Africa and the Caribbean; books by and about him are required reading on university campuses.

Arguments still roil over what might have been, had Marcus Garvey ever managed to fulfil his dream. He inspires both ambivalence and devotion. Writing on Garvey has lately been a polemical tussle between two camps: one that wants to skewer him as a charlatan and the other that seeks to elevate him to the status of a saint. Ultimately, he remains a figure who many, like W. E. B. Du Bois before them, find 'a little difficult to characterise'.

Marcus Garvey's extraordinary ability to provoke extremes of thought in an individual remains as strong today as it did in 1947 when the Jamaican historian, J. A. Rogers, decided to include him in the *World's Great Men of Colour*. Reflecting on the man who, more than anyone, embodied the idea of a Negro Moses, Rogers worried that 'had [Garvey] ever come to power, he would have been another Robespierre', sitting on a throne of blood and presiding over a reign of terror. But almost in the same breath Rogers celebrated Marcus Garvey's sympathetic understanding of black people: 'Like all other messiahs, he was a poet and romancer and knew how to soothe the suffering of his followers with hopes of paradise.'[7]

BIBLIOGRAPHY

Books and Selected Journals

Adams, Ian and Dyson, R.W.: *Fifty Major Political Thinkers*. London: Routledge, 2003

Adi, Hakim and Sherwood, Marika: *Pan-African History: Political Figures from Africa and the Diaspora since 1787*. London: Routledge, 2003

Akpan, A.M.B.: 'Liberia and the UNIA: The background to the abortion of Garvey's scheme for African Colonization', *Journal of African History*, XIV, 1, 1973

Ali, Dusé Mohamed: *In the Land of the Pharaohs*. London: Stanley Paul & Co., 1911

Ali, Dusé Mohamed: 'Leaves From an Active Life'. *The Comet*, 12 June 1937

Allsopp, Richard: *Dictionary of Caribbean English Usage*. Oxford University Press, 1996

Anderson, Jervis: *A. Philip Randolph: A Biographical Portrait*. New York: Harcourt Brace Jovanovich, 1972

Anderson, Jervis: *This Was Harlem: A Cultural Portrait, 1900–1950*. New York: Farrar Straus Giroux, 1982

Aptheker, Herbert (editor): *The Correspondence of W.E.B. Du Bois, Volume 1, Selections, 1877–1934*. University of Massachusetts Press, 1973

Archer-Straw, Petrine: *Negrophilia: Avant-Garde Paris and Black Culture in the 1920s*. London: Thames & Hudson, 2000

Baugh, Edward: *It was the Singing*. Toronto: Sandbury Press, 2000

Blunt, Wilfrid Scawen: *Secret History of the English Occupation of Egypt*. London: T. Fisher Unwin, 1907

Blyden, Edward Wilmot: *Christianity, Islam and the Negro Race*. Edinburgh: Edinburgh University Press, 1967

Bontemps, Arna Wendell (editor): *The Harlem Renaissance Remembered*. New York: Dodd, Mead & Company, 1972

Bourgois, Philippe I.: *Ethnicity at Work: Divided Labour on a Central American Banana Plantation*. Baltimore: The Johns Hopkins University Press, 1989

Bowen, J.W.E.: *Africa and the American Negro. Addresses and Proceedings of the Congress on Africa*. Gammon Theological Seminary: Atlanta, 1896

Boyd, Valerie: *Wrapped in Rainbows: The Life of Zora Neale Hurston*. London: Virago Press, 2003

Bruce, John E.: *Prince Hall, Pioneer of Negro Masonry, Proof of the Legitimacy of Prince Hall*. New York: Hunt Printing Company, 1921

Buckley, N. Roger: *Slaves in Red Coats: The British West India Regiments, 1795–1815*. Yale University Press, 1979

Bundles, A'Lelia: *On Her Own Ground: the Life and Times of Madam C. J. Walker*. New York: Washington Square Press, 2002

Bury, Reverend Herbert: *A Bishop amongst Bananas*. London: Wells Gardner, Darton & Co Ltd., 1911

Caine, Ralph Hall: *The Cruise of the Port Kingston*. London: Collier & Co, 1908

Charters, Ann: *Nobody: The Story of Bert Williams*. New York : Da Capo Press, 1983

Clarke, John Henrik: 'The American Antecedents of Marcus Garvey' [to come]

Clarke, John Henrik (editor): *Marcus Garvey and the Vision of Africa*. New York: Vintage Books, 1974

Coben, Stanley: *A Mitchell Palmer: Politician*. New York: Columbia University Press, 1963

Cobb, Irvin S.:*The Glory of the Coming*. Hodder and Stoughton, 1919

Cobb, Irvin S: *Cobb's Anatomy*. New York: George H. Doran Co., 1912

Coker, Daniel: *Journal of Daniel Coker, a descendant of Africa*. Baltimore: Edward J. Coale, 1820

Cronon, Edmund David: *Black Moses: The Story of Marcus Garvey and the Universal Negro Improvement Association*. Madison: University of Wisconsin Press, 1959

Crowder, Ralph: *John Edward Bruce: Politician, Journalist and Self-Trained Historian of the African Diaspora*. New York: New York University Press, 2004

Cunard, Nancy: *Negro: An Anthology*. New York: Frederick Ungar, 1970

Cundall, Frank: *Historic Jamaica*. Kingston: Institute of Jamaica, 1915

Cunningham, Valentine: *The Penguin Book of the Spanish Civil War*. London: Penguin Books, 1980

Daniel, Vattel E.: 'Ritual and Stratification in Chicago Negro Churches'. *American Sociological Review*, Vol. 7, No. 3, June, 1942

Davies, P.N.: *The Trade Makers: Elder Dempster in West Africa, 1852–1977*. London: George Allen & Unwin Ltd, 1973

Debs, Eugene: *Walls & Bars: Prisons & Prison Life In The "Land Of The Free"*. Chicago: Charles H. Kerr, 1983

De Lisser, Herbert G.: *Jamaica and the Great War*. Kingston: Gleaner Co., 1917

Dixon, Thomas: *The Clansman: An Historical Romance of the Ku Klux Klan*. London: William Heinemann, 1905

Du Bois, W.E.B.: *The Souls of Black Folk*. New York: The Library of America, 1990

Du Bois, W.E.B.: *Selected Writings*. New York: The Library of America, 1986

Du Bois, W.E.B.: *The Autobiography of W.E.B. Du Bois*. New York: International Publishers Co., 1968

Duffield, Ian: *Dusé Mohamed Ali and the Development of Pan-Africanism, 1866–1945*. Edinburgh: University of Edinburgh, 1971

Eisner, Gisela: *Jamaica, 1830–1930: A Study in Economic Growth*. Manchester: Manchester University Press, 1961

Ellis, Scott: *Race, War and Surveillance*. Bloomington: Indiana University Press, 2001

Ellison, Ralph: *Invisible Man*. New York: Penguin Books, 1952

Ellison, Ralph: *The Collected Essays of Ralph Ellison*. New York: The Modern Library, 1995

Evans, Harold: *They Made America*. New York: Little, Brown & Co, 2004

Evans, Harold: *American Century*. New York: Alfred A. Knopf, 1998

Ferris, William: *The African Abroad, or His Evolution in Western Civilization*. New Haven: Tuttle, Morehouse & Taylor Co., 1913

Foley, Barbara: *Spectres of 1919*. Urbana: University of Illinois Press, 2003

Franklin, John Hope: *Race and History: Selected Essays 1938–1988*. Baton Rouge: Louisiana State University Press, 1989

Franklin, John Hope: *George Washington Williams: A Biography*. Durham: Duke University Press, 1998

Franklin, John Hope and Meier, August: *Black Leaders of the Twentieth Century*. Urbana: University of Illinois Press, 1982

Fryer, Peter: *Staying Power: The History of Black People in Britain*. London: Pluto Press, 1984

Garvey, Amy Ashwood: *Portrait of a Liberator*. Unpublished Manuscript

Garvey, Amy Jacques: *Garvey and Garveyism*. London: Collier-Macmillan, 1970

Garvey, Amy Jacques (compiler): *The Philosophy and Opinions of Marcus Garvey, or, Africa for the Africans*. Dover, MA: The Majority Press, 1986

Garvey, Amy Jacques and Essien-Udom, E.U. (editors): *More Philosophy and Opinions of Marcus Garvey*. London: Frank Cass, 1977

Garvey, Marcus: 'Negroes' Greatest Enemy', *Current History*, September 1923

Gates, Henry Louis Jnr and McKay, Neville Y. (editors): *The Norton Anthology of African American Literature*. New York: W.W. Norton & Company, 1997

Gates, Henry Louis Jnr: *Bearing Witness: Selections From African American Autobiography in the Twentieth Century*. New York: Pantheon Books, 1991

Gatewood, Willard B.: *Aristocrats of Color: The Black Elite, 1880–1920*. Bloomington: Indiana University Press, 1990

Geiss, Imanuel: *The Pan-African Movement*. London: Methuen, 1974

Gilroy, Paul: *The Black Atlantic: Modernity and Double Consciousness*. London: Verso, 1993

Green, Jeffrey: *Black Edwardians: Black People in Britain 1901–1914*. London: Frank Cass, 1988

Green, William A.: *British Slave Emancipation: The Sugar Colonies and the Great Experiment, 1830–1865*. Oxford: Clarendon Press, 1976

Hall, James: *An Address to the Free People of Colour of the State of Maryland*. Baltimore: John D. Tony, 1859

Harlan, Louis R.: *Booker T. Washington: The Wizard of Tuskegee, 1901–1915*. New York: Oxford University Press, 1983

Harpelle, Ronald N.: *The West Indians of Costa Rica: Race, Class, and the Integration of an Ethnic Minority*. Montreal & Kingston: McGill-Queen's University Press, 2001

Harris, Stephen: *Harlem's Hell Fighters*. London: Brassey's Inc., 2003

Harrison, Hubert: *When Africa Awakes*. Baltimore: Black Classic Press, 1997

Hill, Robert (editor): *The Marcus Garvey and Universal Negro Improvement Association Papers, Volumes I–X*. Berkley and Los Angeles: University of California Press, 1983–2006

Hill, Robert and Bair, Barbara (editors): *Marcus Garvey: Life and Lessons*. Berkley and Los Angeles: University of California Press, 1987

Hobsbawn, Eric and Terence Ranger (editors): *The Invention of Tradition*. Cambridge: Cambridge University Press, 1983

Holden, Charles: *Inconvenient Material for Lynchers: The Conservative Critique of World War I and the Use of African Soldiers*. Dissertation, St Mary's College of Maryland, South Carolina, 2003

Holder, Calvin: 'Making Ends Meet: Economic Adjustment in New York City, 1900–1952', *Wadabagei: A Journal of the Caribbean and its Diaspora*, Vol. 1, No. 1, Winter/Spring, 1998. New York: Caribbean Diaspora Press

Horton, James Africanus: *West African Countries and Peoples*. Edinburgh: Edinburgh University Press, 1969

Hurley, Edward: *Bridge to France: On the work of the U.S. Shipping Board*. Philadelphia & London: J. B. Lippincott, 1927

Jaffe, Julian: *Crusade Against Radicalism: New York During the Scare, 1914–1921*. Port Washington: Kennikat Press, 1972

James, C.L.R.: *A History of Negro Revolt*. New York: Haskell House Publishers, 1969

James, C.L.R.: *The Black Jacobins*. London: Penguin Books, 2001

James, Winston: *Holding Aloft the Banner of Ethiopia*. London: Verso, 1998

Johnson, James Weldon: *Black Manhattan*. New York: Alfred A. Knopf, 1930

Johnson, James Weldon: *Writings*. New York: The Library of America, 2004

Jonson, Michele A. and Moore, Brian L.: *Neither Led nor Driven*. Kingston: University of the West Indies Press, 2004

Joseph, C.L.: The British West Indies Regiment 1914–1918'. *Journal of Caribbean History*, Vol. 12, May 1971

Julian, Hubert Fauntleroy: *Black Eagle*. London: The Adventurers Club, 1965

Kasinitz, Philip: *Caribbean New York: Black Immigrants and the Politics of Race*. Ithaca: Cornell University Press, 1992

Kennedy, David M.: *Over Here: The First World War and American Society*. New York: Oxford University Press, 1980

Kornweibel, Theodore: *Seeing Red: Federal Campaigns Against Black Militancy 1919–1925*. Bloomington: Indiana University Press, 1998

Legum, Colin: *Congo Disaster*. Harmondsworth: Penguin Books, 1961

Lewis, David Levering: *W.E.B. Du Bois: Biography of a Race, 1868–1919*. New York: Henry Holt, 1993

Lewis, David Levering: *W.E.B. Du Bois: The Fight for Equality and the American Century, 1919–1963*. New York: Henry Holt, 2000

Lewis, David Levering: *When Harlem Was in Vogue*. New York: Alfred A. Knopf, 1981

Lewis, Rupert: *Marcus Garvey: Anti-Colonial Champion*. Trenton: Africa World Press, 1988

Lewis, Rupert and Bryan, Patrick: *Garvey: His Work and Impact*. Trenton: Africa World Press, 1991

Litwack, Leon. F.: *Been in the Storm So Long*. London: Athlone Press, 1980

Litwack, Leon F.: *Trouble in Mind: Black Southerners in the Age of Jim Crow*. New York: Alfred A. Knopf, 1999

Livingstone, William Pringle: *Black Jamaica*. London: Sampson, Low Marston, 1899

Locke, Alain: *The New Negro: An Interpretation*. New York: A. and C. Boni, 1925

Long, Edward: *The History of Jamaica*. London: Frank Cass, 1970

Lumsden, Joyce Mary: *Robert Love and Jamaican Politics*. Kingston, Jamaica: Dissertation, University of the West Indies, 1987

Lusk, Clayton R.: 'Radicalism Under Inquiry', *The Review of Reviews*, February, 1920

Lynch, Hollis R.: *Edward Wilmot Blyden: Pan-Negro Patriot*. London: Oxford University Press, 1967

Makonen, Ras and King, Kenneth: *Pan-Africanism from Within*. New York: Oxford University Press, 1973

Maran, Rene: *Batuola*. London: Heinemann, 1973

Martin, Tony: *Race First: The Ideological and Organizational Struggle of Marcus Garvey and the Universal Negro Improvement Association*. Westport, CT: Greenwood Press, 1976

Martin, Tony: *Marcus Garvey: Hero*. Dover, MA: The Majority Press, 1983

Martin, Tony: *African Fundamentalism: A Literary and Cultural Anthology of Garvey's Harlem Renaissance*. Dover, MA: The Majority Press, 1983

Martin, Tony: *Amy Ashwood Garvey, Pan-Africanist, Feminist and Mrs Marcus Garvey No. 1 or A Tale of Two Amies*. Dover, MA: The Majority Press, 2007

Maxwell, William J. (editor): *Complete Poems, Claude McKay*. Urbana: University of Illinois Press, 2004

McKay, Claude: *A Long Way from Home*. London: Pluto Press, 1985

McKay, Claude: *Harlem: Negro Metropolis*. New York: E. P. Dutton & Co., 1940

McKay, Claude: *My Green Hills of Jamaica*. Kingston: Heinemann Educational Books (Caribbean), 1979

McMurry, Linda: *To Keep the Waters Troubled: the Life of Ida B. Wells*. New York: Oxford University Press, 1998

Mencken, H.L.: *Men Versus the Man: A Correspondence between Robert Rives La Monte, Socialist, and H.L. Mencken, Individualist*. New York: Holt, 1910

Morel, E. D.: *King Leopold's Rule in Africa*. London: Heinemann, 1904

Moses, Wilson Jeremiah: *Creative Conflict in American Thought*. New York: Cambridge University Press, 2004

Mulzac, Hugh: *A Star to Steer By*. New York: International Publishers, 1963

Murray, Robert K.: *Red Scare: A Study in National Hysteria, 1919–1920*. Minneapolis: University of Minnesota Press, 1955

Murray, R.N.: *J.J. Mills. His Own Account of His Life and Times*: William Collins and Sangster (Jamaica) Ltd, 1969

Naipaul, V.S.: *A Way in the World*. London: William Heinemann, 1994

Naipaul, V.S.: *A Turn in the South*. London: Penguin Books, 1989

Nkrumah, Kwame: *Ghana: Autobiography of Kwame Nkrumah*. New York: Thomas Nelson & Sons, 1959

Niven, Alastair (editor): 'The Commonwealth Writer Overseas', *Revue Des Langues Vivantes*, 1976

Nugent, John Peer: *The Black Eagle*. New York: Bantam Books, 1971

Olivier, Sir Sydney: *White Capital and Coloured Labour*. London: The Hogarth Press 1929

Olivier, Sir Sydney: *Jamaica, the Blessed Island*. London: Faber & Faber, 1936

Ottley, Roi: *The Lonely Warrior: The Life and Times of Robert S. Abbott*. Chicago: H. Regnery Co., 1955

Ottley, Roi: *New World A-Coming: Inside Black America*. Boston: Houghton Mifflin, 1943

Ovington, Mary White: *Half a Man: The Status of the Negro in New York*. New York: Longmans, 1911

Ovington, Mary White: *Portraits in Color*. New York: Viking Press, 1927

Palmer, A. Mitchell: 'The Case Against the "Reds"', Part III, Peacemaking, 1919–1920, *Radicalism and the Red Scare*, World War I At Home: Readings on American Life, 1914–1920. New York: John Wiley and Sons, 1931

Parker, Matthew: *Panama Fever: The Battle to Build the Canal*. Hutchinson, 2007

Perry, Jeffrey B. (editor): *A Hubert Harrison Reader*. Middletown, Connecticut: Wesleyan University Press, 2001

Pfannestiel, Todd: *Rethinking the Red Scare: The Lusk Committee and New York's Crusade Against Radicalism, 1919–1923*. New York: Routledge, 2003

Pickens, William: *Bursting Bonds: The Autobiography of A 'New Negro'*. Bloomington: Indiana University Press, 1991

Plummer, Brenda Gayle: *Rising Wind: Black Americans and US Foreign Affairs, 1935–60*. Chapel Hill: University of North Carolina Press, 1996

Powell, Adam Clayton Jnr: *Marching Blacks: An Interpretive History of the Rise of the Black Common Man*. New York: Dial Press, 1945

Rampersad, Arnold: *The Life of Langston Hughes: I, Too, Sing America, Vol.1, 1902–1941*. New York: Oxford University Press, 1986

Redding, Jay Saunders: *On Being Negro in America*. Indianapolis, New York: Bobbs-Merrill Co., 1951

Reed, John: *Ten Days that Shook the World*. London: Modern Books, 1928

Reynolds, David S.: *John Brown, Abolitionist: The Man Who Killed Slavery, Sparked the Civil War, and Seeded Civil Rights*. New York: Alfred A. Knopf, 2005

Richards, Yvette: *Conversations with Maida Springer: A Personal History of Labor, Race and International Relations*. Pittsburgh: University of Pittsburgh Press, 2004

Rogers, Joel A.: *World's Great Men of Colour, Vol.II*. London: Touchstone, 1996

Scott, Emmet J.: *Scott's Official History of the American Negro in the World War*. Washington, DC: War Department, c1919

Schuyler, George: *Black and Conservative: The Autobiography of George S. Schuyler*. New Rochelle, N.Y.: Arlington House, 1966

Schwarz, Bill (editor): *West Indian Intellectuals in Britain*. Manchester: Manchester University Press, 2003

Senior, Olive: *Encyclopedia of Jamaican Heritage*. Kingston: Twin Guinep Publishers Ltd, 2003

Shepherd, Ben: *Kitty and the Prince*. London: Profile Books, 2003

Shotwell, James T.: *At the Paris Peace Conference*. New York: Macmillan, 1937

Slotkin, Richard: *Lost Battalions*. New York: Henry Holt and Co., 2005

Smith, Bolton: 'The Negro in War-Time', *Public*, 31 August, 1918

Smith, Richard: *Jamaican Volunteers in the First World War: Race, Masculinity and the Development of National Consciousness*. Manchester: Manchester University Press 2004

Stoddard, Lorthrop: *The Rising Tide of Colour against White World-Supremacy*. New York: Blue Ribbon Books, 1920

Stowe, Charles Edward: *Harriet Beecher Stowe: the Story of Her Life*. Boston and New York: Houghton Miffin, 1911

Stowe, Harriet Beecher: *Uncle Tom's Cabin: a Tale among the Lowly*. London: Wordsworth Editions, 1995

Smith, Richard: *Jamaican Volunteers in the First World War*. Manchester: Manchester University Press, 2004

Stein, Judith: *The World of Marcus Garvey: Race and Class in Modern Society*. Baton Rouge: Louisiana State University Press, 1986

Stuckey, Sterling: *Slave Culture: Nationalist Theory and the Foundations of Black America*. New York: Oxford University Press, 1987

Tanner, Jo: *Dusky Maidens: The Odyssey of the Early Black Dramatic Actress*. Westport: Greenweed Press, 1992

Taylor, Ula Yvette: *The Veiled Garvey: The Life and Times of Amy Jacques Garvey*. Chapel Hill: University of North Carolina Press, 2002

Tolbert, Emory J.: *The UNIA and Black Los Angeles*. Los Angeles: Centre of Afro-American Studies, University of California, 1980

Townsend, Meredith: *Asia and Europe*. New York: G.P. Putnam's Sons, 1904

Trollope, Anthony: *The West Indies in the Spanish Main*. London: Chapman and Hall, 1860

Trollope, Anthony: *Tales of All Countries*. London: Chapman and Hall, 1864

Tuttle, William M. Jnr: *Race Riot: Chicago in the Red Summer of 1919*. Urbana: University of Illinois Press, 1996

Walker, Charles Rumford: *Steel: the Diary of a Furnace Worker*. Boston: Atlantic Monthly Press, 1922

Walrond, Eric: *Winds Can Wake Up the Dead*. Detroit: Wayne State University Press, 1998

Walrond, Eric: *Tropic Death*. New York: Collier Books, 1972

Walter, John C.: *The Harlem Fox: J. Raymond and Tammany, 1920–1970*. New York: State University of New York Press, 1989

Walworth, Arthur: *Wilson and His Peacemakers: American Diplomacy at the Paris Peace Conference, 1919*. New York: Norton, 1986

Watkins-Owen, Irma: *Blood Relations: Caribbean Immigrants and the Harlem Renaissance*. Bloomington: Indiana University Press, 1996.

Wells, Ida B.: *Crusade for Justice: The Autobiography of Ida B. Wells*. Chicago: University of Chicago Press, 1970

Wiggins, Rosalind Cobb: *Captain Paul Cuffe's Logs and Letters, 1808–1817*. Washington, DC: Howard University Press, 1996

Williams, Alfred Brockenbrough: *The Liberian Exodus. An Account of the Voyage of the First Emigrants in the Bark 'Azor'*. Charleston, SC: The News and Courier Book Presses, 1878

Woodson, Carter Godwin: *The Mis-Education of the Negro*. Trenton, NJ: Africa World Press, 1990

Yard, Lionel M.: *First Amy Tells All*. New York: The Associated Publishers, 1980

Web Sites

In the years of my research the web sites that have proved useful and that appear to remain stable include:

American Heritage: http://www.americanheritage.com/

Booker T. Washington Papers: http:/www.historycooperative.org/btw/index.html

Documenting the American South: http://docsouth.unc.edu/support/about/

FBI: http://www.fbi.gov/

History Matters: http://historymatters.gmu.edu/all.html

Jamaican Family Research: http://www.jamaicanfamilysearch.com/index.htm

NOTES

TNA: PRO   The National Archives Public Records Office, Kew, Surrey, England
            CAB   Records of the Cabinet Office
            CO   Colonial Office
            FO   Foreign Office
            UNIA   Universal Negro Improvement Association

Prologue

1   "Marcus Garvey Dies in London" was the headline on the front page of
     the *Chicago Defender*, Saturday 18 May 1940.

2.   Daisy Whyte recalled the sequence of events leading up to Garvey's death
     in a speech that she later gave at UNIA offices in Kingston, Jamaica on
     24 June 1945. The speech is reproduced in Garvey Papers, VII, pp. 1003–
     1006.

3.   C.L.R. James later eulogised Garvey. In an interview on a BBC Radio 4
     documentary, *Up You Mighty Race*, 1987, James acknowledged that their
     dispute was built on a false premise – on ideological differences that should
     not have obscured their common cause.

1. Bury the Dead and Take Care of the Living

INTERVIEWS AND CORRESPONDENCE: Philippe I. Bourgois, Ronald
Harpelle, Rupert Lewis, Joyce Mary Lumsden. SOURCES: TNA: PRO CO
137/690/3729, FO 288125242, FO 288125250 – from 27 November 1910,
Costa Rica. PUBLICATIONS: Amy Ashwood, *Portrait of a Liberator* (unpub-
lished manuscript); *Associated Press*, 19 January 1907; Edward Baugh, *It was
the Singing*; Edward Wilmot Blyden, *Christianity, Islam and the Negro Race*;
Philippe I. Bourgois, *Ethnicity at Work: Divided Labour on a Central American
Banana Plantation*; The Right Reverend Herbert Bury, *A Bishop Amongst
Bananas*; Ralph Hall Caine, *The Cruise of the Port Kingston*; John Henrik
Clarke, *Marcus Garvey and the Vision of Africa*; E. David Cronon, *Black Moses,
the story of Marcus Garvey*; *Daily Gleaner*, 26 September 1905, 16 February
1907, 21 April 1910, 21 July 1934, 22 January 1935; Gisela Eisner, *Jamaica,
1830–1930: A Study in Economic Growth*; Marcus Garvey, 'The Negroes'
Greatest Enemy', *NYT, Current History* magazine, September 1923; William A.
Green, *British Slave Emancipation: The Sugar Colonies and the Great Experiment,
1830–1865*; Maxwell Hall, *Hurricanes, Earthquakes (and other physical occur-
rences in Jamaica, 1880–1915)*, (National Oceanic and Atmospheric
Administration); Ronald Harpelle, *The West Indians of Costa Rica: Race, Class,
and the Integration of an Ethnic Minority*; Ansell Hart, *Monthly Comments:*

Jamaica, No 23 and 24, Vol 6, October 1969; Robert Hill (ed.), *The Marcus Garvey and Universal Negro Improvement Association Papers* [hereafter *Garvey Papers*]; Robert Hill and Barbara Bair (eds.), *Marcus Garvey, Life and Lessons*; James Africanus Horton, *West African Countries and Peoples*; Amy Jacques, *Garvey and Garveyism*; *Jamaica Journal* (Quarterly of Institute of Jamaica), Vol 20, No. 3, August–October 1987; Michele A. Jonson and Brian L. Moore, *Neither Led nor Driven*; Edward Long, *The History of Jamaica*; Joyce Mary Lumsden, *Robert Love and Jamaican Politics*; Tony Martin, *Race First*; Claude McKay, *Christmas in de Air: Complete Poems*; R. N. Murray, *J. J. Mills: His Own Account of His Life and Times*; Sir Sydney Olivier, *Jamaica, the Blessed Island*; Sir Sydney Olivier, *White Capital and Coloured Labour*; Olive Senior, *Encyclopedia of Jamaica Heritage*; *The Limón Times/El Tiempo* (Costa Rica), 17 March 1911; Anthony Trollope, *'Jamaica – Town': The West Indies in the Spanish Main*

1   Hall, p. 7.
2   Caine, p. 432.
3   *Daily Gleaner*, 16 February 1907.
4   Trollope, p. 15.
5   Sweetenham to Davis. Friction between the Governor and Admiral Davis had begun when the Governor objected to the American's desire for the firing of a salute (in Sweetenham's honour) on the grounds that citizens might mistake the firing for a new earthquake (*Associated Press*, 19 January 1907).
6   Edward Long: *The History of Jamaica*, 3 vols. London: Frank Cass, 1970.
7   Hart, p. 139.
8   Senior, p. 20.
9   *Jamaica Journal* (Quarterly of Institute of Jamaica) Vol. 20, No. 3, August–October 1987, pp. 73–77.
10 Ibid.
11 Ashwood, pp. 5–15.
12 Ibid, p. 31.
13 Thomas Carlyle was particularly vexed on behalf of the slave-owners whom he claimed were not properly compensated for the loss of earnings after the emancipation of the enslaved. In fact, the slave-holders and planters throughout the British Caribbean received £20 million from the British government.
14 *Garvey Papers*, VII, p. 333.
15 Garvey, p. 1.
16 *Garvey Papers*, VII, p. 145.
17 *Garvey Papers*, I, p. 4.
18 Jonson and Moore, pp. 205–209. See also *Daily Gleaner*, 21 July 1934.
19 *Jamaica Journal*, 1987, pp. 73–77.
20 *Daily Gleaner*, 26 September 1905.
21 *Daily Gleaner*, 22 January 1935.

22   *Jamaica Journal*, 1987, pp. 73–77.

23   *Garvey Papers*, I, p. 3.

24   George Fortunatus Judah was the son of Abraham Fortunatus Judah, a local historian who compiled a book on the Jewish presence in Jamaica, *The Jews' Tribute in Jamaica*.

25   *Garvey Papers*, I, p. 5.

26   Hill, p. 35.

27   Ashwood, p. 352.

28   *Garvey Papers*, I, p. 5.

29   For an examination of the corruption of the Jamaican legislative council see Green, pp. 65–95.

30   Sydney Olivier's *White Capital and Coloured Labour* was actually graciously 'dedicated to African Peoples' and sought to scrutinise some of the commonly held perceptions of black people. Summarising the change in attitude brought about by the end of slavery, Olivier noted on p. 108, 'When [the African] was removed from the sanction of force by emancipation, and from that of affection and duty by the substitution of wage labour, he naturally became from the point of view of the employer . . . a very idle and conscienceless person.'

31   Clarke, pp. 33–34.

32   *Daily Gleaner*, 21 April 1910.

33   Interview with Lumsden, 21 November 2005 (telephone). Background information on Robert Love from Lumsden, pp. 1–10.

34   Murray, p. 109, quoted in *Garvey Papers*, I, p. 25.

35   Green, pp. 379–388.

36   McKay, p. 7.

37   Cited in Eisner, p. 311.

38   Bury, pp. 108–110.

39   'Knee-dipping' comes from Baugh; 'all the imaginable dinginess' from Olivier, *Jamaica, the Blessed Island*, p. 442; and 'uncongenial' from TNA: PRO CO 137/690/3729.

40   TNA: PRO FO 288125242.

41   TNA: PRO FO 288125250 – from 27 November 1910, Costa Rica.

42   Jacques, p. 6.

43   *The Limón Times/El Tiempo* (Costa Rica), 17 March, 1911. See also Harpelle, pp. 25–41.

44   Amy Jacques seems to have been the source of these assertions that Garvey's Central and South American journey included Honduras, Ecuador, Colombia and Venezuela. See Jacques, *Garvey and Garveyism*, p. 7; Cronon, p. 15; Martin, p. 5.

45   'Sickened with fever, and sick at heart over appeals for help on their behalf, he decided to return to Jamaica in 1911.' From Jacques, *Garvey and Garveyism*, p. 7.

46   *Daily Gleaner*, 23 January 1935.

2. Almost an Englishman

INTERVIEWS AND CORRESPONDENCE: Hakim Adi, Vivian Crawford, Jeffrey Green, Robert Hill. SOURCES: TNA: PRO CO 351/20, CO 351/21, CO 554/35/55259. PUBLICATIONS: Dusé Mohamed Ali, 'White Women and Coloured Men, the Other Side of the Picture', *New Age*, 21 January 1909; *African Times and Orient Review* (hereafter, *ATOR*); Wilfrid Scawen Blunt, *Secret History of the English Occupation of Egypt*; John H. Clarke, *Marcus Garvey and the Vision of Africa*; W. E. B. Du Bois, *Selected Writing*; Ian Duffield, *Dusé Mohamed Ali and the Development of Pan-Africanism 1866–1945*; William Ferris, *The African Abroad, or His Evolution in Western Civilization*; *Flair* magazine, 17 August 1987; Marcus Garvey, 'Negroes' Greatest Enemy' (*Current History*, September 1923); *The Gleaner*, 1911; Jeffrey Green, *Black Edwardians: Black People in Britain, 1901–1917*; Robert Hill, *Garvey Papers*; *Journal of the Royal African Society*, Vol. 12, No. 8 (July 1913); David Levering Lewis, *W. E. B. Du Bois, Biography of A Race*; *New Jamaican*, August 1932; Alastair Niven (ed.), *The Commonwealth Writer Overseas*; Joel A. Rogers, *World's Great Men of Colour*; Ben Shepherd, *Kitty and the Prince*; *The Tourist*, 19 June 1914: 61–63; Eric Walrond, 'The Negro in London' *Black Man* (March 1936)

1   *Garvey Papers*, I, p. 5.
2   Quoted in Green, p. 92.
3   Walrond, pp. 9–10.
4   *New Jamaican*, August 1932; quoted in Clarke, pp. 38–39.
5   Rogers, Vol. 2, pp. 417–419.
6   Merriman quoted in Green, p. 240.
7   Green, on Isaac Brown's arrest and conviction, p. 84.
8   See Jacques, 'The Early Years of Marcus Garvey', extracted in Clarke, p. 35.
9   *Daily Gleaner*, 1911: Sydney Olivier at the Universal Races Congress.
10   Du Bois, p. 722; Lewis, pp. 439–442.
11   Lewis, p. 442.
12   Ibid.
13   TNA: PRO CO 554/35/55259. See also *Garvey Papers*, I, p. 26.
14   The quotation 'a noxious farce' is in Duffield, extracted in Niven, p. 154.
15   *ATOR*, July 1912.
16   TNA: PRO CO 554/35/55259.
17   *New Age*: 'White Women and Coloured Men, the Other Side of the Picture', 21 January, 1909
18   Blunt, quoted in Duffield, extracted in Niven, p. 152.
19   *ATOR*, July 1912.
20   Ibid.
21   'The British West Indies in the Mirror of Civilization', *ATOR*, October 1913, printed in *Garvey Papers*, I, pp. 27–31.

22   *ATOR*, 14 April 1914.

23   W. B. Yeats's Evening Circle of poets met regularly at his flat in Bloomsbury.

24   The dates of Garvey's arrival in England have not been found and scholars differ as to whether he preceded or followed his sister. According to *Garvey Papers*, I, p. 34, Indiana joined her brother in the summer of 1912. However, according to Rupert Lewis, 'His only surviving sister, Indiana, had paid his passage to England and she helped him during his stay as she herself lived there.' Lewis, *Marcus Garvey: Anti-Colonial Champion*, p. 45.

25   'Garvey's Niece Remembers . . .', *Flair* magazine, 17 August 1987, pp. 12–13.

26   Marcus Garvey to T. A. McCormack, 14 January 1914, printed in *Garvey Papers*, I, pp. 34–35.

27   Marcus Garvey to Alfred E. Burrowes, printed in *Garvey Papers*, I, p. 35.

28   The marriage ended in the divorce courts towards the end of January 1902. Kitty's allegations of brutality against her husband caused a great outpouring of public indignation. The *Daily Express* wrote: 'We pity the misguided girl, but we cannot regret the discouragement her case must bring to any others who might feel inclined to go and do likewise.' And the president of the Divorce Division, Sir Francis Jeune, was not surprised that 'the instincts of the barbarian husband awoke, and [that] blows, kicks, bites and beatings . . . were the portion of this white woman who had abandoned her caste and stooped to marry a savage'. Both quoted in Shepherd, p. 176.

29   *Journal of the Royal African Society*, Vol. 12, No. 8 (July 1913).

30   *Garvey Papers*, I, p. 39.

31   TNA: PRO CO 351/20; CO 351/21. Quoted in Green, p. 58.

32   *The Tourist*, 19 June 1914, pp. 61–63. Printed in *Garvey Papers*, I, pp. 40–43.

33   *Garvey Papers*, I, p. 5; Garvey, p. 3.

34   Ibid, p. 57.

3. In the Company of Negroes

INTERVIEWS AND CORRESPONDENCE: Carolyn Cooper, Vivian Crawford, Cecil Gutmore, Robert Hill, Bernard Jankee, Rupert Lewis, Wayne Modest, Mariamne Samad. SOURCES: BBC Radio 4, *Up You Mighty Race – A Centenary Celebration of Marcus Garvey*, 5 August 1987; TNA: PRO, CO 137/705; PUBLICATIONS: Amy Ashwood, *Portrait of a Liberator*; Edward Wilmot Blyden, *Christianity, Islam and the Negro Race*; Valentine Cunningham, *The Penguin Book of the Spanish Civil War*; *Daily Chronicle*, 26 August 1915; Robert Hill, *Garvey Papers*; *Daily Gleaner*, 23 September 1915 and 25 September 1915; Robert Hill and Barbara Bair (eds.), *Marcus Garvey: Life and Lessons* [hereafter Hill, *L&L*]; Amy Jacques, *The Philosophy and Opinions of Marcus Garvey*, Vols. I and II; Herbert G. de Lisser, *Jamaica and the Great War*; William Pringle

Livingstone, *Black Jamaica*; Richard Smith, *Jamaican Volunteers in the First World War: Race, Masculinity and the Development of National Consciousness*; Lionel M. Yard, *First Amy Tells All*

1　Basutoland, formerly a British Crown Colony, gained its independence in 1968 and was renamed the Kingdom of Lesotho.

2　Jacques, II, p. 126. During his life Garvey offered several subtly different accounts of this 'epiphany'. I have combined the various versions.

3　An abbreviation of Universal Negro Improvement Association and African Communities (Imperial) League.

4　*Christianity, Islam and the Negro Race* was published in 1887, the year of Garvey's birth, and Garvey was so impressed with it that he quoted the book extensively.

5　BBC Radio 4.

6　Letter from Garvey to Booker T. Washington, 8 September 1914, *Garvey Papers*, I, p. 66.

7　Jacques, II, p. 127.

8　Yard, pp. 9–10.

9　Ibid, p. 21.

10　Westwood High School for girls opened in January 1880. It had its origins in the prejudice prevailing at that time which strongly objected to black or darkly coloured girls being educated with those of fairer complexion. This prejudice was manifested a few years earlier, when a well-established school in Falmouth was broken up because they admitted as pupils the daughters of two native ministers.

11　*Jamaica Times*, 17 October 1914, quoted in *Garvey Papers*, I, p. 105.

12　TNA: PRO, CO 137/705, quoted in *Garvey Papers*, I, p. 78.

13　De Lisser, p. 1, quoted in Smith, p. 33.

14　Booker T. Washington Papers, Vol.2, introduction p. xxviii, University of Illinois Press.

15　Ashwood, p. 64.

16　*Garvey Papers*, I, p. 37; Ashwood, pp. 19–20.

17　Yard, p. 24.

18　Ashwood, pp. 70–72.

19　Cunningham, Stephen Spender's 'War Photograph', p. 413.

20　*Jamaica Times*, 17 October 1914, quoted by Smith, p. 71.

21　*Daily Chronicle*, 26 August 1915, printed in *Garvey Papers*, I, pp. 132–136.

22　Exchanges of letters between Garvey and Pink rumbled on throughout September and October in the local papers. *Daily Gleaner*, 23 September 1915 and 25 September 1915.

23　*Garvey Papers*, I, p. 120.

24　Livingstone, pp. 234, 201.

25　Yard, p. 15.

26　Ashwood, chapter 3.

27   'The Tuskegee Machine' was the name given to Booker T. Washington's powerful network through which he and his associates exerted a huge influence over black American life. The 'tools' of the Tuskegee Machine were the vocational college, the Tuskegee Institute, the numerous black papers which uncritically reported Washington's good deeds, and his connections with Southern white politicians who promoted his suggested candidates for patronage appointments to government jobs.

28   Booker T. Washington to Garvey, 17 September 1914, printed in *Garvey Papers*, I, p. 71.

29   Marcus Garvey to Booker T. Washington, 12 April 1915, printed in *Garvey Papers*, I, p. 116.

30   Marcus Garvey to Emmett J. Scott, 4 February 1916, printed in *Garvey Papers*, I, p. 173.

31   Marcus Garvey to Robert Moton, 29 February 1916, printed in *Garvey Papers*, I, pp. 177–183.

32   Ibid.

33   Yard, p. 20.

4. An Ebony Orator in Harlem

INTERVIEWS AND CORRESPONDENCE: Ralph Crowder, Robert Hill. SOURCES: BBC Radio 4, *Harlem Speaks*; PBS, *In the Whirlwind of the Storm*; *History Matters: Burned into Memory*, http://historymatters.gmu.edu/d/67. PUBLICATIONS: Jervis Anderson, *This Was Harlem*; Amy Ashwood, *Portrait of a Liberator*; *Black Man*, October 1937; A'Lelia Bundles, *On Her Own Ground: The Life and Times of Madam C. J. Walker*; *Champion*, January 1917; Ralph Crowder, *John Edward Bruce: Politician, Journalist, and Self-trained Historian of the African Diaspora*; Domingo, 'Tropics in New York', *Survey Graphic*, 1925; Harold Evans, *They Made America*; Amy Jacques, *Garvey and Garveyism*; James Weldon Johnson, *Black Manhattan*; Charles Johnson, 'Black Workers and the City', *Survey Graphic*, 1925; David Levering Lewis, *When Harlem Was in Vogue*; Claude McKay, *A Long Way From Home*; Claude McKay, *Harlem Metropolis*; Frank Moss, *Story of the Riot* (NY: Citizens' Protective League, 1900); *New York News*, 28 August 1926; *New York Times, Current History* magazine, Vol. XVI, No. 2, May 1922; *Opportunity: A Journal of Negro Life*, December 1926; *Survey Graphic*, March 1925 (editorial); Irma Watkins-Owen, *Blood Relations: Caribbean Immigrants and the Harlem Community, 1900–1930*

1   McKay, *A Long Way from Home*, p. 150.

2   Duke Ellington, quoted in BBC Radio 4's *Harlem Speaks*, reflecting on the inspiration for his musical number, 'Harlem Airshaft'.

3   Moss, pp. 1–2.

4   Ashwood, p. 9.

5   *Survey Graphic*, March 1925 (editorial).

6   Anderson, pp. 49–56.

7   Johnson, 'Black Workers and the City', *Survey Graphic*, 1925.

8   Domingo, 'Tropics in New York', *Survey Graphic*, 1925.

9   *Black Man*, October 1937, pp. 8–11, the transcript from a speech delivered at Bethel Church, Halifax (Canada).

10 Lewis, preface, p. xxviii.

11 Jacques, p. 14.

12 *Opportunity: A Journal of Negro Life*, December 1926. (*Opportunity* was the official organ of the Urban League.)

13 *New York Times, Current History* magazine, p. 234.

14 In later life, Garvey set down the history of the UNIA in lesson 20 of his 'School of African Philosophy.' Writing of himself in the third person he recalled:
    '[In 1916], the founder sailed for America, and on his arrival there he visited the Tuskegee Institute on an outstanding invitation from the late Dr Booker T. Washington. He met at the Institute the then Principal, Robert Moton and Professor E. J. Scott, the Secretary-Treasurer. He discussed with them the purposes of the Organization which were similar to the present aims and objects in the constitution. He received very little encouragement and left Tuskegee in continuation of a trip throughout the United States.' – from Hill and Bair, *Marcus Garvey, Life and Lessons*, pp. 319–320.

15 Madam Walker cultivated connections with black churches. In Pittsburgh, church leaders were persuaded to endorse her with a letter stating: 'As a hair grower she has no equal . . . until her advent into this city . . . we did not believe in such a thing as a hair grower.' Cited in Bundles, p. 96; See Evans pp. 254–257 for summary of Walker's spectacular rise.

16 *Champion*, January 1917, pp. 167–168.

17 *History Matters*, 'Burned into Memory'.

18 *New York News*, 28 August 1926, quoted in Watkins-Owen, p. 94.

19 Anderson, p. 78.

20 Ibid, p. 122.

21 Amy Ashwood to Marcus Garvey, printed in *Garvey Papers*, I, p. 204.

22 McKay, *Harlem Metropolis*, p. 135.

23 McKay, *A Long Way From Home*, p. 9.

24 Bruce, 'Impressions of Marcus Garvey', 1922 Bruce papers, B5-14 (#1885), Schomburg centre. Quoted in Crowder, p. 136.

25 James Weldon Johnson, *Black Manhattan*, p. 253.

26 PBS's *In the Whirlwind of the Storm* – Virginia Collins (interviewee).

27 Garvey, 'The West Indies in the Mirror of Truth', *Champion* magazine January 1917, pp. 167–168. Also cited in *Garvey Papers*, I, p. 199.

5. No Flag but the Stars and Stripes – and Possibly the Union Jack

INTERVIEWS AND CORRESPONDENCE: Robert Hill, Judith Stein. SOURCES: AFRC, RG 163, Selective Service Card of Marcus Garvey, Selective Service Act; DNA, RG 165, File 10218–261/36. PUBLICATIONS: Jervis Anderson, *This Was Harlem*; John E. Bruce, 'African American Plea for Organized Resistance to White Men' (speech at undisclosed location, October, 1889) [John E. Bruce Collection, Folder No. 7, Schomburg Centre, New York]; Ann Charters, *Nobody: The Story of Bert Williams*; W. E. B. Du Bois, 'The Black Man in the Great War', *Crisis*, June 1919; W. E. B. Du Bois, 'Close Ranks', *Crisis* 16 July 1918; W. E. B. Du Bois, *Writings*; Scott Ellis, *Race, War and Surveillance*; Stephen L. Harris, *Harlem Hell Fighters*; Robert Hill (ed.), *Garvey Papers*; James Weldon Johnson, *Black Manhattan*; James Weldon Johnson, 'Negro Loyalty in the Present Crisis', *New York Age*, 29 March 1917; James Weldon Johnson, *Writings*; Philip Kasinitz, *Caribbean New York: Black Immigrants and the Politics of Race*; David M. Kennedy, *Over Here: The First World War and American Society*; Claude McKay, *Harlem: Negro Metropolis*; *New York Age*, editorial 8 November 1917; Mary White Ovington, *Half a Man*; Jeffrey B. Perry, *A Hubert Harrison Reader*; Emmet J. Scott, *Scott's Official History of the American Negro in the World War*; Richard Slotkin, *Lost Battalions*

1   Johnson, *Black Manhattan*, p. 232.

2   Du Bois, 'Close Ranks', from *Crisis*, 16 July 1918.

3   Harris, p. 33.

4   Ibid, p. 33. Also reported in *New York Age*, 1 June 1916.

5   AFRC, RG 163. Selective Service Card of Marcus Garvey, printed in *Garvey Papers*, I, p. 206. Under the Selective Service Act, drafted by Brigadier General Hugh Johnson, it was the duty of every male citizen of the United States, and every other male person residing in the United States who was between the ages of twenty-one and thirty, to present himself for, and submit to, registration. Garvey was twenty-nine at the time, two months short of his thirtieth birthday.

6   Du Bois, 'The Black Man in the Great War', *Crisis*, June 1919.

7   Perry, p. 20.

8   *Garvey Papers*, I, p. 311.

9   Anderson, p. 101.

10   *Garvey Papers*, I, p. 214.

11   Johnson, 'Negro Loyalty in the Present Crisis', *New York Age*, editorial, 8 November 1917.

12   Johnson, *Writings*, p. 490.

13   Kennedy, p. 281.

14   Ovington, p. 96, quoted in Anderson, p. 26.

15   Bruce, 'African American Plea for Organized Resistance to White Men'.

16 Revd Charles Martin, 'The Harlem Negro', quoted in Anderson, p. 99.

17 Kasinitz, p. 48.

18 McKay, p. 147.

19 *Garvey Papers*, I, p. 323 – an attachment of a British Military Intelligence report found in DNA, RG 165, File 10218–261/36.

20 Ibid, p. 234 (John E. Bruce to the *New Negro*).

21 Ellis, p. 80, quoting MIB officer from Ohio about the dangers of black morale and suspect loyalty.

22 Anderson, p. 107. The Espionage Act, passed by Congress in 1917, prescribed a $10,000 fine and twenty years' imprisonment for interfering with the recruiting of troops or the disclosure of information dealing with national defence. By the end of 1917 nearly a thousand men were imprisoned under the Espionage Act.

23 Johnson, 'Negro Loyalty in the Present Crisis', *New York Age*, 29 March 1917.

24 Charters, p. 184, quoted in Harris, pp. 67–68.

25 Harris, pp. 101–102.

26 Slotkin, p. 144.

27 Johnson, *Black Manhattan*, p. 235.

28 Slotkin, p. 484.

6. If We Must Die

INTERVIEWS: Ralph Crowder, David Levering Lewis. SOURCES: *The Diary of Ida B. Wells*, Ida B. Wells Papers, Special Collections Research Centre, University of Chicago Library. PUBLICATIONS: John E. Bruce, *Prince Hall, Pioneer of Negro Masonry, Proof of the Legitimacy of Prince Hall*; *Charleston News and Courier*, 22 October 1916; *Cleveland Advocate*, 23 July 1919; Irvin Cobb, *The Glory of the Coming*; Ralph Crowder, *John Edward Bruce: Politician, Journalist, and Self-trained Historian of the African Diaspora*; W. E. B. Du Bois, *Selected Writing*; Ralph Ellison, *Invisible Man*; Barbara Foley, *Spectres of 1919*; Peter Fryer, *Staying Power: the History of Black People in Britain*; Robert Hill, *Garvey Papers*; Charles Holden, *Inconvenient Material for Lynchers: The Conservative Critique of World War I and the Use of African Soldiers*; Amy Jacques, *Garvey and Garveyism*; Amy Jacques, *Philosophy and Opinions of Marcus Garvey*; James Weldon Johnson, *Writings*; Theodore Kornweibel, *Seeing Red*; Claude McKay, *A Long Way From Home*; Claude McKay, *Complete Poems*; Linda McMurry, *To Keep the Waters Troubled: the Life of Ida B. Wells*; Jeffrey Perry, *Hubert Harrison Reader*; Richard Slotkin, *Lost Battalions*; Richard Smith, *Jamaican Volunteers in the First World War: Race, Masculinity and the Development of National Consciousness*; William M. Tuttle Jr, *Race Riot: Chicago in the Red Summer of*

1919; Washington Bee, 20 December 1919; *Washington Post,* 21 July 1919; Ida
B. Wells, *Crusade for Justice: The Autobiography of Ida B. Wells*

1   Cobb, p. 188. See also Slotkin, p. 147.
2   Ibid, p. 295.
3   Wells, *Crusade for Justice,* p. 52. See also Linda McMurry, p. 135.
4   *Charleston News and Courier,* 22 October 1916: 'A Lynching at Abbeville',
     quoted in Holden, p. 9. Holden's dissertation is a shrewd analysis of
     Charleston's progressive approach to race relations in the early part of the
     twentieth century.
5   Walter White was a field officer for the NAACP, who with his fair hair and
     blue eyes and very light skin could pass unmolested through the South posing
     as a white man and collecting vital information for the NAACP on the activ-
     ities of the Ku Klux Klan and the identities of the ringleaders of the lynch
     mobs.
6   Ellison, p. 17.
7   Jacques, *Philosophy and Opinions of Marcus Garvey,* p. 101.
8   *Washington Bee,* 20 December 1919, quoted in Foley, p. 19.
9   Ellison, p. 296.
10   Crowder, interview with author, April 2007 (telephone).
11   Jacques, *Garvey and Garveyism,* p. 29.
12   *Garvey Papers,* I, p. 236.
13   Bruce, pp. 1–12.
14   McKay, *A Long Way from Home,* p. 31.
15   McKay, *Complete Poems,* p. 177.
16   McKay, *A Long Way from Home,* p. 32.
17   Du Bois, 'Returning Soldiers', *Crisis,* May 1919.
18   Smith, pp. 130–131.
19   Tuttle, pp. 6–34.
20   *Washington Post,* 21 July 1919.
21   *Cleveland Advocate,* 23 July 1919.
22   Fryer, p. 297.
23   Johnson, p. 482.
24   Quoted in Kornweibel, p. 37.
25   *Garvey Papers,* I, p. 332, memorandum 11 December 1918.
26   Colonel J. Dunn to Major W. H. Loving, 17 December 1918, printed in
     Garvey Papers, I, p. 326.
27   Major Loving to Director of Military Intelligence, 17 February 1919,
     printed in *Garvey Papers,* I, p. 363.
28   Military Intelligence report from Bethel AME Church, Baltimore, 21
     December 1918, printed in *Garvey Papers,* I, p. 332.
29   Perry, p. 210.
30   Wells, *The Diary of Ida B. Wells,* 12 June 1886.

31 In 1886 there had been an anarchist/labour scare culminating in the Haymarket bombing.

32 John E. Bruce to Major Loving, 13 January 1919, printed in *Garvey Papers*, I, pp. 349–350.

7. How to Manufacture a Traitor

INTERVIEWS AND CORRESPONDENCE: Robert Hill, David Levering Lewis, Arthur Miller. SOURCES: William J. Gordon, *Black Newspapers and America's War for Democracy*; Bolton Smith, *The Negro in War-Time*, Public 21; *Survey Graphic – A Study of Negro Life*, March 1925 special edition, reproduced in *Garvey Papers*, I. PUBLICATIONS: Jervis Anderson, *Portrait of A. Phillip Randolph*; Amy Ashwood, *Portrait of a Liberator*; The *Bible*, Exodus 12:7–14, King James Version, Regency Publishing House, Nashville/New York, 1976; John H. Clarke (ed.), *Marcus Garvey and the Vision of Africa*; *Daily Gleaner*, 15 June 1925; Wilfred Domingo, 'Tropics in New York', *Survey Graphic* 1925; Harold Evans, *American Century*; Barbara Foley, *Spectres of 1919*; Robert Hill, *Garvey Papers*; Amy Jacques, *Garvey and Garveyism*; Julian Jaffee, *Crusade Against Radicalism: New York During the Scare, 1914–1921*; Winston James, *Holding Aloft the Banner of Ethiopia*; James Weldon Johnson, *Black Manhattan*; *Lagos Weekly News*, VI, 16 March 1985; Alain Locke, 'Enter the New Negro', in *Survey Graphic*, 1925; Clayton R. Lusk, 'Radicalism Under Inquiry' in *The Review of Reviews*, February 1920; Hollis R. Lynch, *Edward Wilmot Blyden: Pan-Negro Patriot*; Claude McKay, *A Long Way From Home*; Ras Makonen, *Pan Africanism from Within*; Tony Martin, *Race First*; The *Nation*, 17 April 1920; *Negro World*, 1 March 1919; *Negro World*, 29 March 1919; A. Richard Newman, *African American Quotations* (Oryx Press, Phoenix Arizona, 1998); A. Mitchell Palmer, *The Case Against the Reds*; Jeffrey Perry, *A Hubert Harrison Reader*; Todd Pfannestiel, *Rethinking the Red Scare: The Lusk Committee and New York's Crusade Against Radicalism, 1919–1923*; *Philadelphia Inquirer*, 3 May 1919; John Reed, *Ten Days that Shook the World*; George Schulyer, *Black and Conservative*; Richard Slotkin, *Lost Battalions*; Judith Stein, *The World of Marcus Garvey: Race and Class in Modern Society*; Charles Edward Stowe, *Harriet Beecher Stowe: the Story of Her Life*; Charles Rumford Walker, *Steel: the Diary of a Furnace Worker*; *Washington Bee*, 1919; Lionel M. Yard, *First Amy Tells All*

1 Exodus 12, 7–14.

2 Eugene O'Neill's *The Hairy Ape*, written in 1922, worried the authorities who thought it potentially subversive. The BOI believed *The Hairy Ape* could easily lend itself to radical propaganda, and it is somewhat surprising that it has not already been used for this purpose.

3 Charles Walker was a graduate of Yale who resigned his commission from

the army in the summer of 1919, bought some second-hand clothes and, in disguise as a labourer, found himself in a steelworks near Pittsburgh. He described the pitiable conditions there, as well as the camaraderie of the mainly 'foreign' workforce at the open-hearth furnace.

4   Reed, Chapter IV, The Fall of the Provisional Government, on 7 November 1917, p. 96.

5   Lusk, pp. 167–171. From May 1919 Senator Lusk led the committee to investigate radical activities in New York state, which sanctioned illegal raids and searches of suspected radical institutions in order to secure evidence of violations of the Criminal Anarchy Act of 1901 – a little-enforced law which had been brought in following the assassination of President William McKinley. The act made it a felony to express, either by word of mouth or by writing, the doctrine that organised government should be overthrown by force or violence.

6   Pfannestiel, p. ix (introduction). Between 1919 and 1920, thirty-two states passed criminal syndicalism laws. The loyalty of schoolteachers was screened by local vigilance committees. Hundreds of teachers lost their jobs for reading the wrong books, having the wrong friends, holding the wrong opinions, or joining the wrong groups.

7   'Negroes Get Ready', cited in Martin, p. 92.

8   The 1925 special edition of the *Survey Graphic, A Study of Negro Life*, compared twelve leading black newspapers; routinely the *Chicago Defender* topped the poll as the most rigorous and professional.

9   Clarke, p. 215. Clarke, an impressive African-American scholar, is particularly interested in the American and African antecedents of Marcus Garvey.

10   *Lagos Weekly News*, VI, 16 March 1985. Quoted in Lynch, p. 136.

11   *Garvey Papers*, I, p. 282.

12   Estimations of the *Negro World*'s circulation vary widely. 10,000 was the conservative figure estimated by the conscientious journalist, Hubert Harrison, who became an associate editor in January 1920. Perry, p. 184.

13   *Negro World*, 1 March 1919. Quoted in *Garvey Papers*, I, p. 383.

14   There are a number of biographies of Madam C. J. Walker. Perhaps the most illuminating is by A'Lelia Bundles, *On Her Own Ground: the Life and Times of Madam C. J. Walker*. The author is the great, great grand-daughter of Madam Walker. On her death, Madam Walker was succeeded by her only child, A'Lelia Walker. Her daughter introduced skin-lightening products, for example 'Tan-Off', and Garvey's *Negro World* was at times forced, out of financial necessity, to take adverts for Madam Walker's products. A'Lelia Walker was equally as generous a patron as her mother, most notably towards the arts – opening up her home in Harlem, nicknamed the Dark Tower, as a kind of permanent site for literary and other artistic soirees. The quotation 'kinks out of your mind . . .' is taken from Newman, p. 325.

15   Anderson, p. 80.

16   Domingo, March 1925, pp. 648–650.

17   Johnson, p. 246.

18   Locke, March, 1925, pp. 629–630.

19   The Industrial Workers of the World (IWW) took a pacifist line during the Great War. Its egalitarianism and militancy was more likely to strike a chord with potential black members than the Socialist Party. Hubert Harrison had marched with the IWW's Big Bill Haywood on the Paterson Silk Strike of 1913. Another example of black solidarity with the organisation was witnessed at the start of the Great War, when Ben Fletcher, a prominent African-American member, was arrested along with the other IWW activists under the Espionage Act.

20   McKay, p. 27.

21   Ibid, p. 61.

22   Ibid, p. 109.

23   *Negro World*, 29 March 1919.

24   Marcus Garvey generated an extremely thick FBI file and military intelligence files in the USA and Britain. Many of the memoranda from the surveillance of Garvey are recorded in Robert Hill's exceptional volumes of *Marcus Garvey and the Universal Negro Improvement Association Papers*.

25   *Philadelphia Inquirer*, 3 May 1919. There's a wide selection of similarly hysterical editorials in the *New York Times* and *Tribune* from the same period, 1–3 May 1919. A comprehensive analysis of the Red Scare can be found in Robert K. Murray's *Red Scare: A Study in National Hysteria*. The workings of the Lusk Committee are considered in depth in Todd J. Pfannestiel's *Rethinking the Red Scare*. Richard Slotkin's *Lost Battalions* is insightful on the fear of the black Reds, namely the Black Scare, pp. 429–461.

26   Lusk, pp. 167–171.

27   Garvey often cited Toussaint L'Ouverture in the roll call of black heroes. The slave revolt in Haiti took its cue from the French Revolution. L'Ouverture waged an unremitting campaign which eventually secured Haiti its freedom and independence, an event comprehensively studied in C. L. R. James's seminal work *The Black Jacobins*.

28   Unusually large numbers of Irish immigrants were admitted to mental institutions in the USA at the start of the twentieth century. In the view of Senator Tom Hayden, this was the downside of conformism and assimilation. 'Schizophrenia,' Hayden asserted, 'was commonly called an Irish disease', but more accurately it could have been described as a disease of the immigrant. Medical research conducted throughout the immigrant Norwegian population of Minnesota had shown, for instance, a much greater incidence of schizophrenia than amongst their compatriots back

home. The Norwegian psychiatrist Ornulf Odegaard studied numerous personality types which showed up the discrepancy in the figures. Immigrants were more likely to suffer from schizophrenia than their compatriots who remained at home. The figures were also reflected more generally amongst the Scandinavian population in the census of 1890 who were over-represented in the institutions for the insane. Tom Hayden's *Irish on the Inside* explores mental illness amongst Irish immigrants to America.

29 *Garvey Papers*, II, pp. 634–642, taken from the affidavit of Amy Ashwood on 30 August 1920. Marcus Garvey was then attempting to divorce his first wife.

30 Ashwood, p. 345.

31 Makonen, p. 89.

32 *Garvey Papers*, I, pp. 361–362.

33 The *Nation*, 17 April 1920.

34 Smith, pp. 10–13. Smith's article prompted much discussion amongst black intellectuals. James Weldon Johnson answered for them in the next month's edition of *Public*, observing that Smith had now seen what many black people had been warning of for quite some time. Also quoted in William J. Gordon's *Black Newspapers and America's War for Democracy 1914–20*, pp. 130–131.

35 *Washington Bee*, 20 December 1919, and quoted in Foley, p. 19.

36 Arthur Miller, Interview with author, March 2001 (telephone).

37 Paul Avrich's *The Haymarket Tragedy* provides details on the day of the Haymarket bombing and background on the history of anarchism in America. In the hunt for the culprits of the 1886 bombing, scores of innocent anarchists had been rounded up and several of them were hanged. Their martyrdom later inspired Emma Goldman – the radical writer whose work was alleged to have, in turn, inspired Leon Czolgosz to assassinate President McKinley.

38 *Negro World*, 14 June 1919, printed in *Garvey Papers*, I, p. 415.

39 Palmer, pp. 185–189.

40 The details of the Lusk raids are outlined in Pfannestiel. A brief sketch of Palmer and the Palmer raids is found in Harold Evans's *American Century*.

41 Domingo had been bold enough to write a provocative and unguarded missive in the *Messenger*, 'Socialism: the Negroes' Hope', and signed himself as 'Editor' of the *Negro World* – cited by James in *Holding Aloft the Banner of Ethiopia*, p. 270.

42 Ibid

43 *Garvey Papers*, II, p. 40. Domingo's jaundiced account of the break with Garvey was originally published in the *Daily Gleaner*, 15 June 1925.

44 Ashwood, p. 19.

45 *Garvey Papers*, II, pp. 634–642.

46 'Of the Russian organ of Bolsheviki' from the memo: J. Edgar Hoover,

special assistant to the Attorney General, to Frank Burke. Washington DC, August 12, 1919. Printed in *Garvey Papers*, I, p. 480.

47 Ibid, p. 480.

48 *Garvey Papers*, II, p. 72.

49 The bearded, wild-eyed bomber was a stock character for most of the newspapers. It was an image lampooned in a speech given by Harry Winitsky, executive secretary of the Communist Party of New York, on 22 December 1919 at 175th East Broadway. Winitsky was later arrested and jailed during the wide-scale round-up of radicals in the Palmer raids.

50 Jacques, p. 225, originally printed in the *Negro World*, May 1933.

51 Yard, p. 42. Also quoted in Judith Stein, p. 36.

52 *Garvey Papers*, I, p. 446.

53 The quotations are taken from George Schulyer's autobiography, *Black and Conservative*. As a young man, newly arrived in town, Schulyer was thrilled to find a job with the left-wing *Messenger* whose editors he clearly admired. In a fairly short period, though, Schulyer had moved from the hard left to the far right, upsetting a lot of black folk along the way, particularly with his view that there was nothing special about African-American culture. African-Americans in his view were 'lamp-blacked Anglo-Saxons'.

54 Evans, p. 93.

55 'Radicalism and Sedition Among the Negroes As Reflected in Their Publications', reproduced in *Garvey Papers*, I, p. 488.

56 Stowe, p. 203.

57 *Garvey Papers*, I, p. 376.

8. Harlem Speaks for Scattered Ethiopia

INTERVIEWS: Sylvian Diouf, Howard Dodson, Arnold Rampersad, Mariamne Samad. PUBLICATIONS: Jervis Anderson, *This Was Harlem*; W. E. B. Du Bois, *Collected Writings*; *Crisis,* January 1923; *Crisis,* 20 December, 1920; John Hope Franklin, *George Washington Williams: A Biography*; Robert Hill (ed.), *Garvey Papers*; Eric Hobsbawn and Terence Ranger (eds.), *The Invention of Tradition;* Langston Hughes, 'The Negro Speaks of Rivers', *Crisis*, June 1921; Colin Legum, *Congo Disaster*; Alain Locke, *The New Negro: An Interpretation*; William Roger Louis, 'The US and the African Peace Settlement of 1919: The Pilgrimage of George Louis Beer', *Journal of African History*, 4 (1963); Claude McKay, *My Green Hills of Jamaica*; H. L. Mencken, *Men Versus the Man: A Correspondence between Robert Rives La Monte, Socialist, and H. L. Mencken, Individualist*; E. D. Morel, *King Leopold's Rule in Africa, edition with illustrations and maps*. Heinemann 1904; *New York Daily Tribune*, 8 June 1890; Jeffrey B. Perry, (ed.): *A Hubert Harrison Reader*; Ulrich B. Phillips, *American Negro Slavery: a survey of the supply, employment and control of Negro labour as determined by the plantation regime.* D. Appleton & Co., New York, London, 1918; Brenda Gayle Plummer, *Rising Wind: Black Americans and US Foreign Affairs, 1935–60;* Arnold Rampersad, *Langston Hughes, Vol. I;* Yvette Richards, *Conversations with Maida Springer: A Personal History of Labour, Race and International Relations;* James T. Shotwell, *At the Paris Peace Conference;* Lorthrop Stoddard, *The Rising Tide of Colour against White World-Supremacy* ; Jo Tanner, *Dusky Maidens: The Odyssey of the Early Black Dramatic Actress;* Arthur Walworth, *Wilson and His Peacemakers: American Diplomacy at the Paris Peace Conference;* *Washington Bee,* May 1884; Ida B. Wells, *Crusade for Justice: The Autobiography of Ida B. Wells*

1   Rampersad, p. 39.

2   'The Negro Speaks of Rivers' was published by the *Crisis* magazine in 1921.

3   Grain Coast is the former name of a part of the Atlantic coast of West Africa roughly identical with the coast of modern Liberia. In the fifteenth century 'grains of paradise', i.e. seeds of the melegueta pepper, became a major export item; hence the name Grain Coast.

4   '2 million followers . . .', Garvey Papers I, p. 8; '300,000 paying members . . .', *Crisis,* December, 1920. Three years later Du Bois in *Crisis* was to reduce his estimate of the UNIA membership to fewer than 18,000.

5   Locke, (foreword).

6   The *Communist,* Briggs 1931, quoted in Clarke, p. 175.

7   *Garvey Papers,* II, p. 15.

8   *Washington Bee,* May 1884. Quoted in Tanner, p. 31.

9   Claude McKay, p. 80–81.

10   Richards, p. 20–21.

11   Ulrich B. Phillips's *American Negro Slavery* provides details of the various Maroon treaties with the British. Maroon – the generic name given to runaway slaves is derived from the Spanish *cimaron,* meaning wild or fugitive.

12   A. H. Foote commanded the SS *Perry* off the African coast and was particularly zealous in apprehending slavers; his book, *Africa and the American Flag,* published in 1854, influenced the public against traffic in slaves.

13   Stoddard, citing Meredith Townsend, *Asia and Europe,* G.P. Putnam's Sons, New York, 1904. p. 92

14   Mencken, p. 116.

15   Hobsbawn and Ranger, pp. 211–262. Terence Ranger's chapter on Colonial Africa provides background to the ways in which Europeans utilised their own traditions to assert their authority of their colonial subjects.

16   Legum, pp. 29–30. Morel's book catalogues the Belgian-inspired brutality in the Congo State. The following is a typical entry: 'The hand of Eliba was also cut off and taken away in triumph, to attest that the sentries had done their duty and had punished the "rebel" town, which dared

to fail in supplying the fixed quantity of Indian rubber'. From Morel, p. 377.

17 *New York Daily Tribune*, 8 June 1890. See also Franklin, p. 201.

18 Johnston quoted in Perry, pp. 205–206.

19 Adam Clayton Powell's essay was printed in the *New York Age*, 8 January 1914. See Anderson, pp. 72–91 for an account of the dance craze.

20 In 1915, the US administration had sent 3,000 troops to restore order in Haiti after a bloody coup had led to the assassination of the island's president and members of his government. The temporary American occupation would last for fourteen years.

21 Bishop Reginald Heber, 1819. Heber was the Bishop of Calcutta who became better known as a hymn writer. Each meeting of the UNIA at its headquarters in Harlem began with a rendition of 'From Greenland's Icy Mountains'.

22 'rival and older NAACP . . .', *Garvey Papers*, II, p. 28; Ida B. Wells confirms the nomination of emissaries in her autobiography, Wells, p. 379. The extent of the authorities' antipathy towards the idea of a black delegation was apparent in a flurry of intelligence reports. For example see the Bureau of Investigation report, 5 December 1918, *Garvey Papers*, I, p. 305–306.

23 *Garvey Papers*, II, p. 206.

24 Shotwell, 14 December, 1918.

25 *Garvey Papers*, I, p. 387.

26 British military report, *Garvey Papers*, I, p. 405.

27 *Garvey Papers*, I, p. 408.

28 ' "candour" was quietly changed to "grandeur"', Shotwell, Wednesday 18 December 1918. Background to the events at Versailles is taken from Walworth. The first chapter of Plummer is devoted to the earlier black aspirations at the Paris Peace Conference.

29 *Garvey Papers*, I, p. 409.

30 Du Bois, p. 879.

31 Cadet survived through his skills as a mechanic. He didn't return to the USA until the end of the year for a brief meeting with Garvey.

32 *Garvey Papers*, II, p. 393. First published in *Crisis*, 20 December 1920, pp. 58–60.

33 Louis, pp. 413–33.

9. Flyin' Home on the Black Star Line

INTERVIEWS AND CORRESPONDENCE: Robert Hill, Mariamne Samad.
SOURCES: *History Detectives*, Season 3, episode 2 (2005) 'On the Black Star Line', http://www.pbs.org/opb/historydetectives/investigations/302_blackstar.html
PUBLICATIONS: *American Mercury* magazine, May–August 1926; Jervis

Anderson, *This was Harlem*; Amy Ashwood, *First Amy Tells All, Portrait of a Liberator*; John H. Clarke (ed.), *Marcus Garvey and his Vision of Africa*; W. E. B. Du Bois, *Darkwater: Voices from Within the Veil*; Robert Hill, *Garvey Papers*; Calvin Holder, 'Making Ends Meet: Economic Adjustment in New York City, 1900–1952', from *Wadabagei: A Journal of the Caribbean and its Diaspora*, Vol. 1, No. 1 (Winter/Spring 1998); Amy Jacques, *Garvey and Garveyism*; Amy Jacques, *The Philosophy and Opinions of Marcus Garvey, or Africa for the Africans*; Leon F. Litwack, *Been in the Storm So Long*; Claude McKay, *A Long Way From Home*; Richard Moore, 'The Critics and Opponents of Marcus Garvey', extracted in John H. Clarke, *Marcus Garvey and the Vision of Africa*; Hugh Mulzac, *A Star to Steer By*; *Negro World*, editorials, 6 December 1919, 16 October 1919 and 10 September 1921; *New York Times*, 17 October 1919; *Opportunity*, February, 1926; John Reed, *Ten Days that Shook the World*; George Schulyer, *Black and Conservative*; *Semi-Weekly Louisianan*, 15 June 1871; Ida B. Wells, *Crusade for Justice*

1   Cited in Ashwood, p. 3.

2   *Negro World*, 16 October 1919 and 10 September 1921.

3   McKay, p. 49.

4   Anderson offers an interesting analysis of this attitude.

5   *Opportunity*, February 1926. *Opportunity* was the organ of the Urban League which was founded in 1911 for the welfare of black people, and for their adjustment and assimilation into urban life.

6   Schulyer, pp. 119–122.

7   Wells, pp. 380–382; Ashwood, p. 3.

8   Jacques, *Garvey and Garveyism*, pp. 190–191.

9   Mulzac, pp. 76–77.

10 Ashwood, p. 349.

11 *Garvey Papers*, I, pp. 434–436.

12 *Garvey Papers*, I, p. 449.

13 Samad, interview with author, Kingston, Jamaica, October 2005.

14 *Semi-Weekly Louisianan*, 15 June 1871. Quoted in Litwack, pp. 502–556.

15 Moore, *The Critics and Opponents of Marcus Garvey*, in Clarke, p. 222.

16 Although the analogy of black people impeding each other's progress like crabs in a barrel was often attributed to Booker T. Washington, it almost certainly pre-dates him.

17 Jacques, *The Philosophy and Opinions of Marcus Garvey*, p. 77.

18 *Garvey Papers*, I, pp. 471–472.

19 Ashwood, p. 45.

20 *Garvey Papers*, I, p. 499.

21 Ibid, p. 505.

22 McKay, p. 132.

23 Du Bois, pp. 5–9.

24 Mulzac, p. 77.

25 *Garvey Papers*, II, p. 106.

26 *American Mercury* magazine, May–August 1926, p. 210.

27 Jacques, *The Philosophy and Opinions of Marcus Garvey*, pp. 321–322.

28 *Garvey Papers*, II, p. 68.

29 Jacques, *Garvey and Garveyism*, p. 113.

30 Ibid, pp. 39–40.

31 Holder, pp. 33–35.

32 *New York Times*, 17 October, 1919.

33 Hill, interview with author, October 2006 (Los Angeles) and November 2006 (telephone).

34 *History Detectives*, Season 3, Episode 2 (2005).

35 *Garvey Papers*, II, p. 134.

36 Ibid, p. 124.

37 *Negro World*, editorial, 6 December 1919.

10. A Star in the Storm

INTERVIEWS AND CORRESPONDENCE: Robert Hill, Marian Samad, Edward Seaga. SOURCES: TNA: PRO CO 137/747; TNA: PRO CAB 24/104 rep. No. 18, April 1920, file: 15/D/155; Amy Ashwood Garvey Collection MS 1977, box 7, 'Marcus Garvey', chapter II, 21, National Library of Jamaica, Kingston. PUBLICATIONS: John H. Clarke, *Marcus Garvey and the Vision of Africa*; W. E. B Du Bois, 'The Rise of the West Indian', *Crisis*, September 1920; Du Bois, 'Dusk of Dawn', extracted in *Selected Writings*; Du Bois, *The Souls of Black Folk*; Robert Hill, *Garvey Papers*; Robert Hill and Barbara Bair (eds.), *Marcus Garvey: Life and Lessons*; Amy Jacques, *Garvey and Garveyism*; James Weldon Johnson, *Black Manhattan*; Theodore Kornweibel, *Seeing Red*; David Levering Lewis, *W. E. B. Du Bois: The Fight for Equality and the American Century, 1919–1963*; Claude McKay, *Harlem: Negro Metropolis*; Claude McKay, *A Long Way From Home*; Tony Martin, 'Amy Ashwood Garvey: Wife No. 1', *Jamaica Journal*, 1987; Hugh Mulzac, *Cleveland Gazette*, 6 October 1923; Hugh Mulzac, *A Star to Steer By*; Mary White Ovington, *Portraits in Color*; Jeffrey B. Perry, *Hubert Harrison Reader*; Richard Smith, *Jamaican Volunteers in the First World War*; Ula Yvette Taylor, *The Veiled Garvey: The Life and Times of Amy Jacques Garvey*; UNIA Constitution and Book of Laws, article V, section 2; John C. Walter, *The Harlem Fox: J. Raymond Jones and Tammany, 1920–1970*; *Washington Evening Star*, 5 February 1920; *World Magazine*, 4 December 1921; Lionel M. Yard, *First Amy Tells All*

1 McKay, *Harlem: Negro Metropolis*, p. 90.

2 *Garvey Papers*, II, p. 162.

3 Perry, p. 196.

4 Jacques, p. 39.

5 *Garvey Papers*, II, p. 541. Agent P-138 was Herbert Boulin, president of the Berry and Ross (Black) Toy and Doll Manufacturing Company.

6 Edward Seaga, interview with author, July 2002.

7 Ovington, p. 19. Also cited in Lewis, p. 64.

8 TNA: PRO CAB 24/104 rep. No. 18, April 1920, file: 15/D/155.

9 The under prepared and ill-equipped black troops were sent against the enemy without the benefit of wire cutters to speed their passage through no-man's land but also, more importantly, their offensive had not been preceded by the necessary artillery fire to 'soften up' the German front line. Black troops were stigmatised by the 'failure' of the Muse-Argonne offensive for decades afterwards. See Du Bois's *The Black Man in the Great War* (extracted in Du Bois *Selected Writings*, p. 891).

10 Kornweibel, p. 108. Liberty Hall meeting recorded in the *Negro World*.

11 *Garvey Papers*, II, p. 202 on drilling. 'Pins removed . . .', interview with Mariamne Samad, November 2005.

12 Smith, pp. 2–3. Grant emigrated to the US soon after the Great War, working mostly in restaurants and eventually gravitating towards the UNIA where he was a prominent member of the Tiger Division – a sub-division of the African Legion. He fell out with Garvey over his rough tactics back in Jamaica and was expelled amid much publicity following the 1934 UNIA convention in Kingston.

13 Kornweibel's *Seeing Red* provides extensive background to the BOI agents who infiltrated the UNIA, and the surveillance of other black radical groups following the Armistice of the Great War.

14 Du Bois, *The Souls of Black Folk*, p. 5.

15 Mulzac, *A Star to Steer By*, p. 78.

16 *Garvey Papers*, II, pp. 157–158. See also Perry, p. 186.

17 The rumour would surface a few years later in Garvey's career during his trial for mail fraud. See *Garvey Papers*, VI, p. 497.

18 *Negro World*, 6 December 1919, printed in *Garvey Papers*, II, pp. 159–160.

19 *Garvey Papers*, II, pp. 110–111.

20 Du Bois, 'Dusk of Dawn', *Selected Writings*, p. 757. His article 'The Rise of the West Indian' was printed in *Crisis*, September 1920.

21 McKay, p. 110.

22 Jacques, p. 43.

23 *Garvey Papers*, II, pp. 180 and 636.

24 *UNIA Constitution and Book of Laws*, article V, section 2. See also *Garvey Papers*, I, p. 260.

25 Martin, pp. 32–39.

26 Perry, p. 184.

27 Mulzac, p. 78.

28 Mulzac, *Cleveland Gazette*, 6 October 1923. See also *Garvey Papers*, IV, p. 473.

29 *Washington Evening Star*, 5 February 1920. As well as the missing cases, once the *Yarmouth* arrived back in New York, workmen were apprehended as they loaded stolen bottles of whisky into a small boat. Hill, *Garvey Papers*, II, p. 208. Reverend Jonas maintained that gangsters had plotted to sabotage the ship and rob her of her valuable cargo. Cockburn had saved the day and faced down the plotters with his service revolver.

30 *Garvey Papers*, II, pp. 205–210.

31 Mulzac, *Cleveland Gazette*, 6 October 1923.

32 Mulzac, *A Star to Steer By*, p. 79.

33 Johnson, p. 123. 'When a West Indian gets 10 cents above a beggar, he opens a business which may range from a tailor shop to a Wall Street firm.'

34 Walter, pp. 35–43.

35 PBS TV, *In the Whirlwind of the Storm*.

36 Walter, p. 44. *Esusu* or *sou-sou* (*pardner* in Jamaica) is a friendly cooperative saving scheme in which each member of a small group contributes an equal portion of money each week to a keeper and each member then draws regularly on the total amount in rotation (on their turn). See also Richard Allsopp, *Dictionary of Caribbean English Usage*, Oxford University Press, 1996, p. 540.

37 *Garvey Papers*, II, p. 430.

38 Herbert J. Seligman, *World Magazine*, 4 December 1921. See also *Garvey Papers*, IV, pp. 239–244.

39 McKay, pp. 101–116.

40 Yard, p. 59.

41 Amy Ashwood Garvey Collection MS 1977, box 7, 'Marcus Garvey', chapter II, 21, National Library of Jamaica, Kingston. Also quoted in Taylor, p. 29.

42 Hill and Bair, p. 67.

43 Jacques, p. 43.

44 Samad, interview, November 2005.

45 Hill, interview, October and November 2006.

46 TNA: PRO CO 137/747. See also *Garvey Papers*, II, p. 286.

47 *Negro World*, 31 July 1920, printed in *Garvey Papers*, II, p. 470.

48 *Garvey Papers*, III, p. 7 from Special Agent P-138's report, 4 November 1920.

49 *Garvey Papers*, V, p. 35.

11. He Who Plays the King

SOURCES: 'A Monthly Review of the Progress of Revolutionary Movement Abroad', Home Office, Directorate of Intelligence, report No. 13, 10 November 1919, CAB 24/92; St Vincent Government *Gazette* 52, No. 56, 1 October 1919. PUBLICATIONS: Jervis Anderson, *A. Philip Randolph: A Biography*; *Baltimore Observer*, May 1920; John H. Clarke, *Marcus Garvey and the Vision of Africa*; *Crisis*, 21 December 1920; *Crisis*, January 1921; *Daily Telegraph*, 4 August 1920; W. E. B. Du Bois, 'Dusk of Dawn', extracted in *Selected Writings*; Hubert Harrison's Diary from 31 August 1920, quoted in *Liberator*, April 1922; Hubert Harrison, *When Africa Awakes*; Robert Hill (ed.), *Crusader* Vol. I, August 1919; Robert Hill, *Garvey Papers*; Amy Jacques, *Garvey and Garveyism*; Claude McKay, *A Long Way from Home*; V. S. Naipaul, *A Turn in the South*; *Negro World*, 10 April 1920; *Negro World*, 14 January 1922; *New York Herald*, September 1922; Jeffrey B. Perry, *Hubert Harrison Reader*

1   *Garvey Papers*, II, p. 477.
2   *Negro World*, 14 January 1922.
3   *Garvey Papers*, II, pp. 431–432.
4   Du Bois 'Dusk of Dawn', *Selected Writings*, pp. 276–277. See also Clarke, p. 99.
5   'Needed to take a bath', *Crisis*, December 1920; 'Broadway in a green shirt', *Crisis*, January 1921.
6   Perry, p. 192.
7   Baron Emile de Cartier de Marchienne to Henri Jaspar, 29 June 1921. Printed in *Garvey Papers*, IX, p. 43.
8   *Garvey Papers*, II, pp. 525–526.
9   Ibid, p. 546.
10 Ibid, p. 508.
11 Naipaul, p. 227.
12 *Garvey Papers*, III, p. 724.
13 McKay, p. 113.
14 Perry, p. 184.
15 Hubert Harrison's Diary from 31 August 1920, quoted in Perry, p. 193.
16 Hill, *Crusader* Vol. I, August 1919, pp. 8–9.
17 Perry, p. 194.
18 *Daily Telegraph*, 4 August 1920.
19 *Garvey Papers*, II, p. 188.
20 Ibid, p. 239.
21 'A Monthly Review of the Progress of Revolutionary Movement Abroad', Home Office, Directorate of Intelligence, Report No.13, 10 November 1919, CAB 24/92.
22 St Vincent Government *Gazette* 52, No. 56, 1 October 1919. The same edition also gave notice that the Colonial Postmaster or any person

appointed by him for the purpose, might, without reference to the Administrator, detain or destroy copies of the *Negro World*.

23 *Garvey Papers*, II, p. 345.

24 *Garvey Papers*, IX, p. 54.

25 *Garvey Papers*, II, p. 512.

26 Perry, pp. 377–378.

27 Jacques, p. 189.

28 *New York Herald*, September 1922. Also cited in Anderson, p. 132.

29 Perry, p. 146, extracted from Harrison, pp. 55–60.

30 Ibid.

31 *Garvey Papers*, II, p. 571.

32 'The Bill of Rights', No. 42 stated: 'We declare it an injustice to our people and a serious impediment to the health of the race to deny to competent licensed Negro physicians the right to practise in the public hospitals of the communities in which they reside, for no other reason than their race and colour.' Printed in *Garvey Papers*, II, p. 572.

33 *Crisis*, 21 December 1920.

34 *Garvey Papers*, IV, pp. 1–2.

35 *Baltimore Observer*, May 1920.

36 *Garvey Papers*, II, pp. 622–623.

37 *Garvey Papers*, II, p. 620.

38 *Garvey Papers*, II, pp. 559–560.

39 *Garvey Papers*, III, p. 402. The editorial was originally written by Domingo. The conflict between Domingo and Garvey centred on Domingo's Socialism and his promulgation of Socialist views in the *Negro World*. As the proprietor of the *Negro World*, Garvey sought to use the paper to promote his views about the direction of the UNIA and increasingly about the primacy of race. Domingo demurred. For Domingo, the class struggle came first; he held fast to the doctrine that Socialism would unite the black and white working class. However, in signing his name to the editorial, 'Race First', Domingo adopted a stance at variance with the conventional Socialist line. The editorial appeared in the *Negro World* on 26 July 1919 and chimed with the philosophy of the UNIA. Domingo resigned in July. The editorial was reprinted in the *Negro World* on 10 April 1920, in part to embarrass Domingo who was now attacking Garvey in print.

40 *Liberator*, April 1922.

41 Garvey often spoke admiringly of Bismarck. In his speeches, he regularly invited UNIA audiences to draw lessons from the blood sacrifice of the German people in their quest for unification. Garvey said that he too was satisfied to be a dreamer like Bismarck, and to lead the battle cry for a new African empire. See *Garvey Papers*, I, p. 352, *Garvey Papers*, II, p. 257 and *Garvey Papers*, III, p. 26.

12. Last Stop Liberia

INTERVIEWS AND CORRESPONDENCE: Philippe Bourgois, Ali Mazrui. SOURCES: Journal of Daniel Coker on a *Voyage for Sherbro in Africa*; Phyllis Lewsen, 'Selections from the Correspondence of John X. Merriman, 1890–98', cited in Hollis R. Lynch, *Edward Wilmot Blyden: Pan-Negro Patriot*; United Fruit Company correspondence collected by Philippe Bourgois and Ronlad Harpelle. PUBLICATIONS: A. M. B. Akpan, 'Liberia and the UNIA: The background to the abortion of Garvey's scheme for African Colonization', *Journal of African History*, XIV, I (1973); Philippe Bourgois, *Ethnicity at Work*; J.W.E. Bowen, *Africa and the American Negro*; John H. Clarke, *Marcus Garvey and the Vision of Africa*; *Crisis*, Vol. 22, No. 2, June 1921; E. David Cronon, *Black Moses, the Story of Marcus Garvey*; Du Bois, *Crisis*, September 1920; Scott Ellsworth, *Land of Hope*; Imanuel Geiss, *The Pan-African Movement*; James Hall, *An Address to the Free People of Colour of the State of Maryland*; Robert Hill, *Garvey Papers*; James Africanus Horton, *West African Countries and Peoples*; Edward Hurley, *Bridge to France*; Amy Jacques, *Philosophy and Opinions of Marcus Garvey*; James Weldon Johnson, *Crisis*, July 1921; Olive Lewin, *Rock It: Folk Music of Jamaica*; Hollis R. Lynch, *Edward Wilmot Blyden: Pan-Negro Patriot, 1832–1912*; Tony Martin, *Race First*; Moore and Johnson, *Neither Led Nor Driven*; *York Times*, 7 March 1921, 5 June 1921; Matthew Parker, *Panama Fever: The Battle to Build the Canal*; Jeffrey Perry, *Hubert Harrison Reader*; Monica Schuler, *Alexander Bedward*; *New*; *Sierra Leone Guardian and Foreign Mails*, VII, 16 February 1912; Rosalind Cobb Wiggins (ed.), *Captain Paul Cuffee's, Logs and Letters, 1808-1817* (Howard University Press, 1996); A. B. Williams, *The Liberian Exodus: An Account of Voyage of the First Emigrants in the Bark 'Azor'*

1   *Garvey Papers*, III, p. 50. Garvey had planned to launch the *Phyllis Wheatley* on 1 January 1921.

2   Scott Ellsworth's *Land of Hope* is a comprehensive and compelling account of the Tulsa race riot from 1 June 1921.

3   *New York Times*, 5 June 1921.

4   Johnson, *Crisis*, July 1921. Johnson was critical of the UNIA for allegedly not providing any assistance to the refugees.

5   Journal of Daniel Coker. In the journal Coker, 'a descendant of Africa' gives an account of the search for suitable land for the emigrants, ninety 'persons of colour' aboard the ship, *Elizabeth*.

6   Williams, p. 26. The company was not able to raise funds for another Atlantic crossing despite the continued enthusiasm of the black folk for migrating.

7   *Garvey Papers*, I, Appendix, pp. 536–547.

8   Wiggins, pp. 404.

9   James Hall was the general agent of the Maryland State Colonization Society. The address was printed as a pamphlet by John D. Toy in 1859.

10 Perry, pp. 143–144.

11 Bowen, pp. 195–198. J. W. E. Bowen was the editor of a collection of essays that formed the 'Addresses and Proceedings of the Congress of Africa, 13–15 December 1896'. The section quoted in pp. 195–198 refers to Bishop H. M. Turner's essay, 'The American Negro and the Fatherland'.

12 Horton, p. 243.

13 Hilary Teague's speech in Monrovia, cited in Horton, p. 246.

14 Clarke, introduction, p. xxii.

15 Lewsen, cited in Lynch p. 77.

16 Edward Blyden to William Coppinger (Secretary of the American Colonisation Society), 3 October 1887. Also cited in Lynch, p. 121.

17 *Sierra Leone Guardian and Foreign Mails*, VII, 16 February 1912, quoted in Lynch, p. 139.

18 *Garvey Papers*, III, p. 81.

19 Du Bois, *Crisis*, September 1920.

20 *Garvey Papers*, II, p. 347, Edwin Barclay to Elie Garcia, 14 June 1920.

21 Ibid, p. 346.

22 *Garvey Papers*, III, p. 158, Marcus Garvey to Gabriel Johnson, 1 February 1921.

23 Jacques, p. 366.

24 *Garvey Papers*, III, p. 135, Marcus Garvey to Gabriel Johnson, 18 January 1921.

25 *Garvey Papers*, III, pp. 485–490, Cyril Crichlow to Marcus Garvey, 24 June 1921.

26 Quoted in Martin, p. 124.

27 Ibid.

28 *Garvey Papers*, III, p. 247, 11 March 1921.

29 *Garvey Papers*, III, p. 140, Sir James Willcocks, Governor General of Bermuda to Winston Churchill, the British Secretary of State for the Colonies, 26 January 1921.

30 Ibid, p. 206.

31 *Garvey Papers*, III, p. 219, Gloster Armstrong to Auckland C. Geddes, British Ambassador, Washington, DC, 17 February 1921.

32 Ibid, p. 236, J. Edgar Hoover to William L. Hurley, 24 February 1921.

33 Ibid, p. 249, Alfred Hampton, Assistant Commissioner General, Bureau of Immigration to J. Edgar Hoover, 11 March 1921.

34 *New York Times*, 7 March 1921.

35 Hurley, (foreword).

36 *Garvey Papers*, III, p. 271.

37 Ibid, pp. 371 and 195.

38 Garvey wrote a lengthy rebuttal to Reverend Price published in the *Daily Gleaner*, 5 April 1921. See also *Garvey Papers*, III, pp. 332–339.

39 *Garvey Papers*, III, pp. 344–349.

40   Ibid, p. 418.

41   Jamaican folk song. See Lewin, pp. 33–34.

42   Moore and Johnson, pp. 85–86. 'Sticks to earth . . .', headline from the
     Daily Gleaner, 3 January 1921. For more details on the life of Bedward
     see Monica Schuler's entry on Alexander Bedward in the Encyclopedia of
     African-American Culture and History, published in association with the
     Schomburg Center for Research in Black Culture by MacMillan Reference
     USA, pp. 229–230.

43   Garvey Papers, III, p. 323.

44   Doc No. 210422, G. P. Chittenden, manager, United Fruit Company, Costa
     Rica Division, to V. M. Cutter, vice-president, United Fruit Company,
     Boston.

45   Garvey Papers, III, pp. 536–537.

46   United Fruit Company correspondence, cited in Harpelle, p. 58.

47   Garvey Papers, III, p. 536.

48   DNA, RG 165, 10218–418, and DNA, RG 59 811.108 g 191/11. See also
     Cronon, p. 88. and Bourgois, p. 101.

49   United Fruit Company correspondence, Chittenden to Blair, 20 April 1921.
     See also Harpell, p. 57.

50   UFC, informant's report to Blair, 28 April 1921. See also Harpelle, p. 80.

51   Parker, pp. 188–212.

52   Garvey Papers, III, p. 536.

53   William C. Matthews, the UNIA's lawyer, was believed by the FBI to have
     acted through Henry Lincoln Johnson, the leading black politician in the
     Republican Party, in bribing the immigration official, Harry McBride. The
     black politician, Johnson, had earlier consulted Secretary of State Charles
     Evans Hughes on the matter of Garvey's request for readmission.

54   Crisis, Vol. 22, No. 2, June 1921.

13. Not to Mention His Colour

INTERVIEWS AND CORRESPONDENCE: Valerie Boyd, Henry Louis Gates,
Robert Hill, Arnold Rampersad. PUBLICATIONS: Amy Ashwood, Portrait of
a Liberator; John E. Bruce, Washington's Colored Society; Cincinnati Union, 24
May 1924; Crisis, November 1920, January 1921, December 1929; Du Bois,
'Dusk of Dawn', extracted in Selected Writings, from Crisis, September 1922;
Henry Louis Gates, Bearing Witness: Selections From African American
Autobiography in the Twentieth Century; Robert Hill, Garvey Papers; Langston
Hughes, 'The Negro Artist and the Racial Mountain', published in The Nation,
1926; Amy Jacques, Garvey and Garveyism; Amy Jacques, Philosophy and
Opinions; James Weldon Johnson, Selected Writings; David Levering Lewis, W.
E. B. Du Bois's The Fight for Equality and The American Century; William

Pringle Livingstone, *Black Jamaica*; Claude McKay, *A Long Way From Home*; Claude McKay, *Complete Poems*; Richard Moore 'The Critics and Opponents of Marcus Garvey', extracted in John H. Clarke, *Marcus Garvey and the Vision of Africa*; *Negro World*, 3 September 1921; Hubert Harrison, 'A Tender Point', *Negro World*, 3 July 1920; Hubert Harrison, *When Africa Awakes*; Arnold Rampersad, *The Life of Langston Hughes: I, Too, Sing America, Vol.1, 1902–1941*; J. Saunders Redding, *On Being Negro in America*

1   *Cincinnati Union*, 24 May 1924. Wendell Dabney was both the editor and publisher of the *Cincinnati Union*. See also *Garvey Papers*, V, p. 598.

2   McKay, 'The Mulatto', from *Complete Poems*.

3   Redding, p. 39.

4   Harrison, 'A Tender Point', *Negro World*, 3 July 1920. Harrison eventually fell out with Garvey, and Garvey's name is deleted from the reprint of the article in Harrison, *When Africa Awakes*, pp. 63–66.

5   Zora Neale Hurston, 'How It Feels to Be Colored', published in the anthology *Bearing Witness: Selections From African American Autobiography in the Twentieth Century*, edited by Henry Louis Gates.

6   Jacques, *Garvey and Garveyism*, p. 39.

7   Livingstone, p. 7.

8   Jacques, *Garvey and Garveyism*, p. 197.

9   Walter White's anecdote was quoted by Claude McKay, *A Long Way From Home*, p. 111.

10   Bruce, *Washington's Colored Society*, cited in Crowder, p. 38.

11   The 'upper tens' Negroes referred to Du Bois's unashamed promotion of the talented tenth – the elite 10 per cent of the black population that he postulated would bring about changes to civil rights for the benefit of all black people.

12   *Crisis*, December 1929, January 1921. Du Bois devoted two articles to his early assessment of Garvey.

13   Bishop Charles Spencer Smith had equated Du Bois's approach with that of Garvey's, prompting the editor of *Crisis* to write a corrective to the *New York Age* on 20 June 1921. He followed that up with a letter to the Secretary of State on 23 June. In all, 113 delegates took part in the second Pan-African Congress from 29 August to 6 September 1921.

14   Du Bois, 'Dusk of Dawn', *Selected Writings*, p. 757.

15   *Garvey Papers*, IV, pp. 141–151. Garvey devoted an edition of the *Negro World* to the deconstruction of Harding's speech.

16   *Crisis*, November 1920.

17   Arnold, quoted in Johnson, p. 194.

18   Jacques, *Philosophy and Opinions*, p. 17.

19   Ibid, p. 37.

20   FBI informants alleged that witnesses had seen Jacques and Garvey spend time together in a private compartment on a Pullman sleeper. Jacques was

named as a co-respondent by Amy Ashwood in her alimony claim against Garvey. 'Did not marry for love . . .', author interview with Robert Hill, November 2006.

21   Amy Jacques maintained that Pickens visited them on at least two occasions at their apartment in Harlem and negotiated a firm job offer. Pickens continued to write positively about Garvey in 1921 though rejecting an honorary title that Garvey wanted to bestow upon him.

22   *Garvey Papers*, III, pp. 508–511. Governor Hutson promised not to publish the account of their meeting but he did send a report of it together with reports of Garvey's mass meetings in Belize to the Colonial Secretary, Winston Churchill.

23   According to Robert Hill, the Catechism owed much to the writing of the unusual self-trained scholar and journalist Joel Augustus Rogers. Rogers was a Jamaican friend of Garvey's who wrote occasionally for the *Negro World*. He is best known for his non-fiction work: *From Superman to Man* (1917) and two volumes of profiles of extraordinary black figures from history, *World's Great Men of Colour* (1924). 'Bible that doesn't suit us', speech by Garvey at Guabito, Cuba, on 21 April 1921, reported in *Negro World*, 18 June 1921.

24   *Garvey Papers*, III, p. 398, report from Detective Sergeant J. H. Irving in Jamaica.

25   Rose Pastor Stokes was a founding member of the American Communist Party. Her wealth came from her marriage to the millionaire J. Phelps Stokes. She was initially sentenced to ten years in jail for sedition. She appealed and after two years the sentence was overturned. She had also been arrested during the Palmer raids on 1 January 1920.

26   McKay, in the *Liberator*, April 1922. Also cited in Lewis, p. 64.

27   Cyril V. Briggs to Marcus Garvey, 15 August 1921, *Garvey Papers*, III, pp. 667–668.

28   Quoted in Du Bois, *Selected Writing*, p. 989 from *Crisis*, September 1922.

29   *Garvey Papers*, III, p. 691; Lewis, p. 72.

30   *Garvey Papers*, IV, pp. 74–76.

31   Richard Moore, 'The Critics and Opponents of Marcus Garvey', extracted in Clarke, p. 223.

32   *Garvey Papers*, IV, p. 302.

33   '. . . a little bit of cotton', *Garvey Papers*, III, p. 544. J. E. Spingarn, a member of the NAACP, launched the award in 1914.

34   *Garvey Papers*, III, p. 148.

35   Ashwood, *Portrait*, 2a.

36   Johnson, p. 498.

37   '. . . plaintive wailings', *Garvey Papers*, III, p. 481. '. . . towards Africa and its future', *Garvey Papers*, III, p. 607.

38 The first UNIA Court Reception was reported in microscopic detail by the *Negro World* on 3 September 1921. See *Garvey Papers*, III, pp. 698–707.

39 Hughes, 'The Negro Artist and the Racial Mountain', published in *The Nation*, 1926.

14. Behold the Demagogue or Misunderstood Messiah

INTERVIEWS AND CORRESPONDENCE: Robert Hill, Judith Stein. SOURCES: NAACP files (Library of Congress). PUBLICATIONS: The *Bible*, King James Version, Regency Publishing House, Nashville/New York; W. E. B. Du Bois, *Selected Writings*; *Crisis*, April 1922; *Daily Gleaner*, 11 July 1922; Thomas Dixon, *Clansman*; Robert Hill (ed.), *The Crusader*; Robert Hill, *Garvey Papers*; Amy Jacques, *Garvey and Garveyism*; Colonel Hubert Fauntleroy Julian, *Black Eagle* (Anchor Press, 1965); David Levering Lewis: *When Harlem Was in Vogue*; Rene Maran, *Batouala: A True Black Novel*; Tony Martin, *Race First*; *Messenger*, July 1922; *Negro World*, 21 January 1922; *Negro World*, 10 May 1924; *New Yorker*, 11 July 1931; John Peter Nugent, *The Black Eagle* (Bantam Books, 1971); *New York Times*, 7 August 1922; *New York World* September 1921; Jeffrey Perry, *Hubert Harrison Reader*

1   *Birth of a Nation* was based on the novels *The Clansman* (1905) and *The Leopard's Spots* (1902) by Thomas Dixon. The Klan was formed in Tennessee in 1866 in the aftermath of the Civil War; after that group fell into decline, a more organised Knights of the Ku Klux Klan came to prominence in Atlanta in 1915.

2   Du Bois, 'Dusk of Dawn', *Selected Writings*, p. 602.

3   *Garvey Papers*, IV, p. 916.

4   *Garvey Papers*, IV, p. 13.

5   'Because it welcomes . . .', *Crusader*, vol., IV, December 1921. *Garvey Papers*, IV, p. 73 (on Crichlow's report) and p. 301 (on Rush Memorial Church meeting).

6   *Garvey Papers*, IV, p. 307.

7   'Risked his future . . .', *Garvey Papers*, IV, p. 317. Jacques, p. 44.

8   *Garvey Papers*, IV, pp. 342–352.

9   *Negro World*, 21 January 1922.

10 *Crisis*, April 1922.

11 *Garvey Papers*, IV, p. 348.

12 'Time will tell . . .', Perry, p. 194. 'Appropriated every feature . . .', Perry, introduction, p. 6 and p. 197.

13 *Garvey Papers*, IV, pp. 474–477.

14 'Believing oneself to be a great man', *Garvey Papers*, IV, p. 621, also cited

in *Crisis*, September 1922. In the *Crisis* article the Black Star Line had been lauded as a brilliant suggestion and Garvey's only contribution to solving the race problem. Ultimately, the article was a careful deconstruction of Garvey's failings as a businessman.

15 Jacques, p. 137.

16 *Garvey Papers*, IV, p. 373.

17 Ibid, p. 590.

18 Ibid, p. 650.

19 Ibid.

20 Ibid, p. 660.

21 Ibid, p. 180.

22 Ibid, p. 610.

23 Egypt gained independence on 22 February 1922. *Batouala: A True Black Novel* was based on René Maran's experience working for the Colonial Service in French Equatorial Africa. *Batouala* won France's most prestigious literary honour, the Prix Goncourt, in 1921. Maran was the first black man to do so.

24 *Garvey Papers*, IV, pp. 625–626.

25 *Garvey Papers*, IV, p. 679. Edward Young Clarke was the Imperial Kleagle (chief organiser) of the KKK and was responsible for recruitment into the organisation. He was also a proprietor of the Southern Publicity Association which proved a useful tool in advertising the Klan.

26 *Daily Gleaner*, 11 July 1922. The quote about KKK buying stocks in the Black Star Line was attributed to Garvey's secretary, Charles McElderry.

27 *Garvey Papers*, IV, pp. 747–749.

28 *New York World*, September 1921.

29 Walter White to Leavis R. Gravis, 28 August 1924, Library of Congress – NAACP files.

30 *Messenger*, July 1922.

31 Ibid.

32 *New York Times*, 7 August 1922.

33 A paraphrase of 'Joy shall be in heaven over one sinner that repenteth more than over ninety and nine just persons which need no repentance', Luke 15:7.

34 *Garvey Papers*, IV, pp. 844–845.

35 'The bite, bitterness ...', *New York World*, Seligman, *Garvey Papers*, IV, pp. 243 and *New York World* magazine, 4 December 1921. 'Kernel of truth ...', *Crisis*, April 1922.

36 *Negro World*, 10 May 1924. Also cited in Martin, *Race First*, pp. 303–304.

37 *Garvey Papers*, IV, p. 841.

38 'Colonel' Julian's claim of being the first black pilot in the western hemisphere was disputed. He may have been the first black male pilot but the first black pilot was 'Brave' Bessie Coleman who returned to the

USA in 1921 having obtained her pilot's licence in Paris. Her dream of founding a black aviation school ended when she fell to her death from her plane during an aviation exhibition. Quoted in *Garvey Papers*, IV, p. 948.

39 Julian, pp. 58–65. See also Lewis, pp. 111–112 and Nugent, pp. 26–35 and the *New Yorker*, 'The Black Eagle', 11 July 1931.
40 *Garvey Papers*, IV, p. 1040.
41 Ibid, p. 1041.
42 Ibid, p. 946.
43 Ibid, p. 985.
44 Ibid, p. 1047.

15. Caging the Tiger

INTERVIEWS AND CORRESPONDENCE: Ralph Crowder. SOURCES: *Oral History of the American Left*, Tamiment Library, NYU, for the public radio programme *Grandma Was an Activist*. PUBLICATIONS: Jervis Anderson, *A. Philip Randolph: A Biographical Portrait*; *Baltimore Afro-American*, 29 September 1922; *Chicago Whip*, 21 October 1922; John H. Clarke, *Marcus Garvey and the Vision of Africa*; *Crisis*, September 1922 and February 1928; Ralph Crowder, *John E. Bruce*; *Daily Negro Times*, 20 June 1923; Robert Hill, *Garvey Papers*; *New York Journal*, 18 January 1922; Robert Hill and Barbara Bair (eds.), *Life and Lessons*; Amy Jacques, *Garvey and Garveyism, Philosophy and Opinions*; James Weldon Johnson, *Black Manhattan*; *Messenger*, October 1922 and March 1923; *New York Age*, 27 January 1923; *New Orleans Times-Picayune*, 2 January 1923; *New York Times*, 6 September 1922 and 4 February 1925; Jeffrey B. Perry, *A Hubert Harrison Reader*; Samuel Redding, *On Being a Negro in America*; Emma Lou Thornborough, 'T. Thomas Fortune: Militant Editor in the Age of Accommodation', in John Hope Franklin and August Meier (eds.), *Black Leaders of the Twentieth Century*

1 *Messenger*, October 1922. *New York Times*, 6 September 1922.
2 *New York Age*, 9 September 1922. See also Anderson, pp. 129–137.
3 'Inculcated into the minds of Negroes . . .', *Messenger*, September 1921. 'Against the emotional power . . .', Anderson, p. 137.
4 *Garvey Papers*, V, pp. 6–9.
5 *Garvey Papers*, IV, p. 869.
6 Ibid, pp. 939–940.
7 Johnson, pp. 186–189.
8 Thornborough, in Franklin and Meier, pp. 19–37. 'An old friend of Bruce Grit', see *Crowder*, pp. 59–60.
9 *Garvey Papers*, V, p. 128. *Chicago Defender*, report from 29 October 1922.

10 *Negro World*, 17 March 1923.

11 *Messenger*, March 1923.

12 Domingo resigned from the editorial board of the *Messenger*. In his letter of resignation he first praised the *Messenger* which had 'prided itself upon its internationalism', but in its attack on West Indians the journal had 'fallen from its former high estate'. Cited by Anderson, p. 134.

13 *Garvey Papers*, V, pp. 10, 30, 50.

14 *Oral History of the American Left*, Tamiment Library, NYU.

15 *Garvey Papers*, IV, pp. 690–699, Marcus Garvey speech, Liberty Hall, 4 July, 1922.

16 Jacques, *Garvey and Garveyism*, p. 266.

17 *Garvey Papers*, V, p. 46.

18 Ibid, p. 245.

19 *Chicago Whip*, 21 October 1922, cited in *Garvey Papers* V, p. 57.

20 *Baltimore Afro-American*, 29 September 1922.

21 *New York Age*, 27 January 1923. See also *Garvey Papers* V, p. 188.

22 *Garvey Papers*, V, pp. 133, 142, 153.

23 *New Orleans Times-Picayune*, 2 January 1923 on the fatal shooting of Eason.

24 *Garvey Papers*, V, p. 201, Anderson to Poston, 31 January 1923.

25 *Garvey Papers*, V, p. 169.

26 Ibid, p. 172.

27 Ibid, p. 298.

28 DNA, RG 60, file 198940–282, printed in *Garvey Papers*, V, pp. 182–187.

29 *Garvey Papers*, V, p. 221.

30 Jacques, *Philosophy and Opinions*, p. 294.

31 *Garvey Papers*, V, p. 213.

32 *Crisis*, September 1922.

33 *Garvey Papers*, V, p. 232.

34 Hill and Bair, p. 83.

35 *Garvey Papers*, V, p. 284.

36 *Garvey Papers*, VI, p. 64.

37 Ibid, p. 317.

38 Jacques, *Garvey and Garveyism*, p. 114.

39 *Garvey Papers*, VI, p. 175.

40 Jacques, *Philosophy and Opinions*, p. 155.

41 *Garvey Papers*, VI, p. 366.

42 *Garvey Papers*, V, p. 339.

43 *Daily Negro Times*, 20 June 1923. See also Jacques, *Philosophy and Opinions* and *Garvey Papers*, VI, p. 366.

44 Prior to his trial, Garvey had spoken approvingly of Jewish people. He believed that in its quest for an African homeland, his movement had much in common with Jewish Zionism. Garvey also benefited from Jewish

patronage, especially in Jamaica (from Abraham Judah and Lewis Ashenheim). In at least one speech, at Liberty Hall, in February 1921, Garvey did repeat some aspects of the conspiracy theory of international Jewish dominance, espoused by Henry Ford. However, the overall tone and gist of Garvey's speech 'The Rise of the Jews' is one of admiration of Jewish achievement. In this respect, he notes that black people do not compare favourably with Jewish people. Jewish achievement is put forward as a worthy benchmark.

45   *Garvey Papers*, VI, p. 387. See also *Financial World*, 30 June 1923.
46   Perry, p. 195.
47   *Crisis*, February 1928.
48   *New York Times*, 4 February 1925. Also printed in *Garvey Papers*, VI, p. 87.
49   Redding, pp. 35–36.
50   *New York Journal*, 18 January 1922.
51   Jacques, *Philosophy and Opinions*, p. 248.
52   *New York Times*, 30 June 1929.
53   *Garvey Papers*, V, p. 12.
54   *Garvey Papers*, IV, p. 638.
55   Clark, p. 142.
56   Hill and Bair, p. 93.
57   Jacques, *Garvey and Garveyism*, p. 124.
58   *Garvey Papers*, V, p. 464.
59   Ibid.
60   Ibid, p. 481.
61   Jacques, *Philosophy and Opinions*, p. 71.
62   *Garvey Papers*, V, p. 267.
63   Ibid, p. 461.
64   Redding, pp. 40–41.
65   Jacques, *Garvey and Garveyism*, p. 136.
66   *Crisis*, May 1924, pp. 8–9.
67   *Garvey Papers*, X, p. 148.
68   Ibid, p. 152.
69   Ibid, p. 156.
70   Ibid, p. 158.
71   *Garvey Papers*, X, p. 558.
72   Ibid, p. 249.
73   *Garvey Papers*, II, p. 292.
74   *Garvey Papers*, VI, p. 690.

16. Into the Furnace

PUBLICATIONS: *Baltimore Afro-American*, 13 August 1927; John H. Clarke, *Marcus Garvey and the Vision of Africa*; *Daily Gleaner*, 19 December 1926; Eugene Debs, *Walls & Bars: Prisons and Prison Life in the 'Land of the Free'*; Robert Hill, *Garvey Papers*; Robert Hill and Barbara Bair (eds.), *Life and Lessons*; Amy Jacques, *Garvey and Garveyism*; *New Republic*, 31 August 1927; *New York Amsterdam News*, March 1927; *New York Times*, 3 December 1927; Mary White Ovington, *Portraits in Color*

1   *Garvey Papers*, V, pp. 603, 625.
2   Jacques, pp. 136–137.
3   Ibid, p. 163.
4   Debs, pp. 76–77.
5   *Garvey Papers*, VI, pp. 96–98.
6   Clarke, pp. 191–192.
7   *Garvey Papers*, VII, p. 12.
8   *Garvey Papers*, VI, p. 517.
9   *New York Amsterdam News*, March 1927.
10   Ovington, pp. 18–19.
11   *Garvey Papers*, VI, p. 380.
12   Ibid, p. 271.
13   Ibid, p. 166.
14   Jacques, p. 166.
15   *Garvey Papers*, VII, p. 517.
16   Ibid, p. 166.
17   Ibid, p. 164.
18   Ibid, p. 450.
19   Ibid, p. 275.
20   Ibid, p. 431.
21   Ibid, p. 438.
22   Ibid, p. 464.
23   *Daily Gleaner*, 19 December 1926.
24   Hill and Bair, p. 117.
25   *Garvey Papers*, VI, p. 561.
26   *Baltimore Afro-American*, 13 August 1927.
27   *Garvey Papers*, VI, p. 553.
28   *New Republic*, 31 August 1927.
29   *Garvey Papers*, VI, pp. 607, 608.
30   *New York Times*, 3 December 1927.

17. Silence Mr Garvey

INTERVIEWS AND CORRESPONDENCE: Dr Julius Garvey, Robert Hill, Mariamne Samad, Edward Seaga, Judith Stein. SOURCES: BBC Radio 4, *Up You Mighty Race – A Centenary Celebration of Marcus Garvey*, 5 August 1987. PUBLICATIONS: *Black Man*, 3 November 1938; *Chicago Defender*, 10 December, 1927; John Henrik Clarke, *Marcus Garvey and his Vision of Africa*; *Daily Gleaner*, 11 February 1925, 2 August 1929, 31 January 1930, February 1930; Nancy Cunard, *The Negro: An Anthology*, 1934; *Flair* magazine, 17 August 1987; Robert Hill, *Garvey Papers*; Robert Hill and Barbara Bair (eds.), *Marcus Garvey, Life and Lessons*; Amy Jacques, *Garvey and Garveyism, Portrait of a Liberator*; *Jamaica Journal, Quarterly of the Institute of Jamaica*, August–October, 1987; David Levering Lewis, *When Harlem was in Vogue*; *Negro World*, 22 October 1927, 14 January 1928, November 1928; *New Jamaican*, 8 April 1933; *New York Age*, 24 November 1934

1   *Chicago Defender*, 10 December 1927.
2   BBC Radio 4.
3   *Daily Gleaner*, 11 February 1925. See also *Jamaica Journal*, 1987, pp. 58–65.
4   *Garvey Papers*, VII, pp. 23–24.
5   Ibid, p. 41.
6   Ibid, p. 35.
7   Ibid, p. 43.
8   Ibid, p. 61.
9   Jacques, *Garvey and Garveyism*, p. 190.
10   *Garvey Papers*, VII, p. 45. See also Jacques, p. 190.
11   *Daily Gleaner*, 23 December 1927.
12   *Garvey Papers*, VII, p. 84.
13   *Jamaica Journal*, 1987, pp. 73–76.
14   *Negro World*, 14 January 1928.
15   Ibid, 22 October 1927.
16   *Garvey Papers*, VII, p. 304.
17   Ibid, pp. 145–146.
18   Meriweather Walker, Governor, Panama Canal Zone, to Dwight Davis, Secretary of War, 9 December 1927. Printed in *Garvey Papers*, VII, pp. 9–10.
19   Ibid, p. 136.
20   Ibid, p. 275.
21   Ibid, p. 184. 'gartered flunkeys' from Jacques, *Garvey and Garveyism*, p. 191.
22   *Garvey Papers*, VII, p. 186. '. . . Auxiliary formed for them', from Jacques, *Garvey and Garveyism*, p. 192.
23   *Negro World*, November 1928. See also *Garvey Papers*, VII, p. 279.

24   Jacques, p. 193.
25   *Garvey Papers*, VII, p. 248.
26   Ibid, p. 267.
27   Ibid, p. 288.
28   'Garvey's Niece Remembers', *Flair* magazine, Monday 17 August 1987, pp. 12–13.
29   *Black Man*, 3 November 1938.
30   *Daily Gleaner*, 2 August 1929.
31   *Garvey Papers*, VII, p. 316.
32   Ibid, p. 333.
33   Ibid, p. 364.
34   *Daily Gleaner*, 1 February 1930.
35   *Garvey Papers*, VII, p. 368.
36   Ibid, p. 309. See also *New York Age*, 24 November 1934.
37   Ibid, p. 145.
38   *Daily Gleaner*, 31 January 1930.
39   *Garvey Papers*, VII, p. 503.
40   Clarke, p. 282.
41   *Garvey Papers*, VII, p. 414.
42   Jacques, *Garvey and Garveyism*, pp. 222–223.
43   *Garvey Papers*, VII, p. 453.
44   Ibid, p. 365.
45   Ibid, p. 538.
46   *New Jamaican*, 8 April 1933. See also Hill and Bair (introduction), p. xxxiii.
47   Jacques, *Garvey and Garveyism*, p. 231.
48   *Garvey Papers*, VII, p. 614.
49   BBC Radio 4.

18. Gone to Foreign

INTERVIEWS: Robert Hill, Rupert Lewis, Mariamne Samad. SOURCES: Diary entry of Ralph Bunche, Howard University, Washington, DC; Garvey's speech at Menelik Hall, Sydney, Nova Scotia, Canada 1 October 1937. PUBLICATIONS: Amy Ashwood, *Portrait of a Liberator*; *Black Man*, July 1935, July–August 1937; *Chicago Defender*, 18 May 1940; *Daily Gleaner*, 10 June 1935; Robert Hill, *Garvey Papers*; Amy Jacques, *Garvey & Garveyism*; C. L. R. James, *The Black Jacobins*; Rupert Lewis, *Garvey, Anti-Colonial Champion*; Claude McKay, *Harlem: Negro Metropolis*; *New York Amsterdam News*, 30 January 1937; Joel A. Rogers, *Additional Facts on Marcus Garvey*, Negroes of New York Writers' Program, New York, 1939; *Sunday Guardian*, 29 August 1937; *Time* magazine, November 1934; *West Indian Crusader*, London, 27 November 1937

1   *Garvey Papers*, VII, p. 652.

2   *Daily Gleaner*, 10 June 1935.
3   Marcus Garvey to Vivian Durham, 18 January 1938. Printed in Garvey Papers, VII, p. 817.
4   *Time* magazine, November 1934.
5   *Black Man*, June 1935.
6   *Black Man*, October 1935.
7   Rogers, 7.
8   *Black Man*, July 1935.
9   Ibid.
10 Ibid.
11 Ibid.
12. *Black Man*, July–August 1936.
13. *Black Man*, March–April, 1937.
14 *Garvey Papers*, VII, p. 741.
15 McKay, p. 175–176.
16 *Garvey Papers*, VII, p. 663.
17 *Chicago Defender*, 18 May 1940
18 Diary entry of Ralph Bunche.
19 Jacques, pp. 236–237.
20 Garvey's speech at Menelik Hall, Nova Scotia. The reggae singer, Bob Marley was impressed and borrowed elements of the speech for 'Redemption Song'. Along with many Rastafarians, Marley revered Marcus Garvey. The origins of that reverence date back to the coronation of Haile Selassie and an article Garvey wrote, eulogising Selassie on 8 November 1930 in his Jamaican paper, *Blackman* (later replaced by *Black Man*). The article, often referred to in Rastafarian circles as 'The Prophecy', concludes: 'The Psalmist prophesied that Princes would come out of Egypt and Ethiopia would stretch forth her hands unto God. We have no doubt that the time is now come. Ethiopia is now really stretching forth her hands. This great kingdom of the East has been hidden for many centuries, but gradually she is rising to take a leading place in the world and it is for us of the Negro race to assist in every way to hold up the hand of Emperor Ras Tafari.'
21 *Sunday Guardian*, 29 August 1937. Quoted also in Lewis, p. 271.
22 *West Indian Crusader*, London, 27 November 1937.
23 Jacques, pp. 245–248.
24 Ibid, pp. 248–249.
25 Ibid, p. 250.
26 *Garvey Papers*, VII, p. 901.
27 Ibid, pp. 926–927.
28 *New York Amsterdam News*, 30 January 1937.
29 Ashwood, p. 295.
30 Ibid, p. 297.
31 *Garvey Papers*, VII, p. 930.

32   Ibid, p. 935.
33   Ibid, p. 936.
34   Ibid, Appendix XII, p. 1003.
35   Ashwood, p. 298.

Epilogue

INTERVIEWS: Robert Hill, Mariamne Samad. PUBLICATIONS: Robert Hill, *Garvey Papers*; C. L. R. James, *A History of Negro Revolt*; David Levering Lewis, *W. E. B. Du Bois: Biography of a Race, 1868–1919*; Kwame Nkrumah, *Ghana: Autobiography of Kwame Nkrumah*; Joel A. Rogers, *World's Great Men of Colour*, Vol. 2

1   *Garvey Papers*, VII, p. 948. Garvey's memorial service on 21 July 1940 was organised by Bishop Edward Collins of the Coptic Church.
2   *Garvey Papers*, VII, pp. 950–953.
3   Nkrumah, p. 37. 'Garvey the source', Adu Boahen quoted in Lewis, p. 568.
4   Burning Spear, 'Old Marcus Garvey', from the album *Marcus Garvey/ Garvey's Ghost*.
5   Interview with Samad, November 2005.
6   James, p. 69. C. L. R James believed Garvey was, 'an opportunist to the bone . . . but the Negroes wanted a lead and they took the first that was offered them'.
7   Rogers, pp. 429, 427.

ACKNOWLEDGEMENTS

MARCUS Garvey seemed a distant and mythic figure during my childhood. That all changed a decade ago when I made a radio documentary with my mother, Ethlyn, on her return to Jamaica. Negotiating the back streets of Kingston, she was fired by memories of the UNIA processions and the great outpouring of grief and affection that had followed the passing of this extraordinary and idiosyncratic man. I owe the telling of his story to Ethlyn.

Jo Alderson should be singled out for her attentiveness and enthusiasm for the project; and my children, Jasmine, Maya and Toby for embracing the Garvey story.

Splendid and thorough research was carried out by Sonia Grant. Viv Adams drove me on with his witty provocations. Friends who read and made suggestions to early drafts include: Maggie Gee, Nick Rankin, Gabriel Gbadamosi, Hilary Alderson and Emma Dyer.

I was especially delighted to meet Dr Julius Garvey who gave unique insights into the UNIA Movement and the legacy of his father.

The exemplary *Marcus Garvey and UNIA Papers* have proved to be vital in the construction of this book. It was hugely beneficial to interview Robert Hill, the editor of the *Papers*, and to be exposed to the knowledge that he has accumulated over several decades of assiduous research. I am also grateful to Robert Hill for inviting me to California to read the rare copy of the unpublished manuscript of Garvey's first wife, Amy Ashwood.

Philippe Bourgois and Ronald Harpelle were extraordinarily generous in sharing the rich collection of correspondence from the United Fruit Company and other primary source material. I would like to thank all of the other friends, writers and researchers who have given me their time. They include: Hakim Adi, Ralph Crowder, Howard Dodson, Jeffrey Green, Cecil Gutmore, Rupert Lewis, Joy Lumsden, Mariamne Samad, Edward Seaga and Patrick Walsh.

Vivian Crawford and colleagues at the Institute of Jamaica have been particularly helpful and supportive. Early on I was fortunate to stumble across the Marcus Garvey Library in north London; the librarians Lee Francis and Selma Ibrahim have carefully steered me towards their exhaustive collection of books on Garvey. The staff at the Schomburg Centre for Research in Black Culture in New York, and at Fisk University in Nashville, Tennessee all deserve my praise.

The production of Negro with a Hat has been a thrilling process and for that I have to thank especially my astute and clear-eyed editor, Ellah Allfrey. Finally, my agent, Kevin Conroy-Scott, has been a great enthusiast and shrewd judge of character and story; his indomitable spirit has carried this book forward.

INDEX